The Dublin annals of Prior John de Pembridge OP and his Dominican continuator

For my grandchildren,
Conor and Dylan Baxter, and
Freya and Casper Williams

The Dublin annals of Prior John de Pembridge OP and his Dominican continuator

An account of Irish affairs, 1162–1370

Edited and translated, with an introduction, by

BERNADETTE WILLIAMS

Trinity Medieval Ireland Studies: 6

FOUR COURTS PRESS

Set in EhrhardtMTPro 10.5pt on 12.5pt by
Carrigboy Typesetting Services for
FOUR COURTS PRESS LTD
7 Malpas Street, Dublin 8, Ireland
www.fourcourtspress.ie
and in North America for
FOUR COURTS PRESS
c/o IPG, 814 N Franklin St, Chicago, IL 60610.

© Bernadette Williams and Four Courts Press 2024

A catalogue record for this title is available
from the British Library.

ISBN 978-1-84682-965-9

All rights reserved. No part of this publication may be reproduced, stored in or introduced into a retrieval system, or transmitted, in any form or by any means (electronic, mechanical, photocopying, recording, or otherwise), without the prior written permission of both the copyright owner and publisher of this book.

SPECIAL ACKNOWLEDGMENT

This publication has been financially supported by
Trinity Trust and Dublin City Council.

Printed in England
by CPI Antony Rowe Ltd, Chippenham, Wilts.

Contents

LIST OF FIGURES	vi
LIST OF ABBREVIATIONS	vii
ACKNOWLEDGMENTS	xiii
The Dublin annals: authorship, text and manuscripts	1
The primacy of the Trinity copy	2
The annals' Dominican provenance	3
The first author: Friar John de Pembridge OP	9
The second author: Pembridge's anonymous continuator	12
The Trinity copy: MS 583 (T)	14
The Bodleian copy: Laud Misc. MS 526 (L)	25
T and L compared	28
Pembridge examined	33
The continuator examined	42
Antiquarians and the annals	46
THE ANNALS	55
EDITORIAL CONVENTIONS	57
GLOSSARY	59
LATIN TEXT AND ENGLISH TRANSLATION	60
NOTES TO THE ENGLISH TRANSLATION OF THE ANNALS	205
APPENDIX: LIST OF MARGINAL ILLUSTRATIONS	275
INDEX	279

Figures

Fig.	Folio in T	Description	
1	1r	The opening of the Dominican annals, which commence in the year 1162. The first capital *A* is enlarged and decorated in blue and red ink.	19
2	5v	Marginal head in profile next to the entry for 1240; rubrication visible on the pointed hat and detail of the face (lips and cheek).	20
3	34r	The foot of this folio, following the conclusion of year 1347, marks where Pembridge's authorship ends. This is noted in T with the phrase, 'Here ends the chronicle of Pembridge' (*hyc finitur cronica Pembrig'*).	21
4	36v	The folio, a portion of the continuator's annals, shows two zoomorphic, dragon-like, creatures which form part of the *A* for the years 1362 and 1368.	22
5	37r	The conclusion of the Dublin annals, showing where the work of the Dominican continuator ends in the year 1370.	23

Abbreviations

AC	Annála Connacht: the annals of Connacht (AD 1224–1544), ed. A.M. Freeman (DIAS, Dublin, 1944)
Account roll Holy Trinity	Account roll of the priory of the Holy Trinity, Dublin, 1337–1346; with the Middle English moral play 'The pride of life', ed. James Mills (Dublin, 1891, repr. 1996)
AClon	The annals of Clonmacnoise, being the annals of Ireland from the earliest period to AD 1408 translated into English AD 1627 by Conell Mageoghagan, ed. D. Murphy (Dublin, 1896)
AClyn	The annals of Ireland by Friar John Clyn, ed. Bernadette Williams (Dublin, 2007)
Admin. Ire.	The administration of Ireland, 1172–1377, ed. H.G. Richardson and G.O. Sayles (IMC, Dublin, 1963)
ADR	Annales Dominicani de Roscoman (https://celt.ucc.ie/published/L100015A/index.html)
Affairs Ire.	Documents on the affairs of Ireland before the king's council, ed. G.O. Sayles (IMC, Dublin, 1979)
AFM	Annala rioghachta Eireann: annals of the kingdom of Ireland by the Four Masters, from the earliest period to the year 1616, ed. J. O'Donovan, 7 vols (Dublin, 1851)
AFP	Archivum Fratrum Praedicatorum
AH	Analecta Hibernica, including the report of the Irish Manuscripts Commission (IMC, 1930–)
AI	The annals of Inisfallen (MS Rawlinson B. 503), ed. Seán Mac Airt (DIAS, Dublin, 1951)
ALC	The annals of Loch Cé: a chronicle of Irish affairs from AD 1014 to AD 1590, ed. W.M. Hennessy, 2 vols (RS, London, 1871; repr. IMC, Dublin, 1939)
AMF	The 'Annals of Multyfarnham': Roscommon and Connacht Provenance, ed. Bernadette Williams (Dublin, 2012)
AMisc.	Miscellaneous Irish annals, AD 1114–1437, ed. Séamus Ó hInnse (DIAS, Dublin, 1947)
AMultyfarnham	The 'Annals of Multyfarnham': Roscommon and Connacht provenance, ed. Bernadette Williams (Dublin, 2012)
ARoss	Annals of Ireland by Friar John Clyn and Thady Dowling, together with the annals of Ross, ed. R. Butler (Dublin, 1849)
Archiv. Hib.	Archivium Hibernicum (1912–)

AU	*Annala Uladh ('Annals of Ulster'), otherwise Annala Senait ('Annals of Senat'): a chronicle of Irish Affairs AD 431 to AD 1540*, ed. W.M. Hennessy and B. MacCarthy, 4 vols (Dublin, 1887–1901); *The annals of Ulster (to AD 1131)*, ed. Seán Mac Airt and Gearóid Mac Niocaill (Dublin, 1983)
BL	British Library, London
Bodl.	Bodleian Libraries, Oxford
Brooks, *Knights' fees*	Eric St John Brooks (ed.), *Knights' fees in counties Wexford, Carlow and Kilkenny, 13th–15th century* (IMC, Dublin, 1950)
CARD	J.T. Gilbert (ed.), *Calendar of the Ancient Records of Dublin*, 19 vols (Dublin, 1889–1944)
CCD	*Calendar of Christ Church deeds*, ed. M.J. McEnery and Raymond Refaussé (Dublin, 2001)
CChR	*Calendar of the charter rolls [...], 1226–1516*, 6 vols (PRO, London, 1903–27)
CDI	*Calendar of documents relating to Ireland, 1171–1307*, ed. H.S. Sweetman and G.F. Handcock, 5 vols (PRO, London, 1875–86)
CIRCLE	*CIRCLE: A calendar of Irish chancery letters, c.1244–1509*, ed. Peter Crooks (https://virtualtreasury.ie/gold-seams/circle)
CJRI	*Calendar of the justiciary rolls of Ireland*, ed. James Mills et al., 3 vols (Dublin, 1905–56)
Co.	county [modern][1]
COD	*Calendar of Ormond deeds, 1172–1603*, ed. Edmund Curtis, 6 vols (IMC, Dublin, 1932–43)
Colony and frontier	*Colony and frontier in medieval Ireland: essays presented to J.F. Lydon*, ed. T.B. Barry, Robin Frame and Katharine Simms (London and Rio Grande, 1995)
Connolly, 'Ancient petitions (SC 8)'	Philomena Connolly, 'Irish material in the class of ancient petitions (SC 8), in the Public Record Office, London', *AH*, 34 (1987), 1–106
Connolly, 'Chancery files (C.260)'	Philomena Connolly, 'Irish material in the class of Chancery files (Recorda) (C.260) Public Record Office London', *AH*, 31 (1984), 3–18
Connolly, 'Chancery warrants (C81)'	Philomena Connolly, 'Irish material in the class of Chancery warrants series I (C81), in the Public Record Office, London', *AH*, 36 (1995), 135–61

---

1 'County' written in full refers to the medieval shire.

Connolly, 'Memoranda rolls'
> Philomena Connolly, 'List of Irish entries on the memoranda rolls of the English Exchequer, 1307–27', *AH*, 36 (1995), 163–218

CPL   *Calendar of entries in the papal registers relating to Great Britain and Ireland: papal letters* (London, 1893–)

CPR   *Calendar of the patent rolls [...], 1232–[1509]*, 53 vols (PRO, London, 1911)

CPR Ire., Hen. VIII–Eliz.   *Calendar of the patent and close rolls of chancery in Ireland Henry VIII to 18th Elizabeth*, ed. James Morrin (Dublin, 1862)

CR   *Close rolls of the reign of Henry III*, 14 vols (London, 1902–38)

Crooks (ed.), *Government*   Peter Crooks (ed.), *Government, war and society in medieval Ireland: essays by Edmund Curtis, A.J. Otway-Ruthven and James Lydon* (Dublin, 2008)

Crooks & Duffy (eds), *The Geraldines*
> Peter Crooks and Seán Duffy (eds), *The Geraldines and medieval Ireland: the making of a myth* (Dublin, 2016)

d.   died

DIAS   Dublin Institute for Advanced Studies

DIB   *Dictionary of Irish biography*, ed. James McGuire and James Quinn, 9 vols (Cambridge, 2009)

Duffy (ed.), *Princes, prelates & poets*
> Seán Duffy (ed.), *Princes, prelates and poets in the medieval Ireland: essays in honour of Katharine Simms* (Dublin, 2013)

EHR   *English Historical Review* (1886–)

Flanagan, *Irish society*   M.T. Flanagan, *Irish society, Anglo-Norman settlers, Angevin kingship: interactions in Ireland in the late twelfth century* (Oxford, 1989)

Flanagan, *Transformation*
> Marie Therese Flanagan, *The transformation of the Irish church in the twelfth century* (Woodbridge, 2010)

Frame, *Eng. lordship*   Robin Frame, *English lordship in Ireland, 1318–61* (Oxford, 1982)

Frame, *Ire. & Brit.*   Robin Frame, *Ireland and Britain, 1170–1450* (London, 1998)

Gilbert, *Hist. & mun. docs*
> J.T. Gilbert (ed.), *Historic and municipal documents of Ireland, AD 1172–1320, from the archives of the city of Dublin* (RS, London, 1870)

Gilbert, *Viceroys*   J.T. Gilbert, *History of the viceroys of Ireland with notices of the castle of Dublin and its chief occupants in former times* (Dublin, 1865)

Giraldus, *Expug.* Giraldus Cambrensis, *Expugnatio Hibernica: the conquest of*
Hib. *Ireland*, ed. and tr. A.B. Scott and F.X. Martin (RIA, Dublin, 1978)
Giraldus, *Topog.* Giraldus Cambrensis, *The topography of Ireland*, tr. J.J.
Hib. O'Meara (Dundalk, 1951)
Given-Wilson, *Chronicles*
        Chris Given-Wilson, *Chronicles: the writing of history in medieval England* (London, 2004)
Gwynn, Aubrey Gwynn, 'Some unpublished texts from the Black Book
'Black Book' of Christ Church, Dublin', *AH*, 16 (1946), 281–337
Gwynn & Hadcock, *MRHI*
        Aubrey Gwynn and R.N. Hadcock (eds), *Medieval religious houses: Ireland* (Dublin, 1970; repr. Dublin, 1988)
Hagger, Mark S. Hagger, *The fortunes of a Norman family; the de Verduns*
Fortunes *in England, Ireland and Wales, 1066–1316* (Dublin, 2001)
Harris, *Dublin* Walter Harris, *The history and antiquities of the city of Dublin, from the earliest accounts* (Dublin, 1766)
HBC *Handbook of British chronology*, 3rd edn (Cambridge, 1996)
Hinnebusch, *Dominican order*
        W.A. Hinnebusch, *The history of the Dominican order*, 2 vols (New York, 1966–73)
Hinnebusch, *English friars preachers*
        W.A. Hinnebusch, *The early English friars preachers*, Institutum historicum Ff. Praedicatorum ad S. Sabinae (Rome, 1951).
HMC Historical Manuscripts Commission (Royal Commission on Historical Manuscripts)
HR *Historical Research* [formerly *BIHR*] (1987–)
IER *Irish Ecclesiastical Record* (1864–)
IExP *Irish exchequer payments, 1270–1446*, ed. Philomena Connolly (IMC, Dublin, 1998)
IHS *Irish Historical Studies: The Joint Journal of the Irish Historical Society and the Ulster Society for Irish Historical Studies* (1938–)
IMC *Coimisiún Láimhscríbhinní na hÉireann* (The Irish Manuscripts Commission)
Inquisitions & *Inquisitions and extents of medieval Ireland*, ed. P. Dryburgh and
extents B. Smith, List and Index Society (London, 2007)
Ir. parl. H.G. Richardson and G.O. Sayles, *The Irish parliament in the Middle Ages* (Philadelphia, 1952)
ITS Irish Texts Society (vol. 1–, London, 1899–)
JGAHS *Journal of the Galway Archaeological and*
JLAHS *Journal of the County Louth Archaeological and Historical Society* (1904–)

JRSAI	*Journal of the Royal Society of Antiquaries of Ireland*
Kilkenny chronicle	Robin Flower, 'Manuscripts of Irish interest in the British Museum', *AH*, 2 (1931), 33
L	The Bodleian copy of the Dublin annals in Bodleian MS Miscellaneous S21
Lawlor, 'Liber Niger'	H.J. Lawlor, 'Calendar of the Liber Niger and Liber Albus of Christ Church, Dublin, *PRIA*, 27C (1908), 1–93
Liber antiquissimus	*The great parchment book of Waterford: liber antiquissimus civitatis Waterfordiae*, ed. N.J. Byrne (IMC, Dublin, 2007)
Liber primus Kilkenniensis	*Liber primus Kilkenniensis*, ed. Charles McNeill (IMC, Dublin, 1931)
Llanthony cartularies	*The Irish cartularies of Llanthony prima and secunda*, E. St John Brooks (IMC, Dublin, 1953)
Mac Niocaill, 'Cáipéisí'	Gearóid Mac Niocaill, 'Cáipéisí ón gceathrú céad déag', *Galvia* 5 (1958), 32–42
Milne, *Christ church*	Kenneth Milne (ed.), *Christ church cathedral, Dublin: a history* (Dublin, 2000)
NAI	National Archives of Ireland [formerly PROI], Dublin
NHI, i	*A new history of Ireland*, i: *prehistoric and early Ireland*, ed. Dáibhí Ó Cróinín (Oxford, 2005)
NHI, ii	*A new history of Ireland*, ii: *medieval Ireland, 1169–1534*, ed. Art Cosgrove (Oxford, 1987; repr. with bibliographical supp., 1993)
NHI, ix	*A new history of Ireland*, ix: *maps, genealogies, lists. A companion to Irish history, part II*, ed. T.W. Moody, F.X. Martin and F.J. Byrne (Oxford, 1984)
NLI	National Library of Ireland, Dublin
ODNB	*Oxford dictionary of national biography: from the earliest times to the year 2000*, ed. H.C.G. Matthew and B.H. Harrison, 61 vols (Oxford, 2004)
Orpen, *Normans*	G.H. Orpen, *Ireland under the Normans*, 4 vols (Oxford, 1911–20; new ed., 4 vols in 1, Dublin, 2005)
Otway-Ruthven, *Med. Ire.*	A.J. Otway-Ruthven, *A history of medieval Ireland, with an introduction by Kathleen Hughes* (London, 1968; rev. ed., 1980)
Parls and councils	*Parliaments and councils of mediaeval Ireland*, ed. H.G. Richardson and G.O. Sayles (IMC, Dublin, 1947)
PRIA	*Proceedings of the Royal Irish Academy*
PRO	Public Record Office, London [now included within TNA]
PROI	Public Record Office of Ireland, Dublin [now NAI]
PRONI	Public Record Office of Northern Ireland, Belfast
RCI	Record Commission of Ireland

Red bk Kildare	The red book of the earls of Kildare, ed. Gearóid Mac Niocaill (IMC, Dublin, 1964)
Red bk Ormond	The red book of Ormond [...], ed. N.B. White (IMC, Dublin, 1932)
Reg. Alen	A calendar of Archbishop Alen's register, c.1172–1534, ed. Charles McNeill (RSAI, Dublin, 1950)
Reg. Gormanston	Calendar of the Gormanston register, ed. J. Mills and M.J. McEnery (RSAI, Dublin, 1916)
Reg. St Thomas	Register of the abbey of St Thomas the Martyr, Dublin, ed. J.T. Gilbert (RS, London, 1889)
Regs Christ Church	The registers of Christ Church cathedral, Dublin, ed. Raymond Refaussé with Colm Lennon (Dublin, 1998)
Rep. DKPRI	Reports of the deputy keeper of the public records in Ireland (Dublin, 1869–)
RIA	Royal Irish Academy, Dublin
Röhrkasten, *Mendicant London*	
	Jens Röhrkasten, *The mendicant houses of medieval London, 1221–1539* (Münster, 2004)
RS	*The chronicles and memorials of Great Britain and Ireland during the Middle Ages*, published under the direction of the Master of the Rolls ('Rolls Series'), 99 vols (London, 1858–96)
RSAI	Royal Society of Antiquaries of Ireland
Sayles, 'Rebellious first earl'	
	G.O. Sayles, 'The rebellious first earl of Desmond' in J.A. Watt, J.B. Morrall and F.X. Martin (eds), *Medieval studies presented to Aubrey Gwynn, SJ* (Dublin, 1961), pp 203–27
Sayles, 'Legal proceedings'	
	G.O. Sayles, 'Legal proceedings against the first earl of Desmond', *AH*, 23 (1966), 3–47
ser.	Series
SHR	*Scottish Historical Review* (1903–28; 1947–)
SP Hen. VIII	*State papers, Henry VIII*, 11 vols (London, 1830–52)
Studies	*Studies: An Irish Quarterly Review* (1912–)
T	The Trinity copy of the Dublin annals in TCD MS 583
TCD	Trinity College, Dublin
TCE	*Thirteenth Century England* (Woodbridge, 1985–)
TNA	The National Archives (UK)

Acknowledgments

When I had at last completed the research on Pembridge, I sent the draft to Seán Duffy and Peter Crooks as an extremely large volume with a vast number of footnotes. I knew that the work would need extensive culling! Then, at this stage, Covid arrived, my husband fell ill, and I was hospitalized with heart failure all of which necessitated a move to an apartment. It was now that Seán Duffy and Peter Crooks extremely compassionately took over the next stage (despite their already huge workloads) and prepared the work for publication. Consequently, this work would never have reached fruition had it not been for Seán Duffy and Peter Crooks to whom I owe an immeasurable debt of gratitude for their constant support, encouragement, and invaluable help.

While these annals cover a comparatively short period of time (1162–1370), they range over a major historical period. A staggering amount of great scholarship is available to the researcher, and this is both wonderful and daunting as, necessarily, footnotes must be restricted. I am incredibly grateful to all those historians whose writings have helped me so significantly. I am always struck by the kindness of the historians of medieval Ireland and their readiness to share their knowledge. And, as always, my thanks go to all those numerous scholars whose works have helped me to identify entries. Many eminent historians have also responded with great enthusiasm to my email inquiries, and some of these are, alphabetically: Howard Clarke, Peter Crooks, Seán Duffy, Marie Therese Flanagan, Helen Nicholson, Colmán Ó Clabaigh, Seymour Phillips, Brian Scott, Roger Stalley and Colin Veach.

Historians build on the work, research and insights of other historians and in my case, I am eternally grateful to both the late Professor James Lydon and the late Dr Philomena Connolly, for their inspirational and lasting friendship. I should also like to acknowledge the many hours that my patient friends and colleagues, Dr Colmán Ó Clabaigh OSB, and Dr Arlene Hogan listened, as I sounded out my ideas, and for the thoughtful feedback they supplied.

I should like to express my thanks to all the library staff of Trinity College Dublin, and, in this respect, I would especially like to thank Mary Higgins in the Berkeley Library and Jane Maxwell and the staff of the Department of Manuscripts, who supplied me with such an excellent digital copy of the Pembridge annals. My thanks also go to the authorities and staff of the Bodleian Library, Oxford.

I gratefully acknowledge the assistance and expertise of Martin Fanning, Anthony Tierney and the team at Four Courts Press who have produced this volume to their house's usual high standard. Dr Áine Foley provided the index and expert editorial assistance.

Last, but definitely not least, my husband of 59 years, Graham, and my children Emma, Anna and Gavin who have, as always, applauded my endeavours.

Bernadette Williams

The Dublin annals: authorship, text and manuscripts

The Dublin annals of Prior John de Pembridge OP and his continuator were written in medieval Latin in the fourteenth century. John de Pembridge wrote the first and major section, ceasing in 1348. The annals were then continued by the second author until 13 September 1370. These two men were Dominican friars living in St Saviour's priory of the Friars Preachers in Dublin, situated where Gandon's Four Courts building was later constructed, that is, on Inns Quay on the north side of the River Liffey. The entire work covers the period 1162–1370 but all entries up to $c.1315$ are derived from earlier writers and consequently not quite as reliable as entries of which the principal author Pembridge might be assumed to have personal knowledge (although even the act of selecting from, omitting from, and manipulating earlier sources can reveal something of the interests and biases of the annalist and thus have value).

This important historical source has been known variously as, the 'annals of Ireland', the 'Laud annals', the 'St Mary's annals', and 'Pembridge's annals.' From these confusing and contradictory titles alone, it is evident that our annals have had a chequered past and a new analysis and edition is long overdue. Sadly, the original manuscript written by Pembridge and his continuator is no longer extant but, very fortunately, two medieval copies survive: one a late fourteenth-century copy in Trinity College Dublin, Trinity MS 583 (*hereafter* **T**) and the other an early fifteenth-century copy in the Bodleian Library, Oxford, Laud Miscellaneous MS 526 (*hereafter* **L**). Hence we can say that, although only two copies survive, there were actually four persons involved in what has been passed down to us:

i) John Pembridge, prior of the Dublin Dominicans ($c.1329$–$c.1333$ and $c.1341$–$c.1343$): responsible for entries between 1162 and 1347.
ii) The Dublin Dominican continuator: responsible for entries between 1348 and 1370.
iii) The copyist of **T**: internal evidence indicates that he too was a Dublin Dominican.
iv) The copyist of **L**, who declared that he produced his copy for the Preston family (who later procured the title Viscount Gormanston).

THE PRIMACY OF THE TRINITY COPY (T)

I have accepted the Trinity copy (T) as the prime source and noted the variances in the Laud copy (L). This editorial decision was justified by detailed analysis of both manuscripts (discussed more fully below) in order to arrive at the closest version of the original text. On palaeographical evidence alone, T is the earlier copy, and, what is more, it is clear that the copyist of T worked directly from the original manuscript. As far back as 1922 the significance of T was noted, Olive Armstrong astutely observing:

> Pembridge is admittedly the highest authority among Anglo-Norman annalists. It is not right that he should be known to us only through a transcript made for Viscount Gormanston (Laud 526) when we have the exemplar from which it was made in perfect preservation, clearly written with coloured and decorated capitals, among the muniments of our own University. The script of the TCD MS may be compared with that of the Bodleian MS ... from which it would appear that the TCD MS is of an earlier date.[1]

Armstrong was correct in most respects, but not in her belief that L was a transcript of T because internal evidence indicates that it too was copied independently from the original. This being so, we know that we have the best possible medieval version of these annals.

Although there is no title at the beginning of either copy, the decoration in T makes it quite clear that the year 1162, for whatever reason, is the beginning of the annals (Fig. 1). Both copies begin and end with the same year, namely 1162 and 1370. Both also have the same number of years missing which are as follows: 1163, 1164, 1165, 1173, 1181, 1182, 1184, 1188, 1192, 1196, 1197, 1201, 1207, 1209, 1212, 1214, 1215, 1216, 1217, 1218, 1221, 1222, 1223, 1226–9, 1232, 1333, 1235–40, 1242, 1244, 1245, 1247, 1249, 1252, 1253, 1254, 1256, 1257, 1258, 1263, 1265, 1266, 1288, 1324, 1334, 1335, 1336, 1344, 1353, 1354, 1363, 1366. These missing years are not indicated on the manuscript in either T or L as there is no interruption in the flow of the written account and no gaps are left on the page. Therefore, these years were not in the original manuscript. This is an additional corroboration that both copies are fundamentally the same.

However, one major and immensely important difference is that the name of the author, Pembridge, the man who was responsible for the first and by far the largest section of the work (1162–1347), is only to be found in T where there is a very distinctive notice, with first letter rubricated, stating 'hyc finitur cronica Pembrig' at the end of the year 1347 (Fig. 3). Crucially, after this notice, T begins a new page while L, without that vital information, just continues without any break, both copies ceasing in 1370 (Fig. 5).

1 Olive Armstrong, *Edward Bruce's invasion of Ireland* (London, 1923), pp 73–4 fn. 1.

THE ANNALS' DOMINICAN PROVENANCE

These are Dominican annals, the two authors and at least one of the two copyists being members of that order. Having said that, they are not concerned in any way with describing or discussing the Dominican order as such; there is, for example, no mention of the Dublin priors or any members of the priory,[2] although we do hear about gifts made to it by eminent and wealthy Dubliners.

The Dominican order (officially the order of Friars Preachers, and often known as Black Friars) was founded by the Spanish Augustinian Dominic de Guzman in the context of attempts to halt the rapid growth of the Cathar heresy in southern France in the early decades of the thirteenth century.[3] From the beginning, study was at the core of the Dominican life, Dominic vigorously seeking to attract the best academic minds to his new order.[4] The early *Constitutions* provided that select students be sent to the great university centres and that every priory should have a brother appointed as *lector* to continue the education of the brethren throughout their lives.[5] Such houses required a good library.[6] It is not surprising therefore that our annals report the establishment of a university in Dublin in 1320 with a real sense of gravitas, beginning with very momentous opening words, 'In the time of Pope John XXII and of the Lord

---

2 It is the same with Clyn. Apart from Clyn's personal information, which only comes in 1348, a cursory reading of the annals does not immediately result in the overwhelming recognition of it as the work of a Franciscan: *AClyn*. Antonia Gransden also notes that the fourteenth-century chronicler of the Franciscans of Lynn mentions his own house only once and Chris Given-Wilson notes that it is surprising 'how little some of these chronicles tell us about religious life in their monasteries': Antonia Gransden, 'A fourteenth-century chronicle from the Grey Friars at Lynn', *EHR*, 72 (1957), 273, 278; Given-Wilson, *Chronicles*, p. 95.
3 Hinnebusch, *Dominican order*; idem, *English friars preachers*; Ernest Barker, *The Dominican order and convocation: a study of the growth of representation in the church in the thirteenth century* (Oxford, 1913); Bede Jarrett, *The English Dominicans* (New York, 1921); Röhrkasten, *Mendicant London*; for Dominican Ireland, see Thomas Burke, *Hibernia Dominicana; sive, historia provinciae Hiberniae Ordinis Praedicatorum* (Farnborough, 1970); M.H. MacInerny, *A history of the Irish Dominicans*, vi, *Irish Dominican bishops, 1224–1307* (Dublin, 1916); B. O'Sullivan OP, *Medieval Irish Dominican studies*, ed. Hugh Fenning OP (Dublin, 2009). For a general overview, see Colmán Ó Clabaigh OSB, *The friars in Ireland, 1224–1540* (Dublin, 2012).
4 Hinnebusch, *Dominican order*, ch. 1. 'He had a consuming zeal for study', Barker, *The Dominican order and convocation*, p. 10. See also, Michèle Mulchahey, *'First the bow is bent in study ...': Dominican education before 1350* (Toronto, 1998); M. O'Carroll, 'The educational organization of the Dominicans in England and Wales, 1221–1348: a multi-disciplinary approach', *AFP*, 50 (1980), 23–62.   5 K.W. Humphreys, *The book provisions of the medieval friars* (Amsterdam, 1964), p. 18 n1; Tugwell, 'The evolution of Dominican structures of government, III', *AFP*, 71 (2001), 30; Hinnebusch, *Dominican order*, p. 86; Hinnebusch, *English friars preachers*, p. 9; Little, 'Educational organization of mendicant friars in England (Dominicans and Franciscans)', *TRHS*, new ser. 8 (1894), 50–63; Mulchahey, *'First the bow is bent in study'*, p. 39.   6 For the library regulations of the Dominicans, see K.W. Humphreys, *The book provisions of the medieval friars* (Amsterdam, 1964), pp 18–45; Hinnebusch, *English friars preachers*, pp 180–6.

Edward, son of King E. (this Edward was the 25th king after the coming of St Augustine to England), and also under Alexander Bicknor, then the said archbishop of Dublin, the Dublin citizens began the university'. It is only from our annals that we learn the names of the four founding teachers at the newly instituted university, two of whom were Dominican (Friars William de Hardits and Edmund de Kermerdyn).[7]

We are very fortunate in having unequivocal contemporary evidence of the date that the Dominican order entered Ireland. The thirteenth-century Franciscan Annals of Multyfarnham records 1224 as the year of their arrival, as does the Franciscan Kilkenny Chronicle,[8] the *Annales Dominicani de Roscoman*,[9] and the Gaelic Annals of Ulster.[10] However, nowhere in any of these sources is there any mention of where the friars preachers first settled in Ireland, although it is most likely that their first convent was in Dublin.[11] As to who initiated the Dublin foundation, we cannot say.[12] Tantalizingly, in the eighteenth-century Walter Harris refers to 'the registry of the Dominicans of Dublin', but sadly it is no longer extant, and his words are the only reference to the document.[13] Our

---

7 For the identification of Friar Edmund de Kermerdyn as a Dominican, see *The whole works of Sir James Ware, vol. II, Antiquities and writers*, ed. Walter Harris (Dublin, 1745), p. 244; Fitzmaurice and Little, *Franciscan province of Ire.*, p. 108 fn. 1. 8 *AMultyfarnham*, p. 150; *Kilkenny chronicle*, p. 331. 9 *Annales Dominicani de Roscoman*, Benjamin Hazard and Kenneth W. Nicholls (eds), CELT (2012). 10 This is most significant as it is the only medieval Gaelic annals to record the arrival in Ireland; the year 1224 is also found in extracts from annals of St Mary's made by Sir James Ware (*CStM*, ii, p. 288), and in two other seventeenth-century transcripts containing notes from two Dominican medieval Latin annals which sadly are no longer extant (the annals of Ross, not to be confused with the Franciscan annals of Ross, and the annals of Trim: TCD MS 579/2 ff 343–5; Bodl. Rawlinson B 484; Clarendon MS BL Add 4789 ff 206v–207v). Williams, 'The arrival of the Dominicans in Ireland in 1224', pp 157–8. The transcripts are only very brief, *Chronicle of Ross*, Bodl. MS Rawl. B 479, ff 68r–69r; this transcript has as its title *Annales*, but Ware appended this note, *Anonymi Hibernici forte ord fratrum Praedicatorum Ross* in Bodl. Rawlinson B 484; Clarendon MS BM Add 4789 ff 206v–207v. The reason for assigning the annals to Ross is clearly the entry in 1267 which states that the Dominicans entered Ross and gives the date 13 Kal November (68v). This identification is strengthened by an entry in 1293 concerning Thomastown in Ossory (68v). From the beginning of the annal in the year 184 to 1259, every entry present is, in the great majority of the cases, virtually identical with the entries in the Annals of Multyfarnham and this might account for the entry concerning the arrival of the Dominicans in Ireland, *AMultyfarnham* p. 150; The Chronicle of Trim, BL MS Add 4789, ff 206v–207v; this transcript has as its title *Annal Coenob Dominic Trim* and *Chron cuiusdam fratris ord Praedicatorum*. The chronicle is preceded by the list of thirteenth-century Dominican foundation dates ending with Kilmallock in 1291 and a list of Dominican chapters (of the Irish vicariate) ending in 1347 (f. 206r). 11 B. Williams, 'The arrival of the Dominicans in Ireland in 1224 and the question of Dublin and Drogheda: the sources re-examined' in Seán Duffy (ed.), *Medieval Dublin, XIII* (Dublin, 2013), pp 150–82. 12 On this, see Williams, 'The arrival of the Dominicans in Ireland in 1224', pp 169–77. 13 Harris, *Dublin*, p. 258. Hugh Fenning, OP, 'Irish material in the registers of the Dominican masters general (1390–1649), *AFP*, 39 (1969), 251. The case is similar in England. Also as a mendicant order, the Dominicans did not normally own property

only extant Dublin Dominican medieval source are the annals presented in this volume, which have only incidental comments about the Dublin priory. Hugh Fenning discovered a manuscript in Rome, albeit from 1647, which states *a civibus fundatus*,[14] and Ambrose Coleman in 1902, using a seventeenth-century manuscript, also says that the Dublin convent and church were built by the citizens of Dublin.[15] The consensus of historical opinion, especially by the seventeenth-century historians, is that the Cistercian abbey of St Mary gave the Dominicans their site on the north bank of river Liffey on which they built St Saviour's priory.[16]

The location directly opposite the Liffey from Dublin with a bridge connecting it with the walled city meant that anyone who wanted to leave Dublin and go to Oxmantown, to Meath, to Ulster or to the northwest had to cross the bridge and pass the priory. There can be little doubt that important messengers and the great and lesser magnates would call in to the priory to pay their respects, either coming or going, and accordingly impart news. The location ensured that the whole of Dublin, situated on the high ground across the water, was in full view. This was made noticeably clear in 1337 by the primary author John Pembridge when he related the incident of the seven partridges who left the open field and settled on the top of the brew house belonging to the canons of Holy Trinity in Christ Church: Pembridge tells how the Dubliners came running out and wondered at so strange a sight, and one can almost visualize the friars coming out of their priory to watch what was going on just across the river. Then follows the fascinating human insight: some boys caught two alive and killed a third and the rest flew off and escaped over the fields. This was so strange that Pembridge declares that he cannot tell what it portends. This entry follows a gap of three years; perhaps Pembridge had been away attending chapter meetings and then came back to this strange sight.

outside their priories, and, consequently, at their dissolution they had very few, if any, title deeds. The Dominicans generally held the property rights to their own priory: Röhrkasten, *Mendicant London*, p. 239. Before the dissolution, each convent had records of its own, as for instance, the *obituaria*, the calendar for the commemoration of the obits of its former members and friends but only one *obituaria* has survived in England, that of Guildford. The *obituaria* were compiled to serve as calendars for the commemoration of the obits of its former members and friends. Only one has survived A.B. Emden, *A survey of Dominican in England based on the ordination lists in episcopal registers (1268 to 1538)* (Rome, 1967) pp 15–16. The chattels were worth £37 8s. 6d., and there is also mention of 'a chalice, parcell of the goods and chattels pertaining to the late house of friars preachers of Dublin; for that chalice was given and demised to the late prior of that house for celebrating mass in the chapel of Blessed Mary at the foot of Dublin Bridge': C. McNeill (ed.), 'Accounts of sums realized by sales of chattels of some suppressed Irish monasteries', *JRSAI*, 52 (1922), 23, 26.   14 This list also states that Galway Waterford, Cashel, Kilmallock and Drogheda were also *a civibus fundatus*: Hugh Fenning OP, 'Founders of Irish Dominican friaries: an unpublished list of *c.*1647', *Collectanea Hibernica*, 44/5 (2002–3), 59, 60, 62.   15 *Epilogus Chronologicus*, O'Heyne and Coleman, p. 23.   16 See Williams, 'The arrival of the Dominicans in Ireland in 1224', pp 174–7.

Beyond Christ Church, almost within sight of the priory, stood Dublin Castle and it is from there that, on Saturday 6 January 1329, Pembridge tells us Domhnall Mac Murchadha (MacMurrough), the king of Leinster, escaped by a rope that Adam Naungle brought to him; Adam was later drawn and hanged. Pembridge does not mention the similar attempt to escape by William de Bermingham on 2 July 1332 and perhaps the explanation lies in the support given by the de Berminghams for the Dominicans.[17] Hence, when reporting the execution of William de Bermingham in 1332, Pembridge declares 'William [was] a noble knight, among thousands of knights, the most noble and best in military skill. Alas, alas, ah grief! Who recalling his death is able to contain tears?' Not surprisingly we hear that he was buried in Dublin 'among the friars preachers'.

In 1308 John le Decer, mayor of the city of Dublin, built the marble cistern which was to supply water to the city. He also gave active support to the Dominicans of Saviour's in Dublin, providing a stone buttress in the church and an altar stone for the high altar together with its ornaments, and both acts of patronage are recorded in these annals. Apart from le Decer, other Dominican benefactors also feature prominently. There are numerous records of burials in Dominican priories and, interestingly, these are usually accompanied by precise dating. The first burial reported is that of Theobald Butler, who died in Arklow Castle on 26 September in 1285, and we are informed that he was buried in the Dominican priory at Arklow, which Butler himself had founded.[18] There are another nineteen such notices of burials scattered throughout. Geoffrey de Geneville, lord of Meath (who retired to the Dominican friary of Trim), and his family, are featured prominently: we hear of Geoffrey's marriage, his return from the Holy Land, his period as justiciar, the death of his wife Matilda in 1304,[19] and his death and burial in that priory in 1314. The death of Nicholas de Geneville, son and heir of Simon de Geneville, is mentioned in 1324, as is his subsequent burial among the Dominicans of Trim. The death of Joanna fitz Leones, wife of Simon de Geneville, is also reported, as is the burial in the convent of the Dominicans at Trim in 1347. The le Poers were important benefactors and, when fire burned the Dominican church on 12 June 1304, we are told that on the 2 February following, Eustace le Poer laid the first stone of the choir of the Dominicans. Consequently, the Dominicans proved very loyal to the le Poers. In 1328 when Arnold le Poer was in disgrace and died in Dublin Castle, he lay with the Dominicans without burial: they were evidently willing to take his body and hold it even though he was subject to ecclesiastical censure.

---

17 The de Berminghams co-founded Athenry: *Regestum monasterii fratrum praedicatorum de Athenry* (ed.), Ambrose Coleman, *Archiv. Hib.*, 1 (1912), 201–21.   18 'Ware tells us that he was bury'd there, and that his statue cut in stone was to be seen on his tomb', *Monasticon Hibernicum*, p. 216.   19 There is, however, a problem about the year of her death as it is mentioned twice in the annals (1302 and 1304). This was before Geoffrey de Geneville became a friar in Trim in 1308. Geoffrey de Geneville is assumed by some to be the founder of Trim

Other Dominican benefactors also feature prominently in these annals, for example the de Berminghams are praised by both Pembridge and his continuator. Meiler de Bermingham had founded Athenry priory, and it was his daughter Basilia who forced her husband Jordan de Exonia to oust the friars minor from Strade (Co. Mayo) and replace them with the friars preachers.[20] In 1308 in these annals Peter de Bermingham is pronounced the noble vanquisher of the Irish. In 1332 William de Bermingham's execution was greeted with the sad lament 'Alas, alas, ah grief! Who recalling his death is able to contain tears?'. He was described by Pembridge as most renowned and excellent in arms. After such partisanship we are not surprised to learn that William de Bermingham was buried in St Saviour's Dominican church in Dublin. The death of Walter de Bermingham in 1349 is accompanied by the comment that he was the best justiciar Ireland ever had. These annals also tell us that Margaret de Bermingham, wife of Robert Preston, was buried with the friars preachers in Drogheda in 1361. She is one of the very few women whose burial is noted in the annals; two of the others are de Geneville women. Under the year 1316, Pembridge has a long tale about the battle of Athenry where John Husse decapitated Ó Ceallaigh and two others and took their heads to Richard de Bermingham, for which action he was then knighted and given lands, 'as he well deserved'. Why this story is included is not clear; it is either that it shows a de Bermingham rewarding loyal service, or it may be that John Husse was related to the Dublin Husse family and as such was of interest to a Dublin chronicler.[21] When Thomas Butler died in 1329 Pembridge considers it a disaster for Ireland and furthermore relates that his body, brought to Dublin, was placed with the Dominicans until he was carried by the citizens with great honour and buried in the Dominican cemetery, after which his wife held a feast that same day.

One final indication of the text's Dominican provenance is the fact that, the Dominicans having been founded to combat the Albigensian heresy, Pembridge was naturally interested in any case of heresy coming to his ears. Pembridge's first mention of heresy is in 1287 where he includes in his annals a long entry about the king of Hungary to the effect that he apostatized, retribution followed and the Christian Hungarians were victorious and then crowned the king's son while the 'apostate king' went off with the Saracens.[22] While this entry is clearly historically inaccurate and distorted, the sentiment is quite clear: heresy never triumphs.[23] Much closer to home was the trial of the Templars.[24] The Dominican

but, if he had founded Trim, one would expect that it would be mentioned and it is not mentioned by Thomas Case, nor by the Ware fragment, nor by the Rome document (*CStM*, ii, p 281, *CStM*, ii, p. 293). **20** '*Regestum de Athenry*', pp 204–5. Paul Mohr, 'The de Berminghams, barons of Athenry: a suggested outline lineage from first to last', *Journal of the Galway Archaeological and Historical Society*, 63 (2011), 43–56. **21** We do know that as early as *c*.1185, Hugh Hose had land which was 'situate between the stone gate near Dublin bridge

Pembridge has it that the Templars 'in parts beyond the sea, having been condemned of certain heresies, as was said, were seized and imprisoned by papal mandate'. England and Ireland followed suit,[25] and Pembridge connects the Templar crisis with an omen, stating that 'on Thursday the day after St Lucy, virgin (Thursday 14 December 1312), in the sixth year of King Edward there was seen an astonishing moon of different colours in which [day] it was decided that the order of Templars should be abolished forever'.[26] It is unusual for Pembridge to include the regnal year; he only does so at very important moments such as the foundation of the university at Dublin.

As with the Templars, one cannot talk about accusations of heresy in this period without mentioning the situation in Kilkenny and the Kyteler case. In 1324, Richard Ledrede, bishop of Ossory, accused Alice Kyteler and her associates of sorcery and heresy. Naturally, Pembridge is interested in the case, but he is reporting it from a physical distance and from a year later, so he has a far more sensational twist to it than the Kilkenny-based chronicler Clyn. His report may well have been imported into his annals from another source because, unusually for these annals, there are two separate entries for the year 1325, the second of which is given entirely to the Kyteler affair. This entry has extra

on the side of the water towards Meath ... towards Castleknock' (*Christ church: deeds*, p. 124; Lawlor, 'Liber Niger', 50). It is likely that he or his family were Dominican benefactors as in 1418 a Matthew Husse, baron of Galtrim, is named as a great benefactor of Trim. The foundation 'is attributed to Baron Galtrim, whose family name is Hussey', but also to Geneville, *Epilogus Chronologicus*, O'Heyne and Coleman, p. 41. In 1418 Matthew Hussey, baron of Galtrim, was buried at Trim friary: *Epilogus Chronologicus*, O'Heyne and Coleman (Coleman), p. 32; however, Coleman erroneously gives his reference as Pembridge. Burke, *Hibernia Dominicana*, p. 264.   22 In June 1286, Ladislas held a diet at Rákos: Z.J. Kosztolnyik, *Hungary in the thirteenth century* (New York, 1996), p. 292.   23 Upon the murder of Ladislas IV, the barons of the realm made Andrew ('of Venice'), a nephew of Ladislas IV, king. His widow Izabella died as a member of the order of St Dominic in 1304: Kosztolnyik, *Hungary in the thirteenth century*, p. 296. After the murder of Ladislas, who died childless, the last of the Árpád dynasty, Andrew III, grandson of Andrew II, became king: Pál Engel, *The realm of St Stephen: A history of medieval Hungary, 895–1526* (London, 2001), p. 110.   24 After the justiciar John Wogan received the order for the suppression in Ireland, they were seized and imprisoned but not treated with undue harshness. Lawlor, 'Liber Niger', 48.   25 Malcolm Barber, *The trial of the Templars* (Cambridge, 1978); Malcolm Barber, 'Propaganda in the Middle Ages: the charges against the Templars', *Nottingham Medieval Studies*, 17 (1973), 42–57. In January 1308 Edward II ordered the seizure of all Templars in England, Scotland and Ireland: Gearóid Mac Niocaill (ed.), 'Documents relating to the suppression of the Templars in Ireland', *AH*, 24 (1967), 193–226. Richard de Babylin, Hugh de St Leger and Philip de Slane, lector of the order of preachers in Dublin were conducting trial; Philip de Slane was 'the earliest known instance we have of an unofficial councillor who received a fee' (*Ir. parl.*, pp 30); 'five marks yearly for life', *CCR, 1318–1323*, p. 161. There is a claim that in 1312 a John de Slane was vicar general of the Dominicans in Ireland, but the reference is to Pembridge, which is incorrect: Mervyn Archdall, *Monasticon Hibernicum*, vol. ii (Dublin, 1876), p. 70.   26 The date, 14 Dec. 1312, is about nine months after the bull *Vox in excelso* suppressed the order.

information about Kyteler not to be found in either Clyn's annals or in Bishop Ledrede's contemporary *Narrative*, no doubt the result of rumours and exaggerations reaching Dublin, Pembridge being inclined to believe tall tales.[27]

THE FIRST AUTHOR: FRIAR JOHN DE PEMBRIDGE OP

Only in T is it obvious that these annals are the work of two individuals and that the first writer was named Pembridge. This note by the copyist adds credence to the premise that he was also a member of the Dublin Dominican priory dedicated to St Saviour. The note was probably written by the Dominican continuator because, if it were in the original manuscript, one would expect this most important notice to have been copied in L, which does not identify the primary author nor indeed the fact that there were two authors, Pembridge and his continuator.

Although the name Pembridge had been linked to the annals for centuries, no individual of that name was every identified in a contemporary source until the late Philomena Connolly discovered a Friar John de Pembridge who was prior of the Dominicans in Dublin $c.1329$–$c.1333$ and $c.1341$–$c.1343$.[28] His career as prior was contemporaneous with the composition of the Dublin annals by a hitherto-unknown 'Pembridge', making the identification of the Dominican annalist with this John de Pembridge almost certain. It is necessary to emphasize the certainty of this identification because of earlier antiquarian confusion about the first name of the author.[29] The only other Pembridge whose name occurs in connection with Ireland was of later date when, in 1372, a Richard Pembridge, one of the first knights of the garter, refused the offer of the lieutenancy of Ireland, and never did come to the country.[30] The surname Pembridge, otherwise unknown in medieval Ireland, is associated with the Welsh Marches, the Pembridge family having been established in Herefordshire from the reign of Stephen. There is a Pembridge Castle just north of Welsh Newton,

---

[27] Only in this Pembridge report do we find the information that Alice put ointment on a stick called a *coultree* which she could then ride on throughout the world. And the statement, 'she would clean out the neighbourhood of Kilkenny between compline and the curfew-bell and, sweeping the filth all the way up to the house of William Outlawe her son and swearing an oath, she said that all the prosperity of Kilkenny would come to this house'; this later became the doggerel, 'Unto the house of William my son – Hie all the wealth of Kilkenny town'. If Ledrede had this probably spurious information it would have been in his *Narrative* (*A contemporary narrative of the proceedings against Dame Alice Kyteler, prosecuted for sorcery in 1324, by Richard de Ledrede, bishop of Ossory*, ed. Thomas Wright (London, 1843), pp 179, 262–4). It is far more likely to be just an example of how quickly rumour can add to and distort truth. [28] These are the dates noted but he could have been the prior from $c.1329$–43 at least, see *IExP*, pp 337, 342, 345, 351, 357, 408. [29] See below p. 47. [30] Otway-Ruthven, 'Chief

Herefordshire, and there is a place-name Pembridge just on the English side of the Welsh border between Kington and Leominster.[31] Although many of the English who arrived in Ireland from the twelfth century came from this general area, it is impossible, on the available evidence, to determine whether a Pembridge family member came to Ireland in the entourage of any great English magnate. In the early twelfth century, the manor of Pembridge was in the hands of William de Braose. The de Braose family were overlords to the Pembridge family and remained so until the de Braose heiress married Roger Mortimer of Wigmore in 1247 at which point the manor of Pembridge passed to the Mortimer family.[32] But to link our author John de Pembridge with the Mortimer family, so prominent in Ireland at the time of composition of his annals, would be entirely conjectural: there is no indication in his annals that Pembridge was familiar with that area in England, or indeed any area in England (though he does mention both de Braoses and Mortimers) and he shows little knowledge of or interest in any country other than Ireland.

That John de Pembridge was well educated is beyond question. Perhaps Pembridge was the librarian before becoming prior.[33] Whether he was educated under the auspices of his own priory or elsewhere is impossible to determine. From the inception of the order, it had been decreed that every Dominican province should have a college or convent for the education of youth.[34] When considering a possible university that Pembridge might have attended, the short-lived university (*universitas*)[35] at Dublin cannot be ignored as Pembridge, as we have seen, gave the notification of that foundation a particular emphasis in his annals. The movement for the establishment of a university in Ireland was launched in the early fourteenth century under the auspices of Alexander Bicknor, archbishop of Dublin, so that students should not be subjected to the risk of a sea crossing in order to gain their education.[36] Sir James Ware (1594–1666) claims that the first bull was dated 13 July 1311.[37] Bicknor looked to the existing theological schools of the Dominicans and Franciscans in Dublin to provide the first four masters; these were a Dominican, a Franciscan, the dean of St Patrick's cathedral and Edmund de Kermerdyn, who has also been

---

governors', p. 86. 31 Coincidentally, there was a Dominican priory in Hereford since the mid-1240s: Peter Brinkley, 'John Bromyard and the Hereford Dominicans' in Jan Willem Drijvers and Alasdair A. MacDonald (eds), *Centres of learning: learning and location in pre-modern Europe and the near East* (Leiden, 1995), pp 255–64. 32 Herbert Wood, 'The muniments of Edmund de Mortimer, third earl of March', *PRIA*, 40C (1932), 325. 33 The office of librarian was created by 1246: K.W. Humphreys, *The book provisions of the medieval friars* (Amsterdam, 1964), pp 31–2, 33, 136. 34 For the estimated number (3,000) of Dominican students in the fourteenth century, see Humphreys, *The book provisions of the medieval friars*, p. 19 n7. 35 Clyn also uses the word *universitas*: *AClyn*, p. 173. 36 Aubrey Gwynn, 'The medieval university of St Patrick's, Dublin', *Studies*, 27 (1938), 199–212, 437–54; Fergal McGrath, *Education in ancient and medieval Ireland* (Dublin, 1979), pp 216–19. 37 *The whole works of Sir James Ware, vol. II, Antiquities*, ed. Walter Harris (Dublin, 1745), p. 242.

identified as a Dominican.³⁸ Despite the fact that it never prospered, there is some suggestion that, for a period of time, qualifications were conferred,³⁹ but the university appears to have withered away by 1348 when the prior of the Augustinian order stated that 'there is no university or place of study of arts or theology in Ireland'.⁴⁰ Of course, that might reflect irritation at the lack of Augustinian involvement in the Dublin university but the Franciscan friar John Clyn also disparaged it.⁴¹ There is a suggestion that another university was founded in Ireland in 1358,⁴² but it is difficult to imagine that the Dominican continuator would not note this event, if indeed it happened, especially as he had Pembridge's manuscript in front of him and would have been familiar with the entry concerning the 1320 Dublin university. One indication, perhaps, that Pembridge attended this new university at Dublin is the fact that, had he attended a university outside Ireland, one would expect hints of this in the annals, whereas there are none.

The question now arises as to Pembridge's age and how this can be estimated. The importance of the position of prior of Dublin would clearly have required someone of a certain seniority. Chris Given-Wilson states that a characteristic of late medieval chroniclers is that 'they nearly all seem to have been either middle-aged or elderly' and he states that he cannot point with confidence to any chronicle written by a young man in fourteenth-century England.⁴³ But in fact, we have an exception to that rule in Ireland. In 1270 the Franciscan, Stephen de Exonia, was writing the Annals of Multyfarnham when he was aged only twenty-two.⁴⁴ The Kilkenny Franciscan chronicler, Friar John Clyn, has a surmised age of about 50 years when he wrote his annals.⁴⁵ In order to attempt to calculate Pembridge's age, an entry for 1308 is important. In this year we are informed that John le Decer fed the friars at his table on the sixth day or 'so the elders had told the juniors'. Therefore, one could postulate that Pembridge was not in the priory in 1308. We know that he was prior in Dublin c. 1329 and we can extrapolate backwards. If we take a possible date of birth as c. 1296, then entry to the order in 1314, becoming a priest by 1321 and getting a degree by 1329 at the point at which he became prior, this is certainly feasible, albeit entirely conjectural.⁴⁶ Therefore he could have been in his late teens or early twenties in the Dublin priory during the Bruce invasion. In that case some information about that event would be his

---

38 See E.B Fitzmaurice, and A.G. Little, *Materials for the history of the Franciscan province of Ireland, 1230–1450* (Manchester, 1920), p. 108, n. 1; James Ware, *The antiquities and history of Ireland* (Dublin, 1705), p. 244.   **39** McGrath, *Education in ancient and medieval Ireland*, pp 217–18.   **40** Philomena Connolly (ed.), 'Irish material in the class of chancery warrants series I (C81), in the Public Record Office, London', *AH*, 36 (1995), 158.   **41** *AClyn*, p. 172.   **42** Linne R. Mooney, 'An English record of the founding of a university in Dublin in 1358', *IHS*, 28:111 (1993), 225–7;   *FL*, p.109.   **43** Given-Wilson, *Chronicles*, pp 61–2.   **44** *AMultyfarnham* pp 56–7.   **45** *AClyn*, p. 57.   **46** The usual practice was to become a priest at age twenty-five and to gain a degree at age thirty-three to thirty-seven: A.B. Emden, *A survey of Dominicans in England based on the ordination lists in episcopal registers (1268–1538)*

own personal knowledge, supplemented by the memory of the older friars. From the years *c.* 1330, when he was prior, he might have been in his mid-to-late thirties and it is noticeable that from that time the given dates in the annals have both a day and month rather than just a feast day.

THE SECOND AUTHOR: PEMBRIDGE'S ANONYMOUS CONTINUATOR

The break in authorship after 1347 is very apparent. Up to and including the year 1347, each year was only identified by the words *Anno domini* followed by the year number in Roman numerals. But in 1348, for the first time, the year is additionally identified by the regnal year, for example, the twenty-second year of the reign of King Edward III (*et anno xxii R. R. E. tertii*). Furthermore, when the continuator began with the year 1348, he stated 'as previously written', indicating that he had the earlier section of the annals before him.

This second section of the annals, which covers the years 1348 to 1370, was clearly also written by a Dominican friar as the nature of the annals is mendicant in tone. The *raison d'être* of the Dominican order was, as noted, preaching and combating heresy and hence didactic comments occur in these annals, and do so in both the section written by Pembridge and that by his continuator. For example, Pembridge himself, under the year 1317, decries the actions of the men of Ulster because they had eaten flesh in Lent, the result being that such tribulation by way of famine and other disasters came upon them that they ate each other and here appeared the vengeance of God. In 1318, after the notice that Roger Mortimer had sailed to England without paying for the food he had taken from Dublin to the value of £1,000, Pembridge reports that, by the mercy of God, around the feast of St James (25 July), new bread was made with new corn, a thing that had seldom been seen before in Ireland, a sign of God's tender mercy. And Pembridge sees the hand of God too in the death of the unpopular justiciar Ralph Ufford on 9 April 1346. But this kind of sentiment carries through to the section written by his continuator, never more so than in his account of Richard fitzRalph, archbishop of Armagh, a man renowned for his opposition to the mendicant orders:[47] in 1357, the report is that 'a great controversy began between Master Richard fitz Ralph, archbishop of Armagh and the four orders of mendicants; but finally they [the friars] prevailed and silence was imposed on Armagh by the pope.'[48] It was while pursuing his suit against the mendicants

---

(Rome, 1967), p. 22.   **47** Katherine Walsh, *A fourteenth century scholar and primate: Richard FitzRalph in Oxford, Avignon and Armagh* (Oxford, 1981).   **48** He had preached a sermon at the Dominican General Chapter at Avignon in 1342: Michael Dunne and Simon Nolan (eds) *Richard FitzRalph: his life, times and thought* (Dublin, 2013); Michael Dunne, 'Richard FitzRalph of Dundalk (*c.*1300–1360) and the new world', *Archivium Hibernicum*, 58 (2004), 243–58; Janet Coleman, 'FitzRalph's antimendicant '*proposicio*' (1350) and the politics of the

that the archbishop died at Avignon in 1360; the continuator reports this and then informs us that his bones were conveyed to Ireland by Stephen, bishop of Meath, for burial in the parish church of St Nicholas, Dundalk, where he was born, after which statement our mendicant annalist adds the dismissive rider, 'but it is doubted whether they were his bones or those of some other man'.

Internal evidence proves unquestionably that the annals remained in Dublin Dominican hands after Pembridge ceased writing. One instance of Dublin Dominican interest is the report in 1351 of the death of Kendrick Sherman, formerly mayor of Dublin, accompanied by the information that he was buried under the Dublin Dominicans' campanile, which we are told he erected. Additionally, we are informed that Sherman glazed the window in the chapter choir and roofed the church. A decade later in 1361 we have the report of the death of the Dublin citizen Maurice Doncreef, perhaps due to the second plague, that he had given forty pounds to glaze the church of the Dublin Dominicans and was also buried in their cemetery. Entries relating to Dominican benefactors and the references to burial notices alone would be sufficient reason for the conclusion that the continuator was a Dominican of this house. A suggestion has previously been made that the continuator was a Dominican in Trim but since burial notices and information about the Dominican priory of St Saviour's in Dublin continue to predominate after 1348, and indeed increase as regards information about the fabric of the priory, then it is unquestionably of Dublin provenance.[49] The suggestion of Trim arose from the statement in 1368 that the church of St Mary's of Trim was burnt but, in fact, this St Mary's is the Augustinian church not the Dominican church. When a Dominican church is mentioned by either Pembridge, or indeed the continuator, the identification is quite clear: the phrases used are *always* the 'church of the friars preachers', 'the church of the order of preachers', 'cemetery of the preachers', and so on.[50]

Even without the notice in T indicating the end of Pembridge's contribution to the annals, and the novel inclusion of the regnal year in the dating, an internal examination of the entries would have raised the strong probability of a break in authorship at this point. This is partly to do with the fact that Ireland during the years 1349–70 was crowded with incidents that would have interested Pembridge but did not interest his continuator, who often ignores the deaths of important ecclesiastics, the actions of chief ministers of the crown, the holding of parliaments, and instances of heresy that Pembridge would surely have noted. The Dublin Dominican continuator is, therefore, a quite different man from

---

papal court at Avignon', *Journal of Ecclesiastical History*, 35 (1984), 376–90; M.J. Haren, 'Friars as confessors: the canonist background to fourteenth-century controversy', *Peritia*, 3 (1984), 503–16.   **49** There are many flaws in this section by Gwynn, especially stating that the continuator was responsible for 1341–5: A. Gwynn, 'Some unpublished texts from the Black Book of Christ Church, Dublin', *AH,* 16 (1946), 321 fn. 22.   **50** Hugh Fenning 'The Dominicans of Trim, 1263–1682', *Ríocht na Midhe*, 3 (1963), 17.

Pembridge. The continuator was very partisan towards certain individuals and families, including the de Berminghams, and the first earl of Desmond, Maurice fitz Thomas, whose corpse, following his death in Dublin Castle in 1355, was first buried in the choir of Dublin Dominicans and then returned for re-interment with the Dominicans of Tralee. In 1360 another Geraldine, this time the fourth earl of Kildare, was of great interest to the continuator who first announced that Maurice fitz Thomas was made justiciar of Ireland, and then copied the text of his actual letters patent of office, dated 30 March 1361, something unique in these annals. An English justiciar who merits praise by the continuator is Thomas de Rokeby because he subdued the Irish and, perhaps more importantly for Dublin, 'he paid well for his provisions and said, "I wish to eat and to drink only from vessels of wood, and to pay gold and silver for food and for clothes and for wages".'[51] This was an extraordinary change of behaviour from previous justiciars, such as Roger Mortimer and later Ufford's wife (who we are told had left Ireland with vast debts unpaid). It is interesting to speculate whether the Dublin Dominicans knew of Rokeby before he came to Ireland; he had been keeper of Stirling Castle and Edinburgh both of which had Dominican priories.[52]

THE TRINITY COPY: MS 583 (T)

TCD MS 583 has several former library shelf marks on the first folio (Fig. 1).[53] The press mark E.4.6. refers to the Lyon catalogue.[54] The number 630 refers to Bernard's Catalogue of 1688 which states '583 *fol. partim membr., s. xvi. Pembrigii Annales rerum Hibernicarum ab ann. 1162 ad 1370*'.[55] It was marked as GGG.72 in the Ussher catalogue and as F.60 in the Foley catalogue and in *c.*1670 it was catalogued as N.1.20. There are 73 leaves, foliated 1 to 37. It is in a single hand throughout. It averages 26 to 33 lines to a page and each *Anno* begins a new line, but not each *Item*. It is paper with the central and outside sheets being of parchment.[56] Parchment was more often saved for a religious book, thereby

---

51 Gilbert, *Viceroys*, pp 205–6, 541–2. *CStM*, ii, p. cxxxviii fn 2; R. Frame, 'English officials and Irish chiefs in the fourteenth century', repr. in Frame, *Ire. & Brit.*, pp 249–78. 52 R. Frame, 'Thomas Rokeby, sheriff of Yorkshire, justiciar of Ireland', *Peritia*, 10 (1996), 274–96. Frame, *Lordship*, p. 295. Roland and Catherine Page, 'Blackfriars of Stirling', *Proceedings of the Society of Antiquaries of Scotland*, 126 (1996), 881–98. William Moir Bryce, *The Blackfriars of Edinburgh* (Edinburgh, 1911). 53 TCD MS GGG 7.2; n 20; f (?) 60; E-4 Rufia (?). 1166 in library .... ? 54 T.K. Abbott, *Catalogue of the manuscripts in Trinity College, Dublin* (Dublin, 1900), p. xx. 55 Abbott, *Catalogue*, p. xiii (second last col 5 up). 584 fol. chart., *c.*1600. Annals of Ireland from 1162 to 12 13 (a translation of the above.); *Chronica Hiberniae auct. Phil. Flatisbury de Johnyston juxta le Naas a.d. 1517* (formerly belonged to Tho. Messingham, President of Boncourt College, Paris.): Abbott, *Catalogue*, p. 97. 56 Extremely helpful is Raymond Clemens and Timothy Graham (eds), *Introduction to manuscript studies* (London, 2007), pp 6–8: 'Books made of a mixture of paper and parchment are not infrequently found.

giving greater permanence and prestige. Parchment was stronger than paper so when the outside sheets were parchment this would protect the more fragile inner paper sheets. In the late Middle Ages, paper was cheaper than parchment, although without the status that parchment conferred. According to Andre Blum, paper in Italy in 1382 was about one-sixth the price of parchment.[57] The paper for English manuscripts tended to come from France or the Low Counties. The paper of T has a unicorn watermark.[58] It was leather bound in 1830. Binding did not always occur immediately after the production of the document and sometimes books circulated unbound. Binding was an extra cost, and the outside leaves of parchment would in any case protect the more fragile interior. Therefore, a slightly worn outer folio of a medieval manuscript is often a sign that it circulated without bindings for a considerable period; this description fits T (Fig. 1).[59] In Kilkenny, Clyn's annals (written at about the same time as Pembridge) were placed at the end of the friary community book and perhaps this happened also in the case of our annals.[60] But if so, it is odd that Walter Harris, writing in the mid-eighteenth century, had had sight of what he calls 'the registry of the Dominicans of Dublin',[61] but never mentions the Dominican annals, suggesting that they were no longer or never had been part of the register of the priory.

The pages of T are ruled in a typical pattern (though some pages have only border ruling) and, as there are no visible pricking marks, a plummet may have been used.[62] The page format is a single column inside outer ruled lines. The copyist did not always follow the practice established by the end of the thirteenth century of beginning the text below the top ruled line.[63] There are only a few instances of catchwords written on the lower margin.[64]

T is contained in a single volume and is written in a single, very uniform, hand. There is no title but the decoration of the first letter in *Anno* 1162 demonstrates indisputably that 1162 is the beginning of the annals (Fig. 1). The

One reason for this is that paper is not as strong as parchment and could be torn or deteriorate over time'; see Rodney Thomson, 'Technology of production of the manuscript book' in Nigel Morgan and Rodney Thomson (eds), *The book in England*, vol. 2 (Cambridge, 2008), p. 78. There were firm rules governing parchment-makers and their apprentices in Dublin: Phyllis Gaffney and Yolande de Pontfarcy Sexton, '"The laws and usages of Dublin": a complete translation of *Les leys et les uages de la cite de Diveline*' in Seán Duffy (ed.), *Medieval Dublin XVII* (Dublin, 2019), p. 199. **57** Referenced by Raymond Clemens and Graham, *Introduction to manuscripts studies* (Ithaca, 2007), p. 7. **58** M.L. Colker, *Trinity College Library, Dublin: descriptive catalogue of the mediaeval and renaissance Latin manuscripts*, vol. i (London, 1991), p. 1041; Clemens and Graham, *Manuscripts studies*, pp 8, 122–3. Watermark recognition is extremely complex but, if a close match could be found, it would, in theory, give an approximate date of manufacture. The acknowledged expert source is C.M. Briquet, *Les Filigranes* (1907, repr. Amsterdam, 1968). **59** Clemens and Graham, *Manuscripts studies*, pp 51–3. **60** *AClyn*, p. 20. **61** Harris, *Dublin*, p. 258. **62** Clemens and Graham, *Manuscripts studies*, pp 15–17. **63** Ibid., p. 21. **64** T, ff 28, 56; Clemens and Graham, *Manuscripts studies*, p. 49.

final page is written in the same uniform hand demonstrating that the transcript can unquestionably be taken as a single unit and that the same copyist copied both Pembridge and his continuator (Fig. 5). Neil Ker emphasized that all assessments of the date of a script are no more than approximations and that, when dating a manuscript on palaeographical ground, one should factor in a possible margin of error of a quarter of a century or so.[65] Marvin Colker states that 'the hand is mid-fifteenth century secretary with some *anglicana* forms and having an Irish flavour.'[66] However, a date within the range 1370 to 1408 is far more acceptable for this transcript because of the condition of the last page (Fig. 5) recording the events of 1370. An abortive attempt, in a later hand and different ink, to add entries relating to 1408 which were then crossed out follows. The bottom of the final folio of the manuscript folio is also torn.

The copyist's Dominican provenance

The copy of Pembridge in T has all the appearance of being copied by a Dominican in the Dublin priory of St Saviour. It is perfectly logical to assume that the copyist is a Dominican as all the internal evidence indicates that he was a man of religion. This claim is borne out by the presence of the letters *IHC* (*iesus christus*) which are present at the top of the first folio and throughout the work as an invocation to God to bless the work. The thirty-seven examples of the Christogram symbol are mostly at the top of a page, but in two instances they are to be found three times on one page (top, middle and last line). Dr Colmán Ó Clabaigh OSB has suggested that these may indicate a new day's work and indeed the erratic nature of the placing of *IHC* makes this a very logical proposition.[67] As a Dominican friar, the copyist would not necessarily have a whole day of uninterrupted time to write as he would have pastoral care to take into consideration.[68] Also present is the word *Maria*.[69] The words *Ave Maria gratia plena* together with *IHC* are also present on page 29. Also, in T, there is a verse in the Irish language on the bottom of page 60, in the same hand and ink, referring to the blood of Christ. Furthermore, and most importantly, the copyist knows which section was written by Pembridge, a former head of his priory, and he indicated this by a rubricated first letter of the words 'hyc finitur cronica Pembrig' at the end of the year 1347 (Fig. 3). Moreover, he emphasized this item on that page by leaving about five vacant lines around the important note. Also, in the first entry by the continuator in 1348 there is the statement *ut prius scribitur*

---

[65] Clemens and Graham, *Manuscripts studies*, p. 121. [66] Colker, *Descriptive catalogue*, p. 1041; the secretary hand emerged in late fourteenth century, Clemens and Graham, *Manuscripts studies*, p. 167. [67] See appendix, p. 275. [68] A dedicated monk would probably have copied between 150 and 200 lines of text a day: Clemens and Graham, *Manuscripts studies*, p. 23. [69] Ibid., p. 89.

The Dublin annals: authorship, text and manuscripts 17

('as previously written'), and so it is clearly evident that the continuator had the manuscript written by Pembridge in his possession as he wrote this entry. All these points support the proposition that the copyist was himself a Dominican friar in their Dublin priory.

Decorations and scribal marks

It is clear from the beginning that the copyist intended some decoration and indeed it was probably intended that rubricated capital *A*s were to be present throughout the work. Perhaps he was intending to copy what was before him in the original Pembridge manuscript. Any illustration is expensive, especially if different coloured inks are to be used although, in the case of T, apart from the first parchment folio, the only extra ink used is red. It has been stated that, in the early days of the Dominican order, books were to be plain and not highly ornamented.[70] Throughout the manuscript the initial letter *A* of *Anno* is either over one or two lines.[71] On the first folio, the first capital *A* is larger than the rest and is the only letter *A* to be decorated with two colours, blue and red, and on that first page the sequence of decoration of the *A* of *Anno* that follows is red, blue, red, red, followed by a small green *A* and then lastly a larger green *A* — the only green found in the manuscript (Fig. 3). After the first page, only red ink is used.[72] The first entry on the next page has a double line space left empty for an intended decorated capital *A*. Other early capital *A*s are left blank, the space also covering two lines.[73] Frequently, scribes left spaces for coloured initials and other forms of decoration, but often these were never filled in for various reasons.[74] It is possible that a *confrère* who was intended to decorate the manuscript did not become available. Whatever the answer, it seems clear that the copyist himself took over that function. Halfway down the second side he makes a black decorated *A* and by page 7 he has rubricated one *A*. By page ten he is beginning to place a line of red pigment beside some black initial letters. By folio 3 the copyist begins to use crude flourishes and droll heads in profile. One unusual head appears to have a beard and, as this one is highlighting the genealogy of the Marshal family, the long stringy beard may imply descent. Droll heads are also found in the section by the Dominican continuator, but the last head has a different cap of a later style. In this section, there are also three instances of zoomorphic initials (an initial composed of animal forms). In this instance, they are rather crude 'dragon'-type decoration (see Appendix for a list of these decorations and other scribal marks).[75] The fact that a significantly

70 K.W. Humphreys, *The book provisions of the medieval friars* (Amsterdam, 1964), p. 42. 71 Clemens and Graham, *Manuscripts studies*, p. 21. 72 For rubrication and initials, see ibid., pp 24–9. 73 See illustration 2–10, ibid., p. 21. 74 Nigel Morgan, 'Illumination – pigments, drawing and gilding' in Nigel Morgan and Rodney Thomson (eds), *The book in England*, vol. 2 (Cambridge, 2008), p. 84. 75 Clemens and Graham, *Manuscripts studies*, p. 45.

different decoration is used in the section covered by the continuator suggests that the copyist may be following the original illustrations (Figs 4, 5).

Marginalia

When considering a copy, the question arises as to whether the marginal additions and decorations are the work of the original scribe or of the copyist. If two copies differ in their marginalia this may indicate either that one copyist independently added the marginalia or that the other, likewise independently, ignored the original marginalia. In this instance, T includes decorations and marginalia, and these are often rubricated (see Appendix for a list of these). The copyist may either have been true to the original decorations and marginalia or may have created them himself. There are no decorations in L, which was planned just as a working copy. When marginalia are present it is designed to draw the attention of the reader to a significant passage. T often rubricates these passages and encloses the note in a red square, beginning the note with an abbreviated *nö* for *note*. Were these present in the original manuscript? There are 28 marginalia by the fourteenth-century copyist, including the two *maniculae* (hand with index finger extended) and the three 'dragons'. The first *manicula* is rubricated, the second is not, but both have the instruction *note* above the *manicula*.[76] Many of these fourteenth-century marginalia display an interest in the earls of Kildare and their family.[77] There are also, throughout T, approximately 25 seventeenth-century marginalia in a different hand; these are always in very faint ink and it is sometimes difficult to decipher the content, although an approximation can often be determined by examining the context of the adjacent text. These later marginalia display an interest in the archbishops of Dublin.

T has all the appearance of a work by a non-professional; mistakes are made and when these are noticed by the copyist they are then removed by two different methods of deletion. The first is expunctuation or subpunctuation (where dots are placed beneath a letter or a word to indicate deletion); the second is just crossing out.[78] Occasionally both methods are used.[79] With a transcript there is also the problem of determining whether an error was made by the original scribe

---

76 T, ff. 12, 32. Clemens and Graham, *Manuscripts studies*, pp 44, 45, 128, 267.   77 We know that chroniclers sometimes wrote for a patron. The Dominican Nicholas Trevet, for example, wrote one of his chronicles for Mary, daughter of Edward I, who was a nun at Amesbury: John Taylor, *English historical literature in the fourteenth century* (Oxford, 1987), p. 13.   78 Clemens and Graham, *Manuscripts studies*, pp 35–8.   79 For research on errors, see Daniel Wakelin, *Scribal correction and literary craft: English manuscripts, 1375–1510* (Cambridge, 2014); Kato Takako, 'Corrected mistakes in Cambridge University Library MS Gg.4.27' in Margaret Connolly and Linne R. Mooney (eds), *Design and distribution of late medieval manuscripts in England* (York, 2008), pp 61–87. Errors often occur in transcripts. P.D.A. Harvey, *Editing historical records* (London, 2001), pp 33–4, describes the difficulty in achieving accuracy in simple transcribing.

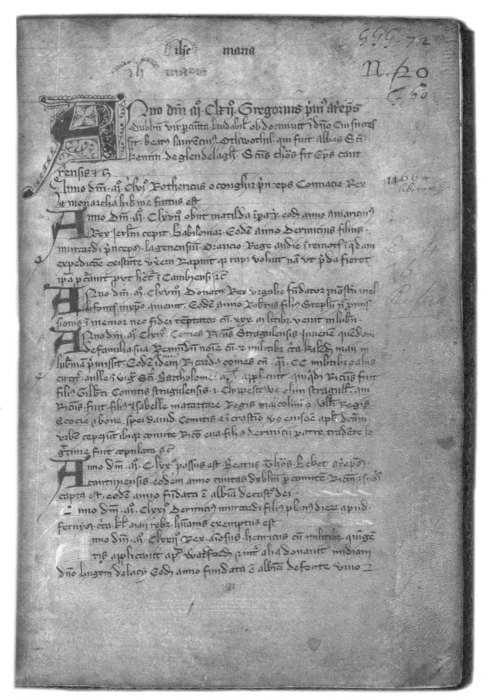

Figure 1. Folio 1r. The opening of the Dominican annals, which commence in the year 1162. The first capital *A* is enlarged and decorated in blue and red ink.

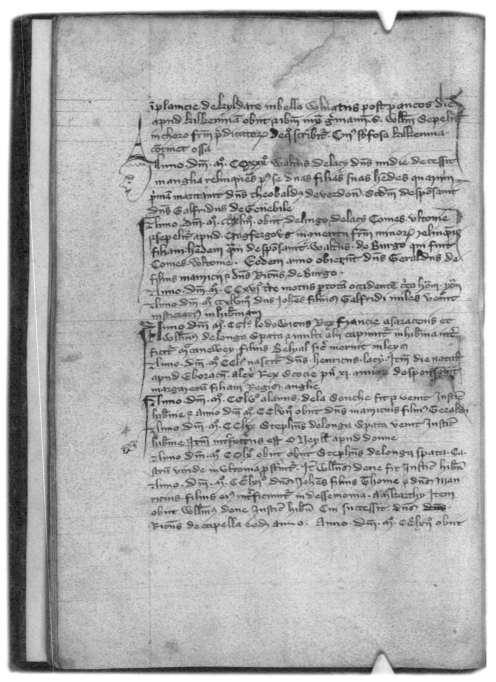

Figure 2. Folio 5v. Marginal head in profile next to the entry for 1240; rubrication visible on the pointed hat and detail of the face (lips and cheek).

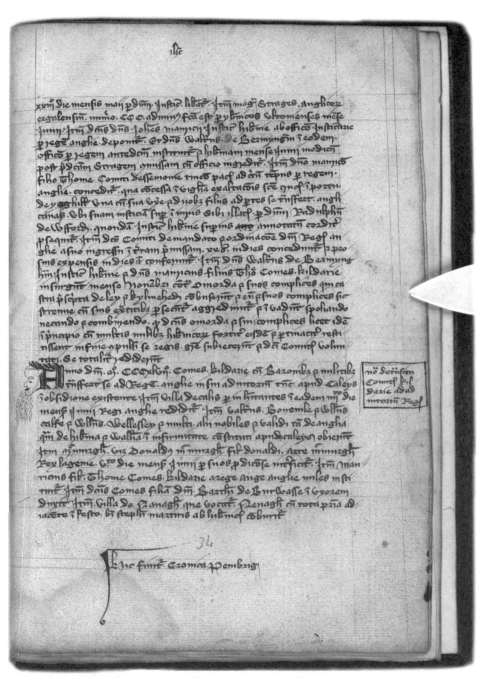

Figure 3. Folio 34r. The foot of this folio, following the conclusion of year 1347, marks where Pembridge's authorship ends. This is noted in **T** with the phrase, 'Here ends the chronicle of Pembridge' (*hyc finitur cronica Pembrig*). The first letter of *hyc* rubricated. A face with a beard is visible forming part of the *A* of year 1347, while in the right-hand margin, a rubricated box highlights a note concerning the earl of Kildare.

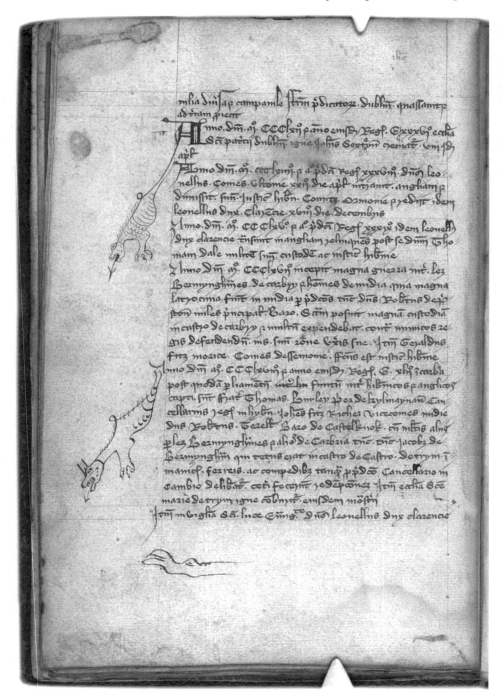

Figure 4. Folio 36v. The folio, a portion of the continuator's annals, shows two zoomorphic, dragon-like, creatures which form part of the *A* for the years 1362 and 1368.

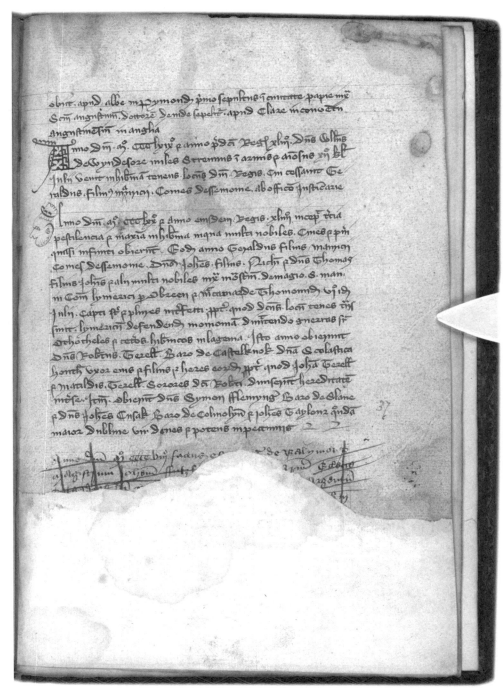

Figure 5. Folio 37r. The conclusion of the Dublin annals, showing where the work of the Dominican continuator ends in the year 1370. Sitting beneath this entry is an abortive attempt, in a later hand and different ink, to add an annal relating to 1408: this text is crossed out. The bottom of this folio is torn.

or by the copyist. Corrected errors are clearly the mistakes by the copyist: for example, on one occasion he places *comes* in the wrong place, *eodem anno* ~~comes~~ *Gilbertus de Clare, comes Gloucestrie*. The copyist (or the original scribe) is inconsistent with spelling, and this is understandable especially with surnames; even place-names are often given different spellings in the same entry. It is easy for errors to creep in and, also, 'a major shift in script was taking place in the fourteenth century and a young copyist ... might have increasing difficulties in reading a manuscript written decades before'.[80]

The identity of the copyist of T

It is impossible to suggest the exact identity of the copyist. What we can say is that he copied between 1370 and 1408. We know that he was a Dublin Dominican, but only a very few names of Dominicans are known from this period, although recently the names of some of the Dublin Dominican priors of this period have been uncovered from Connolly's *Irish exchequer payments*.[81]

T and the Kildare Geraldines

T is plentifully supplied with marginalia both in the same hand as the copyist and in a later hand, with many being rubricated, and a significant number of these are concerned with the Kildare Geraldines. The Kildare interest begins in 1285 with the first manicula (*Nö*) where the top of the finger is level with the words *captus est,* beside the information that Gerald fitz Maurice was captured by the Irish in Offaly.[82] Then, at the year 1294, the copyist places the rubricated words 'Note the acquisition of Kildare with its appurtenances by John fitz Thomas' inside a decorated and rubricated box. The marriage of the earl of Kildare to the daughter of the earl of Ulster in 1312 was also highlighted by a note inside a decorated and rubricated border and this Kildare interest continues throughout. It is evident, for example, in the 1323 report of the death of the earl's eldest son John, aged nine: there are only two other occasions in these annals when the age of a boy is given, the first being when the eleven-year-old King Alexander III of Scotland married the king of England's daughter (1251) and the second when Alphonso, son of King Edward I, died aged twelve (1284). And then of course there is, as we have seen, the transcription under the year 1361 of a full transcript of Maurice fitz Thomas's letters of appointment as justiciar of Ireland, the only chancery letter in this entire set of annals. It could have come from the muniments of the earl of Kildare himself or from the administration but either way the significance is its inclusion.

80 *Vita Edwardi secundi*, pp xviii–xix. 81 See *IExP*, index. 82 Gerald Fitz Maurice III, fourth baron of Offaly came of age in 1285: *Red bk Kildare*, no. 136; Orpen, 'The Fitz Geralds, barons of Offaly', *JRSAI*, 6th ser., iv (1914), 110.

As the earls of Kildare grew in importance and confidence, so inevitably would their interest in any historical report concerning their lineage.[83] Any readily available document that told of the history of the immediate family and the important families to which they were related by marriage would be a desirable acquisition. The Kildares were collectors and patrons and had a famous library that had three copies of Cambrensis, and Pembridge quotes Cambrensis several times at the beginning of his annals; perhaps he went to Kildare to read one.[84] It is worth noting too that, while details about the Kildares are present in both T and L, the former has additional Kildare marginalia either ignored by L who (as we shall discuss presently) was copying for Preston, or perhaps independently added by the copyist of T. Therefore, the planned recipient of T of these Dublin Dominican annals could possibly be either Maurice fitz Gerald, fourth earl of Kildare (c. 1322–90), justiciar of Ireland, or his son Gerald, fifth earl of Kildare (1390–1432), an associate of Sir Christopher Preston (whose family, as we just noted, commissioned L). However, it appears that the copy – if indeed a copy was ever sent to Kildare (perhaps Earl Maurice's death negated the commission?) – did not remain in Kildare ownership as a history of the Kildare family written by the marquis of Kildare in 1858 makes no mention of Pembridge, although constantly referencing Clyn, Grace, Ware and Camden.[85]

A curious point worth noting is the name of one Dublin Dominican prior during this period: John son of Gerald, who was prior of Dublin c. 1355–6. It is tempting to claim him as a Geraldine and possibly a kinsman of the earl of Kildare, but regrettably there is no solid justification for such a claim. If indeed he were a member of the family, it is intriguing to speculate that he could have either undertaken the task (as continuator) for his kinsman himself or designated a member of his priory to do so.

THE BODLEIAN COPY: LAUD MISC. MS 526 (L)

The second copy of these annals is the Bodleian MS Laud Misc. 526 (L). There are 42 folios, part paper and part membrane, plus the first and last pages which contain bibliographical information. It was bound in plain calf for George Carew,

---

[83] Colm Lennon, 'The Fitzgeralds of Kildare and the building of a dynastic image, 1500–1630' in W. Nolan and T. McGrath (eds), *Kildare history and society. Interdisciplinary essays on the history of an Irish county* (Dublin, 2006), pp 195–8; Colm Lennon, 'The making of the Geraldines: the Kildare FitzGeralds and their early historians' in P. Cosgrove, T. Dooley and K. Mullaney-Dignam (eds), *Aspects of Irish aristocratic life: essays on the FitzGeralds and Carton House* (Dublin, 2014), p. 71. [84] There is a late medieval inventory for the library of the later earls of Kildare: Aisling Byrne, 'The earls of Kildare and their books at the end of the Middle Ages', *The Library*, 14 (2013), 129–53; Aisling Byrne, 'The Geraldines and the culture of the wider world' in Crooks & Duffy (eds), *Geraldines*, pp 278–91. [85] Marquis of Kildare, *The earls of Kildare and their ancestors from 1057 to 1773* (Dublin, 1858).

earl of Totnes (d. 1629), and was part of four volumes relating to Irish affairs collected by Carew and bequeathed to Sir Thomas Stafford.[86] The condition of L is moderately good, although there are several very dark pages. The hand is a small chancery hand of the mid-fifteenth century with an average of thirty-one lines to a page and, like T, each *Anno* begins a new line, but not each *Item*. The pages are not ruled. We have some information about the provenance of L. On the first page a different hand to the copyist gives a title in Latin: *Annales Hiberniae ab Anno Christi 1162 usque ad annum 1370*. This is followed by a statement in English:

> The author of this book is unknown, it was brought as is supposed out of Ireland by the Lord Thomas Howard, duke of Norfolk, lord treasurer and earl marshal of England, when he was earl of Surrey and lord lieutenant of that realm in the 11th regnal year of king Henry VIII, and of late years, given by the Lord William Howard, youngest son to Thomas, late duke of Norfolk, unto the learned and judicious antiquary Mr William Camden, who put the same in print, inserting it into his Britannia, and by him given to George, Lord Carew, in anno 1619.

A large gap follows and near the end of the page is a note, in Latin, stating that the book was the property of William Laud, archbishop of Canterbury and chancellor of the university of Oxford, 1636.

At the top of the last page is a note also in Latin which states that this book was the property of Lord William Preston, *vicecomes* of Gormanston; this is William Preston, second Viscount Gormanston who died in 1532. The Prestons were an extremely ambitious family from Lancashire who arrived in Ireland in the late thirteenth century and quickly rose to prominence.[87] Since the title Viscount Gormanston was created in 1478, the note was written after that date.[88] The note is very elaborate with many letters having extra-long descenders and ascenders. For example, the *I* of *Iste* covers five lines and the *P* and *S* of Preston descend four lines. There is nothing else on that page.

---

86 H.O. Cox, *Bodleian Library quarto Catalogues II, Laudian manuscripts* (repr. with corrections and additions by R.W. Hunt (Oxford 1973), pp xxii, xxxvii, xxxxi, 380–1, 658.   87 For an account of the Preston family, see the preface to *Gormanston reg.*, pp iii-xix; James Moynes, 'The Prestons of Gormanston, c.1300–1532: an Anglo-Irish gentry family', *Ríocht na Mídhe*, 14 (2003), 26–55. For this period see P. Crooks, '"Representation and dissent: parliamentarianism" and the structure of politics in colonial Ireland, c.1370–1420', *EHR*, 125 (2010), 1–34; Crooks, 'The background to the arrest of the fifth earl of Kildare and Sir Christopher Preston, a missing membrane', *AH*, 40 (2008), 1–15; Otway-Ruthven, 'The background to the arrest of Sir Christopher Preston, pp 71–94. Between 1325 and 1332 Richard de Preston was constable of Drogheda castle, *IExP*, pp 314, 325, 363. At the same period Roger de Preston, a burgess of Drogheda, appears, from 1327 to 1343, in the list of justices of the common bench and on the list of justices of the justiciar's Bench from 1329, *Admin. Ire.*, index, p. 295.   88 *Vicecomes* in the medieval period meant sheriff, but in this case

L is neat and of uniform appearance throughout and has the air of a professional copy with any errors left uncorrected. There are two types of marginalia, a few in the original hand and a later hand, probably seventeenth-century. The later hand is in light ink and thinner nib and displays an eclectic interest. L is identical with T in having no title and covering the years 1162 to 1370; the missing years are also identical with T. As with T, each year begins on a new line, but L has the date of each year entered twice, once in the body of the text and repeated again in the wide margin. The last three words of the annals, *potens in pecuniis*, are placed on their own in the middle of an additional line on the last page, thus clearly indicating that the scribe knew that the annals had ended at that point.

Laud and the Prestons of Gormanston

On the last page of L is the information that the book was the property of William Preston, *Vicecomiti de Gormanstoun*; there is nothing else on that page. His father Robert Preston (II) was awarded the title in 1478 but William Preston, second Viscount Gormanston, did not become viscount until 1503 and died in 1532.[89] Therefore that note was written between those years. Robert Preston (I), who appears in the annals, was a lawyer who, in 1353, married Margaret, the daughter of Walter de Bermingham of Castlecarbury and Kells in Ossory.[90] Walter de Bermingham had recently been justiciar (1346–9) and so Robert was now allying himself with a top-rank family – a clear indication of upward mobility.[91] From the annals we know that Robert's wife, Margaret de Bermingham, died in 1361 aged 21 (probably as a result of the 1361 plague) and was buried with the Dominicans of Drogheda. Her son was Christopher. It was in 1363, two years after the death of Margaret, that Robert bought from Amaury St Amand the estate at Gormanston from which the title Viscount Gormanston (1478) was taken.[92] Robert continued to flourish professionally and by the end of his career in 1392 he had served as keeper of the great seal of Ireland and chancellor. On his death in 1396 he was succeeded by his son Christopher who added to the wealth and importance of the family by marrying Elizabeth, daughter and co-heiress of William de London, baron of Naas, and by this marriage the family acquired most of the lands that had belonged to the barons of Naas.

The Prestons were frequently in Dublin and, between 1359 and 1361, they acquired a stone house there near Fishamble Street (later probably Preston's

---

the designation was intended as viscount. 'Viscount Gormanston' is the oldest such title in either Britain or Ireland.   89 Moynes, 'Prestons of Gormanston', pp 40, 46.   90 *Gormanston reg.*, p. vii.   91 Moynes, 'Prestons of Gormanston', p. 33. In 1384/5 he was proctor of Maurice Bermingham, clerk, prebendary of Newcastle Lyons, *IExP*, p. 544. For a connection with de Bermingham in 1322, see P. Connolly (ed.), 'List of Irish entries on the memoranda rolls of the English Exchequer, 1307–27', *AH*, 36 (1995), 200.   92 In 1358 Robert was paid for

Inns).⁹³ Christopher, who died before 1445, could have sought, and easily obtained, permission from the Dublin Dominicans to make a copy of their annals. We know that Christopher's mother, Margaret de Bermingham, was buried with the Drogheda Dominicans; we also know that the de Berminghams had been great Dominican patrons since the founding of Athenry in 1241.⁹⁴ Christopher had an interest in documents – one of his first acts when he inherited in 1396 was to examine the contents of the family muniments chest and gather them together to produce the *Register of Gormanston*,⁹⁵ which contains documents that indicate an interest in antiquarian matters – and would probably have known of the annals held by the Dublin Dominicans. We are told that Preston 'may have borrowed one of the clerks of the Chancery to commence the transcription of the title deeds' in the *Register*,⁹⁶ so it would have been comparatively easy for him to authorize a copy of these annals. It is of course not surprising to find the Prestons interested in annals that referred to their family and the great families into which they married, as was true of the Kildare Geraldines, as we have seen. Not only were the Kildares and Prestons interested in the annals of Pembridge, but they also had mutual political interests that were well-documented.⁹⁷ On one famous occasion a report spoke of Kildare, Preston, and their adherents intercommuning (*entrecomonantz*), which is to say that they 'confabulated with each other ... they acted furtively and, it would seem, behind closed doors':⁹⁸ these two men may well have been interested in acquiring copies of these annals as much for political as or familial reasons.

T AND L COMPARED

T and L manuscripts are not the original, so how much reliance can we place on them? The annals of Pembridge and his continuator begin with the year 1162. Despite the oddity of the choice of opening year – not an especially noteworthy one – all evidence points to 1162 as the true beginning (Fig. 1), both T and L

accompanying the justiciar Rokeby to Munster and Leinster, *IExP*, pp 472–3.   93 Moynes, 'Prestons of Gormanston', p. 32; for Preston's inn, see Harris, *Dublin*, pp 84–5; for information concerning property in Dublin, see *Gormanston Reg.*, pp vii, 84–6.   94 Milo de Bermingham was heavily involved in the foundation of Athenry: Ambrose Coleman (ed.), '*Regestum monasterii fratrum praedicatorum de Athenry*', *Archiv. Hib.*, 1 (1912), 201–21.   95 *Gormanston reg.*, pp x–xi.   96 *Gormanston reg.*, pp x–xi; for the suggestion of an 'inter-institutional scribal network' in Dublin, see Alan Fletcher, 'The *Liber albus* of Christ Church Cathedral' in *Christ church: manuscripts*, p. 156. Christopher did not just preserve charters but included miscellaneous items of antiquarian interest and the muniments chest contained Geraldine, Lacy, London and Bermingham documents: *Gormanston reg.*, pp x–xi, xii, xiv.   97 Crooks, 'Background to the arrest', 1–15; Otway-Ruthven, 'Background to the arrest', 71–94.   98 Crooks, 'Representation and dissent'; P. Crooks, 'The structure of politics in theory and practice: colonial Ireland, 1210–1541' in Brendan Smith (ed.), *The Cambridge history of*

beginning in this same year. If two independent copies are virtually identical in years and content, then we can be fairly confident that we are looking at original entries without any additions by the copyist. Both scribes have produced a straightforward copy. There is one extra insertion by the copyist of L that is the foundation of a Cistercian house. This could be a personal addition by the L copyist or, given the fact that Cistercian abbey foundation dates are included in the early section, this entry could have been omitted in error by the copyist of T. This is not a problem in need of serious consideration.

But then we come to the question of marginalia and decoration, which are plentiful in T, but very sparse in L. Any copyist has important decisions to make when he sees marginalia in the manuscript in front of him: to copy it faithfully; to move it from the margins to the main text; to select some according to his own preference; or to ignore it. What decision was made by both our copyists? L has a small number of marginalia while T has many. So how can we resolve the question as to whether the marginalia were in fact in the original manuscript and not just the product of the copyist? Clearly one item, *hyc finitur cronica Pembrig*, was not in the original manuscript as L would not have ignored this. A second major item to resolve is the Irish language quatrain referring to the blood of Christ at the foot of folio 30r.[99] Here the copyist of L could have decided to ignore it as it was not in any way an item of history, plus it was in Irish, and the copy was made for Preston. The most likely explanation for the quatrain in Irish is that it was a religious invocation made as an addition by the copyist of T. There are only five times when both T and L have the same marginalia. In 1338, 1348, 1350, 1360 and again in 1360. This leads to the hypothesis that at least these five marginalia were in the original. Then the question is whether the extra ones in T were also in the original, and ignored by L, or were a personal addition. This is virtually impossible to answer.

As regards the decoration, present only in T, it is possible to conjecture that the copyist was in fact replicating the manuscript in front of him. The decoration is crude, especially the 'dragons' on pages 71 and 72 (Fig. 4). The copyist was clearly not a skilled artist and did not copy accurately from the original. The first 'dragon' is difficult even to identify as a dragon; the next two are clearer but that page also includes what appears to be a pen trial of the dragon on the foot of the page.[100] Also on the last page, the hat is different and of a later style than the earlier droll heads, which all have a conical hat with a swirl at the top, typical of the fourteenth century called a *chaperon* (hood covering head and draped over shoulders) with a long *liripipe* (a long, trailing point often added to a hood)

Ireland, i: *1000–1550* (Cambridge, 2017), pp 457–60.   **99** Clemens and Graham, *Manuscripts studies*, p. 45.   **100** 'Often the manuscript artist would make preliminary sketches of their more ornate initials before entering the final version of the initial': ibid., p. 45.

attached.[101] The last hat is different. But the copyist would be unlikely to change the hat style unless the manuscript in front of him had changed styles. On balance the answer may perhaps be that T copied original decorative material; nothing else explains the quite different and individual decoration in the continuator section.

While the language is predominantly Latin throughout, there are a few anomalies. There is a French entry in both manuscripts concerning the formal complaint made to the king in 1341. There are also three English words. The first is in 1186 where the entry states that the subject of the entry was killed with an iron instrument namely a *pykays* (i.e., 'pickaxe'); here the scribe is probably using a word for which he has no Latin equivalent. The second occasion is in 1352 where the scribe states *et dixit in vulgari melius est castrum de* bones *quam de* stones, *scilicet, de ossibus quam de lapidibus*. He is in effect already translating the Latin *de ossibus quam de lapidibus* for us. Anglo-Norman is likewise present in occasional words. As we have seen, the copyist of T also has a quatrain in Irish as a marginal note in the same ink, which at the very least indicates that he was comfortable with that language: it is not found in L.

Similarities between T and L

There are many parallels between the two copies, the most obvious being the years present and years missed. Another particularly important similarity is that of errors. In 1199 both have the impossible *xviii ides* April as the date of King Richard's death, which should be *viii ides*, i.e., 6 April. In 1279 both give Robert de Fulbourne the incorrect forename Stephen.[102] In 1291 both copies name the pope as Martin instead of Nicholas.[103] Both give the deaths of Margaret wife of John Wogan and Matilda de Lacy in 1302 and erroneously again in 1304. There are also occasions when both have entered the same incorrect date, for example in 1246. There is also a remarkably interesting similarity connected with numerals. In the years 1331, 1332, 1337, and 1340 both T and L use Arabic numerals for *19, 13, 17,* and *13*. In 1339, T uses Arabic 2, but L uses *secundo*. Arabic numerals came to Europe from the Islamic world around 1100. From the thirteenth century on, the use of Arabic numerals increased, partially supplanting Roman numerals but were not in general use until the fifteenth century. As stated above, there are a few marginalia that are virtually identical in both transcripts

---

[101] See similar head in P. Connolly and G. Martin (eds), *The Dublin guild merchant roll, c.1190–1265* (Dublin, 1992), pp 57, 72, 73; see also face in Bernard Meehan, 'A fourteenth-century historical compilation from St Mary's Cistercian abbey, Dublin' in Seán Duffy (ed.), *Medieval Dublin XV* (Dublin, 2016), p. 373; *HMDI*, p. xxxvii, n2. [102] The error in T is corrected in the margin in the same ink, but possibly a different hand by three small dots in a triangle above *Robertum* indicating the error. L has Robertum. Both L and T use the correct name, Stephen, in 1281. [103] Pope Martin IV, 1281–5; Pope Nicholas IV, 1288–92: Pope

which suggests that those items were present in the original document. A few of these items have the full note in **T** but just the mark *nö* (note) in **L**. In 1337 **T** has a black note inside a rubricated box (referring to the subject of partridges) while **L** merely has *nö*. Additionally, in 1337 **T** has a black note in a rubricated box (referring to the death of the first earl of Ormond) while **L** again just has a note beside the entry saying *nö*. In 1338 **T** has a rubricated note in a rubricated box (referring to the snow in Dublin) while **L** again just has a note beside the entry saying *nö*. It is when we come to the work of the continuator that we find four, virtually identical, marginalia, which must indicate that these were in the original manuscript. In 1348 **T** has a note in a rubricated box (referring to the grant of Kells in Ossory) and **L** has the same note in the scribe's own hand. This is followed by the notice of the death of Walter de Bermingham in 1350 where again **T** has a note in a rubricated box and **L** just has the information. Similarly, in 1360 the death of Richard Fitz Ralph is noted by both with **T** having just an extra phrase *de morte*. Finally, both **T** and **L** note the killing of the Irish by Robert Savage.

The years 1334, 1335 and 1336 are absent in both copies of the annals (despite being not without incident) and significantly there is no gap in either manuscript. Perhaps Pembridge was absent from Ireland at the time. He could have been at a general chapter of the friars preachers or even at a provincial chapter in England.[104] The general chapters were at Limousine in 1334, London in 1335 and Bruges in 1336.[105] We know that the provincial priors went to the general chapters: for example, in March 1322 there was a 'safe conduct … for John de Bristoll, prior provincial of the friars preachers in England, going with divers friars to their general chapter to be held at Vienna in the duchy of Austria'.[106] As the prior provincial of England was also the prior provincial of Ireland, Irish friars may well have gone separately. The Irish and Scottish houses were formed into two separate administrative districts, known as vicariates; the Irish vicariate was already formed by 1256 when a papal mandate was addressed to it.[107] A Dublin friar could have been one of the 'divers friars' in 1322. Pembridge could also have been at Vitry in 1331,[108] and at the London general chapter of 1335. However, if he had attended any of those general chapters, one might expect an indication in the annals, but Pembridge does not indicate any specific knowledge of the world beyond Ireland, and certainly not anything that might indicate that he had been on the Continent.[109]

Martin V, 1417–31.   **104** In April 1285 a Walter de Kilkenny went to the general chapter at Bologna and was presumably from Ireland, *CPR, 1281–1292*, p. 156.   **105** *Acta*, ii, pp 222–43.   **106** *CPR, 1321–1324*, p. 76. *ACTA 1321–1322*, p. 138.   **107** We know of an early vicar, Friar Geoffrey de Blund, from the *Liber exemplorum* written between 1275 and 1279. Hinnebusch, *English friars preachers*, p. 209. There was also a Nicholas Hill in 1390, ibid., p. 210n4.   **108** *CCR, 1330–1333*, p. 283.   **109** We might compare this with Friar John Clyn's presence at a Franciscan general chapter at Marseilles in 1343 which can be deduced from

Differences between the T and L copies

However, despite the similarities, it is the differences that are of the utmost significance. The first entry of T (1162) is the most decorated capital in the manuscript, larger than any other and the only capital, or indeed only decoration, to have two colours. The first entry of L (1162) is simply the same as all the other entries. L also lacks two additional items present in T. The first one is the Irish marginalia previously noted. Even if this was in the original manuscript, the copyist of L may nevertheless have just ignored it as it was not an intrinsic part of the narrative historical tale. The second one, also previously noted, is more crucial; there would be no excuse for ignoring rubricated words of the highest importance, that is the words '*hyc finitur cronica Pembrig*'. It is highly unlikely that the copyist of L would have ignored such words. This most important and most obvious difference between T and L is strengthened by the fact that the Laud copy has no indication of any break or separation at the end of year 1347 where T asserts that Pembridge's contribution ends (pls 2, 3). L has no pause in the handwriting, or any space left to suggest that there was a gap in the original manuscript. Therefore, it appears that *hic finitur chronica Pembrig* was not in the original manuscript. The answer must be that the copyist of T was the person who placed this information in the centre of the page and rubricated it with a flourish and this is additional proof that the copyist was a Dublin Dominican and knew of Pembridge and knew this statement to be true.[110]

There are other differences, but the one that makes it highly unlikely that L copied from the T is the fact that in 1343 the original manuscript must have had an error in date. The copyist of T realized the error and wrote *Anno domini m. ccc̶l̶ cccxliii*. The error *ccc̶l̶* was erased by underdotting and furthermore it was also crossed out. The Laud scribe did not notice the error and wrote *m. ccc[ ]liii* (with the '*x*' omitted). If L had copied from T, then he could not have failed to notice an error cancelled by not one but two methods. Therefore, the error was in the original. In the year 1352 T omits the *m* for *milia* (*Anno domini [m.] ccc lij*), but L has no problem with that year giving it correctly as *Anno domini m. ccc lij*. Under the year 1361 the L has an important additional phrase that is not in T: *quod nullus nativus de Hibernia appropinquaret exercitui suo* ('that no native of Ireland would come near to his army'). As will be discussed further below, L appears to be correct. Other important differences are that there are no religious invocations and no illuminated capitals or rubrication in L.

These several differences indicate the strong probability that both copyists independently transcribed from the original. Therefore, the mistakes present in

---

unusual entries in his annals after that year: *AClyn*, pp 45–9.   110 Another possibility is that the original version included the *hyc finitur cronica Pembrig* statement as marginalia and the copyist of T might have moved the statement into a more prominent position in his copy, while the Laud copyist, who included fewer marginalia in any case, might have ignored it altogether.

both are the result of both copying mistakes in the original manuscript. L did not copy T, both being separate but remarkably faithful copies of the original work of Pembridge and his Dominican continuator. There is also a strong probability that the original manuscript remained in the Dublin priory while it was being copied and, indeed, we may suppose that the original remained in the Dublin priory until the Dissolution.

PEMBRIDGE EXAMINED

When did Pembridge write?

The Dominican Friar John de Pembridge wrote the section of the annals covering the years 1162–1347. Pembridge was also prior for several years and as there would be numerous calls on his time it is not surprising that there are several indications that, in the section dealing with the events of his own day, he often wrote after the event he recounted. From internal evidence, we can estimate when Pembridge was writing. The 1308 entry concerning John le Decer indicates that he was not present as a friar in the Dublin priory at that point, as he tells us that the story was one told to the juniors by the seniors: here Pembridge also states that le Decer was *later* buried with the Franciscans and, as John le Decer died in 1332, this means that Pembridge was writing the 1308 entry in, or after, 1332.

Even though the annals begin in 1162, the first mention of crops and prices comes only in 1310. The Dominicans, like any institution then or now, needed to keep financial accounts and so there is a possibility that this early information came from the priory accounts. This is the same entry that also records that the bakers of Dublin, 'for their false weight of bread', were punished by being drawn on hurdles tied to the tails of horses through the streets of the city. This information about the bakers' punishment would still have been well known in the priory and could even have been used to illuminate a sermon.

It is when we come to the period of the Scottish invasion under Edward Bruce that we begin to reach the point when Pembridge was telling the story in part at least from within his own memory and certainly within that of his *confrères*. It was an extremely dramatic period not only because of the war situation but also because of the acute famine.[111] In 1316 Pembridge tells us that in the middle of Lent wheat was selling for eighteen shillings and in the following Easter for eleven shillings; hence, that 1316 item was written after 1317. These though are the kind of details that rely on more than memory and it is clear that Pembridge had material in front of him from earlier notes made either by himself or another of the priory's scribes. Furthermore, as will be discussed presently, his synopsis of

---

111 There were 'many afflictions in all parts of Ireland: very many deaths, famine and many strange diseases, murders, and intolerable storms as well': *AConn*, p. 241.

the future course of the Bruce invasion makes this abundantly clear. When Pembridge recounts that Robert de Nottingham, the mayor of Dublin, gave orders for the citizens to destroy the Dublin Dominican priory and to use the stones to enlarge part of the quay walls against Robert Bruce, he can state, in that specific entry, that *later* the king of England ordered the same mayor and community to restore the priory as before. The request clearly went to the king after 1317.[112]

A strong claim can be made for the year 1331 as the beginning of the actual task, using existing annals, notes or memory for the earlier section. In this year, the period when Pembridge was prior of Dublin, a new form of dating enters the annals; for example, an overthrow of the Irish in Uí Cheinnsealaigh by the English 'on ninth day of the month of April', and the capture of Arklow Castle by the Irish 'on the twenty-first day of the month of April'. There are twenty-five such instances of giving the date in days and months until the last one in 1347, 'on the fifth day of the month of July'. This means that Pembridge was writing while he was prior of the Dublin Dominicans and even afterwards. But even in the section when Pembridge is writing contemporaneously there are hints of retrospection. The entry for the year 1332 must have been written on or after 1334 as Pembridge recounts that on 11 July 1332 William de Bermingham was hanged in Dublin by the justiciar and Walter his son was set free; but Walter was not freed until 1334.[113] In 1343, when Pembridge was writing his extremely dramatic account of Ralph Ufford's time in Ireland, he reported Ufford's arrival on 13 July but, importantly, he then stated that the weather became bad on Ufford's arrival and did not improve until after his death on 9 April 1346: hence, the 1343 entry was completed in or after 1346.

We know Pembridge ceased writing after Wednesday 26 December 1347. The Black Death may well be the reason as Dublin was overwhelmed by the effect of plague. In Kilkenny Friar John Clyn reports that 'in Dublin alone ... fourteen thousand men died' and specifically that twenty-three of the Dublin Franciscan friars died.[114] The mendicant friars were particularly susceptible to the plague as they lived in the towns and ministered to the people: as Clyn puts it, in Kilkenny the confessor died with the confessed.[115] If Pembridge was in Dublin he was in great danger. However, Pembridge could also have been in Drogheda as in 1348 the chapter of the friars preachers was held there.[116] Again, from Clyn, we hear that 'the cities of Dublin and Drogheda were almost destroyed and wasted of inhabitants and men'.[117] The odds of Pembridge surviving in either place were not good. Pembridge's entries cease before he can report the Black Death. It is

---

112 For it, see *Affairs Ire.*, p. 87.   113 On 11 July, 'William de Bermingham, a vigorous and military knight, bold and intrepid, was hanged in Dublin': *AClyn*, p. 208; *Kilkenny chronicle*, p. 340; Connolly, 'An attempted escape from Dublin castle', p. 102.   114 *AClyn*, pp 246, 250.   115 Ibid., p. 250.   116 BL, MS Add. 4789, f. 206r.   117 *AClyn*, p. 246.

also possible, though perhaps less likely, that Pembridge may just have been moved to another region because of the depletion of some priories by that plague.

One curious point worth noting is that both Pembridge in Dublin and Clyn in Kilkenny were writing their annals in the same decade. It is certainly possible that they had met as they shared a common interest in history. We would need to look at the chapters of both orders to see if there was an overlap when they could both be in the same place at the same time but unfortunately there is a gap in our knowledge of Dominican chapters between 1315 and 1340.[118] However, we do know that there was a Franciscan provincial chapter at Dublin in 1324 and the Dominican provincial chapter was held at Kilkenny in 1346. So, they may well have met on at least one of those occasions.

Pembridge's sources and approach to writing

Annals were important, for how else could one have a record or knowledge of the past? This was acknowledged by the rulers of the land. In 1291 Edward I asked thirty monastic houses for evidence about the legality of the English claim to rule Scotland.[119] The *Chronica Buriensis* makes a similar point in 1300 when the validity of an argument was proved 'by the chronicles of Malmesbury, Marianus, Master Henry of Huntingdon and Hovenden'.[120]

When a history begins, as our annals do, with a somewhat arbitrary date that is nearly two centuries before the scribe's lifetime, then the work is clearly bipartite: the first part being the product of assembling of sources and the second the contemporary and original material. When compiling from other sources scribes, as a rule, copied what was in front of them without making too many changes or alterations. Before beginning his task, the scribe had three key decisions to make. First, with what year to begin: it could be the dawn of creation, the beginning of Christianity or any other date he personally considered to be significant. Second, he had to decide when the year began, 1 January, 25 March, or even the start of the regnal year. Third, when writing contemporaneously, was the scribe to enter events as he heard about them, or wait for the year end and sort the various bits of information that had come his way so that he could present them in strict chronological order?[121]

---

118 Ireland was a vicariate not a province, so these were chapters of the Irish vicariate and not provincial chapters. 119 In 1291 royal letters were sent asking for historical precedents to the claim of overlordship of Scotland: Lionel Stones, 'English chroniclers and the affairs of Scotland, 1286–1296' in R.H.C. Davis and J.M. Wallace-Hadrill (eds), *The writing of history in the Middle Ages* (Oxford, 1981), p. 329; R.A. Griffiths, 'Edward I, Scotland and the chronicles of English religious houses', *Journal of the Society of Archivists*, 6 (1979), 191–9; E.L.G. Stones and Grant G. Simpson (eds), *Edward I and the throne of Scotland, 1290–1296: an edition of the record sources for the Great Cause*, 2 vols (Oxford, 1978). 120 *Chronica Buriensis*, p. 156. 121 John Taylor, *English historical literature in the fourteenth century*, pp 47–50.

Rather curiously, the first decision made by John de Pembridge was to begin with the year 1162. At first glance this appears as an odd choice. The brief account of that year begins with a report on the death of Gréne (Gregory), the first archbishop of Dublin, and the information that he was succeeded by 'Blessed' Lorcán Ó Tuathail (Laurence O'Toole), abbot of Glendalough. The peculiar decision to start with Gréne's death rather than his appointment as Dublin's first archbishop was perhaps linked to the complication that he was already bishop of Dublin before the diocese was elevated to archiepiscopal status; so, in effect the first man elected as archbishop and duly consecrated as such in Dublin by his superior, the archbishop of Armagh, was in fact Lorcán Ó Tuathail in 1162.

The second decision was to begin each year on 25 March, the feast of the Annunciation, a fairly standard choice made by most scribes:[122] as the Ghent Annals put it: 'note that the years of our Lord which follow are always to be begun on the feast of the Annunciation of the Blessed Virgin, that is to say, on March 25'.[123] Accordingly, entries would progress from 25 March, past the December year end, and forward to 24 March of the following calendar year. This is the dating system used by Pembridge. Thus, for our purposes, all dates which refer to January, February, and 1–24 March, should be understood to belong to the following calendar year.

The third decision, which arose when a scribe was living through the events he was recording, was at what point he should enter the items of news he received. He had two options, as mentioned above. He could wait for the year to end and fill in all the entries in a chronological manner. Or he could enter items of news as they came to him, in which case the chronology would not be so precise because events that occurred at a distance might be quite late in becoming known (an example being when Berwick was taken by the Scots on 1–2 April 1318, news of which, Pembridge tells us, only reached Ireland a full three weeks later).[124] Annalistic material like this, whether compiled by a young Pembridge or another friar, may have been collected and available in the priory before Pembridge began to write his annals but, when he starts to write contemporaneously, it seems that Pembridge, who generally presented events in the correct chronological order, wrote each year as one exercise, probably using notes which could have been made throughout the year on slates or scraps of parchment or paper.[125] For recent events, he would also have relied on his memory as we sometimes underestimate the 'craft of memory training' which had an important place in medieval education.[126]

---

122 Cheney, *Handbook of dates*, p. 12. See also Given-Wilson, *Chronicles*, pp 121–2; R.L. Poole, 'The beginning of the year in the Middle Ages', *Proceedings of the British Academy* (1922), 113–37. 123 Hilda Johnstone (ed. and trans.), *Annales Gandenses* (Oxford 1985), p. 1. 124 G.W.S. Barrow, *Robert Bruce and the community of the realm of Scotland* (Edinburgh, 1976), p. 463. 125 For a particularly useful account, see Dauvit Broun, 'Creating and maintaining a year-by-year chronicle: the evidence of the chronicle of Melrose' in E. Kooper (ed.), *The Medieval Chronicle VI* (Amsterdam, 2009), pp 141–52, for an account of keeping notes, see ibid., p. 142. 126 M.

For events before his time, writing as he was in the mid-fourteenth century, Pembridge's main task was to find a source on which he could rely. Apart from an acknowledgement that he used Giraldus Cambrensis from 1167 to 1179 ('*in Cambrensi et cetera*' and '*ut patet in Cambrensi*'), he reveals no other authority. The obvious solution would be to look to other pre-existing Dublin annals. In this case Pembridge had a source readily available to him adjoining his own priory, the annals of the Cistercian abbey of St Mary's, Dublin. There were many connections between the Cistercians and Dominicans from the earliest foundation of the Dominican order, and there was also the convenience of the close physical proximity of the Cistercian and Dominican houses in the transpontine suburb of Dublin. That Pembridge did indeed have access to Cistercian annals is suggested by the initial section of his own work which has several references to new Irish Cistercian foundations up to and including the year 1211 when Richard Tuyt founded the abbey of Granard, Co. Longford. There is no mention of the 1225 foundation of a Cistercian house at Tracton, Co. Cork, and hence we might conclude that the Cistercian source ceases at some point between 1211 and 1225.

What might these Cistercian annals have been? The only surviving sources of St Mary's historical material are brief extracts from annals of St Mary's made in the seventeenth century by Sir James Ware.[127] Significantly, there are two entries in Ware's notes that are not present in Pembridge's annals, these being the arrival of the order of preachers in Ireland in 1224, and the information that on the kalends of May 1238, the Dominican church of St Saviour was founded in Dublin (by this is presumably meant that the house, in development for a number of years, was formally dedicated).[128] Of all things, one might have assumed that these important Dominican events would be recorded in Pembridge's annals but presumably the absence of this detail is accounted for by the information being common knowledge in the priory, written into another book there, and therefore not required in the annals. The other surviving Dublin annals of any significant substance are those of Thomas Case, though these, if not actually written later, were certainly copied at a later date.[129] Case begins with the birth of Christ while Pembridge, as we know, begins in 1162. If Case and Pembridge were both using the same original source, then one might expect Pembridge at least to have some entries before and after 1162 which are present in Case's text.

From around 1224, when the Dominicans arrived in Dublin, there must have been an attempt at least to note events of importance. Certainly, in Pembridge's annals, by 1274 the Dominican interest begins to emerge with the coronation

Carruthers, *The book of memory: a study of memory in medieval culture* (Cambridge, 2008), pp x, 193. **127** For Sir James Ware's brief extracts from St Mary's annals, see *CStM*, ii, pp 287–92. **128** *CStM*, ii, pp 288–9. **129** Case tells us that he ceased copying on 25 May 1427: *CStM*, ii, p. 286.

oath of Edward I and the significant fact that Edward was crowned by the Dominican archbishop of Canterbury, Friar Robert Kilwardby.[130] From 1282 more specific dates occur and from 1304 more information about the priory is included; for example, on Monday 8 June Dublin was burned as was 'the church of the friars preachers, and the church of the monks', i.e., the Dominican priory and the Cistercian abbey. In 1308 the memory of the older friars in the priory is being cited as Pembridge relates his story of John le Decer feeding the friars. A Dominican interest is evident in 1313 when we learn that Friar Roland Jorz, the Dominican archbishop of Armagh, arrived in Howth with his cross but was then chased out of Leinster by the men of the archbishop of Dublin (part of the long-running dispute between Dublin and Armagh regarding the latter's claim to primacy). But in general, as previously remarked, the Dominican information that Pembridge includes is mostly related to its benefactors and what they contributed to the fabric of the priory.

Pembridge's sources for the Bruce invasion

There are a few hints in the text that help to clarify the development of these annals. The cessation of Cistercian information after 1221 is followed by a definite Dominican input from the 1270s/1280s and a definite Dublin Dominican input from 1304. Then we come to the extremely long entries of 1315 to 1318. Reading his account of the years of the Bruce upheaval, it is evident that Pembridge has some personal knowledge of the events of that time. At what stage Pembridge's own personal memory and knowledge began to contribute to the annals can only be conjectured but a date around 1315 must be seriously considered. His knowledge of these events ranges from his note on the price of wheat at Eastertide 1315 to the start of the use of phrases like 'three weeks after Easter, there came news to Dublin', or 'on Sunday after the feast of St Michael, news came to Dublin that the Lord Alexander Bicknor had landed in Youghal', or 'news came from Connacht', 'news arrived from England', 'rumour states', or 'rumour came to Dublin'.

One might speculate that only a chronicler who had experienced that period first-hand could write in such a manner but of course he would also have the opinions and memories of his *confrères* to consult. Also, Pembridge would have information from other Dominican priories when they met for their chapters. Chapters were held, for example in Arklow, Athenry, Athy, Cashel, Coleraine, Cork, Drogheda, Galway, Kilkenny, Limerick, Naas, Waterford and Youghal and these places are all mentioned in the annals: in 1316, for example, Pembridge tells us that after the battle of Skerries several of the slain Scots were buried in the convent of the friars preachers in Athy.[131] Also, the Cistercian abbey of St

---

130 B. Williams, 'The lost coronation oath of King Edward I: rediscovered in a Dublin manuscript?' in Seán Duffy (ed.), *Medieval Dublin IX* (Dublin, 2009), pp 84–90. 131 J.R.S.

Mary was adjacent to Pembridge's own house, and had vast lands and widespread interests and so would have information gathered from their daughter-houses and granges: for example, under November 1315 the information that Bruce burnt the Cistercian house at Abbeylara, Co. Longford (Granard) and robbed it of all its goods may well have been obtained from St Mary's. We might expect Pembridge to know and note the capture of the earl of Ulster in February 1317 when the earl had been staying in St Mary's abbey, but the additional information that 'the chamber in which he was kept was burnt and seven of the men of the same earl were killed there', is specific.[132] Furthermore the entry has a rubricated note in a box and the capital N (for the sheriff Robert de Nottingham) was also rubricated. Another point worth noting is that, since most of the action during the invasion took place north of Dublin, the Dominican priory being at the bridge into Dublin from the north, all messengers had to pass the house; instinctively they would call in to impart news and pay their respects, especially if seeking a blessing on their way back to the hostilities. We should not discount the possibility either that Dominican friars were with the army, something they were encouraged to do, bringing portable altars with them.[133]

Apart from these general sources of information, another very significant source could have been John de Hothum who had been active in Dublin as early as 1291.[134] John was the nephew of William de Hothum, provincial prior of the English Dominicans and therefore also provincial prior of the Irish Dominicans during the years 1282–7 and 1290–6.[135] Although William de Hothum was elected archbishop of Dublin, he never managed to take up the office as he died at Dijon in 1298 while John de Hothum was with him. As the nephew of that most important Dominican, it is highly probable that when John de Hothum was in Dublin he stayed in the Dominican priory; certainly, he would have visited.[136] John was similarly important and trusted, being one of Piers Gaveston's attorneys and one of Edward I's administrators and receiving the castle and town of Leixlip

Phillips, 'Documents on the early stages of the Bruce invasion of Ireland, 1315–1316', *PRIA*, 79C (1979), 247–70.   132 'On Monday around the hour of vespers 18 February', '*Cáipéisí ón gCeathrú céad déag*', p. 34. 'The Bruce invasion of Ireland: an examination of some problems' in Seán Duffy, *Robert the Bruce's Irish wars: the invasions of Ireland 1306–1329* (Stroud, 2002), p. 80.   133 D.S. Bachrach, 'The friars go to war: mendicant military chaplains, 1216–*c*.1300', *Catholic Historical Review*, 90 (2004), 621, 627; Hinnebusch, *English friars preachers*, pp 435, 470.   134 Phillips, 'The mission of John de Hothum to Ireland, 1315–1316' in J.F. Lydon (ed.), *England and Ireland in the later Middle Ages; essays in honour of Jocelyn Otway-Ruthven* (Dublin 1981), pp 62–85; J.R.S. Phillips (ed.), 'Documents on the early stages of the Bruce invasion of Ireland, 1315–1316', *PRIA*, 79C (1979), 247–70; S. Duffy, 'The "Continuation" of Nicholas Trevet: a new source for the Bruce invasion', *PRIA*, 91C (1991), 303–15. 135 Hinnebusch, *English friars preachers*, pp 386–9, 497; William Hinnebusch, 'Diplomatic activities of the English Dominicans in the thirteenth century', *Catholic Historical Review*, 28 (1942), 309–39, at 327–34. MacInerny, *Irish Dominicans*, pp 378–476.   136 John de Hothum represented William de Valence, earl of Pembroke, and by 1305 he was a baron of the Irish exchequer: *39th rep. DKPRI*, p. 25; *38th rep. DKPRI*, p. 54.

from the king in 1302; in August 1314 John de Hothum was sent to Ireland to see how much money could be raised for the king and Pembridge recounts that de he was again sent to Ireland during the Bruce invasion 'to shape peace and greater security with the king of England'. Many magnates came to de Hothum swearing to stay faithful to the king and to destroy the Scots and giving hostages as pledges, but Pembridge shows his pro-Hothum bias by adding that, if other magnates of the land were not willing to do this, they must be deemed enemies of the king.

Overall, reading Pembridge's account of the years of the Bruce upheaval it is evident that his is an account derived from word-of-mouth news: in 1316 'rumours came to Dublin that Lord Robert de Bruce king of Scotland entered Ireland'; and 'news came from Connacht that Ó Conchobhair killed many English' and in 1317 'news came to Dublin that the Scots were at Kells in Ossory'. We are even told how the news reached Dublin in July 1317: 'Nicholas de Balscote came from England and brought news'. There are thirteen specific mentions of news arriving during the Bruce years. Only an on-the-ground observer could write in such terms.

But, as previously remarked, one of Pembridge's most difficult problems was to attempt to establish (and then relate) the events in the correct sequence, not an easy task as he must have had scraps of notes and memories from several persons with which to contend. On balance, his chronology bears up extremely well under scrutiny. When Pembridge's initial entries about the Bruce invasion are examined, an interesting structure emerges. In his opening entry in 1315 Pembridge reports the result of the battle of Stirling that occurred in the previous year and makes the statement that 'the Scots became audacious' and began to attack Northumberland and then moved on to attack Carlisle.[137] The attack on Carlisle was beside the Dominican priory and this fact could well be the source of the specific item of news that James Douglas was crushed by a falling wall, something verified by the Chronicle of Lanercost.[138] After this information Pembridge begins, first, with what we could call a preamble to the Bruce invasion to the effect that 'the said Scots, not content with their own land' arrived in the north of Ireland at a place called Clondonne. Then second, Pembridge gives a synopsis of future major events and identifies the opening battles listing what he calls the first, second, and third conflicts, namely, the gathering at the River Bann (in September 1315), then Kells in Meath (in December 1315) and then Skerries

---

137 Stirling led to Bannockburn.   138 Lanercost tells us that Douglas 'stationed himself ... on the west side opposite the place of the canons and preaching friars where no attack was expected because of the height [of the wall] and the difficulty of access': *Lanercost*, vol. ii, p. 215. Among the defenders of Carlisle were forty Irish archers; and among the force which eventually relieved the city was a large contingent of Irish hobelars (light cavalry) under the earl of Pembroke: J.R.S. Phillips, *Aymer de Valence, earl of Pembroke, 1307–24: baronial politics in the reign of Edward II* (Oxford, 1972), pp 89, 91, fn. 4.

near Ardscull (in January 1316). This suggests that he had the loose material in front of him, either in notes or in his well-trained memory. Only at that point did he begin his proper chronological account of the Bruce invasion with the information that on Sunday 29 June 1315 the Scots took Dundalk. He then proceeds in what is a fairly accurate chronological narrative of events, ending with the defeat of Edward Bruce at Faughart on 14 October 1318.

During the Bruce years Pembridge praises the local magnates, most of these in the north of the country. There is praise, therefore, for Drogheda when Thomas de Mandeville successfully fought the Scots at Carrickfergus 'with many men of Drogheda' and 'eight ships of Drogheda were fitted out to [go to] Carrickfergus with provisions'. Drogheda is praised again in 1317 when we hear that the men of Ulster took plunder from the town, but the men of Drogheda went and captured the plunder back. And of Faughart Pembridge relates that Walter de la Pulle brought around twenty armed men of Drogheda to the battle with John Maupass and that it was a man of Drogheda, John Maupass, who 'with great honour courageously killed' Edward Bruce and was found dead on Bruce's body. This all looks like information that might have come his way from the Dominican priory at Drogheda, and also of course from the arrival of victorious men into Dublin.

Overall, we see in Pembridge an attempt to record the Bruce invasion of Ireland as truthfully as possible. It cannot be claimed that his account is entirely precise as to date and day, but it is nevertheless remarkably near to it. It is the account of a man living at the bridge leading into Dublin from the north and gleaning as much information as he can and then doing his best to present an honest account, as it was known at that time. After the end of the Bruce crisis Pembridge recounts very few entries between 1319 and 1326; either there was little happening, or he was just weary.

Pembridge: conclusion

The identification of the main author as John de Pembridge, head of the Dublin Dominican house, who lived in St Saviour's priory across the River Liffey from the walled city of Dublin is beyond doubt. All people entering Dublin from the north and even northwest would pass the priory. Pembridge was a reporter of news and from an examination of other primary sources, English, Scottish and Irish, it is clear that he does report the news faithfully (as it was then currently believed). He was aware of the parliaments that took place in Ireland and perhaps this interest might reflect the constitutions of the Dominican order. He was critical of those English settlers in Ireland who ignored the public good for their own personal agenda. He saw the hand of God in the events that happened around him and he also had a lively interest in omens and strange tales.

He also emerges as somewhat cynical. When in 1310 Pembridge tells us that many arrangements 'as if like statutes' were promulgated, the entry ends with a

slightly scornful note, 'if they should be heeded'. In 1317 we hear that when the men of Ulster came with an army of about 2,000 and asked for the king's aid in order to destroy the Scots, he ends with the words 'as they said': his lack of sympathy is apparent when this is followed by his description of the actions of that army, which he said did greater damage than the Scots and furthermore they ate meat throughout Lent, 'from which abuse they felt the curse of men'. He is critical when armies do not fulfil their function as, for example, in 1317, when Edmund Butler, Richard de Clare and other magnates had gathered, Pembridge recounting that they tarried for a whole week and did nothing despite the fact that the army numbered 30,000 well-armed men. Roger Mortimer landed at Youghal in 1317 replacing Butler but when Mortimer and the magnates were at Kilkenny 'in order to dispose of Bruce, there they did nothing'.[139] Mortimer then held a parliament at Kilmainham, just outside Dublin, where 'nothing was done' except discussion concerning the release of the earl of Ulster. In general, Pembridge does not have a high opinion of the management of the invasion.

And such strong views continue into the period when he was writing fully contemporaneously. The omen of bad weather for the two years of Ralph Ufford's time as chief governor of Ireland from 1343 to 1345 reflects Pembridge's intense dislike of him and his wife, although he did exhibit a modicum of sympathy for her final exit. Pembridge ceased writing after Wednesday 26 December 1347. It is possible that he died during the plague.[140]

THE CONTINUATOR EXAMINED

Date of composition

The continuator takes over from 1348. In 1352, when recording an entry about Robert Savage, he declares that *subsequently* 'the Irish destroyed all that neighbourhood because of the absence of castles'. This comment discloses that the continuator was writing later than 1352. But in fact he begins his contribution to the chronicle with a sentence about the 'first and greatest' plague in 1348, a phrase signalling that he knows there were further plagues, some less severe. As the second incidence of the plague took place in 1361, the continuator must have been writing the 1348 entry at least after that point. In 1361 he mentions the second plague almost in passing but, with the third plague in 1370, he begins with the words 'the third and greatest plague began in Ireland in which many

---

139 The Dominican convent in Youghal was used as the location for the parliament: P. Connolly, '"The head and comfort of Leinster": Carlow as an administrative capital of Ireland, 1361–1394' in T. McGrath (ed.) *Carlow: history and society: interdisciplinary essays on the history of an Irish county* (Dublin, 2008), p. 328 fn. 46.   **140** In enclosed places such as monasteries and prisons, the infection of one person usually meant all; in Marseilles, 'of 150 Franciscans, not one survives': Philip Ziegler, *The Black Death* (London, 1982), p. 66.

nobles, citizens, and almost innumerable children, died'. His last sentence is the report of the deaths of Simon Fleming, baron of Slane, John Cusack, baron of Culmullin and John Taillour, 'a powerful and wealthy man and formerly mayor of Dublin'. This final entry finishes halfway down f. 37r of T. The continuator was living through this plague and may even have died at this point. Both T and L end here, and indeed L places the last three words in the middle of a fresh line. In T, a later rough annalistic entry written in 1408 follows: it is crossed out and the last third of the folio roughly torn away (Fig. 5).

Initially it had appeared, from internal evidence, that the continuator was writing after c.1377. This was because in 1368, the continuator correctly reported the death in Italy on Tuesday 17 October 1368 of Lionel, duke of Clarence, but then added that, although Lionel died at Alba in Piedmont and was first buried in Italy, later his heart and bones were returned to England and re-interred at Clare priory in Suffolk (alongside his first wife, Elizabeth de Burgh). Historians have stated that the date of his burial at Clare was 1377. If this were indeed the case, it would cause a problem here: why would the annals end in 1370 when the continuator's knowledge ran as late as 1377? However, it transpires that the only evidence for that assumed date of burial in 1377 is in the Clare cartulary. The deed is dated 12 September 1377 in in fact states only that 'in 1377 his commissary arbitrated in an internal dispute in the convent concerning the funeral expenses of Lionel, duke of Clarence',[141] and hence it does not actually state that Lionel's interment at Clare took place in 1377 but that a dispute relating to its costs occurred at that time. In truth, it is extremely unlikely that it would take seven years for the remains of the king's son to arrive back in England. We do not know the precise year of the Clare burial of his heart and bones, but probably only a year at the very maximum. Therefore, from the entry about the reburial of Lionel, we know that the continuator was writing that item at least a year after 1368. Fortuitously, the last entry of 1370 includes the notice of the death of Simon Fleming of Slane. And, even more fortuitously, we have a record of the inquisition of Simon Fleming's lands taken by the escheator at Slane on 3 March 1371 which states that Simon Fleming died on 13 September 1370.[142] So the continuator ceased writing after 13 September 1370.

What happened in 1370?

The continuator may well have died because of the plague in 1370, but if so he can only have died after 13 September 1370. Another possibility was that he might have been transferred to a different priory because of a shortage of friars elsewhere due to the plague.[143] The least likely is that he may have just lost

141 Christopher Harper-Bill (ed.), *The Cartulary of the Friars of Clare* (11) (Suffolk Charters) (Woodbridge, 1991), pp 74–5; K.W. Barnardiston, *Clare Priory* (Cambridge, 1962), pp 16, 20–1, 77. 142 *Inquisitions & extents*, p. 200. 143 In 1397 John Pole was transferred from

interest in the annals, although this cannot be rejected as he did not display a great attentiveness to current affairs. This was also at a time of another crisis in the Dublin administration surrounding William of Windsor but, as the continuator had never evidenced the slightest interest in political affairs, it is highly unlikely that he would have been sent to England on the king's affairs, as the Dominican Friar Philip of Slane had been in earlier decades.[144] Another theory can be promulgated. Perhaps the continuator went to a general chapter, the supreme authority within the Dominican order. From 1370 the general chapter was held every two years and in 1372 it took place in Toulouse and in 1374 in Florence. The general chapter of 1374 was especially important for Ireland. It was here that the master general presented his report on the affairs of the English province and a number of developments resulted. The first was a proposal that the Irish vicariate should be erected as an independent province of the order. Although this proposal was approved, the Dominican constitutions required the consent of three consecutive chapters for motions of this nature and so it only marked the start of a process that could subsequently be reversed. In 1376 and 1378, legislation was still ongoing to establish Ireland as a province but it failed to receive the final ratification.[145] Perhaps the continuator and indeed the whole Irish vicariate became immersed in preparing for the 1374 general chapter and annals became perceived as less relevant.

Was the continuator a member of the Savage family?

The most intriguing fact about the continuator is his interest in and indeed profound admiration for Robert Savage, a minor lord in the Ards and Lecale, Co. Down, and seneschal of Ulster.[146] The continuator has two long entries concerning Robert. The first, in 1352, is a very lengthy anecdote about his decision to build new castles in many places on his manors in Ulster. The continuator relates that Robert advised his son and heir, Henry, that they should

---

the Dominican friary of Trim to Lincolnshire, Fenning, 'The Dominicans of Trim: 1263–1682', p. 18.   **144** Peter Crooks, 'Negotiating authority in a colonial capital: Dublin and the Windsor crisis, 1369–78' in Seán Duffy (ed.), *Medieval Dublin IX* (Dublin, 2009), pp 131–51; Hinnebusch, 'Diplomatic activities of the English Dominicans'.   **145** In the general chapter of 1376 at Bituricum (Bourges): '*Approbamus hanc : quod insula Sicilie et nacio Hibernie pro provinciis habeantur cum iuribus aliarum provinciarum , et sic vocate in suis locis debitis post alias provincias in nostris constitucionibus adnotentur... ; secunda vero videlicet nacio Hibernie usque ad sequens generale capitulum sub regimine provincialis Anglie perseveret*'. In 1378 at Carcassone General Chapter: '*Confirmamus hanc: quod insule Sicilie et Hibernie sint provincie cum iuribus aliarum provinciarum. Et hec habet iii capitula*' (*ACTA*, ii, pp 427, 442).   **146** Katharine Simms, *Gaelic Ulster in the Middle Ages: history, culture and society* (Dublin, 2020), pp 123–4; Robin Frame, 'A register of lost deeds relating to the earldom of Ulster, *c*.1230–1376' in Duffy (ed.), *Princes, prelates & poets*, p. 94; K.W. Nicholls, 'Anglo-French Ireland and after', *Peritia*, 1 (1982) 386, 386 n3. For the later Savages, see Katharine Simms, 'The Ulster revolt of 1404– an anti-Lancastrian Dimension?' in Brendan Smith (ed.), *Ireland and the English world in the*

surround themselves with strong walls against the Irish or otherwise they would be shamed. His son disagreed with him and argued that as long as there were strong men then, in essence, there were castles, and there was no need to build stone ones. His father was angry and stopped work and swore that he would never build 'a castle from stones and mortar, but he would hold an excessively good house and great household'. In other words, he would spend well and live a luxurious life, but he prophesized that his sons would be sorry. The continuator then says that 'the Irish destroyed all that neighbourhood because of the absence of castles'.[147]

The continuator returns again to Robert Savage in 1360, his portrait being elaborated with an account of an episode when Savage in one day, with only a few Englishmen, killed three thousand Irish near Antrim.[148] The continuator then adds a long comment about Robert's liberality, a trait much admired in the medieval period.[149] Before the battle, we hear that Robert ordered that his soldiers be given wine or ale and moreover, evidently anticipating victory, he ordered a huge feast to be prepared for their return: Savage said in effect that he would be shamed if guests should come and have nothing to eat or drink. Of more significance perhaps, we are then given a list of the foods supplied at the banquet. And when God gave victory to the English, Savage invited them all to eat and he himself said 'I give thanks to God'. Perhaps one of the reasons for the praise lavished on Robert Savage becomes clear as the second entry ends with the statement that he was buried with the Dominicans of Coleraine.[150]

Details like this are very unusual for a somewhat obscure family as such anecdotes tend to be about important individuals and lineages. The reason for the inclusion of the Savage family is exceedingly difficult to determine. Pembridge has no interest in the family and indeed it is from Clyn in Kilkenny, not Pembridge in Dublin, that we hear about the death of a William Savage in Ulster in 1317.[151] Was the continuator a member of the Savage family? Certainly, we can assume that such tales would not have been included unless the continuator knew Robert Savage or at least knew the family.

The only hint of the Savage family in Dublin at this time is the mention of a Brother John Savage in Dublin in 1344 recorded in the well-known account roll of the priory of Holy Trinity: *Item lib. Fratri Johanni Savage pro xviii imaginibus cindendis et depictandis pro feretro, xvii s* ('to Brother John Savage, 17 shillings for carving and painting 18 images for the portable shrine/reliquary').[152] The question is whether this brother or friar John Savage was an Augustinian member

---

late Middle Ages (Basingstoke, 2009), pp 143–4, 157.   **147** McNeill, *Anglo-Norman Ulster*, pp 118–19.   **148** In 1360 'Sir Robert Savadge and Dermot O'Hanly died', and 'Art, son of Gillareagh Magennis, was treacherously slain by the sons of Savadge': *AFM*, pp 617, 619.   **149** Generosity was highly valued; see eulogy for Fulk II: *AClyn*, p. 252.   **150** In 1333 Robert de Savage, knight and John le Savage were free tenants in Coleraine: *Inquisitions & extents*, p. 148. Robert, *IExP*, pp 240, 244, 247, 249.   **151** *AClyn*, p. 166.   **152** *Account Roll, Holy*

of Holy Trinity, or was just employed by them. It seems very unlikely that he is an Augustinian as one does not pay a member of one's own community for work done on its behalf. It is of course possible that the payment of seventeen shillings was only for materials. However, looking at the other entries, it appears that when the money is specifically for a material, the accounts itemize that clearly. A Dominican friar could make an artistic object for a church as it was considered to bring honour to God and helped as a teaching device.[153] Whatever the solution may be, it is significant that a member of the Savage family can be identified among the religious in Dublin in 1344.[154] If by chance, the friar/brother John Savage making the reliquary for Holy Trinity was a Dominican, he could also have been charged with the task of continuing the annals in the priory and, if so, it might also explain the 'artistic' dragons on his section of the manuscript that T clumsily attempts to replicate.

ANTIQUARIANS AND THE ANNALS

Given the amount of interest shown by John de Pembridge's annals in one of the greatest families in English Ireland, the Kildare Geraldines, one might assume that the earls of Kildare knew of these annals. But, if they had indeed known of them, they appear to have lost that knowledge by 1858 when the marquis of Kildare published his famous history of the family, *The earls of Kildare and their ancestors from 1057 to 1773*. Here there are constant references Clyn, Grace, Ware and Camden but no mention whatsoever of Pembridge and perhaps most interesting of all is that there is no mention of the patent of appointment in 1361 of his ancestor, the fourth earl, Maurice fitz Thomas, which is preserved in the Pembridge continuation.[155] From L we know that the Prestons knew about the annals, as did both Thomas Howard, duke of Norfolk and Archbishop Laud himself. Apart from these, it is difficult to determine who exactly, among the early antiquarians of Ireland in the sixteenth and seventeenth centuries, had actually viewed these annals.

Trinity, p. 98; *Christ Church deeds*, p. 79; Raghnall Ó Floinn, 'The late medieval relics of Holy Trinity church, Dublin' in John Bradley, Anngret Simms and Alan J. Fletcher (eds), *Dublin in the medieval world: studies in honour of Howard B. Clarke* (Dublin, 2009), pp 369–89. **153** For comparison with costs of some religious artefacts in Athenry, see Rachel Moss, 'Records of art and architectural patronage at Athenry Friary', and 'Select handlist of artists and craftsmen' in Rachel Moss (ed.), *Art and Architecture of Ireland*: vol. I: *Medieval* (Dublin, 2015), pp 511–43, 544–7. I thank Colmán Ó Clabaigh for this reference. **154** In 1488 there was a John Savage, citizen of Dublin, *Cal. Lib. Niger and Lib. Albus*, p. 34; John Savage, *quondam maior ciuitatis Dublin*, died in 1499 and was buried in Christ Church, *Christ Church: reg*, pp 69, 85, 86, 120. R. Gillespie, 'The coming of reform, 1500–58' in *Christ Church: history*, p. 156. **155** Marquis of Kildare, *The earls of Kildare and their ancestors from 1057 to 1773* (Dublin, 1858), p. 34.

The Dublin annals: authorship, text and manuscripts 47

Among these early antiquarians, it became accepted that Pembridge's first name was Christopher (it is only the discovery by Dr Philomena Connolly of a Friar John de Pembridge as prior of the Dublin Dominicans at exactly the correct time that allows us to conclude that his name was actually John). An explanation for the error may be that a note was misinterpreted by both Ussher and Harris. I would suggest that instead of writing '*Cronica Pembrig*', it was abbreviated to '*C.*' or perhaps '*Ch.*' or even '*Chr. Pembrig*' and hence became misinterpreted as Christopher. But in 1639, Ware makes no mention of a Christopher Pembridge as he writes, '*Pembrigiis (Dubliniensis opinor) claruit anno 1347. Scripsit longe majorem partem annalium Hiberniae ... nempne usqua ad 1347*',[156] and hence it is only later that the name Christopher is erroneously attached to Pembridge.[157]

Who had knowledge of these annals?

The most important man with certain knowledge of the annals is William Camden, who in his 1607 work *Britannia*, states that,

> Thus far forward was the Printers presse a-going when the Honourable Lord William Howard of Naworth, ... willingly imparted unto me the Manuscript Annales of Ireland from the yere of our Salvation MCLII[158] unto the yere MCCCLXX. Which I thought good to publish ... And albeit they are penned in a style somewhat rude and barrain (as those times required), yet much matter is therein contained that may illustrate the Irish Historie, and would have given good light unto me if they had not come to my hands so late. Take them heere therefore truely and faithfully exemplified, even as I found them, with all their imperfections and faults; ... Thus far forth were continued the Annales of Ireland which came to my hands, and upon which I have bestowed these few pages to gratifie them that may delight therein.[159]

The title page of L reveals that it then just known as the Annals of Ireland, and hence it is the manuscript which Lord William Howard of Naworth in Cumberland (son of Thomas, duke of Norfolk) gave to Camden. Camden duly added them to the end of his *Britannia*, with errors. These errors may be accounted for by the rush to publish which Camden himself mentioned. One of the oddities is that he translates Kalendar or Ides dating as calendar dates; in 1362 his 'the 8th of April,' should be 8 Id. April (6 April); in 1369 it is not 12 July but 12 Kal July (21 June).[160]

---

156 Ware, *De Scriptoribus Hiberniae* (Dublin, 1639) (bk I), p. 68. **157** Sir James Ware, *The whole works of Sir James Ware concerning Ireland* (London, 1654), vol. ii, 'The writers of Ireland', p. 83. **158** *Recte* 1162. **159** William Camden, 1551–1623: *Britannia* (ed.), Dana F. Sutton, trans. by Philemon Holland (HTML at the Philological Museum), p. 149. **160** There are many such errors.

Many antiquarians used Camden, the Irish antiquarians appearing only to use him or L. Philip Flattisbury's (*fl.* 1503–26) principal claim to fame is that in 1503 he compiled the Red Book of the Earls of Kildare. Later in 1517 he made a collection of annals in Latin, terminating in 1370. He added extra material and praise of the earl of Kildare.[161] In Kilkenny James Grace (1537–9) after a short preamble concerning fabled Irish prehistory, began his annals with the permission given by the pope to Henry II to subdue Ireland and the next entry is the foundation of St Mary's Cistercian abbey.[162] From 1162 there are similarities to Pembridge but sometimes with extra material, sometimes with less material and often with different material. For example, regarding the death of King Richard in 1199 he has no mention of the long and dramatic entry in Pembridge; he just states, 'death of King Richard'. He ignores dates as given in Pembridge. Grace continues after 1370 but with much reduced entries to the year 1504. In the 1570s the Book of Howth has some annalistic entries that are somewhat similar to items in Pembridge's annals. However, those entries are confused. Some are fairly accurate, some have arbitrary inclusions, and the errors are too numerous to note. It appears likely that Christopher St Lawrence, seventh baron of Howth, had seen an historical compilation sourced from L. He cannot have seen **T** as there is no mention of *hyc finitur cronica Pembrig*. The editor of the Book of Howth tells us that the source for the annalistic entries 'as appeareth in this book, [were] found with the Justice Plunket, 1569'.[163] The St Lawrence family was related by marriage to the Plunkets.[164] The 'book' in question is mentioned again under the year 1327 when we are told that Henry Traane 'brought him to one *Salois* [*recte Saltus*] *Salmone* [Leixlip], so termed in the Book'.[165] So the inference is that St Laurence had gleaned his entries from Justice Plunket's chronicle. The entries similar to Pembridge begin on f. 62 of the Book of Howth, but not immediately after the notice about Justice Plunket's book.[166] There are two points to note here. First, Christopher St Lawrence, first Baron of Howth, was sheriff of the county of Dublin in 1456 and had married Elizabeth Bermingham of Athenry, so there is a Dominican connection here which is magnified by the information that, when Christopher St Lawrence died in

---

161 TCD, MS 584.   **162** *Annales Hiberniae* James Grace, Kilkenniensis ed. and trans. Richard Butler (Dublin, 1842).   **163** John S. Brewer and William Bullen (eds), *Calendar of the Carew manuscripts preserved in the archiepiscopal library at Lambeth, Book of Howth; Miscellaneous* (London, 1871), p. 120; Valerie McGowan-Doyle, *The book of Howth: Elizabethan conquest and the Old English* (Cork, 2011).   **164** In 1546 Christopher had married Elizabeth, daughter of John Plunket of Beaulieu, Co. Louth and in 1562 Christopher had travelled with John Plunket, chief justice of the Queen's Bench, to London in late 1562 to present a petition to the queen. *DNB*.   **165** *Calendar of the Carew manuscripts ... Book of Howth; Miscellaneous*, p. 149; Sparky Booker, 'The Knight's Tale' in Sparky Booker and Cherie N. Peters (eds), *Tales of medieval Dublin* (Dublin, 2014), pp 135–48.   **166** For the annalistic entries, see *Calendar of the Carew manuscripts, ... Book of Howth; Miscellaneous,* pp 120–69. McGowan-Doyle, *The*

The Dublin annals: authorship, text and manuscripts 49

London, he was buried with the Dominicans there. Second, John Plunket was the eldest son of Christopher Plunket of Finglas and Catherine Bermingham, and he married Elizabeth Preston.[167] Fascinating as the Book of Howth is, it does not further our understanding of Pembridge. Possibly John Plunket had taken notes from the annals in the Dominican priory, or he had taken notes from the Preston copy and these he then passed on to Christopher St Lawrence.

Subsequently, the eminent James Ussher wrote a letter to his uncle Richard Stanihurst and he declared that he had not seen a copy of 'Christopher' Pembridge's chronicle:

> But especially I would entreat you to let me have a copy of Philip Flatsebury's Chronicle, for hitherto I could never get a sight of it; as neither of ... Christopher Pembridg his Abstract of the Irish chronicles, &c.

The letter must have been written in or before 1618 when Stanihurst died.[168] This is the earliest mention of the name Christopher being associated with Pembridge. Later, in the 1705 edition of Ware's *The antiquities and history of Ireland*, when considering the infamous Anglo-Norman archbishop of Dublin, Henry of London, the following comment occurs: 'the reason why he was nicknamed ScorchVilleine, may be found in *Camden's* Annals of *Ireland*, at the year 1212'.[169] No mention here of Pembridge. Clearly Ware had never seen Pembridge or even L and must only have used Camden. There are several reasons for this assumption. Firstly, what is very notable is that Ware penned two-and-a-half lines on the Dublin writer Pembridge (and those lines refer to the Camden edition), whereas he produced eleven and a half lines on the Kilkenny writer Clyn.[170] Ware's statement, in his account of the writers of Ireland, is as follows:

> *Christopher Pembrige* (a native of Dublin I think) flourished in the year 1347. He writ the much larger Part of those *Annals* of Ireland which Cambden [sic] published at the End of his *Britannia* Anno 1607, *i.e.* he carried the said annals down as far as the year 1347.

Ware then continues with the erroneous statement 'from the year 1161. They are continued by *Henry* of *eburg* to the Close of the year 1421'.[171] Only T mentions Pembridge: L, the version appended to Camden's work, made no mention of Pembridge and is his ending his contribution in 1347, so how would Ware have known about this unless it was known to some Dublin antiquarians? Third, Ware

---

book of Howth, pp 41–2, 44, 135.   **167** F. Elrington Ball, *The judges in Ireland, 1221–1921* (London, 1926), p. 208.   **168** C.R. Elrington and J.H. Todd (eds), *The whole works of the Most Rev. James Ussher, D.D.*, 17 vols (Dublin, 1847–64), vol. xv, p. 4.   **169** For a wonderful description of the reason for his name, see Sir James Ware, *The antiquities and history of Ireland* (Dublin, 1705), pp 4–5 and 43–4.   **170** For Clyn, see ibid., pp 20–1.   **171** Sir James Ware, *De scriptoribus Hiberniae. Libri dvo.*, pp 61–2, 68; Sir James Ware, *Antiquities and history of*

apparently had no knowledge of the work of Pembridge's continuator who was responsible for the section 1348 to 1370. Fourth, Ware repeats the curious tale told by Pembridge of the banishment of the de Lacy brothers from Ireland in 1210 (whereupon they fled to France and worked as gardeners) but the reference Ware gives is not to the manuscript annals but to the extracts from them that found their way into The Book of Howth. Fifthly and most significantly, in 1283 he states that 'it is remembered in Clyn and others,' that a great part of Dublin was burned; if he had known Pembridge at the very least he would have stated it here.[172] Finally, Ware constantly refers to Clyn, Dowling, Grace, and others, which suggests, very firmly indeed, that he did not have access to Pembridge's annals.

J.T. Gilbert's Latin edition and its problems

Lastly, in 1884, the distinguished nineteenth-century historian, J.T. Gilbert produced two volumes for the Rolls Series called *Chartularies of St Mary's Abbey, Dublin: with the Register of its house at Dunbrody, and Annals of Ireland (CStM)*.[173] This St Mary's abbey was the Cistercian abbey situated on the north bank of the river Liffey just opposite the medieval walled city of Dublin on the south bank. The abbey had vast wealth and prestige and was indeed the wealthiest Cistercian house in Ireland.[174] In the second volume of *CStM*, Gilbert included a miscellany of materials belonging to St Mary's. Also, in that second volume, Gilbert arbitrarily included four sets of annals that appeared to him to have a Dublin connection. These four annals have been frequently and erroneously referred to as 'the annals of St Mary's', and therefore often assumed to be Cistercian. They are in fact four separate and distinct texts. Gilbert himself identified these four annals as:

(i) *Annales Monasterii Beate Marie Virginis, juxta Dublin*. This is not entirely accurate as Thomas Case identifies himself on the last page, at the year 1427, by the words '*scripta per manus Thome Case, clerici ecclesie Sanctae Warburge, Virginis*.[175] The entries begin with the birth of Christ and the final entry in the

Ireland, pp 20–21; *The whole works of Sir James Ware, vol II antiquities and writers*, ed. Walter Harris (Dublin, 1745), p. 83. **172** Ware, *Antiquities and history of Ireland*, p. 59. **173** *Chartularies of Saint Mary's Abbey, Dublin*, ed. J.T. Gilbert, 2 vols (RS, London, 1884–6). **174** For St Mary's, see Colmcille Ó Conbhuí [Conway], 'The lands of St Mary's abbey, Dublin', *PRIA*, 62C (1962), 21–86; Colmcille Ó Conbhuí, 'The lands of St Mary's Abbey, Dublin, at the dissolution of the abbey: the demesne lands and the grange of Clonliffe', *Reportorium Novum*, 3 (1961), 94–107; Gwynn, 'The origins of St Mary's abbey, Dublin', pp 115–25; G. Stout, 'The topography of St Mary's Cistercian abbey and precinct, Dublin' in Sean Duffy (ed.), *Medieval Dublin XII* (Dublin, 2012), pp 138–60; G. Stout, 'St Mary's Abbey, Dublin, and its medieval farm suppliers' in Sean Duffy (ed.), *Medieval Dublin XIV*, pp 146–62; Linda Doran and Bill Doran, 'St Mary's Cistercian abbey, Dublin: a ghost in the alleyways' in Bradley (ed.), *Dublin in the medieval world*, pp 188–201. **175** *CStM*, ii, p. 286. Thomas

annals is for 25 May 1427.[176] There are several breaks in these Case annals; the most serious of which is that of forty-five years between 1316 and 1361. While there is no problem with associating the early part of these annals with a Cistercian affiliation (despite the fact that St Mary's abbey is only mentioned specifically four times), the Cistercian entries cease in 1221.[177] The latter section of Thomas Case, though undoubtedly Dublin annals, cannot be claimed to show any affiliation to any specific order.

(ii) Excerpts by Sir James Ware, who identified them as belonging to St Mary's; these excerpts are merely notes covering a scant six pages from the year 684 to the year 1434.[178] Given the frequent references to Cistercian matters, there is no need to challenge his title.

(iii) Two fragmentary annals labelled by Gilbert as first, 'Annals of Ireland; Fragment: A.D. 1308–1310 and 1316–1317' and these cover ten pages. The second fragment covers the year 1316–1317 and is familiar to anyone working on the Bruce invasion of Ireland.[179] The entries for latter years have a great similarity with the entries in Pembridge for that period and an examination proves that the fragment is more similar to L than T. There are three leaves of fourteenth-century parchment in the British Library, BL Add. MS 4792, fols 211–13; entitled *Annals of Ireland, 1308–1310, 1316–1317*. These are the two fragments printed by J.T. Gilbert in his second volume of the *Chartularies of Saint Mary's Abbey, Dublin*.[180]

(iv) The fourth set of annals covering ninety-five pages is called 'Annals of Ireland, A.D. 1162–1370'.[181] Gilbert does not mention that these last annals (our annals) are in fact by two authors, John de Pembridge and his Dominican continuator. Gilbert tells us that his Latin edition of Pembridge was sourced from Bodleian MS Laud Misc., 526. Evidently, Gilbert, although living in Dublin, must have been unaware at that time of the earlier source, that of TCD MS 584.[182] Gilbert states that 'Sir James Ware in 1639 attributed these [Laud]

Case is not mentioned in H.F. Twiss, 'Some ancient deeds of the parish of St Werburgh, Dublin, 1243–1676', *PRIA*, 35 (1918–20), 282–315; nor in H.F. Berry, 'Ancient deeds of St Werburgh's 1243–1676', *JRSAI*, 45 (1915), 32–44; nor in A. Empey (ed.), *The proctors' accounts of the parish church of St Werburgh, Dublin, 1481–1627* (Dublin, 2009). Colker, *Descriptive catalogue*, pp 330–1. **176** *CStM*, ii, pp 241–86. **177** Ibid., p. 281 (there is one mention of St Mary's in 1370, idem p. 283). **178** BL MS Add. 4787 f 30–34; TCD MS 804 pp 309–14. These very brief notes cover initially only the years 684, 1095, 1180 and 1186 and then brief entries of mostly one-line from 1187 to 1319. There are three final additional entries for the years 1337, 1361, and 1434: *CStM*, ii, pp 287–292. Ware frequently mentions the annals of St Mary's: Sir James Ware, *The antiquities and history of Ireland* (Dublin, 1705), pp 3, 11, 12, 62, 77. **179** BL MS Add. 4792 (on three leaves of parchment). St Mary's is only mentioned once (capture of the earl of Ulster from the abbey); the Dominicans are mentioned once; the Franciscans are mentioned three times and, with four references, these annals in fact show a far greater interest in Holy Trinity affairs. **180** *CStM*, ii, pp 293–302. **181** Ibid., pp 303–98. **182** When Gilbert was discussing Camden's 1607 edition of *Britannia* (which included a rough copy of this manuscript), he noted that Sir James Ware made corrections to

Annals to "*Pembrigius*" or *Pembrige*, whom he conjectured to have been a Dublin writer.[183] Had Gilbert used T, he would have seen, at the conclusion of the year 1347, the most important stand-alone rubricated note discussed above, which states, '*Hyc finitur cronica Pembrig*'. As a result, since 1884, Pembridge's annals have suffered under the disadvantage of being included together with the three other sets of annalistic material under the incorrect heading of the Dublin annals of St Mary's Cistercian abbey.[184]

A great debt of gratitude is due to J.T. Gilbert for his massive historical effort. Nevertheless, a new and completely unabridged edition of these Dublin annals is long overdue. His Latin edition has many problems, and his mistakes need to be identified and rectified. Flaws in Gilbert's other works have been noted by other historians. Mary Clark observes that

> in recent years scholars have begun again to read the original medieval manuscripts in the Dublin City Archives and have discovered several mistakes and a number of strange omissions in the versions which Gilbert published. Words, phrases, and even entire sentences were occasionally omitted from the transcripts and consequently from the published versions, changing the meaning of the texts.[185]

In his introduction, for example, the list Gilbert gives of missing years is confusing and has errors of omission.[186]

However, the most vexing aspect of Gilbert's edition of Pembridge, and therefore the major difficulty facing the reader, is his failure to give the entire text of these annals. Consequently, Gilbert's Latin edition is not complete. When Gilbert found sections in Pembridge similar to Thomas Case's annals or to James Ware's notes or to the fragmentary annals, he decided that, if they were similar enough to an entry already in one of the three previous annals, he would not repeat the entry but only refer the reader back to the relevant page in the earlier chronicle. This is clearly most unsatisfactory as Gilbert just stated *ante* and gave a page number referring the reader back to one of the other previous three annals. To exacerbate the problem, even then he was not clear in indicating how much of that material in the other annals was to be used. The first example of this

---

Camden and among his corrections he included the statement, '*1347. Pro Monaghan lege Nanagh; et post comburitur adde: Hic finitur Chronica Pembrig*', *CStM*, ii, p. cxviii footnote 2. 183 'Ware, however, did not state the grounds for ascribing the work to him, nor are particulars accessible relative to any writer named Pembridge connected with Ireland': *CStM*, ii, p. cxviii. 184 B. Williams, 'The arrival of the Dominicans in Ireland in 1224 and the question of Dublin and Drogheda: the sources re-examined' in Seán Duffy (ed.), *Medieval Dublin XIII* (Dublin, 2013), pp 150–182. 185 For a full account of Gilbert's life and works see Mary Clark, Yvonne Desmond and Nodlaig P. Hardiman (eds), *John T. Gilbert 1829–1898: librarian, historian and archivist: a centenary celebration* (Dublin, 1999). See, Clark, 'Local archives and Gilbertian reforms' in Clark (ed.), *John T. Gilbert*, p. 87. 186 *CStM*, ii, pp cxl, cxli.

anomaly is in 1174 where Gilbert begins the entry with the words *Gelesius, Armachanus ... vir sacer, senex*. After the word *senex* he states *ante*, p. 274 which refers the reader back to the annals of Thomas Case where there is a similar entry. The problem is that unless one has access to the manuscripts, one cannot know how much of that entry to take as being present in the later manuscripts. Also confusing is the habit of using differing font sizes in the text.[187] These problems occur very many times, indeed too many to list, and there are many errors of transcription and occasional omissions of important entries. He has a more satisfactory approach after 1317 because Thomas Case has a lacuna from 1316 to 1361 and Ware's notes end in 1317 and hence the editorial approach of referring the reader to their earlier entries has to cease. But this does little to remedy matters: the fact is that in order for us to get a full appreciation of Pembridge and his continuator, a modern re-examination of both Latin manuscripts, **T** and **L**, has been required, and a full new edition of the Latin text with, for the first time, a modern English translation.

---

187 For example, see Pembridge, *CStM*, ii, p. 307.

THE ANNALS

Editorial conventions

This work has no original title in the manuscript. It was a composite work of John de Pembridge, compiler and author of the section covering the years 1162–1347, and his anonymous Dominican continuator, who contributed the entries for the period 1348–70.[1] One might query the very description of the work as 'annals'. A recent study condemned the tendency to distinguish between annals and chronicles as a modern development that should be abandoned.[2] As the entries in the work below are arranged under individual years, some quite brief, it seems logical to follow Antonia Gransden's recommendation that the word chronicle be applied to 'general, serious historical writing', reserving the term annals for a narrative of very short annual entries.[3] Hence, we may perhaps think of our work as *The Dublin annals of Prior John de Pembridge OP and his Dominican continuator*.

The text given below is based on TCD MS 583 (T), with variant readings from Bodleian, Laud Misc MS 526 (L) indicated in notes to the text.

The foliation given throughout the edition in square brackets refers to T. Minimum modern punctuation has been introduced to facilitate understanding.

Editorial interventions in the text are indicated with square brackets: [...]. Supplied letters are placed in round brackets.

Marginal notes are shown here enclosed within braces: {...}, and placed immediately before the entry to which they brought attention. These marginal notes are often introduced by the abbreviation 'nō': this is extended to 'No*ta*'.

The apparatus identifies the different scribal hands, and also records marginal notes dating from seventeenth century.

Interlineations are shown in superscript between two carets, thus: ^...^. Cancelled words are printed with a horizontal strike through the letters. Where scribe cancels words with a strike through, this is shown without further editorial comment. On occasion, the scribe uses other scribal marks, such as under-dotting, and these are recorded in the apparatus.

T includes a number of scribal features including faces, manicules, flourishes and other scribal marks. These are indicated at the appropriate point in the text using symbols, enclosed by braces if the symbol appears in the margin, or angled brackets if the symbol appears in line within the text. A black dot {•} indicates a

---

1 For full discussion, see pp 9–14. 2 R.W. Burgess and Michael Kulikowski, 'Medieval historiographical terminology: the meaning of the word *Annales*', *The Medieval Chronicle*, 8 (2013), 167–9, 174–5, 181. 3 Antonia Gransden, 'The chronicles of medieval England and Scotland' in A. Gransden (ed.), *Legends, traditions and history in medieval England* (London, 1992), pp 199–201; see also Christopher Given-Wilson, *Chronicles: the writing of history in medieval England* (London, 2004), p. 1.

'face'; the asterisk {*} indicates a scribal flourish or decoration; a double dagger {‡} indicates a zoomorphic design, such as a dragon. The scribe included a Christogram in the abbreviated form IHC on many folios, possibly indicating the commencement of a new day of copying. After the first occurrence of this device on f. 1r, the appearance of the Christogram is denoted using the <†> symbol.

Nomenclature

The Latin text gives fore-names and surnames as rendered in the chronicle. These names are standardized in the translation.[4] When translating the Irish names, I have sought to use the nearest form to that which was used in the fourteenth century. Such a form is closest phonetically to the Latin interpretation of Irish names by the scribe. I am grateful to Prof. Seán Duffy for his assistance on matters of Gaelic orthography.[5]

Apparatus

The endnotes that accompany the translation are used to verify, where possible, the events described by Pembridge drawing on the reports of other chroniclers in Ireland, and where relevant in England and Scotland.

Footnotes to the Latin edition record variant readings.

I have usually placed references to reports in contemporary Irish annals first, followed by relevant reports in English and Scottish annals. The Franciscan Friar John Clyn in Kilkenny (writing contemporaneously in the 1330s–1340s) is vital in this respect because he frequently provides an independent source, in Ireland, of the same item of news.[6] Also from Kilkenny are short annals which are also useful for the purpose of verification of news.[7]

I have noted when a Dominican priory was located in, or near, the area mentioned in the annals. There is no doubt that reports of local importance would be related at the regular Dominican chapters and indeed by visitors to Dublin and it is for that reason that, where relevant, I have recorded the location where a Dominican chapter was held that year.[8]

4 The standardized name-forms employed in *IExP*, index, pp 633–718, are followed here. 5 Robin Frame points out that as 'we see the MicMhurchadha ... mostly through the eyes of Dublin; it can be difficult even to identify the dozens of members ... their names crudely Latinized': Frame, 'Two kings in Leinster: the crown and the MicMhurchadha in the fourteenth century' in *Colony and Frontier*, p. 157.   6 He began writing his section of the annals *c*.1333, *AClyn*, p. 37.   7 Robin Flower (ed.), 'Kilkenny chronicle in Cotton MS. Vespasian B XI' in 'Manuscripts of Irish interest in the British museum', *AH*, 2 (1931), 330–40. For correction to these annals, see Bernadette Williams, 'The "Kilkenny Chronicle"' in *Colony and frontier*, pp 75–95.   8 For a list of all the provincial chapters, see Bede Jarrett, *The English Dominicans* (Oxford, 1921), appendix II, p. 228. Also 'a visitor was appointed every year to visit and report on each visitation to the provincial chapter': A.G. Little 'The administrative divisions of the mendicant orders in England', *EHR*, 34 (1919), 206.

Glossary

Term	Definition
caput (Lat.)	Literally the 'head' or 'capital', this refers to the primary seat or centre of a noble estate
crannock (Eng.)	Measure for grain, peas, beans, woad, coals, salt, etc.[1]
dominus (Lat.)	'lord', applied generally as a term of respect to a superior in rank or station ('the lord king'), and specifically as an honorific for knights (typically encountered in the form 'Sir Maurice fitz Thomas')
familia (Lat.)	family, household, military force, dependants[2]
Item (Lat.)	Not translated: the word is intended as a heading of a section
parlement (Fr.)	Translated into modern French to distinguish the '*parlement*' of Paris from the English and Irish parliaments
regulus/-i (Lat.)	Ruler(s) of a small kingdom, petty king(s), under-king(s)
vill (Eng.)	any small settlement

---

[1] *HMDI*, p. xxxiv. [2] For a discussion of the term *familia*, see Grant G. Simpson, 'The *familia* of Roger de Quincy, earl of Quincy and constable of Scotland' in K.J. Stringer (ed.), *Essays on the nobility of medieval Scotland* (Edinburgh, 1985), pp 102–29, see especially p. 123 fn. 17.

|Folio 1r| **Ihc   maria**[a]

ANNO[b] **DOMINI M⁰ CLXII**[c]
Gregorius primus archiepiscopus Dublin, vir per cuncta laudabilis, obdormivit in domino, cui successit beatus Laurentius Othwothil, qui fuit abbas Sancti Kevini de Glendelagh. Sanctus Thomas fit episcopus[d] Canturiensis, et cetera.[e]

ANNO DOMINI M⁰ CL[X]VI[f]
Rothericus o conghir, princeps connacie, rex et monarcha Hibernie factus est.

ANNO DOMINI M⁰ CLXVII
Obiit Matilda Imperatrix.
   Eodem anno, Amaricius, rex Jerusalem, cepit Babiloniarum.
   Eodem anno, Dermicius, filius Murcardi, princeps Lagenensium, Oraricio, rege Midie, in remotis in quadam expeditione existente, uxorem rapuit, quia rapi voluit, nam ut preda fieret ipsa procuravit, prout habetur in Cambrensi et cetera.[g]

ANNO DOMINI M⁰ CLXVIII
Donatus, rex Urgalie, fundator monasterii Mellifontis, in Christo quievit.[h]
   Eodem anno, Robertus filius Stephani, nec promissionis immemor, nec fidei temptator, cum xxx militibus venit in Hiberniam.

ANNO DOMINI M⁰ CLXIX
Comes Ricardus Stragulensis juvenem quendam de familia sua, Remundum nomine, cum x militibus circa kalends Maii in Hiberniam premissit. Eodem ^anno^,[i] idem Ricardus comes, cum quasi cc militibus et aliis circiter mille, in vigilia sancti Bartolomei, apostoli applicuit. Qui quidem Ricardus fuit filius Gilberti, comitis Stragulensis, id est, Chipestowe, olim Stragull. Qui Ricardus fuit filius[j] Isabelle, matartare regis Malcolmi, et Willelmi, regis Scotie, et bone spei David Comitis, et in crastino vero eiusdem Apostoli, dictam urbem ceperunt, ibique Comiti Ricardo Eva, filia Dermicii, patre tradente, legitime fuit copulate etc.[k]

---

[a] *decorated* H. *Another* IH *and* MARIA *beneath in fainter ink.*   [b] *decorated capital over four lines.*
[c] *The x is odd, compared to other examples of x from the scribe, but clear in* L.   [d] archiepiscopus L.   [e] et cetera *omitted* L.   [f] *missing x, but marg. note in later hand in Arabic numerals supplied* 1166; x *supplied* L.   [g] et cetera *omitted* L.   [h] *marg. note in same hand*: Donatus rex fundator mellifontis L.   [i] *interlined in later hand.*   [j] filius fuit L.   [k] etc *omitted* L.

1162

Gregory, first archbishop of Dublin, a man praised by all, slept in the Lord.[1] Blessed Laurence Ó Tuathail, who was the abbot of St Kevin of Glendalough, succeeded him.[2] St Thomas was made bishop [*recte* archbishop] of Canterbury, *et cetera*.[3]

1166

Ruaidrí Ó Conchobhair, prince of Connacht, was made king and sole ruler of Ireland.[4]

1167

The Empress Matilda died.[5]

In the same year Almeric, king of Jerusalem, took Babylon.[6]

In the same year, while Ó Ruairc, king of Meath, had withdrawn on a certain military expedition, Diarmait Mac Murchadha, prince of Leinster, abducted his wife because she wished to be abducted, for she gave herself in order that she might be the prey, according as it is in Cambrensis, *et cetera*.[7]

1168

Donnchadh, king of Airgialla, founder of the monastery of Mellifont, rested in Christ.[8]

In the same year, Robert fitz Stephen, neither unmindful of promises nor a despiser of faith, came to Ireland with thirty knights.[9]

1169

Around the Kal. May [Thurs., 1 May 1169] Earl Richard of Strigoil had sent ahead into Ireland a certain young man of his familia named Raymond, with ten knights.[10] In the same year, the same Earl Richard with about two hundred knights and around a thousand others, landed on the eve of St Bartholomew, apostle [Sat., 23 Aug. 1169]. Indeed this Richard was the son of Gilbert, earl of Strigoil, that is Chepstow (formerly Strigoil). This Richard was the son of Isabella, maternal aunt of King Malcolm and of William, king of Scotland, and of Earl David, of good hope.[11] And in fact on the day after the same apostle [Mon., 25 Aug. 1169], they captured the said city and there Earl Richard was legitimately joined in marriage to Eva, the daughter of Diarmait, [she] having been given by the father, *et cetera*.[12]

Anno domini M⁰ CLXXᵃ
Passus est Beatus Thomas Beket, archiepiscopus Cantuariensis.ᵇ
    Eodem anno, civitas Dublin per Comitem Ricardum et suos capta est.
    Eodem anno, fundata est Abbatia de Castro Dei.

Annoᶜ **domini M⁰ CLXXI**
Dermicius Murcardi filius, plenus dierum apud Fernys, circa kl Maii, rebus humanis exemptus est.

Anno domini M⁰ CLXXII
Rex animosus Henricus cum militibus quingentis, applicuit apud Waterford, et inter alia donavit Midiam domino Hugoni de Lacy.ᵈ
    Eodem anno, fundata est Abbatia de Fonte Vivo.

|Folio iv| [–]**nno**ᵉ **domini M⁰ CLXXIIII**
Gelesius, Armachanus archiepiscopus, primus Primas Hibernie, vir sacer, senex plenus dierum in Christo quievit. Hic primus archiepiscopus dicitur qui primo pallio usus est. Alii vero ante ipsum sole nomine archiepiscopi et primates vocabantur, ob reverentias et honorem Sancti Patricii tanquam apostoli illius gentis, cuius sedes in tanta ab initio cunctis veneratione habebatur, ut non modo episcopi et sacerdotes et qui de clero sunt, sed eciam regum ac principum universitas subiecta est illiᶠ episcopo in omni obedientia, cui successit in archiepiscopatu bone memorie Gilbertus.

Anno domini M⁰ CLXXV
Captus est Willelmus, rex Scotie, apud Alnewike.

Anno domini M⁰ CLXXVI
Bertram de Verdon fundavit abbathiam de Crokisdenne et cetera.ᵍ

Anno domini M⁰ CLXXVII
Comes Ricardus, circa klʰ Maii, apud Dubliniam obiit; in ecclesia Sancte Trinitatis Dublinie sepilietur.
    Eodem anno, Vivianus, presbyter cardinalis, tituli Sancti Stephani in Monte Cellio, apostolice sedis legatus, venit in Hiberniam, missus ab Alexandro papa.

Annoⁱ **domini M⁰ CLXXVIII**
ix kl Decembris fundata est ~~ecca~~ʲ abbathia de Samaria. Eodem anno, fundatur Rosea Vallis, id est, Rosglas.

ᵃ *erased space with* ᵒ *above* M. CLXXI L.   ᵇ *marg. note in same hand*: Sanctus Thomas Archiepiscopus Cantuariensis, passus est L.   ᶜ *slightly smaller initial* A.   ᵈ *marg. note in same hand*: Henricus rex donavit Midiam domino Hugoni de Lacy L.   ᵉ *initial missing, space left for decorated capital over two ruled lines.*   ᶠ *illius* L.   ᵍ *et cetera omitted* L.   ʰ *tentative underdotting.*   ⁱ *initial* A *decorated with a fine linear embellishment but not rubricated.*   ʲ *ecca underdotted, error for* ecclesia.

1170

Blessed Thomas Becket, archbishop of Canterbury, was martyred.[13]

In the same year the city of Dublin was captured by Earl Richard and his [men].[14]

In the same year the abbey of *Castrum Dei* was founded.[15]

1171

Diarmait Mac Murchadha, full of days, was taken from human life at Ferns around Kal. May [Sat. 1 May].[16]

1172

King Henry [II], full of courage, landed at Waterford with five hundred knights and, among other things, he gave Meath to lord Hugh de Lacy.[17]

In the same year the abbey of *Fons Vivus* was founded.[18]

1174

Gelasius, archbishop of Armagh, the first primate of Ireland, a holy man and old of days, rested in Christ. He was proclaimed the first archbishop (he used the pallium first).[19] For others before him were only being called by the name of archbishop and primate because of reverence and honour of St Patrick as apostle of that nation. The see from the beginning was held with all great veneration, so that not only bishops and priests and those of the clergy but also kings and princes were universally subject to that bishop in all obedience. He was succeeded in the archbishopric by Gilbert of good memory.[20]

1175

William, king of Scotland, was captured at Alnwick.[21]

1176

Bertram de Verdun founded the abbey of Croxden, *et cetera*.[22]

1177

Around Kal. May [Sun. 1 May 1177], Earl Richard died at Dublin and was buried in the church of the Holy Trinity, Dublin.[23]

In the same year Vivian, cardinal priest (by title St Stephen at Monte Celio), legate of the apostolic see, sent by Pope Alexander, came into Ireland.[24]

1178

On 9 Kal. December [Thurs. 23 Nov. 1178] the abbey of *Samaria* was founded. In the same year *Rosea Vallis*, that is Rosglas, was founded.[25]

Anno domini M° CLXXIX
Interfectus est Milo Coganensis et Radulphus, filius Stephanidis, gener ipsius, inter Waterfordiam et Lysmore et cetera, ut patet in Cambrensi.

Eodem anno, Herienus[a] de Monte Marisco[b] intravit monasterium Sancte Trinitatis Cantuarie, qui fundavit monasterium Sancte Marie de Portu, id est, Donbrothy.

{•}
Anno domini M° CLXXX
Fundata est abbathia de Choro Benedicti.[c]

Eodem anno, Laurentius, archiepiscopus Dubliniensis, xviii kl Decembris apud Normanniam in ecclesia Sancte Marie Augensis feliciter obdormivit in domino. Cui successit Johannes de Cemino, vir Anglicus natione, et in Anglia apud Evesham a clero Dublinensi, regia procurante industria, consone satis et concorditer electus, et a Papa confirmatus, qui Johannes postmodum fundavit ecclesiam Sancti Patricii, Dublin.

Anno domini M. CLXXXIII
Ordo Templariorum et Hospitalariorum confirmatur. Eodem anno, fundata est Abbathia de Lege Dei.

[–]nno[d] domini M. CLXXXV
Johannes, filius regis, dominus Hibernie, de dono patris, venit in Hiberniam anno etatis sue duodecimo, ab adventu patris sui in insulam xiii, ab adventu Stephanidis xv, ab adventu comitis Ricardi xiiii, et eodem anno xv revertitur.

Anno domini M. CLXXXVI
Cartusiensis et Grandiensis confirmatur. Eodem anno, Hugo de Lacy apud Derwath fuit occissus dolose ab |Folio 2r| Hibernico, quia ibidem predictus Hugo voluit edificare castrum, et sicut docuit Hibernicum laborare cum instrumento ferreo, scilicet, *pykays*;[e] et quando Hugo inclinavit se percutiendo in terram cum ambabus manibus capite demisso, Hibernicus cum securi amputavit capud Hugonis de Lacy, et ibi cessavit conquesta.

Eodem anno,[f] Christianis, Lismorensis episcopus, quondam legatus Hibernie, emulator virtutum quas viderat et ad[g] audierat a patre sancto suo Bernardo, summoque pontifice, viro venerabili, Eugenio, cum quo fuit in probabtorio, apud Clarevallem, qui et eum legatum in Hibernia constituit, post peractam obedientiam in monasterio de Kyrieleyson feliciter migravit ad Christum.

---

[a] Herveus L. [b] *marg. note in same hand*: Herveus de Monte Marisco, fundator monasterii de Portu, id est Dunbrothy L. [c] Eodem anno, fundata est Abbathia de Geripount *added* L. [d] *initial* A *missing but space left for decorated capital over two ruled lines.* [e] *marg. note (very faint, seventeenth century) in English* [- lost following - Lacy Castle?]. [f] *new line.* [g] *underdotted and struck through.*

1179

Miles Cogan and Ralph fitz Stephen, his son-in-law, were killed between Waterford and Lismore, *et cetera*, as is revealed in Cambrensis.[26]

In the same year Hervey de Montmorency entered the monastery of Holy Trinity, Canterbury.[27] He had founded the abbey of *Portus St Marie*, that is, Dunbrody.[28]

1180

The abbey of *Chorus Benedicti* was founded.[29]

In the same year on 18 Kal. December [Fri. 14 Nov. 1180] Laurence, archbishop of Dublin, slept happily in the lord, in the church of St Mary at Eu in Normandy.[30] He was succeeded by John de Cumin, a man of the English nation.[31] And he was elected at Evesham in England by the clerics of Dublin, with satisfactory agreement and accord (with the king procuring by his effort) and was confirmed by the pope.[32] This John afterwards founded the church of St Patrick, Dublin.[33]

1183

The order of Templars and Hospitallers was confirmed.[34] In the same year the abbey of *Lex Dei* was founded.[35]

1185

John, son of the king, lord of Ireland by gift of the father, came to Ireland, aged twelve, the thirteenth year from the coming of his father to the island, fifteen from the coming of fitz Stephen, fourteen from the coming of Earl Richard. And he returned in the same fifteenth year.[36]

1186

The Carthusian order, and the order of Grandmont, were confirmed.[37] In the same year Hugh de Lacy was treacherously killed by an Irishman at Durrow because the aforesaid Hugh wished to build a castle there. And just as he instructed the Irishman to work with an iron tool, namely a *pykays*, and when Hugh himself bent in order to strike into the earth with both hands, with head lowered, the Irishman cut off the head of Hugh de Lacy with the axe.[38] And here the conquest ended.

In the same year, Christian, bishop of Lismore, formerly legate of Ireland, a follower of the virtues which he saw and heard from his holy father, Bernard, and from the most high pope, the venerable man, Eugene, with whom he was a novice at Clairvaux and who also ordained him to be legate in Ireland., after the vow of obedience was successfully completed, went to Christ in the monastery of *Kyrie Eleison*.[39]

Eodem anno[a] Jerusalem capta est[b] a Soldono et a Saracenis, interfectis multis christianis.

ANNO DOMINI M. CLXXXVII
Kl Julii fundata est Abbathia de Ynes in Ultonia.

[–]NNO[c] DOMINI M. CLXXXIX
Obiit Rex Henricus, filius imperatricis, cui successit Ricardus filius eius, et apud Fontem Evbradi sepelitur.

Eodem anno, fundata est Abbathia de Colle Victorie, i.e. Cnokmoy.

ANNO DOMINI [M][d] C NONAGESIMO
Ricardus et Philippus, reges, vadunt in Terram Sanctam.[e]

ANNO DOMINI M. C NONAGESIMO PRIMO[f]
Civitas Dublin combusta est.[g]

ANNO DOMINI M. C NONAGESIMO[h]
In monasterio Clarevallis translatio Sancti Malachie, episcopi Ardmachani[i] honorifice celebratur.

{•}

ANNO DOMINI M. C NONAGESIMO III
Ricardus, rex Anglie, rediens a Terra Sancta, per ducem ~~austerie~~ Austrie[j] capitur, fecit que finem cum Imperatore pro redemptione sua pro c millibus marcarum, cum Imperatrice pro xxx millibus, et cum predicto duce pro xx millibus marcarum, pro obligatione quam fecerant eis pro Henrico, duce Saxonie. Fuit autem in carcere Imperatoris anno uno, mensibus vi et tribus diebus,[k] pro cuius redemptione calices totius Anglie fere fuere venditi.

Anno eodem, fundata est Abbathia de Iugo Dei.

ANNO DOMINI M. C L[l] NONAGESIMO IIII
Reliquie Sancti Malachie episcopi, de Clarevalle in Hiberniam sub adducte et in monasterio Mellefontis, et ceteris monasteriis ordinis cisterciensis, cum maximo honore sunt recepte.

---

[a] eodem anno *omitted* L.   [b] cum cruce domini *added* L.   [c] *initial* A *missing but space left for decorated capital* L.   [d] m *missing.*   [e] *marg. note (very faint) in different hand on bottom of page* L.   [f] ~~primo~~ *is struck through by a later hand and ink and* 2[do] *inserted.*   [g] *marg. note (same hand):* combusta prima civitatis Dublin L.   [h] ii *added* L.   [i] episcopi Ardma *missing due to damaged manuscript over first three lines* L.   [j] *spelling error underdotted and struck through.*   [k] sex et iii diebus L.   [l] l *error.*

In the same year Jerusalem was captured by Saladin and by the Saracens, with many Christians killed.[40]

1187
On the Kal. July [Wed. 1 July 1187] the abbey of Inch was founded in Ulster.[41]

1189
King Henry [II], son of the Empress, died and was buried at Fontevrault. Richard, his son, succeeded.[42]

In the same year the abbey of *Collis Victoriae*, that is Knockmoy, was founded.[43]

1190
The kings, Richard and Philip, went to the Holy Land.[44]

1191
The city of Dublin was burnt.[45]

1192
In the monastery of Clairvaux, the translation of St Malachy, bishop of Armagh, was celebrated with honour.[46]

1193
Richard, king of England, returning from the Holy Land, was captured by the duke of Austria, and he made a fine with the emperor for his ransom for a hundred thousand marks [and] with the empress for thirty thousand, and with the aforesaid duke for twenty thousand marks, for a guarantee which they made with them on behalf of Henry, duke of Saxony. He was however in the emperor's prison for one year, six months and three days. For his ransom almost all the chalices in the whole of England were sold.[47]

In the same year the abbey of *Jugum Dei* was founded.[48]

1194
The sacred relics of St Malachy, bishop, were brought from Clairvaux to Ireland and were received with the greatest honour in the monastery of Mellifont and other monasteries of the order of the Cistercians.[49]

Anno Domini M. C nonagesimo V

Mattheus, archiepiscopus Cassellensis, Hibernie legatus, et Johannes, archiepiscopus Dublinie, corpus Hugonis de Lacy, conquestoris Midie, ab Hybernicis reportaverunt, et in monasterio de Beatitudine, id est, Becty, solemniter sepelierunt. Caput vero eiusdem Hugonis positum est in monasterio Sancti Thome Dublin.

{•}
Anno Domini M. C nonagesimo VIII

Ordo fratrum predicatorum incepit in | Folio 2v | †[a] in[b] partibus Tolosanis per Sanctum Dominicum.

[–]nno Domini M. C nonagesimo IX

Obiit Ricardus, rex Anglie, cui successit Joannes, frater eius, qui fuit dominus Hibernie et comes Mortonie, qui Johannes interfecit Arthurum, legitimum heredem, filium Galfridi, germani sui. Sic autem Ricardus obiit. Cum autem ~~rex obsideret~~ Ricardus rex obsideret castellum de Gallicis in Britania Minori a quodam existente in castello, Bertrame de Gourdon nomine, sagitta, letaliter vulneratus est. Cum vero de vita desparet dimisit fratri suo regnum Anglie et omnes alias terras suas custodiendas. Et omnia iocalia sua et quartam partem thesauri sui dedit Otham, nepoti suo, aliam vero quartam partem thesauri sui dedit et precepit servientibus suis et pauperibus erogari. Comprehenso autem dicto Bertramo, et coram rege adducto, interrogavit eum rex, 'Quid tibi male feci, quod me occidisti?' Cui ille, intrepidus, respondit, 'Tu interemisti patrem meum, et duos fratres meos, manu propria, et eciam nunc me interimere voluisti. Sume, igitur, de me vindictam qualemcumque volueris, quia non est michi cura dummodo tu interficiaris, qui tot mala mundo intulisti'. Tunc rex condonavit eidem mortem suam, precipiens eum dimitti liberum et dari ei c[c] solidos sterlingorum. Sed mortuo rege, quidam de ministris dictum Bertramum excoriatum suspendunt. Obiit autem rex xviii idus Aprilis,[d] quarta feria ante Dominicam in Ramis Palmarum, xi die postquam vulneratus est, et sepultus apud Fontem Enbrardi ad pedes patris sui, de cuius morte quidam versificator ait.

> Istius in morte perimit formica leonem
> pro dolor[e] in tanto funere mundus obit.

Cuius corpus Ricardi Regis in tres partes dividitur. Unde versus.

> viscera Carleolum, corpus Fons servat Enbrardi,
> Et Rothomagum, magne ecce, tuum.

---

[a] *first new* IHC, *at top of page, possibly implying the beginning of the second day's work.* [b] in *repeated as catchword.* [c] centum L. [d] xviii *error common to* T, L. [e] et *added* L.

1195

Matthew, archbishop of Cashel, legate of Ireland, and John, archbishop of Dublin, brought back the body of Hugh de Lacy, conqueror of Meath, from the Irish and he was solemnly buried in the monastery of Beatitude, which is Bective. However, the head of the same Hugh was placed in the monastery of St Thomas in Dublin.[50]

1198

The order of the Friars Preachers was founded by St Dominic in the area of Toulouse.[51]

1199

Richard, king of England, died. John, his brother, who was lord of Ireland and count of Mortain, succeeded. This John killed Arthur, the legitimate heir, the son of his full brother Geoffrey.[52] Also, Richard died in this way. When King Richard besieged a French castle in Brittany,[53] he was fatally wounded by an arrow from a certain man living in the castle named Bertrand de Gourdon, who fatally wounded him with an arrow. When however, he despaired of life, he demised to his brother the kingdom of England and the custody of all his other lands. And all his jewels and a quarter part of his treasury he gave to Otto his nephew. However another quarter part of his treasure he gave and asked to be distributed in advance to his servants and to the poor. Now, when the said Bertram was taken and brought before the king, the king asked him, 'What harm have I done to you that you would kill me?' To that, he replied calmly, 'You destroyed my father and two of my brothers by your own hand and furthermore now you wish to destroy me. Take therefore from me whatever kind of vengeance you wish, because it is not a concern to me so long as you, who brought such evil to the world, are dying'. Then the king (ordering him to be given his freedom and a hundred shillings sterling) gave way to his death.[54] But when the king had died, some of the ministers flayed [and] hanged the said Bertram. However, the king died on the 18 [*recte* 8[55]] Id. April [Tues. 6 April 1199], the fourth day before Palm Sunday, eleven days after he was wounded, and he was buried at Fontevrault at the feet of his father. Concerning whose death, a certain composer of verse stated of him:

> In death an ant destroyed the lion.
> Ah sadness! In such burial the world died.

The body of King Richard was divided into three parts; whereupon the verse:

> The entrails to Charroux; Fontevrault kept the body.
> And behold to Rouen your great [heart].[56]

Defuncto Ricardo rege, Johannes, frater eius, per archiepiscopum
Rothomagensem, vii kl Maii post mortem predicti Regis accinctus est gladio
ducatus Normanie. Qui archiepiscopus posuit in capite eius ducis circulum,
rosas aureas habentem in summitate per circuitum, sed et vi kl Junii,
presentibus omnibus magnatibus Anglie in ecclesia Sancti Petri
Westmonasterii, die Ascensionis Domini unctus est in Regem Anglie et
coronatus. Et postmodum vocatus est Johannes, rex Anglie, ad parliamentum
Francie per Regem Francie, ad respondendum de morte Arthuri, nepotis sui,
et quia non venit privavit eum de Normannia.

Eodem anno, fundata est Abbathia de Commere.

ANNO DOMINI M. CC[a]
Cathorolus Croverg, rex Connacie, fundator monasterii de Colle Victorie, i.e.
Cnokmoy[b] eicitur de Connacia.

Eodem anno, fundatur monasterium de Voto, id est, Tynterne, per
Willelmum Mareschall, comitem Mareschall et Pembrochie, qui fuit dominus
Lagenie, scilicet, quatuor comitatuum, Wey[–] | Folio 3r | Weyford,[c] Ossorie,
Carlochie et Kyldarie, racione et iure uxoris sue, quia disponsavit filiam
comitis Ricardi Strogulensis et Eve, filie Dermicii Murcardi; sed quia
predictus Willelmus, comes mareshall, fuit in maximo periculo in mari die
noctuque votum vovebat domino ihus Christo, quod si liberaretur a
tempestate, et veniret ad terram, faceret monasterium Christo et Marie,
matrique eius et sic factum est cum pervenisset secure ad WeyFord, fecit
monasterium de Tynterne ex voto, et vocatur monasterium Devoto.

Eodem anno, fundatum est monasterium de Flumine Dei.

ANNO DOMINI M. CCII
Restitutio Catholi Croverg, vel Crorobdir, regis Connacie, in regno suo.

Eodem anno, domus Sancte Marie canonicorum de Connall fundatur per
dominum Meilerum filium Henrici.

ANNO DOMINI M. CCIII
Fundatur Abbathia de Sancto Salvatore, id est Dowisky, isto anno et sequenti
edificatur.

[–]NNO DOMINI M. CCIIII
Commissum est bellum inter Johannem Courcy, primum comitem Ultonie, et
Hugonem de Lacy apud Doune, in quo bello corruerunt ex utraque parte.[d]
Sed Johannes Courcy prevaluit in bello, sed postmodum feria vi[e] in parasceve

---

[a] *decorated capital – not rubricated.*   [b] i.e. Cnokmoy *omitted* L.   [c] 'Wey' *repeated from previous folio as catchword*; Weyford L.   [d] *marg. note (seventeenth century)*: bellum inter Johannes de Courcy et Hugoni de Lacy.   [e] et *added* L.

After King Richard was dead, his brother John was girded with the sword of the duchy of Normandy by the archbishop of Rouen on the 7 Kal. May [Sun. 25 April 1199], after the death of the said king [Richard]. The archbishop placed a circle, which had gold roses on the top, on the head of his duke.[57] And, what is more, on 6 Kal. June [Thurs. 27 May 1199], when all the magnates of England were present, he was anointed into the kingdom of England and crowned in the church of St Peter, Westminster, on the day of the Ascension of Our Lord [Thurs. 27 May 1199]. And afterwards John, king of England, was called to the *parlement* of France by the king of France to answer concerning the death of Arthur, his nephew.[58] And, because he did not come, he deprived him of Normandy.[59]

In the same year the abbey of Comber was founded.[60]

1200

Cathal Crobderg, king of Connacht, founder of the monastery of *Collis Victoriae*, that is Knockmoy, was driven out from Connacht.[61]

In the same year the monastery of the vow, that is Tintern, was founded by William Marshal, earl Marshal and [earl] of Pembroke, who was lord of Leinster (namely of the four counties, Wexford, Ossory, Carlow and Kildare), by reason and by right of his wife, because he married the daughter of Earl Richard Strigoil and of Eva, the daughter of Diarmait Mac Murchadha. But, because the aforesaid William, earl Marshal, was in the greatest danger in the sea by day and by night, he vowed a vow to the lord Jesus Christ that if he should be freed from the storm and should come to land, he would build a monastery to Christ and to Mary His mother. When he reached Wexford safely this was done. He built the monastery of Tintern because of the vow and the monastery was called 'of the vow'.[62]

In the same year the monastery of *Flumen Dei* was founded.[63]

1202

Cathal Crobderg, or Crorobdyr, king of Connacht, was restored into his kingdom.[64]

In the same year, the house of St Mary of the canons of Greatconnell was founded by lord Meiler fitz Henry.[65]

1203

The abbey of St Saviour, that is Duiske, was founded in this year and was built in the following year.[66]

1204

A battle began at Down between John Courcy, first earl of Ulster,[67] and Hugh de Lacy in which battle many fell on both sides.[68] But John Courcy prevailed in

quando fuit inermis Johannes antedictus, et nudis pedibus et in lineis in peregrinatione visitando limina ecclesiarum, ut mos est, iret, capitur a suis proditiose pro mercede data ac maiori danda in futura et remunerandis, traditur Hugoni de Lacy. At ille ducit illum ad regem Anglie, qui rex dedit Hugoni de Lacy comitatum Ultonie et dominium Connacie que fuerunt Johannis Courcy. Tunc Hugo de Lacy, comes, remuneravit et dedit aurum et argentum omnibus proditoribus Johannis Courcy multum et minus, sed statim suspendit omnes predictos proditores et accepit omnia bona illorum, et sic Hugo de Lacy dominatur in tota Ultonia, et Johannes Courcy iudicatur carceri perpetuo, quia fuit ante rebellus Johanni, regi Anglie, et noluit sibi facere homagium, et vituperavit eum de morte Arthuri legii heredis; sed dummodo fuit in carcere in maxima egestate, et modicum habuit et vile ad manducandum et bibendum, et dixit, 'O tu Deus, quare sic facis mecum qui tot monasteria edificavi et reedificavi tibi et sanctis tuis?' Qui cum multis vicibus sic eiularet et obdormiret, affuit ei Sancta Trinitas dicens,^{a} 'Quare me eiecisti de sede mea, et de ecclesia Dunensi et posuisti servum meum Patricium, patronum Ibernie'? Quia Johannes Courcy expulsit seculares canonicos de ecclesia cathedrali Dunensi, et adduxit monachos nigros de Cestria, et posuit in eadem ecclesia, et Sancta Trinitas fuit ibidem in^b sede magnitudinis, et ipse Johannes deposuit eum de ecclesia, et ordinavit | Folio 3v | † capellam pro ea ymagine, et in magna ecclesia posuit ymaginem Sancti Patricii, quod non placuit Deo altissimo, et^c ideo Deus dixit sibi,^{d} 'Scies quod nunquam intrabis in dominium tuum nec in Yberniam, sed, ^propter^^{e} alia bona que fecisti, cum honore liberaberis de carcere', quod et sic^f factum est. Nam contentio facta est inter Johannem, regem Anglie, et regem Francie, propter dominium quoddam et quedam castella, lite pendente, rex Francie obtulit gigantem seu pugilem ad pugnandum pro iure suo. Tunc rex Anglie, memor viri sui fortissimi, Johannis Courcy, quem misit ante in carcere ad informatores aliorum; tunc rex misit pro Johanne Courcy, et quesivit ab eo si posset iuvare in duello, et tunc Johannes respondit et dixit, 'Non propter te pugnabo, sed propter iusticiam regni tui'. Et postmodum accepit pugnam in duello, et tunc recreatus est in esculentis et poculentis et balneis, et accepit virtutem fortitudinis sue, et dies assignata est inter istos gigantes seu pugiles, scilicet, inter Johannem Courcy et alium; sed quando gigas Francie audivit de nimia commestione et maxima fortitudine noluit pugnare, et tunc datum est dominium regi Anglie. Tunc rex Francie pepetivit^g videre ictum a manu Johannis Courcy; tunc posuit galeam fortissimam plenam loricis super truncum magnum seu lignum, et predictus Johannes accipiens pugionem^h sive gladium, et respiciens torvo vultu

---

^{a} sibi *added* L. ^{b} et L. ^{c} et *omitted* L. ^{d} sibi *omitted* L. ^{e} *inserted above the line by the scribe.* ^{f} sic *omitted* L. ^{g} *the letters* pe *are at the end of line and the next line commences again with* pe petevit L. ^{h} *a gap of three letters here with a faint mark* L.

the battle. But afterwards on the sixth day, Good Friday [23 April 1204], when the aforesaid John was going unarmed and barefoot and in linen cloth, on a pilgrimage visiting the lintels of the churches, as is the custom, he was treacherously captured by his men and for the reward he was handed over to Hugh de Lacy (for money given and more to be given in the future).[69] And he [de Lacy] led him to the king of England and that king gave the earldom of Ulster and the lordship of Connacht, which had been [held] by John Courcy, to Hugh de Lacy.[70] Then Earl Hugh de Lacy rewarded and gave gold and silver, more and less, to all the treacherous [men] of John Courcy but immediately hanged all of the aforesaid traitors and took all of their goods.[71] And thus Hugh de Lacy ruled in all of Ulster.[72] And John Courcy was judged to be imprisoned forever, because he was previously a rebel of John, king of England, and he did not wish to make homage to him and had blamed him concerning the death of Arthur, the lawful heir. But, now while he was in prison in the greatest need with only limited and poor food to eat and drink, he said, 'Oh God, why do you do this to me, I who built and rebuilt so many monasteries to you and to your saints?'[73] Having repeated this many times, he lamented and slept and the Holy Trinity came to him saying, 'Why am I ejected from my seat and from the church of Down and my servant Patrick, patron of Ireland, placed there?'[74] [This was] because John Courcy drove out the secular canons from the cathedral church of Down and brought the black monks of Chester and placed them in the same church.[75] And the Holy Trinity was there and in the great seat, and John himself deposed him from the church and appointed a chapel for his image, and in the great church he placed the image of St Patrick,[76] which did not please the most high God. And therefore, God said to him, 'Know that you shall never enter into your lordship nor into Ireland, but, because of other good things that you have done, you will be freed from prison with honour'; and this was done. For a dispute began between John, king of England, and the king of France concerning a certain lordship and certain castles.[77] While the suit was pending, the king of France offered a champion or pugilist to fight for his right.[78] Then the king of England, was remembering his strongest man, John Courcy, whom he had sent to prison before, at the instigation of others.[79] The king then sent for John Courcy and asked of him if he was able to fight in a duel.[80] And then John [Courcy] replied and said, 'I will not fight because of you, but because of justice for your kingdom'.[81] Then, after he had undertaken to fight in the duel [and] when he was restored both in food and drink and bathing, he accepted his good fortune. And the day was assigned between the said champions or pugilists, namely between John Courcy and the other. But when the champion of France heard of the excessive eating and greatest strength, he was not willing to fight, and then the lordship was given to the king of England. Then the king of France requested to see a stroke by the hand of John Courcy. He then placed a full hauberk upon a great trunk or timber and the aforesaid John, accepting the weapon or sword,

circumquaque, et percussit galeam a sumo usque deorsum in truncum, et stetit gladius in ligno fixus, ita quod nullus alius ^preter^*a* eum posset extraere gladium. Tunc interrogatus Johannes a regibus leviter extraxit. Tunc reges quesierunt a Johanne predicto quare ita torvo vultu respexit ante percussionem; tunc respondit, quod si defecisset in ictu, omnes interfecisset tam reges quam alios. Et reges dederunt sibi munera magna, sed et rex Anglie dedit sibi dominium suum, scilicet, Ultoniam. Sed Johannes Courcy temptavit xv vicibus venire per mare in Ybernias, sed semper fuit in periculis et continue ventus fuit contrarius sibi, ~~qm~~ ^quapropter^*b* exspectavit paulisper inter monachos Cestrie. Tandem reversus in Gallias et ibi quievit in Domino.

[–]NNO DOMINI M. CCV
Fundata est Abbathia de Wethneia in comitatu Lymerici per Theobaldum, filium Walteri de Pincerna, dominum de Karryk.

ANNO DOMINI M. CCVI
Ordo fratrum minorum incepit incepit*c* prope civitatem Assisam per Sanctum Franciscum.*d*

| Folio 4r | ANNO DOMINI M. CCVIII
Willelmus de Brewes expellitur de Anglia, et venit in Hiberniam. Anglia interdicta est propter tirannidem Johannis regis Anglie.
    Item, strages magna apud Thurles in Momonia super homines Justiciarii Hibernie per dominium Galifridum Marege.*e*

ANNO DOMINI M. CCX
Johannes, rex Anglie, venit in Hiberniam, cum magna classe et ingenti exercitu, filiosque Hugonis Lacy, scilicet, dominum Walterum, dominum Midie, et Hugonem, fratrem eius, propter tirannidem quam exercuerunt in plebem, et maxime quia*f* interfecerunt dominum Johannem de Courson,*g* dominum de Rathenny et Kilbarrok, qui*h* ipsi audierunt quod eos predictus Johannes accussavit ad regem; ideo rex ~~predictos~~ predictos*i* eiecit de terra. At illi in Franciam fugerunt, et servierunt in monasterio Sancti Taurini, ignoti in operibus luti et latrinis, et aliquando in orto sicut ortolani. Sed tandem cogniti ab Abbate eiusdem monasterii, rogavit idem Abbas pro eis ad Regem quia levavit filios suos de sancto lavacro et fuit compater illius multociens, et Walterus Lacy solvit duo milia marcaro et dimidium mille, et Hugo Lacy solvit magnam summam pecunie Regi, et pro redemptione et pro rogatu dicti

---

a inserted above the line by the scribe. *b* scribe (same ink) corrected in margin. *c* incepit repeated. *d* marg. note (seventeenth century, very faint, illegible): possibly referring to St Francis? *e* Mareys L. *f* quod L. *g* Courson repeated L. *h* quia L. *i* underdotted as error and then entered again.

and looking back and around with fierce expression, he split the hauberk from the top up downwards to the trunk of the tree and at once the sword stuck in the wood, fixed so that none except him was able to draw out the sword. Then John, having been asked by the kings, extracted it easily.[82] Then the kings questioned the aforesaid John, 'Why had he looked around before the stroke in such a way, with fierce expression?' Then he replied that if he failed in the stroke, he would kill all, both kings and others. And the kings gave great reward to him and indeed the king of England gave his lordship to him, namely Ulster. But John Courcy tried fifteen ways to come by sea to Ireland but always he was in danger and the wind continued contrary for him. Meanwhile, he waited a little while among the monks of Chester.[83] At last he returned to France and there he rested in the Lord.[84]

1205

The abbey of Wetheney was founded in the county of Limerick by Theobald, the son of Walter de [*sic*] Pincerna [Butler], lord of Carrick.[85]

1206

The Order of Friars Minor was founded by St Francis near the city of Assisi.[86]

1208

William de Briouze was driven out from England and came to Ireland.[87] England was under interdict because of the tyranny of John, king of England.[88]

Item, there was a great slaughter upon the men of the justiciar of Ireland at Thurles in Munster by lord Geoffrey de Marisco.[89]

1210

John, king of England, came to Ireland with a great fleet and an enormous army,[90] both [because of] the sons of Hugh Lacy namely, lord Walter, lord of Meath, and Hugh his brother (because of the tyranny which they exercised on the people),[91] and especially because they killed lord John de Courson, lord of Raheny and Kilbarrack (because they had heard that the aforesaid [Courson] had accused them to the king).[92] Therefore, the king ejected the aforesaid [de Lacys] from the land.[93] And so they fled to France and they worked, unknown, in the monastery of St Taurin, in the washing places and the latrines and sometimes in the garden just like gardeners.[94] But at last having been discovered by the abbot of the same monastery, the abbot asked the king for them [de Lacys] because he had baptised their sons with holy water and was godfather of them many times. And Walter Lacy paid two and a half thousand marks and Hugh Lacy paid a great sum of money to the king for ransom.[95] And, also at the request of the said abbot, they were restored to their former state and lordship.[96] And Walter Lacy brought with him John fitz Alured (that is fitz Acory), son of the brother of the said abbot and

Abbatis restituti sunt ad gradum et dominium pristinum. Et Walterus Lacy secum adduxit Johannem filium Aluredi, id est, fitz Acory, filium germani predicti Abbatis, et fecit eum militem et sibi dedit dominium de Dengle et alia et alia multa dominia.

Item, adduxit monachos de eodem monasterio, et dedit eis predia multa et cellam que vocatur Foure, intuitu caritatis et gratitudinis, et consimilia fecit Hugo de Lacy, comes Ultonie, et fecit cellam pro monachis, et ditavit eos in Ultonia in loco qui vocatur <... ... ...>.[a] Sed Johannes, rex Anglie, captisque obsidibus plurimis, tam Anglicorum quam Hibernicorum, malificusque multis in patibulis suspensis, stabilitaque terra, in Angliam est reversus eodem quo venerat.

ANNO DOMINI M. CCXI
Dominus Ricardus Tuyt apud Alone, turre cadente, compressus et comminutus occubuit. Iste Ricardus fuit fundator monasterii de Grenard.[b]

Eodem anno, obiit Johannes Comyn, archiepiscopus Dublinie, et in choro ecclesie Sancte Trinitatis sepelitur, qui fuit fundator ecclesie Sancti Patricii, Dublin. Cui successit Henricus Lonndres, qui vocatur[c] |Folio 4v| † Scorchewilleyn a quo facto suo, quia quodam die vocavit suos tenentes ad respondendum sibi quomodo tenerent.[d] At illi tenentes ostenderunt literas ac cartas suas ac ille iussit incendi cartas rusticorum, et tunc liberi tenentes continue vocabant eum Henricum Scorchewilleyn, qui Henricus archiepiscopus Dublin fuit justiciarius Hibernie et construxit castrum Dublin.[e]

ANNO DOMINI M. CCXIII
Obierunt Willelmus Petyt et Petrus Mysset. Iste Petrus Messet fuit baro de Luyn iuxta Trym; sed quia obiit sine masculo herede transiit hereditas ad tres filias, quarum primam maritavit dominus de Vernaill, secundam Talbot, aliam Loundres, et dividebant inter se hereditatem.

ANNO DOMINI M. CCXIX
Civitas Damiete, nonas Septembris, intempesta noctis silencio, miraculose capta est, ita quod in captione eius ipsius[f] nec unus de christianis occubuit.

{•}
ANNO DOMINI M. CCXIX[g]
Willelmus Mareshall, senior, comes mareshall et Pembrochie generavit, ex filia Ricardi Strangbowe comitis Strogulensis, quinque filios et v filias. Nomen quiq

---

[a] *remainder of line blank in* T; *blank space of approximately eight letters* L.   [b] *additional entry follows in*: Anno domini m cc xii, fundata est Abbathia de Grenard L.   [c] *marg. note (seventeenth century, very faint): possibly* obit Johannes [Comyn] archiepiscopus Dublinie.   [d] de eo L.   [e] *marg. note (seventeenth century, very faint): possibly* construxit castrum Dublin.   [f] euis *erased, corrected to* ipsius.   [g] Anno domini M CC XIX *omitted;* anno eodem obit *added* L. Title *on top of page in later hand:* Genealogia Wm Mareschalle L.

he knighted him and gave the lordship of Dengle to him, and many other lordships.[97]

Item, he [Walter] brought monks of the same monastery and he gave many lordships and the cell which was called Fore to them, in consideration of [their] charity and in gratitude.[98] And Hugh de Lacy, earl of Ulster, did similar things and he made a cell for the monks and enriched them in Ulster in a place which was called <........>.[99] But John, king of England, after many hostages were seized, both English and Irish,[100] and many evil doers hanged on pillories and, with the land stabilized, he [John] returned to England in the same [year] that he came.

1211

Lord Richard Tuyt, after he was squashed and crushed by a falling tower at Athlone, rested in the grave. Richard was the founder of the monastery of Granard.[101]

In the same year John Cumin, archbishop of Dublin, died and was buried in the choir of the church of the Holy Trinity; he was the founder of the church of St Patrick, Dublin.[102] He was succeeded by Henry London who was called Scorchvillain because of an act of his.[103] For on a certain day he called his tenants to answer to him by how they held [their lands] of him. And those tenants showed their deeds and charters; and he ordered the charters of those villeins to be burnt. And then the free tenants were forever calling him Henry Scorchvillain.[104] This Henry, archbishop of Dublin, was justiciar of Ireland and built Dublin castle.[105]

1213

William Petit[106] and Peter Messet died.[107] This Peter Messet was the baron of Lune, near Trim, but because he died without male heirs, the inheritance was transferred to the three daughters; the first married the lord de Vernoyl, the second Talbot, the other Loundres, and they divided the inheritance among them.[108]

1219

On Non. September [Thur 5 Sept. 1219] the city of Damietta itself was miraculously captured, silently in the dead of night so that in the capture not one of the Christians was killed.[109]

1219

William Marshal, the elder, earl marshal and [earl of] Pembroke [died].[110] He had five sons and five daughters by the daughter of Richard Strongbow, earl of Strigoil.[111] The name of the first son, William;[112] the name of the second, [*recte* fourth] Walter;[113] the name of the third, Gilbert;[114] the name of the fourth [*recte* fifth], Anselm; the name of the fifth, [*recte* second] Richard who was killed in the

primi filii, Willelmus; nomen secundi, Walterus; nomen tercii, Gilbertus; nomen quarti, Anselimus; nomen quinti, Ricardus, qui cecidit in bello Kyldarie. Et quilibus*a* istorum quinque filiorum fuit comes post patrem per successionem hereditate paterna, et nullus istorum generavit prolem, quapropter hereditas transsivit ad sorores,*b* filias patris eorundem. Nomen prime, Matildis le Mareschall; secunda, Isabella de Clare; tertia, Eva de Breous; iiij^{ta}, Johanna de Mount genesey; v^{ta}, Ysibilla, comitissa de Ferreye. Hugo Bygod, comes Norfolgie, desponsavit Matildam Mareschall, qui fuit comes mareschallus Anglie, iure uxoris sue, qui Hugo generavit Radulphum Begod, patrem Johannis Bygod, qui fuit filius Domine Berte de Furnyvall, et Isabelle de Lacy, uxoris Domini Johannis Fitz GerFerky, et quando*c* Hugo Bygod, comes de Northfolk, fuit mortuus, Johannes de Garenne, comes de Surrey, ex filia filium nomine Ricardum et sororem Isabellam de Albeney, comitissam de Arondell. Gilbertus de Clare, comes de Clovernia, disponsavit Isabellam, secundam sororem, qui genuerunt Ricardum de Clare, |Folio 5r| comitem de Clovernia, que fuit mater Avise, comitisse de Avernia, que fuit Isabelle, matris domini Roberti de de Breous, comitis de Carryk in Scotia, et fuit rex eiusdem Scocie. De Eva de Bryoues, tertia sorore, generata est Matilldis, que fuit mater domini Edmundi de Mortimer; et mater domine Eve de Cauntelowe, mater domine Milsont de Mohune, que mater*d* Alianore, matris comitis Herford. Dominus Garenne de Mountgenesey desponsavit Johannam*e* Mareschal, quartam sororem, de qua venit Johanna de Valens. De Sibilla, comitissa de Ferreys, scilicet, quinta sorore, fuerunt vii filie. Prima, Agnes de Vescy.*f* Secunda, Isabella Basset. Tertia, Johanna Mohun, uxor domini Johannis de Mohun, le filia*g* dominus Reginaldi; Quarta, Sibilla de Bohun, uxor domini Francissci de Bohun, dominus de Midhurst; v, Alionora de Varis, que fuit uxor domini*h* comitis Winton; vi Agas de Mortimer, uxor domini Hugonis de Mortimer; vii, Matildis de Kyme, domina de Carbry. Omnes predicti, tam masculi quam femine, sunt de genealogia dicti Willelmi, comitis Mareschall.

Anno domini M. CCXX
Translacio Sancti Thome Cantuariensis.*i* Anno eodem, obiit dominus Meilerus filius filius*j* Henrici, fundator domus de Connall qui sepelitur in domo capitulari eiusdem domus.

Anno domini M. CCXX IIII
Castrum de Bedford obsessum est, et castrum de Trym in Hibernia.

---

a quilibet L.   *b* cilicet *added* L.   *c* quandam L.   *d* Domine *added* L.   *e* de *added* L.   *f added*, mater domini Johannis et domini Willelmi de Vesey L.   *g* T *and* L [*sic*].   *h* domini *omitted* L.
i marg. note (seventeenth century, very faint): *possibly* translation St Thom martyris.

battle of Kildare.¹¹⁵ And all of those five sons (by hereditary paternal succession) were earl after the father and none of those produced a descendant.¹¹⁶ Therefore the inheritance crossed over to the sisters, the daughters of their father.¹¹⁷ The name of the first, Matilda le Marshal; the second, Isabella de Clare; the third, Eva de Briouze; the fourth, Joan de Munchensi; the fifth Sibyl, countess of Ferrers. Hugh Bigod, earl of Norfolk, married Matilda Marshal; he was earl marshal of England, by right of his wife. This Hugh produced Ralph Bigod (the father of John Bigod, who was the son of lady Bertha de Furnivall), and Isabella de Lacy (wife of lord John fitz Geoffrey). And, when Hugh Bigod, earl of Norfolk, died [Matilda married] John [recte William V] de Warenne, earl of Surrey, [and] from the daughter [Matilda Marshal] a son by name Richard [recte John] and a sister Isabel de Albeney, countess of Arundel [sic]. Gilbert de Clare, earl of Gloucester, married Isabel (the second sister) who produced Richard de Clare, earl of Gloucester; [Isabella] was the mother of Amicia, countess of Avernia [Devonia], who was [the mother] of Isabelle mother of lord Robert de Bruce, earl of Carrick in Scotland, and was king of the same Scotland. From Eve de Briouze, the third sister, was produced Matilda, who was the mother of lord Edmund de Mortimer, and the mother of lady Eve de Cantilupe [who was in turn] mother of lady Millicent de Mohun, who was the mother of Eleanor, mother of the earl of Hereford. Lord Warin de Munchensi married Joan Marshal the fourth sister from whom came Joan de Valence. From Sybil, countess of Ferrers, namely the fifth [recte fourth] sister, there were seven daughters. First Agnes de Vescy, second, Isabella Basset, third, Joan Mohun, wife of lord John de Mohun, *le filia* [sic] of lord Reginald. Fourth, Sibyl de Bohun, wife of lord Francis de Bohun, lord of Midhurst. Fifth, Eleanor de Vaux, who was the wife of the lord earl of Winchester. Sixth, Agatha de Mortimer, wife of lord Hugh de Mortimer. Seventh, Matilda de Kyme, lady of Carbury. All the aforesaid, both masculine and feminine, are of the genealogy of the said William, earl marshal.

1220

Translation of St Thomas of Canterbury.¹¹⁸ In the same year lord Meiler fitz Henry, founder of the house of Greatconnell, died; he was buried in the chapter house of the same house.¹¹⁹

1224¹²⁰

The castle of Bedford was thrown down, and the castle of Trim in Ireland.¹²¹

Anno domini m. cc[xx]^a v

Obiit Rogerus Pyppard, et anno domini m cc [xx]^b viii obiit Willelmus Pyppard, quondam dominus de Saltu Salmonum.

Item, eodem ~~eodem~~ anno^c obiit Henricus Londres, scilicet^d Scorchewylleyn, archiepiscopus Dublin, et sepelitur in ecclesia Sancte Trini^ta^tis, Dublin.^e

Anno domini m. ccxxx

Henricus, rex Anglie, dedit Huberto de Burgo, iusticiariam, et tertium denarium Cancie, et fecit eum comitem Cancie. Et postea idem Hubertus incarceratus est, et facta est perturbatio inter regem et suos, quia magis adhessit extraneis quam suis.

Anno domini m. ccxxxi

Obiit Willelmus Mareschall, iunior, comes mareschall et Pembrochie, qui sepelitur in choro fratrum predicatorum Kylkennie.^f

Anno domini m. ccxxxiiii

Ricardus, comes mareschall et Pembrochie et Stragulensis, primo idus Aprilis, in planicie | Folio 5v | in planicie^g de Kyldare in bello vulneratus, post paucos dies apud Kilkenniam obiit, et ibidem iuxta germanum, scilicet, Willelmum, sepelitur in choro fratrum predicatorum, de quo scribitur, Cuius, sub fososa Kylkenia continet ossa.

{•}
Anno domini m. cc[x]xxx^h

Walterus de Lacy, dominus Midie, decessit in Anglia, relinquens post se duas filias, suas heredes, quarum primam maritavit dominus Theobaldus de Verdon, secundam desponsavit dominusⁱ Galfridus de Genevile.

*Anno domini m. ccxliii

Obiit de^j Hugo de Lacy, comes Ultonie, et sepelitur apud Cragfergous in conventu fratrum minorum, relinquens filiam heredem, quam desponsavit Walterus de Burgo, qui fuit comes Ultonie.

Eodem anno, obierunt dominus Geraldus de^k filius Mauricii et dominus Ricardus de Burgo.

---

^a xx missing, T, L.   ^b xx *missing*, T, L.   ^c *Eodem anno omitted* L.   ^d vel L.   ^e *marg. note (very faint), seventeenth-century: possibly* obiit Henricus Lond ... Dublin....   ^f Kylkennie *placed on line below*.   ^g in planicie *repeated as catchword*.   ^h *appears as if the extra* x *inserted; reads* M CCXXXI L.   ⁱ dominus *omitted* L.   ^j de *omitted* L.   ^k de *omitted* L.

1225

Roger Pippard died.[122] And, in the year of Our Lord 1228, William Pippard, formerly lord of Salmon Leap [Leixlip], died.[123]

Item, in the same year Henry London, namely Scorchvillain, archbishop of Dublin, died and was buried in the church of Holy Trinity, Dublin.[124]

1230

Henry, king of England, gave the [English] justiciarship and the third penny of Kent to Hubert de Burgh, and made him earl of Kent. And later the same Earl Hubert was imprisoned.[125] And there was great trouble between the king and his [subjects] because he adhered more to strangers than his own.[126]

1231

William Marshal, the younger, earl Marshal and [earl of] Pembroke, died and was buried in the choir of the Friars Preachers of Kilkenny.[127]

1234

On the first Id. April, Richard, earl Marshal [and earl of] Pembroke and Strigoil, was wounded in battle on the plain of Kildare and died after a few days at Kilkenny and there, next to his brother, namely William, he was buried in the choir of the Friars Preachers. Concerning whom it was written: 'whose bones remain under the foss of Kilkenny'.[128]

1240 [recte 1241]

Walter de Lacy, lord of Meath, died in England, leaving after him two daughters [recte granddaughters] as his heirs, of whom the first married lord Theobald [recte John] de Verdun and the second married Geoffrey de Geneville.[129]

1243

Hugh de Lacy, earl of Ulster, died, and was buried at Carrickfergus in the convent of the Friars Minor, leaving as heir a daughter who married Walter de Burgh who was earl of Ulster.[130]

In the same year lord Gerald fitz Maurice and lord Richard de Burgh died.[131]

ANNO DOMINI M. CCX[L] VI*a*
Terre motus per totam occidentem circa horam nonam.

ANNO DOMINI M. CCXLVIII
Dominus Johannes filius Galfridi, miles, venit iusticiarius in Hiberniam.

* ANNO DOMINI M. CCL
Lodovicus, rex Francie, a Saracenis, et Willelmus de Longa Spata et multi alii capiuntur.
 In Hibernia interficitur McCanewey, filius Belyal, sicut*b* meruit, in Leys.

ANNO DOMINI M. CCLI
Nascitur dominus Henricus Lacy.
 Item, die natali apud Eboracum, Alexander, rex Scotie, puer xi annorum, desponsavit Margaretam, filiam regis Anglie.

* ANNO DOMINI M. CCLV
Alanus de la Souche fit et venit justiciarius Hibernie; et anno Domini M CC LVII obiit dominus Mauricius filius Geraldi.

ANNO DOMINI M. CCLIX
Stephanus de Longa Spata venit Justiciarius Hibernie.
 Item, interfectus est Oneyll, apud Doune.

ANNO DOMINI M. CCLX
Obiit ~~obiit~~*c* Stephanus de Longa Spata.
 Castrum Viride in Ultonia prosternitur.
 Item, Willelmus Dene fit justiciarius Hibernie.

ANNO DOMINI M. CCLXI
Dominus Johannes filius Thome et dominus Mauricius, filius eius, interficiuntur in Dessemonia a Mc Karthy.
 Item, obiit Willelmus Dene, justiciarius Hibernie. Cui succcessit dominus ~~dominus~~*d* Ricardus de Capella, eodem anno. Anno domini M. CCLXII obiit
|Folio 6r| †

ANNO DOMINI M. CCLXII
Obiit*e* Ricardus de Clare, comes Glovernie.
 * Item, obiit Martinus demaun de bile in crastino Sancti*f* Benedicti.

---

a T *and* L. *both have* l *missing - should be* m. cc xlvi.   *b* bene *added* L.   *c* obiit *repeated and struck through.*   *d* dominus *repeated and struck through.*   *e* Anno domini m cc lxij, obiit, *repeated- but now rubricated.*   *f* sancti *omitted* L.

1246
There was an earthquake through the whole of the west around the ninth hour.[132]

1248
Lord John fitz Geoffrey, knight, came as justiciar of Ireland.[133]

1250
Louis, king of France, and William de Longespée, and many others, were captured by the Saracens.[134]
   In Ireland, Mac Anmchadha, the son of Belial, was killed in Laois, as he well deserved.[135]

1251
Lord Henry Lacy was born.[136]
   Item, at Christmas at York, Alexander, king of Scotland, a boy of 11 years, was married to Margaret, daughter of the king of England.[137]

ANNO[138] DOMINI 1255
Alan de la Zouche was appointed and came [as] justiciar of Ireland.[139] And in the year of Our Lord 1257 lord Maurice fitz Gerald died.[140]

1259
Stephen de Longespée, justiciar of Ireland, came.[141]
   Item, Ó Néill was killed at Down.[142]

1260
Stephen de Longespée died.[143]
   Greencastle in Ulster was destroyed.[144]
   Item, William Dene was appointed justiciar of Ireland.[145]

1261
Lord John fitz Thomas and his son, lord Maurice, were killed in Desmond by Mac Cárthaigh.[146]
   Item, William Dene, justiciar of Ireland, died. Lord Richard de la Rochelle succeeded in the same year.[147]

1262
Richard de Clare, earl of Gloucester, died.[148]
   Item, Martin de Mandeville died the day after the feast of St Benedict.[149]

* Anno domini M. CCLXIIII
Mauricius filius Geraldi et Mauricius filius Mauricii ceperunt Ricardum de Capella et*[a]* dominum Theobaldum Botiller et dominum Johannem Cogan, apud Tristeldermot.*[b]*

Anno domini M. CCLXVII
David de Barry fit justiciarius Hibernie.

Anno domini M. CCLXVIII
Dominus Mauricius filius Mauricii submergitur.
    Item,*[c]* Robertus Ufford fit justiciarius Hibernie.

* Anno domini M. CCLXIX
Castrum de Roscaman fundatur.
    Ricardus de Exoniis fit justiciarius itinerans.

Anno domini M. CCLXX
Dominus Jacobus de Audely venit justiciarius iusticiarius*[d]* in Hiberniam.

Anno domini M. CCLXXI
Henricus, filius regis de Almania, interficitur in curia Romana.
    Eodem anno, pestis, famis et gladius, et maxime in Midia.
    Item, interficitur Nicholaus*[e]* Verdon et Johannes, frater eius. Obiit Walterus de Burgo, comes Ultonie.

Anno domini M. CCLXXII
Interficitur dominus Jacobus de Audeley, justiciarius Hibernie, cadendo de equo suo in Thothomonia. Cui successit*[f]* Mauricius filius Mauricii in officio capitalis justiciarie.

* Anno domini M. CCLXXIII
Dominus Galfridus de Genebile rediit de Terra Sancta, et justiciarius Hibernie.

Anno domini M. CCLXXIIII*[g]*
Edwardus, filius Regis Henrici, per Fratrem Robertum Kilwardby, ordinis predicatorum, archiepiscopum Cantuariensis, die Sancti Magni, martiris, in ecclesia Westmonasteriensi unctus est in regem Anglie, et coronatus est, presentibus magnatibus totius Anglie, cuius professio sive iuramentum tale

---

[a] et *omitted* L.   *[b]* *very faint seventeenth century Marginalia* [*possibly* Mauricius filius Geraldi … filius Maurice …].   *[c]* dominus *added* L.   *[d]* justiciarius *repeated but not deleted.*   *[e]* de *added* L.   *[f]* dominus *added* L.   *[g]* *marg. note (hand B)*: Sacramentum Regis.

1264
Maurice fitz Gerald and Maurice fitz Maurice captured Richard de la Rochelle, lord Theobald Butler and lord John Cogan at Tristledermot [Castledermot].[150]

1267
David de Barry was justiciar of Ireland.[151]

1268
Lord Maurice fitz Maurice was drowned.[152]
    Item, lord Robert d'Ufford was appointed justiciar of Ireland.[153]

1269
The castle of Roscommon was founded.
    Richard de Exonia was appointed itinerant justice.[154]

1270
James de Audley, justiciar to Ireland, came.[155]

1271
Henry, son of the king of Germany, was killed in the Roman Curia.[156]
    In the same year, plague, famine, and death by the sword and [it was] greatest in Meath.[157]
    Item, Nicholas de Verdun was killed and John his brother.[158] Walter de Burgh, earl of Ulster, died.[159]

1272
Lord James de Audley, justiciar of Ireland, was killed falling from his horse in Thomond;[160] Maurice fitz Maurice succeeded in the office of chief justiciar.[161]

1273
Lord Geoffrey de Geneville returned from the Holy Land and [was appointed] justiciar of Ireland.[162]

1274[163]
Edward, son of King Henry, was anointed into the kingdom of England, by Friar Robert Kilwardby, of the Order of Preachers, archbishop of Canterbury, on the feast day of St Magnus, martyr [Sun. 19 Aug. 1274], in the church of Westminster and was crowned with all the magnates of England being present.[164] His profession or oath was the following: I, Edward, son and heir of King Henry, vow, acknowledge and promise in the presence of God and His angels, from henceforth and in the future, to watch over and preserve the law, justice and the

fuit. Ego, Edwardus,[a] filius et heres Henrici regis, profiteor, confiteor, et promitto, coram Deo et Angelis eius, amodo et deinceps legem et iustitiam, pacemque Sancte Dei Ecclesie, populoque dei[b] michi subiecto respectu sicut cum consilio fidelium nostrorum invenire poterimus; Pontificibus quoque Ecclesie Dei condignum et[c] canonicum honorem exibere atque[d] ab imperatoribus et regibus ecclesie sibi commissis collata sunt inviolabiliter conservare, abbatibus et vasis dominicis congruum honorem secundum fidelium nostrorum sicut Deus me adiuvet et Sancta Dei ewangelia.

Eodem anno, obiit dominus Johannes de | Folio 6v | de[e] Verdona.

Item, dominus Thomas de Clara venit in Hiberniam.

Item, Willemus filius Rogeri, prior Hospitaliorum, et multi alii capiuntur apud Glyndelory, et plures interficiuntur ibidem.

*Anno domini m. cclxxv
Castrum de Roscaman[f] iterum erigitur.

Eodem anno, Moridach captus erat apud Norragh per dominum Walterum Lefauntte.

Anno domini m. cclxxvi
Robertus Dufford fit justiciarius Hibernie iterato; cessit Galfridus de Genebile.

Anno domini m. cclxxvii[g] Obrene interficitur.

*Anno domini m. cclxxviii
Obiit dominus David de Barry.

Item, obiit dominus Johannes de Cogan.

Anno domini m. cclxxix[h]
Dominus Robertus Dufford intravit Angliam, et constituit in[i] loco suo Fratrem Robertum[j] de Fulborne, episcopum Waterford, cuius tempore mutata est moneta.

Item, tabula rotunda tenta est apud Kenylworth per dominum Rogerum de Mortuo mari.

*Anno domini m. cclxxx
Robertus Dufford rediit de Anglia justiciarius ut prius.

Item, obiit uxor domini Roberti Ufford.

---

[a] E *for* Edwardus L.   [b] Dei *underdotted.*   [c] *marg. note (very faint), seventeenth-cent.: possibly* [... coronat].   [d] at L.   [e] *repetition of* de L.   [f] Roscoman; *underdotted, and struck through, unidentified letter* L.   [g] *continuation of previous AD instead of new line.*   [h] *continuation of previous AD instead of new line.*   [i] in *omitted* L.   [j] *error corrected in margin:* Steph, *but possibly different hand?* ∴ *above* Robertum *indicating the error. The correct name,* Stephen, *in 1281 below.* .Robertum L.

peace of the holy church of God and to protect the people subject to me [without] distinction of persons according as we will be able to find [ways of doing so] with the counsel of our faithful [men]. And to show towards the bishops of the church of God that honour which is worthy of them and is lawfully due [to them], as has been conferred upon the churches entrusted to them by emperors and kings; and to preserve intact for abbots and the vessels of the lord the honour appropriate to them, in accordance with the counsel of our faithful men. So, may God and the holy gospels of God help me.[165]

In the same year lord John de Verdun died.[156]

Item, lord Thomas de Clare came to Ireland.[167]

Item, William fitz Roger, prior of the Hospitallers, and many others, were captured at Glenmalure and many were killed there.[168]

1275
The castle of Roscommon was built again.[169]

In the same year Muircheartach was captured at Norragh by lord Walter Lenfaunt.[170]

1276
Robert d'Ufford was again appointed justiciar of Ireland.[171] Geoffrey de Geneville ceased.

1277
Ó Briain was killed.[172]

1278
Lord David de Barry died.[173]

Item, lord John de Cogan died.[174]

1279
Lord Robert d'Ufford entered England and established in his place Friar Robert [*recte* Stephen] de Fulbourne, bishop of Waterford, in whose time money was changed.[175]

Item, a round table was held at Kenilworth by lord Roger de Mortimer.[176]

1280
Robert d'Ufford returned from England, justiciar as before.

Item, the wife of lord Robert d'Ufford died.[177]

ANNO DOMINI M. CCLXXXI
Adam Cusak, minor, interfecit Willelmum Baret et plures alios, in Connacia.
   Item, Frater Stephanus Fulborne fit justiciarius Hibernie.
   Item, dominus Robertus Dufford rediit in Angliam.

{•}
ANNO DOMINI M. CCLXXXII
Interfectus est Moritagh et Arte McMurgh, frater eius, apud Arclowe in vigilia Sancte Marie Magdalene.
   Item, obiit dominus Rogerus de Mortuo mari.

ANNO DOMINI M. CCLXXXIII
Combusta civitas Dublin, pro parte, et campanile ecclesie Sancte Trinitatis, Dublin, iii. nonas Januarii.

{•}
ANNO DOMINI M. CCLXXXIIII
Captum est castrum de Ley a regulis Offoliensium, et combustum est in crastino Sancti Barnabe, apostoli.
   Obiit Alfonsius, filius regis E., etate xii annorum.

ANNO DOMINI M. CCLXXXV
Obiit Dominus Theobaldus le Botiller, vi kl Octobris, et^a castello de Arclo et sepultus in^b conventu predicatorum ibidem.^{c}
{No*ta*} Item,^{d} captus est Geraldus filius Mauricii a suis Hibernicis in Ofalia, et R. Petyt, et S. Doget, cum multis aliis, et strages magna apud Rathode.

ANNO DOMINI M. CCLXXXVI
Combusta ^est^ le Norragh et Arscoll, cetereque ville continue per Philippum Staunton, xvi kal. Decembris.
   In hiis diebus, Alianora, regina Anglie, mater Regis Edwardi, religionem suscepit apud Ambresbury, die Translacionis Sancti Thome, dote sua in regno Anglie a perpetuo possidenda per Summum Pontificem confirmata.
   Item, |Folio 7r| † Calwagh capitur apud Kildare.
   Obiit dominus Thomas de Clara.

ANNO DOMINI M. CCLXXXVII
Fratre^f Stephanus Fulborne, archiepiscopus Tuamensis, obiit, cui successit in officio justiciarie, ad tempus, Johannes Sampford, archiepiscopus Dublin.
   * Eodem anno rex Hungarie, fide christianorum relicta, apostatavit, et convocatis, quasi ad parliamentum, fraudolenter potencioribus sue terre,

---

^{a} in L. ^{b} in *omitted* L. ^{c} ibidem predicatorum conventu L. ^{d} *first manicula here: top of finger level with* captus est. ^{e} *Sign for insertion* ^ *and* est. ^{f} fratre *omitted* L.

1281

Adam Cusack, the younger, killed William Barrett and many others in Connacht.[178]

Item, Friar Stephen Fulbourne was appointed justiciar of Ireland.[179]

Item, lord Robert d'Ufford returned to England.

1282

Muircheartach and Art Mac Murchadha, his brother, were killed at Arklow on the eve of St Mary Magdalen [Tues. 21 July 1282].[180]

Item, lord Roger de Mortimer died.[181]

1283

On 3 Non. January [Mon. 3 Jan. 1284], the city of Dublin was partly burnt, and the campanile of the church of Holy Trinity, Dublin.[182]

1284

The castle of Lea was captured and was burnt on the day following St Barnabas, apostle [Mon., 12 June 1284] by the kinglets of Offaly.[183]

Alphonso, the son of King E. [Edward I], died aged 12 years.[184]

1285[185]

On 6 Kal. October [Wed. 26 Sept. 1285] lord Theobald Butler died in the castle of Arklow and was buried in the convent of the Preachers there.[186]

{**Note**} Item, Gerald fitz Maurice[187] was captured by his Irish in Offaly and [also] R. Petit[188] and S. Doget, with many others; and a great massacre at Ratoath.[189]

1286

On 16 Kal. December [Sat. 16 Nov. 1286], Norragh and Ardscull, together with other vills, were burnt in succession by Philip Staunton.[190]

In these days Eleanor, queen of England, mother of King Edward, accepted religion at Amesbury on the day of the translation of St Thomas [Sun. 7 July], while her dowry in the kingdom of England, [held by her] in lasting possession, was confirmed by the supreme pontiff.[191]

Item, Calbhach was captured at Kildare.[192]

Lord Thomas de Clare died.[193]

1287

Friar Stephen de Fulbourne, archbishop of Tuam, died. John Sandford, archbishop of Dublin, succeeded in the office of the justiciar at that time.[194]

In the same year the king of Hungary, deserter of the Christian faith, apostatised.[195] And he called together, fraudulently, as if to a parliament, the

supervenit Miramomelius, Saracenns potens, cum xx milibus bellatorum, regem cum omnibus christianis ibidem congregatis, in vigilia Sancti Johannis Baptiste, secum adducens, Itinerantibus itaque christianis, tempus clarum in nubulum est conlisum,[a] subitoque grandiosa tempestas multa millia incredibilium continue occidit, et christiani ad sua sunt conversi, solo rege apostata cum Saracenis gradiente. Hungarii[b] eius filium coronantes in fide catholica permanserunt.

Anno domini m. cc * lxxxix
Tripolis, civitas famosa, solo tenus, non sine magna sanguinis effussione christiani complanatur per Soldanum Babilonie, qui iussit ymagines sanctorum ad caudas trahi equorum, in contemptum nominis Ihus Christi, per civitatem distructam.

*Anno domini mcc nonagesimo
Inclita stirps regis sponsis datur ordine legis. Dominus Gilbertus de Clare duxit in uxorem dominam Johannem de Acon, filiam domini Regis Edwardi, in conventuali ecclesia Westmonasteriensi, nuptiis solempniter celebratis mense Maii, et Johannes, filius ducis Brabancie, Margaretam, dicti regis filiam, duxit in uxorem, in predicta ecclesia mense Julii. Eodem anno, dominus Willelmus Wescy fit justiciarius Hibernie, eam intrando die Sancti Martini.

Item, Omolaghelyn, rex Midie, interficitur.[c]

Anno domini m. cc nonagesimo i
Gilbertus de Clare, filius Gilberti et domine Johanne de Acon, xi die Maii intrante, natus est.

Item, exercitus ductus est in Ultoniam, contra Ohanlon et ceteros regulos pacem impedientes, per Ricardum, comitem Ultonie, et Willelmum de Wescy, justiciarium Hibernie.

Item, obiit domina Elianora, regina quondam Anglie, et mater Edwardi Regis, in festo Sancti Johannis Baptiste, que in habitu religionis desiderato, per annos iiij et menses xi et vi dies laudabilem vitam duxit in cenobio Ambrisbury, ubi fuit monialis.

Item insonuerunt rumores in auribus domini Pape Martini,[d] in vigilia Beate Marie Magdalene, de civitate Acon in Terra Sancta, que sola fuit refugium christianorum, quod illa[e] a Milkadar, Soldano Babilonie, et suis infinitis fuit obsessa, et quasi xliiii[or] diebus fortissime impugnata, scilicet, ab viii idus Aprilis usque xv kl Julii. Tandem ab impugnantibus Sarasenis dirutus est murus, et

---

[a] conversum L.   [b] igitur added L.   [c] Added on end of next line and underlined in red.   [d] T and Martin [sic] L.   [e] in added L.

magnates of his land.¹⁹⁶ Miramomelius, a mighty Saracen arrived, with twenty thousand warriors, on the eve of St John the Baptist, they came upon the king, with all the Christians collected there, bringing them along with him.¹⁹⁷ And, when the Christians were journeying, the clear weather turned cloudy and suddenly an incredible hailstorm killed many thousands at once. And the Christians returned to their [home], only the apostate king going with the Saracens.¹⁹⁸ The Hungarians, crowning his son king, remained in the Catholic faith.

1289

Tripoli, the renowned city, was levelled as far as the ground by the sultan of Babylon, [and] not without great flowing of Christian blood. He ordered the images of the saints to be drawn at horse's tails, through the destroyed city, in contempt of the name of Jesus Christ.¹⁹⁹

1290²⁰⁰

The illustrious offspring of the king were legally given in marriage. Lord Gilbert de Clare married lady Joan of Acre, daughter of the Lord King Edward, in the convent church of Westminster, the wedding was solemnly celebrated in the month of May. And John [II], son of the duke of Brabant, married Margaret, daughter of the said king, in the aforesaid church in the month of July.²⁰¹

    In the same year lord William Vescy was appointed justiciar of Ireland; he arrived on the feast of St Martin [Pope/ 10 Nov.; apos/ 11 Nov. 1290].²⁰²

    Item, Ó Maoilsheachlainn, king of Meath, was killed.²⁰³

1291

Gilbert de Clare, the son of Gilbert and of lady Joan of Acre, entered the world; he was born on the eleventh day of May [Fri. 11 May 1291]²⁰⁴

    Item, Richard earl of Ulster and William de Vescy justiciar of Ireland, led the army into Ulster against Ó hAnluain and other kinglets obstructing peace.²⁰⁵

    Item, Lady Eleanor, formerly queen of England and mother of King Edward, died on the feast of St John the Baptist [Sun. 24 June 1291]. For four years, eleven months and six days she had led a praiseworthy life in the monastery of Amesbury where she was a nun in the desired religious habit.²⁰⁶

    Item, on the eve of Blessed Mary Magdalen [Sat., 21 July 1291], reports came to the ears of the lord Pope Martin [*recte* Nicholas IV] concerning the city of Acre in the Holy Land (which was the only refuge of Christians) that it was besieged by Milkadar, sultan of Babylon, and an infinite [number] of his men, and it had been fiercely assaulted for almost forty-four days, namely, from 8 Id. April [Fri., 6 April 1291] right up to 15 Kal. July [Sun. 17 June 1291]. At last the wall was demolished by the Saracens' attack and the Saracens entered in great numbers and many Christians were killed. Some people, through fear, drowned

intraverunt Saraceni in numero infinito, pluribusque Christianis | Folio 7v | interfectis, quibusdam in mari pre timore submerses. Periit eciam mare patriarcha, cum suis et rex Cipri et Oto de Grandisano, cum suis, miserabiliter per navigium evaserunt.

Item, concessum est*a* domino E. R.*b* Anglie, per dominum*c* Martinum*d* decima pars omnium proventuum beneficiorum ecclesiasticorum per septennium in Hibernia, in subsidium Terre Sancte.

Item, senex*e* filius Comitis de Clare nascitur.

Anno domini m. cclxx*f* nonagesimo ii

Rex E. Anglie iterum intravit Scociam, et electus est in regem Scocie dominus Johannes de Bailoll, comes de Galweya, totum regnum Scocie iure hereditario acquisivit, et dominus E. R.*g* Anglorum, apud Novum Castrum super Tyne, die Sancti Stephani, homagium fecit, Florencio, comite de Holand, Roberto de Bruce, comite de Carrik, Johanne Hastynges, Johanne Comyn, Patricio de Dunbarre, Johanne de Wescy, Nicholo de Sawles et Willelmo de Roos, qui omnes calumpniati sunt ius in dicto regno, sed submiserunt se iudicio domini Regis E.

Item, xv pars bonorum secularium concessa domino regi Anglie in Hibernia, termino ea colligendo in festo Sancti Michaelis.

Item, obiit dominus Petrus de Genevile, miles.

Item, Rice Omereduk ductus est Eboracum, et ibidem ad caudas equorum distractus.

Anno domini m. cc nonagesimo iii

Bellum navale fit Normanis generale.

Item, interfecti sunt Normani non modico numero per bellum navale a baronis de partibus*h* Anglie, et aliis coadiutoribus, inter pascha et pentecosten, qua de causa mota est guerra inter Angliam et Francos, unde rex Francorum, Philippus, direxit regi Anglorum literas creditorias, ut personaliter ad parliamentum suum accederet*i* responsurus questionibus quas idem rex erat propositurus versus eum. Cuius mandato minime completo, mox ipsum regem Anglie extorrem per consilium Francorum rex Francie iudicans condempnavit.

Item, Gilbertus de Clare, comes Glovernie, cum uxore sua intravit Hiberniam circa festum Sancti Luce.

Anno domini m.cc nonagesimo iiii

W. de Monte forti, in consilio regis, Westmonasterii coram rege subito exspiravit. Qui Willelmus fuit decanus Sancti Pauli, London. In cuius ore pontifices et clerus verba sua ponentes et hesitantes quantum rex a quolibet ipsorum affectaret, inde volentes certificari, in quo et rex maxime confidebat.

---

a est *omitted* L.   *b* regi L.   *c* papam *added* L.   *d* *and* Martinum [sic] L.   *e* senior L.   *f* lxx *is error and underlined.*   *g* rege L.   *h* ptibus L *could be* partibus *or* portibus L.   *i* accordaret L.

in the sea. Additionally, the patriarch, with his men, perished in the sea. Both the king of Cyprus and Otto de Grandison with their men, dejectedly escaped by ship.[207]

Item, the tenth of all the profits of ecclesiastical benefices in Ireland was granted for seven years as a subsidy for the Holy Land, by the lord Martin [*recte* Nicholas IV] to the lord E. [Edward], k [king] of England.[208]

Item, the first son of the earl of Clare was born.[209]

1292

King E[dward I] of England, entered Scotland and lord John de Balliol, earl of Galloway, was elected into the kingdom of Scotland.[210] He [Balliol] acquired the whole kingdom of Scotland by right of inheritance and he made homage to lord E[dward] K[ing] of England, at Newcastle upon Tyne on the feast of St Stephen [Fri. 26 Dec. 1292].[211] [Then], Florence, count of Holland, Robert de Bruce, earl of Carrick, John Hastings, John Comyn, Patrick de Dunbar, John de Vescy, Nicholas de Soules and William de Ross, who all had claimed a right in the said kingdom, submitted themselves to the judgment of the lord King E[dward].[212]

Item, a fifteenth of all the secular goods in Ireland was granted to the lord king of England, to be collected at the term of the feast of Saint Michael.[213]

Item, lord Peter de Geneville, knight, died.[214]

Item, Rhys ap Maredudd was led to York, and there he was pulled apart at the tails of horses.[215]

1293

There was a general naval battle in Normandy.[216]

Item between Easter and Pentecost [29 March to 17 May 1293], in the course of the naval battle a large number of Normans were killed by the barons from the [Cinque] ports of England and with others assisting.[217] Because of this, a war was incited between England and France, whereupon Philip, king of the French, directed letters of citation to the king of the English that he should personally come to his *parlement* to answer questions that the same king would put to him. With very little of the command fulfilled, later the same king of England was banished by the council of the French, the king of France judging him convicted.[218]

Item, Gilbert de Clare, earl of Gloucester, entered Ireland with his wife around the feast of St Luke [Sun. 18 Oct. 1293].[219]

1294

W[illiam] de Montfort died suddenly in front of the king, in the king's court at Westminster. This William was the dean of St Paul's, London. Both the bishops and clerics had placed their words into his mouth (because the king had the greatest trust in him). They were uncertain (and wishing to know for certain),

Ad regem reversus et appropians ante regem, ut conceptum sermonem exprimeret, repente obmutescens labit ad terram, extractus a regis ministris in ulnis eorum miserabiliter. Quapropter visum quod accidit dixerunt viri timorati, vere iste homo procurator fuerat * |Folio 8| ut decime ecclesiasticorum et beneficiorum regi persolverentur. Scrutinii facti in ovile Christi alter instigator ut Willelmus clamabat,*a* post modum regi concesse.

Item, civitas Burdugalie, cum terra Vasconie adiacente, occupata a ministris regis Francie est conditionaliter, sed iniuste proditioseque detenta est ^per^ regem Francie. Cuius causa Johannes, archiepiscopus Dublin, et quidam alii magnates in Almania sunt missi ad regem ejusdem, et habito responso in Tordran, reversus*b* dominus archiepiscopus in Angliam, diem claudendo extremum die Sancti Leodegarii. Cuius Johannis Sampford ossa traduntur sepulture in ecelesia Sancti Patricii, Dublin, x kl Martii.

{Nota de acquisicione Kildarie cum suis pertinenciis per Johanni filium Thome}

Eodem anno,* oriebatur contentio inter dominum Willelmum de Vescy, tunc justitiarium Hibernie, et dominum Johannem filium Thome, et dominus Willelmus appellavit eum de felonia, et et*c* dominus Willelmus de Vescy transfretavit in Angliam, et dimisit dominum Willelmum de la Hay loco suo justitiarium Hibernie. Sed cum venissent ambo coram rege ut pugnarent sub appellatione pro prodicione, fugit in Franciam predictus Willelmus Vescy, et noluit pugnare. Tunc rex Anglie dedit dominia que fuerunt domini Willelmi de Vescy domino Johanni filio Thome, scilicet, Kyldare et Rathemgan et multa alia.

Eodem anno comes*d* Gilbertus de Clare, comes Gloucestrie, rediit de Hibernia in Angliam.

Item, Ricardus, comes Ultonie, cito post festum Sancti Nicholai captus est per dominum Johannem filium Thome, et in castro de Lega, id est, Ley, detentus est usque ad festum Sancti Gregorii Pape, cuius liberatio facta fuit tunc per consilium domini regis in parliamento de Kilkenny. Pro cuius captione predictus dominus Johannes filius Thome dedit omnes terras suas, scilicet, Slygo, in connacia cum pertinenciis, quas habuit in Connacia.

{Nota de combustione de Kykdarie et castri}

Item, castrum Kildarie capitur. Kildaria et patria circumstans ab Anglicis et Hibernicis spoliatur. Calvagh combussit rotulos et tallias comitatus.

Magna caristia et pestilentia per Hiberniam isto anno et duobus annis sequentibus.*e*

Item, dominus Willelmus Doddyngzele fit justiciarius Hibernie.

---

a contributionis added **L**. *b* est **L**. *c* repeated in MS: *the first* et *is the usual abbreviation; the second is written in full.* *d* cancelled by underdotting. *e* stray I (*initial letter for* Item) *at end of line, anticipating* Item *of next entry.*

how much the king wanted from each of them. He [William] returned to the king and approaching before the king in order that he might force out the prepared speech, suddenly became speechless, and faltering he began to sink to the earth. And sadly, he was carried out by the king's ministers in their arms. Wherefore, at the sight that happened, [and] for that reason, men spoke fearfully. For this man was the proctor of what they might pay to the king as a tithe of the churches and benefices after an examination had been made among the flock of Christ. Another instigator, as William was being called, yielded afterwards to the king.[220]

Item, the city of Bordeaux, with the adjacent land of Gascony, was occupied by the ministers of the king of France conditionally (but unjustly and treacherously held by the king of France).[221] For which reason John, archbishop of Dublin, and certain other magnates were sent to Germany to the king of the same.[222] And after having an answer in Tordran [Nuremberg], the lord archbishop returned to England and ended his days on the feast of St Leger [Sat., 2 Oct. 1294].[223] The bones of this John Sandford were handed over for burial in the church of St Patrick, Dublin, on 10 Kal. March [Sun., 20 Feb. 1295].[224]

{Note the acquisition of Kildare with its appurtenances by John fitz Thomas}
In the same year a quarrel arose between lord William de Vescy, then justiciar of Ireland, and lord John fitz Thomas. And lord William accused him concerning a felony. And lord William de Vescy crossed to England and left lord William de la Hay in his place as justiciar of Ireland.[225] But when they had both come before the court of the king, in order that they might fight under the appeal for treason,[226] the aforesaid William Vescy fled into France and would not fight.[227] Then the king of England gave the lordships which belonged to William de Vescy to lord John fitz Thomas, namely Kildare and Rathangan and many others.[228]

In the same year Gilbert de Clare, earl of Gloucester, returned from Ireland to England.[229]

Item, soon after the feast of St Nicholas [Mon., 6 Dec. 1294][230] Richard, earl of Ulster, was captured by lord John fitz Thomas and was held in the castle of Lega, that is Ley [Lea].[231] He was detained right up to the feast of St Gregory, pope [Sat., 12 March 1295]. His release was then made by the council of the lord king in the parliament of Kilkenny.[232] Because of his capture, the said lord John fitz Thomas gave [up] all his lands, namely Sligo, with appurtenances, which he had in Connacht.[233]

{Note the burning of Kildare and the castle}
Item, the castle of Kildare was captured. Kildare, and the surrounding countryside, was plundered by the English and Irish. Calbhach burnt the rolls and tallies of the county.[234]

There was great shortage and pestilence through Ireland this year, and for the following two years.[235]

Item, lord William d'Oddingeseles was justiciar of Ireland.[236]

ANNO DOMINI M.CC NONAGESIMO V
Edwardus, rex Anglie, edificavit castrum de Bello Marisco, id est, Bewemarys*a*
in Venedocia, que mater Cambrie vocatur, ^et^ a vulgo Anglisia, eam intrando
cito post pascha, et Venodotes, id est, homines valensens*b* Anglesie, suo imperio
subiugando et cito post istam tempestatem, videlicet, circa festum Beate
Margarete, Madocus, tunc temporis Wallie electus, gratie regis se supponens,
per dominum Johannem de Havergnges London est adductus, et ibidem in
turri inclusus, gratiam et benevolentiam | Folio 8v | † regis expectando.

 Isto anno, obiit ^d(omi)n(us)^ Willelmus Dudyngzele, justiciarius Hibernie, in
crastino Sancte Marie Egyptiace. Cui successit Dominus Thomas, filius
Mauritii, in justiciaria.

 Item, circa eundem*c* tempestatem, Hibernici Lagenienses Lageniam
vastaverunt, Novum Castrum, cum aliis villis, comburendo.

 Item, Thomas de Torbelile, seductor regis et regni, convictus trahitur per
medium London, super pellem prostratus vallatusque quatuor tortoribus
larvatis, improperantibus ei convicia, et sic ultimo patibulo affigitur ut
sepulture non daretur corpus eius, wlvis*d* et corvis exequias celebrantibus. Fuit
iste Thomas unus eorum qui, in obsidione castri de Rions capti, Parisius
ducebantur. Qui locutus est ad principes Francorum quod illis regem Anglie
traderet. Relinquens ibi duos filios obsides, rediit de partibus transmarinis, et
regi Anglie et suo consilio se iunxit, enarrans omnibus quod caute evasit de
carcere, et cum de consilio regis et ordinatione regni certificaretur, omnia in
scriptis redigens, preposito Parisiensi direxit. Super quo demum convictus,
predictam subiit sententiam.

 Item,*e* circa eandem tempestatem Scoti, rupti pacis vinculo quod cum ligeo
domino regie Anglie pepigerant, cum rege Francie novum foedus inierunt, et,
conspiratione facta, in regem proprium eorum, dominum Johannem Baillol,
insurrexerunt, et eum in quodam castro altis montibus circumcepto in
interiora loca Scotie incluserunt. Elegerunt sibi, more Francie, xii pares,
videlicet, quatuor episcopos, quatuor comites,*f* iiij^or^ proceres, quorum nutu
cuncta regni negotia sencerentur. Et hoc factum est in ignominiam regis*g* quia
reclamantibus Scotis, dictus Johannes per regem Anglie eis preficebatur.

 Item, rex Anglie iterum versus Scotiam, in xl*h* sequente, ducit exercitum ad
temerariam arrogantiam et presumptionem Scotorum degenerum in patrem et
regem proprium compescendam.

 Item,*i* Johannes Wogan factus est justiciarius Hibernie, domino Thoma filio
Mauricii cedente eidem.

---

a Bewmarys L.   *b* valences L.   *c* eandem L.   *d* milvis *meaning kites makes more sense here* L.
e Item *inserted in the outside margin before* circa.   *f* et *added* L.   *g* Anglie *added* L.   *h* i.e.,
Quadragesima.   *i* dominus L.

1295

Edward, king of England, built the castle of *Bello Marisco*, that is Beaumaris, in Gwynedd (which was called the mother of Wales, and by the common people, Anglesey). He entered there soon after Easter [Sun. 3 April] making the Venedotians (that is the Welshmen of Anglesey) subdued to his rule.[237] And soon after that time, namely around the feast of Blessed Margaret [Fri. 8 or Wed. 20 July 1295], Madog, then at that time the chosen one of Wales, submitting himself to the grace of the king, was brought to London by lord John de Havering and there he was imprisoned in the tower, awaiting the grace and favour of the king.[238]

In this year lord William d'Oddingseles, justiciar of Ireland, died on the day after the feast of St Mary the Egyptian [Easter Sunday 3 April].[239] Lord Thomas fitz Maurice succeeded him in the justiciarship.[240]

Item, around the same period of time the Irish of Leinster laid waste to Leinster, burning Newcastle with other vills.[241]

Item, after he was convicted, Thomas de Turberville, traitor of the king and the kingdom, was dragged through the middle of London prostrate on a hide and guarded by four masked torturers taunting abuses at him. And thus in the end he was fixed to a pillory so that no one dared to bury his body: kites and ravens celebrated his funeral. This Thomas was one of those who was captured in the siege of the castle of Rheims and taken to Paris. He said to the nobles of France that he would hand the king of England over to them. Leaving two sons there as hostages, he returned from across the sea and, uniting himself with the king of England and council, he was recounting to all how he escaped furtively from the prison. And when he was informed, concerning the council of the king and the arrangements of the kingdom, he put it all in writing and directed it to the provost of Paris. Upon this in the end he was convicted and received the aforesaid sentence.[242]

Item, around the same time the Scots, having broken the chains of peace which they had fastened with the liege lord king of England, made a new alliance with the king of France.[243] And, conspiring, they rose against their own king, lord John Balliol, in their own kingdom and confined him in a certain castle surrounded with high mountains, in an inner place in Scotland,[244] electing to themselves, in the manner of the French, twelve peers namely four bishops and four earls and four magnates by whose command all of the business of the kingdom should be advised.[245] And this was done, in dishonour of the king because, with the Scots protesting, the said John had been set over them by the king of England.

Item, the king of England went to Scotland again in the following Lent. He led an army to restrain the shameful arrogance and presumption of the degenerate Scots towards their own father and king.[246]

Item, lord John Wogan was appointed justiciar of Ireland, after lord Thomas fitz Maurice had yielded the same.[247]

Item,*a* Johannes Wogan, justiciarius Hibernie, fecit pacem inter comitem Ultonie et Johannem filium Thome, et Geraldinos, per biennium duraturam, ac induciam.

Item, hiis diebus, circa Nativitatem Domini, dominus Gilbertus de Clare, comes Glovernie, diem clausit extremum.

Item, rex Anglie mittit Edmundus, fratrem suum, cum exercitu, in Vastoniam.

|Folio 9r| ANNO DOMINI M. CC NONAGESIMO VI
Dominus rex Anglie tertio kl Aprilis, scilicet, die Veneris, tunc temporis in septimana pasche, cepit Berwicum, in quo interfecti fuerunt de Scotis circa septem millia, de Anglicis unum quidem militem scilicet, dominus Ricardus de Cornubia, et vii homines pedestres tantum.

{No*ta* de magna occisione scotorum}
Item, * cito post, scilicet, iiii die Maii, intravit castrum de Donboe,*b* et cepit de inimicis suis circa xli milites, qui omnes se gratie regis supposuerunt, confecto prius toto exercitu Scotorum, scilicet, septingentis hominibus equestribus et xl milia pedibus ex hiis interfectis, x milia et l tam de equestribus quam de peditibus; nec fuerunt occisi de Anglicis*c* nisi homines pedites tantum.

Item,*d* die Sancti Johannis ante Portam Latinam, Wallenses, in numero non modico, circa xv milia hominum, ad mandatum regis Scociam adierunt eandem pugnaturi. Et eodem temporo magnates Hibernie, scilicet, Johannes Wogan, justiciarius Hibernie, Ricardus de Burgo, comes Ultonie, Theoballdus Pincerna, et Johannes filius Thome, cum multis aliis inerunt, similiter in adiutorium transfretando in Scociam. Rex etiam Anglie eos recipiens tercio idus Maii, scilicet, die pentecostes, in castro de Rokesburgh eis et aliis militibus Anglie magnum fecit convivium et solempne.

Item, die Mercurii proximo ante festum beati Barnabe, Apostoli, intravit villam de Edynburgh et cepit castrum ante festum beati Johannis Baptiste, et cito post in eadem estate omnia castra infra ambitum Scotie contenta ad eius nutum fuerunt reddita.

Item, idem dominus Johannes Balloil, rex ~~Anglie~~*e* Scotie, venit licet invitus die Dominica proxima post festum Translacionis Sancti Thome, archiepiscopi, ad regem Anglie, cum comitibus, ^episcopis^, et aliis militibus plurimis, et supposuerunt se*f* gratie domini regis et voluntati, salvis sibi vita et membris, et dominus Johannes de Ballol resignavit totum ius suum Scocie in manu regis Anglie, quem dominus rex missit versus partes Londonie in salvo conductu ad perhendinandum.

Item, Edmundus, frater regis Anglie, obiit in Wastonia.

---

a idem L.   *b* Donbar L.   *c* in eadem confectione *added* L.   *d* Item *in margin.*   *e* *cancelled by underdotting.*   *f* se *omitted* L.

Item, lord John Wogan, justiciar of Ireland, made peace, to be spread over a two-year duration, between the earl of Ulster and John fitz Thomas and the Geraldines.[248]

Item, in these days, around Christmas, lord Gilbert de Clare, earl of Gloucester, closed the last day.[249]

Item, the king of England sent his brother Edmund to Gascony with an army.[250]

1296

On 3 Kal. April [Fri. 30 March] namely Friday then in the time of Easter week [Easter Sun. 25 March], the lord king of England took Berwick, where around seven thousand of the Scots were killed; of the English only one (a certain knight, namely lord Richard de Cornwall) and only seven footsoldiers.[251]

{Note the great killing of the Scots}

Item, soon after, namely the 4th day of May, he [Edward] entered the castle of Dunbar and he captured around forty-one knights of his enemies, who all submitted themselves to the grace of the king.[252] Before he had finished, from the whole army of the Scots, he had killed namely seven hundred horsemen and forty thousand foot soldiers. And, in the same conflict, none were killed of the English only foot soldiers.[253]

Item, on the feast day of St John before the Lateran Gate [Sun. 6 May], by the command of the king, the Welsh, in number not a few (around fifteen thousand men), went to fight against the same [Scots]. At the same time [Sun. 6 May] the magnates of Ireland, namely John Wogan, justiciar of Ireland, Richard de Burgh, earl of Ulster, Theobald Pincerna [Butler] and John fitz Thomas, with many others, similarly began the journey to assist, passing over the sea to Scotland.[254] Now the king of England received them on 3 Id. May, namely Whitsunday [13 May], and a great and solemn feast was held in the castle of Roxburgh for them and other knights of England.[255]

Item, on the Wednesday next before the feast of blessed Barnabas apostle [Wed. 6 June 1296] he entered the town of Edinburgh and before the feast of [the nativity of] blessed John the Baptist he took the castle. And soon after, in the same summer, all the castles within the borders of Scotland he bound to his command.[256]

Item, the same lord John Balliol, king of Scotland, although unwilling, came to the king of England on the Sunday next after the feast of the translation of St Thomas, archbishop [Sunday 8 July], with earls, bishops and many other knights and they submitted themselves to the will and grace of the lord king, saving to themselves life and limb. And lord John de Balliol resigned all his right to Scotland into the hands of the king of England, which lord king sent him to stay in the region of London, under safe conduct.[257]

Item, Edmund, brother of the king of England, died in Gascony.[258]

Anno Domini M. CC nonagesimo vii
Dominus Edwardus, rex Anglie, transfretavit in Flandriam manu armata contra regem Francie propter guerram inter eos motam, ubi post graves expensas et altercationes quedam forma pacis inita inter eos in hac conditione quod se supponerent ordinationi domini pape. Hync inde missi fuerunt certi nuncii ad curiam Romanam. |Folio 9v| Sed Rege Edwardo existente in Flandria, Willelmus le^a Walleys, cum magno exercitu, per commune consilium Scotorum venit ad pontem de Scrilegium, et dedit bellum contra dominum Johannem Warent,^{b} in quo bello ex utraque parte multi corruerunt, multique erant submersi. Sed discomfitura erat super Anglicos. Quo facto commoti sunt omnes Scoti, tam comites quam baroni, contra regem Anglie. Et mota fuit discordia inter regem Anglie et Rogerum Bigoid, comitem marescallum, et cito post concordaverunt.

Et Sanctus Lodowicus, filius regis Cecilie, archiepiscopus Colonie, frater minor, obiit. Et filius et heres regis de Maliagre, id est Marioritacorum, intravit ordinem fratrum minorum ad informationem Sancti Lodowici, qui dixit, 'Vade et fac sic'.

Item, in Hibernia combusta fuit Lethilina, cum aliis aliis^c villis, per Hibernicos de Slemergy.

Item, Calwagh Ohanlan et Ybegus McMathan^d interficiuntur in Urgalia.

[–]nno Domini M. CC nonagesimo viii
Papa Bonifacius iiii,^{e} in crastino Apostolorum Petri et Pauli, ordinavit et confirmavit, omni sedato tumultu guerre, pacem inter regem Anglie et regem Francie, cum certis condicionibus subsecutis.

Item, Rex E. Anglie duxit exercitum iterum in Scociam ad subiugandum Scotos rebelles periuros sue ditioni.

Item, interfecti sunt in eodem exercitu, circa festum Sancte Marie Magdalene, de Scotis lx milia et amplius apud Fowkirk, alii scr^i^bunt circa xxiiii milia. Et sol in illo die rubens instar sanguinis per totam Hiberniam, dum bellum fuerit apud Fowkirk predictum.

Item, circa idem tempus feofavit dominus rex Anglie suos milites de comitatibus et baroni^i^s Scotorum peremptorum.

Item, in Hibernia pax et concordia inite sunt inter comitem Ultonie et dominum Johannem filium Thome, circa festum Apostolorum Simonis et Iude.

Item, in crastino Sanctorum vii Dormientium, radius solaris mutatur in colorem fere sanguineum, ab hora matutina, ita quod hoc videntes admirarentur universi.

---

^{a} de L. ^{b} *marg. note (unfinished), covered in possible ink blot on upper right margin, may read* Nö Dub[....]. ^{c} *repeated, but cancelled.* ^{d} Yvegus mcmaghon L. ^{e} [*sic*] quartus L.

1297

Lord Edward, king of England, crossed over to Flanders with armed men against the king of France, because of the war that had arisen between them.[259] There, after great cost and debate, a certain form of peace was arranged between them; on this condition, that they should submit themselves to the arrangement of the lord pope.[260] Then, from here certain messengers were sent to the Roman Curia.[261] But while King Edward was in Flanders, William Wallace with a great army, by the common council of the Scots, came to the bridge at Stirling and gave battle against lord John Warenne, in which battle from both sides many fell, and many were drowned.[262] But defeat was upon the English. So, because of this, all the Scots, both earls and barons, rose up violently against the king of England.[263] And discord arose between the king of England and Roger Bigod, earl Marshal, but soon after they came to an agreement.[264]

And St Louis, son of the king of Sicily, a friar minor and archbishop of 'Colonie' [*recte* bishop of Toulouse] died.[265] And the son and heir of the king of *Maliagro* that is *Marortcarum* [Majorca] entered the order of Friar Minors at the instruction of St Louis who said, 'Go and do likewise'.[266]

Item, in Ireland, Leighlin, with other vills, were burnt by the Irish of Slievemargy.[267]

Item, Cú Uladh Ó hAnluain and Aonghus Mac Mathghamhna were killed in Airghialla.[268]

1298

When all the tumult of war was settled, on the day after the apostles Peter and Paul [Mon. 30 June], Pope Boniface IIII [*recte* VIII][269] ordained and confirmed peace between the king of England and the king of France, with certain conditions to follow.[270]

Item, King E[dward] of England again led an army into Scotland to subdue the rebel Scots, oath-breakers to his sovereignty.[271]

Item, around the feast of St Mary Magdalen [Tues. 22 July], in the same army of the Scots around sixty thousand and more were killed at Falkirk; others write around twenty-four thousand.[272] And, while the aforesaid battle was taking place at Falkirk, through the whole of Ireland on that day the sun was red, the image of blood.[273]

Item, around that time, the lord king of England enfeoffed his knights with the earldoms and baronies of the slaughtered Scots.[274]

Item, in Ireland around the feast of the apostles Simon and Jude [Tues. 28 October 1298[275]] peace and agreement was entered between the earl of Ulster and lord John fitz Thomas.

Item, from the hour of matins on the day after the Seven Sleepers, saints [Mon. 28 July 1298] the rays of the sun were changed in colour almost to blood, so that all seeing it admired it.[276]

Item, obierunt dominus Thomas filius Mauricii, miles, et dominus Robertus Bagod, quondam justiciarius in Banco.

Item, in Artha civitate, et etiam Reate in partibus Ytalie, Papa Bonifacio tunc temporis ibidem existente, tantus erat factus terre motus, quod turres et palatia sub solo tenus corruerunt. Papa autem cum cardinalibus a civitate fugit, territus pre timore.

|Folio 10r| Item, in die Epiphanie, terremotus licet non tam violentus factus est in Anglia, a Cantuaria usque Hamptoniam.

Anno domini M. CC nonagesimo nono
Obiit dominus Theobaldus le Botiler, iunior, in manerio de Turby, secundo idus Maii, cuius corpus delatum est[a] versus Weydeneam, id est Wayney in comitatu Limerici, x kl Junii.

Item, E, Rex Anglie, duxit in uxorem dominam Margaretam, sororem illustris regis Francie, in ecclesia Sancte Trinitatis, Cantuarie, circa festum Sancte Trinitatis.

Item, confectus est Soldonus Babilonie, cum exercitu Saracenorum per Cassanum, regem Tartarorum.

Anno domini M. CC nonagesimo IX[b]
In die post festum Purificationis Beate Marie Virginis, interfecti fuerunt numeri cm Saracenorum equestrium, exceptis hominibus pedestribus, quorum numerus fuit infinitus.

Item, eodem anno, fuit bellum canum in Burgundia apud castrum Genelon, et fuit numerus canum tria millia, et quilibet interfecit alium, et nullus canis evasit nisi solummodo[c] unus.

Item, eodem anno, plures Hibernici venerunt ad gravandum dominum Theobaldum de Verdon et[d] ad castrum de Roche, ante festum Annunciacionis.

Anno domini M. CCC
{No*ta* histör decambus}
Numissma pallardorum prohibetur in Anglia et in Hibernia.
Item, in auptomno sequenti[e] Edwardus, rex Anglie, intravit iterum in Scotiam in manu armata, sed ad mandatum Bonifacii Pape impeditus est, et direxit nuncios solempnes ad Curiam se ab iniuria excusando.

Item, Thomas, filius regis Anglie, nascitur apud Brothirton, ultimo die Maii, de Margareta, sorore regis Francie.[f]

Item, Edmundus,[g] comes Cornubie, obiit sine herede de corpore suo relicto, et in abbatia de Hailes traditus est sepulture.

---

[a] est *omitted* L.   [b] *repetition of year in: second 1299 with* ix *instead of* nono L.   [c] solomodo *and margin no:* de bello canum L.   [d] et *omitted* L.   [e] sequenti *omitted* L.   [f] *marg. note (hand B)*: Thomas Brotherton natus 31 May A.dm 1300 L.   [g] Edwardus L.

Item, lord Thomas fitz Maurice, knight died, and lord Robert Bagod died, formerly justice of the Common Bench.[277]

Item, in parts of Italy, in the city of Orte, and even Rieti where Pope Boniface was living at that time, there was such an earthquake that towers, and large residences fell down beneath the ground. Furthermore, the pope with the cardinals fled from the city terrified through fear.[278]

Item, on the feast day of the Epiphany, [Tues. 6 January 1299] there was an earthquake, though not so violent, in England from Canterbury to Hampton.[279]

1299

On 2 Id. May [Thurs. 14 May] lord Theobald Butler, the younger, died in the manor of Turvey and on 10 Kal. June [Sat. 23 May] his body was taken to Weydeneam that is Wayney in the county of Limerick.[280]

Item, around the feast of Holy Trinity [Sun. 14 June] E[dward] king of England married lady Margaret sister of the illustrious king of France, in the church of Holy Trinity, Canterbury.[281]

Item, the sultan of Babylon, with the army of Saracens, was defeated by Cassanus, king of the Tartars.[282]

1299[283]

On the day after the feast of the purification of Blessed Virgin Mary [Tues. 3 Feb] Saracen horsemen, by number nine hundred, were killed, besides the number of men on foot, of whom the number was boundless.[284]

Item, in the same year there was a war of dogs in Burgundy at castle Genelon and the number of dogs was three thousand and each killed the other and none of the dogs survived merely one.[285]

Item, in the same year, before the feast of the Annunciation [25 Mar.], many Irish came to harass lord Theobald de Verdun and Castle Roche.[286]

1300[287]

{Note account of change of money}

Pollard money was prohibited in England and Ireland.[288]

Item, in the following autumn, Edward, king of England, again entered Scotland with armed men, but this was forbidden by the mandate of Pope Boniface and he [Edward] sent religious messengers to the Curia excusing himself from wrongdoing.[289]

Item, Thomas, son of the king of England, [and] of Margaret, sister of the king of France was born at Brotherton on the last day of May.[290]

Item, Edmund, earl of Cornwall, died without leaving a legal heir of his body and was taken for burial to Hailes abbey.[291]

Anno Domini M. CCCI

Edwardus, rex Anglie, intravit Scotiam cum exercitu, ad quem transfretavit dominus Johannes Wogan, justiciarius Hibernie, et dominus Johannes filius Thome, et*[a]* Petrus Bermyngham, et multi alii in auxilium regis Anglie.

Item, comburitur magna pars civitatis Dublin, cum ecclesia Sancte Werberge, nocte Beate Columbe.

Item, dominus de Genibile desponsavit filiam domini Johannis de Monteforte. Et dominus Johannes de Mortuo mari desponsavit filiam et heredem domini Petri de Genibile. Et dominus Theobaldus de Verdon desponsavit filiam domini Rogeri de Mortuo mari.

| Folio 10v | Eodem tempore, Lagenienses moverunt guerram in hyeme, villam de Wykynlo, et Rathdon, et cetera comburendo; sed non impunes evaserunt, quia major pars sustentationis fuerat combusta, et armenta eorum per depredationem amissa; et iidem Hibernici fere in xl consumpti fuissent, nisi seditio quorundam Anglicorum impedivisset.

Item, confectio facta in autumno per Felanos*[b]* super conventulum Bremorum,*[c]* in qua occisi sunt fere ccc latrones.

Item, Walterus ~~Pw~~ Power magnam partem Momonie devastavit, plurima predia incendendus.

{•}

Anno Domini M. CCCII

Obierunt domina Margareta, uxor domini Johannis Wogan, justiciarii Hibernie, iii*[d]* idus Aprilis, et*[e]* ebdomada sequenti Matildis de Lacy, uxor domini Galfridi de Genebile.

Item, Edmundus le Botiler recuperavit*[f]* manerium de Sancto Bosco cum pertinenciis, de domino R. de Feringes, archiepiscopo Dublin, per concordiam factam inter eos in Banco R. post festum Sancti Hilarii.

Item*, confectio facta apud Courtenay in Flandria per Flandrenses super exercitum Gallicorum, die Mercurii proximo post festum Translationis Sancti Thome, in qua {†} occisi fuerunt comes Arthosie, comes Albemarlie, comes de Hue, Radulphus de Noel, constabularius Francie ~~Francie~~ *[g]*Guido de Nevil, marescallus Francie, filius comitis Hennaud, Godfridus de Brabang, cum filio, Willelmus de Fenlys, cum filio. Jacobus de Sancto Paulo, Petrus de Flore comes de Sancto Paulo*[h]* amisit manum, et xl baroneti eodom die fuerunt interfecti, cum militibus et armigeris et ceteris sine numero.

Item, decime omnium beneficiorum ecclesiasticorum in Anglia ^et^ in*[i]* Hibernia exacta est a Bonifacio Papa, per triennium, in subsidium ecclesie Romane contra regem Arroganum.

---

[a] et *omitted* L. *[b]* folanos L. *[c]* capital B. *[d]* L *and not clear if* in *or* iii. T *and* L *usually have an* º *above the* iii *but not here* L. *[e]* in *added* L. *[f]* reparavit L. *[g]* *repeated, underdotted.* *[h]* *hole in ms and* Petrus de Flore comes de Sancto Paulo *omitted* L. *[i]* in *omitted* L.

1301

Edward, king of England, entered Scotland with an army.[292] Lord John Wogan, justiciar of Ireland, and lord John fitz Thomas and Peter Bermingham and many others crossed over in aid of the king of England.[293]

Item, the greater part of the city of Dublin, with the church of St Werburgh, was burnt on the night of blessed Columba [Fri. 9 June].[294]

Item, lord de Geneville married the daughter of lord John de Montfort, and lord John de Mortimer married the daughter and heir of lord Peter de Geneville, and lord Theobald de Verdun married the daughter of lord Roger de Mortimer.[295]

In winter, at the same time, the men of Leinster went to war, burning the vills of Wicklow and Rathdown and others. But they did not escape without punishment because the greater part of their supplies was burnt and their arms lost by plunder and the same Irish should have been almost destroyed in Lent, except that certain of the English had seditiously hindered it.[296]

Item, there was a victory[297] in autumn by the Uí Fhaeláin over a gathering of the Berminghams[298] in which almost three hundred robbers were killed.

Item, Walter Poer devastated the great part of Munster, burning many farms.[299]

1302

Lady Margaret, wife of lord John Wogan, justiciar of Ireland, died on 3 Id. April [Wed. 11 April] and in the following week [11 to 17 April] Matilda de Lacy, wife of lord Geoffrey de Geneville.[300]

Item, Edmund Butler regained the manor of Holywood with appurtenances from lord R[ichard] de Ferings, archbishop of Dublin, by an agreement made between them in the court of common pleas after the feast of St Hilary [13 January 1302/1303?].[301]

Item, on the next Wednesday after the feast of the translation of St Thomas [Wed. 11 July], victory at Courtrai in Flanders by the Flemings over the French army.[302]

Here the count of Artois, the count of Aumale, the count of Eu, Raoul de Nesle, constable of France, Guy de Nesle, marshal of France, the son of the count of Hainault, Godfrey of Brabant and his son, William de Fenlys and his son, James de St-Pol were killed. Peter de Flore, the count of St-Pol lost a hand and on the same day forty barons were killed, plus knights and squires and others without number.[303]

Item, the tithe of all ecclesiastical benefices in England and Ireland was demanded by Pope Boniface for three years in a subsidy to the Roman church against the king of Aragon.

Item, in die Circumsicionis,^{a} Hugo de Lacy depredavit Hugonem Vernaill.

{•} Anno eodem, dominus^b Robertus le Bruys, tunc comes de Carryk, desponsavit Elizabeth, filiam domini Ricardi de Burgo, comitis Ultonie.

Item, Edmundus Botiller desponsavit filiam domini Johannis filii Thome.

Item,^{c} Burdegallie, cum ceteris circumiacentibus civitatibus, que per seditionem Francorum aliquo tempore ab Edwardo, rege Anglie, fuerant alienate, eidem sunt reddite, in vigilia Sancti Andree, per industriam domini Johannis de Hastinges.

|Folio 11r| † XPC^d ANNO DOMINI M. CCCIII

Comes Ultonie, scilicet, Richardus de Burgo, et dominus Eustacius le Power, cum magna potencia intraverunt Scotiam, sed factis primo ab ipso comite in castro Dublin xxxiii^e militibus, sed in adiutorium regis Anglie transivit in Scotiam.

{No*ta* de morte Geraldi filii et heredis domini Johannis filii Thome}
Item obiit Geraldus, filius et heres domini Johannis filii Thome.
Eodem^f anno, Papa Bonifacius regem Francie et reginam, et liberos eorundem, excommunicavit, et renovavit omnia privilegia universitati Parisius concessa quocunque tempore; et statim post Papa fuit captus, et tentus quasi in carcere tribus diebus integris. Et cito post Papa obiit.

Item, obiit comitissa Ultonie.

Item, Walranus de Wellysley et dominus Robertus de Percevall interfecti sunt, xi kl Novembris.

ANNO DOMINI M. CCCIIII

Magna pars Dublin comburitur, scilicet, vicus pontis, cum magna parte keye, et ecclesia fratrum predicatorum, et ecclesia monachorum, cum magna parte monasterii, scilicet, idus Junii, in festo sancti Medardi.^{g}

Item, primarius lapis chori fratrum predicatorum Dublin ponitur per dominum Eustacium le Power, in festo Sancte Agathe, Virginis.

Item, domina Margareta Wogan, uxor domini Johannis Wogan,^{h} justiciarii Hibernie, obiit^i domina Matildis Lacy, uxor domini Galfridi Genebile, iii^j idus Aprilis.

Item,^{k} post festum Purificationis Beate Marie Virginis, dominus rex Francie iterum invasit Flandrenses in propria persona, cum magna multitudine exercitus. Tum se bene habuit in bello, et viriliter pugnavit donec duo dextrarii vel tres sub illo interfecti fuerunt; sed ad ultimum capicium amissit, quod sub galea capiti ejus imponebatur, quod Flandrenses capientes, in lancea tanquam

---

^{a} dominus *added.* ^{b} dominus *omitted* L. ^{c} civitas *added* L. ^{d} *faint.* ^{e} xxx *on inner edge of page, but* iii *not visible* L. ^{f} *decorated* E. ^{g} *marg. note (seventeenth century)*, combustio Dublin. ^{h} *hole in ms* L. ^{i} *catchword bottom of page* Item obiit. ^{j} tertio L. ^{k} *long trailing* I.

Item, on the feast of Circumcision [Thurs. 1 Jan. 1303] lord Hugh de Lacy plundered Hugh Vernoyl.

In the same year lord Robert Bruce, then earl of Carrick, married Elizabeth, daughter of lord Richard de Burgh, earl of Ulster.[304]

Item, Edmund Butler married the daughter of lord John fitz Thomas.

Item, on the eve of St Andrew [29 Nov. 1302], Bordeaux with the other surrounding cities, which for some time by the sedition of the French were alienated from Edward, king of England, by the diligence of lord John de Hastings the same were returned.[305]

1303

The earl of Ulster, namely Richard de Burgh, and lord Eustace le Poer, entered Scotland with great strength indeed, but first thirty-three knights were knighted by the same earl in Dublin castle before he crossed into Scotland to assist the king of England.[306]

{Note the death of Gerald, the son and heir of lord John fitz Thomas}
Item, Gerald, son and heir of John fitz Thomas, died.[307]

In the same year[308] Pope Boniface excommunicated the king and queen of France and their children, and he restored all the privileges of the University of Paris to whatever had been granted before. And immediately after the pope was captured and held (as if in prison) for three whole days. And soon after the pope died.[309]

Item, the countess of Ulster died.[310]

Item, on 11 Kal. November [Tues. 22 October] Walerand de Wellesley and lord Robert de Percival were killed.[311]

1304

The greater part of Dublin was burnt, namely the street of the bridge with a great part of the quay and the church of the Friars Preachers, and the church of the monks with a great part of the monastery,[312] namely on the [VI] Id. June [Mon. 8 June] on the feast of blessed Medardus [Mon. 8 June].[313]

Item, the first stone of the choir of the Friars Preachers was laid by lord Eustace le Poer on the feast of St Agatha, virgin [Fri. 5 Feb. 1305?].[314]

Item, Lady Margaret Wogan, wife of lord John Wogan, justiciar of Ireland, died. Lady Matilda Lacy, the wife of lord Geoffrey de Geneville, on 3 Id. [11 April].[315]

Item, after the feast of the Purification of Blessed Virgin Mary [Tuesday 2 February 1305?] the lord king of France, in his own person, once again invaded Flanders with an army of great multitude. While he was holding himself well in battle and fighting strongly, two or three destriers were killed under him. But at the end he lost his hood that was placed on his head under his helmet,[316] which, being seized by the Flemings, they carried it on a lance, with derision, just as if

vexillum derisorie portaverunt, et in omnibus nundinis Flandrie famosis ad altam fenestram alicuius palatii, tanquam signum tabernale, in signum victorie ostenderunt.

ANNO DOMINI M. CCCV
Jordanus Comyn, cum complicibus, interfecit Maritagh O Conchuir, regem de Offaly, et Calwagh, germanum eius, et quosdam alios in curia domini Petri Bermyngham, apud Carryk in Carbria.

Item; interfectus est dominus Gilbertus de Sutton, senescallus Weyfordie, ab Hibernicis prope villam Hamundi de Grace, qui quidem Hamundus in dicto bello viriliter se habuit, sed strenue |Folio 11v| evasit.

Item, in Scotia dominus Robertus de Brus, comes de Carryk, immemor iuramenti domino regi Anglie, interfecit dominum Johannem[a] Rede Comyn infra septa fratrum minorum de Dunfres, et[b] post se fecit coronari in regem Scotie per manus duorum episcoporum, scilicet, Sancti Andree et Glasco, in villa de Scone, ad suam confucionem et multorum aliorum.

{•} ANNO DOMINI M. CCCVI
Confectio facta fuit in Offalia iuxta castrum de Gesehil, idus Aprilis, super Ochonchuir per Odympcyes, in qua occisus est Odymcy dux Reganorum, cum magna comitiva.

Item, obiit Obrene, rex Tothomonie.

Item, Donaldus Oge M^ccarthy interfecit Donaldum Ruffum, regem Desmonie.

Item, confectio dolenda cecidit super partem domini Petri Bermyngham, iiii idus Maii, in confinio Midie.

Item, Balymore in Lagenia comburitur ab Hibernicis, interfecto tunc ibidem Henrico Calfe, et commota est guerra inter Anglicos et Hibernicos in Lagenia, ob quam causam[c] convocatus est magnus exercitus de diversis partibus Hibernie ad refrenandam malitiam Hibernicorum Lagenie, in qua expeditione dominus Thomas Maundibile, miles egregius, iniit gravem conflictum cum Hibernicis iuxta Glenfell, in quo conflictu se viriliter gessit donec dextrarius eius occisus est, ad laudem et honorem adquirendo, et plures salvavit et seipsum.

Item, Magister Thomas Cantok, cancellarius Hibernie, consecratus est in episcopum Ymelasensem in ecclesia Sancte Trinitatis Dublin, cum magno honore, cuius consecrationi interfuerunt maiores natu totius Hibernie, tali contento convivio, primo divitibus, postea de pauperibus, quale in Hibernia temporibus retroactis fuerat inauditum.[d]

---

[a] Jo L.   [b] cito *added* L.   [c] causam *omitted* L.   [d] *marg. note (later hand)*: fit archipiscopus Dublin L.

a banner. And, in all the famous marketplaces of Flanders, they hung it out of the high window of some big residence, just as if a sign of a tavern, showing it as a token of victory.[317]

1305

Jordan Comyn, with accomplices, killed Muircheartach Ó Conchobhair, king of Offaly, and Calbhach his whole brother, and certain others, in the house of lord Peter Bermingham at Carrick in Carbury.[318]

Item, lord Gilbert de Sutton, seneschal of Wexford, was killed by the Irish near the vill of Hamon de Grace, indeed that Hamon carried himself bravely in the said battle but boldly escaped.[319]

Item, in Scotland lord Robert de Bruce, earl of Carrick, unmindful of the oath to the lord king of England, killed lord John Rede Comyn within the cloister of the friars minor of Dumfries.[320] And soon after, in the town of Scone, he [Bruce] had himself crowned king of Scotland by the hands of two bishops, namely [those] of St Andrews and Glasgow, to the ruin of himself and of many others.[321]

1306

On Id. April [Wed. 13 April], a victory was gained in Offaly near the castle of Geashill, upon Ua Conchobhair by the Uí Dhíomusaigh, in which Ó Duinn, chief of Uí Riagáin, was killed with a great following.[322]

Item, Ó Briain, king of Thomond, died.[323]

Item, Domhnall Óg Mac Cárthaigh killed Domhnall Ruadh, king of Desmond.[324]

Item, on 4 Id. May [Thurs. 12 May 1306)] in the region of Meath, a lamentable defeat was inflicted upon the side of lord Peter de Bermingham.[325]

Item, Ballymore Eustace in Leinster was burnt by the Irish,[326] with Henry Calf being killed there,[327] and war arose between the English and Irish in Leinster. [And] for that reason a great army was called together from different parts of Ireland to restrain the malice of the Irish of Leinster.[328] In that expedition, lord Thomas Mandeville, a distinguished knight, entered a heavy armed conflict with the Irish near Glenfell.[329] He carried himself courageously in that conflict, until his horse was killed, amassing praise and honour and saving himself and many [others].[330]

Item, in the church of Holy Trinity, Dublin, Master Thomas Cantok, chancellor of Ireland, was consecrated into the bishopric of Emly, with great honour. All the great noble-born of Ireland attended at this consecration with such a generous feast of a kind unheard of in Ireland in times past; first the rich ate and afterwards the poor.[331]

Item, Ricardus de Feringes, archiepiscopus Dublin, obiit in vigilia Sancti Luce evangeliste.*a* Cui successit Magister Ricardus de Haveryinges, qui occupavit archiepiscopatum fere per quinquennium ex dispensatione*b* apostolica. Qui et cessit archiepiscopatum cui successit Johannes de Leche.*c* Causa cessionis eius, et*d* bone memorie archidiaconus Dublin, nepos eiusdem, retulit, quod fuit quadam nocte et videbat in sompnis quoddam monstrum universo mundo ponderacius super pectus eius eminenter stare, de cuius ponderositate liberari maluit quam totius orbis bona solus habere, sed |Folio 12r| evigilans cogitabat hoc nichil aliud esse quam Dublinensis ecclesia, cuius fructus recipiebat, nihil pro eisdem laborando. Et quam cito potuit accedens ad Dominum Papam, a quo multum fuit dilectus, archiepiscopatum renuntiavit. Habuit enim, ut idem archidiaconus asseruit, uberiora beneficia archiepiscopatu.

Item, Edwardus, Rex Anglie, fecit Edwardum, filium suum, militem in festo Pentecostes, London, in quo festo neoptolizati fuerunt milites circa cccc, et Edwardus de Carnarban, novus miles, fecit cccc milites de predictis, et tenuit festum, London, apud Novum Templum, et pater suus dedit sibi ducatum Acquietanie.

Item, eodem anno, in festo Sancte Potentiane, episcopus Wyntoniensis et episcopus Wygorniensis, de mandato Domini Pape, excommunicaverunt Robertum Brus, pretensum regem Scotie, et suos socios, pro morte domini Johannis Rede Comyn.

Eodem anno, die Sancti Bonifacii, Adomarus de Valentia, comes Pembrock, et dominus Guido, comes … … …,*e* interfecerunt plures Scotos, et confectus fuit dominus Robertus Brus extra villam Sancti Johannis.

Eodem anno, ad festum Nativitatis Sancti Johannis Baptiste, Rex Edwardus ivit versus*f* Scotiam per aquam de Newerk usque ad*g* Lincolniam.

Item, eodem anno, comes de Asceles et dominus Symon Freysell, et comitissa de Carryk, pretensa regina Scotie, filia comitis Ultonie, fuerunt capti. Et comes de Asceles et dominus Symon Freysell fuerunt suspensi London, et dominus Symon Freysell fuit*h* prius dilaceratus, et comitissa remansit cum rege in magno honore, ceteri, vero, in Scotia miserabiliter diem clauserunt extremum.

Item, circa festum Purificationis Beate Marie Virginis, duo fratres Roberti Brus, vitam piraticam agentes, exierunt de galleis suis super terram ad depredandum,*i* qui capti fuerunt, cum aliis xvi Scotis, et ipsi duo dilacerati fuerunt apud Carlele, ceteris in patibulis suspensis.

---

a evangeliste *omitted* L. *b* *stain over two lines here. It is possible that a substance called 'tower water', made from iron gall, caused this stain. Gilbert was known to use iron gall, see* Mary Clark, 'Local archives and Gilbertian reforms', in Mary Clark, Yvonne Desmond and Nodlaig P. Hardiman, *John T. Gilbert 1829-1898: librarian, historian and archivisa centenary celebration* (Dublin, 1999), p. 89. *c* *marg. note (later hand)*: nö sompnis. *d* [?]tot L. *e* *space left for name, approximately ten letters.* *f* *ink blot covering* Scotiam *and therefore* Scotiam *repeated.* *g* ad *omitted* L. *h* fuit *omitted* L. *i* ad predandum L.

Item, Richard de Ferings, archbishop of Dublin, died on the eve of St Luke, evangelist [Mon. 17 Oct.].[332] Magister Richard de Haverings succeeded; he occupied the archbishopric for almost five years, by the dispensation of the Apostolic [See].[333] And when he ceased to be archbishop he was succeeded by John de Leche. The cause of his [de Haverings'] resignation (as his nephew of good memory, the archdeacon of Dublin, related), was that on a certain night, in dreaming, he was seeing a certain monster heavier [than] the whole world standing prominent upon his chest, [then] he chose to be free from that weight, than to have all the goods of the world. But wakening, he was thinking this was to be nothing other than the church of Dublin, whose fruits he had received and not labouring for the same. And when soon he was able to come to the lord pope, by whom he was much beloved, he renounced the archbishopric. Indeed, he had, as the same archdeacon asserted, more abundant benefices [than] the archbishopric.

Item, in London on the feast of Pentecost [Sun. 22 May] Edward, king of England, made his son Edward a knight. In this feast around four hundred knights were made. And the new knight, Edward de Caernarvon, made sixty of the aforesaid knights, and he held a feast in London at the New Temple and his father gave the duchy of Aquitaine to him.[334]

Item, in the same year, on the feast of St Potentiana [Thurs. 19 May], the bishop of Winchester and the bishop of Worcester, by the mandate of the lord pope, excommunicated Robert Bruce, the pretender king of Scotland, and his companions for the death of lord John Rede Comyn.[335] In the same year on the feast of St Boniface [Sun. 5 June], Aymer de Valence, earl of Pembroke, and lord Guy, earl of ...., killed many Scots,[336] and defeated lord Robert Bruce outside the vill of St John [Perth].[337]

In the same year, on the feast of the nativity of St John the Baptist [24 June], King Edward journeyed to Scotland by water, from Newark up to Lincoln.[338]

Item, in the same year the earl of Athol and lord Simon Fraser and the countess of Carrick, pretender queen of Scotland, daughter of the earl of Ulster, were captured. And the earl of Athol and lord Simon Fraser were hanged in London and lord Simon first was torn to pieces.[339] The countess remained with the king with great honour, but the rest died miserably in Scotland.[340]

Item, around the feast of the Purification of the Blessed Virgin Mary [Thurs. 2 Feb. 1307], two brothers of Robert Bruce, engaging in a life of piracy, left their galleys to prey on the land. They were captured with sixteen other Scots, and those two were torn apart at Carlisle and the rest were hanged on gallows.[341]

Item, in Hibernia, die Sancti Patricii, captus est Ricardus M^caochy*^a* cum duobus filiis, iuxta Novum Castrum, per Thomam de Sueterby,*^b* decollato ibidem Lorcano Obony, fure fortissimo.

Anno Domini M. CCCVII

Kl Aprilis,*^c* decollatus est Murcod Ballagh, iuxta Marton, per dominum David Caunton, militem strenuum, et cito | Folio 12v | † post interfectus est Adam Dan.

Item, confectio et interfectio gravis cecidit super Anglicos in Connacia, facta per Oscheles, die Apostolorum Philippi et Jacobi.

Item, predones de Offaly diruerunt castrum de Geschil,*^d* et in vigilia Translationis Sancti Thome combuserunt villam de Lega, id est, Lye, castrum obsidendo; sed cito post amoti sunt per Iohannem filium Thome et Edmundum Botiller.

Item, obiit Edwardus, rex Anglie, cui suceessit in regno Edwardus, filius eius, qui solempnissime sepilivit patrem suum apud Westmonasterium, cum magna reverentia et honore.*^e*

Item, dominus Edwardus, iunior, duxit in uxorem dominam Isabellam, filiam regis Francie, in ecclesia Sancte Marie Bononie, et cito post coronati ambo in ecclesia Westmonasteriensi.

Item, Templarii in partibus transmarinis, quadam heresi dampnati, ut dicebatur, capti sunt et incarcerati per papale mandatum. In Anglia, similiter, omnes eiusdem generis*^f* capti fuerunt et incarcerati*^g* in crastino Epiphanie. Et in Hibernia capti fuerunt in crastino Purificationis, et incarcerati.

Anno Domini M. CCCVIII

II idus Aprilis, obiit dominus Petrus de Bermyngham, nobilis debellator Hibernicorum.

Item, iiij idus Maii, comburitur castrum Kevini, quibusdam custodibus*^h* interfectis per Willelmum McVabther, et Cuygnissimo Otothiles, et suos fautores.

Item, comburitur villa de Courcouly per eosdem malefactores.

Item, vi idus Junii, confectus fuit dominus Johannes W^ogan*ⁱ* justiciarius Hibernie, † cum suo exercitu, prope Glyndelory, interfectis ibidem Johanne dicto Hogelyn, Johanne de Nortan, Johanne de Breton, cum multis aliis.

Item, xvi kl Iulii combusta est Donlovan, Tobir, et alie ville contermine per prefatos malefactores.

Item, in Anglia cito post tentum est magnum parliamentum London, in quo oriebatur discensio et fere mortalis conflictus inter regem et barones,

---

^a Ricardus *omitted and then* M^cnochi L.   *^b and* Sneterby? L.   *^c* iii *or* in? kl Aprilis.   *^d* cashil L.   *^e marg. note (hand B):* nō obiit R.E.   *^f* eiusdem generis *omitted* L.   *^g* et incarcerati *omitted* L.   *^h* in eo *added* L.   *ⁱ* o *of* Wogan *inserted above line.*

1307

Item, in Ireland on the feast day of St Patrick [Fri. 17 March 1307], Richard (Mac Eochaidh) Ó Tuathail with two sons was captured by Thomas de Suerterby near Newcastle being beheaded there with Lorcán Ó Broin, a most powerful thief.[342]

1307

On Kal. April [Sat. 1 April] Murchadh Ballach [Mac Murchadha] was beheaded near Marton by lord David Caunteton, an active knight.[343] And soon afterwards Adam Dan was killed.[344]

Item, on the feast of the apostles Philip and James [Mon. 1 May], a defeat and grievous slaughter was inflicted by the Uí Cheallaigh upon the English in Connacht.[345]

Item, the plunderers of Offaly threw down the castle of Geashill and on the eve of the feast of the translation of St Thomas [Thomas Beckett, 7 July, or Thomas, apostle, 3 July] they burnt the vill of Lega, that is Lea, in order to besiege the castle.[346] But soon after they were removed by John fitz Thomas and Edmund Butler.

Item, Edward, king of England, died. His son Edward succeeded in the kingship; he buried his father at Westminster most solemnly, with great reverence and honour.[347]

Item, lord Edward, the younger, married lady Isabella, daughter of the king of France, in the church of Notre Dame at Boulogne and soon after they were both crowned in the church of Westminster.[348]

Item, in parts beyond the sea the Templars, condemned of certain heresies, as was said, were seized and imprisoned by papal mandate.[349] Similarly, in England all of the same order was captured and imprisoned on the day after the Epiphany [Sun. 7 January 1308]. And in Ireland they were captured on the day after the Purification and imprisoned [Sat. 3 February 1308].[350]

1308

On 2 Id. April [Good Friday 12 April], lord Peter de Bermingham, noble subduer of the Irish, died.[351]

Item, on 4 Id. May [Sun. 12 May] Castlekevin was burnt, certain guards being killed by William mac Walter[352] and Cuygnismio Ó Tuathail[353] and his accomplices.

Item, the vill of Courcouley was burnt by the same malefactors.[354]

Item, on 6 Id. June [Sat. 8 June] lord John de Wogan, justiciar of Ireland, was defeated with IHC[355] his army near Glenmalure. John, called Hogelyn,[356] John de Northon, John de Bretton with many others were killed there.[357]

Item, on 16 Kal. July [Sun. 16 June] Dunlavin, Tober and other adjoining vills were burnt by the aforesaid malefactors.[358]

Item, in England, shortly after a great parliament was held in London, there arose a disagreement and an almost mortal combat between the king and barons,

occasione domini Petri de Gavuston, qui proscriptus est a regno Anglie in crastino Natalis Beati Johannis Baptiste, et transfretavit in Hiberniam circa festum Sanctorum Quirite et Julite, cum uxore et sorore, comitissa Glovernie, ad Dublin, cum pompa vehementi et ibidem traxit moram.

Item, Willelmus M^cbaltor, fortis latro et incendiarius, in curia domini regis, Dublin, coram capitali justiciario, domino Johanne Wogan, {†} condempnatus et iudicatus xii kl vii ^bris^,*a* distractus est ad caudas equorum | Folio 13r | ad calofurcium, et ibi suspensus, prout merita sua exigerunt.

Item, in eodem anno, erecta est quedam cisterna marmorea ad recipiendam aquam de aquaductuli in civitate Dublin,*b* qualis ante nunquam fuit ibidem, per dispositionem et providentiam domini Johannis le Decer, tunc maiore*c* civitatis predicte,*d* qui de propria pecunia ad eandem structuram invenit, et idem Johannes parum ante idem tempus construi fecit quendam pontem ultra Aniliphiam juxta prioratum Sancti Wlstani. Capellam Sancte Marie fratrum minorum, et ibidem sepilitur. Capellam Sancte Marie Hospitalis Sancti Johannis, Dublin.

Item, idem Johannes Decere multa bona fecit in conventu fratrum predicatorum, Dublin, videlicet, unam columpnam lapideam in ecelesia, et lapidem unum latum super altare magnum, cum ornamentis eius.

Item, oĩ,*e* vi feria recepit fratres ad mensam suam, ista dicunt seniores iunioribus intuitu caritatis.

Item, in autumno transfretavit dominus Iohannes Wogan ad parliamentum Anglie, in cuius loco dominus Willelmus de Burgo factus est custos Hibernie.

Item, eodem anno, in vigilia apostolorum Symonis et Iude, dominus Rogerus de Mortuo mari applicuit in Hiberniam, cum sua consorte, recta herede Midie, filia domini Petri, filii domini Galfridi Genebile intraverunt Hiberniam, et se^i^sinam ceperunt de Midia, domino Galfrido do Genenible cedente eisdem, et intrante ordinem fratrum predicatorum apud Trym, in crastino Sancti Edmundi, archiepiscopi.

Item, Dermot Odymcy occisus est apud Tully per servientes domini Petri de Gaveston.

Item, Ricardus de Burgo, comes Ultonie, tenuit magnum festum in Pentecosten, apud Trym et fecit Walteram de Lacy et Hugonem de Lacy milites. Et, in vigilia Assumptionis, comes Ultonie venit contra Petrum Gaveston, comitem Cornubie, apud Drogheda. Et eodem tempore remeavit passagium in Scociam.

Item, dicto anno, Matildis, filia comitis Ultonie, transfretavit versus Angliam ad maritagium contrahendum cum comite Glovernie. Et cito post infra mensem comes et ipsa fuerunt desponsati.

Item, Mauricius de Caunton interfecit Ricardum Talon, et Rupenses interfecerunt predictum Mauricium.

---

a [sic] *in* T; Septembris L.   *b* seventeenth century *Marginalia*, Nö de edificatione cisterne.   *c* maioris L.   *d* predicte *omitted and* Dublin *added*.   *e* oĩ. *not present* L.

caused by lord Peter de Gaveston.³⁵⁹ He was banished from the kingdom of England on the day after the feast of the Nativity of blessed John the Baptist [Tues. 25 June] and around the feast of saints Ciricus and Julitta [Sun. 16 June] he crossed to Ireland with his wife and sister, the countess of Gloucester [and came] to Dublin with great ostentation, and there he remained.³⁶⁰

Item, in the court of the lord king at Dublin, before the chief justiciar lord John Wogan, William mac Walter, a powerful thief and arsonist, was judged and condemned and on 12 Kal. September [Wed. 21 Aug] he was drawn at the tails of horses to the gallows and there hanged as his deeds had demanded.³⁶¹

Item, in the same year a certain marble cistern was erected to receive water from the aqueduct in the city of Dublin, such as never before, by the arrangement and foresight of the lord John le Decer, then mayor of the aforesaid city, which structure he provided for with his own money.³⁶² And the same John shortly before that time instigated the construction of a certain bridge over the Liffey near the priory of St Wolfstan,³⁶³ the chapel of St Mary of the Friars Minor (and there he was buried),³⁶⁴ [and] the chapel of the St Mary of the Hospital of St John, Dublin.³⁶⁵

Item, the same John Decer did many good things for the convent of the Friar Preachers Dublin, namely, one stone column in the church and one broad stone upon the high altar with its ornaments.³⁶⁶

Item, on the sixth day he [le Decer] received the friars at his table; this was for the sake of charity, the elders said to the juniors.³⁶⁷

Item, in autumn, lord John Wogan crossed to the parliament in England; lord William de Burgh was appointed custodian of Ireland in his place.³⁶⁸

Item, in the same year, on the eve of the apostles of Simon and Jude [Sun. 27 Oct.], lord Roger de Mortimer landed in Ireland with his wife the legal direct heir of Meath, the daughter of lord Peter, son of lord Geoffrey de Geneville.³⁶⁹ They entered Ireland and took seisin of Meath, with Geoffrey de Geneville ceding the same.³⁷⁰ And, on the day after the feast of St Edmund, archbishop [Mon. 17 Nov.], he [Geoffrey] entered the order of Friars Preachers at Trim.³⁷¹

Item, Diarmuid Ó Díomusaigh was killed at Tullow by the followers of lord Peter de Gaveston.³⁷²

Item, Richard de Burgh, earl of Ulster, held a great feast in Trim at Pentecost [June 1308] and made Walter de Lacy and Hugh de Lacy knights.³⁷³ On the eve of the Assumption [Wed. 14 Aug. 1308] the earl of Ulster came against Peter de Gaveston, earl of Cornwall, at Drogheda.³⁷⁴ And at the same time he took passage to Scotland.

Item, in the said year, Matilda, daughter of the earl of Ulster, crossed to England in order to contract marriage with the earl of Gloucester. And soon after, within the month, she and the earl were married.³⁷⁵

Item, Maurice de Caunteton killed Richard Talon and the Roches killed the aforesaid Maurice.³⁷⁶

Item, dominus David de Caunton suspenditur Dublin.

Item, Odo, filius Catholi, Yconghir inter[a] |Folio 13v| interfecit Odonem Oconghir, regem Connatie.

Item, Atby comburitur ab Hibernicis.

Anno domini m. cccix

Petrus de Gaveston subiugavit Obrynnes Hibernicos, et reedificavit Novum Castrum M^{c}kyngan, et et[b] castrum Kevini et amputavit et mundavit passum inter castrum Keyvini et Glydelagh, invitis Hibernicis, et abiit et optulit in ecclesia Sancti Keyvini. Eodem anno, dominus Petrus de Gaveston transfretavit in Angliam in vigilia nativitatis Sancti Johannis Baptiste.

Item, uxor filii comitis Ultonie, filia comitis Glovernie, xv die Octobris applicuit in Hiberniam.

Item in vigilia Nativitatis Domini, rediit comes Ultonie de Anglia, et applicuit apud portum de Drogheda.

Item, in die Purificationis, Beate Marie virginis interficitur dominus Johannis Bonebile prope villam de Arscoll per dominum Arnaldum Pover et suos fautores et sepultus apud Athy in ecclesia praediciatorum.

Item parliamentum tentum est apud Kylkennie in octavo purificationis beate Marie per comitem Ultonie et Johannem Wogan justicarium Hibernie et ceteros magnates, in quo fit cedata magna discordia orta inter quosdam magnates Hibernie, et multe provisiones, tanquam statuta, providebantur multum utiles terre Hibernie si fuissent observate.

Item, cito post illud tempus rediit dominus Edmundus le Botiller de Anglia, qui ibi antea London factus est miles.

Item, transfretaverunt in Angliam de Hibernia comes Ultonie, Rogerus de Mortuo mari, et dominus Johannes filius Thome.

Item, obiit dominus Theobaldus de Verdon.

Anno domini m. cccx

Dominus[c] Rex Edwardus et dominus Petrus de Gaveston iter suum versus Scotiam arripuerunt ad pugnandum versus[d] versus Robertum de Brus.

Item, dicto anno, magna caristia blade in Hibernia, cranca frumenti vendita pro xx solidis et ultra.[e]

Item, pistores Dublinie pro sua falso pondere panis subiererunt novum genus tormenti ibidem non prius visum eo quod die Sancti Sampsonis episcopi tracti fuerunt super crates per vicos civitatis ad caudas equorum.

Item, in abbathia Sancti Thome, martiris, Dublin, obiit dominus Nigellus le Bruyn, miles, escaetor domini regis in Hibernia, cuius corpus Nigelli fuit

---

[a] interfecit *continued on next page.*   [b] et *repeated at end and beginning of line.*   [c] dominus *omitted* L.   [d] *omitted* L.   [e] *marg. note (seventeenth century)*: de vendit frumeti.

Item, lord David de Caunteton was hanged in Dublin.[377]

Item, Aodh, son of Cathal Ó Conchobhair, killed Aodh Ó Conchobhair, king of Connacht.[378]

Item, Athboy was burned by the Irish.[379]

1309

Peter de Gaveston subdued the Uí Bhroin Irishmen, and rebuilt Newcastle McKinegan and Castlekevin, and cleared and ordered the pass between Castlekevin and Glendalough, despite the Irish; and he went and made offerings in the church of St Kevin.[380] In the same year, lord Peter de Gaveston crossed to England on the eve of the nativity of St John the Baptist [Monday 23 June].[381]

Item, the wife of the son of the earl of Ulster, daughter of the earl of Gloucester, landed in Ireland on the 15th day of October.[382]

Item, on Christmas Eve the earl of Ulster returned from England and landed at the port of Drogheda.[383]

Item on the day of the purification of the Blessed Mary, virgin, [Mon. 2 Feb. 1310] lord John Boneville was killed near the vill of Ardscull by lord Arnold Poer and his accomplices. And he was buried at Athy in the church of the Preachers.[384]

Item, a parliament was held at Kilkenny in the octave of the purification of the Blessed Mary [c. 2 Feb. 1310] by the earl of Ulster and John Wogan justiciar of Ireland, and other magnates.[385] By this, a great conflict which had arisen between certain magnates of Ireland was calmed and many arrangements, as if they were statutes, were provided with many benefits for the land of Ireland if they should be heeded.[386]

Item, soon after that time, lord Edmund Butler returned from England; before [he left] he was made a knight in London.[387]

Item, the earl of Ulster, Roger de Mortimer, and lord John fitz Thomas, crossed to England from Ireland.

Item, lord Theobald de Verdun died.[388]

1310

The lord King Edward and lord Peter de Gaveston started on their journey towards Scotland to fight against Robert de Bruce.[389]

Item, in the said year there was a great shortage of grain in Ireland; a crannock of grain was selling for 20 shillings and more.[390]

Item, the bakers of Dublin, for their false weight of bread, have received a new kind of torment at that time not seen before, because on the feast day of St Sampson the bishop, [Tues. 28 July] they were drawn upon hurdles at horse tails through the streets of the city.[391]

Item, in the abbey of St Thomas the martyr, in Dublin, lord Nigel le Brun knight, escheator of the lord king in Ireland, died. The body of this Nigel was

sepultum |Folio 14r| † in monasterio*ᵃ* fratrum minorum de*ᵇ* Dublini cum tanta reverencia cereorum qualis ante^a^ in Hibernia non videbatur.

Eodem anno, parliamentum apud Kyldare, ubi dominus Arnaldus Povere de morte domini Johannis Bonevile acquietatur, quia hoc fecerat se defendendo.

Item, in die Sancti Patricii, unanimi assensu capitulorum, dominus Alexander de Bigenore elictus est in archiepiscopum Dublin electus.*ᶜ*

Item, dominus Rogerus de Mortuo mari rediit in Hiberniam infra octavam be*ᵈ* Nativitatis Beate Marie Virginis.

Item, eodem anno, dominus Henricus de Lacy, comes Lincolnie, obiit.

[–]NNO DOMINI M. CCCXI

In Thomond, apud Bonnorathe, mirabilis*ᵉ* et miraculosa disconfectio facta per dominum Ricardum de Clare super partes comitis Ultonie, quia predictus dominus Ricardus cepit in bello dominum Willelmum de Burgo et*ᶠ* Johannem, filium domini Walteri de Lacy, et multis aliis*ᵍ* et multos alios; quo quidem bello multi corruerunt, tam de Anglicis quam de Hibernicis, xiii kl Junii.

Item, Tassagard et Rathcoule invaserunt latrones, scilicet, Obrynnes et Othothiles,*ʰ* in crastino Nativitatis Sancti Johannis Baptiste. Unde cito in autumno collectus est magnus exercitus in Lagenia ad impugnandum dictos latrones, in Glyndelory et in aliis locis nemorosis latentes.

Item, parliamentum tentum Londonie, in Augusto, inter regem et barones ad tractandum de statu regni et de familiam regis, per ordinationem sex episcoporum, sex comitum et sex baronum qualiter utilius regno poterunt providere.

Item, ii idus Novembris,*ⁱ* Ricardus de Clara interfecit de Galagleghes vi centum.

Item, die Omnium Sanctorum precedente, proscriptus fuit Petrus de Gaveston de regno Anglie per comites et barones, et multa bona statuta rei publice necessaria per eosdem sunt confecta. Qui Petrus abiuravit regnum Anglie circa festum Omnium Sanctorum, et ibat*ʲ* in Flandriam iiii^or mensibus post et rediit et dictus Petrus cito post Epiphaniaus furtive intravit Angliam, adherens lateri regis, quia*ᵏ* et*ˡ* barones non poterant faciliter ad eum appropinquare. Et adivit Eboracum cum rege ibidem moram faciendo xl unde episcopi, comites, et barones Anglie London pervenerunt ad tractandum de statu regni, per*ᵐ* dicti Petri redditum res publica commoveretur.

ᵃ in monasterio *omitted* L.   *ᵇ* de *omitted* L.   *ᶜ* electus *omitted; marg. note (seventeenth century)*: Alexander archiepiscopus.   *ᵈ* be *(initial letters of* beate*) cancelled by underdotting.*   *ᵉ* *gap left and later insertion* mirabilis; mirabilis L.   *ᶠ* *different shorthand for* et *for a few entries.*   *ᵍ* repetition et multis aliis *omitted* L.   *ʰ* *marg. note (seventeenth century)*: Tassagard et Rathcoule.   *ⁱ* dominus *added* L.   *ʲ* ivit L.   *ᵏ* quod L.   *ˡ* et *omitted* L.   *ᵐ* ne per L.

buried in the monastery of the friars minor of Dublin with great tokens of respect, [and] candles such as had never before been seen in Ireland.³⁹²

In the same year a parliament at Kildare, where lord Arnold Poer, because he was defending himself, was acquitted of the death of lord John de Boneville.³⁹³

Item, on the feast of St Patrick [Wed. 1311] lord Alexander de Bicknor, with the unanimous assent of the chapters, was elected to the archbishopric of Dublin.³⁹⁴

Item, lord Roger de Mortimer returned to Ireland within the octave of the nativity of Blessed Virgin Mary [*c.* Sept. 1310 or 11].

Item, in the same year lord Henry de Lacy, earl of Lincoln, died.

1311

At Bunratty in Thomond on 13 Kal. June [20 May 1311] lord Richard de Clare made a wonderful and miraculous defeat upon the supporters of the earl of Ulster, so that the aforesaid lord Richard captured lord William de Burgh and John, son of lord Walter de Lacy, and many others in the battle. In which battle many fell, both of the English and of the Irish.³⁹⁵

Item, on the day after the Nativity of St John the Baptist [Fri. 25 June] Saggart and Rathcoole were assaulted by robbers, namely the Uí Bhroin and Uí Thuathail.³⁹⁶ Therefore, soon after, in autumn, a great army was collected in Leinster to fight the said robbers in Glenmalure and other concealed woody places.

Item, in August a parliament was held in London between the king and the barons, by ordinance of six bishops, six earls, and six barons, to discuss the state of the kingdom and the *familia* of the king, in order to be able to provide for the benefit of the kingdom.³⁹⁷

Item, on 2 Id. November [Fri. 12 Nov.] lord Richard de Clare killed six hundred galloglass.³⁹⁸

Item, on the preceding feast day of All Saints [Mon. 1 Nov.] Peter de Gaveston was outlawed from the kingdom of England by the earls and barons, and many good statutes necessary for the public good were made by them.³⁹⁹ He, Peter, abjured the kingdom of England around the feast of All Saints and went to Flanders for four months and after he returned.⁴⁰⁰ And the said Peter, soon after Epiphany [Thursday 6 January 1312?], secretly entered England, adhering to the side of the king, where the barons were not able to approach him easily. And he went to York with the king making a stay there in Lent. Whereupon the bishops, earls and barons of England went to London to treat of the state of the kingdom, about the return of the said Peter [which] might agitate the state.

Item, abierunt*a* dominus Johannes de Cogan, dominus Walterus Lefaunte |Folio 14v| † et dominus Johannes, filius Rery, milites, et sepelitur in ecclesia*b* predicatorum, Dublin.

Item, Johannes M*c*goghedan interficitur per Omolmoy.

Item, obiit Willelmus de Rupe, Dublin, de ictu sagitte unius Hibernici montani.

Item, obiit dominus Eustacius le Power, miles.

Item, in vigilia Cathedre Sancti Petri, incepit riota Urgalie per Robertum de Verdon.

Item, interficitur Donatus Obrene per suos tradisiose in Tothamonia.

Anno domini M. CCCXII

Dominus Petrus de Gaveston intravit castrum de Scardeburgh, baronibus resistendo. Sed, cito post kl Junii, se reddit domino Adomaro de Valencia, per quem fuerat obsessus, certis tamen condicionibus prelocutis, qui eum duxit versus London, sed itinerando captus est apud Dedyiniton per comitem Warwici, et ductus est ad Warewik, unde inito consilio comitum*c* baronum decollatur, xiii kl Julii, cuius corpus sepelitur in conventu de Langley in ecclesia fratrum predicatorum.

Item, exercitus ductus per Iohannem Wogan, justiciarium Hibernie, ad refrenandam malitiam Roberti de Verdon et suorum fautorum, miserabiliter confectus est vi idus Julii, interfectis ibidem domino*d* Nicholao Avenel, Patricio de Rupe, et multis aliis, ob quod dictus Robertus de Verdon et multi suorum fautorum se reddiderunt carceri regis, in castro*e* Dublin, gratiam expectando.

Item, die Jovis in crastino Sancte Lucie, Virginis, anno regni R. E. vi luna videbatur mirabiliter de diversis coloribus, in quo diffinitum*f* quod ordo templariorum de medio deleatur in eternum.

Item, sancti Martini natus est Edwardus filius regis E. in castro de Windesora.*g*

Item, in Hibernia dominus Edmundus le Botiler factus est locum tenens domini Johannis Wogan, justicarii Hibernie, qui Edmundus in xl sequente obsessit Obreynnes et*h* Glyndelory, et ipsos compulit ad deditionem et fere ad confucionem, nisi citius ad pacem domini regis redissent.

{Maritagium inter comitem Kyldarie et filiam comitis Ultonie scilicet Iohannis}

Item, eodem anno, in crastino Sancti Dominici, dominus Mauricius filius Thome desponsavit Katherinam, filiam comitis Ultonie, ad Viride Castrum. Et Thomas filius Johannis desponsavit aliam filiam ejusdem comitis, in crastino Assumptionis, in eodem loco.

---

a obierunt L.   *b* fratrum *added* L.   *c* m et *added* L.   *d* domino *omitted* L.   *e* in castro *omitted* L.   *f* est *added* L.   *g* Item, sancti Martini natus est Edwardus filius regis E. in castro de Windesore - *omitted*.   *h* in L.

Item, lord John de Cogan, lord Walter Lenfaunt and lord John fitz Rery, knights, died and were buried in the church of Friars Preachers, Dublin.[401]

Item, John Mag Eochagáin was killed by Ó Maoil Mhuaidh.[402]

Item, William de Roche died in Dublin by a stroke of a single arrow from a mountain Irishman.[403]

Item, lord Eustace le Poer, knight, died.[404]

Item, on the eve of the feast of St Peter's chair [17 Jan/21 Feb. 1312] Robert de Verdun began a riot in Uriel.[405]

Item, Donnchadh Ó Briain was killed treacherously by his own in Thomond.[406]

1312

Lord Peter de Gaveston entered the castle of Scarborough, resisting the barons.[407] But soon after the Kal. June [Thurs. 1 June] he delivered himself to lord Aymer de Valence (by whom he had been besieged), certain conditions having been spoken of before, who led him towards London.[408] But while journeying he was captured at Deddington by the earl of Warwick, and he was led to Warwick. Whereupon, counsel having been taken by the earls and barons, he was beheaded on 13 Kal. July [Mon. 19 June 1312]. His body was buried in the convent of Langley in the church of the Friars Preachers.[409]

Item, on the 6 Id. June [Thurs. 8 June] an army led by John Wogan, justiciar of Ireland, to repress the malice of Robert de Verdun and his accomplices, and he was miserably defeated, lord Nicholas Avenal, Patrick de Roche, and many others being killed there, because of which the said Robert de Verdun and many of his accomplices surrendered themselves to the king's prison in Dublin castle, awaiting grace.[410]

Item, On Thursday the day after St Lucy, virgin [Thurs. 14 Dec.], in the sixth year of K. E. [King Edward] there was seen an astonishing moon of different colours, on which [day] it was determined by writ that the order of Templars should be abolished forever.[411]

Item, on the feast of St Martin [11 Nov.], Edward, the son of King E[dward] was born in Windsor castle.[412]

Item, in Ireland lord Edmund Butler was appointed the *locum tenens* of lord John Wogan, justiciar of Ireland,[413] which Edmund, in the following Lent, besieged the Uí Bhroin at Glenmalure and threatened almost their complete ruination unless they speedily returned to the peace of the lord king.

{The marriage between the earl of Kildare and the daughter of John the earl of Ulster}

Item, in the same year on the day after the feast of St Dominic [Saturday 5 August] lord Maurice fitz Thomas married Katherine, daughter of the earl of Ulster, at Greencastle and in the same place, after the feast of the Assumption [Wednesday 16 August], Thomas fitz John married another daughter of the same earl.[414]

Item, die Dominica post festum Exaltacionis Sancte Crucis, filia comitis Glovernie, uxor domini Johannis de Burgo, peperit filium.

Anno domini M. CCCXIII
Frater Rolandus Joce, primas Ardmachanus,*a*

{applicuit}
|Folio 15r| **Ave Maria gratia plena †** applicuit in insula de Houtes, in crastino Annunciationis Beate Marie, de nocte surgens furtive levando crucem suam, illam portavit usque ad*b* prioratum de Gratia Dei. Cui occurrebant quidam de familiaribus archiepiscopi Dublin illam crucem deponendo, et ipsum Armachanum tanquam confusum a Lagenia effugarunt.

Item, tentum est parliamentum London, in quo nichil vel modicum de pace est expeditum. De quo parliamento discessit rex, tendens in Franciam, ad mandatum regis Francie ut interesset in die Pentecostes ad neaptoluzionem suorum duorum filiorum in quo festo rex Francie*c* et rex Anglie et multi nobiles sunt cruce signati.

Item, dominus*d* filius Thome fecit milites Nicholaum filium Mauritii et Robertum de Clanhull, apud Adare in Momonia.

Item, ultima die Maii, Robertus de Brus misit quasdam*e* ad partes Ultonie cum suis piratis ad *de*predandum, illos*f* quibus restiterunt Ultonienses, viriliter eos effugando, dicitur tamen quo*g* idem Robertus applicuit per licenciam comitis treugas capiendo.

Item, in eadem estate, dominus Johannes de*h* le Decer, civis Dublin, construi fecit pontem necessarium extra villam de Balyboght usque calcidum stagni molendini de Clontarf, ubi primum imminebat maximum periculum transeuntibus. Sed gravibus expensis positis, propter inundationem aque, pons cum arcubus corruit.

{No*ta* de submersione mare [?]}
Item, dominus Johannes de Leck, archiepiscopus Dublin, in festo Sancti Laurentii diem suum clausit extremum.*i* Tunc electi sunt in discordia in archiepiscopum Dublin, dominus Walterus Thornbury, cancellarius domini regis in Hibernia, et dominus Alexander Biggenore, thesaurarius Hibernie; sed dominus Walterus Thornbury submersus est, et alii plures, circiter centum quinquaginta sex, mare ingressi sunt et nocte sequenti omnes fuerunt submersi. Tempore cuius mortis, scilicet, predicti Walteri, Alexander Begenore expectavit gratiam Summi Pontificis. Archiepiscopus Dublin factus est idem Alexander.*j*

---

a rubricated box added here: text black. Applicuit *is catchword for the next page.*   *b* ad *missing* L.   *c* ut interesset in die Pentecostes ad neaptoluzionem suorum duorum filiorum in quo festo Rex Francie omitted.   *d* Johannes *supplied* L.   *e* galeas *supplied* L.   *f* illos *omitted* L.   *g* quod L.   *h* de *omitted* L.   *i marg. note (seventeenth century, very faint): possibly* John de Leck [...]
j marg. note (seventeenth century, very faint): possibly Alexander archiepiscopus.

Item, on the Sunday after the feast of the exaltation of the Holy Cross [Sun. 17 Sep 1312], the daughter of the earl of Gloucester, wife of lord John de Burgh, gave birth to a son.[415]

1313

Friar Roland Jorz, primate of Armagh[416] {landed} (Hail Mary full of grace)[417] landed secretly at the island of Howth on the day after the Annunciation of the Blessed Virgin Mary [Mon. 26 March]. Getting up in the night, then raising his cross, he carried that as far as the priory of Grace Dieu. There certain of the household of the archbishop of Dublin hurried to meet him, to make him put down that cross, and drove the same [archbishop of] Armagh himself from Leinster shamefully.[418]

Item, a parliament was held in London where little or nothing was done about peace.[419] The king departed from this parliament heading for France at the command of the king of France, to attend the knighting of his two sons on the feast day of Pentecost. At which feast the king of France and the king of England, and many nobles were signed with the cross.[420]

Item, lord John fitz Thomas knighted Nicholas fitz Maurice and Robert de Clohull at Adare in Munster.[421]

Item, on the last day of May [Thurs. 31 May] Robert de Bruce sent certain [galleys[422]] with his pirates to parts of Ulster to plunder it; the men of Ulster manfully resisted them, putting them to flight. It is said, however, that the same Robert landed by the authority of the earl to make truces.[423]

Item, in the same summer, lord John le Decer, citizen of Dublin, caused to be constructed an essential bridge outside the vill of Ballybough up to the causeway of the mill-pond of Clontarf, where for the first time, it lessened the great danger to those crossing. But after serious expense having been incurred, because of the flood of water, the bridge with its arch fell down.[424]

{Note the drowning in the sea}

Item, lord John de Lech, archbishop of Dublin, ended his days on the feast of St Lawrence [10 Aug. or 3 Feb. 1313].[425] Then lord Walter Thornberry, chancellor of the lord king in Ireland, and lord Alexander Bicknor, treasurer of Ireland, were elected in discord, into the archbishopric of Dublin. However, lord Walter Thornberry was drowned, and many others (around one hundred and fifty-six) went into the sea, and the following night all were drowned.[426] At the time of that death (namely, of the aforesaid Walter's), Alexander Bicknor awaited the grace of the pope. The same Alexander was made archbishop of Dublin.[427]

Item, dominus Milo de Verdon desponsavit filiam domini Ricardi de de*a* Oxoniis.

Item, eodem anno, dominus Robertus de Brus prostravit castrum de Manne, et cepit*b* dominum Danegan Odowyll, die Sancti Barnabe apostoli.*c*

Et dominus Johannes de Burgo, heres comitis Ultonie, Ricardi, obiit apud Galby in festo Sanctorum Marcelli et Marcelliani.

Item, dominus Edmundus le Botiler fecit xxx milites in castro Dublin in die Dominica et Sancti Michaelis archangli*d*.

|Folio 15v| [–]NNO DOMINI M. CCCXIIII
Hospitalarii receperunt terras templariorum Hibernie.

Item, dominus Johannes Parice interficitur apud Pontem.

Item, dominus Theobaldus de Verdon venit justiciarius Hibernie in die Sancti Silvestri.

Item, dominus ac Frater Galfridus de Genevile obiit xii kl Novembris; sepultus in suo ordine fratrum predicatorum de Trym, qui fuit dominus libertatis Midie.

Item, eodem anno, et die Sancti Matthie, apostoli, Loghseudy fuit succensa. Et die Veneris sequenti, dominus Edmundus le Botiler recepit suam comissionem, quod esset justiciarius Hibernie.

{•} ANNO DOMINI M. CCCXV
In die Sancti Johannis Baptiste, obiit interfectus comes Glovernie, cum multis aliis, quasi sine numero, interficiuntur, in Scotia, et plures capiuntur per Scotos; qua de causa Scoti in audacia erecti, terram bonam et tributa de Northumbeland ceperunt.

Item, cito post hec venerunt Scoti, et villam de Carlele obsiderunt, ubi oppressus fuit Jacobus de Douglas per infortunium cuiusdam muri cadentis.

Eodem*e* anno, dicti Scoti, terra propria non contenti, prenimia superbia Hiberniam in parte boriali apud Clondonne applicuerunt, sex millibus pugnatorum et in bellis peritorum scilicet, dominus Edwardus le Brus, germanus Roberti, regis Scotorum, et cum eo comes de Morreth, Johannes de Weriteth,*f* Johannes Styward, dominus Johannes Cambell, Thomas Randolfe, Fergus de Ardressan, Johannes de Bosco et Johannes Bysset Ultoniam manciparunt, et dominum Thomam de Mandebile, ceterosque fideles a terra propria expulerunt. Scoti primo Hibernia intraverunt die Sancti Augustini Anglorum, mense Maii, juxta Cragfergus in Ultonia, inter quos et Anglicos primus conflictus habebatur juxta le Banne, in quo fugatur comes Ultonie, capiuntur ibi*g* Willelmus de Burgo, Johannes de Stantona, et multi alii,

---

a de *repeated at end and beginning of a line.*   *b* deperdidit L.   *c* apostoli *omitted* L.   *d* archangli *omitted* L.   *e* *new line.*   *f* Meneteth L.   *g* ibi *omitted* L.

Item, lord Milo de Verdun married the daughter of lord Richard de Exonia.[428]

Item, in the same year, lord Robert de Bruce demolished the castle of Man and on the feast day of St Barnabas, apostle [Mon. 11 June], seized lord Duncan O Dowell.[429]

And on the feast of saints Marcus and Marcellianus [Mon. 18 June 1313], lord John de Burgh, heir of Richard, earl of Ulster, died at Galway.[430]

Item, on the Sunday the feast of St Michael, archangel [29 Sept. 1313] lord Edmund Butler made thirty knights in Dublin castle.[431]

1314

The Hospitallers received the lands of the Templars in Ireland.[432]

Item, lord John Parys was killed at Drogheda.[433]

Item, on the feast day of St Sylvester [Tues. 31 Dec.] lord Theobald de Verdun [II] arrived as justiciar of Ireland.[434]

Item, Geoffrey de Geneville, lord, and friar, died on 12 Kal. November [Mon. 21 Oct.] and was buried in his order of Friars Preachers of Trim; he was the lord of the liberty of Meath.[435]

Item, in the same year and on the feast day of St Matthew, apostle [Tues. 4 Feb. 1315], Lough Sewdy was set on fire.[436] And on the following Friday [Fri. 7 Feb. 1315] lord Edmund Butler received his commission, that he was to be justiciar of Ireland.[437]

1315

On the feast of St John Baptist [Nativity of John the Baptist Tues. 24 June], the earl of Gloucester was killed with many others, almost without number.[438] They were killed in Scotland, and many were captured by the Scots. For this reason the Scots became audacious; they seized land, goods, and tribute from Northumberland.[439]

Item, soon after this the Scots came and besieged the town of Carlisle where James de Douglas was crushed by the misfortune of the collapse of a certain wall.[440]

In the same year,[441] the said Scots, not content with their own land,[442] [and] with too much arrogance, landed in the northern part of Ireland at Clondonne[443] with six thousand fighters skilled in battle,[444] namely lord Edward le Bruce, full brother of Robert, king of Scots, and with him the earl of Moray, John de Menteith, John Stewart, lord John Campbell, Thomas Randolph, Fergus de Ardrossan, John de Bosco, and John Bisset[445] and took Ulster into their hands. And lord Thomas de Mandeville and other faithful [men] were expelled from their own lands.[446] The Scots first entered Ireland near Carrickfergus in Ulster on the feast of St Augustine of the English, in the month of May [Monday 26 May 1315],[447] and had their first conflict with the English near the [river] Bann, in which the earl of Ulster was put to flight, and there William de Burgh, John

multisque Anglicis interfectis, prevaluerunt Scoti. Secundus conflictus apud Kenlys in Midia, in quo fugatur Rogerus de Mortuo mari cum sequela sua. Tertius conflictus est apud Sketheris juxta Arscoll, in crastino Conversionis Sancti Pauli, in quo fugantur Anglici, Scoti prevaluerunt. Et predictus Edwardus le Brus, cito post festum Philippi et Jacobi fecit se coronari in regem Hibernie |Folio 16r| et Castrum Viride receperunt, et suos ibidem reliquerunt, quos Dublinienses cito post expellerant, et dictum castrum ad manum domini regis receperunt, et dominum Robertum de Coulrach, custodem castri ibidem invenientes, secum Dublin adduxerunt, qui incarceratus ad dietam positus expiravit.

Item, ^die^*a* Apostolorum Petri et Pauli, venerunt Scoti apud Dondalk, et villam ceperunt, spoliaverunt, conbusserunt, eisdem resistentes interfecerunt, et magna pars Urgalie comburitur a Scotis. Ecclesia Beate Marie Virginis de Atrio Dei, plena viris,*b* mulieribus et parvulis, comburitur a Scotis et Hibernicis.

Eodem anno, dominus Edmundus le Botiler, justiciarius Hibernie, circa festum Sancte Marie Magdalene, magnum exercitum de Momonia et Lagenia, et aliis partibus collegit, et comes Ultonie, cum exercitu innumerabili, quasi in adverso, de partibus Conacie veniens ad partes de Dondalk, simul venerunt, et mutuo consulebant ut Scotos interficerent et quomodo ignoratur fugerent; aliter, ut sperabatur, capti essent, quo facto, dominus comes Ultonie, cum iusticiario predicto et aliis magnatibus ibidem manucepit, Scotis interfectis, dominum Edwardum le Brus vivum vel mortuum Dublin adducere, qui comes eos sequebatur usque ad aquam de Banne, et postea dictus comes retraxit se versus Coyners; quod percipiens dictus Brus caute dictam aquam transivit sequens eum, quem cum quibusdam in parte comitis in fugam convertit, vulneratis Georgio de Rupe et aliis interfectis, scilicet, domino Johanne Staunton, Rogero de Sancto Bosco, similiter ex parte Brus multi ceciderunt, et dominus Willelmus de Burgo captus fuit x die mensis Septembris, et comes confectus est iuxta Coyners.

Et tunc Hibernici de Connacia et de Midia insurrexerunt contra Regem et contra comitem Ultonie, et conbuserunt castrum de Athlon, et de Randon, et multa alia castra.

In dicto ~~castra de~~*c* bello de Conyners Baro de Donull ibi strenue fecit, sed multa bona ibi amissit et dicti Scoti viriliter*d* fugabant usque ad Cragfergus, ibique fugerunt ex parte comitis, et quidam castrum intraverunt et viriliter tenuerunt, et postea venerunt naute de portibus Anglicorum, et quadam nocte supervenerunt Scotos, et quadraginta |Folio 16v| ex eis occiderunt, et tentoria eorum et multa alia abstulerunt.

---

a ^ and die *above the line.* *b* et *added* L. *c* *corrected by underdotting and strike through.* *d* ~~eos~~ *added* L.

de Stanton and many others were captured, and many English killed, and the Scots prevailed. The second conflict was at Kells in Meath in which Roger de Mortimer and his following fled. The third conflict was at Skerries near Ardscull on the day after the conversion of St Paul [Mon. 26 January 1316][448], in which the English fled and the Scots prevailed.[449] And soon after the feast of Phillip and James [soon after 1 May 1316], the aforesaid Edward le Bruce had himself crowned king of Ireland,[450] and took Greencastle and left his men there.[451] The men of Dublin soon after drove them out and recovered the said castle into the hand of the lord king; and, finding there lord Robert de Coulrach, custodian of the same castle, they led him to Dublin with them, and he was imprisoned and he died of the diet.[452]

Item,[453] on the feast day of the apostles Peter and Paul [Sun. 29 June 1315] the Scots came and took Dundalk and plundered and burnt the vill and killed those resisting.[454] And a great part of Uriel was burnt by the Scots. The church of the Blessed Virgin Mary of Ardee, full of men, women, and little children, was burnt by the Scots and the Irish.[455]

In the same year, around the feast of St Mary Magdalen [c. Tues. 22 July 1315], lord Edmund Butler, justiciar of Ireland, gathered together a great army of men of Leinster and Munster and other parts. And the earl of Ulster, almost against them, with a countless army from parts of Connacht likewise came to the district of Dundalk. And they consulted mutually how the Scots might be killed. They were unaware they [the Scots] were fleeing, otherwise it is believed they would have been captured.[456] After this happened, then the lord earl of Ulster, with the aforesaid justiciar and other magnates undertook that when the Scots were killed, lord Edward le Bruce would be brought to Dublin, dead or alive. The earl followed them [the Scots] to the water of the Bann and afterwards the said earl himself returned towards Connor.[457] Learning this, the said Bruce carefully crossed the said water following him, and certain [men] on the side of the earl turned to flight, George de Roche was wounded and others killed, namely lord John Staunton, Roger de St Bosco.[458] Similarly on the side of Bruce many fell and lord William de Burgh was captured on the tenth day of September [Wed. 10 Sept. 1315], and the earl was defeated near Connor.[459]

And then the Irish of Connacht and Meath rose against the king and against the earl of Ulster and burnt the castles of Athlone and of Rindoon and many other castles.

In the said battle of Connor the baron of Dunoil made a strong stand there but lost many goods there and the said Scots were chasing [the English] vigorously right up to Carrickfergus.[460] And there, they fled the earl's side, and they entered a certain castle and vigorously held it. And later sailors came from the English ports, and on a certain night came upon the Scots and killed forty of them and carried away their tents and many other things.[461]

Et in crastino Exaltacionis Sancte Crucis, comes de Morreth transfretavit in Scotiam, et duxit dominum Willelmum de Burgo secum, querendo plures bellicosos et armatos homines cum quatuor piratis plenis bonorum terre Hibernie, quarum una submersa est; quo tempore dictus Brus castrum de Cragfergus obsidebat.

Eodem anno,[a] Cathil Rothe tria castra comitis Ultonie in Connacia fregit et plures villas in eadem Connacia conbussit et spoliavit.

Et eodem tempore dicti naute dictum castrum adierunt, et domini ibidem preliabantur, et interim plures Scotos interfecerunt, quo tempore Ricardus de Lan de Oferwill[b] quodam Hibernico de mid^i^a[c] occisus est.

Item, die ^Sancti^[d] Nicholai, postea dictus le Brus recessit de Cragfergus, ad quem comes de Murreth cum quingentis venit ad partes de Dundalk pariter venerunt, ad quos multi fugerunt et dextram aliqui dederunt, et inde apud Nobre transeunt, ubi multos de suis relinquunt, circa festum Sancti Andree, apostoli. Et ipse Brus conbussit Kenlys in Midia et Grenard et dictum monasterium spoliavit de omnibus bonis, et Fynnagh et Novum Castrum conbussit et totam illam patriam, et tenuerunt eorum natale apud Loghsudy et conbusserunt. Et postea transierunt per Totmoy usque Rathymegan et Kyldare, et partes de Tristeldermot et de Athy et de Ribane, non sine dampno hominum suorum. Et tunc venit le Brus ad Skethir, juxta Arscol in Lagenia. Ibi occurrerunt ei in pugnam dominus Edmundus le[e] Botiler, justiciarius Hibernie, et dominus Johannes filius Thome, et dominus Arnaldus Power, et alii magnates Lagenie et Momonie; ita quod unus predictorum dominorum, cum exercitu ^sue^,[f] sufficeret eundem Edwardum et exercitum suum debellare.

{no*ta* discordia}
Sed discordia orta est inter eos; confusi campum eidem Edwardo relinquunt, juxta illud quod scriptum est. Omne regnum in se [ipsum] divisum desolabitur. Ibi interfectus est armiger nobilis et fidelis regi et regno, Haymundus le Grace, et dominus Willelmus Prendregast, miles. Occiduntur ex parte Scotorum dominus Fergus Andressan, dominus Walterus de Morrey, et multi alii interficiuntur, quorum corpora sepulta sunt apud Athy, in conventu fratrum predicatorum. Postea, dictus Brus, in redditu suo versus Midiam, castrum de Ley cremavit, et tunc transiunt dicti Scoti ad[g] Kenlys in Midia, ad quos dominus[h] |Folio 17r| de Mortimer d̶e̶ ᶜᵘᵐ[i] magno exercitu, venit fere cum xv millibus, non fidelibus, ut creditur, inter se, nec cum domino Rogero confederatis, qui quasi hora tertia fugam ceperunt, et terga verterunt, et principaliter de Lacyes, domino Rogero, solo, cum paucis, quem oportebat fugere versus Dublin, et dominum Walterus Cusak, fugebat[j] ad castrum de Trym, relicta cum Scotis patria illa et villa de Kenlys.

---

[a] eodem tempore L.   [b] *word* a *added: see footnote to translation.*   [c] de Midia *omitted.*   [d] ^ *and* sancti *above the line.*   [e] le *omitted.*   [f] ^ *and* sue *above the line.* suo L.   [g] de L.   [h] Rogerus *supplied* L.   [i] de *corrected by underdotting and* cum *inserted above line.*   [j] fugebat *omitted* L.

And on the day after the Exaltation of the Holy Cross [Mon 15 Sept. 1315] the earl of Moray crossed into Scotland and took lord William de Burgh with him,⁴⁶² seeking many warlike and armed men, with four pirates ships full of goods of the land of Ireland, of which one was sunk.⁴⁶³ At which time the said Bruce was besieging Carrickfergus castle.⁴⁶⁴

In the same year Cathal Ruadh threw down three castles of the earl of Ulster in Connacht and he burnt and plundered many vills in the same Connacht.⁴⁶⁵

And at the same time the said sailors went to the said castle [Carrickfergus] and the lords there were fighting and meanwhile many Scots were killed.⁴⁶⁶

At which time Richard de Lan was killed by Ó Fearghail, a certain Irishman of Meath.⁴⁶⁷

Item, afterwards, on the feast day of St Nicholas [11 Nov. 1315],⁴⁶⁸ the said Bruce withdrew from Carrickfergus. The earl of Moray came to him with five hundred [men] and they came together to the area of Dundalk.⁴⁶⁹ Many fled to them, and some gave their pledge and then, around the feast of St Andrew, apostle, [c.30 Nov. 1315] they crossed to Nobber where they left many of their men. And Bruce himself burnt Kells in Meath and Granard and he plundered the said abbey of all its goods. He burnt both Finnea and Newcastle and all of that country.⁴⁷⁰ And they held their Christmas [1315] at Loughsewdy and burnt it.⁴⁷¹ And afterwards they crossed by Tethmoy as far as Rathangan and Kildare and then to the area of Tristledermot [Castledermot] and Athy and Reban, but not without loss of their men.⁴⁷² And then Bruce came to Skerries near Ardscull in Leinster.⁴⁷³ Here they met in battle lord Edmund le Butler, justiciar of Ireland, and lord John fitz Thomas and lord Arnold Poer and other magnates of Leinster and Munster,⁴⁷⁴ so that any one of the aforesaid lords with his army was enough to defeat the same Edward [Bruce] and his army.

{Note discord}

But discord arose among them [and] they left the field in confusion to the same Edward, according to which was written, 'a kingdom divided among itself shall be desolate'.⁴⁷⁵ Hamon le Gras (that noble and faithful squire of the king and kingdom), was killed here and lord William Prendergast, knight.⁴⁷⁶ On the Scots side, lord Fergus Ardrossan,⁴⁷⁷ lord Walter de Moray, and many others were killed there, the bodies of whom were buried at Athy in the convent of the Friars Preachers.⁴⁷⁸ Afterwards the said Bruce, in returning his men towards Meath, burnt the castle of Lea.⁴⁷⁹ And then the said Scots crossed to Kells in Meath. Lord [Roger]⁴⁸⁰ de Mortimer came there with a great army (almost fifteen thousand as believed), neither faithful among themselves, nor loyally joined with lord Roger. At about the third hour they took flight and turned back, primarily the de Lacys,⁴⁸¹ lord Roger, alone with only a few, having to flee towards Dublin. And lord Walter Cusack fled to the castle of Trim, leaving that land and the vill of Kells to the Scots.⁴⁸²

Item, eodem tempore, Hibernici australes, Othothiles et Obrynnes cremaverunt totam patriam australem, scilicet, Arclowe, Novum Castrum, Bree et omnes villas adiacentes. Et Omorghes cremabant et devastabant partem de Leye in Lagenia, quosᵃ Edmundus Botiler, ^iusticiarius Hibernie^,ᵇ in magna parte occidit quorum capita quasi octinginta ad castrum Dublin deportata sunt.

Item, eodem anno, circa festum Purificationis Beate Marie Virginis, quidam magnates Hibernie vsᶜ dominus Johannesᵈ filius Thome, dominus Ricardus de Clara, dominus Johannes le Power, et dominus Arnaldus le Pover, ratione pacis et maioris securitatis cum rege Anglie formande, venerunt ad dominum Johannem de Hothom, per dictum regem Anglie ibi assignatum, qui dicti magnates simul pro morte et vita ad tenende cum rege Anglie et pacem in terra pro posse eorum facere et Scotos interficere iuraverunt. Quo facto complendo, mediante Deo, obsides dederunt et sic redierunt. Quam formam si alii magnates terre tenere noluerunt, tanquam inimici regis puplice tenebantur.

Item, obiit dominus Johannes Bysset. Et ^ecclesia^ nove ville de Leys, cum campanile, a Scotis comburitur etᵉ castrum de Norghkuryhᶠ in Ultonia capitur a Scotis.

Item, Fedelmicus Ochonchure, rex Connacie, interfecit Roricum Roricum,ᵍ filium Catholi Ychonghure.

Item, obiit dominus Willemus Mandibile et episcopus Conerensis fugit ad castrum de Cragfergus et supponitur episcopatus eius interdicto. Et dominus Hugo de Antona interficitur in Connacia.

Item, in die Sancti Valentini eodem anno, Scoti moram fecerunt prope Gesyl inʰ Offalia, et exercitus Anglicorum juxta partes de Kyldare, et Scoti tantam famem patiebantur quod plures eorum fame moriebantur, et eadem de causa iter occulte arripuerunt versus Fowr in Midia Dominica sequenti taliter debilitati fuerunt, quid de fame quid de labore plures eorum moriebantur.

|Folio 17v| Et postea venerunt magnates ad Parliamentum et nichil ibi fecerunt, sed totam patriam redeundo spoliaverunt. Et dominus Walterus de Lacy venit Dublin ad ^in^-famamⁱ sibi impositam purgandam, et obsides domino regi offerre sicut alii magnates fecerunt. Et eodem tempore Edwardusʲ Brus in Ultonia pacifice morabatur.

Item, Otothilesᵏ Obrynnes, Archibauldes et Haroldes coniurati fuerunt et villam de Wikelowe cum tota patria devastaverunt. Et prima septimana xl, comes de Morreth transfretavit in Scotiam, et le Brus placita tenuit in Ultonia et plures suspendi fecit.

Item, in medio xl, Brus tenuit placita et occidit les Logans, et cepit dominum Alanum filium Warini et duxit eum in Scotiam.

Item, eodem anno, Fennyn Oconghor occidit Cale Rothe, et cum eo deˡ gallogloghes et aliis circa trecentos.

ᵃ dominus *added* L. ᵇ ^ *and* justiciarius Hibernie *above the line.* ᶜ et L. ᵈ Johannes *omitted* L. ᵉ et *omitted* L. ᶠ Northburgh L. ᵍ Roricum *repeated but not deleted.* ʰ et L. ⁱ ^ *and* in *above the line.* L in *omitted* = famam. ʲ de *added* L. ᵏ et *added* L. ˡ de *omitted* L.

Item, at the same time the Irish of the south, the Uí Thuathail and Uí Bhroin, burnt all the land to the south namely Arklow, Newcastle, Bray and all the adjacent vills.[483] And the Uí Mhórdha burnt and devastated the area of Lea in Leinster; of those Edmund Butler, justiciar of Ireland, killed the most part; almost eighty of their heads were carried to the castle of Dublin.[484]

Item, in same year around the feast of the Purification of blessed Virgin Mary [c.Fri. 2 Feb. 1316][485] certain magnates of Ireland and lord John fitz Thomas, lord Richard de Clare, lord John le Poer and lord Arnold le Poer, came to lord John de Hothum, he having been assigned there by the said lord king, in order to shape the peace and greater security with the king of England.[486] These said magnates swore together, for death and life, to hold with the king of England and to make peace in the land to the best of their ability, and to kill the Scots. When this was done, with the help of God, they gave hostages and thus returned [home]. If other magnates of the land were not willing to hold these terms, they were to be publicly considered enemies of the king.[487]

Item, lord John Bisset died.[488] And the New Town of Leys was burnt by the Scots.[489] And the castle of Northburgh in Ulster was captured by the Scots.[490]

Item, Feidhlim Ó Conchobhair, king of Connacht, killed Ruadhrí son of Cathal Ruadh Ó Conchobhair.[491]

Item, lord William Mandeville died.[492] And the bishop of Connor fled to the castle of Carrickfergus and his bishopric was put under interdict.[493] And lord Hugo de Antona was killed in Connacht.[494]

Item, in the same year on the feast of St Valentine [Sat. 14 Feb. 1316] the Scots delayed near Geashill in Offaly, and the English near parts of Kildare.[495] And the Scots suffered such famine that many of them perished from the famine. And the same [Scots] because of this, secretly began a journey towards Fore in Meath. On the following Sunday [Sun. 15 or 22 Feb. 1316] they were so weakened, both from hunger and from travel, very many of them died.[496]

And afterwards the magnates came to the parliament and did nothing there,[497] but as they returned, they plundered the whole countryside. And lord Walter de Lacy came to Dublin in order to clear himself of an accusation placed on him and he offered hostages to the lord king just as other magnates had done.[498] And at the same time [22 Feb. 1316], Edward Bruce remained peacefully in Ulster.[499]

Item, the Uí Thuathail, Uí Bhroin, Archebolds and Harolds conspired together and devastated the town of Wicklow with all the countryside.[500] And, in the first week of Lent [Ash Wednesday 25 February 1316] the earl of Moray crossed to Scotland. And Bruce held pleas in Ulster, and many were hanged.[501]

Item, in the middle of Lent [Lent: 25 Feb–11 April 1316] Bruce held pleas and killed the Logans and captured lord Alan fitz Warin and led him to Scotland.[502]

Item, in the same year Finghin Ó Conchobhair killed Cathal Ruadh, and with him around three hundred galloglass and others.[503]

Eadem xl, in medio, frumentum vendebatur pro xviii solidis, et in*ᵃ* Pascha sequenti ~~et ad sequens~~*ᵇ* pro xi solidis.

Anno domini m. cccxvi

Dominus Thomas de Maundevile, cum pluribus de Drogheda, venit ad*ᶜ* Cragfergus, die Jovis in Cena Domini, et bellum commiserunt cum Scotis, et eos in fugam converterunt, et circa xxx Scotorum occiderunt. Et, postea, in vigilia Pasche, dictus dominus Thomas, cum suis, insultum fecit contra Scotos, et plures eorum occidit circa lx et ibi occisus erat dictus dominus Thomas*ᵈ* in propria patria pro iure suo.

Item, in partibus Connacie multi Hibernici occisi fuerunt per dominum Ricardum de Clare,*ᵉ* Ricardum Bermyngham.

Item, die Sabbatbi post Ascensionem Domini, per dominum Willelmum Comyn et suos sequaces, custodes pacis, occisus erat Donneyn Obrynne, fortis latro, cum xii de suis sociis, quorum capita Dublin portata fuerunt.

Item, homines de Dondalk exierunt versus Ohanlan, et de Hibernicos occiderunt circa cc et occisus erat Robertus de Verdon, armiger bellicosus.

Item, ad festum Pentecostes eodem anno, Ricardus de Bermyngham occidit de Hibernicis in Momonia circa ccc vel magis.*ᶠ*

Et postea ad festum Nativitatis Beati Johannis Baptiste |Folio 17v| venit le Brus ad castrum de Cragfergus, et precepit custodibus castrum sibi reddi sicut conventio inter eos facta fuit, ut dixit. Qui responderunt quod eos oportebat hoc facere, et preceperunt eum mittere triginta de suis et concederet eis vitam et membrum, qui sic fecit. Et receptis triginta Scotis castro eos incluserunt et in carcere detenuerunt.

Eo tempore, Hibernici de Omayll inierunt ad*ᵍ* partes de Tullagh*ʰ* bellum commiserunt, unde de Hibernicis occisi fuerunt circa cccc quorum capita Dublin missa fuerunt, et mirabilia postea ibi videbantur quod mortui surrexerunt et invicem pugnaverunt et *Finnok Abo* signum eorum, exclamaverunt.

Et, postea, circa festum Translationis Beati Thome, parate erant viii naves de Drogheda versus Cragfergus cum victualibus, que per comitem Ultonie perturbate fuerunt, propter deliberacionem Willelmi de Burgo, qui cum Scotis captus erat, et die sabbati sequente coadiunati fuerunt Dublin comes Ultonie et dominus Johannes filius Thome, et plures magnati coniurati et confederati fuerunt pro vita et morte, pro pace terre Hibernie sustinenda.

Eodem anno venerint nova de Connacia quod Oconghur occidebat plures Anglicos videlicet dominum Stephanum de Exoniis, Milonem de Cogan et plures de Barries et de Laweles circa octoginta.

ᵃ ad *instead of* in.   *ᵇ* *struck through, underdotted.*   *ᶜ* apud L.   *ᵈ* de Maundevile *added* L.
ᵉ dominum *added* L.   *ᶠ* plures L.   *ᵍ* versus L.   *ʰ* et *added* L.

In the middle of the same Lent wheat was selling for eighteen shillings and in the following Easter for eleven shillings.

1316[504]

On Thursday in the second Sunday of Lent [Thurs. 11 March 1316] lord Thomas de Mandeville with many men of Drogheda came to Carrickfergus and they commenced battle with the Scots and put them to flight and killed around thirty of the Scots.[505] And afterwards, on the day before Easter [Sat. 10 April 1316] the said lord Thomas [de Mandeville] with his men made an assault upon the Scots and he killed many of them, around sixty. And there the said lord Thomas was killed in his own land while defending his property.[506]

Item, many Irish were killed in parts of Connacht by lord Richard de Clare and Richard Bermingham.[507]

Item, on the Saturday after the Ascension of the lord [Sat. 22 May 1316] Dúnlaing Ó Broin, a powerful thief, was killed with twelve of his associates by lord William Comyn and his following, keepers of the peace.[508] Their heads were taken to Dublin.

Item, the men of Dundalk went forth against Ó hAnluain and around two hundred of the Irish were killed and Robert de Verdun, a warlike squire, was killed.[509]

Item, on the feast of Pentecost in the same year [Sun. 30 May 1316] Richard de Bermingham killed around three hundred or more of the Irish in Munster.

And afterwards, at the feast of the Nativity of the blessed John the Baptist [Thurs. 24 June], Bruce came to Carrickfergus castle and commanded the custodians to hand over the castle to him, as he claimed that an agreement had been made between them.[510] They replied that they ought to do this. And they begged him to send thirty of his men, and they insisted that they would grant them life and limb, and he did this. When receiving the thirty Scots in the castle they imprisoned them and kept them in prison there.[511]

At that time, the Irish of Imaal entered the parts of Tullow to commence battle, from where around four hundred of the Irish were killed, whose heads were sent to Dublin.[512] And wonders were afterwards seen there because the dead arose and in turn they fought and cried out their signal '*Fennok Abo*'.[513]

And afterwards, around the feast of the translation of Blessed Thomas [Wed. 7 July], eight ships of Drogheda were fitted out to [go to] Carrickfergus with provisions.[514] These were thrown into confusion by the earl of Ulster (because of handing over of William de Burgh, who had been taken by the Scots).[515] And on the following Saturday [Sat. 10 July 1316] the earl of Ulster and John fitz Thomas and many nobles, united, came to Dublin and they swore and joined [together] for life or death to support the peace of the land of Ireland.

In the same year news came from Connacht that Ó Conchobhair killed very many English, namely lord Stephen de Exonia, Milo de Cogan and many, around eighty, of the Barrys and of the Lawlesses.[516]

Item, in septimana post festum Sancti Laurentii, in Connacia surrexerunt iiii^{or} regegeos^a Hibernici in bellum contra Anglicos, contra quos venerunt dominus Willelmus de Burgo, dominus Ricardus de Bermygham, dominus de Anry, cum sequela sua de patria, et de eisdem Hibernicis occiderunt circa xi millia juxta Anry, que villa muratur postmodum per arma et spolia que fuerunt Hibernicorum, quia quilibus Anglicos qui habuit duplicia arma de Hibernicis, medietatem dedit ad muros ville Anry.^{b} |Folio 18r| † Ibi interficiebatur Fedelmicus Oconghur, rex Connacie, et Okelly et plures alii reguli. Ibi dimicavit Johannes Huse, carnifex de Anry {no*ta* **crudelitatem carnificis qui vocatur Husee**}, qui eadem nocte ad rogatum domini sui de Anry stetit inter^c mortuos, ut exploraret Okellay, qui Okelly, cum suo armigero de latebulis surrexit et clamavit ad predictum virum, scilicet, Johannes^d Hussee^e dicens^f ^o^^{g} venias mecum, et ego faciam te magnum dominum in terra mea. Et Husee,^{h} Non ibo tecum, sed tu ibis ad dominum meum, Ricardum Bermyngham. Tunc dixit Okelly, Tu non^i nisi unum famulum tecum, et ego habeo armigerum probum; ideo venias mecum, ut diteris. Cui etiam famulus Johannis dixit, Consentias et transeas cum Okelly ut salvemur et dItemur, quia fortiores nobis sunt. At ille Johannes Hussee primo interfecit famulum proprium^j et Okelly et suum armigerum et amputavit eorum tria capita, et portavit ad^k domini suum^l Bermyngham, et ille Bermyngham dedit predicto Johanni Hussee amplas terras, et fecit illum militem, ut bene meruit.

Eodem anno, circa festum Sancti Laurentii, venit Ohanlayn apud Dondalk ad distringendum et homines de Dondalk cum suis hominibus plures occiderunt.

Item, die Lune proximo ante festum Nativitatis Sancte Marie, venit Davit David^m Othothil cum xxiiii^n et occulte se abscondit tota nocte in bosco de Calyn. Quod percipientes Dublinenses et dominus Willelmus Comyn exierunt et ipsos viriliter fugaverunt usque ad vi leucas, et de eisdem occiderunt circa xvii, et plures usque ad mortem vulneraverunt.

Item, rumores venerunt Dublin quod dominus Robertus de Brus, rex Scotie, intravit Hibeniam ad confortandum^l Edwardum Brus, fratrem suum, et castrum de Cragfergus in Ultonia obsessum est a predictis Scotis. Monasteria Beati Patricii de Duno et de Saballo |Folio 19r| † et diversa alia tam monachorum quam canonicorum, predicatorum et minorum spoliantur in Ultonia a Scotis.

---

^{a} regegorum [?]; reges L. ^{b} Ihc *on top of next page and also in middle again. End of page 35 looks very rushed.* ^{c} in L. ^{d} Johannes *omitted* L. ^{e} Husea. *insert of letter* o L. ^{f} dicens *omitted* L. ^{g} o *above omission arrow after* dicens. dicens *and* o *omitted* L. ^{h} respondit *supplied* L. ^{i} habes L. ^{j} proprium famulum L. ^{k} ad *omitted* L. ^{l} domino suo Richardo *supplied* L. ^{m} David *repeated* (Davit *first, not deleted*). ^{n} iiii^{xx} L. ^{l} *looks like 3 circles followed by* fortandum. adiuvandum L.

Item, in the week after the feast of St Laurence [Martyr 10 Aug. 1316], four Irish kings in Connacht rose in battle against the English; against whom came lord William de Burgh, lord Richard de Bermingham, lord of Athenry, with his following of the country. And about eleven thousand of the same Irish were killed near to Athenry.[517] This vill was afterwards walled by the arms and spoils of the Irish, because every one of the Englishmen who had double arms from the Irish gave one half to [build] the walls of the town of Athenry.[518] Feidhlim Ó Conchobhair, king of Connacht and Ó Ceallaigh and many other *reguli* were killed here. John Husse, the butcher of Athenry, fought here.[519]

{Note the cruel butcher who was called Husse}

He [Husse] on the same night (at the request of his lord of Athenry) stood among the dead in order to search out Ó Ceallaigh. That Ó Ceallaigh, with his squire, rose up from his hiding place and called to the aforesaid man, namely John Husse, saying, 'Come with me and I will make you a great lord in my land'. And Husse [replied], 'No, I will not go with you, but you will come with me to my lord Richard Bermingham'.[520] Then Ó Ceallaigh said, 'You have only one servant with you, and I have a strong squire, therefore you come with me that you will be enriched.' To which also the servant said to John, 'Agree and cross over to Ó Ceallaigh [so] that we will be safe and enriched because they are stronger than we are'. At that, John Husse first of all killed his own servant, and then Ó Ceallaigh and his squire, and cut off all three heads and carried them to his lord Bermingham.[521] And that Bermingham gave to the aforesaid John Husse many lands and made him a knight as he well deserved.[522]

In the same year, around the feast of St Laurence [Tues. 10 Aug. 1316] Ó hAnluain came to Dundalk in order to seize it, and the men of Dundalk killed many of his men.[523]

Item, on the Monday next before the feast of the nativity of St Mary [Mon. 6 Sept. 1316], David Ó Tuathail, with twenty-four [men] came and they concealed themselves secretly all night in the wood of Cullen.[524] Discovering this, the men of Dublin and lord William Comyn went out and they courageously routed them as far as six leagues.[525] And they killed about seventeen of them and wounded many unto death.[526]

Item, rumours came to Dublin that lord Robert de Bruce, king of Scotland, had entered Ireland to help his brother Edward Bruce, and Carrickfergus castle in Ulster was besieged by the aforesaid Scots.[527] The monasteries of Blessed Patrick at Down, and of Saul and many others, both monks and canons [and] preachers and minors, were plundered by the Scots in Ulster.[528]

Item, Dominus Willelmus de Burgo, relicto filio suo obside in Scotia, liberatur. Ecclesia in*ᵃ* de Brught in Ultonia, quasi plena utriusque sexus hominibus, comburitur a Scotis et Hibernicis Ultonie. Eodem tempore, venerunt nova de Cragfergus quod custodes, pro defectu victualium corea comederunt, et circa viii Scotos, qui ante capti fuerunt, unde dolendum fuit quod nemo talibus succurreret. Et die Veneris sequenti, venerunt nova quod Thomas, filius Comitis Ultonie, moriebatur.

{de dormitone domini Iohannis filii Thome primi comitis Kyldarye}
* Et die dominica sequenti, scilicet, post festum Nativitatis Beate Virginis, moriebatur dominus Johannes filius Thome, apud Laragbryne juxta Maynoth, et sepultus est apud Kyldare inter fratres minores. De quo domino Johanne filio Thome dicitur modicum ante mortem suam factus est comes Kyldarie, cui successit filius ejus dominus Thomas, filius Johannis filius*ᵇ* et heres, vir prudens. Et postea venerunt nova quod castrum de Cragfergus Scotis redebatur, et concessa erant custodibus vita et membra. Et die Exaltacionis Sancte Crucis occisus*ᶜ* Conghor Mᶜ Kele cum quingentis Hibernicis per dominum Willelmum de Burgo et Ricardum Bermyngham in Connacia.

Item, die Lune ante festum Omnium Sanctorum facta fuit magna occisio Scotorum in Ultonia per Johannem Loggan, et*ᵈ* domini Hugonem Bysset, circa centum cum dupplicibus armis, et cc cum solis armis, - summa occisorum ccc preter pedales. Et postea in vigilia Sancti Edmundi, regis, erat tempestas magna venti et pluvie, que prosternebat plures domos et campanile Sancte Trinitatis, Dublin et plura dampna fecit in terra et in mari.*ᵉ*

Item, in vigilia Sancti Nicholai, dominus Alanus Styward |Folio 19v| † iii*ᶠ* qui captus fuit in Ultonia per Johannem Loggan et dominum Johannem Sandale, ductus fuit ad castrum Dublin. Eodem*ᵍ* anno, venerunt nova de Anglia quod*ʰ* rex Anglia et comes Lancastrie fuerunt in discordia, quia unusquisque eorum voluit alium capere. Qua de causa tota terra diu in magna tribulacione fuit.

Item, eodem anno, circa festum Sancti Andree Apostoli, missi fuerunt ad curiam Romanam dominus Hugo le Despencer et dominus Bartolomeus de Baldesmere, episcopus Vigorniensis, et episcopus Heliensis, pro arduis negociis Domini Regis Anglie, pro terra Scotie, qui reversi sunt in Angliam circa festum Purificacionis Beate Marie.

Item, post dictum festum venerunt le Lacies Dublin, et procuraverunt inquisicionem quod Scoti in Hiberniam ^per eos^ non venerunt que inquisicionem eos acquietavit. Unde habuerunt cartam Domini Regis de pace et prestito sacramento iurarunt*ʲ* pacem Domini Regis Anglie tenere et Scotos

---

ᵃ in *deleted by underdotting.*   *ᵇ* filius *omitted* L.   *ᶜ* erat *added* L.   *ᵈ* et *omitted* L.   *ᵉ faint seventeenth century. Marginalia, (possibly ... prosternebat campanile St Trin ...).*   *ᶠ Pen trial?*   *ᵍ* et *added before* eodem L.   *ʰ* dominus L.   *ⁱ* ^ *and* per eos *above the line.*   *ʲ* iuraurunt? L.

Item, lord William de Burgh was freed, leaving his son as hostage in Scotland. The church of Bright in Ulster, almost full of people of each sex, was burnt by the Scots and the Irish of Ulster.[529] At the same time news came concerning Carrickfergus, that the keepers, because of lack of provisions, were eating leather and around eight Scots who had previously been taken prisoner (in respect of which it is to be lamented that no one was able to assist).[530] And on the following Friday [Fri. 10 Sept. 1316] news came that Thomas, son of the earl of Ulster, was dead.

{Concerning the falling asleep [death] of lord John fitz Thomas first earl of Kildare}

And on the Sunday following, namely after the feast of the nativity of the blessed Virgin [12 Sept. 1316], lord John fitz Thomas died at Laraghbryne near Maynooth and was buried at Kildare among the Friars Minor.[531] Concerning this lord John fitz Thomas, it is said that a short time before his death he was created earl of Kildare.[532] He was succeeded by his son, lord Thomas fitz John, son and heir, a wise man. And afterwards news came that Carrickfergus castle was surrendered to the Scots and the custodians were granted life and limb.[533] And on the day of the Exaltation of the Holy Cross [Tues. 14 Sept. 1316] Conghor McKele with five hundred Irishmen was killed by lord William de Burgh and Richard Bermingham, in Connacht.[534]

Item, on the Monday before the feast of All Saints [Mon. 25 Oct. 1316], there was a great slaughter of the Scots in Ulster by John Logan and lord Hugh Bisset (around a hundred with double armour and two hundred with single armour). The number killed in all was three hundred, besides foot [soldiers]. And afterwards on the eve of St Edmund, king [Fri. 19 Nov. 1316], there was a great storm of wind and rain which threw down many houses, and the campanile of Holy Trinity in Dublin, and did great damage on land and sea.[535]

Item on the eve of St Nicholas [prob. Mon. 1c Nov. 1316] lord Alan Stewart, who was captured in Ulster by John Logan and lord John Sandal, was led to Dublin castle.[536] In the same year, news arrived from England that the king of England and the earl of Lancaster were in discord because each of them wished to capture the other. Because of this all the land was in great tribulation for a long time.[537]

Item, in the same year, around the feast of St Andrew apostle [Tues. 30 Nov. 1316], lord Hugh le Despenser and lord Bartholomew de Badlesmere, the bishop of Worcester, and the bishop of Ely, were sent to the Roman Curia on important affairs of the lord king of England, concerning the land of Scotland. They returned to England around the feast of the Purification of Blessed Mary [Wed. 2 Feb. 1317].

Item, after the said feast [Wed. 2 Feb. 1317] the Lacys came to Dublin to undergo an inquisition, to prove that the Scots did not come into Ireland by their help. The inquisition acquitted them.[538] Whereupon they had a charter of the

pro posse destruere. Et post, eodem anno post festum Carniprivii venerunt Scoti occulte usque ad*ᵃ* Slane cum viginti millibus armatis et exercitus Ultonie cum*ᵇ* illis et depredaverunt ante ipsos totam patriam.

{De capcione comitis Ultonie in abbacia beate Marie in Dublin}
Et postea, die Lune ante festum Sancti Mathie, Apostoli, captus erat Comes Ultonie in Abbatia Beate Marie per maiorem civitatis Dublin, scilicet, Robertum Notyngham,*ᶜ* et ductus fuit ad castrum Dublin et ibi diu detentus erat*ᵈ* et camera in qua erat combusta fuit, et vij de hominibus dicti Comitis ibidem occisi. Eadem septimana, in vigilia Sancte Mathie, venit le Brus, cum exercitu suo, versus Dublin, et quam cito audivit de capcione dicti Comitis, iter suum arripuit versus Castrum Cnok, et dictum castrum intravit et cepit dominum baronem ejusdem, scilicet, Dominum*ᵉ* Hugonem Tirell, et uxorem suam, qui pro pecunia deliberati fuerunt. Et eadem |Folio 20r| nocte, per assensum concivium, per Dublinenses, pro timo^{re/f} Scotorum, fuit vicus Sancti Thome combustus et per dictum ignem fuit ecclesia Sancti Johannis, cum capella Beate Marie Magdalene, cremata per infortunium, et omnia suburbana comburuntur*ᵍ* una cum monasterio beate Marie, et ecclesia Sancti Patricii, Dublin, per dictos villanos spoliatur.

Item, ecclesiam Sancti Salvatoris, qui est locus fratrum predicatorum, dictus maior cum communitate destruxit, et lapides eiusdem loci asportavit ad faciendum muros civitatis, quia tunc ampliavit in parte boriali super keyam, quia muri primo transierant iuxta ecclesiam Sancti Audoeni, ubi apparet turris ultra portam, et in vico tabernariorum vini apparet alia porta. Sed postea rex Anglie iussit eisdem maiori et communitati ut facerent conventum ut prius. Et post festum Sancti Mathie intellexit le Brus civitatem esse premunitam, iter suum arripuit versus Saltus Salmonum, et ibi fixerunt tentoria sua, videlicet, Robertus le Brus, rex Scocie, Edwardus le Brus, comes de Morrey, Johannes de Meneteth, dominus Johannes Styward, dominus Philippus*ʰ* Mortbray et ibidem iiij dies moram fecerunt et partem ville combusserunt, et ecclesiam fregerunt et spoliaverunt. Et postea perrexerunt versus le Naas et les Lacyes contra sacramentum eorum ipsos duxerunt et consiliaverunt et dominus Hugo Canon ordinavit Wadinum White fratrem uxoris sue ipsos per patriam conducere et venit usque le Naas et villam depredaverunt et ecclesias fregerunt archas abstraxerunt et fregerunt et sepulturas in cimiterio aperierunt ad querendum thesaurum et multa mala fecerunt per duos dies perhendinantes. Et postea perrexerunt usque Trestildermote in secunda septimana xl et fratres minores destruxerunt libros ac vestimenta*ⁱ* asportaverunt et inde |Folio 20v| † recesserunt usque Baligaveran et de Baligaveran dimissa villa de Kelkenni venerunt usque ad*ʲ* Callan circa festum Sancti Gregorii pape. Eodem tempore

---

ᵃ ad *omitted* L.   *ᵇ* coram L.   *ᶜ slight rubrication of first letter.*   *ᵈ* erat *omitted* L.   *ᵉ slight rubrication of first letter.*   *ᶠ* ∧ *and* re *above the line.*   *ᵍ* Dublin *added* L.   *ʰ* Johannis L.   *ⁱ* et alia arnamenta *added* L.   *ʲ* ad *omitted* L.

lord king of England regarding peace, and they took an oath on the sacraments to hold the peace of the lord king and, as far as possible, to destroy the Scots. And afterwards, in the same year, after the feast of *Carniprivii*,[539] the Scots came secretly as far as Slane with twenty thousand armed men (and the army of Ulster with them)[540] and they plundered the whole country before them.

{Concerning the capture of the earl of Ulster in the abbey of Blessed Mary Dublin}

And afterwards, on the Monday before the feast of Mathias apostle [Mon. 21 Feb. 1317], the earl of Ulster was captured in the abbey of blessed Mary by the mayor of the city of Dublin, namely Robert Nottingham, and led to Dublin castle and he was kept there for a long time.[541] And the chamber in which he was kept was burnt, and seven of the men of the same earl were killed there.[542] In the same week, on the eve of St Matthias [Wed. 23 Feb. 1317], Bruce came with his army towards Dublin and, when he heard about the capture of the said earl, he quickly started his journey towards Castleknock and entered the said castle and captured the lord baron of the same, namely Lord Hugh Tyrell, and his wife, who were ransomed for money.[543] And the same night, by consent of the citizens (for fear of the Scots), St Thomas's Street was burnt by the men of Dublin. And by the said fire the church of St John with the chapel of Blessed Mary Magdalen was burnt by misfortune.[544] And all the suburbs were burned together with the monastery of blessed Mary, and the church of St Patrick was plundered by the said villains.[545]

Item, the church of St Saviour, which is the heart[546] of the Friars Preachers, was destroyed by the said mayor together with the community.[547] The stones of this place were transported in order to build the walls of the city,[548] because it was then enlarged in the north part upon the quay, because the former wall crossed next to the church of St Audeon (where can be seen a tower above the gate, and in Winetavern Street another gate was evident).[549] But later the king of England ordered that the same mayor and community should make the convent as before.[550] And after the feast of St Matthias [after 24 Feb. 1317] Bruce, understanding that the city was strongly fortified, made his journey towards Leixlip.[551] And there they fixed their tents, namely lord Robert Bruce, king of Scotland, Edward Bruce, the earl of Moray,[552] John de Menteith,[553] lord John Stewart, lord Philip Mowbray.[554] And there they delayed for four days and burnt part of the town and they plundered and broke the church. And afterwards they pressed on towards Naas.[555] And, the Lacys, against their oath, led them and gave them counsel.[556] And lord Hugh Canon appointed Wadin White, his wife's brother, to lead them through the land.[557] And they came right up to Naas, and they sacked the vill, and they destroyed the churches. And for the duration of two days broke money chests and broke and opened the tombs of the cemetery in order to seek treasure and did much damage.[558] And afterwards in the second week of Lent [20–26 Feb], they passed on up to Tristledermot [Castledermot]

venerunt littere per dominum Edmundum le Botiler tunc justiciarum Hibernie, et*[a]* dominum Thomam filium Johannis*[b]* comitem Kildarye, dominum Ricardum de Clara, dominum Arnaldum le Power et dominum Mauricum filium Thome ad deliberandum comitem Ultonie per manucapionem et per breve domini regis. De quo tunc nichil factum fuit. Et postea, venerunt Ultonienses cum exercitum circa m.m. et petierunt auxilium domini regis ad destruendum Scotos, ut dixerunt. Qua de causa liberatum fuit eis vexillum domini regis. Cum hoc habuerint magis dampnum fecerunt quod Scoti et carnes per totam xl comedrunt et totam patriam fere vastaverunt per que maledictionem*[c]* hominium perceperunt.

{no*ta* dedacorie[?] vexilli regis Ultoniensibus}

Item, strages magna super Hibernicos, juxta Desertum Dermicii, id est, Trestildermote per Edmundum Pincernam*[d]* tunc justiciarum Hibernie. Tunc le Brus cum Scotis usque Lymericum penetrarunt; congregatis autem exercitibus Anglicorum Hibernie pulcherrimis, apud Ledyn de castro Connyny de nocte latenter reversi sunt. Et circa Dominicam in Ramis Palmarum venerunt nova Dubline, quod Scoti fuerunt apud Kenlis in Ossoria, et magnates Hibernie fuerunt apud Kilkenny, et ibi congregaverunt exercitum ad pergendum versus le Brus. Et die Lune sequenti, preceptum fuit Ultoniensibus per dominum regem, quod se festinarent versus Scotos, quorum ductor et caput ordinatus fuit comes de Kildare scilicet, Thomas filius Johannis, et sic perrexerunt, et tunc fuit le Brus apud le Cashell, et exinde de*[e]* perrexit usque Nathnath, et ibidem moram fecit, et omnes terras domini pincerne*[f]* combussit et destruxit.

Anno domini M. CCCXVII

Die Jovis, in cena domini, congregati fuerunt dominus Edmundus le Botiller, tunc justiciarius Hibernie, dominus Thomas filius Johannis, comes Kyldarie, quia rex dedit sibi iurisdictionem et libertatem |Folio 21r| comitatus Kildarie, Ricardus de Clare, cum exercito Ultonie, dominus Arnaldus Power, baro de Donnoyll, Mauricius de Rupe forti, Thomas filius Mauricii et les Conntones cum sequela sua et omnes*[g]* congregati fuerunt circa Scotos et*[h]* per totam septimanam circa ipsos moram traxerunt et nichil fecerunt quorum exercitus numeratus fuit*[i]* xxx milia hominum bene armatorum. Et postea die Jovis in septimana Pasche applicuit le Mortimer apud Yoghill cum potestate regis qui justicarius fuit et*[j]* die Lune sequente iter suum arripuit versus exercitum et literas misit Edmundo Botiller qui fuit iusticiarius ut dicebatur quod nichil faceret erga Scotos ante suum adventum. Et antequam le Mortumer venit per quosdam le Brus premunitus fuit quod abinde discederet qui nocte sequenti

---

[a] et *omitted* L.   *[b]* tunc *added* L.   *[c]* et *added* L.   *[d]* strages magna super Omorghe, apud Balilethan, per eundum Edmundum Pincernam *added* L.   *[e]* de *omitted* L.   *[f]* integre *added* L.   *[g]* predicti *added* L.   *[h]* et *omitted* L.   *[i]* circa *added* L.   *[j]* festinanter *added* L.

and destroyed the [friary of] the Friars Minor and took away books and vestments.[559] And then they withdrew to Gowran and, from Gowran (leaving [aside] the town of Kilkenny), they came as far as Callan around the feast of St Gregory, pope [2 March 1317].[560] At the same time letters came at the hands of lord Edmund Butler, then justiciar of Ireland, and lord Thomas fitz John, earl of Kildare, lord Richard de Clare, lord Arnold le Poer and lord Maurice fitz Thomas, to deliver the earl of Ulster by mainprise and by the king's writ, about which nothing was done then. And afterwards the men of Ulster came with an army of about two thousand and asked the [feudal] aid of the lord king, in order to destroy the Scots, as they said. In that way the banner of the lord king was made free to them. With this, they made and did greater damage than the Scots, and they were eating meat through the whole of Lent and devastating almost the whole country, from which abuse they felt the curse of men.[561]

{Note disgracing of royal standard by the Ulstermen}
Item, there was a great massacre upon the Irish near Castledermot, that is, Tristledermot, by Edmund *Pincerna* [Butler], then justiciar of Ireland. Then Bruce, with the Scots, made their way as far as Limerick.[562] However, with the most excellent army of the English of Ireland assembled together at Ludden, they [the Scots] left secretly at night from the castle at Connell.[563] And around about Palm Sunday [*c*.27 March 1317] news came to Dublin that the Scots were at Kells in Ossory, and the magnates of Ireland were at Kilkenny, and the army gathered there to proceed against Bruce.[564] And the Monday following [28 March 1317] a command was given by the lord king to the men of Ulster that they should hasten themselves against the Scots. The earl of Kildare, namely Thomas fitz John, was their leader and chief, and they proceeded in this way. And then Bruce was at Cashel and from there he went out right up to Nenagh and there he stayed, and he burnt and destroyed all the lands of the lord *Pincerna* [Butler].[565]

1317
On Maundy Thursday [31 March], lord Edmund Butler, then justiciar of Ireland, lord Thomas fitz John, earl of Kildare (because the king gave the jurisdiction and the liberty of the county of Kildare to him),[566] [and] Richard de Clare, were assembled together with the army of Ulster [and] lord Arnold le Poer, baron of Dunohill, Maurice de Rocheford, Thomas fitz Maurice, and the Cauntetons with their *sequela*, and all assembled together around all the Scots. And for a whole week they tarried around them and did nothing; the army numbered thirty thousand well-armed men. And afterwards, on the Thursday in Easter week [Thurs. 7 April], le Mortimer, with the power of the king because he was the justiciar, landed at Youghal.[567] And the following Monday [Mon. 11 April], he quickly made his journey towards the army, and sent letters to Edmund Butler (who was the justiciar of Ireland, as was said), that he should do nothing about the Scots before his arrival.[568] And before Mortimer arrived, Bruce was

iter suum cepit versus Kyldare et postea in sequenti septimana unusquisque Anglicorum repatriavit et exercitus Ultonie venit le Naas. Et eodem tempore duo nuncii de civitate Dublin transfretaverunt versus regem Anglie ad consulendum et ostendendum de statu Hibernie et deliberacione comitis Ultonie. Et eodem tempore dominus Rogerus Mortimer justiciarum Hibernie et magnates terre Hibernie fuerunt apud Kilkenny ad disponendum pro le Brus qui tunc ibi nichil fecerunt. Et circa mensem post Pascha venit le Brus cum exercito suo circa iiii^{or} leucas prope Trym in quodam bosco et ibidem moram fecit per septimanam et amplius ad perhendinandum homines suos qui fame et labore fere perierunt quam plures; ibidem moriebantur. Et postea die Apostolorum Philippi et Jacobi[a] dictus Brus iter suum versus Ultoniam in cepit et post dictum festum venit dominus Rogerus Mortuum justiciarum Hibernie ad Dublin, cum domino Johanne Wogan et domino Fulcone Filio Warini, cum xxx militibus et eorum sequela et tenuerunt Parliamentum cum omnibus magnatibus terre apud Kylmaynan. Nichil ibi fecerunt nisi ~~deliberacione~~[b] tractando de deliberacione comitis Ultonie. Et, die Dominica ante festum Ascencionis Domini |Folio 21v| enerunt iterum magnates terre ad parliamentum Dublin, et ibi deliberaverunt comitem Ultonie per manucapcionem et hostages[c] et per sacramentum, et dictus comes, prestito sacramento, iuravit, quod nunquam occasione sue captionis, per se vel per suos ullam malestiam[d] dampnum, seu gravamen civibus Dublin de cetero faceret seu procuraret, sed quod ipsum de transsgressoribus per legem impetraret, et inde habuit diem usque festum Nativitatis Beati Johannis Baptiste, ad quem diem non venit.

Item, eodem anno, fuerunt ^blada^[e] et alia victualia valde cara. Cronocus frumenti vendebatur pro xxiiii[f] solidis, avene pro xvi solidis, et vinum pro viii denariis, et tota patria fere devastata per Scotos et Utonienses, et plures patres familias, et qui plures homines sustinuerunt, mendicantes fuerunt, et fame[g] perierunt, et tanta erat pestilencia et fames quod pauperes infamierunt,[h] et plures moriebantur. Eo tempore, nuncii Dublin venerunt de Anglia cum impetracionibus quas ad voluntatem habuerunt, sed ante ipsorum adventum deliberatus erat comes predictus, et ad festum Pentecostes le Mortuum, justiciarius, iter suum arripuit versus Droghda et abinde usque Trym, et literas misit pro les Lacies ut ad ipsum venirent, qui venire contempserunt. Et, postea, dominus Hugo de Croftes, miles, missus fuit ad les Lacies ad tractandum de pace, qui per eosdem ibidem occissus fuit, unde dolendum fuit. Et postea le Mortuum Justiciarius exercitum suum congregavit versus les Lacyes, et bona sua et animalia et thesaurum cepit, et ipsos omnino destruxit, et plures de eorum hominibus occidit, et eos fugavit in partibus Connacie. Et

---

[a] Johanni L. [b] deliberacione *struck through and repeated later* L. [c] [sic]. [d] molestiam L.
[e] ^ *and* blada *inserted in margin* L. [f] xxiii L. [g] plures *added* L. [h] infamuerunt L.

warned by some that he should depart from that place. On the following night he made his way to Kildare and afterwards, in the following week, every one of the Englishmen returned home and the army of Ulster came to Naas. And at the same time two messengers were sent from the city of Dublin; they crossed the sea to the king of England to ask advice and to discuss the affairs of Ireland and in order to consult about the earl of Ulster. And at the same time lord Roger Mortimer, justiciar of Ireland, and the magnates of the land of Ireland were at Kilkenny in order to dispose of Bruce – there they did nothing.[569] And around a month after Easter [*c*.3 May 1317], Bruce advanced with his army around four leagues near Trim to a certain wood and there they delayed a week and more in order to rest his men; very many had almost perished from hunger and travel. They were dying here.[570] And afterwards, on the feast day of the apostles Philip and James. [Sun. 1 May] the said Bruce took his journey to Ulster and, after the said feast day, lord Roger Mortimer, as justiciar of Ireland, came to Dublin with lord John Wogan and lord Fulk fitz Warin with thirty knights and their *sequela*; and they held a parliament at Kilmainham with all the magnates of the land.[571] There nothing was done except to conduct [measures] concerning the release of the earl of Ulster.[572] And on the Sunday before the feast day of the Ascension of the Lord [Sun. 8 May], the magnates of the land went again to the parliament at Dublin and there released the earl of Ulster by mainprise, and hostages, and by oath.[573] And the said earl took an oath on the sacraments that never henceforth would he himself or his men molest, damage, or injure the citizens of Dublin (because of his capture), unless henceforth he could make legal claim, concerning the transgressors. To which end he had a day until the feast of the nativity of John the Baptist [Fri. 24 June] – to which day he did not come.

Item, in the same year corn and other provisions were very expensive. A crannock of wheat was selling for twenty-four shillings, oats for sixteen shillings and wine for eight pence, and the whole land was almost wasted by the Scots and men of Ulster. And many heads of households, who had supported very many men, were beggars and died of hunger. And there was such pestilence and hunger that paupers were starving and very many were dying.[574] At that time messengers came to Dublin from England with the petitions which they had wished to have had, but the aforesaid earl [of Ulster] was released before their arrival. And at the feast of Pentecost [Sunday 22 May] le Mortimer, justiciar, made a journey to Drogheda and thereafter right up to Trim and sent letters to the Lacys that they should come to him.[575] They scorned to come. And, afterward, lord Hugo de Croft, knight, was sent to the Lacys to treat concerning peace – he was killed there by them, which is to be lamented. And afterwards le Mortimer, justiciar, assembled his army against the Lacys and seized their goods and animals and treasure, and he destroyed them entirely. And he killed very many of their men

dicebatur quod dominus Walterus de Lacy perrexit usque Ultoniam ad petendum le Brus.

Item, in villa Sancti Omeri, in Flandria, circa festum Pentecostes, captus fuit dominus Adamarus de Valencia et filius eius, et ducti fuerunt in Almania. Et, eodem anno, die*[a]* proximo post festum Nativitatis Beati |Folio 22r| Johannis Baptiste, congregati fuerunt magnates Hibernie ad parliamentum Dublin, et*[b]* ibidem deliberatus fuit comes Ultonie, qui, prestito sacramento, iuravit ~~quod~~*[c]* et manucaptores invenit ad respondendum mandatis legis et quod fugaret inimicos domini regis de Hibernicis et Scotis.

Item, in die Sanctorum Processi et Martiniani, dominus Johannes de Athy in mari obviavit Thome Don, fortissimo latroni, et eum cepit, et circa xl bene armatos de suis occidit, et caput suum secum tulit Dublin.

Item, die Translacionis Sancti Thome, dominus Nicholaus de Balscot venit de Anglia, et detulit nova, quod duo cardinales venerunt de curia Romana in Angliam ad tractandum de pace, et tulerunt bullam ad excommunicandum omnes perturbatores pacis domini regis Anglie.

Item, die Jovis proximo ante festum Sancte Margarete, dominus Hugo et Walterus de Lacy exclamati fuerunt seductores et felones domini regis, quia vexilium tulerunt contra pacem domini regis Anglie.

Item, die Dominica sequenti, dominus Rogerus Mortuum, Justiciarius,*[d]* iter suum arripuit versus Drogheda, cum omnibus militibus suis. Eodem tempore, Ultonienses ceperunt unam predam iuxta Drogheda, et gentes de Drogheda exierunt et predam reverterunt et ibi occisus est Milo Logan cum fratre.*[e]* Et vi alii magnates de Ultonia capti fuerunt et ducti ad castrum Dublin. Et postea le Mortuum, justiciarius, congregavit exercitum suum versus Ofervill, et scindere fecit passum malum, et destruxit omnia*[f]* habitacula*[g]* eorum*[h]* et postea dictus Offerwill se paci reddidit et dedit obsides.

{Occisio Hugonis Canon iusticarii}

Item, Dominus Rogerus de Mortuo mari, justiciarius iter arripuit versus Clony, et cepit inquisitionem de Domino Johanne Blound, scilicet, White, de Rathregan, que inquisicio dictum Johannem accusavit, unde oportebat ipsum finem facere pro cc marcis, et postea, Dominica post festum Nativitatis Beate Marie predictus Mortimer cum magno exercitu iter suum arripuit versus Hibernicos de Omayll et |Folio 22v| venerunt apud Glynsely, et ibi*[i]* occisi sunt*[j]* tam de Hibernicis quam de Anglicis, sed peior pars cum Hibernicis remansit. Et cito post venit Morgh Obrynne et reddidit se paci domini regis et pro se et suis venit ad castrum Dublin. Et die Apostolorum Symonis et Iude

---

[a] lune added L. *[b]* x intended for 'and' here. *[c]* quod cancelled by underdotting. *[d]* Hibernie supplied L. *[e]* suo supplied L. *[f]* omnes L. *[g]* habitaculos suos added L. *[h]* eorum omitted L. *[i]* L shows a stain in the centre of the 5 last lines on fols 24v and 25r make these lines difficult to read but appears similar to T. The stain 'appears to have existed in the MS in 1607' (CStM, ii, p. 356. n. 3). *[j]* plures L.

and chased them into the parts of Connacht. And it was said that lord Walter de Lacy went right up to Ulster to seek le Bruce.[576]

Item, around the feast of the Pentecost [c.22 May 1317], lord Aymer de Valence and his son were captured in the vill of St Omer in Flanders and were taken into Germany.[577] And, in the same year, on the day next after the feast of the nativity of blessed John Baptist [Sat. 25 June], the magnates of Ireland gathered together to a parliament in Dublin and the earl of Ulster was discussed.[578] He took an oath and found mainpernors to answer the legal writs and he swore to pursue the enemies of the lord king, both Irish and Scots.[579]

Item, on the day of the saints Processus and Martian [Sat. 2 July 1317], lord John de Athy met Thomas Don, the strongest thief, at sea and captured him and he killed around forty of his well-armed men and brought his head to Dublin with him.[580]

Item, on the day of the Translation of St Thomas [Thurs. 7 July 1317] lord Nicholas de Balscote came from England and brought news that two cardinals had come from the Roman Curia to England to treat concerning peace; and they brought a bull to excommunicate all troublemakers of the peace of the lord king of England.[581]

Item, on Thursday next before the feast of St Margaret [Thurs. 14 July 1317], lord Hugh and Walter de Lacy, because they had raised a banner against the peace of the lord king of England, were proclaimed traitors and felons of the lord king.[582]

Item, on the following Sunday [17 July], lord Roger Mortimer, justiciar, with all of his knights, made a journey to Drogheda. At the same time, the men of Ulster took one plunder near Drogheda and the men of Drogheda went out and captured the plunder back.[583] And there Milo Logan with his brother was killed; and six other magnates of Ulster were captured and led to Dublin castle.[584] And afterward Mortimer, the justiciar, gathered his army against Ó Fearghail and caused the evil pass to be cut and he destroyed all of their habitations. And afterwards the said Ó Fearghail returned himself to peace and gave hostages.

{The killing of Hugh Canon, justice}

Item, lord Roger de Mortimer, justiciar, made a journey towards Clonee and took an inquisition concerning lord John Blound (namely White) of Rathregan.[585] This inquisition accused the said John, whereupon he himself was required to make a fine for two hundred marks. And afterwards, on the Sunday after the feast of the nativity of the Blessed Virgin Mary [Sun. 11 September] the aforesaid Mortimer with a great army marched towards the Irish of Imaal and came to Glenealy and there both the Irish and English were killed, but the Irish endured the worst share. And soon after Murchadh Ó Broin came to Dublin castle and, for himself and for his men, returned himself to the peace of the lord king.[586] And on the day of the apostles Simon and Jude [Fri. 28 October], the Archebolds had peace, by mainprise of the earl of Kildare. And at the feast of St Hilary

les Archevoldes habuerunt pacem per manucapciones comitis Kildarie. Et ad festum Sancti Hillarii sequens erat parliamentum apud Lincolnni ad tractandum de pace inter dominum regem Anglie et comItem Lancastrie, et inter Scotos, et Scoti[a] in pace tenuerunt, et causa illius parliamenti dominus archiepiscopus Dublin et comes Ultonie moram in Anglia per preceptum domini regis fecerunt. Et circa festum Epiphanie Domini venerunt nova Dublin quod dominus Hugo Canon, justiciarius domini regis in banco, occissus erat per Andream Bermyngham inter le Naas et Castelmartyn.[b]

Item, ad festum Purificationis Beate Marie venerunt bulle quod Dominus Alexander de Bigenore confirmatus fuit et consecratus Archiepiscopus Dublin,[c] et ille bulle lecte fuerunt in ecclesia Sancte Trinitatis. Et eodem tempore, lecta fuit alia bulla, quod dominus papa ordinavit diem inter regem Anglie et Dominum Robertum de Brus, regem Scotie, per duos annos, ad quem diem dictus Brus acquiescere recusavit et[d] ista facta fuerunt circa festum Sancti Valentini.

Item, Dominica sequenti, venit dominus Rogerus Mortuum Dublin, et fecit dominum[e] Mortuum militem cum iiii^{or} sociis, et eodem die le Mortuum tenuit magnum convivium in castro Dublin.

Item, eodem tempore, facta fuit magna Hibernicorum occisio in Connacia inter duos reges, et occisi erant ex utraque parte circa iiii^{or} mille homines, et postea venit mirabilis vindicta de Ultoniensibus, qui tempore quo Scoti depredaverunt in Hibernia magna dampna fecerunt, et carnes in xl sine necessitate comederunt, idcirco venit super eos tribulatio magna quod unusquisque eorum alium comedit, ita quod de decem millibus eorum non remanserunt nisi circa ccc qui fere pro vindictam evaserunt,[f] | Folio 23r | et hoc patet vindictam Dei.

Item, dicebatur vere quod quidam predictorum malefactorum ita fame destructi erant quod corpora sepultorum a cimiteriis extraxerunt et in capitibus eorum corpora coxerunt et comederunt, et mulieres pueros suos pro fame comederunt.

Anno Domini M. CCCXVIII

Circa[g] vigilias Pasche venerunt nova de Anglia in Hiberniam, quod villa de Berewik capta fuit per Scotos per seductionem, et postea eodem anno applicuit magister Walterus de Islep, thesaurarius domini regis in Hibernia, et detulit literas domino Rogero de Mortuo mari quod domino regi se pararet, qui sic fecit, et posuit dominum Willelmum, archiepiscopum cancellensem, custodem Hibernie, qui simul et semel fuit justiciarius Hibernie, cancellarius, et

---

[a] inter Scotos, et Scoti *underlined (seventeenth century.)*   [b] *underneath is an illegible later marg. note possible referring to Bicknor.*   [c] *marg. note (seventeenth century, very faint)*: alexander arch...   [d] et *omitted* L.   [e] Johannes *supplied* L.   [f] *stain in centre of 5 last lines fols 24v, 25r make these lines difficult to read* L.   [g] circa *omitted*; in vigilia L.

following [Hilarius 13 Jan. 1318/not Hilarion 21 Oct.)],[587] there was a parliament at Lincoln to treat concerning the peace between the lord king of England and the earl of Lancaster, and the Scots; and the Scots held the peace. And by reason of that parliament, [both] the lord archbishop of Dublin and the earl of Ulster stayed in England by the command of the lord king.[588] And around the feast of the Epiphany of the Lord [c.Fri. 6 Jan. 1318], news came to Dublin that lord Hugh Canon, justice of the king's bench, was killed by Andrew Bermingham between Naas and Castlemartin.[589]

Item, at the feast of the Purification of the Blessed Virgin Mary [Thurs. 2 Feb. 1318], the bull came that lord Alexander de Bicknor was confirmed and consecrated archbishop of Dublin and that bull was read in the church of Holy Trinity.[590] And at the same time another bull was read saying that the lord pope ordered a day between the king of England and lord Robert de Bruce, king of Scotland, for two years, to which day the said Bruce refused to concede; and this thing happened around the feast of St Valentine [Tues. 14 Feb. 1318].[591]

Item, on the following Sunday [Sun. 19 Feb. 1318], lord Roger Mortimer came to Dublin and made lord [L: John] Mortimer a knight with four of his friends, and the same day Mortimer held a great feast in the castle of Dublin.[592]

Item, at the same time a great slaughter of the Irish was made in Connacht between two kings, and around four thousand men were killed there on both sides. And afterwards there was an extraordinary punishment of the men of Ulster – who, at the time when the Scots were plundering in Ireland, did great damage and had eaten meat in Lent without necessity – for that reason great tribulation came upon them – that every single one of them ate another – so that of ten thousand of them none remained only around three hundred – who just escaped punishment – and this revealed the vengeance of God.

Item, truly, they were saying, that certain of the aforesaid evildoers were so destroyed with hunger that they extracted the bodies of the buried in the cemeteries and in the heads of their bodies they cooked and ate, and women ate their own children from hunger.[593]

1318

Around the eve of Easter, news arrived from England to Ireland that the town of Berwick was captured treacherously by the Scots.[594] And afterwards in the same year Master Walter de Istlip, treasurer of the lord king in Ireland,[595] landed and brought letters to lord Roger de Mortimer that he should make himself ready [to go] to the lord king, which he thus did.[596] And he placed lord William, archbishop of Cashel, as custodian of Ireland (he, at one and the same time, was justiciar of Ireland, chancellor and archbishop).[597] And afterwards, three weeks after Easter [c.14 May 1318], news came to Dublin that lord Richard de Clare was killed on the feast of the saints Gordianus and Epimachus [Wed. 10 May], and with him four knights namely, lord Henry de Capella, lord Thomas de Naas,

archiepiscopus. Et postea, iii septimana post Pascha, venerunt nova Dublin, quod dominus Ricardus de Clare occisus erat*a* et cum eo iiii*or* milites, scilicet, dominus Henricus de Capella, dominus Thomas de Naas, dominus Jacobus de Caunton et*b* dominus Johannes de Caunton, et Adam de*c* Apilgard, cum aliis lxxx hominibus, per Obrene et M*c*carthy, in festo Sanctorum Gordiani et Ephimachi. Et dicebatur quod dictus dominus minutis peciis pro odio scindebatur. Sed reliquie eius sepulte in Lymerico inter fratres minores.

Item, die Dominica in mense Pasche ductus fuit Johannes Lacy de castro Dublin usque ad*d* Trym ad audiendum et ibi iudicium suum recipiendum, qui adiudicatus fuit ad dietam et in carcere moriebatur.

Item, die Dominica ante Ascensionem Domini, dominus Rogerus de Mortuum transfretavit versus Angliam, et nichil solvit pro victualibus que cepit in civitate Dublin nec alibi, ad valentiam mille ~~marcarum~~*e* librarum.

Item, eodem anno, circa festum Sancti Johannis Baptiste gracia Dei ostendebatur, inter gentes*f* quod frumentum quod*g* ante vendebatur ante pro xvi solidis non valebat nisi in vij solidis, et avene pro v solidis, vini et salis habundantia et piscium, similiter, ita quod circa festum Sancti Jacobi |Folio 23v| novus panis de novo blado habebatur, quod nunquam vel raro ante videbatur in Hibernia; et hoc erat signum indulgencie Dei, et hoc per orationes pauperum et aliorum fidelium.

Item, die Dominica post festum Sancti Michaelis venerunt nova Dublin, quod dominus Alexander de Beykenore,*h* tunc justiciarius domini regis in Hibernia et archiepiscopus Dublin, applicuit apud Yoghill. Die Sancti Dionisii venit Dublin cum processione et magno honore religiosorum et aliorum tam clericorum quam laycorum receptus erat.

{nota de bello inter anglicos Hibernie et Scotos}

Item, die Sabbathi in festo Sancti*i* Kalixti Pape, commotum erat bellum inter Scotos et Anglicos de Hibernia duas leucas a villa de Dondalk, ad quod bellum venit de Scotis dominus Edwardus de Brus qui se regem Hibernie dixit, dominus ~~de Moun,~~ Philippus de Mounbray, dominus Walterus de Sules,*j* dominus Alanus Styward, cum tribus fratribus suis, dominus Walterus de Lacy, dominus Hugo de Lacy, dominus Robertus et Almoricus de Lacy, Johannes Kermerdyne, et Walterus Albus, et circa tria millia aliorum, contra quos venerunt de Anglicis, dominus Johannes de Bermyngham, qui caput fuit exercitus, dominus Richardus Tuyt, dominus Milo de Verdon, dominus Hugo de Tripeton, dominus Herebertus de Sutton, dominus Johannes de Cusak, domini Edmundus et Willelmus de Bermyngham, Walterus Bermyngham, et primas Ardmachanus, qui omnes absolvit. Dominus Walterus de la Pull, et

---

a erat *omitted* L.   *b* et *omitted* L.   *c* de *omitted* L.   *d* ad *omitted* L.   *e* *cancelled and underdotted.*   *f* inter gentes *omitted* L.   *g* ante *added* L.   *h* *marg. note (seventeenth century)*: Alexander archiepiscopus.   *i* sancti *omitted* L.   *j* *faint insertion mark then top of fol 26r*, Dominus Alanus Styward, cum tribus fratribus suis.

lord James de Caunteton, lord John de Caunteton and Adam de Apilgard, [and] with eighty other men, by Ó Briain and Mac Cárthaigh.[598] And they were saying that the said lord [de Clare] was being torn to small pieces by hatred. But his remains were buried in Limerick among the Friars Minor.[599]

Item, on Sunday in the month of Easter [Easter Sunday 23 April 1318], John Lacy was led from Dublin castle and brought to Trim to be heard, and there to receive his judgment, which judgment was to be put to a diet and he died in prison.[600]

Item, on the Sunday before the Ascension of the Lord [28 May], lord Roger de Mortimer crossed to England and he did not pay for the food which he took in the city of Dublin nor elsewhere to the value of a thousand pounds.[601]

Item, in the same year, around the feast of St John Baptist [Nativity of John 24 June rather than 29 Aug], it was seen among people that, by the grace of God, grain which was selling before for sixteen shillings was only selling for seven shillings and oats for five shillings, and similarly an abundance of wine and salt and fish so that around the feast of St James [Tues. 25 July], new bread was being made with new corn, which never or rarely was seen before in Ireland. And this was a sign of the indulgence of God and this by the prayers of the poor and other faithful people.[602]

Item, the Sunday after the feast of St Michael [1 Oct.], news came to Dublin that lord Alexander de Bicknor, then justiciar of the lord king in Ireland and archbishop of Dublin, had landed in Youghal.[603] On the feast day of St Dionysius [9 Oct.], he came to Dublin with a great procession and was received with great honour by the religious and by others, both of the clergy and of the laity.

{Note the battle between the English of Ireland and the Scots}

Item, on Saturday the feast of St Calixtus, pope, [14 Oct.], a battle began between the Scots and the English of Ireland two leagues from the vill of Dundalk.[604] To which battle of the Scots there came lord Edward de Bruce (who called himself king of Ireland), lord Philip de Mowbray, lord Walter de Soules, lord Alan Stewart with his three brothers, lord Walter de Lacy, lord Hugo de Lacy, lord Robert and Armoricus de Lacy, John Kermedyn and Walter White,[605] and around three thousand others.[606] Against those came lord John de Bermingham (who was the head of the army of the English), lord Richard Tuyt,[607] lord Milo de Verdun,[608] lord Hugo de Turpilton,[609] lord Herbert de Sutton,[610] lord John de Cusack,[611] the lords Edmund and William de Bermingham, Walter Bermingham, and the primate of Armagh [Roland Jorse] who absolved them all. Lord Walter de la Pulle[612] and certain [men] of Drogheda, around twenty well-armed and chosen, came to the said battle, with whom came John Maupas.[613] They fought hand to hand, and the English with great number and with great vigour first entered the scaling ladder [first pierced the attack],[614] and the said John Maupas with great honour courageously killed the said lord Edward le Bruce in the same battle.[615] This John was found dead upon the body of the said

quidam de Drogheda venerunt circa xx bene armati et electi, cum quibus venit Johannes Maupas ad dictum bellum. Immiscuerunt, et Anglici cum magno numero*a* et cum magno vigore primam scalam penetraverunt, et dictus Johannes Maupas dictum dominum Edwardum le Brus in eodem bello viriliter, cum magno honore, occidit, qui Johannes supra corpus dicti Edwardi occisus inventus erat, et omnes Scoti fere occisi erant, circa duo millia, unde pauci Scotorum evaserunt, praeter dominum Philippum de Montbray, qui vulneratus erat usque ad mortem, et dominus Hugo de Lacy,*b* et pauci alii, qui secum erant, vix evaserunt. Hoc accidit inter Dondalk |Folio 24r| † et Fighird. Capud vero predicti Edwardi dictus dominus Johannes Bermyngham attulit dicto domino regi Anglie, cui rex ad tunc contulit comitatum de Louth, sibi et heredibus suis masculis, baroniam de Atrio Dei. Et quarterium, mannus et cor predicti Edwardi partata fuerunt Dublin et cetera quarteria divisa ad alia loca.

ANNO DOMINI M. CCCXIX
Dominus Rogerus de Mortuo mari de Anglia rediit et fit Justiciarius Hibernie. Eodem anno, ad festum Omnium Sanctorum, venit bulla de papa ad excommunicandum Robertum de Brus, regem Scotie, ter ad quamlibet missam.

Item, villa de Athisell et magna pars patrie per dominum Johannem filium Thome, germanum domini Mauricii filii Thome, comburitur. Isto anno, predictus Johannes Bermyngham factus est comes Loueth.

Item, pons de*c* lapideus de Kylcolyn construitur per Magistrum Mauritium Jak, canonicum ecclesie cathedralis Kildarie.

ANNO DOMINI M. CCCXX
{No*ta* de universitate Dublin}
Temporibus Johannis Pape XXII et domini Edwardi, filii regis E., qui Edwardus post adventum Sancti Augustini in Angliam vicesimus quintus rex fuerat, necnon sub Alexandro Bikenore, tunc archiepiscopo Dublin, dicte civitatis Dublinensis universitas incepit. Primus magister in eadem universitate fit Frater Willelmus de Hardits, ordinis praedicatorum, qui Willelmus sub dicto archiepiscopo in sacra theologia solempniter incepit. Secundus magister in eadem facultate fit Frater Henricus Cogry, ordinis minorum. Tertius magister fit Willelmus de Rodyard, decanus Dublin ecclesie cathedralis Sancti Patricii, qui in iure canonico solempniter incepit. Iste fit primus cancellarius dicte universitatis. iiij^{us} magister in sacra theologia fit Frater Edmundus de Kermerdyn.

Item, Rogerus de Mortuo mari, justiciarius Hibernie, ad Angliam est reversus, domino Thoma filio Johannis, tunc comite Kyldarie in loco suo dimisso.

---

a cum magno numero et *omitted* L.   *b* Dominus Walterus de Lacy *added* L.   *c* de *cancelled by underdotting.*

Edward. And almost all the Scots were killed, around two thousand. Few of the Scots escaped from here, except lord Philip de Mowbray who was fatally wounded; and lord Hugh de Lacy, and a few others who were with them, barely escaped.[616] This happened between Dundalk and Faughart.[617] The said lord John Bermingham brought the head of the said Edward to the said lord king of England.[618] At the same time this king bestowed the earldom of Louth and the barony of Ardee on him and his male heirs.[619] And one quarter [of the body] with the hands and the heart of the aforesaid Edward were carried to Dublin and the other quarters divided [and sent] to other places.[620]

1319[621]

Lord Roger de Mortimer returned by sea from England and was justiciar of Ireland.[622] In the same year on the feast of All Saints [Thurs. 1 Nov.], a bull came from the pope to excommunicate Robert de Bruce, king of Scotland, [read] three times at each Mass.[623]

Item, the vill of Athassel and the greater part of the countryside was burnt by lord John fitz Thomas, full brother of lord Maurice fitz Thomas.[624] In this year the aforesaid John Bermingham was made earl of Louth.[625]

Item, the stone bridge of Kilcullen was constructed by Master Maurice Jak, canon of the cathedral church of Kildare.[626]

1320

{Note the university of Dublin}

In the time of Pope John XXII and of the lord Edward, son of King E[dward] (this Edward was the 25th king after the coming of St Augustine to England), and also under Alexander Bicknor, then the said archbishop of Dublin, the Dublin citizens began the university.[627] The first master in that university was Friar William de Hardits of the Order of Preachers; this William solemnly commenced in sacred theology under the said archbishop. The second master in the same faculty was Friar Henry Cogry of the Order of Minors. The third master was William de Rodyard, dean of the Dublin cathedral church of St Patrick, who commenced solemnly in canon law; he was the first chancellor of the said university. The fourth master, in sacred theology, was Friar Edmund de Kermerdyn.[628]

Item, Roger de Mortimer, justiciar of Ireland, returned to England, leaving lord Thomas fitz John, then earl of Kildare, in his place.[629]

Item, Dominus Edmundus de Pincerna Angliam intravit, et inde ad Sanctum ~~Petri~~[a] Jacobum accessit.

Item, pons ville de Leghelyn construitur per Magistram Mauricium Jak, canonicum ecclesie cathedralis Kyldarie.

{•} Anno domini m. cccxxi

Maxima strages Oconghors apud Balybegan facta est, nono die Maii, per Laginienses et Midenses.

Item, obiit Dominus Edmundus Botiller apud London, et sepilitur apud Balygaveran, in Hibernia.

Item, Johannes Bermyngham, comes Loueth, fit |Folio 24v| † justiciarius in Hibernia.

Item, obiit Johannes Wogan.

Anno domini m. cccxxii

Andreas Bermyngham et Nicholaus de la Lond, miles, et multi alii interficiuntur per Onolane, die Sancti Michaelis.

Anno domini m.cccxxiii

Treuga capitur inter regem Anglie et dominum Robertum Brus, regem Scocie, xiiii annis.

Item, Dominus Johannes Doroy venit capitalis justiciarius Hibernie.[b]

Item, obiit Johannes, primogenitus domini Thome filii Johannis, comitis Kyldarie, nonum etatis sue agens annum.

Anno domini m. cccxxv[c]

Obiit Nicholaus de Genebile, filius et heres domini Symonis de Genebile, et sepultus apud praedicatores de Trym.

Item, magnus ventus fuit in nocte Epiphanie.[d]

Item, communis morticina[e] bouum et vaccarus in Hibernia.

Anno domini m.ccc^{xx}v[f]

Ricardus Lederede, episcopus Ossoriensis, citavit dominam Aliciam Ketyll de heretica pravitate, et ipsam coram se comparere fecit, et de sortilegiis examinata per inquisitionem invenit, quod sortilegia commiserat; inter que unum fuit maleficium quod quidam demon incubus nomine Robyn Artyson concubuit cum ea, et ipsa offerebat demoni novem gallos rubeos, apud quendam pontem lapideum, in quodam quadrivio.

Item, ipsam mundare vicos Kilkennie scopis inter completorum et ignitegium, et scopando sordes usque ad domum Willelmi Utlawe, filii sui,

---

[a] *cancelled and underdotted.* [b] *marg. note (hand B): hand B (foot of page).* Johannes Darcy Justiciarius L. [c] *error for 1324 in* T; Anno domini M CCC XXIIIJ [1324], L. [d] domini *added* L. [e] morina L. [f] *Two faint* xx *inserted above line.*

Item, lord Edmund de *Pincerna* entered England and from there approached towards St James [de Compostela].⁶³⁰

Item, the bridge of the vill of Leighlin was built by magister Maurice Jak, canon of the cathedral church of Kildare.⁶³¹

1321

A great massacre of the Uí Chonchobhair by the men of Leinster and Meath occurred at Balibegan on the ninth day of May [Sat. 9 May 1321].⁶³²

Item, lord Edmund Butler died in London and was buried at Gowran in Ireland.⁶³³

Item, John Bermingham, earl of Louth, was appointed justiciar of Ireland.⁶³⁴

Item, John Wogan died.

1322⁶³⁵

On the feast day of St Michael [Wed. 29 Sept. 1322], Andrew Bermingham and Nicholas de la Launde, knight, and many others, were killed by Ó Nualláin.⁶³⁶

1323

A truce for fourteen years, was taken between the king of England and lord Robert Bruce, king of the Scots.⁶³⁷

Item, lord John Darcy arrived as chief justiciar of Ireland.⁶³⁸

Item, John, the first-born son of lord Thomas fitz John, earl of Kildare, died aged nine years.⁶³⁹

1325

Nicholas de Geneville, son and heir of lord Simon de Geneville, died and was buried with the Preachers at Trim.⁶⁴⁰

Item, there was a great wind on the night of the Epiphany.⁶⁴¹

Item, a common murrain of oxen and cows in Ireland.⁶⁴²

1325⁶⁴³

Richard Ledrede, bishop of Ossory, issued a summons to lady Alice de Kyteler for heretical depravity, and he made her appear in person before him in public.⁶⁴⁴ When she had been examined about witchcraft he found that she had perpetrated acts of witchcraft among which one evil act was that a certain demon by the name of Robyn Artysson lay with her; she was also in the habit of sacrificing to the demon nine red roosters near a certain stone bridge at a certain crossroads.

Item, she would clean out the neighbourhood of Kilkenny between compline and the curfew-bell and, sweeping the filth all the way up to the house of William Outlawe her son and swearing an oath, she said that all the prosperity of Kilkenny would come to this house. The accomplices of the aforesaid Alice and those

coniurando dixit, tota felicitas Kilkennie veniat ad domum hanc. Complices vero dicte Alicie et consentientes huic miserie fuerunt Petronilla de Midia et Basilia, filia ejusdem Petronille. Prefata vero Alicia super predictis per inquisitiorem fedata, Episcopus predictus primo eam per penam peccuniariam punivit, et fecit eam penitus sortilegium abiurare. Sed cum postea super eodem crimine fuisset convicta, ipsa cum prefata[a] Petronilla Kilkennie fuit combusta, sed cum morti esset proxima, dixit quod dictus Willelmus tantum meruit mortem sicut et ipsa asserendo quod ipse per unum annum et diem utebatur zona dyaboli super nudum corpus suum. Unde prefatus episcopus capi fecit predictum Willelmum et carceri mancipari per viii septimanas vel novem in castro Kilkennie et decreto episcopi habuit duos |Folio 25r| † homines ad ministrandum, quibus preceptum fuit ne loquerentur ei, nisi semel in die, et ne[b] comederent nec biberent cum ^eo^[c] tandem dictus Willelmus per iuramentum domini Arnaldi Poer, senescalli comitatus Kilkennie, fuit a carcere liberatus, et prefatus Willelmus predicto Arnaldo magnam summam pecunie,[d] ut predictum episcopum incarceraret. Predictus dominus Arnaldus fecit incarcerari prefatum episcopum circa tres menses. Inter res dicte Alicie inventa fuit quedam hostia in qua nomen diaboli erat scriptum, inventa fuit etiam quedam biix[e] pixis in qua fuit unguentum in[f] quo perungi consuevit quedam trabes vocata Cowltre, qua peruncta posset predicta Alicia cum suis sequacibus sub[g] ipsam trabem ferrei quocunque vellent per mundum sine aliqua lesione seu impedimento. Et quia predicta fuerunt ita notoria, predicta Alicia fuit iterum citata quod compareret Dublin coram domino decano ecclesie Sancti Patricii,[h] ad maiorem favorem habendum. Que ibidem comparuit et petiit diem ad respondendum in crastino, ut[i] cum dies in crastino sibi data fuisset ad respondendum sub sufficienti manucapcione ut putabatur, ipsa ulterius[j] non comparuit, sed de consilio filii sui et aliorum ignotorum absconsa fuit in villa quousque habuit ventum versus Angliam, et sic transivit, et sic nescitur quo devenit. Et quia inventum fuit per inquisitionem et recognitionem dicte Petronille, incendio dampnate, quod Willelmus Utlawe concensiens sortilegio matris, episcopus predictus fecit eum capi per breve regis, et carceri mancipari, qui tandem ad supplicationem magnatum ^de^liberatus[k] fuit, conditione tamen quod cooperire faceret ecclesias Beate Marie Kilkennie plumbo, et alias elymosinas plures faceret infra certum tempus, quas elymosinas si[l] infra dictum terminum non compleret, quod esset in eodem statu quo fuit quando captus fuit per breve regium.

---

[a] Basilia fugit, sed nunquam postea fuit inventa. Dicta vero *added in* L.   [b] ne *omitted*.   [c] *Insertion mark and* eo *above* L.   [d] dedit *added* L.   [e] [sic]; biix *omitted* L.   [f] in *omitted* L.   [g] super L.   [h] Dublin *added* L.   [i] et L.   [j] ulterio L.   [l] si *omitted* L.

agreeing to this wretchedness were Petronilla de Midia and Basilia, the daughter of the same Petronilla. When the aforementioned Alice had been disgraced by the inquiry concerning the abovementioned matters, the aforesaid bishop first punished her with a monetary fine and made her thoroughly abjure her witchcraft. But when she had later been convicted again of the same crime she fled along with the aforesaid Basilia; she was however never found again. The aforesaid Petronilla was burnt at Kilkenny but when she was near death she said that the aforesaid William deserved death as much as she did, claiming that he had used the devil's belt on his naked body for a year and a day. The aforesaid bishop caused the aforesaid William to be arrested and confined in prison for eight or nine weeks in Kilkenny castle.[645] By decree of the bishop William had two men to serve him, these had been commanded not to speak to him more than once a day. Nor were they to eat or drink with him. At length the aforesaid William was freed from prison on the guarantee of Arnold le Poer seneschal of the county of Kilkenny and the aforesaid William gave a great sum of money to the aforesaid Arnold so that he would imprison the aforesaid bishop. The aforesaid lord Arnold imprisoned the bishop for three months. Among the belongings of the aforesaid Alice there was found a certain piece of Eucharistic bread on which the name of the devil was written. Also a certain pyx was found containing an ointment with which a certain beam of wood called a *cowltre* was accustomed to be anointed. When it had been anointed the aforesaid Alice and her followers were able to be carried wherever in the world they wished to go without let or hindrance.[646] And because these aforesaid things were so well known the aforesaid Alice was again summoned to appear publicly in Dublin before the lord dean of St Patrick's church, Dublin in order to have greater support. She appeared in that very place and requested that on the morrow a date should be set for her response and when on the morrow a day was set for her response on what was felt to be adequate bail, she did not in fact appear, either then or at any later time, but on the advice of her son and of other persons unknown she fled to a town where she obtained a favourable wind to England and so crossed over. It is not known where she landed. Since it was discovered by inquiry and confession from the said Petronilla following her condemnation to the flames, that William Outlawe had been a party to his mother's witchcraft, the bishop had him arrested by royal writ and confined in prison. He was at length freed in consequence of the intercession of magnates, but on the condition that he have the church of St Mary at Kilkenny covered with lead and that he should perform many other acts of charity within a certain time. If he did not perform these acts of charity within a stipulated time he was to be put back in the same place where he had been held when he was arrested by royal writ.

Anno Domini M. CCCXXVI

Tentum*a* parliamentum apud Kilkenniam, ad festum Pentecostes, ad quod parlyamentum venit dominus Ricardus de Burgo, tunc comes Ultonie, licet aliquantulum infirmus. Venerunt omnes magnates Hibernie, ibique dictus comes fecit magnum ac famosum convivium magnatibus et populo. Postea dominus comes, accipiens licentiam suam a magnatibus ivit apud Athisel, ubi diem suum clausit extremum. Modicum ante festum Sancti Johannis Baptiste ibidem sepelitur. Dominus Willelmus*b* fuit*c* heres suus.*d*

|Folio 25v| ## Anno Domini M. CCCXXVII

Orta fuit contentio inter dominum Mauricium filium Thome et dominum Arnaldum le Pover, et dominus Mauricius filius Thome*e* habuit in comitiva dominum le Botiller et dominum Willelmum Bermyngham; et dominus Arnaldus habuit in comitiva sua le*f* Burkeyns quorum plures dictus dominus Mauricius filius Thome interfecit et quosdam in Connaciam fugavit. Eodem anno, post festum Sancti Michaelis, quia dominus Arnaldus venit ad auxiliandum les Burkeyns, et propter enormia verba que dictus*g* Arnaldus dixerat, vocando eum Rymoure.*h*

Item*i* dictus ~~Arnald~~*j* Mauricius collegit exercitum et cum le Botiller et dicto Willelmo Bermyngham cum magno exercitu cremavit terras dicti*k* Arnaldi in Offath.

Item, dictus Willelmus Bermyngham terras et maneria domini Arnaldi le Pover in Momonia et Kenlys in Ossoria combussit, ita quod oportuit dictum Arnaldum cum barone de Donnoyll fugere Waterford, et ibi fuerunt per unum mensem, quousque comes Kildarie, tunc justiciarius Hibernie, et alii de consilio domini regis diem ceperunt inter eos, quem diem dominus Arnaldus non tenuit, sed venit apud Dublin et transfretavit in Angliam, circa festum Purificationis. Et postquam dominus Arnaldus transfretavit dictus dominus Mauricius et le Botiller et dominus Willelmus Bermyngham venerunt cum magno exercitu,*l* depredaverunt et combusserunt terras dicti Arnaldi, et propter magnum exercitum quem duxerant et plura mala que fecerunt, ministri regis de eius consilio timuerunt quod obsiderent civitates, unde civitates*m* plures providentias et vigilias medio tempore. Et quando*n* dictus dominus Mauricius, le Botiller et Willelmus audierunt quod civitates fecerunt providentiam, mandaverunt consilio domini regis quod venirent ad Kilkeniam, et quod ibi purgarent se quod nullum malum cogitaverunt facere super terras*o* regis, sed vindicare se de inimicis suis. Ad quod parliamentum comes Kildarie, tunc justiciarius Hibernie, prior de Kilmanian scilicet, Rogerus Outlawe, cancellarius Hibernie, Nicholaus Fastoll, justiciarius in Banco, et alii de

---

a fuit *added* L. *b* de Burgo *supplied* L. *c* fit L. *d* *On the space below the last line*: fuit heres suus. *e* filius Thome *omitted* L. *f* les L. *g* dominus L. *h* *marg. note (hand B)*, Mauricius filius Thome dictus Le Rimour L. *i* iterum L. *j* *cancelled*. *k* domini *added* L. *l* venerunt *added* L. *m* fecerunt fec*er*unt *added* L. *n* quando L. *o* domini *added* L.

1326[647]

A parliament was held at Kilkenny at the feast of Pentecost [Sun. 11 May].[648] Lord Richard de Burgh, then earl of Ulster, came to this parliament, although he was somewhat infirm.[649] All the magnates of Ireland came and there the said earl held a great and celebrated feast for the magnates and people. Afterwards the lord earl, accepting his leave to depart from the magnates, went to Athassel where he ended his days. He was buried there a short time before the feast of St John Baptist [prob Nativity, so 24 June not 29 Aug.].[650] Lord William was his heir.[651]

1327[652]

A struggle arose between lord Maurice fitz Thomas and lord Arnold le Poer. And, on his side, lord Maurice had lord Butler and lord William Bermingham; and, on his side, lord Arnold had the Burghs. The said lord Maurice fitz Thomas killed many of those and he chased others to Connacht.[653] In the same year, after the feast of St Michael [Tue 29 Sept. 1327], because lord Arnold went to the aid of the Burghs, and because of outrageous words which the said Arnold said (calling him a *rymoure*), once again the said Maurice collected an army and, with Butler and the said William Bermingham with a great army, burnt the lands of the said lord Arnold in Ossory.[654]

Item, the said William Bermingham burnt the lands and manor of lord Arnold le Poer in Munster, and Kells in Ossory, so that he forced the said Arnold, with the baron of Dunohill, to flee to Waterford and they were there for one month – until the earl of Kildare, then justiciar of Ireland, and others of the council of the lord king, arranged a day between them.[655] Lord Arnold did not hold this day but, around the feast of the Purification [2 Feb. 1328], he came to Dublin and crossed to England. And after lord Arnold had crossed, the said lord Maurice and Butler and lord William de Bermingham came with a great army and sacked and burnt the lands of the said Arnold.[656] And because of the great army which they led, and many evils which they committed, the ministers of the king and his council feared that they would besiege cities. Whereupon in the midst of that time, the cities made many preparations and vigils. And when the said lord Maurice, Butler, and William [de Bermingham] heard that the cities made preparation, they asked the council of the lord king if they might come to Kilkenny and that there they would clear themselves – that they had not intended any evil upon the lands of the king – but to vindicate themselves concerning their enemies.[657] To this parliament came the earl of Kildare, then justiciar of Ireland, the prior of Kilmainham, namely, Roger Outlawe, chancellor of Ireland,[658] Nicholas Fastolf, justice of the common bench[659] and others of the council of the lord king, and the aforesaid [Maurice] sought a charter of peace of the lord king.[660] However, they of the council of the lord king replied warily [and] they

consilio domini regis, et predicti petierunt cartam |Folio 26r| † de pace domini regis; sed illi de consilio domini regis caute respondentes, ceperunt diem usque mensem post Pascha, ut possint cum sociis de consilio super hoc tractare.

    Eodem anno, ante xl, Hibernici de Lagenia colligerunt se, simul, et fecerunt quemdam regem, videlicet, Donaldum filium Arte M^{c}murgh. Qui, cum rex factus fuerat, ordinavit ponere vexillum suum ad duo milliaria Dublin, et postea transire per omnes terras Hibernie. Cujus superbiam ac malitiam videns Deus permisit eum cadere in manibus domini Henrici Trahran, qui duxit eum ad Saltus Salmonum, et habuit pro eo centum libras de ransona, et duxit eum ad Dublin, et posuit eum in castro, ut ibi expectaret quousque consilium domini regis possit providere quid sit faciendum de eo. Et post ejus capcionem plura infortunia contigerunt Hibernicis de Lagenia, videlicet, quod dominus Johannes de Wellesley cepit David Otothil; et plures interfecti sunt de Hibernicis.

    Eodem^a anno Adam Duff, filius Walteri Duff de Lagenia de cognatione Othothiles convictus fuit quod contra fidem Catholicam negavit incarnationem Jhesu Christi, et dixit quod non poterant esse tres persone et unus^b, et asseruit beatissimam Mariam, matrem domini, esse meretricem, et negavit resurrectionem mortuorum et asseruit sacram scripturam fabulas esse et nichil aliud; et sacrosancte Apostolice Sedis falcitatem. Propter que^c et eorum quodlibet, idem Adam Duff hereticus et blasfemus fuit pronuntiatus, unde idem Adam per decretum ecclesie, die Lune post octavas Pasche, anno Domini, m ccc xxviii, combustus fuit apud le Hoggis, juxta Dublin.

Anno Domini m. cccxxviii

Dei Martis in ebdomada Pasche, dominus Thomas filius Johannis, comes de Kildare et justiciarius Hibernie, obiit. Cui successit in officio justiciarie Frater Rogerus Outlawe, prior de Kilmaynan. Eodem anno, David Otothil, fortis latro, inimicus Regis, succensor ecclesiarum, et distructor populi, ductus fuit de Castro Dublin ad tholoneum civitatis, coram Nicholao Fastok et Elia Assheborne, justiciariis in Banco, qui justiciarii dederunt ei judicium quod primo tractaretur ad cau * † |Folio 26v| caudas^d equorum per medium civitatis usque ad furcas, et postea suspenderetur in patibulo, quod et factum est.

    Item, eodem anno, dominus Mauricius filius Thome collegit magnum exercitum ad distruendum les Burkeyns et le^e Poers. Eodem^f Willelmus de Burgo, comes Ultonie, factus est miles London, in die Pentecostes, et rex dedit sibi dominium suum.

    Item, eodem anno, Jacobus Botiller disponsavit in Anglia filiam comitis Herfordie et factus est comes Ormonie,^{g} qui prius vocabatur Tiperarie. Eodem

---

^{a} *new line.* ^{b} deus *added.* ^{c} que *inserted above line.* ^{d} *full word completed on new page.* ^{e} les L. ^{f} anno, dominus *added* L. ^{g} *marg. note (different hand)*: prima [comes?] Ormonie.

chose a day – up to the month after Easter – that they might be able, with the members of the council, to deal with this.

Before Lent in the same year [probably 1328 Ash Wed. 17 Feb; a leap year], the Irish of Leinster gathered themselves together at the same time and a made a certain person king, namely Domhnall son of Art Mac Murchadha, who, when he was made king, ordered his banner to be placed two miles from Dublin, and afterwards to cross through all the lands of Ireland.[661] God, seeing his pride and malice, allowed him to fall into the hands of Henry Treharne who led him to Salmon Leap [Leixlip] and had a hundred pounds of ransom for him. And he led him to Dublin and placed him in the castle. There he waited until the lord king's council would be able to see what they must do with him.[662] And after his capture much misfortune fell upon the Irish of Leinster, namely that lord John de Wellesley captured David Ó Tuathail and very many of the Irish were killed.[663]

In the same year Adam Dubh, son of Walter Dubh from Leinster, of the *cognomine* of Uí Thuathail, was convicted that, against catholic faith, he denied the incarnation of Jesus Christ, and he said that it was not possible to have three persons and one [God] and he asserted that the most Blessed Mary, mother of the Lord, was a harlot and he denied the resurrection of the dead and asserted that sacred scriptures were fables and no more than that; and that the holy Apostolic See was false. Because of this and other things, Adam Duff was pronounced a heretic and blasphemer. For this reason, the same Adam, by decree of the church, was burned at Hoggen Green in Dublin on the Monday after the octave of Easter in the year of the lord 1328 [Mon. 11 April 1328].[664]

1328

On Tuesday in Easter week [Tues. 5 April 1328] lord Thomas fitz John, earl of Kildare and justiciar of Ireland, died.[665] He was succeeded in the office of justiciar, by Friar Roger Outlawe, prior of Kilmainham.[666] In the same year David Ó Tuathail, a powerful thief, enemy of the king, a burner of churches and destroyer of people, was taken from Dublin castle to the Tholsel of the city in the presence of Nicholas Fastolf and Elias Ashbourne, justices of the common bench.[667] These justices gave to him the judgment that first he should be dragged at the tails of horses through the middle of the city right up to the fork shaped gallows, and afterwards he should be hanged on the gallows, and that was done.[668]

Item, in the same year, lord Maurice fitz Thomas collected a great army to destroy the de Burghs and the le Poers.[669] In the same [year], on Whit Sunday, William de Burgh, earl of Ulster, was made a knight in London and the king gave to him his lordship.[670]

Item, in the same year, in England, James Butler married the daughter of the earl of Hereford and was made earl of Ormond (previously called Tipperary).[671] In the same year, a parliament was held at Northampton where the greater part of the magnates of England had gathered and peace was reestablished between

anno, tentum est parliamentum apud Northampton,[a] ubi magna pars magnatum Anglie congregata fuit, et pax reformata est inter Scotiam et Angliam et Hiberniam per maritagia inter eos, et ordinata fuit quod comes Ultonie cum pluribus magnatibus Anglie irent apud Berewicum super Twedam ad sponsalia. Eodem anno, post predicta sponsalia facta apud Berwek, dominus[b] le Brus, rex Scotie, et dominus Willelmus de Burgo, comes Ultonie, comes de Meneteth, et plures magnates Scotie applicuerunt apud Cragfergus pacifice, et miserunt Justiciario Hibernie et consilio quod venirent ad Viride Castrum, ad tractandum de pace Scotie et Hibernie, et quia dicti justiciarius et consilium non venerunt sicut voluit, accepit licentiam a comite Ultonie et rediit in patriam suam post[c] Assumptionis Beate Marie. Et comes Ultonie venit Dublin ad parliamentum et ibidem morabatur per vi dies, et tenuit magnum convivium et postmodum ivit in Connaciam.

Eodem anno,[d] circa festum Sancte Katerine, virginis,[e] Ossoriensis mandavit consilio domini regis quod dominus Arnaldus Pover coram eo convictus fuit super diversis arti^culis^ heretice pravitatis. Unde ad sectam dicti episcopi, dictus dominus Arnaldus per breve regium captus fuit, et positus fuit in Castro Dublin, et dies datus fuit dicto episcopo quod veniret Dublin ad prosequendam causam predictam versus predictum dominum Arnaldum, qui excusavit se tunc quod non potuit venire quia inimici sui fuerunt insidiantes ei in via. Unde consilium regis nescivit ponere finem isto negotio, et sic dominus Arnaldus mancipatus fuit custodie Castri Dublin usque ad sequens parliamentum quod |Folio 27r| fuit in medio xl, ubi omnes magnates Hibernie fuerunt.

Item, eodem anno, frater Rogerus Utlawe, domus ^hospitalis^ Johannis[g] Baptiste Jerusalem in Hibernia, prior, justiciarius et cancellarius Hibernie, diffamatus fuit per dictum episcopum, quod fuit fautor heresis et consiliarius et adiutor dicti domini Arnaldi in heretica pravitate. Et quia persona ita indigne fuit diffamata, dictus prior ivit ad consilium domini regis et petiit quod posset purgare se, unde illi de consilio domini regis acceperunt consilium et concesserunt ei quod posset habere purgationem suam. Et fecerunt clamare per tres dies, quod si esset aliquis qui vellet prosequi versus predictum Fratrem Rogerum quod prosequeretur, sed nullus fuit inventus. Unde ad procurationem domini Fratris Rogeri exiit breve regium ad summoniendum maiores Hibernie videlicet, episcopos, abbates, priores, et iiii^or^ maiores iiii^or^ civitatum, videlicet, Dublin, Cork, Lymric et Waterford, et Droghda, ac etiam vicecomites et senescallos, et milites comitatuum, cum melioribus liberis hominibus comitatuum, ad veniendum Dublin; et fuerunt electi sex examinatores in dicta causa, videlicet, Magister Willelmus Rodyard, decanus ecclesie cathedralis Sancti Patricii, Dublin, abbas Sancti Thome,

---

[a] *marg. box (hand B), nö* L.   [b] Robertus *added* L.   [c] festum *added* L.   [d] a *for* Anno, *inserted above line* L.   [e] episcopus *added* L.   [f] hospitalis *placed above the top line of the folio.*   [g] sancti Johannis L.

Scotland and England and Ireland by marriages between them.[672] And it was arranged that the earl of Ulster, with very many magnates of England, should go to Berwick-upon-Tweed to the espousals.[673] In the same year, after the aforesaid marriage was made at Berwick, lord le Bruce, king of the Scots and lord William de Burgh, earl of Ulster, the earl of Menteith and many magnates of Scotland landed peacefully at Carrickfergus and sent word to the justiciar of Ireland and the council that they should come to Greencastle to treat concerning the peace of Scotland and Ireland. And because the said justiciar and council did not come just as he [Bruce] wished, he took leave from the earl of Ulster and, after the assumption of the Blessed Virgin Mary [Mon. 15 Aug. 1328], returned into his country.[674] And the earl of Ulster came to Dublin to the parliament and there he delayed for six days and held a great feast and afterwards went to Connacht.[675]

In the same year, around the feast of St Catherine, virgin [Fri. 25 Nov.], [Ledrede, bishop of] Ossory reported to the council of the lord king that lord Arnold Poer had been convicted before himself upon diverse charges of heretical depravity.[676] Whereupon, on the suit of the said bishop, the said lord Arnold was taken by royal writ and was placed in Dublin castle; and a day was given for the said bishop that he should come to Dublin to pursue the aforesaid case against the aforesaid lord Arnold. The bishop then excused himself [on the grounds] that he was not able to come because his enemies would have ambushed him on the way. Whereupon the king's council did not know [how] to place an end to this business. And thus, lord Arnold was detained in custody at Dublin castle right up to the following parliament, which was held in the middle of Lent, where all the magnates of Ireland were present.[677]

Item, in the same year Friar Roger Outlawe, of the house of the Hospital of John of Jerusalem in Ireland, prior, justiciar and chancellor of Ireland, was defamed by the said bishop [saying] that he was a supporter of heresies and a counsellor and advisor of the said lord Arnold in heretical depravity. And because his character was so shamefully defamed, the said prior went to the council of the lord king and asked that he should be able to purge himself. Whereupon those of the council of the lord king took advice and conceded to him that he should be able to purge himself.[678] And they made a proclamation for three days – that if it should be [found that] anyone who wished to pursue against the aforesaid Friar Roger – that they should pursue. But no one was found. Whereupon, at the instigation of the lord Friar Roger, a royal writ was issued to summon the leaders of Ireland, namely the bishops, abbots, priors, and the four mayors of the four cities, namely Dublin, Cork, Limerick and Waterford and of Drogheda, and furthermore the sheriffs and seneschals and knights of the counties, with the best free men of the counties to come to Dublin.[679] And six examiners were elected in the said case, namely Master William Rodyard, dean of the cathedral church of St Patrick, Dublin,[680] the abbot of St Thomas, the abbot of Blessed Mary, the

abbas Beate Marie, prior ecclesie Sancte Trinitatis, Dublin, Magister Elias Laules et Magister Pe[a] Petrus Walleby.[b] Qui examinatores fecerunt venire eos qui fuerunt citati, et examinaverunt quemlibet per se. Quibus iuratis, omnes dixerunt eum esse probum, et[c] fidelem et zelatorem fidei et paratum mori pro fide, et pro magna purgationis sue solempnitate dictus Frater Rogerus tenuit magnum convivium omnibus qui ~~venerunt~~ voluerunt venire.

Item, eodem anno, in xl obiit dictus dominus Arnaldus le Pover in castro Dublin et diu iacuit cum Predictatoribus sine sepultura.

Anno domini m. cccxxix

Post festum Annunciacionis Beate Marie Virginis, venerunt magnates Hibernie ad parliamentum Dublin, videlicet, comes Ultonie, dominus Mauricius filius Thome; comes Loueth, Willelmus Bremynhgam; et ceteri domini, et ibi fuit pax refor[-] |Folio 27v| † [-]mata inter dominum comitem Ultonie et dominium Mauricium filium Thome, et dicti magnates cum consilio regis ibidem statuerunt summam pacem domini regis teneri, ita quod quilibet magnatum castigaret parentelam suam et homines suos. Et dictus comes Ultonie tenuit magnum convivium in castro Dublin et dominus Mauricius filius Thome in[d] crastino tenuit magnum convivium in ecelesia Sancti Patricii, Dublin, et Frater Rogerus Utlawe, justiciarius Hibernie, tenuit magnum convivium apud Kylmaynan, tertio die, et sic recesserunt.

nota de tribus convivis[e]
{nota de occissione Johannis de Bermyngham, comitis Loueth}
Eodem anno, in vigilia Sancti Barnabe, apostoli, dominus Johannes de Bermyngham, comes Loueth, apud Balybragan, in Urgallia, ab illis de Urgalia interfectus fuit, et, cum eo, Petrus de Bermyngham, frater dicti comitis, et germanus legitimus, Robertus de Bermyngham, frater ejusdem comitis putativi, dominus Johannes Bermyngham, filius fratris Ricardi, domini de Anry, Willelmus Fynne Bermyngham, filius a[f] avunculi predicti domini de Anry, Symon de Bermyngham, filius eiusdem Willelmi, Thomas Bermyngham[g] de Connaccia, Henricus Bermyngham de Connacia,[h] Ricardus Talbot de Malaghyde, validus in armis, et cc cum ipsis, quorum nomina ~~ip~~[i] ignorantur.

Item, post predictam stragem, homines domini Symonis de Genevile intraverunt patriam de Carbry ad depredandum[j] propter furta et homicidia eorum multociens super Midia facta, et antiquam discencionem et insurrexerunt illi de Carbry, et interfecerunt de hominibus dicti Symonis lxxvi homines.

---

[a] Pe; [*beginning of* Petrus?]. [b] Willeby L. [c] et *omitted* L. [d] in *omitted* L. [e] *marg. note (same hand no box, black ink)*. [f] *scribe began* avunculi *at line end with* a *and then repeated it with full word*. [g] filius Roberti de Connacia Petrus Bermyngham, filius Jacobi de Connacia, L. [h] et *added* L. [i] *cancelled* L. [j] eos *added* L.

prior of the church of Holy Trinity, Dublin, Master Elias Laweles,[681] and Master Peter Wileby.[682] These examiners appointed those who were summoned to come, and they examined each of them by themselves. When all these had sworn oaths, everyone said that he [Roger] was an upright man and faithful and zealous supporter of the faith and prepared to die for the faith. And for his great purgation the said Friar Roger formally held a great feast for all who wished to come.

Item, in the same year in Lent [Tues. 14 March 1329] the said lord Arnold le Poer died in Dublin castle and lay for a long time with the Preachers without burial.[683]

1329[684]

After the feast of the Annunciation of the Blessed Virgin Mary [Sat. 25 March 1329], the magnates of Ireland, namely, the earl of Ulster, lord Maurice fitz Thomas, the earl of Louth [John de Bermingham], William Bermingham, and other lords came to a parliament at Dublin.[685] There peace was established between the lord earl of Ulster and lord Maurice fitz Thomas.[686] And the said magnates, with the council of the king in the same place, established the highest peace of the lord king to be held – so that each magnate would punish his *parentela* and his men. And the said earl of Ulster held a great feast at Dublin castle and the next day Maurice fitz Thomas held a great feast in the church of St Patrick, Dublin, and on the third day Friar Roger Outlawe, justiciar of Ireland, held a great feast at Kilmainham and thus they departed.

[Note the three feasts]
{Note the killing of John de Bermingham earl of Louth}

In the same year on the vigil of St Barnabas, apostle, [Whitsunday 11 June 1329] lord John de Bermingham, earl of Louth, was killed, by those of Uriel, at Balybragan in Uriel. And with him [was] Peter de Bermingham, brother of the said earl and his full legitimate brother, Robert de Bermingham, presumptive brother of the same earl, lord John Bermingham, son of his brother Richard, lord of Athenry, William Fynn Bermingham, son of the uncle of the aforesaid lord of Athenry, Simon de Bermingham, son of the same William, Thomas Bermingham of Connacht [L: adds: 'the son of Robert of Connacht, Peter Bermingham son of James of Connacht'], Henry Bermingham of Connacht and Richard Talbot of Malahide, strong in arms, and with them two hundred of whom the names are unknown.[687]

Item, after the aforesaid slaughter, the men of lord Simon de Geneville entered the country of Carbury in order to plunder, because of their robberies and multiple murders made upon Meath, and ancient dispute. And those of Carbury rose up and killed seventy-six men of the said Simon.[688]

Item, eodem anno, in crastino Sancte Trinitatis, venerunt Dublin Johannes Gernon ac Rogerus Gernon, frater ejus, ex parte eorum de Urgalia, et supplicaverunt quod possent stare ad communem legem. Et die Martis, in crastino dicti[a] Johannes et Rogerus, audientes quod dominus Willelmus de Bermyngham veniret, recesserunt de Dublin. Eodem anno, in vigilia Sancti Laurencii, dominus Thomas le Botiller ivit cum magno exercitu versus partes de Ardnorwicher, et ibi obviit dicto domino Thome Willelmus M^{c}goghdan exercitu suo, et ibi interfectus fuit dictus dominus Thomas |Folio 28r| † ad dampnum magnum terre Hibernie, et cum eo interfecti fuerunt Dominus Johannes de Ledewiche, Rogerus Ledewiche, Thomas Ledewiche, Johannes Nangle, Meilerus Petyt, Simon Petyt, David Nangle, dominus Johannes Waryng, Jacobus Terell, Nicolaus Albus, Willelmus Freynes, Petrus Kent, Johannes Albus, et cum illis cxl viri, quorum nomina ignorantur. Et die Martis, proxima ante festum[b] Bartholomei, corpus dicti ^domini^[c] Thome le Botiller delatum fuit Dublin; et positum apud Fratres Predicatores, adhuc non sepultum. Et die Dominica, proxima post festum Decollationis Beati Johannis Baptiste, corpus dicti Domini Thome portatum fuit per civitatem cum magno honore et sepultum apud Fratres Predicatores. Et uxor dicti Domini Thome illo die tenuit convivium. Eodem anno, Dominus Johannes Darcy venit Justiciarius Hibernie, secundo, et idem Dominus Johannes desponsavit Dominam Joannam de Burgo, comitissam Kildarie, iii die Julii, apud Maynoth.

Item, Philippus Staunton interficitur.

Item, Dominus Henricus Traharn capitur prodiciose in domo sua apud Kilbeg per Ricardum filium Philippi Onolane.

Item, eodem anno[d] dominus Jacobus le Botiller, comes Ormonie, conbussit Foghaird super Onolane, propter predictum Dominum Henricum, et fratrem Pincerne.

Eodem anno, die Mercurii, proxima post festum Assumptionis Beate Marie, Dominus Johannes Darcy, Justiciarius Hibernie, ivit versus partes de Novo Castro de M^{c}kynghan et de Wikelowe super les Obrynnes, et in[e] die lune sequenti, fuerunt quidam de Law^{e}les interfecti et plures vulnerati et Robertus Locun fuit vulneratus et de Hibernicis meliores fuerunt interfecti et plures vulnerati et ceteri fugerunt. Sed Murkud Obrynne reddidit se obsidem cum filio suo et avunculo et filio avunculi sui. Et ducti fuerunt ad Castrum Dublin. Sed postea liberati fuerunt pro aliis obsidibus, scilicet, melioribus de eorum parentela.

Eodem anno, Justiciarius, scilicet, Dominus Johannes Darcy, et illi qui fuerunt de consilio domini regis in Hibernia, circa festum Circumcisionis Domini, mandavit Domino Mauricio Filio Thome de Dessemond, quod ipse veniret cum exercitu suo ad debellandum inimicos regis, et dominus rex

---

[a] sancti L.   [b] sancti added L.   [c] domini added in margin with insert mark L.   [d] eodem anno omitted L.   [e] in omitted L.

Item, in the same year on the day after Holy Trinity [Mon. 19 June 1329], John Gernon and Roger Gernon his brother came to Dublin on behalf of those of Uriel and begged that they should be able to stand to common law.[689] And on Tuesday the day after the said [L: saint], [Tues. 20 June 1329], John and Roger hearing that lord William de Bermingham might come, retreated from Dublin. In the same year, on the eve of St Laurence [Wed. 9 Aug. 1329], lord Thomas Butler went with a great army towards parts of Ardnurcher and there William Mag Eochagáin with his army faced Lord Thomas. And there, to the great damage of the land of Ireland, the said Thomas was killed.[690] And with him were killed lord John de Ledweiche, Roger Ledewiche,[691] Thomas Ledewiche, John Naungle, Meiler Petit, Simon Petit,[692] David Naungle,[693] lord John Waring, James Tyrell,[694] Nicholas Albus [White],[695] William Freigne, Peter Kent, John Albus [White], and with them one hundred and forty men of whom the names are unknown.[696] And on the Tuesday next before the feast of Bartholomew [Tuesday 22 August 1329], the body of the said lord Thomas Butler was brought to Dublin and placed at the Friars Preachers, still not buried.[697] And on the Sunday next after the feast of the beheading of Blessed John the Baptist [Sun. 23 Sept], the body of the said Thomas was carried by the citizens with great honour and buried at Friars Preachers. And the wife of the same lord Thomas held a feast that day. In the same year, lord John Darcy, justiciar of Ireland, came the second time, and on the third day of July [Mon. 3 July], the same lord John married the lady Johanna de Burgh, countess of Kildare, at Maynooth.

Item, Philip Staunton was killed.[698]

Item, lord Henry Treharne was treacherously captured in his house at Kilbeg by Richard, son of Philip Ó Nualláin.[699]

Item, lord James Butler, earl of Ormond, burnt Forth against Ó Nualláin, because of the aforesaid lord Henry and the brother of the *Pincerna*.[700]

In the same year, on Wednesday next after the feast of the Assumption of Blessed Virgin Mary [Wed. 16 Aug. 1329], lord John Darcy, justiciar of Ireland, journeyed towards the parts of Newcastle McKinegan and to Wicklow against the Uí Bhroin. And, on the following Monday [21 Aug. 1329], certain of the Laweleses were killed and many wounded and Robert Locun[701] was wounded, and more of the Irish were killed, and many wounded and others fled. But Murchadh Ó Broin returned himself as hostage with his son and uncle, and the son of his uncle, and they were led to Dublin castle.[702] But afterwards they were freed for other hostages, namely, the seniors of their *parentela*.

In the same year, around the feast of the Circumcision of the Lord [Mon. 1 Jan. 1330], the justiciar, namely, lord John Darcy and those who were of the council of the lord king in Ireland, gave an order to lord Maurice fitz Thomas, [earl] of Desmond,[703] that he should come himself with his army in order to end the war of the enemies of the king, and the lord king would provide concerning expenses for him and his army. And the said lord Maurice came with his army

provideret sibi et exercitu suo de sumptibus. Et dictus dominus Mauricius*a* cum exercitu suo |Folio 28v| †*b* venit et Briene Obrene fuit cum eo, et fuit *nns* eorum*c* exercitus x millia virorum, et dictus dominus Mauricius, cum exercitu suo, primo ivit super Onolanes et debellavit eos, et accepit predam magnam, et cremavit terras eorum, et les Onolanes fugerunt; et postea liberaverunt obsides qui missi fuerunt ad castrum Dublin. Et postea dictus dominus Mauricius ivit super les Omorhes, qui dederunt obsides ad firmam pacem Regis tenendam. Eodem tempore, castrum de Ley, quod Odymcy ceperat et tenuerat, redditum fuit dicto domino Mauricio. Eodem anno, post Epiphaniam Domini, Donaldus Donaldus*d* Arte Macmurgh evasit de castro Dublin, per cordam quam quidam Adam Nangle emat*e* ei qui Adam postea distractus fuit et suspensus.

Anno Domini M. CCCXXX
Venti validi diversi in festis Sancte Katerine, Sancti Nicholai, et Nativitatis Domini, per quem ventum pars muri cujusdam domus coruens oppressit uxorem domini Milonis de Verdona, cum filia, in vigilia Sancti Nicholai; quales etiam venti nunquam fuerant visi in terra Hibernie.

    Item, inundatio aque de Boyn, qualis nunquam fuerat visa antea, per quam inundationem omnes pontes tam lapidei quam lignei super dictam aquam existentes funditus diruti sunt, preterquam pontem Babe. Aqua etiam asportavit diversa molendina, et multa alia mala*f* intulit fratribus minoribus de Trym et de Drogheda, quia fregit domes eorum. Eodem anno, circa festum Beati*g* Johannis Baptiste, magna caristia bladi incepit esse in Hibernia, et duravit usque ad festum Sancti Michaelis.

    Item, cranocus frumenti vendebatur pro xx solidis.

    Item, cranocus avenarum pro viii solidis; pise, fabe, et ordini i cranocus pro viii solidis. Et ista caristia contigibat*h* propter magnam habundantiam pluvie, ita ut magna pars bladi non posset meti ante festum Sancti Michaelis.

    Eodem anno, Anglici de Midia interfecerunt de Hibernicis, scilicet, de M*c*goghdanes, circa xl, iuxta Laghynerthy, unde dictus M*c*goghdan iratus conbussit in partibus*i* xv parvas villatas, et depredavit {eas}

|Folio 29r| † eas; quod videntes Anglici, colligerunt contra ipsum, et de hominibus suis centum et x interfecerunt, inter quos fuerunt interfecti tres filii regulorum Hibernicorum.

    Item, Dominus Willelmus de Burgo, comes Ultonie, duxit exercitum de Ultonia ad Momoniam, super Brene Obrene.

    Item, Domina Johanna, comitissa Kyldarie, peperit apud Maynoth Willelmum, filium domini Johannis Darcy, per ipsam primum, ipso domino Johanne tunc*j* in Anglia existente.

---

a venit *added here also* L. *b* L. *c* nns eorum *omitted* L. *d* Donaldus *twice* L. *e* emerat L. *f* mala *omitted* L. *g* beati *omitted* L. *h* accidit L. *i* illis *omitted* L. *j* tunc *omitted* L.

and Brian Ó Briain was with him and [the least] of the army was ten thousand men.[704] And with his army the said lord Maurice first went against the Uí Nualláin and waged war with them and accepted great plunder and burnt their lands and the Uí Nualláin fled. And afterwards they delivered hostages which were sent to Dublin castle. And afterwards the said lord Maurice went against the Uí Mhórdha, who gave hostages to hold firm the peace of the king. At the same time, the castle of Lea, which Ó Díomusaigh had taken and held was returned to the said lord Maurice.[705] In the same year, after the Epiphany of the Lord [Sat. 6 Jan. 1330], Domhnall [son of] Art Mac Murchadha escaped from the castle of Dublin, by a rope which a certain Adam Naungle brought to him. This Adam was later drawn and hanged.[706]

1330[707]

On the feasts of St Katherine, St Nicholas, and the Nativity of the Lord [25 Nov., 6 Dec., 25 Dec.. 1330], there was a strong wind in different places; on the eve of St Nicholas [5 Dec. 1330] this wind threw down to the ground part of a wall of a certain house; it collapsed [on] the wife and the daughter of lord Milo de Verdun. Also, such a wind had never been seen in the land of Ireland.[708]

Item, there was a deluge of water of the Boyne, such as never was seen before, by which flood all the bridges, both stone and wood being upon the said water were utterly breached (apart from the bridge of Babe). Furthermore, the water carried away many mills and it inflicted many other damages to the Friars Minor of Trim and of Drogheda, because it demolished their houses. In the same year, around the feast of Blessed John the Baptist [perhaps Nativity of John, 24 June, rather than 29 Aug], a great shortage of grain began in Ireland and lasted right up to the feast of St Michael [29 September 1330].

Item, a crannock of wheat was selling for twenty shillings.

Item, a crannock of oats for eight shillings. peas, beans and barley one crannock for eight shillings. And this scarcity happened because of great abundance of rainwater so that the great part of grain was not able to be gathered before the feast of St Michael [29 Sept. 1330].

In the same year, the English of Meath killed around forty of the Irish near Laghynerthy, namely the Mic Eochagáin. Whereupon the said Mag Eochagáin, being angry, burnt fifteen small vills in those parts and sacked them. The English, seeing this, gathered against him and killed a hundred and ten of his men and among those who were killed [were] three sons of the kinglets of the Irish.

Item, lord William de Burgh, earl of Ulster, led an army of Ulster to Munster against Brian Ó Briain.[709]

Item, lady Johanna, countess of Kildare, gave birth at Maynooth to William, son of lord John Darcy, the first by the same (the same lord John then being in England).

Item, Remundus Laules interficitur apud Wikelowe, prodiciose.

Item, Parliamentum tentum apud Kilkeniam, per Fratrem Rogerum Utlawe, priorem de Kylmaynan, tunc locum tenentem justicarii, ubi fuerunt Alexander Dublin archiepiscopus, dominus Willelmus, comes Ultonie, dominus Jacobus, comes Ormonie, et dominus Willelmus Bermyngham, et Walterus de Burgo de Connacia, quilibet eorum cum magno exercitu iverunt ad expellendum Brene Obrene de Urlyse juxta Casshell.

Item, Walterus de Burgo, cum exercitu suo de Connacia, tunc depredavit terras domini Mauricii filii Thome, reducens secum predam ad Urkyff.

Item, Dominus comes Ultonie, et comes Dessemonie, scilicet, dominus Mauricius filius Thome, quia nunc primo voco eum comitem, custodie marescalli, apud Lymerik, deputantur per Fratrem Rogerum Utlawe, justiciarium Hibernie. Comes, vero, Dessemonie de custodia dicti marescalli calide fugit ^et recessit^*a*

ANNO*b* DOMINI M. CCCXXXI

Dominus Hugo Lacy, cum pace Regis Hiberniam intravit.

Item, Comes Ultonie Angliam intravit.

Item, strages Hibernicorum in O Kensely per Anglicos, ix die mensis*c* Aprilis.

Item, castrum de Arclo capitur prodiciose per Hibernicos, xxi die mensis Aprilis.

Item, eodem die, in vigilia Sancti Marcii evangeliste, Ototheles venerunt apud Tauelaght et depredaverunt Alexandrum, archiepiscopum Dublin, de ccc ovibus, et occiderunt Ricardum White, et alios probos in sua comitiam. Tunc venerunt rumores Dublin de illa predatione et occissione et Dominus Philippus Bryt, miles, et Frater Mauricius Filius Geraldi, miles de ordine*d* Hospitaliorum, Hamundus Archedekyn, Johannes Camerarius, Robertus Tirell, et duo filii Reginaldi Bernewall, et multi alii, et maxime de familia domini archiepiscopi Dublin, interficiuntur per David Otohill per incidias in Culiagh.

Item, Dominus Willelmus Bermyngham duxit magnum exercitum super predictos Hibernicos, et multa mala fecit, et maiora fecisset nisi impeditus fuisset per falsa promissa Hybernicorum.

Item, Dominus Antonius de Lacy,*e* miles, venit capitalis justiciarius Hibernie, iii die Junii.

Item, strages magna Hibernicorum super Brene Obrene per Anglicos terre, apud Thurles, in mense Maii.

Item, apud Fynnagh in Midia, strages |Folio 29v| † Hibernicorum per Anglicos ejusdem terre xi die mensis Junii.

---

a *Placed on the line underneath after* pace.   *b* *rubricated capital* A *has a very long tailed decoration over 9 lines.*   *c* mensis *omitted* L.   *d* ordine *omitted* L.   *e* Lucy L.

Item, Raymond Lawlees was treacherously killed at Wicklow.

Item, a parliament was held at Kilkenny by Friar Roger Outlawe, prior of Kilmainham, then holding the place of the justiciar.[710] Present there were Alexander, archbishop of Dublin, lord William, earl of Ulster, lord James, earl of Ormond, and lord William Bermingham and Walter de Burgh of Connacht.[711] Each of them [went] with a great army to drive out Brian Ó Briain from Thurles near Cashel.[712]

Item, Walter de Burgh, with his army of Connacht, then plundered the lands of lord Maurice fitz Thomas [earl of Desmond]. leading the prey back with him to Thurles.[713]

Item, the lord earl of Ulster and the earl of Desmond (namely, lord Maurice fitz Thomas because he was first called earl now[714]) are appointed by Friar Roger Outlawe, justiciar of Ireland to the custody of the marshal at Limerick. But the earl of Desmond promptly fled and retreated from the custody of the said marshal.[715]

1331[716]

Lord Hugh de Lacy entered Ireland with the king's peace.

Item, the earl of Ulster entered England.[717]

Item, on ninth day of the month of April [Tues. 9 April 1331], the Irish in Uí Cheinnsealaigh were defeated by the English.

Item, on the twenty-first day of the month of April [Sun. 21 April 1331], the castle of Arklow was captured treacherously by the Irish.[718]

Item, on the same day, on the eve of St Mark, evangelist [Wed. 24 April 1331], the Uí Thuathail came towards Tallaght and plundered Alexander, archbishop of Dublin, of three hundred sheep and they killed Richard White and other upright [men] in his retinue.[719] Then reports of that slaughter and killing came to Dublin, and lord Philip Bryt, knight, and Friar Maurice fitz Gerald, knight of the order of Hospitallers, Hamund the Archdeacon, John the Chamberlain, Robert Tyrell, and two sons of Reginald Barnwell and many others, and the greatest of the household of the lord archbishop of Dublin, were killed by ambush by David Ó Tuathail in Coillach.[720]

Item, lord William Bermingham led a great army upon the aforesaid Irish and did great harm – and greater would have been done except they were hindered by the false promises of the Irish.

Item, on third day of June [Mon. 3 June 1331], lord Anthony de Lucy, knight, came as chief justiciar of Ireland.[721]

Item, in the month of May [May], at Thurles a great defeat of the Irish (and of Brian Ó Briain) by the English of the land.[722]

Item, on eleventh day of the month of June [Tues. 11 June 1331], there was a defeat of the Irish at Finnea in Meath by the English of the same place[723]

Item, fame nimia et*ᵃ* valescente in Hibernia, disponente divina miseratione, xxvii die mensis Junii, ingens*ᵇ* marinarum bellinarum, scilicet tharlhedis,*ᶜ* qualis nunquam a pluribus retroactis seculis videbatur, qui secundum estimationem plurium, quingentenum numerum excedebant, et hoc accidebat juxta le Connyng et aquam que vocatur Dodir, in portu Dublin, circa horam vesperarum, et dominus Antonius de Luscy, tunc justiciarius Hibernie, cum suis et quibusdam civibus Dublin, inter quos*ᵈ* Philippus Cradok, et occiderunt de predictis piscibus plusquam cc, et nullus prohibitus facere et asportare, eodem justiciario precipiente.

Item, Dominus Antonius de Lucy, justiciarius Hibernie, statuit commune parliamentum Dublin, in octavis Sancti Johannis Baptiste, ad quod non venerunt quidam terre maiores. Deinde transtulit se dictus justiciarius usque ad*ᵉ* Kylkenniam, continuando dictum Parliamentum ad*ᶠ* predictis octavis usque ad festum Sancti Petri quod dicitur Ad Vincula. Ad quem locum venit dominus Mauricius filius Thome et multi alii nobiles terre qui prius non venerunt, subicientes se gratie Regis. Rex vero mala per predictos commissa in terra, quantum sibi incumbebat, sub certa forma eis gratiose remisit.

Item, castrum de Fernys per Hibernicos capitur prodiciose, et comburitur mense Augusti.

Item, dictus dominus Mauricius filius Thome, comes Dessemonie, de consilio capitur apud Lym^e^ricum per dictum justiciarium, in crastino Assumptionis Beate Marie, et ducitur cum justiciario ad castrum Dublin vii die mensis Octobris.

Item, Henricus Mandevile capitur, mense Septembris, ad castrum Dublin ducitur, de mandato Symonis filii Ricardi, justiciarii in Banco.

Item, Walterus de Burgo, cum duobus germanis suis, capiuntur in Connacia per comitem Ultonie, mense Novembri, et ducuntur per eundem ad castrum de Northburgh, mense scilicet Februarii.

Item, Dominus Willelmus de Bermyngham, cum filio suo, domino Waltero de Bermyngham, apud Clonmell capiuntur per dictum justiciarium mense Februarii, non obstante carta domini regis eis prius data per justiciarium annotatum, et ducunter ad castrum Dublin, 19*ᵍ* die mensis Aprilis.

Item, Hibernici de Lagenia depredaverunt*ʰ* et conbusserunt ecclesias, et in ecclesia de Freynestoun conbusserunt circa lxx homines et mulieres, et quendam capellanum dicte ecclesie, indutum sacris vestibus cum corpore Dominico volentem exire, repulerunt cum lanceis suis et ipsum cum ceteris in predicta ecclesia conbusserunt. Et*ⁱ* isti rumores venerunt ad dominum papam, qui misit bullam suam domino archiepiscopo Dublin, precipiendo quod dictos Hibernicos et omnes eis adherentes cum eorum sequela excomnumicaret, et

---

ᵃ in L. *ᵇ* multitudo added L. *ᶜ* thurlhedis; *and marg. note (same hand)*: thurlhedis L. *ᵈ* fuit added L. *ᵉ* ad omitted L. *ᶠ* a L. *ᵍ* Arabic '19' T, L. *ʰ* Anglicos added L. *ⁱ* et omitted L.

Item, on twenty-seventh day of the month of June [Thurs. 1331], when there was a very great and worsening famine in Ireland. By the dispensation of divine mercy, enormous monsters of the sea, namely *tharlhedis*,[724] of a kind never seen formerly in this lifetime, which according to estimates of most were exceeding the number five hundred. And this happened near le Connyng and the water which is called Dodder in the port of Dublin around the hour of vespers.[725] And lord Anthony de Lucy, then justiciar of Ireland, with his men and with certain citizens of the city of Dublin, among whom was Philip Craddock,[726] killed more than two hundred of the aforesaid fishes and, by order of the same justiciar, no one was prohibited to exploit and carry away.[727]

Item, lord Anthony de Lucy, justiciar of Ireland, held a common parliament in Dublin on the octave of St John the Baptist [must be nativity 24 June not August, hence Mon. 1 July 1331], to which certain of the magnates of the land did not come.[728] Then the said justiciar transferred himself up to Kilkenny to continue the said parliament (to the aforesaid octave right up to the feast of St Peter which is called ad Vincula [Thurs. 1 Aug. 1331]).[729] Lord Maurice fitz Thomas and many other nobles of the land (who previously had not come), came to this place, submitting themselves to the grace of the king.[730] In fact, under certain terms, the king was himself inclining that he would send back his pardon, for the evil committed by the aforesaid in the land.

Item, in the month of August, the castle of Ferns was captured treacherously by the Irish and burnt.[731]

Item, on the day after the Assumption of the Blessed Virgin Mary [Fri. 16 Aug], the said lord Maurice fitz Thomas, earl of Desmond, by the [order of] council, was captured at Limerick by the said justiciar.[732] And on seventh day of the month of October [Mon. 7 October], he was led by the justiciar to Dublin castle.[733]

Item, Henry Mandeville was captured in the month of September, by the mandate of Simon fitz Rery, justice of the common bench, and led to the castle of Dublin.[734]

Item, in the month of November, Walter de Burgh, with two of his full brothers, was captured in Connacht by the earl of Ulster and, namely in the month of February [1332], was led by the same to the castle of Northburgh.[735]

Item, notwithstanding the charter of the lord king given to him previously (having been noted by the justiciar), lord William de Bermingham, with his son, lord Walter de Bermingham, was captured at Clonmel by the said justiciar in the month of February and led to Dublin castle on the nineteenth day[736] of the month of April [Sunday 19 April 1332].[737]

Item, the Irish of Leinster plundered [L: the English] and burned churches, and they burnt around eighty men and women in the church of Freynestown.[738] When the certain chaplain of the said church was putting on sacred vestments (wishing to leave with the body of the Lord), they drove [him] back with their lances and he was burnt with others in the aforesaid church.[739] And this report

terras eorum interdiceret. Archiepiscopus vero mandatum domini pape coplevit,[a] sed dicti Hibernici dictam bullam, excommunicationem et interdictionem, et coercionem ecclesie contempnentes, ^et^ in malitia sua perseverantes, iterum se in |Folio 30r| vicem collegerunt et iverunt per comitatum Wexford usque Carcornan,[b] et totam patriam depredaverunt. Quibus obviantes Anglici, videlicet, Ricardus Whitey et Ricardus filius Henrici, cum burgensibus de Wexford [et] aliis Anglicis, de predictis Hibernicis circa cccc interfecerunt, et multi alii ex eis fugientes submersi fuerunt in aqua que vocatur Slane.

ANNO DOMINI M. CCCXXXII [c]
{no*ta* de morte Willelmi Bermyngham}
Dominus Willelmus Bermyngham morti traditur, et suspenditur Dublin, per eundem iusticiarium, xi die mensis Julii, et dominus Walterus filius ejus est deliberatus. Predictus dominus Willelmus nobilis miles inter milia milium militum in opere militari nobilissimus et optimus. Heu, heu, prohdolor, quis ejus necem commemorans lacrimas continere potest. Sed tandem sepultus est Dublin inter fratres predicatores.

Item, castrum de Banrat capitur et ad terram prosternitur per Hibernicos Totomonie, mense Julii.

Item, castrum de Arclo per dictum justiciarium, cum civibus Dublin et cum adiutorio Anglicorum de terra, capitur ab Hibernicis in manu Regis, viij die mensis Augusti, et pro parte erigitur.

Item[d] Dominus Antonius de Lucy, justiciarius Hibernie, ab officio deponitur et ad Angliam redit, una cum sua consorte et liberis, mense Novembri in[e] cuius etiam loco dominus Johannes Darcy, justiciarius Hibernie instituitur, et Hibernian intravit 13[f] die mensis Februarii.

Item, strages magna Hibernicorum in partibus Momonie super Brene[g] Obrene et M[c]karthy per Anglicos de terra.

Item, obiit Johannes Decer, civis Dublin, et sepelitur apud fratres minores, qui multa bona fecit. †

Item, infirmitas que dicitur mauses per totam Hiberniam tam in senibus viris et mulieribus, quam in iuvenibus et parvulis.

Item, obsides existentes in castro de Lymeryk occiderunt constabularium ejusdem castri, et ceperunt castrum, sed recuperato castro per cives civitatis in manu forti, iidem obsides interfecti sunt in ore gladii.

Item, obsides ceperunt castrum[h] de Nenagh, et eiusdem porta combusta recuperatum est, obsidibus reservatis.

---

[a] complevit L.   [b] Carcarne L.   [c] *box and text rubricated.*   [d] *slight rubrication to capital* I.   [e] et omitted L.   [f] *same use of Arabic number* 13 T *and* L.   [g] *slight rubrication to capital* B.   [h] similiter *added* L.

had come to the lord pope who sent his bull to the lord archbishop of Dublin to command that the said Irish and all their adherents with all of their *sequela* should be excommunicated and their lands placed under interdict.[740] Truly the archbishop fulfilled the mandate of the lord pope. But the said Irish, contemptuous of the said bull, excommunication, interdict and church restraint, continued steadfastly in their ill-will. Again assembling themselves, one after the other, again they went through the county of Wexford right up to Carnsore Point and they plundered the whole countryside.[741] Meeting the English, namely Richard White[742] and Richard fitz Henry, with the burgesses of Wexford and other English, around four hundred of the aforesaid Irish were killed and many others, while fleeing from them, were drowned in the water which is called the Slaney.

1332[743]
{Note the death of William Bermyngham}
On the eleventh day of the month of July [Sat], lord William Bermingham was delivered to death and hanged in Dublin by the same justiciar, and lord Walter his son was freed.[744] The aforesaid lord William [was] a noble knight – among thousands of knights, the most noble and best in military skill. Alas, alas, ah grief! Who recalling his death is able to contain tears?[745] But finally he was buried in Dublin among the Friars Preachers.

Item, in the month of July, the castle of Bunratty was captured and razed to the ground by the Irish of Thomond.[746]

Item, the castle of Arklow was captured from the Irish by the said justiciar with the citizens of Dublin, and, with the help of the English of the land, [taken] into the hands of the king on the eighth day of the month of August [Sat. 8 Aug] and rebuilt on behalf of [the king].[747]

Item, in the month of November, lord Anthony de Lucy, justiciar of Ireland, was deposed from the office and returned to England together with his consort and children. In which place lord John Darcy was instituted as justiciar of Ireland and entered Ireland on 13th[748] day of the month of February [Sat. 13 Feb. 1333].[749]

Item, a great massacre of the Irish in parts of Munster upon Brian Ó Briain and Mac Cárthaigh by the English of the land.[750]

Item, John Decer, citizen of Dublin, died and he was buried at the Friars Minor. He did many good deeds.[751]

Item, the sickness which is called *maures* through the whole of Ireland both in older men and women, and in young and children.[752]

Item, the hostages being [kept] in the castle of Limerick killed the constable of the same castle and took the castle. But, by the strong hands by the citizens of the city, the castle was recovered; the same hostages were killed by the edge of the swords.[753]

Item, the hostages took the castle of Nenagh and burnt the gate of the same. It was regained, and the hostages were brought back.[754]

Item, j pecke frumenti, circa Natale Domini, pro xxii solidis et cito post Pascha, et deinceps pro xii denariis communiter vendebatur.

Item, villa Novi Castri de Lyons per Ototheles comburitur et depredatur.

Anno domini M. CCCXXXIII

Dominus Joannes Darcy applicuit Dublin, Justiciarius Hibernie.

Item, Oconghors perdiderunt magnam predam, duo millia vaccarum et ultra per les Bermyngehames de Carbria.

Item, Dominus Joannes Darcy, Justiciarius Hibernie, fecit scindi passum apud Ethergonyll in Offalia super Oconghir.

{nota derede ... dominus Mauricius filius Thome comites Desmonia [?]}
Item*a* Dominus Mauricius filius Thome, comes Dessemonie, educitur de carcere Dublin, postquam incarceratus est per unum annum cum dimidio, multis manucaptoribus, maioribus et nobilioribus terre inventis prius pro eodem, sub ^foris^factura vite omniumque bonorum suorum admissis, si tunc dictus dominus Mauricius contra Regem | Folio 30r | aliquid attemptaret, et suam personam Regi non presentarent pro suis demeritis nobiles antedicti.

Item*b* Dominus Willelmus de Burgo, comes Ultonie, inter novam villam et Cragfergows in Ultonia a suis prohdolor, prodiciose interficitur anno etatis sue xx | vi*c* die mensis Junii; Roberto filio Martini Maundevile ipsum primo percutiente. Quibus auditis rumoribus, uxor dicti comitis, tunc in dictis partibus Ultonie existens cum filia sua et herede navem statim ascendit, et ad partes se transtulit Anglicanas; post cuius interfectionem dominus Joannes Darcy, capitalis justiciarius Hibernie, vindicaturus mortem dicti comitis de consilio omnium maiorum terre existentium tunc in dicto parliamento, statim cum exercitu suo iter suum arripuit, et navigio applicuit apud Cragfergows, primo die mensis Julii. Patriote vero de adventu justiciarii gaudentes, et audaciam ex hoc assumentes, contra interfectores dicti comitis Ultonie et eius interfectioni assentientes insurrexerunt, et in bello campestri victoriam obtinentes quosdam ceperunt, alios gladio occiderunt. Hiis peractis, dictus justiciarius cum dicto exercitu ad Scotiam se transtulit, Magistro Thoma Burgh, tunc thesaurario Hibernie, in suo loco dimisso.

Item, multi terre nobiles et comes Ormonie cum eorum sequela ad domum carmelitarum Dublin congregati xi die mensis Junii et tempore dicti parliamenti in eorum exite arcea*d* dictorum fratrum subito infra populi pressuram, Murcardus sive Mauricius, filius Nicholai Otothil; inibi interficitur, super cuius subitanea interfectione omnes terre maiores prescripti prodicionem timentes et computantes, insolito timore concutiuntur et conturbantur, necnon et eiusdem Murcardi interfector illorum*e* omnium strenue manus evasit,*f* cuius nomen et notitia ab eisdem penitus ignorabatur.

---

a slight rubrication to capital I. box and text both rubricated.   *b* marg. note (same hand): nota de morte Willelmus comitibus Ultonie.   *c* an upright line has been inserted between the xx and vi – to separate the age and date.   *d* area L.   *e* eorum L.   *f* strenue manus strenue L.

Item, around Christmas, one peck of wheat was commonly selling for twenty-two shillings – and soon after Easter and thereafter for twelve pence [Easter 4 April 1333].

Item, the vill of Newcastle Lyons was burnt and plundered by the Uí Thuathail.[755]

1333

Lord John Darcy, justiciar of Ireland, landed in Dublin.

Item, Ó Conchobhair lost a great prey, two thousand cows and more, at the hands of the Bermingham of Carbury.

Item, lord John Darcy, justiciar of Ireland ordered the pass at Ethergonyll[756] in Offaly to be cut against Ó Conchobhair.

{Note... lord Maurice fitz Thomas earl of Desmond [?]}

Item, lord Maurice fitz Thomas, earl of Desmond, after he was incarcerated for one year and a half, was taken from the prison of Dublin by many mainpernors, magnates and nobles of the land (finding previously for him under forfeiture of life and all of their goods), accepting that if then the said lord Maurice should attempt anything against the king, and if the aforesaid nobles did not present his person to the king for his faults.[757]

Item, lord William de Burgh earl of Ulster, was killed treacherously by his men between Newtown and Carrickfergus in Ulster – ah grief – with Robert, son of Martin Mandeville, wounding him first.[758] He was aged 20 years on the sixth day of the month of June [Sun. 6 June].[759] The wife of the said earl, then being in the said parts of Ulster with her daughter and heir, when she heard of these reports, at once took ship and crossed to English parts.[760] After whose murder, lord John Darcy, chief justiciar of Ireland (by the counsel of all the magnates of the land being then in the said parliament[761]), at once made his journey with his army and landed by ship at Carrickfergus on the first day of the month of July [Thurs. 1 July], to revenge the death of the said earl. Truly, the local inhabitants were rejoicing at the coming of the justiciar, and taking courage from this, and assenting, they rose against the murderers of the said earl of Ulster, and in an open battlefield they fought, taking victory; some they captured, others they killed by the sword. Once this had been accomplished, the said justiciar himself, with his said army, crossed to Scotland leaving Master Thomas Burgh, then treasurer of Ireland, in his place.[762]

Item, on the eleventh day of the month of June [Sat. 11 June] the earl of Ormond and many nobles of the land with their *sequela*, gathered at the house of the Carmelites of Dublin. And, at the time of the said parliament, when leaving the open area of the said friars – suddenly within the throng of the people – Murchadh, or Maurice, son of Nicholas Ó Tuathail was killed nearby. Upon which unexpected killing, all the above-named magnates of the land, fearing and calculating treachery, were agitated and confused with unaccustomed fear. Indeed, the killer of the same Murchadh quickly escaped their hands. They were ignorant of his name and identity.[763]

Item, prefatus dominus Joannes Darcy rediit justiciarius Hibernie.

Item, Dominus Walterus de Bermyngham, filius domini Willelmi de Bermyngham de castro Dublin liberatur mense Februarii.

Item, Dominus Mauricius filius Thome, comes Dessemonie, casu palfridi sui fregit tibiam suam.

Item, Estas vero tota pulchra et sicca, ita quod in festo Ad Vincula Sancti Petri comedebatur panis novi frumenti, et vendebatur pecke frumenti pro vi denariis in Dublin.

Item, Dominus Remundus Archedekeyn, miles, et multi alii de eadem cognatione interficiuntur in Lagenia.*a*

Anno domini m. cccxxxvii
{no*ta* de perdicibus}
In vigilia Sancti Kalixti, pape, vii perdices, et nescitur quo spiritu agitante, campum deserentes, recta linea ad civitatem Dublin convolarunt et fori loca citissime transvolantes in summitate pandaxatorii canonicorum Sancte Trinitatis Dublin concederunt. Ad quod spectaculum nonnulli cives Dublin concurrerunt, prodigium illud plurimum admirantes. Pueri autem de civitate duas ex illis apprehenderunt vivas, tertiam peremerunt. Cetere ex hoc territe altiora petentes ad campos oppo[-]

*Niroibh ar dhacorp a coimdhe cneadh arnem asnarsil cru. fuil as da taeb oguin ghallga saeib is nac duil tharla thu.*b

|Folio 31r| [-]sitos volatu pervici affugerunt. Quod autem portendit casus iste, retro seculis inauditus, peritorum arbitrio relinquatur.

Item, Dominus Johannes Charleton, miles et baro, cum sua uxore et filiis et filiabus suis, cum tota familia sua venit, in festo Sancti*c* Kalixti, pape, capitalis justiciarius Hibernie, et de filiis et familia sua quidam mortui sunt.

Item, Dominus d*d* Thomas Charleton, episcopus Herfordensis et germanus dicti justiciarii, venit, eodem die cum suo germano, cancellarius Hibernie, una cum Magistro Joanne Rees, thesaurario Hibernie et magistro in decretis, ducentes secum multos Wallicos numero cc et omnes in portu Dublin applicaverunt.

Item, Domino Johanne Charleton existente justiciario et tenente parliamentum Dublin, Magister David Ohirraghty, archiepiscopus Ardmachanus, vocatus ad parliamentum, fecit providentiam in monasterio Beate Marie, juxta Dublin, sed impeditus fuit per Archiepiscopam et clerum, quia voluit portare crucem ante eum et noluerunt permittere eum.*e*

---

a 4 very faint manks L.   *b verse in Irish at bottom of page.*   *c* sancti *omitted* L.   *d* d *underdotted as error.*   *e very faint and in a later hand* nō archiepiscopus Ardmachanus …portat crucem[?]. *marg. note (same hand)*: nō de armachano et cruce *in* L.

Item, the aforesaid lord John Darcy justiciar of Ireland returned.

Item, in the month of February, lord Walter de Bermingham, son of lord William de Bermingham was freed from Dublin castle.⁷⁶⁴

Item, lord Maurice fitz Thomas, earl of Desmond, broke his tibia because of his palfrey.

Item, the summer was totally beautiful and dry so that on the feast of St Peter ad Vincula [i.e. Sunday 1 August 1333?] bread was being made of new wheat and a peck was selling for six pence in Dublin.⁷⁶⁵

Item, lord Raymond Archdeacon, knight, and many others of the same name were killed in Leinster.

1337⁷⁶⁶

{Note the partridges}

On the eve of St Calixtus, pope [Mon. 13 Oct. 1337], seven partridges leaving the field (and it is not known what spirit agitated [them]), flew in a direct line to the city of Dublin and flying most swiftly over the marketplace they went on to the top of the brew-house of the canons of Holy Trinity in Dublin. At this sight several of the citizens of Dublin came together very much admiring that wonder. However, the boys of the city seized two of them alive and a third they destroyed. The rest, frightened, flew away from this highest place desiring to gain the fields opposite by flight.⁷⁶⁷

> [*There was not on your body, Lord, a [highly] poisonous wound from which blood did not flow, blood from your side from the wounding of a foreign spear, even though you were not formed of blood.*]⁷⁶⁸

However, what this event predicts (unheard of before in this age) I leave to expert judgment.⁷⁶⁹

Item, on the feast of St Calixtus pope [Tues. 14 Oct.] lord John Charlton, knight and baron, came with his wife and sons and daughters, with all his *familia* as chief justiciar of Ireland, and of his sons and his *familia* certain ones died.⁷⁷⁰

Item, lord Thomas Charlton, bishop of Hereford, and the full brother of the said justiciar, came on the same day with his brother [Tues. 14 Oct.], as chancellor of Ireland – together with Master John Rhys, treasurer of Ireland and master in decretals.⁷⁷¹ [Charlton] brought with him many Welshmen, two hundred in number, and all landed in the port of Dublin.⁷⁷²

Item, while lord John Charlton was being justiciar and holding a parliament in Dublin, Master David Mág Oireachtaigh, archbishop of Armagh, having been called to the parliament,⁷⁷³ made his stay in the monastery of the Blessed Mary near Dublin, but he was impeded by the archbishop [Bicknor] and clerk, because he wished to carry his cross before him and they would not allow him.⁷⁷⁴

Item, eodem anno obiit idem David, Archiepiscopus Ardmachanus, cui successit Magister Ricardus filius Radulphi, Decanus Lychefeldensis, clericus loculentus, qui natus fuit in villa de Dundalk.[a]

{no*ta* de obitu domini Jacobus primus Comitis Ormonie}
Item,[b] obiit dominus[c] Jacobus Pincerna, primus Comes Ormonie, in $1\Lambda^d$ die mensis Januarii, et sepelitur apud Baligaveran.

• Anno domini M. CCCXXXVIII

Dominus Johannes Charleton, ad instigationem germani sui, videlicet, domini Thome, episcopi Herfordensis, per regem ab officio deponitur, et cum tota sua familia, uxore et liberis, ultimo die Julii ad Angliam revertitur. Et dictus dominus Thomas, episcopus Herfordensis, in custodem et iustitiarium Hibernie per regem instituitur.

Item, dominus Eustacius Power, et dominus Johannes Power, eius avunculus, per dictum justiciarium de Momonia ducuntur ad Dublin, et in castro detinentur, tertio die mensis Februarii.

{No*ta* de gelu}
Item,[e] in partibus Hibernie gelu tam intensum fuit, quod fluvius Dublin Anelifius congelebatur in tantum, quod plurimi super glaciem eiusdem fluvii tripudiabant, ludebant ad pilam, et currebant; focum inde super eandem glaciem de lignis et glebis terreis succendunt et super focum ~~allicia~~[f] allecia assarunt. Hec glacies per dies plurimos duravit; de nive quoque in partibus Hibernie eidem gelu comitante non oportet[g] amplius os aperire, cum fuisset profunditate mirabili insignita. A $2^{o\,h}$ die mensis Decembris usque ad x diem mensis Februarii illa tempestas duravit, retro seculis in Hibernia maxime inaudita.

Anno domini M. CCCXXXIX

Guerra generalis per totam Hiberniam.

Item, |Folio 31v| † maxima strages et submersio Hibernicorum, ad minus m cc corpora, per dominum Mauricium filium Thome, comitem Dessemonie, et ceteros Geraldinos in partibus Kernigie.

Item, Dominus Mauricius filius Nicholai, dominus Kernigie, per dominum Mauricium filium Thome, comitem Dessemonie, capitur et incarceratur, et in carcere moritur, positus ad dietam, pro eo quod contra dominum regem Anglie et contra dominum comitem cum dictis Hibernicis palam se exposuit et surrexit.

Item, strages et submersio magna de Odympcies et aliorum Hibernicorum in aqua de Barrowe per Anglicos comitatus Kyldarie, eos valide persequentes.

---

[a] *marg. note*: nö L.   [b] *rubricated box, text black* T. *marg. note*, nö L.   [c] dominus *omitted* L.   [d] *Arabic numeral for* $17 - 1\Lambda$ T *and* L.   [e] *rubricated box and text* T; *marg. note*, nö L.   [f] *cancelled by underdotting.*   [g] opertus? L.   [h] *Arabic* 2°. a secundo L.

Item, in the same year, the same David, archbishop of Armagh, died, to whom succeeded Master Richard fitz Ralph, dean of Lichfield, a distinguished clerk who was born in the town of Dundalk.[775]

{Note the death of lord James Pincerna fist earl of Ormond}
Item, James *Pincerna* [Butler], first earl of Ormond died on 1∧ [17][776] of the month of January [Tues. 17 Jan. 1338] and was buried at Gowran.[777]

1338
Lord John Charlton, at the prompting of his brother, namely, lord Thomas, bishop of Hereford, was deposed from his office by the king and returned to England on the last day of July, with all his *familia*, wife and children. And the said lord Thomas, bishop of Hereford, was instituted in the custody and justiciarship of Ireland by the king.[778]

Item, lord Eustace Poer, and lord John Poer, his uncle, were led from Munster to Dublin by the said justiciar and detained in the castle on third day of the month of February [Wed. 3 Feb. 1339].[779]

{Note the freezing}
Item, in parts of Ireland the frost was so intense that the Dublin river, the Anna Liffey, thoroughly froze over in such a way that many were dancing, playing with a ball and running upon the ice of the same river. Then, upon the same ice, they kindled a hearth of wood and peat and they roasted herrings upon the hearth.[780] This ice lasted for many days. As regards to other parts of Ireland, concerning the snow and also the same frost, it is not necessary to say more verbally, when it had been noted by the extraordinary depth. This storm lasted from the 2nd day of the month of December [Wed. 2 Dec. 1338] right up to the tenth day of the month of February [Ash Wed. 10 Feb. 1339]. [This was] formerly unheard of in this age and had never been known in Ireland.

1339[781]
A general war through the whole of Ireland.[782]

Item, a great massacre and drowning of the Irish by lord Maurice fitz Thomas, earl of Desmond, and other Geraldines in the parts of Kerry (one thousand, two hundred bodies at the least).[783]

Item, lord Maurice fitz Nicholas, lord of Kerry, was captured and imprisoned by lord Maurice fitz Thomas, earl of Desmond, and, having been placed on a diet, died in prison. For he had openly placed himself against the lord king of England and against the lord earl – and openly he cast himself out and rose with the said Irish.[784]

Item, a great massacre and drowning of the Uí Dhíomasaigh, and of other Irish, in the water of the Barrow, by the English of the county of Kildare, who were pursuing strongly.[785]

Item, magna preda animalium diversorum generum, qualis non fuerat visa in partibus Lagenie, per dictum dominum Thomam, episcopum Herfordensem, justiciarium Hibernie, cum adiutorio Anglicorum ejusdem terre capitur ab Hibernicis in partibus de Odrone in fine mensis Februarii.[a]

Anno domini M. CCCXL
Dictus episcopus Herfordensis et iusticiarius Hibernie per regem vocatus reddit in Angliam, x die mensis Aprilis, Fratre Rogero Outlawe, priore de Kylmaynan, in loco suo dimisso.

Item, obiit dominus Rogerus Utlawe, prior de Kylmaynan ac justiciarius et cancellarius dicte terre, 13[b] die mensis Februarii.

Item, Rex Anglie concessit Johanni Darcy officium Justiciarii Hibernie ad totam vitam suam.

Anno[c] domini M. CCCXLI
Dominus Johannes Moris, miles, venit Justiciarius Hibernie, mense Maii, tenens[d] Johannis Darcy in terra predicta.

Item, prodigium[e] subsequens admirandum,[f] nostris retro seculis inauditum, contigit in comitatu Leycestrie, ubi quidam vir, iter faciens in publica strata, unum par cirotecarum reperit aptum suis usibus, ut credebat, quas suis manibus imponens, concito loco loquele humane ~~loquele~~ more canino latratus mirabiles proferebat, et extunc per eundem comitatum senes et adulti ac mulieres tanquam canes magni, parvuli vero tanquam parvi catuli, elatrarunt. Peste igitur illa perdurante apud aliquos per xliii,[g] apud alios per mensem, apud quosdam per duos menses. Pestis etiam predicta comitatus alios vicinos intravit et populum pari modo latrare coegit.

Item, Rex Anglie omnia per eum et patrem suum collata modo quocunque quibuscunque personis Hibernie, tam libertates quam terras et alia bona, revocavit, ob quorum revocatiorum magna briga orta fuit in terra, et a manibus regis Anglie terra Hibernie in punctu perditionis extitit.

Item, commune parliamentum Hibernie, de consilio regis, mense Octobris Dublin[h] extitit ordinatum. Ad idem parliamentum dominus Mauricius filius Thome, comes Dessemonia |Folio 32r| non pervenit, ante quod tempus nunquam inter Anglicos in Anglia ~~orind~~ oriundos[i] ita nobilis[j] et manifesta divisio habebatur. Maiores insuper civitatum regalium ejusdem terre, una cum nobilioribus dicte terre et fornicibus universis, unanimes existentes, habito consilio deliberato, in ceteris conclusionibus decreverunt et statuerunt parliamentum ~~eom~~ commune Kilkennie mense Novembri, ad utilitatem et

---

[a] *faint note* no E xiiii – *later hand* – *probably Edward's regnal year 14* L.   [b] *Arabic numeral* 13 T, L.   [c] *less decorated* A.   [d] *locum added* L.   [e] *very faint different later hand* nö prodigium —. *marg. note* (*same hand*): nö prodigium maximum *in* L.   [f] *et added* L.   [g] xviii L.   [h] Dublin *omitted but enough space for the word at line end* L.   [i] *et Anglicos in terra Hibernie oriundos added* L.   [j] notabilis L.

Item, in the parts of Idrone, at the end of the month of February [1340], a great plunder of various kinds of animals [i.e., heads of cattle], such as had not been seen in the parts of Leinster, were captured by the said lord Thomas, bishop of Hereford, justiciar of Ireland, from the Irish with the help of the English of the same land.[786]

1340

On the tenth day of the month of April [Mon. 10 April], the said bishop of Hereford and justiciar of Ireland was called by the king to return to England. Friar Roger Outlawe, prior of Kilmainham, was left in his place.[787]

Item, lord Roger Outlawe, prior of Kilmainham and justiciar and chancellor of the said land, died on the '13' day of the month of February [Tues. 13 Feb. 1341].[788]

Item, the king of England gave the office of justiciar of Ireland to John Darcy for his whole life.[789]

1341[790]

Lord John Morris, knight, justiciar of Ireland, came in the month of May holding [the place] of John Darcy in the aforesaid land.[791]

Item, there was an astonishing portent unheard of before in our generation. It happened in the county of Leicester, where a certain man, making a journey on the public way, came upon one pair of gloves, suitable for his use, as he thought. Which, placing on his hands, it brought forward in place of human speech the marvel of barking in the character of a dog. And thereafter throughout the same county the old, and full grown and women barked out as if great dogs, the children however barking like young dogs. This pestilence therefore was lasting among them for [eighteen] days,[792] among others for a month among some for two months. And also the aforesaid pestilence entered in other nearby counties and now forced the people brought together equally to bark.[793]

Item, the king of England revoked both liberties and lands and other things granted by him and by his father, now in whatsoever mode to whomsoever persons in Ireland.[794] By which revocation great dispute arose in the land, and the land of Ireland, from the hands of the king of England, appeared on the point of destruction.[795]

Item, in the month of October in Dublin, a common parliament of Ireland was being ordained by the council of the king.[796] Lord Maurice fitz Thomas, earl of Desmond, did not come to that parliament.[797] Before that time, never, between the English born in England [L: and the English born in the land of Ireland] was there existing such notable and visible division.[798] In addition, the mayors of the royal cities of the same land, together with the most noble of the said land and with all the rest, all being unanimous, they held a counsel to deliberate. Among other conclusions, they decreed and established a common parliament at Kilkenny in the month of November, for the advantage and profit of the king and

profectum regis et prefate terre, consilio justiciarii et regalium predictorum irrequisito penitus in hac parte. Justiciarius autem et ceteri ministri regis ad idem parliamentum Kilkennie accedere nullatenus presumpserunt. Maiores igitur terre prenotate una cum maioribus civitatum ordinaverunt de solempnibus nunciis regi Anglie quamtocius destinandum*a* pro statu terre relevando et conquerendo de eius ministris in Hibernia, de iniquo et iniusto regimine eorundem, et non de cetero tollerarent quod terra Hibernie per suos ministros more solito regeretur. Conqueruntur modo pro parte de predictis ministris modo prout sequitur.

{No*ta* ^de^ **France**}

*b *Treis choses sount ademaundere du Consaill le Roie en Engleterre. Ore primer wil* ~~me~~*c* *nosmer la quele est mowe de seure a tere, coment part terre gaverner qui rien nad ne seit de guerre. A ceo lour please respounce daner quare tiel demaund ne doit displere. Le movere de cest matier prie que la secound soit monstre, de home quest myse en baileie,*d* *et est bien*e *pover en son entre, coment il est riche del office que laure est bailie. Et ne rent a la service son seignor montaunt un darre; la tiers. Nous tenons du Roie, ses subiectis sumes et s serrouns, et vous disums en bone foy que de nous teres profitz prenouns. Ore nos dies la cause pur quey il quest Seignor de nous tous prent riens est ceo la ley monstre la que nos ne savouns. Cestis demaundis deincetis quant des sagis serount confutes.*

*Et ceux que sount de Roie prive a pleine le avera entendus. Dieus vous doit pour sa pite que fauxime en sait conuse et ceux quei agment*f *laialte ne saient par faux gent deceus.*

***Anno domini m. cccxlii**g

xj die Octobris, luna xi existente, vise sunt Dublin*h* due lune bene ante diem in firmamento a multis viris. Quarum una fuit juxta cursum nature in occidente et clara, alia vero ad quantitatem unius rotundi panis tenui modicum splendens in oriente existebat.

***Anno domini m. ~~cccl~~ cccxliii**i

Vicus Sancti Thome Dublin comburitur cum igne proprio in festo, videlicet, Sancti Valentini, Martiri.

|Folio 32v| *j Item, xiii die mensis Julii, dominus Radulphus de*k* Wffcrd, cum sua consorte, comitissa Ultonie, venit capitalis justiciarius Hibernie, in quorum ingressu aura pulchra in aeris intemperie subito mutatur, ac et exinde ymbrium ~~hah~~ habundancia, et tepestatum*l* affluencia, usque ad vite sue exitum copiose sequebatur. Nullus suorum predecessorum temporibus retroactis sibi, prohdolor, extitit comparabilis. Hic enim justiciarius justiciarie officium

---

a destinandis L.   *b* L.   *c* cancelled by 2 methods L.   *d* baalie L.   *e* biene L.   *f* ayment L.   *g* m ccclii, x omitted L.   *h* marg. note (same hand): de duabus lunis m.ccclii.   *i* m ccc liii with x omitted. error ~~cccl~~ cancelled by underdotting and strike through. Error in original therefore L.   *j* L.   *k* de omitted L.   *l* tempestatum L.

of the aforesaid land (with the council of the justiciar and the aforesaid jurisdiction wholly unsought in this matter).[799] However, the justiciar and other ministers of the king did not at all presume to approach to the same parliament at Kilkenny.[800] Therefore, the most important of the pre-named land, together with the mayors of the cities, appointed eminent messengers to go to the king of England as soon as possible to disclose and complain (on behalf of the state of the land) concerning his ministers in Ireland about their unjust and excessive governance of them. And henceforth they will not tolerate that the land of Ireland should be ruled by his ministers as before accustomed.[801] They now complain in front of the aforesaid ministers, just as it now follows.[802]

{Note concerning French}[803]

There are three things to be asked of the King's Council in England. Firstly, I want to mention the most critical in the land: how can a country be governed where there is nothing but war? Please respond to them in this matter, for such a question should not offend. The pleader in this case requests that the second matter be explained: concerning a man who is endowed with a bailiwick and is poor at the beginning, how can he be rich from the position granted to him and not render service to his lord worth even a penny? The third: we hold land from the king, are and will remain his subjects, and tell you in good faith that we claim right to the benefits of our lands. So, tell us why he who is lord of us all takes anything. Is this the law? Show it, for we do not know it. Dismiss these requests if they are refuted by experts and when those close to the king have fully heard them. May God grant you that fraud be recognised as such and that those who love loyalty not be deceived by treacherous persons.[804]

1342

On the eleventh day of October [Fri. 11 Oct.], well before the daybreak, when the moon was eleven [days old], two moons were seen in the sky in Dublin by many men. One of which was near the natural course in the west, and bright, however the other, appearing to shine only a little in the east, was the size of one round loaf.

1343

St Thomas's Street in Dublin was burnt with a spontaneous fire, namely on the east, of St Valentine, martyr [Fri. 14 Feb. 1343 or 1344].

Item, on the thirteenth day of the month of July [Sun. 13 July 1343], lord Ralph de Ufford, chief justiciar, came to Ireland with his wife, the countess of Ulster.[805] Upon their coming, the beautiful wind in the air suddenly changed to intemperate weather and from then on, right up to the end of his life, an abundance of very heavy rain and copiously bad weather followed. None of his predecessors, from times past to himself – ah grief – was comparable. For this justiciar, holding the office of justiciar, appeared as a usurper of the people of the land, a plunderer of the goods of the clerics, of the laity, of rich and poor.

gerens, populi terre extitit invasor, clericorum, laycorum, divitum et pauperum bonorum depredator, sub colore ~~bonorum depredator~~*ᵃ* boni multorum defraudator. Jura ecclesie non observans, legem regni non custodiens,*ᵇ* iniurias irrogans, paucis ac nullis iustitiam tribuens, indigenis, paucis dumtaxat exceptis, totaliter diffidens. Hec et alia faciens et attemptans, sue consortis consilio ductus.

Item, dictus justiciarius ingrediendo Ultoniam mense Martii, per passum qui vocatur Emerdullan, insultum gravem passus est a M*ᶜ*cartan ibidem; quiquidem M*ᶜ*cartanus cum dicto justiciario congressus est eundem*ᶜ* pannis, pecunia, utensilibus argenteis, et equis inibi spoliavit, et quosdam de suis interfecit. Demum autem, justiciarius antedictus, cum adiutorio Ergallencium victoria potitus, Ultonie partes intravit.

Anno Domini M. cccxlv

vij die mensis*ᵈ* Junii commune parliamentum, Dublin, ad quod non venit dominus Mauritius filius Thome, comes Dessemonie.

Item, ~~dictus~~*ᵉ* dominus Radulphus de Ufford, justiciarius Hibernie post festum Beati Johannis Baptiste, cum vexillo regis, sine tamen assensu maiorum terre, levato contra dominum Mauricium filium Thome, comitem Dessemonie, ad Momoniam progreditur, et ibidem terras comitis in manum*ᶠ* regis cepit, et terras captas pro uno certo annuatim domino regi portando aliis contulit.

Item, dictus justiciarius in partibus Momonie existens, domino Willelmo Burton, militi, duo brevia contulit, quorum unum dictus Willelmus traderet domino Mauricio filio Thome, comiti Kildarie, in quo continebatur, quod sub forisfactura omnium terrarum suarum manu forti in regis et sui auxilium celeriter ad eum veniret; in alio autem brevi continebatur quod dictus dominus Willelmus dictum comitem Kildarie caperet, et captum incarceraret. Dominus autem Willelmus videns quod hoc affectui debito per se non poterat mancipari verbis subornatis suasit dicto comiti cum fuerat parando se cum suo exercitu et exercitum colligendo ad justiciarium antedictum quod ante suum recessum de terra ad consilium regis Dublin veniret, et de unanimi eorundem consilio sic ageret, quo ad terrarum suarum custodiam in sua absentia, quo |Folio 33r| † si ex tunc mali aliquid terris suis ipso absente contingeret,*ᵍ* regis consilio*ʰ* imputaretur et non sibi. Comes igitur fidem adhibens verbis militis, et nullam prodicionem estimans in hac parte, disposuit se Dublin venire. Quo igitur veniente, et prodicionem penitus ignorante, ac ipso ~~insa~~ in Scaccario unacum aliis de consilio regis in consilio sedente, subito proditiose per dictum Willelmum attachiatur, seu arrestatur, et capitur, et ad Castrum eiusdem civitatis ducitur et incarceratur.

ᵃ cancelled by underdotting and crossing out **L**. *ᵇ* indigenis added **L**. *ᶜ* justiciarius ad~~lec~~ **L**. *ᵈ* mensis omitted **L**. *ᵉ* cancelled by underdotting and crossing out. *ᶠ* manu **L**. *ᵍ* contigere **L**. *ʰ* consilio regis **L**.

Under the appearance of good, he was a defrauder of many. He was neither observing the rights of the church, nor guarding the laws of the kingdom. Inflicting damage on the poor and assigning justice to none; entirely distrusting, except for a few, the locally born.[806] Doing these things, and attempting others, he was led by the counsel of his consort.[807]

Item, in the month of March [1344–5], the said justiciar, entering Ulster through a pass called Emerdullan, was harshly attacked by Mac Artáin in the same place.[808] This Mac Artáin, having fought with the same justiciar, robbed the same of clothes, money, appurtenances, and silver and plundered horses in that place and killed some of his men. At last however the aforesaid justiciar, with the help of the men of Uriel, obtained victory and entered into the parts of Ulster.[809]

1345

On the seventh day of the month of June [Tues. 7 June] a common parliament was held in Dublin; Maurice fitz Thomas, earl of Desmond, did not come to this.[810]

Item, after the feast of Blessed John the Baptist [24 June], lord Ralph de Ufford, justiciar of Ireland, marched to Munster with the standard of the king raised against lord Maurice fitz Thomas, earl of Desmond (without however the assent of the magnates of the land). And there he took the lands of the earl into the hand of the king.[811] And he bestowed the lands he seized for one fixed yearly payment to be conveyed to the lord king.[812]

Item, while the said justiciar was in the parts of Munster, he gave to lord William Burton, knight, two writs. One of which, the said William should deliver to lord Maurice fitz Thomas, earl of Kildare, in which it was enclosed that, under forfeiture of all of his lands, he should come quickly to him for the king with a strong force, and his feudal aid.[813] On the other hand, in the other writ, it was enclosed that the said lord William [Burton] should seize the said earl of Kildare and imprison the captured [earl].[814] However, lord William [Burton], seeing that he would not be able to deliver this obligation by himself, urged the said earl with secret words, that when he [Kildare] himself with his army, was preparing and assembling his army for the aforesaid justiciar, that, before withdrawal from his land, he should go to the council of the king in Dublin. And by the unanimous agreement of the council he should do this, in order that the custody of his lands in his absence [should be protected]. If thereafter any evil should happen to his lands in his absence, it should be charged to the council of the king and not to himself. Therefore, the earl, extending trust to the words of the knight, and not estimating treachery on his part, arranged to come to Dublin himself. When therefore he had come and he himself was in the exchequer court together with others of the king's council sitting in council, and wholly ignorant of any treachery, he was suddenly betrayed by the aforesaid lord William. He was distrained or arrested and captured and was led to the castle of the said city and imprisoned.[815]

Item, dictus Justiciarius partes Oconnill in Momonia,^{a} et partes Kernigie, cum suo exercitu, intravit, et duo castrum comitis Dessemonie, scilicet, castrum de Ynyskysty, et castrum de Insula proditiose cepit, in quo castro de Insula,^{b} milites in eodem castro existentes, videlicet, dominus Eustacius le Poer, dominus Willelmus Graunte, dominus Johannes Coterell, primo tracti, deinde suspensi, mense Octobris, morti exponuntur.

Item, dictus comes Dessemonie, cum quibusdam aliis de suis militibus, per dictum justiciarium exulant. Hiis igitur factis, justiciarius, antedictus de Momonia cum suis ad suam consortem, tunc pregnantem,^{c} apud Killmaynan, que est iuxta Dublin, commorantem, rediens mense Novembris, preter illa que contra laycos^d extiterant facta, quosdam illorum indictando et incarcerando, et eas^e bonis suis spoliando; verum viros ecclesiasticos, tam sacerdotes quam clericos nonnullos, indictari fecit et indictatos cepit et incarceravit, ac pecunias non modicum ab eisdem extorsit.

Item, concessiones terrarum illorum, videlicet, quos prius eis de terres privaverat, et diversis contulit, ut dictum est, necnon literas super concessis sic per eum et sigillo Regio sigillatas, revocavit, et illas ab eis cepit, et fregit et penitus a nullavit.^{f}

{no*ta* de nominibus militum}

Item, omnes manucaptore dicti comitis Dessemonie numero viginti sex, tam comitum quam baronum et militum et aliorum de terra quorum nomina sunt hec, videlicet, dominus Willelmus de Burgo, comes Ultonie, dominus Jacobus le Botiler, comes Ormonie, Ricardus le Tuyt, miles, Nicholaus de Verdon, miles, Mauricius de Rupe Forti, miles, Eustacius le Power, miles, Geraldus de Rupe Forti, miles, Joannes filius Roberti ^le Pover^g^, miles, Robertus le^h Barry, miles, Mauricius Filius Geraldi, miles, Joannes le^i Wellesley, miles, Walterus Lenfaunte, miles, Ricardus de la Rokell, miles, Henricus Traharne, miles, Rogerus le Power, miles, Johannes Lenfaunt factus^j miles, Rogerus le Power, miles, Matheus filius Henrici, miles, Ricardus le Walleys, miles, Edmundus de Burgo, miles, filius comitis Ultonie, David de Barry, |Folio 33v| Willelmus filius Geraldi, Fulco de Fraxinis, Robertus filius Mauricii, Henricus filius^k de Berkeley, Joannes filius Georgii de Rupe, Thomas de Lees de Burgo. Non obstantibus laboribus et propriis expensis quas illorum aliqui cum dicto Justiciario in sua guerra fecerant, dictum comitem Dessemonie prosequendo, eorum terris sentencialiter in iudicio^l privavit et exheredavit, et Regis voluntati eorum corpora applicavit, iiii^or^ personis de predictis duntaxat exceptis, quarum nomina personarum sunt hec, videlicet, Willelmus de Burgo, comes Ultonie, Jacobus le Botilier, comes Ormonie.

---

^{a} *marg. note (same hand)*: nö L. ^{b} capto *added* L. ^{c} rediens mense Novembris *added here, struck through and repeated on next line (eyeskip error?)*. ^{d} laicos L. ^{e} eos L. ^{f} a *end of line*: nullavit *beginning of next line*. adnullavit L. ^{g} *inserted in margin*. ^{h} de L. ^{i} de L. ^{j} factus *omitted* L. ^{k} *cancelled by underdotting and crossing out* L. ^{l} in judicio *omitted* L.

Item, the said justiciar with his army entered the district of Uí Chonaill in Munster and parts of Kerry and he treacherously seized two castles of the earl of Desmond (namely the castle of Askeaton and Castleisland).[816] In Castleisland, in the month of October, the knights, namely lord Eustace le Poer, lord William Grant and lord John Coterel[817] being in the same castle, were first drawn then hanged [and] put on display in death.[818]

Item, the said earl of Desmond with certain others of his knights, was exiled by the said justiciar. In the month of November, after this was done, the aforesaid justiciar with his men were returning from Munster to his wife then pregnant and remaining at Kilmainham, which is near Dublin, in addition to that which had been done against the laity (some of them he had indicted and imprisoned and he plundered their goods), he also caused several ecclesiastical men, both priests and clerics, to be indicted and, standing indicted, took and imprisoned and extorted not a little money from the same.

Item, the grants of their lands (namely those who before had been deprived of their lands), he bestowed on various [men], as was said. And also he revoked the deeds on those grants. And with the seal of the king signed by him, he took those from them and completely broke into pieces and ruined.

{Notes the names of the knights}

Item, all the [previous] mainpernors of the said earl of Desmond[819] in number twenty six, both earls and barons and knights and others of the land of which the names are these: namely, lord William de Burgh, earl of Ulster, lord James Butler, earl of Ormond, Richard le Tuyt, knight, Nicholas de Verdun, knight, Maurice de Rocheford, knight, Eustace le Poer, knight, Gerald de Rocheford, knight, John, son of Robert le Poer, knight, Robert de Barry, knight, Maurice fitz Gerald, knight, John le Wellesley, knight, Walter Lenfaunt, knight, Richard de la Rochelle, knight, Henry Traharne, knight, Roger le Poer, knight, John Lenfaunt, having been made a knight, Roger le Poer, knight, Matthew fitz Henry, knight, Richard le Waleys, knight, Edmund de Burgh, knight (son of the earl of Ulster), David de Barry, William fitz Gerald, Fulk de la Freigne, Robert fitz Maurice, Henry de Berkeley, John, son of George de Roche, Thomas de Lees de Burgh. Notwithstanding their efforts and their own payments that some of them had made with the said justiciar in his war pursuing the said earl of Desmond, he judicially stripped and disinherited them of their lands. And he placed their bodies to the will of the king – merely excepting four of the aforesaid persons of whom the names of the persons are these, namely, William de Burgh, earl of Ulster, lord James Butler, earl of Ormond [L: adds etc].[820]

*Anno[a] domini M. CCCXLVI

Dominica in Ramis, que fuerat ix die mensis Aprilis, dominus Radulphus Ufford,[b] justiciarius Hibernie prenominatus, viam ingreditur[c] universe carnis. In cuius in[d] morte in mesticiam non modicam sui vertuntur, unacum uxore. De cuius etiam morte turba fidelium letatur Hibernie, ac clerus populusque terre pre gaudio ex hac[e] vita migrationis sue cum cordis tripudio solempne festum celebrat Paschale. In eius morte cessaverunt flumina, aeris intemperies, unde filium Dei laudat plebs fidelis. Mortuo igitur justiciario, in capsa plumbea fortiter incluso, comitissa antedicta cum thesauro predicto, inter tamen sanctorum reliquias minime collocando, cum diro dolore cordis, viscerium in Anglia humando ad partes predictam transtulit se denuo mense Maii. Mensis etiam ejusdem dieque secundo, en[f] prodigium non dubium a superis miraculose monstratum, illa enim que prius in suo ingressu cum signis Regiis, magnaque constipata milicia, per valvas Dublin in civitatem eandem gloriose est ingressa, exindeque cum suis licet brevi tempore vitam ducens regiam in Hibernie insula, in eiusdem vero egressu a civitate predicta clam per posticum castri ville premisse vulgi clamorem vitans, super debitis contractis vulgo reddendo ferre non posse, cum signis mortis, meroris[g] tristicie, ad propria remeando, cum suis inglorie mesteque est ingressa.

Item, post mortem dicti[h] justiciarii Hibernie, dominus Rogerus Darcy, de assensu et ordinatione regalium et aliorum ejusdem terre in justiciarie officio ad tempus ponitur.

Item, castra de Ley et Kilmehede per Hibernicos capiuntur et conburuntur, mense Aprili.

Item, Dominus Johannes filius[i] Mauricius venit capitalis justitiarius Hibernie, xv die mensis Maii.

Item, Mauricius filius Thome, comes Kildarie, inventis xxiiii[or] manucaptoribus, a carcere Dublin | Folio 34r | † xxiii die mensis[j] Maii, per dominum justiciarium liberatur.

Item, magna strages Anglicorum Ergalensium, numero ccc ad minus, facta est per Ybernicos Ultonienses, mense Junii.

Item, dictus dominus Johannes Mauricii, justiciarius Hibernie,[k] ab officio justiciarie per regem Anglie deponitur, et dominus Walterus de Bermyngham in eodem officio per regem antedictum instituitur, et Hiberniam mense Junii, modicum post predictam stragem commissam, cum officio ingreditur.

Item, Domino Mauricio filio Thome, comiti Dessemonie, tuitio pacis ad[l] certum tempus per regem Anglie conceditur. Qua concessa, in vigilia Exaltationis Sancte Crucis, in[m] portu de Yoghill, unacum sua uxore et duobus filiis, ad partes se transfert Anglicanas, ubi suam iusticiam super iniuriis sibi

---

[a] T; L. [b] *margin*, Nota de obitu Raldulphi Ufford L. [c] ingreditur *omitted* L. [d] in *omitted* L. [e] hac *omitted* L. [f] [?]heu L. [g] et *added* L. [h] predicti L. [i] filius *omitted*; Laud is correct see footnote in translation. [j] mensis *omitted* L. [k] marg. note (same hand): nö. [l] et L. [m] de L.

1346[821]

Palm Sunday, which was the ninth day of the month of April, [Palm Sunday 9 April 1346] lord Ralph Ufford, the aforenamed justiciar of Ireland, went the way of flesh.[822] At whose death many of his [men] together with the wife, retreated in sadness.[823] Also, concerning the same death, the multitude of loyal subjects of Ireland rejoiced. And first the clergy and the people of the land rejoiced from his death, [then] with hearts dancing, they solemnly celebrated that feast of Easter [16 April]. On his death the floods and wild air ceased, whereupon the faithful people praised the son of God. Therefore, after the death of the justiciar, the aforesaid countess, with the aforesaid treasure (scarcely to be reckoned among the relics of saints) – in a casket strongly enclosed with lead with the entrails to be interred in England, she herself – with awful grief of heart – crossed over to the said region, again in the month of May. Also, in the same month and on the second day [Tuesday 2 May 1346?] behold [there was] without doubt a wonder shown miraculously from above. For she, that in her first coming (with the standard of the king and great crowd of soldiers) gloriously entered through the doors of Dublin in the same city, and from then (even if for this brief time) living the life of a queen in the island of Ireland, now she left secretly the aforesaid city by the postern gate of the castle of the town avoiding the clamour of the ordinary people (for she was not able to pay the debts contracted with the people). With the sign of death, sorrowful and disconsolate, she returned to her own and sad she entered without glory.[824]

Item, after the death of the said justiciar of Ireland, lord Roger Darcy, with the assent and decree of the *regalium* and others of the said land, was, for the period, placed in the office of justiciar.[825]

Item, in the month of April the castles of Lea and Kilmohide were captured and burnt by the Irish.[826]

Item, on the fifteenth day of the month of May [Mon. 15 May 1346], lord John fitz Maurice came as chief justiciar of Ireland.[827]

Item, on twenty-third day of the month of May [Tues. 23 May 1346], Maurice fitz Thomas, earl of Kildare, finding twenty-four mainpernors, was released from the prison of Dublin by the lord justiciar.[828]

Item, in the month of June, a great massacre of the English of Uriel (of number at least three hundred) by the Irish of Ulster.[829]

Item, the said lord John Maurice, justiciar of Ireland, was discharged from the office of justiciar by the king of England. And lord Walter de Bermingham was placed in the same office by the aforesaid king. And he entered the office in Ireland in the month of June, a little after the aforesaid massacre began.[830]

Item, the protection of the peace was granted by the king of England to lord Maurice fitz Thomas, earl of Desmond, for a fixed time. After this was granted, on the eve of the exaltation of the Holy Cross [Wed. 13 Sept. 1346], from the port of Youghal, he himself together with his wife and two sons crossed over into

illatis per dominum Radulphum de Wfford, quondam justiciarium Hibernie, superius ~~ano~~ annotatum, corditer prosequitur.

Item, dicto comiti, de mandate et ordinacione domini regis Anglie, a suo ingressu in terram premissam xx solidi indies conceduntur et pro suis expensis indies etiam conferuntur.

Item, Dominus Walterus de Bermyngham, justiciarius Hibernie, et dominus Mauritius filius Thome, comes Kildarie, insurgunt mense Novembri contra Omorda et suos complices qui castra prescripta de Ley et Kylmehede conbusserunt, et eum et suos complices sic strenue cum suis exercitibus, prosequuntur, aggrediuntur et invadunt spoliando, necando, et comburendo quod dictus Omorda et sui complices, licet idem in principio cum multis millibus Hibernicorum fortiter eisdem et pertinaciter restitissent, in fine compulsi se Regis gratie subiecerunt, et dicti comitis voluntati se totaliter reddiderunt.

•*a* A**NNO DOMINI** M. CCCXLVII
{No*ta* **de transit comitis Kildarie ad adiutiorum regis**}
Comes Kildarie cum baronibus et militibus transfert se*b* ad regem Anglie, in sui adiutorium tunc apud Caleys in obsidione existente.

Item, villa de Calis per inhabitantes in eodem iiii^{to} die mensis Junii regi Anglie redditur.

Item, Walterus Bonevile et*c* Willelmus Calfe, et Willelmus Wellesley, et multi alii nobiles et validi, tam de Anglia quam de Hibernia et Wallia, in infirmitate constituti apud Caleys obierunt.

Item, M^cmurgh, videlicet, Donaldus M^cmurgh, filius Donaldi Arte M^cmurgh, rex Lagenie, v die mensis Junii per suos proditiose interficitur.

Item, Mauricius filius Thome, comes Kildarie, a rege ange*d* Anglie miles instituitur.

Item, dictus comes filiam Domini Bartholomei de Burwasse in uxorem duxit.

Item, villa de Nanagh, que vocatur Nenagh, cum tota patria adiacente, in festo Beati Stephani, martiris, ab Hibernicis comburitur.*e*

Hyc finitur cronica Pembrig*f*

|Folio 34v| * Item obiit domina Iohanna fitz Leones, quondam uxor domini Simonis Genevile, sepulta in conventu fratrum predicatorum apud Trim ii idus Aprilis.

---

a additional words et Edwardi tercii xxi *added another hand in* L.   *b mense Maii added* L.   *c* et *omitted* L.   *d* ange *probably an uncorrected spelling error for next word* Anglie.   *e* T; *last line written underneath the last ruled line.*   *f not present* L.

the region of England, where he wholeheartedly pursued his own justice upon wrongs inflicted by lord Ralph Ufford, formerly justiciar of Ireland, as noted above.[831]

Item, by command and order of the lord king of England, twenty shillings daily was allowed to the said earl from his permitted entry to the land; and for his daily expenses he was granted the same.[832]

Item, in the month of November lord Walter de Bermingham, justiciar of Ireland, and lord Maurice fitz Thomas, earl of Kildare, rose in arms against Ó Mórdha and his accomplices (who burnt the above-noted castles of Lea and Kilmohide).[833] And they, with their forces (thus strong with their armies), pursued, attacked and entered in order to plunder, kill and burn. The said Ó Mórdha and his forces, with many thousands of Irish, although they strongly and steadfastly resisted in the beginning, were compelled to make a fine and they submitted themselves to the grace of the king – and returned themselves freely and totally to the said earl.[834]

1347

{Note the crossing of the earl of Kildare to the help of the king}

The earl of Kildare himself crossed with the barons and knights to the king of England, to his assistance at Calais which was besieged [L: adds in the month of May].[835]

Item, on the fourth day of the month of June [Wed. 4 June 1347], the town of Calais was given up to the king of England, by the inhabitants of the same.[836]

Item, Walter Boneville[837] and William Calf, and William Wellesley[838] and many other nobles and strong [men], both of England and Ireland and Wales, died of sickness present at Calais.[839]

Item, Mac Muchadha, namely Domhnall Mac Murchadha, son of Domhnall [son of] Art Mac Murchadha, king of Leinster, was treacherously killed by his [men] on the fifth day of the month of July [Thurs. 5 July].[840]

Item, Maurice fitz Thomas, earl of Kildare, was created a knight by the king of England.

Item, the said earl married the daughter of lord Bartholomew de Burghersh.

Item, on the feast of Blessed Stephen martyr [Wed. 26 Dec. 1347], the vill of Nanagh (which is called Nenagh), with all the adjacent country, was burnt by the Irish.[841]

Here ends the chronicle of Pembridge[842]

Item, lady Joanna fitz Leon, formerly wife of lord Simon de Geneville, died and was buried in the convent of the Friars Preachers at Trim on 2 Id. April [Easter Sunday 12 April 1348?].[843]

ANNO DOMINI M. CCCXLVIII ET ANNO XXII R. R.[a] E. TERTII
Prima pestilentia et maxima in Hibernia que inceperat antea in aliis terris.

{Concessio baronie de Kenlys in Osseria}

Item,[b] isto anno, dominus Walterus Bermyngham, justiciarius Hibernie, intravit Angliam et dimisit Fratrem Johannem Archere, priorem de Kylmaynan, loco suo suum locum-tenentem. Et iterum revertitur eodem anno justiciarius ut prius, et rex contulit baroniam de Kenlys eidem Walthero, que est in Osseria, quia duxit grandem exercitum contra comitem Dessemonie cum Radulpho Ufford, ut prius scribitur, que baronia quondam fuit domini Eustacii le Pover, qui fuit tractus et suspensus apud castrum de Iland.

ANNO DOMINI M. CCCXLIX [NO REGNAL YEAR]
Cessit dominus Walterus de Bermyngham, optimus justiciarius ab officio justiciarie, cui successit dominus de Carreve, miles ac Baro.

ANNO DOMINI M. €€€[c] CCCL ET ANNO R R EIUSDEM[d] PREDICTI[e] XXIIII
Dominus Thomas Rokisby, miles, factus est justiciarius Hibernie.

{Nota de obitu domini Walteri de Bermyngham}

Item,[f] obiit dominus Walterus Bermyngham, miles, quondam optimus justiciarius Hibernie, in vigilia Sancte Margarete, virginis, in Anglia.

*ANNO DOMINI M. CCCLI ET DICTI REGIS XXV
Obiit Kenwricus Sherman, quondam maior civitatis Dublin, sub campanili Fratrum Predicatorum eiusdem civitatis, quod campanile ipse erexit, et vitreavit fenistram in capite chori, et fieri fecit tectum ecclesie et multa bona. In eodem conventu vi kl Marcii obiit. In fine vite sue condidit testamentum suum ad valorem trium mille marcarum, et legavit multa bona ecclesie, sacerdotibus et[g] religiosis et secularibus per xx miliaria circa civitatem.

*ANNO DOMINI [M.][h] CCCLII ET ANNO EJUSDEM R. R. XXVI [i]
Dominus Robertus Savage, miles, in Ultonia incepit edificare nova castella in diversis locis ac in maneriis suis, qui, dum construeret, dixit filio suo et heredi, Domino Henrico Savage, 'Faciamus muros fortes circa nos, ne forte veniant Hibernici et tollent nostrum locum et gentem nostram destruant, et erimus in opprobium cunctis gentibus'. Tunc respondit filius, 'Ubicunque fuerint homines fortes, ibi est castrum vel castellum, iuxta illud, 'filii ca[–]
|Folio 35r| † [–]strametati sunt, id est, fortes ordinati sunt ad bellum, ideo, semper ero inter fortes homines, sic ero in castro, et dixit in vulgari melius est

---

[a] et anno xxii R E iii L. [b] T; *marg. note (same hand)*, concessio baronie de Kenlys in Osseria in L. [c] *struck through.* [d] *underdotted.* [e] et anno regni regis predicti ^E iiii. *The* ^E *is a later addition.* [f] *red box, black text,* T; *marg. note (same hand)*, nō de obitu Walter Bermyngham L. [g] et *omitted* L. [h] m *omitted* L. [i] et anno ejusdem regis xxvj; *marg. note (same hand)*: nō de Roberto savage milite L.

1348 and the 22nd year of the reign of King Edward III[844]
The first and greatest plague in Ireland – which previously began in other lands.[845]

{Grant of the barony of Kells in Ossory}

Item, in this year lord Walter de Bermingham, justiciar of Ireland, entered England and left in his place as his deputy Friar John Archer, prior of Kilmainham. And he returned again in the same year, justiciar as before.[846] And the king conferred the barony of Kells (which is in Ossory) to the same Walter, because he led a large army against the earl of Desmond with Ralph Ufford, as previously written.[847] This barony was formerly [the property] of lord Eustace le Poer who was drawn and hanged at Castleisland.[848]

1349
Lord Walter de Bermingham, the very best justiciar, departed from the office of justiciar,[849] to whom succeeded lord [John] de Carew, knight and baron.[850]

1350 and in the 24th year of the reign of the aforesaid king
Lord Thomas Rokeby, knight, was made justiciar of Ireland.[851]

{Note the death of lord Walter de Bermingham}

Item, lord Walter Bermingham, knight, once the very best justiciar of Ireland, died in England on the eve of [the feast] of St Margaret, virgin [Mon. 19 July].[852]

1351 and 25th of the said king
Kendrick Sherman, formerly mayor of the city of Dublin, died.[853] And [was buried] under the campanile of the Friars Preachers of the same city, which campanile he himself erected and he glazed the window in the chapter choir[854] and he was responsible for the roof of the church and many other good [things]. In the same convent he died on 6 Kal. March [Thurs. 24 February 1351].[855] At the end of his life he made his will to the value of three thousand marks, and he left many goods to the church, to the priests, both religious and secular, within twenty miles around the city.[856]

1352 and in the year of same reign of the king 26
Lord Robert Savage, knight, began to build new castles in many places in Ulster and on his manors.[857] While he was building, he said to his son and heir, lord Henry Savage, 'Let us make strong walls around us, lest strong Irish should come and take away our place and destroy our people and we shall be in disgrace to all of the people'.[858] Then his son answered, 'Wherever there may be strong men, there is a castle or fort near them: "The sons pitched camp, that is, were bravely arranged for battle".[859] Therefore I want to be among strong men always; thus I will be [as if] at a castle' and he said in the common tongue, 'Better is a castle of

castrum de bones quam de stones, scilicet, de ossibus quam de lapidibus'. Et tunc pater cessavit ab operibus, ira commotus, et iuravit quod nunquam construeret castrum*a* ex lapidibus et cemento, sed teneret ~~bonn~~*b* bonam domum et familiam multam nimis, et prophetavit de futuro quod filii dolerent et luerent. Quod et factum est, nam Hibernici destruxerunt totam illam patriam propter defectum castellorum.

Anno Domino M. CCCLV et eiusdem regis anno XXX
Dominus Thomas Rokesby, miles, cessit ab officio Justiciarie, xxvi die Julii, cui successit Mauricius filius Thome, comes Dessemonie, et duravit*c* usque ad mortem.

Item, in die Conversionis Sancti Pauli, obiit*d* dominus Mauricius filius Thome, in castro Dublin, justiciarius Hibernie, non sine magno suorum merore, et aliorum*e* pacem diligentium, Hibernicorum timore et tremore. Primo sepultus in choro predicatorum Dublin, ultimo humatus in conventu predicatorum de Traly. Hic justus ~~est~~*f* erat in officio in tantum quod suspendebat suos consanguineos pro furto, et rapina, et malefactis eorum, sicut alienos, et bene castigavit*g* Hibernicos.*h*

{*}
Anno Domini MCCCLVI et predicti regis anno XXXI
Iterum dominus Thomas Rokesby factus est justiciarius Hibernie, qui bene expugnavit Hibernicos, et bene solvebat pro victualibus suis, et dixit, '<u>Ego volo</u>*i* comedere et bibere de vasis ligneis tantum, et solvere aurum et argentum pro victu et vestitu et stipendiariis'.

Eodem anno, obiit predictus*j* dominus Thomas justiciarius Hibernie, in castro de Kylka.

{*}
{•} ### Anno Domini M⁰ CCCLVII et ejusdem regis anno XXXII*k*
Dominus Almaricus de Sancto Amando factus est capitalis justiciarius Hibernie, et eam intravit. Isto tempore, incepit magna controversia inter magistrum Ricardum FitzRowe, archiepiscopum Ardmachanum, et iiij ordines mendicantium, sed tandem prevaluerunt*l* imposito silentio Ardmachano per papam.*m*

Anno Domino M⁰ CCCLVIII et anno eiusdem regis XXXIII
Dominus Almaricus de Sancto Amando, justiciarius Hibernie, transivit.*n*

---

a castrum *omitted* L.   *b* *underdotted* L.   *c* in officio *added* L.   *d* idem *added* L.   *e* omnium *added* L.   *f* *Underdotted and struck through.*   *g* castigans L.   *h* *marg. note (later hand, illegible), plus a few lines down a possible pen trial.*   *i* Ego volo *underlined in same ink.*   *j* idem L.   *k* et ejusdem regis^ anno xxxii [^ primo *in another hand*].   *l* fratres *added* L.   *m* T; *marg. note (later hand)*: iiij oro[–].   *n* in Angliam *supplied. Note plenty of room online for* T.

bones than of *stones*', namely *de ossibus quam de lapidibus*'. And then the father, provoked by anger, ceased from the works, and swore that never would he build a castle from stones and mortar, but he would hold an excessively good house and great household and he prophesised in the future that sons should grieve and lament. And this happened for the Irish destroyed all that neighbourhood because of the absence of castles.[860]

1355 and the 30th year of the same king[861]

On the twenty-sixth day July [Sun. 26 July], lord Thomas Rokeby, knight, ceased from the office of justiciar;[862] to whom succeeded Maurice fitz Thomas, earl of Desmond, and he continued right up to death.[863]

Item, on the day of the Conversion of St Paul [Tues. 25 Jan. 1356], lord Maurice fitz Thomas, justiciar of Ireland, died in the castle of Dublin, not without the great grief of his men and of others loving peace [and the cause of] the fear and trembling of the Irish.[864] He was first buried in the choir of the Preachers of Dublin, lastly interred in the convent of the Preachers of Tralee. He was just in office such that he hanged his kinsmen, as well as others, for their theft and rape and evil deeds and he punished the Irish well.

1356 and the 31st year of the aforesaid king[865]

Lord Thomas Rokeby was appointed justiciar of Ireland again. He subdued the Irish well and he paid well for his provisions and said, 'I wish to eat and to drink only from vessels of wood – and pay gold and silver for food and for clothes and for wages'.[866]

In the same year the aforesaid lord Thomas [Rokeby], justiciar of Ireland, died in the castle of Kilkea.[867]

1357 and the 32nd year of the same king

Lord Almeric de St Amand was appointed chief justiciar of Ireland and he entered it [Ireland].[868] At this time a great controversy began between Master Richard fitz Ralph, archbishop of Armagh, and the four orders of mendicants;[869] but finally they prevailed, and silence was imposed on Armagh by the pope.

1358 and the 33rd year of the same king

Lord Almeric de St Amand, justiciar of Ireland, crossed the sea [to England].[870]

ANNO DOMINO M⁰ ~~CCCL~~ CCCLIX[a] ET ANNO DICTI REGIS XXXIIII
Jacobus le Botiler, comes Ormonie, factus est capitalis justiciarus Hibernie.

 Item, obiit domina Johanna de Burgo, comitissa de Kildare, in die Sancti Georgii |Folio 35v| sepulta est in ecclesia fratrum minorum de Kildare, juxta dominum Thomam filium[b] Johannis, comitem Kildarie, consortem suum.

ANNO DOMINI M⁰ CCCLX ET PREDICTI REGIS ANNO XXXV
 {No*ta* de morte et de obitu Ricardi Fitz-Rowe, primatis}
Obiit Magister Ricardus filius Radulphi,[c] archiepiscopus Armachanus, in Aviniona xvi kl Decembris. Cujus ossa per venerabilem patrem Stephanum, episcopum Midie, in Hiberniam dilata sunt ad recondendum in ecclesia Sancti Nicholai de Dondalk, unde fuit oriundus, sed dubium[d] est aliquibus si sunt ossa illius vel alterius.

 Item[e] _____

{No*ta* de laudabali [?] confectione [?] Hibernicorum per Robertum Savage}
Anno eodem,[f] dominus Robertus Savage,[g] miles strenuus, in Ultonia manens, qui cum paucis Anglicis uno die interfecit de Hibernicis tria millia juxta Antrum, sed antequam transivit ad illud bellum ordinavit dari unicuique Anglico unum bonum haustum seu potum de vino sive[h] de servicia, quibus doliis ~~plenus~~ plenis habundabat, et residuum servavit usque ad adventum suorum, et fecit occidi oves et boves, volatilia, altilia, volucres celi et cervos de venatione, ut essent parata victoribus redeuntibus de prelio, quicunque essent. Quia dixit, obprobrium esset sibi, si hospites venirent et non haberent quod manducarent vel biberent. Sed Deo dante victoriam Anglicis, optinentibus[i] omnes invitavit ad cenam, et letati sunt cum gratiarum actione, et dixit, Deo gratias ago, quia sic melius servare est quam effundere in terram ut quidam consueverant.[j] Sepultus est in conventu fratrum predicatorum de Coulrath, juxta aquam de Banne.

 Item, Comes Ormonie, justiciarius Hibernie, intravit Angliam, in cujus loco Mauricius filius Thome, comes Kildarie, factus est justiciarius Hibernie, per cartam et commissionem, ut patet.

> Omnibus ad quos litere pervenerint, salute. Sciatis quod commisimus dilecto et fideli nostro Mauricio, comiti de Kildare, officium justiciarie nostre terre nostre Hibernie et terram nostram Hiberniam, cum castris et omnibus pertinenciis suis custodiendis quamdiu nobis placuerit. Recipiendo ad scaccarium nostrum Dublin per annum, quamdiu in officio

---

[a] M CCC LV *followed by a small gap.*   [b] filius L.   [c] *black box and text*, T. nota de obitu ricardi fitz rowe primate L.   [d] dublinum L.   [e] Item *placed halfway on the line with rest of line a gap-in mistake for* Anno.   [f] anno eodem *omitted; sentence begins*: Item obit dominus Robertus Savage.   [g] *Black box here and text. margin* nota de laudabili confeccione Hibernicorum per Robertum Savage *in* L.   [h] seu L.   [i] optinentibus *omitted* L.   [j] consulerunt L.

1359 and the 34th year of the said king
James Butler, earl of Ormond, was appointed chief justiciar of Ireland.⁸⁷¹

Item, lady Johanna de Burgh, countess of Kildare, died on the feast day of St George [Tues. 23 April]. She was buried in the church of the Friars Minor of Kildare next to lord Thomas fitz John, earl of Kildare, her husband.⁸⁷²

1360 and the 35th year of the aforesaid king⁸⁷³
{Note the death and *de obitu* of Richard fitz Ralph Primate}
Master Richard fitz Ralph, archbishop of Armagh, died in Avignon on 16 Kal. December [Mon. 16 Nov.]. His bones were carried to Ireland by the venerable Father Stephen, bishop of Meath, to be buried in the church of St Nicholas of Dundalk where he originated; but it is doubted by some if they are the bones of him or another.⁸⁷⁴

{Note the praiseworthy (?) defeat (?) of the Irish by Robert Savage}
Item, in the same year lord Robert Savage, a vigorous knight living in Ulster, who with a few of the English, in one day killed three thousand of the Irish near Antrim.⁸⁷⁵ But before he went to that battle he ordered each Englishman to be given one good draught or pot of wine or of ale, of which he had many casks. And the rest he saved until the arrival back of his [men]. And he ordered sheep and oxen, fowl, fattened poultry, flying birds of the skies, and hunting stags to be killed – in order that they should be prepared for the victorious returning from battle, whosoever they might be. Because he said, 'It would be shame to himself if guests should come and they had nothing to eat or drink'. And indeed, God gave victory to the English and all of the most noble were invited to the feast and they were rejoicing with gratitude at the giving of thanks. And he said, 'I give thanks to God because it is better in this way to preserve, than to waste/shed in the earth as some are accustomed'. He was buried in the convent of the Friars Preachers of Coleraine, near the water of the Bann.⁸⁷⁶

Item, the earl of Ormond, justiciar of Ireland, entered England; Maurice fitz Thomas, earl of Kildare, was appointed justiciar of Ireland in his place by charter and commission as it is manifest:

> To all to whom these letters shall come, greeting. Know that we have entrusted to our beloved and faithful Maurice, earl of Kildare, the office of justiciar of our land of our [*sic*] Ireland, to keep our land of Ireland with castles and all their appurtenances, as long as it pleases us. To receive at our exchequer at Dublin each year, as long as he remains thus in that office, five

illo sic steterit, quingentas libras, pro quibus officium illud et terram custodiet; et erit vicesimus de hominibus ad arma cum tot equis coopertis, commissione continue durante nostra supradicta. In cujus rei testimonium, etc. Datum per |Folio 36| manus dilecti nostri in Christo, Fratris Thome de Burley, prioris*a* Sancti Johannis Ierusalem in Hibernia, cancellarii nostri Hibernie, apud Dublin, xxx die Martii, anno regni nostri xxxv.

Item iterum venit dominus Jacobus le Botiller, comes Ormonie, de Anglia in Hiberniam justiciarius Hibernie ut prius, cui cessit comes Kildarie ab officio iusticiarie.

‡
Anno domini m^o ccclxi
Leonellus, comes Ultonie, iure hereditario uxoris sue, et filius domini regis Anglie, venit in Hiberniam, tenens locum Domini Regis, et applicuit apud Dublin in octava die Nativitatis Beate Virginis, ducens secum uxorem suam, Elizabeth, filiam et heredem domini Willelmi de Burgo, comitis Ultonie. Eodem anno, pestilentia secunda.*b* Obierunt in Anglia Henricus, dux Lancastrie, comes Marchie, comes Northamonie.*c*

Item, vi idus Januarii, Mauricius Doncref, civis Dublin, sepultus in cimeterio predicatorum ejusdem civitatis, cui conventui dedit xl libras ad vitreandam ecclesiam.

Item, obierunt domina Johanna Flemyng, uxor domini Galfridi Trevers, et domina Margareta Bermyngham, uxor domini Roberti Preston, in vigilia Sancte Margarete, sepulte in conventu predicatorum de Drogheda.

Item, Dominus Walterus Bermyngham junior obiit in die Sancti Laurencii qui divisit hereditatem suam sororibus, quarum unam partem accepit predictus Preston.

Item, predictus Dominus Leonellus, postquam intraverat Hiberniam et requievit paucis diebus, fecit gueram cum Obrenne, et clamavit in exercitu suo*d* et centum de stipendiariis suis interfecti sunt. Statim hoc videns, Leonellus, redegit totum populum, tam de Anglia quam de Hibernia, in unum et bene prosperatur, et fecit plura bella circumquaque cum Hibernicis cum adiutorio Dei et populi Hibernie et fecit plures milites de Anglia et Hibernia, inter quos Robertum Preston, Robertum Holywod, Thomam Talbot, Walterum Cusak, Jacobum de la Hyde, Joannem de Fraxinis, Patricium et Robertum de Fraxinis, et plures alios.

Item, transtulit Scaccarium de Dublin ad Carlagh, et dedit quingentas libras ad murandam eandem villam.

Item, in festo*e* Sancti Mauri, abbatis, fuit ventus vehemens, pinnacula, camina, et cetera eminentiora, arbores ultra numerum, et campa[–]

---

a hospitalis *added* L.   *b marg. note (same hand)*: 2n pestilentia.   *c* Northantoine L.   *d* quod nullus nativus de Hibernia appropinquaret exercitui suo *added. There is no gap in* T   *e* in *omitted* L.

hundred pounds – for which he shall keep that office and land. And he shall have twenty men-at-arms with as many covered horses during the continuance of our aforesaid commission.[877] In testimony of which thing *et cetera*. Given by our hand to our beloved in Christ, Friar Thomas de Burley, prior of St John of Jerusalem in Ireland, our chancellor of Ireland,[878] at Dublin 30th day March in the 35th year of our reign [30 March 1361].[879]

Item, James Butler, earl of Ormond, returned again from England to Ireland, justiciar of Ireland as before, to whom ceded the earl of Kildare from the office of justiciar.

1361[880]
Lionel, earl of Ulster (by right of the inheritance of his wife), and son of the lord king of England,[881] came to Ireland, as lieutenant of the lord king.[882] And he landed at Dublin on the octave day of the nativity of the Blessed Virgin [Wed. 15 Sept], bringing with him his wife Elizabeth, daughter and heir of lord William de Burgh, earl of Ulster.[883] In the same year, the second plague.[884] Henry, duke of Lancaster, the earl of March and the earl of Northampton, died in England.[885]

Item, on 6 Id. January [Fri. 8 January] Maurice Doncref, citizen of Dublin, died [and] was buried in the cemetery of the Preachers of the same city; to which convent he gave forty pounds to glaze the church.[886]

Item, lady Johanna Fleming, wife of lord Geoffrey Travers, and lady Margaret Bermingham, wife of lord Robert Preston, died on the eve of St Margaret [Margaret, virgin and martyr, Mon. 19 July or Queen Margaret 7 July] [and] they were buried in the convent of the preachers of Drogheda.[887]

Item, lord Walter Bermingham, the younger, died on the day of St Laurence [10 August or 3 Feb]; he divided his inheritance [among] his sisters, of which the aforesaid Preston received one part.[888]

Item, the aforesaid lord Lionel, after he had entered Ireland and rested for a few days, made war with the Uí Bhroin.[889] And he claimed in his army [L: that no native of Ireland would come near to his army], and a hundred of his paid soldiers were killed.[890] Immediately, seeing this, Lionel brought back all the people, both of the English and of the Irish, into one and he truly prospered and, with the help of God and the people of Ireland, brought about many battles on all sides with the Irish.[891] And he made many knights, both of England and of Ireland, among whom was Robert Preston,[892] Robert Holywood,[893] Thomas Talbot, Walter Cusack,[894] James de la Hyde, John de Freigne, Patrick and Robert de Freigne,[895] and many others.

Item, he transferred the exchequer from Dublin to Carlow and he gave five hundred pounds to wall that town.[896]

Item, on the feast of St Maurice, abbot [Sat. 15 Jan. 1362] there was a furious wind. Spires, chimneys, and other lofty building, trees beyond number, and

|Folio 36v| † [–]nilia diversa, et campanile fratrum predicatorum, Dublin, quassavit et ad terram proiecit.

‡
ANNO DOMINI M⁰ CCCLXII ET ANNO EJUSDEM REGIS E. XXXVJ
Ecclesia Sancti Patricii, Dublin, igne Johannis Sext^ae^yn, crematur viii idus Aprilis.

ANNO DOMINI M⁰ CCCLXIIII ET ANNO PREDICTI REGIS XXXVIII
Dominus Leonellus, comes Ultonie, xxii die Aprilis intravit Angliam et dimisit suum Justiciarium Hibernie, comitem Ormonie, et idem Leonellus rediit, dux Clarencie, xviii*ᵃ* die Decembris.

ANNO DOMINI M⁰ CCCLXV ET ANNO PREDICTI REGIS XXXIX
Idem Leonellus, Dux Clarencie, transivit in Angliam, relinquens post se Dominum Thomam Dale, militem, suum custodem ac iusticiarium Hibernie.

ANNO DOMINI M⁰ CCCLXVII
Incepit magna guerra inter les Bermynghames de Carbry et homines de Midia, quia magna latrocinia fiunt in Midia per predictos. Tunc Dominus Robertus de Preston, miles, Principalis Baro Scaccarii, posuit magnam custodiam in castro de Carbry, et multum expendebat contra inimicos Regis, defendendum*ᵇ* ius suum ratione uxoris sue.

    Item, Geraldus Fitz Morice, Comes Dessemonie, factus est iusticiarius Hibernie.

‡
ANNO DOMINI MO CCCLXVIII ET ANNO EIUSDEM REGIS E. XLII
In Carbra, post quoddam parliamentum ~~inter hi~~ finitum inter Hibernicos et Anglicos, capti sunt Frater Thomas Burley, prior de Kylmaynan, cancellarius regis in Hibernia, Johannes Fitz Richer, vicecomes Midie, dominus Robertus Terell, baro de Castelknok, cum multis aliis per les Bermynghames et alios de Carbria, tunc tunc*ᶜ* Jacobus de Bermyngham, qui tentus erat in castro de Castro*ᵈ* de Trym, in manicis ferreis ac compedibus, tanquam*ᵉ* pro predicto Cancellario in cambio deliberatur; ceteri fecerunt redempciones.

    Item, ecclesia Sancte Marie de Trym igne conburitur ejusdem monasterii*ᶠ*
    Item, in vigilia Sancti Luce, Evangeliste, dominus Leonellus, dux Clarencie*ᵍ* |Folio 37r| obiit apud Albe in Pymond, primo sepultus in civitate Papie juxta Sanctum Augustinum doctorem, deinde sepelitur apud Clare, in conventu Augustinencium in Anglia.

ᵃ viii L.   *ᵇ* defendendo L.   *ᶜ* tunc *repeated.*   *ᵈ* capital C *on this second* castro.   *ᵉ* proditor *added* L.   *ᶠ* gap of about 9 letters.   *ᵍ* possible pen trial here in shape of snake.

various campaniles, and the campanile of the Friars Preachers, Dublin were flung to the ground.[897]

1362 and in the 36th year of the same king E. [Edward]
The church of St Patrick's, Dublin, was destroyed by the fire of John Sexton on 8 Id. April [Wed. 6 April 1362].[898]

1364 and in the 38th year of the aforesaid king
Lord Lionel, earl of Ulster, on 22 day of April [Mon. 22 April] entered England and left the earl of Ormond as his justiciar in Ireland.[899] And the same Lionel, returned on the eighteenth day[900] of December [as] duke of Clarence [Wed. 18 Dec.].[901]

1365 and in the 39th year of the aforesaid king
The same Lionel, duke of Clarence, crossed to England; leaving behind him lord Thomas Dale, knight, custodian and justiciar of Ireland.[902]

1367
A great war began between the Berminghams of Carbury and the men of Meath, because of the great robberies in Meath made by the aforesaid. Then lord Robert de Preston, knight, chief baron of the exchequer, placed a great ward in the castle of Carbury and spent much against the enemies of the king – to defend his right by reason of his wife.[903]

Item, Gerald fitz Maurice, earl of Desmond, was appointed justiciar of Ireland.[904]

1368 and the 42nd year of the same king
After a certain parley ended between the Irish and the English,[905] Friar Thomas Burley, prior of Kilmainham, chancellor of the king in Ireland, John fitz Richer, sheriff of Meath, lord Robert Tyrell, baron of Castleknock, with many others were captured in Carbury by the Berminghams and others of Carbury.[906] Then James de Bermingham, who was held in the castle of Trim Castle in iron handcuffs and shackles like a [L: traitor], was exchanged for the aforesaid chancellor.[907] The others were to make a ransom.

Item, the church of St Mary's of Trim was burnt by the fire of the same monastery.[908]

Item, on the eve of St Luke the evangelist [Tues. 17 Oct.] lord Lionel, duke of Clarence, died at Alba in Piedmont. First he was buried in the city of Pavia near St Augustine, doctor, then he was buried at Clare in the convent of the Augustinians [friars] in England.[909]

ANNO DOMINI M⁰ CCCLXIX ET ANNO PREDICTI REGIS XLIII
Dominus Willelmus de Wyndesore, miles strenuus in armis et animosus, xii kal Julii venit in Hiberniam tenens locum domini Regis, cui cessavit Geraldus filius M^a^uricii comes Dessemonie, ab officio Justicarie.

{•} **ANNO DOMINI M⁰ CCCLXX ET ANNO EJUSDEM REGIS XLIIII**
Incepit tercia pestilentia et maxima in Hibernia, in qua multi nobiles, cives, et pueri quasi infiniti obierunt.ᵃ Eodem anno Geraldus filius Mauricii, comes Dessemonie, dominus Johannes filiusᵇ Nicholai, et dominus Thomas filius Johannis, et alii multi nobiles, juxta monasterium de Magio, scilicet, Maii in comitatu Lymerici, per Obreen et M^camar de Thomond, vi idus Julii capti sunt, et plures interfecti, propter quod dictus locum tenens transivit Lymericum defendendam Momoniam, dimittendo guerras super Othotheles et ceteros Hibernicos in Lagenia. Isto anno, obierunt Dominus Robertus Terell, Baro de Castelknok, Domina Scolastica Houth, uxor ejus, et filius et heres eorundem, propter quod Johanna Terell et Matildis Terell, sorores dicti Roberti, diviserunt hereditatem inter se.

Item, obierunt dominus Symon Flemyng, baro de Slane, et dominus Johannes Cusak, baro de Colmolyn, et Johannes Taylour, quondam maior Dublin, vir dives et potens in pecuniis.ᶜ

ANNO DOMINI MCCCVIII ᵈ
~~Factus est~~ ———————————— ~~de Balymore~~
~~per magistrum (?) Johannem fitz~~——————————

ᵃ margin tertia pestilentia L.   ᵇ filius *omitted* L.   ᶜ *the last 3 words*, potens in pecuniis, *are two thirds indented in middle of last line of page thus clearly indicating that the scribe knew that the chronicle had ended* L.   ᵈ *The ending is the same in both manuscripts, but* T *has an entry, in a different and later hand, for 1408, four lines subsequently struck through and page ripped and torn.*

1369 and the 43rd year of the aforesaid king
On 12 Kal. July [Wed. 21 June] lord William de Windsor, a knight strong in arms and courageous, came to Ireland as deputy of the lord king; Gerald fitz Maurice, earl of Desmond yielded to him from the office of justiciar.[910]

1370 and the 44th year of the same king
The third and greatest plague began in Ireland in which many nobles, citizens, and almost innumerable children, died.[911] In the same year on 6 Id. July [Wed. 10 July 1370] Gerald fitz Maurice, earl of Desmond, lord John fitz Nicholas and lord Thomas fitz John and many other nobles, were captured near the monastery of Maigue (namely Maio) in the county of Limerick,[912] by Ó Briain and Mac Conmara of Thomond and many were killed. Because of this, the said deputy, giving up the wars against Ó Tuathail and other Irish in Leinster, crossed to Limerick to defend Munster.[913] In this year lord Robert Tyrell, baron of Castleknock, lady Scholastica Houth, his wife, and their son and heir died.[914] Because of this Joan Tyrell and Matilda Tyrell, sisters of the said Robert, divided the inheritance between themselves.

Item, lord Simon Fleming, baron of Slane,[915] and lord John Cusack, baron of Culmullin[916] and John Taillour, a powerful and wealthy man and formerly mayor of Dublin, died.[917]

Notes to the English translation of the Annals

1 Ob. Oct. 1161. Consecrated at Canterbury, Gregory (Gréine) received the pallium as Dublin's first archbishop in March 1152: Aubrey Gwynn, *The Irish church in the eleventh and twelfth centuries*, ed. Gerard O'Brien (Dublin, 1992), pp 65, 220; Flanagan, *Transformation*, pp 6–7.
2 *AMF*, p. 136; *CStM*, ii, pp 265–6; Lorcán Ó Tuathail (*c.*1128–80) was related through marriage to Diarmait Mac Murchada: Flanagan, *Irish society*, pp 30, 31, 46.
3 Use of the phrase *et cetera* suggests that Pembridge was quoting Giraldus. *AMF*, p. 136; called archbishop in *AClyn*, p. 134; for his cult in Ireland, see Colmán Ó Clabaigh and Michael Staunton, 'Thomas Becket and Ireland' in Diarmuid Scully and Elizabeth Mullins (eds), *Listen, O isles, unto me: studies in medieval word and image in honour of Jennifer O'Reilly* (Cork, 2011), pp 87–101.
4 Flanagan, *Irish society*, pp 79, 240; for Ó Conchobhair donations to St Mary's, see *CStM*, ii, p. xiv.
5 Empress of Germany, daughter of Henry I, mother of Henry II; she died at Rouen 10 September 1167: Marjorie Chibnal, *The Empress Matilda: queen consort, queen mother and lady of the English* (Oxford, 1991), p. 173.
6 *AMF*, p. 136; Almeric captured Bilbeis in 1169: Steven Runciman, *A history of the crusades*, 3 vols (London, 1978), ii, pp 362–81.
7 Tigernán Ó Ruairc was king of Bréifne; the Latin agrees with Giraldus, *Expug. Hib.*, p. 24; see also, Evelyn Mullally, *The deeds of the Normans in Ireland: La geste des Engleis en Yrlande* (Dublin, 2002), pp 53–6. For Giraldus in a St Mary's manuscript, see Bernard Meehan, 'A fourteenth-century historical compilation from St Mary's Cistercian abbey, Dublin' in Seán Duffy (ed.), *Medieval Dublin XV* (Dublin, 2016), p. 268; also, a Cistercian interest here as Ó Ruairc's wife Derbforgaill was a benefactor of Mellifont, buried there in 1193 aged 85 (*AFM*, iii, p. 97; Flanagan, *Transformation*, p. 201).
8 *AMF*, p. 136; Donnchadh was Ó Cerbaill, king of Airgialla (Donncha[dh] Ó Corráin, *Ireland before the Normans* (Dublin, 1972), pp 159–60, 164–9); Mellifont was the first Cistercian abbey in Ireland (Colmcille Conway (Ó Conbhuí), *The story of Mellifont* (Dublin, 1958); Flanagan, *Transformation*, pp 149–51, 202).
9 The Latin agrees with Giraldus, *Expug. Hib.*, pp 30, 31–3; for a description of fitz Stephen, ibid., p. 87; see also, M.T. Flanagan, 'Robert fitz Stephen (d. before 1192), adventurer', *ODNB*.
10 Richard fitz Gilbert de Clare (Strongbow), for whom, see Flanagan, *Irish society*, part II; Raymond le Gros, a cousin of Giraldus (*Expug. Hib.*, pp xxi, 57), married Basilia, *sororem comitis* (*CStM*, i, p. 260); see Orpen, *Normans*, p. 66.
11 Michael Altschul, *A baronial family in medieval England: the Clares, 1217–1314* (Baltimore, 1965), table III, at p. 332; Keith Stringer, *David of Huntingdon, 1152–1219: a study in Anglo-Scottish history* (Edinburgh, 1985).
12 The city was Waterford (Giraldus, *Expug. Hib.*, pp 64, 67); Flanagan, *Irish society*, pp 79–111.
13 Correct title of archbishop this time; Giraldus, *Expug. Hib.*, pp 73–5; *AClyn*, p. 134; Anne Duggan, 'Becket is dead! Long live Saint Thomas' in Paul Webster and M.P. Gelin (eds), *The cult of Saint Thomas Becket in the Plantagenet world, c.1170–c.1220* (Woodbridge, 2016), pp 25–52.

14 Giraldus, *Expug. Hib.*, pp 67–9; *CStM*, ii, pp 269; Mullally, *Deeds of the Normans*, pp 94–6; Seán Duffy, 'Ireland's Hastings: the Anglo-Norman conquest of Dublin' in Christopher Harper-Bill (ed.), *Anglo-Norman studies XX* (Woodbridge, 1998), pp 79–80.
15 Fermoy O.Cist. (*CStM*, ii, p. 234). For the Cistercian abbeys, see Roger Stalley, *The Cistercian monasteries of Ireland: an account of the history, art and architecture of the white monks in Ireland from 1142–1540* (London, 1987), pp 240–50.
16 Same words and date as Giraldus, *Expug. Hib.*, p. 74; *AClyn*, p. 134; he died 'without unction, without Body of Christ, without penance, without a will' (*AU* 1171); Emmett O'Byrne, 'The MacMurroughs and the marches of Leinster, 1170–1340' in Linda Doran and James Lyttleton (eds), *Lordship in medieval Ireland: image and reality* (Dublin, 2007), pp 160–2; he was a significant benefactor to many religious orders: Flanagan, *Transformation*, p. 202.
17 Hugh de Lacy, 'a transnational aristocrat', accompanied Henry II to Ireland in October 1171 and was granted the kingdom of Mide (Meath): see Colin T. Veach, *Lordship in four realms: the Lacy family, 1166–1241* (Manchester, 2014), pp 26–30; idem, 'Henry II's grant of Meath to Hugh de Lacy in 1172: a reassessment', *Ríocht na Mídhe*, 18 (2007), 67–94.
18 Abbeymahon, O.Cist. (*CStM*, ii, p. 235).
19 Gelasius is Gilla meic Liac (Flanagan, *Transformation*, pp 98, 110–11, 166–7, 182–3). He received the *pallium* at the synod of Kells in 1152; the title *totius Hiberniae primas* dates only from the latter synod (Gwynn, *Irish church*, p. 233). On the role of primate, see Flanagan, *Transformation*, pp 55, 58, 243.
20 Gillebertus was Gilla an Choimded Ó Caráin, archbishop of Armagh, 1175–80 (*CStM*, ii, pp 274), although Pembridge makes no mention of the fact that he was briefly preceded by Conchobar mac Meic Concaille, who died in France in 1175 on the journey home from Rome to receive his pallium: Flanagan, *Transformation*, p. 231.
21 *AMF*, p. 138; *Melrose*, pp 135–6; William supported the rebellion of Henry II's sons but was ultimately forced by Henry to accept the Treaty of Falaise (1174) by which he became his 'liegeman': Michael Brown, *The wars of Scotland, 1214–1371* (Edinburgh, 2004), p. 19.
22 Croxden O.Cist., Staffordshire; the words *et cetera* suggest a source; Bertram de Verdun was a signatory of the Lord John's charter to St Mary's abbey (*CStM*, i, 85, 87; Gearóid Mac Niocaill, 'The charters of John, lord of Ireland, to the see of Dublin', *Reportorium Novum*, 3:2 (1964), 286–7); for patronage, see Hagger, *Fortunes*, pp 45, 207–10; for Bertram's Court in Dublin, see Linzi Simpson, 'Forty years a-digging: a preliminary synthesis of archaeological investigations in medieval Dublin' in Seán Duffy (ed.), *Medieval Dublin I* (Dublin, 2000) p. 59.
23 Giraldus, *Expug. Hib.*, p. 167; *CStM*, ii, p 274; Orpen, *Normans*, pp 134–6.
24 *AMF*, p. 140; *AClyn*, p. 134; *Kilkenny chronicle*, p. 331; *AFM*, iii, p. 29; Vivian presided over a council at Dublin where he 'proclaimed the right of the king of England over Ireland and the pope's confirmation of these rights' (Giraldus, *Expug. Hib.*, pp 181–3, 335, n. 323; cf. M.T. Flanagan, 'Hiberno-papal relations in the late twelfth century', *Archiv. Hib.*, 34 (1976–7), 58–60).
25 Assaroe and Monasterevin, O.Cist. (*CStM*, ii, pp 230, 234).
26 'Miles and Ralph fitz Stephen's son, who had lately become Miles' son-in-law, set out towards Lismore ... were killed' (Giraldus, *Expug. Hib.*, pp 187); Orpen, *Normans*, pp 166–7.
27 Giraldus, *Expug. Hib.*, pp 189; in May 1169 Montmorency accompanied Robert fitz Stephen to Ireland and took part in the capture of Wexford: Orpen, *Normans*, pp 121–2.

28 O.Cist., *CStM*, ii, pp 151–4; 'Register of Dunbrody', ibid., pp 97–216; Aubrey Gwynn, 'The origins of St Mary's abbey, Dublin', *JRSAI*, 4th ser., 79 (1949), 117; H.G. Richardson, 'Some Norman monastic foundations in Ireland' in J.A. Watt, J.B. Morrall and F.X. Martin (eds), *Medieval studies presented to Aubrey Gwynn* (Dublin, 1961), pp 31–2.

29 L adds: 'the abbey of Jerpoint was founded'; Middleton and Jerpoint, O.Cist. (*CStM*, ii, pp 232, 234, 287).

30 *CStM*, ii, p. 287; buried in the habit of a regular canon (Flanagan, *Transformation*, p. 200); Laurence was a signatory to the foundation charter and also a benefactor of the abbey (*Reg. St Thomas*, pp xi, xii).

31 Aubrey Gwynn, 'Archbishop John Cumin', *Reportorium Novum*, 1 (1955–6), 285–310; Margaret Murphy, 'Balancing the concerns of church and state: the archbishops of Dublin, 1181–1228' in *Colony and frontier*, pp 43–8.

32 Consecrated Aug. 1182 with the king present (Giraldus, *Expug. Hib.*, 197–9).

33 Margaret Murphy, 'Balancing the concerns of church and state', pp 43, 47–8; Orpen, *Normans*, pp 174–6; he held a synod in March 1186 (Flanagan, *Transformation*, pp 81–2, 113, 182).

34 *AMF*, p. 140; *AClyn*, p. 136; Celestine III confirmed the Hospitallers in 1193; the main house in Ireland was Kilmainham: C.L. Falkiner, 'Hospital of St John of Jerusalem in Ireland', *PRIA*, 26C (1906–7), 275–317; Herbert Wood, 'The Templars in Ireland', *PRIA*, 26C (1907), 327–77; H.J. Nicholson, 'A long way from Jerusalem: the Templars and Hospitallers in Ireland, c.1172–1348' in Martin Browne and Colmán Ó Clabaigh (eds), *Soldiers of Christ: the Knights Hospitaller and the Knights Templar in medieval Ireland* (Dublin, 2015), pp 1–22.

35 Abbeyleix, O.Cist. (*CStM*, ii, p. 231).

36 Giraldus, *Expug. Hib.*, 229; *AMF*, p. 142: *AClyn*, p. 136; with a fleet of 60 ships (*AFM*, iii, pp 67–9); Seán Duffy, 'John and Ireland: the origins of England's Irish problem' in S.D. Church (ed.), *King John: new interpretations* (Woodbridge, 1999), pp 221–45; for men who accompanied John, see W.L. Warren, 'John in Ireland, 1185' in John Bossy and Peter Jupp (eds), *Essays presented to Michael Roberts* (Belfast, 1976), pp 11–23.

37 *AClyn*, p. 136; the Carthusian order, founded by St Bruno of Cologne in 1084, received papal approval in 1133; the date of Grandmont's foundation by St Stephen of Muret is uncertain.

38 For a description of the Irish using an axe, see Giraldus, *Topog. Hib.*; the *pykays* is presumably a pickaxe.

39 Abbeydorney, O.Cist. (*CStM*, ii, p. 288); Gille Críst Ó Connairche, Cistercian abbot of Mellifont; consecrated bishop of Lismore in 1151 and died 1186 (Flanagan, *Transformation*, pp 97, 178, 181–3, 189–9; Aubrey Gwynn, 'Six Irish papal legates, 1101–98' in idem, *Irish church*, pp 134–5).

40 In 1187, *AClyn*, p. 134; in 1186, *AMF*, p. 142; Runciman, *Crusades*, ii, pp 465–7; Christopher Tyerman, *England and the Crusades, 1095–1588* (Chicago, 1988); for the role of the mendicants in preaching the Crusades, see Kathryn Hurlock, *Britain, Ireland and the Crusades, c.1000–1300* (London, 2012), pp 32–4.

41 O.Cist., *Fundavit anno 1188, alias, 1180* (*CStM*, ii, pp 233, 288; Richardson, 'Some Norman monastic foundations in Ireland', 35–8; M.T. Flanagan, 'John de Courcy, the first Ulster plantation and Irish church men' in Brendan Smith (ed.), *Britain and Ireland, 900–1300* (Cambridge, 1999), pp 167–8.

42 In 1188, *AMF*, p. 142; 'Richard, the great hearted', *AClyn*, p. 136; Henry II died at Chinon 6 July and was buried in Fontevrault (Wendover, *Flores historiarum*, trans. C.D. Yonge, *Flowers of history, especially such as relate to the affairs of Britain*, ii (London, 1853), p. 78); W.L. Warren, *Henry II* (Berkeley, CA, 1973), pp 625–6.

43 O.Cist.; founded by Cathal Croibhdhearg Ó Conchobhair who was buried there in 1224 (*CStM*, ii, p. 237); according to Ware founded in 1190 (*CStM*, ii, p. 288).
44 *AClyn*, p. 136; in 1189, 'Richard, king of England, and Philip, king of France, set out for Jerusalem'; in 1170, 'The kings crossed the Greek sea', *AMF*, p. 142; Gillingham, *Richard I*, pp 2–8; the fall of Jerusalem shocked the Christian world: Runciman, *Crusades*, iii, pp 9–11, 36.
45 *Combustio prima civitatis Dublinie*, in the margin of L (*CStM*, ii, p. 306, fn. 3).
46 St Malachy fell ill at Clairvaux in 1148 where he died in the arms of St Bernard on the night of 1/2 November: M.T. Flanagan, 'St Malachy, St Bernard of Clairvaux, and the Cistercian order', *Archiv. Hib.*, 68 (2015), 306.
47 *AMF*, p. 144; he 'was ransomed for 900 pounds' (*AClyn*, p. 136); for a full account, see Gillingham, *Richard I*, pp 222–53.
48 Grey Abbey founded in 1193 by Affreca, wife of John de Courcy and daughter of Gofred, king of Man, and colonized with monks from Holmcultram, Cumbria: Seán Duffy, 'The first Ulster plantation: John de Courcy and the men of Cumbria' in *Colony and frontier*, pp 9–10.
49 *CStM*, ii, p. 276; Bernard of Clairvaux, *The life of St Malachy*, ed. H.J. Lawlor (London, 1920); Bernard of Clairvaux, *The life and death of Saint Malachy the Irishman*, trans. R.T. Meyer (Kalamazoo, MN, 1978); Flanagan, 'St Malachy', pp 294–311.
50 *CStM*, ii, p. 276; Bective, O. Cist., Co. Meath; *Reg. St Thomas*, pp xv, 348–51; probably initially buried at Durrow where he was killed (Orpen, *Normans*, p. 178); in 1195, with the help of the archbishop of Cashel and papal legate, and John Cumin, archbishop of Dublin, his body was interred in Bective abbey, Co. Meath, but his head was buried at St Thomas's abbey, Dublin; further controversy ended in 1205 with a papal judgment in favour of removal of the body to St Thomas's: Joe Hillaby, 'Colonisation, crisis-management and debt: Walter de Lacy and the Lordship of Meath, 1189–1241 , *Ríocht Na Mídhe*, 8:4 (1992–3), 34; Veach, *Lordship*, p. 67; Claire Walsh, 'Archaeological excavations at the abbey of St Thomas the martyr, Dublin' in Duffy (ed.), *Medieval Dublin I*, p. 200.
51 The Order of Friars Preachers also known as Dominicans, founded by St Dominic and confirmed at the Fourth Lateran Council; in 1216, 'The order of Preachers was confirmed', and 1221, 'The Preachers entered England and their founder, blessed Dominic, died' (*AClyn*, p. 138); in 1216, 'order of Preachers was confirmed', and 1221, 'Blessed Dominic died' (*AMF*, pp 148, 150); for the general history, see Hinnebusch, *Dominican order*.
52 *AMF*, p. 144; *AClyn*, p. 138. An early fourteenth-century MS, written in Ireland (Harley MS. 4003), also states that John killed Arthur the legal heir: Robin Flower, 'Manuscripts of Irish interest in the British museum', *AH*, 2 (1931), 314–15, fn. 3; F.M. Powicke, 'King John and Arthur of Brittany', *EHR*, 24 (1909) 659–74. On his deathbed, Richard nominated John: Gillingham, *Richard I*, pp 227–8, 335–6; for his death, see ibid., pp 321–47; John crowned 27 May 1199: W.L. Warren, *King John* (London, 1978), pp 48–50.
53 Château de Chalus-Chabrol, Haute-Vienne, central France.
54 See, e.g. the continuator of Florence of Worcester (Thomas Forester (trans.), *The chronicle of Florence of Worcester with the two continuations; comprising annals of English history, from the departure of the Romans to the reign of Edward I* (London, 1854), p. 310); *Roger of Howden*, pp 452–4; *CStM*, ii, pp 276–7. In March 1199, while besieging the castle of Châlus-Chabrol near Limoges, a bolt from a crossbow was fatal and Richard died of his wounds; for all the medieval accounts, see John Gillingham, 'The unromantic death of Richard I', *Speculum*, 54 (1979), 18–41; Bertrand also named as Peter Basil

(ibid., 33, 35); for the rumour about buried treasure (ibid., pp 18–22, 39–41); Gillingham, *Richard I*, pp 324–5, 329; for Otto IV, king of Germany (ibid., pp 311–12).

55   Richard died 6 April 1199 and therefore should be *viii Id.* (there are only 8 ides).

56   'In this man's death, the lion by the ant was slain. O evil destiny! In a death so great the whole world fell': *Roger of Howden*, p. 454; 'For the especial love which he bore to the Normans, he bequeathed his invincible heart to the church of Rouen': *Flores hist.*, p. 94; his heart at Rouen: *Roger of Howden*, p. 454; Gillingham, *Richard I*, pp 324–5; both Pembridge manuscripts, T and L, have omitted *cor*; it should be *ecce cor meum*, 'behold my heart'; for the layout and punctuation of verse in the Middle Ages, see M.B. Parkes, *Pause and effect: an introduction to the history of punctuation in the West* (Berkeley, CA, 1992), p. 98.

57   'A circlet of gold, having on the top thereof, around the border, roses worked in gold': *Roger of Howden*, p. 457.

58   Philip 'ordered him indignantly to restore to count Arthur all the lands which he held and unjustly retained possession of on the continent, namely Normandy [etc] ... he also required many other things of him, which the king of England declared that he would never do': *Flores hist.*, p. 97.

59   F.M. Powicke, *The loss of Normandy, 1189–1204: studies in the history of the Angevin empire* (Manchester 1960).

60   O.Cist., founded 1199 (*CStM*, ii, 225); colonized from Whitlan in Wales

61   *AMF*, p. 144; Thomas Case, in *CStM* ii, p. 278; *AI* 1200: 'The foreigners took the kingship of Connachta, and Cathal Crobderg was banished, and Cathal Carrach installed by them'.

62   O.Cist. (*CStM*, ii, 226); daughter-house of Tintern in Wales.

63   Abbeyshrule O.Cist. (*CStM*, ii, p. 232).

64   *AI* 1202: 'A great hosting by William [de Burgh] into Desmumu ... Accompanied by the nobles of Munster, he proceeded then into Connachta, and they slew Cathal Carrach Ua Conchobuir and gave the kingship to Cathal Crobderg'.

65   *AClyn*, p. 142; Meiler, grandson of Henry I and justiciar of Ireland, nephew of Robert fitz Stephen, and a Geraldine had married the niece of Hugh de Lacy, but died without legitimate heir: Orpen, *Normans*, p. 176.

66   O.Cist. (*CStM*, ii, p. 231).

67   *CDI, 1171–1251*, pp 39–40; Down here is Downpatrick (Duffy, 'The first Ulster plantation', p. 3, fn. 11); Courcy never held the title of earl (Steve Flanders, *De Courcy. Anglo-Normans in Ireland, England and France in the eleventh and twelfth centuries* (Dublin, 2008) pp 127–65; Flanagan, 'John de Courcy', pp 154–78).

68   *AFM*, iii, p. 137; for Lacy and Courcy 1201–5, see Orpen, *Normans*, pp 204–5; Veach, *Lordship*, pp 116–20; idem, 'King and magnate in medieval Ireland: Walter de Lacy, King Richard and King John', *IHS*, 37 (2010), 195–6, 201–2.

69   *AMF*, p. 146; *AClyn*, p. 138; Flanders, *De Courcy*, pp 164–5.

70   *CDI, 1171–1351*, p. 40; Orpen, *Normans*, pp 206–7; Daniel Brown, *Hugh de Lacy, first earl of Ulster: rising and falling in Angevin Ireland* (Woodbridge, 2016); cf. Flanders, *De Courcy*, pp 164–5.

71   Treachery was abhorred (*AClyn*, pp 91–2).

72   In 1205 the pope authorized the archbishop of Armagh to anathemize de Lacy for his unjust action against de Courcy: Daniel Brown, 'The archbishop and citizens of Dublin during Hugh de Lacy's Irish rebellion, 1223–4' in Duffy (ed.), *Medieval Dublin XV*, p. 255.

73   'Away from the battlefield he was modest and restrained and gave the church of Christ that honour which is its due' (Giraldus, *Expug. Hib.*, p. 181). He is credited with founding

seven new houses in Ireland: Helen Birkett, *The saints' Lives of Jocelin of Furness: hagiography, patronage and ecclesiastical politics* (York, 2010), p. 142, n. 4.

74 He was involved in the production of Jocelin's *Vita Patricii*: Birkett, *Lives of Jocelin of Furness*, pp 141–70; Flanders, *De Courcy*, pp 149–50; for his foundations, see Duffy, 'The first Ulster plantation', pp 8–27.

75 Black monks are Benedictines; see Flanders, *De Courcy*, p. 155.

76 John fostered devotion to the Irish saints: Duffy, 'The first Ulster plantation', pp 8–9; Richardson, 'Some Norman monastic foundations in Ireland', p. 38; 'Flanagan, 'John de Courcy', pp 163–9.

77 Connected with the loss of Anjou and Normandy, 1202–1205; Roger de Lacy defended the castle of Châteaux Gaillard (overlooking Seine) but lost on 6 March 1204: Warren, *King John*, pp 93–7.

78 In 1287 Bury St Edmunds appointed a judicial champion but, as he was killed, they lost the case: *Chronica Buriensis*, ed. Antonia Gransden (London, 1964), pp 88, 89.

79 Perhaps implying that the king was not at fault? 'John was fair-haired and tall ... and he had a very strong physique, immense bodily strength, and an extraordinarily bold temperament' and although brave, he was impetuous, 'and had ... the air of an ordinary soldier rather than that of a leader' (Giraldus, *Expug. Hib.*, pp 179–81).

80 The honour of Courcy was in Normandy: see Flanders, *De Courcy*, pp 37–8; for a legend concerning John fighting a duel for Henry III in the 1220s, see Flanders, *De Courcy*, p. 165; Matthew Strickland, 'Provoking or avoiding battle? Challenge, judicial duel, and single combat in eleventh- and twelfth-century warfare' in idem (ed.), *Armies, chivalry and warfare in medieval Britain and France* (Stamford, 1998), pp 317–43.

81 Authority 'springs from the general body and the officials are rather servants of that body than its lords': Ernest Barker, *The Dominican order and convocation: a study of the growth of representation in the church during the thirteenth century* (Oxford, 1913), p. 17; for comment on political ideas of kingship, resistance, and treason, see *Vita Edwardi secondi*, ed. W.R. Childs (Oxford, 2005), pp lii–lv.

82 This tale has obvious Arthurian parallels: Carmen J. Neale, 'The sword withdrawal in Robert De Boron's Merlin and in the *Queste Del Saint Graal*', *PMLA*, 53 (1938), 593–5; V.H. Galbraith, 'The death of a champion (1287)' in R.W. Hunt et al. (eds), *Studies in medieval history, presented to F.M. Powicke* (Oxford, 1948), pp 283–95; the theory was that the sword was to uphold true law and order; much has been written on the importance of the sword in medieval society both as imagery and fact: see, e.g, Richard Kaeuper, *Chivalry and violence in medieval Europe* (Oxford, 1999), pp 31–3; Ewart Oakeshott, *The sword in the age of chivalry* (Woodbridge, 1994).

83 Flanders, *De Courcy*, p. 165; on 14 Nov. 1207, the king granted him licence to come to England and remain with friends; he must have died before 22 Sept. 1219 (Orpen, *Normans*, p. 207); for the Chester connection, see Duffy, 'The first Ulster plantation', pp 8, 15–17; Birkett, *Lives of Jocelin of Furness*, pp 146–7.

84 For his intended burial place at Ashby, see A.J. Otway-Ruthven (ed.), 'Dower charter of John de Courcy's wife', *Ulster Journal of Archaeology*, 3rd ser., 12 (1949), 77.

85 Abington, O.Cist. (*CStM*, ii, p. 235); see s.a. 1299; for the name *Pincerna* (Butler) and a list of five Theobalds, see Frame, *Eng. Lordship*, pp 30–1.

86 For the Franciscan order, see J.R.H. Moorman, *A history of the Franciscan order from its origins to the year 1517* (Oxford, 1968); Colmán Ó Clabaigh, *The Franciscans in Ireland, 1400–1534: from reform to reformation* (Dublin, 2002).

87 *AMF*, p. 146; *Flores hist.*, p. 111; he died in Paris and was buried in St Victor's: 'Cont. Florence Worcester', p. 314; for the full background, see Colin Veach, 'King John and royal control in Ireland: why William de Briouze had to be destroyed', *EHR*, 129:540

(2014), 1051–78; his wife accused King John of murdering his nephew Arthur: Brock Holden, 'King John, the Braoses, and the Celtic fringe, 1207–1216', pp 6, 7–9, 15.

88 In 1214 'the interdict on England was relaxed' (*AClyn*, p. 138; *AMF*, p. 146; *Flores hist.*, pp 107–8); for the reason for the interdict, see 'Cont. Florence Worcester', pp 313, 316; Peter D. Clarke, *The interdict in the thirteenth century: a question of collective guilt* (Oxford, 2007) pp 42, 49, 88, 89, 169, 226; the interdict did not apply in Ireland: Orpen, *Normans*, p. 275; the interdict was officially lifted on 2 July 1214: Warren, *King John*, pp 163–73, 206–10; C.R. Cheney, 'King John and the papal interdict', *Bulletin of the John Rylands Library*, 31 (1948), 295–317; idem, C.R. Cheney, 'A recent view of the general interdict on England, 1208–1214', *Studies in Church history*, 3 (1966), 159–68.

89 First use of word *Item* and first use of word *justiciarius*. This justiciar was either Meiler fitz Henry or John de Grey (but first mention of John de Gray in Ireland is 2 Jan. 1209: *Admin. Ire.*, p. 75); Veach, 'King John and royal control in Ireland', 1067–70; Eric St John Brooks, 'The family of Marisco', *JRSAI*, 4th ser., 62 (1932), 50–74.

90 Around 700 ships were used to transport his army: S.D. Church, 'The 1210 campaign in Ireland; evidence for a military revolution?' in Christopher Harper-Bill (ed.), *Anglo-Norman studies XX* (Woodbridge, 1997), p. 48; landed 20 June 1210 at Crook (Co. Waterford) and arrived back in Fishguard on 26 August: Seán Duffy, 'King John's expedition to Ireland, 1210: the evidence reconsidered', *IHS*, 30 (1996), 2; for King John's triumph over the de Lacy brothers, see Veach, *Lordship*, pp 141–4.

91 'He ejected the sons of Hugh de Lacy from the land': *Kilkenny chronicle*, p. 331; Walter de Lacy married Margery, daughter of William de Briouze: Colin Veach, 'King and magnate in medieval Ireland: Walter de Lacy, King Richard and King John', *IHS*, 37: 146 (2010), 191; 'By 1209 or early 1210 there is evidence that Walter and Hugh were intriguing against King John with King Philip of France': Veach, *Lordship*, pp 138–9.

92 Grant from St Mary's to '*Albericio de Cursum et heredibus suis totam terram de Rathenni*', *Johannes [de Curçon] frater de Albericii* (*CStM*, i, pp 259–60); Colin Veach has informed me that de Courson never witnessed any known Lacy charter; there is no mention of a Briouze connection: Seán Duffy, 'King John's expedition to Ireland', pp 17–18.

93 'Hugh de Lacy was ejected from the land with his sons': *AMF*, p. 146; Brown, *Hugh de Lacy*, chap. 5; Paul Duffy, 'The exiled earl and soon-to-be saint', *History Ireland*, 24 (2016), 16–19; Simon de Montfort granted Hugh lands near Carcassonne and therefore Hugh was able to disregard Walter's efforts on his behalf: Veach, *Lordship*, p. 150.

94 This is an apocryphal tale; nevertheless, the de Lacys did leave Ireland and did go to France where they had strong French connections; they were patrons of St Taurin (Benedictine, Évreux, Normandy) and Hugh granted the monks the churches and tithes of Fore and the wood and mill of St Fechin: Veach, *Lordship*, pp 140, 144, 244; for Fore, see Rory Masterson, *Medieval Fore, County Westmeath* (Dublin, 2014).

95 Eventually, 'almost four years after Hugh de Lacy began the war to recover his earldom, Ulster was restored to him' but reverted to the crown after his death; the whole account can be followed in great detail in Veach, *Lordship* and Brown, *Hugh de Lacy*.

96 Walter returned to the king's service in England in 1213: Veach, *Lordship*, pp 147–50.

97 The family name 'first appears as fitz Alured' and 'the alleged grant of Dengen seems authentic': G.H. Orpen, 'The earldom of Ulster', *JRSAI*, 4th ser., 50 (1920), 170; idem, *Normans*, p. 254.

98 Masterson, *Medieval Fore*, pp 21–4.

99 Blank in both MSS.

100 *AFM* 1210: 'the King requested O'Conor to deliver him up his son, to be kept as a hostage. O'Conor did not give him his son, but delivered up four of his people instead … The King then returned to England, bringing these hostages with him'.

101 Last Cistercian entry; Abbeylara, OCist.; *CStM*, ii, p. 279; *AMF*, p. 146; *ADR;* in 1210 the king ordered the justiciar 'to erect three castles in Connacht' (*ALC*, i, pp 243–5); Orpen 'Athlone Castle; its early history, with notes on some neighbouring castles', *JRSAI*, 37 (1907), 262–3; *ALC* 1211: 'Richard de Tuit was killed by a stone in Ath-Luain'; Tuit built a castle at Granard, Co. Longford, which was visited by King John: Orpen, *Normans*, pp 185, 263.

102 *Kilkenny chronicle*, p. 331; buried on the south side: Lawlor, 'Liber Niger', 69; Stuart Kinsella, 'From Hiberno-Norse to Anglo-Norman, *c*.1030–1300' in Milne, *Christ Church*, pp 50–51; Gwynn, 'Archbishop Cumin', 285–310.

103 Scorchvillain may derive from the French word '*escorcher*' to flay.

104 Consecrated in 1213; for Dublin complaints against Henry of London in 1223, see Gilbert, *Hist. & mun. docs*, pp 78–9; for an agreement between Henry and the citizens in 1224–5, see *CARD*, i, pp 90–1; he was 'the archetype of the curialist bishop': Murphy, 'Balancing the concerns of church and state' in *Colony and frontier*, pp 49–54; Aubrey Gwynn, 'Henry of London, archbishop of Dublin: a study in Anglo-Norman statecraft', *Studies*, 38 (1949), 297–306, 389–402; Brown, 'The archbishop and citizens and of Dublin', pp 253–63.

105 Appointed justiciar 3 July 1221: *Admin. Ire.*, p. 76; for Archbishop Henry's involvement with the construction of the castle, see Seán Duffy, 'Building King John's castle at Dublin' in idem et al. (eds), *Dublin castle from fortress to palace, Volume 1* (Dublin, 2023), pp 24–42.

106 *AMF*, p. 148; William Petit calls Hugh de Lacy ' my lord' (*CStM*, i, p. 69; Orpen, *Normans*, pp 184, 195); constable of Meath in 1202: Arlene Hogan, *The priory of Llanthony Prima and Secunda in Ireland, 1172–1541* (Dublin, 2008), p. 21; Veach, *Lordship*, pp 63, 259–61.

107 Messet's death is recorded in the Irish annals: *ALC* 1213: 'The victory of Coill-na-gcrann by Cormac, son of Art O'Maelsechlainn, over the Foreigners, in which a great multitude of the Foreigners were slain, along with Perris Messat and Walter Dunel'; Orpen, *Normans*, pp 250, 269; for the Messet family, see Hogan, *Llanthony*, pp 20, 58–9, 224.

108 The husbands were probably Henry de Vernoyl, William de London and Michael Talbot; all involved in a court case in 1288 against Walter de Lacy; Henry's wife was Amice (*CDI, 1285–1292* (no. 891), p. 404), a reference I owe to Colin Veach; Hogan, *Llanthony*, p. 333: *Reg. Gormanston*, pp 151, 170,174.

109 *AMF*, p. 150; *CStM*, ii, p. 280; *Chronica Buriensis*, p. 4; *Flores hist.*, pp 134–5, 136; 'Cont. Florence Worcester', p. 318; Runciman, *Crusades*, iii, pp 152–8.

110 *AMF*, p. 150; he founded the Cistercian houses of Duiske and Tintern in Leinster and was buried at New Temple London; Isabella was buried at Tintern, Wales (*CStM*, ii, pp 140–44); for the Marshals, see *CStM*, ii, pp 140–6; David Crouch, *William Marshal: knighthood, war and chivalry, 1147–1219* (2nd edition, London, 2002), pp 140–2.

111 The order of seniority of the sons is confused here but easily rectified as they each became earl in turn, and all died without issue; to untangle this very difficult Marshal pedigree, see Hamilton Hall, 'The Marshal pedigree', *JRSAI*, 43 (1913), 1–29; Orpen tried to correct errors in Hall, in Orpen, *Normans*, p. 334.

112 *AMF*, p. 152, where Pembridge states that William Marshal II died in 1231 and was buried with the Dominicans of Kilkenny, see s.aa. 1231, 1234. He is credited with founding Kilkenny: E.B. Fitzmaurice and A.G. Little (eds), *Materials for the history of the Franciscan province of Ireland, AD 1230–1450* (Manchester, 1920), p. 3; another claim, perhaps confusing him with his father of the same name, is that he was buried at New Temple London (*CStM* ii, p. 142; Orpen, *Normans*, pp 309–10).

113 *AMF*, p. 156; Walter, the fourth son, and his brother Anselm both died in 1245 with only eleven days between the deaths (Orpen, *Norman*, p. 317; Hall, 'Marshal pedigree', pp 5–6), both buried at Tintern, Wales (*CStM*, ii, p. 143).

114 Gilbert died by accident at a prohibited tournament at Ware in 1242 and was buried at New Temple (*CStM*, ii, p. 143; Orpen, *Norman*, p. 317; Hall, 'Marshal pedigree', pp 4–5). In 1241, *AMF*, p. 154.

115 See s.a. 1234. In 1233, *AClyn*, p. 140; Richard was buried at Kilkenny (*CStM*, ii, p. 142; *AMF*, p. 152); 'One of the worst deeds done in that age' (*AC* 1234); Orpen, *Normans*, pp 310–16; Brendan Smith, 'Irish politics, 1220–1245' in Michael Prestwich et al. (eds), *Thirteenth century England VIII* (Woodbridge, 2001), pp 15–19.

116 The widows of the five brothers were entitled to their dower before the division (Orpen, *Normans*, pp 317–18).

117 Pembridge made mistakes with the daughters; the question of seniority was not legally important as they were all coparceners, except in he case of Matilda/Maud to whose husband the marshalsy title went; Orpen gives the order of seniority as Maud, Joan, Isabella, Sybil and Eve (Orpen, *Normans*, p. 317).

118 *AMF*, p. 150; *Chronica Buriensis*, p. 4; *Flores hist.*, p. 137; 'Cont. Florence Worcester', p. 318; *ADR;* it was 'one of the most splendid state occasions of Henry's reign' (Anne Duggan, 'Becket is dead! Long live St Thomas', p. 42).

119 See above s.a. 1202.

120 The year the Dominicans arrive in Dublin; the last Cistersian foundation noted is in 1211; no mention of that of Tracton in 1225.

121 *AMF*, p. 150; *Kilkenny chronicle*, p. 331; *Chronica Buriensis*, p. 5; 'Cont. Florence Worcester', pp 318–19; *Flores hist.*, p. 145. At Easter 1224, Trim was seized by the king: Michael Potterton, *Medieval Trim: history and archaeology* (Dublin, 2005), pp 67–80; Brown, 'The archbishop and citizens of Dublin', pp 253–63; for the rebellion of Fawkes de Breauté, see F.M. Powicke, *The thirteenth century, 1216–1307* (Oxford, 1962), p. 27.

122 For whom, see Brendan Smith, *Colonisation and conquest in medieval Ireland: the English in Louth, 1170–1330* (Cambridge, 1999), pp 34, 37, 41, 48, 60.

123 *AMF,* pp 150, 152; for Roger and William, see Brendan Smith, 'Tenure and locality in North Leinster in the early thirteenth century' in *Colony and frontier*, pp 32–3, 35, 38–40; Roger Pippard married Alice de Lacy (Hogan, *Llanthony*, p. 50); the male Pippard line ended with William's death: Smith, *Colonisation and conquest*, p. 93.

124 Thomas Case's annals has no derogatory comment in 1212, and Henry's death occurs during the lacuna in Case's annals (*CStM*, ii, 279, 281); buried in a wooden tomb in the north wall of Christ Church but Ware said no physical evidence remains: Walter Harris (ed.), *The whole works of Sir James Ware*, i: *bishops* (Dublin, 1739), p. 319.

125 'Cont. Florence Worcester', p. 320; *Chronica Buriensis*, pp 6–8; *Flores hist.*, pp 145, 165–6, 172. D.A. Carpenter, 'The fall of Hubert de Burgh' in idem., *The reign of Henry III* (London, 2006), pp 45–60. This information could have been heard at the Chapter at Oxford in 1230: Bede Jarrett, *The English Dominicans* (New York, 1921), p. 228. For its effect in Ireland, see Orpen, *Normans*, p. 396.

126 Nicholas Vincent, *Peter Des Roches: an alien in English politics, 1205–1238* (Cambridge, 2002).

127 *AMF*, p. 152; 'Cont. Florence Worcester', p. 320; *ADR*.

128 In 1232 'Richard, earl Marshal, was killed in battle at Kildare by the Geraldines, who were on the side of the king and acting on his behalf': *Clyn*, p. 140; *AMF*, p. 152; *Kilkenny chronicle*, pp 331, 332; *Liber primus Kilkenniensis*, p. 62. Dublin had warned the king of Richard Marshal's arrival in Ireland: Gilbert, *Hist. & mun. docs*, p. 98. For Henry Clement, clerk to Maurice Fitz Gerald, murdered in London by Marshal sympathizers,

see Maurice Powicke, *King Henry III and the Lord Edward* (Oxford, 1947), ii, pp 740–59; Orpen, *Normans*, p. 396; for the situation in Ireland, see Smith, 'Irish politics, 1220–1245', pp 15–19.

129 In 1241, Walter de Lacy died (*AMF*, p. 154); he was 'chief counsellor of the Galls of Ireland' (*AC*, p. 75; *ALC*, p. 355; *AFM*, iii, p. 303); also *filias heredes* and died in England (*CStM*, ii, p. 289); death occurred before 24 February 1241 (Veach, *Lordship*, p. 223; Orpen, *Normans*, p. 412); the great Lacy inheritance was then carved up between his two granddaughters, Margaret/Margery and Matilda, daughters of his son Gilbert; Margaret married John de Verdun (son of Theobald and Rohesia de Verdun) and Matilda married, first, de Geneve, and second, Geoffrey de Geneville (Orpen, *Normans*, p. 412). Both men had interests in Dublin; for Geneville's Tower, see Simpson, 'Forty years a-digging', p. 47; Walsh, 'Dublin's southern town defences, tenth to fourteenth centuries: the evidence from Ross Road' in Seán Duffy (ed.), *Medieval Dublin II* (Dublin, 2001), pp 112–14; Beth Hartland, 'Vaucouleurs, Ludlow and Trim: the role of Ireland in the career of Geoffrey de Geneville (c.1226–1314)', *IHS*, 32 (2001), 457–77; Hagger, *Fortunes*, pp 218–19.

130 *AClyn*, p. 142; *AMF*, p. 154; see s.a 1242. Orpen, *Normans*, p. 412. Younger brother of Walter de Lacy, lord of Meath (who died the previous year); he died before February 1243 and he had a daughter, Matilda but for disagreement with the marriage statement by Pembridge, see Orpen, *Normans*, pp 414–15.

131 *AMF*, p. 154; they died in Gascony (*AClyn*, p. 142. *AFM*, iii, p. 307); Richard's summons to war and subsequent death was mentioned in Irish annals (*AMisc.*, pp 99, 121; *ADR*); Louis IX made his brother count of Poitou in 1241 and Henry III entered Poitou in the winter of 1242–43: Orpen, *Normans*, p. 412; R.T.D. Fitzgerald, 'Discovery of the burial place of Gerald son of Maurice Fitzgerald, justiciar of Ireland, 1232–1245', *The Irish Genealogist*, 5 (1975), 166–8.

132 Many quakes were reported at this period and the dates are confusing. In 1247, 'An earthquake throughout the whole of the west 10 kal. March [20 February] [and] on the vigil of St Lucy [13 December]' (*AMF*, p. 156; *Kilkenny chronicle*, p. 332); in 1247 (*CStM*, ii, p. 289); in 1247 '*circa horam nonam*' (BL, Harley MS 4003, in Flower, 'Manuscripts of Irish interest', pp 314–15, n. 3); on 13 January 1247 (*Flores hist.*, p. 280); 'There were many earthquakes in England, and a very unprecedented extension of the sea' (ibid., p. 313); on 1 March in 1247 ('Cont. Florence Worcester', p. 324); but 1248/9, a great earthquake in Ireland and Wales (*AI*, p. 353); on 1 March 1247 (*Chronica Buriensis*, p. 14); see B.M.S. Campbell and Francis Ludlow, 'Climate, disease and society in late-medieval Ireland', *PRIA*, 120C (2020), 194.

133 Orpen, *Normans*, p. 396; appointed 4 November 1245, but his departure was delayed: *Admin. Ire.*, p 78.

134 *AMF*, p. 156; *Kilkenny chronicle*, p. 332; *Flores hist.*, p. 313; 'Cont. Florence Worcester', pp 325–6; the Dominican chapter was in London and the news might have come from there; *Chronica Buriensis*, pp 16–17; Louis IX was ill when he was captured and had to cede Damietta and pay a huge ransom; Damietta was handed over Friday 6 May 1250: Runciman, *Crusades*, iii, pp 270–74.

135 Harley MS. 4003 is specific, '*xvii kal. Septembris Mackanefyd occisus est*' (Flower 'Manuscripts of Irish interest', pp 314–15n3); in 1248 '*guerra Maccanefy*' (*Kilkenny chronicle*, p. 332); Donnchadh, son of Anmchadh, son of Donnchadh Mac Giollaphádraig of Ossory (I thank Seán Duffy for this identification); *ALC*, pp 389–91: 'He used to go in person as a spy in the market-towns, in the guise of a beggar or carpenter or turner or some other craftsman'; *AC*, p. 101; *AI*, p. 353; *AFM*, p. 339; Mackanfy (*Liber primus Kilkenniensis*, p. 62).

136 Henry de Lacy, fifth earl of Lincoln (1249–1311), was born in December (perhaps on the 19th) 1249.
137 Alexander III (1241–86), only son of Alexander II, who died in 1249; Alexander III was crowned in July 1249 and was knighted (with twenty new knights) by Henry III on Christmas day 1251: 'Cont. Florence Worcester', p. 327; *Flores hist.*, p. 320; *Chronica Buriensis*, p. 18; the day before the marriage 'Henry III raised the question of Alexander's homage for Scotland, but a definite response was politely but firmly declined': Dauvit Brown, 'A second England? Scotland and the monarchy of Britain in the first English empire' in Seán Duffy and Susan Foran (eds), *The English Isles: cultural transmission and political conflict in Britain and Ireland, 1100–1500* (Dublin, 2013), pp 101–2; for the marriage, see Brown, *Wars of Scotland*, pp 10, 44, 47–8; Alexander II favoured the Dominicans, and it is claimed that he invited them to Scotland: Ronald Page and Catherine Page, 'Blackfriars of Stirling', *Proceedings of the Society of Antiquaries of Scotland*, 126 (1996), 881.
138 Rubrication, maybe highlighting the death of Maurice fitz Gerald.
139 No formal appointment but he left for Ireland in April 1256: *Admin. Ire.*, p. 79.
140 *AMF*, p. 158; according to Clyn, he 'died in the habit and as a friar minor': *AClyn*, p. 144; in the habit of the Friars minor at Pentecost: *Kilkenny chronicle*, p. 332; justiciar of Ireland 1232–45: *Admin. Ire.*, p. 77; Coleman claims that he founded the Dominican priory at Sligo: Ambrose Coleman, *The ancient Dominican foundations in Ireland: an appendix to O'Heyne's 'Epilogus chronologicus'* (Dundalk, 1902), p. 97; but the Loch Cé annals only state that a 'monastery was erected, and a cemetery consecrated, for the Friars Preachers at Sligech': *ALC* p. 403; founded Franciscan friary of Youghal, where he was buried: Orpen, *Normans*, p. 418, n. 72.
141 *AMF*, p. 160; married Emeline daughter of Walter de Ridlesford and widow of Hugh de Lacy: Orpen, *Normans*, p. 388; addressed as justiciar on 21 October 1258 but still in England in June 1259: *Admin. Ire.*, p 78.
142 *AMF*, p. 160; on 16 May 1260, *AClyn*, p. 144; *AFM*, iii, pp 375–7; *AC*, pp 131–3; Brian Ó Néill, king of Tír Eoghain, had been accepted as high king but following his defeat his head was sent to London: *AMisc.*, p. 103; Katharine Simms, 'The O Hanlons, the O Neills, and the Anglo-Normans in thirteenth-century Armagh', *Seanchas Ardmhacha*, 9 (1978), 78–81; he was succeeded by Aedh Buidhe Ó Néill; Down did not become Downpatrick until the seventeenth century: Duffy, 'The first Ulster plantation', p. 3, fn. 11.
143 *CStM*, ii, p. 289; *Kilkenny chronicle*, p. 332; 'His body was borne eastwards over sea for burial', *AI*, p. 361; died after 4 March 1260: *Admin. Ire.*, p. 79.
144 *AMF*, p. 160; see above 1259.
145 *AMF*, p. 160; *AClyn*, p. 144; *Kilkenny chronicle*, p. 332; seneschal of Kilkenny, sheriff of Wexford and justiciar of Ireland; he died after the battle of Callan in 1261: Brooks, *Knights' fees*, p. 49; Orpen *Normans*, pp 326–7, 350–1; *Admin. Ire.*, p. 79.
146 'Also killed were Walter de Riddlesford and Thomas de Rocheford': *AMF*, p. 160; *AClyn*, p. 144; *AFM*, iii, pp 381–3; around 1 August: Flower, 'Manuscripts of Irish interest', pp 314–15, n. 3; they were buried with Dominicans of Tralee: *Caithréim Thoirdhealbhaigh*, ed. S.H. O'Grady, ii (Irish Texts Soc., London, 1929), p. 178; See also *ALC*, p. 439; *AMisc.*, p. 105; John Fitz Thomas of Shanid got all of lands of Desmond, the background to the battle of Callan on 24 July 1261: Lydon, 'A land of war', *NHI*, ii, pp 251–2.
147 *AMF*, p. 160; Orpen, *Normans*, pp 327, 350–51; *AMisc.*, p. 105; Dene died after the battle of Callann in 1261; for marriage see Orpen, *Normans*, p. 403 n. 55; Richard de la Rochelle came with his wife and son: *AI*, p. 363; *Admin. Ire.*, p. 79.
148 *AMF*, p. 160; *AClyn*, p. 146; on 22 July, *Chronica Buriensis*, p. 26; on 22 July, 'Cont. Florence Worcester', p. 333; Altschul, *The Clares*, p. 92.

149 St Benedict 21 March or Translation 11 July; witnessed a King John charter for Ratoath: Orpen, *Normans*, p. 250; *Gormanston*, pp 179–80; Robin Frame, 'King Henry III and Ireland: the shaping of a peripheral lordship', repr. in Frame, *Ire. & Brit.*, p. 42, fn. 69; his daughter Joan was married to Hugh de Feypo: *CDI, 1171–1251*, pp 194, 243; possibly part of the army of Greencastle: A.J. Otway-Ruthven, 'Royal service in Ireland' in Crooks (ed.), *Government*, p. 173; for a later Martin, see s.a. 1333.

150 *AMF*, p. 162; *AClyn*, p. 146; *Kilkenny chronicle*, p. 332; they were 'captured ... in a consecrated church': *AC*, p. 143; *ALC*, p. 449; for the business at meeting, see Gilbert, *Hist. & mun. docs*, p. 141; Lea was the Geraldine *caput* in Offaly: G.H. Orpen, 'The Fitz Geralds, barons of Offaly', *JRSAI*, 44 (1914), 109; they were 'captured ... in a consecrated church', *AC*, p. 143; *ALC*, ii, p. 449; *AFM*, iii, p. 395; Connacht appears to have been the centre of the disturbance: Lydon, 'The years of crisis, 1254–1315', *NHI*, ii, pp 183–4; for connection with events in England, see Robin Frame, 'Ireland and the barons' war', repr. in Frame, *Ire. & Brit.*, pp 59–69; they were probably there for a parliament: *Ir. parl.*, pp 58–9; A.J. Otway-Ruthven, 'Chief governors' in Crooks (ed.), *Government*, p. 80; Orpen, *Normans*, p. 396; appointed 4 November 1245: *Admin. Ire.*, p 78; a later John Cogan buried with Dublin Dominicans in 1311; for interfamilial marriages, see Orpen, *Normans*, p. 403 fn.55.

151 In office before Michaelmas 1266: *Admin. Ire.*, p. 80.

152 Drowned between Wales and Ireland: *AMF*, p. 164; drowned on 28 July, 'returning from England': *AClyn*, p. 146; 'died in the sea around the feast of James (July 25) leaving an heir of three and a half years': *Kilkenny chronicle*, p. 332; his heir was 3½ years old: *CStM*, ii, p. 290; 'with all the crew of the ship, as he was coming from the King of England': *AC*, p. 151; *AI*, p. 369; *ALC*, p. 459; *AFM* iii, p 405; a long minority followed during which the custody of Offaly changed hands several times.

153 *AMF*, p. 164; in 1270 'R[obert] de Ufford returned to England and lord Richard de Exonia conducted the duties of justiciar of Ireland': *AMF*, p. 166; *AClyn*, p. 146; possibly in office before 18 November 1267: *Admin. Ire.*, p. 80; *Kilkenny chronicle*, p. 332.

154 'Ufford built Roscommon castle': *AMF*, p. 164; *AFM*, iii, p. 409; built because 'Áed Ó Conchobair was sick ... at this time': *AC*, p. 153; *ALC*, p. 461; *AI*, p. 369; Tadhg O'Keeffe, 'The fortifications of Western Ireland, AD 1100–1300, and their interpretation', *JGAHS*, 50 (1998), 195; Margaret Murphy, 'Roscommon Castle: underestimated in terms of location', *JGAHS*, 55 (2003), 38–49; the army of Roscommon in 1269, Otway-Ruthven, 'Royal service', p. 173; for Richard de Exonia, see *AMF*, pp 72–4; served as deputy from 6 March 1270 to 6 November 1276: *Admin. Ire.*, p. 80.

155 *AMF*, p. 166; *AClyn*, p. 148; *CStM*, ii, p. 290; in office from Michaelmas 1270: *Admin. Ire.*, p. 80.

156 Perhaps discussed at chapter at Northampton; 'Henry of Almain was killed at Viterbo by Guy de Montfort': *AMF*, p. 168; 'Attacked and brutally murdered': *Chronica Buriensis*, p. 49; killed while attending diving service: 'Cont. Florence Worcester', pp 347–8; *Flores hist.*, p. 452; the son of Richard of Cornwall, cousin of Edward I, murdered by Simon and Guy de Montfort in revenge for death of their father at Evesham: Michael Prestwich, *Edward I* (London, 1988), pp 27, 74, 83, 319; Powicke, *The thirteenth century*, p 226.

157 Noted by most annals: *AClyn*, p. 148; 'great scarcity in Ireland and many men died because of hunger': *AMF*, p. 168; *Kilkenny chronicle*, p. 332; Flower, 'Manuscripts of Irish interest', pp 314–15 fn.3; *ADR*; it was so bad that even 'the rich suffered hardship': *AI*, p. 371; noted under 1270: *ALC*, p. 467; *AC*, p. 157; Campbell and Ludlow, 'Climate disease and society', 198–9; for a list of known famines in this period, see E. Margaret

Crawford, 'William Wilde's table of Irish famines, 900–1850' in eadem (ed.), *Famine: the Irish experience, 900–1900: subsistence crises and famines in Ireland* (Edinburgh, 1989), pp 4–6; Mary C. Lyons, 'Weather, famine, pestilence and plague, 900–1500' in Crawford (ed.), *Famine*, pp 31–74; the inevitable insurrection of the Irish was noted in England: *Flores hist.*, p. 453.

158 In 1269, 'Nicholas de Verdun and his brother lord J[ohn] were made knights', but in 1271 they were killed: *AMF*, pp 166, 168; 'N. de Verdun and his brother': *Kilkenny chronicle*, p. 332; not called brothers by Clyn: *AClyn*, p. 148; 'Nicholas son of John de Verdun, lord of Oriel was killed by Sefraid O Fergail': *AC*, p. 159; *ALC*, p. 469; *AFM*, iii, p. 415; *AClon*, p. 249; Hagger, *Fortunes*, pp 97–8, for identification of Nicholas and John as John de Verdun's sons: ibid. p. 233; *CDI, 1252–1284*, p. 524; for de Verdun in Co. Longford: A.J. Otway Ruthven 'The partition of Verdon lands', *PRIAC*, 66 (1968), 413–15.

159 'Such sorrow': *AMF*, p. 168; *AClyn*, p. 148; *Kilkenny chronicle*, p. 332; died in Galway: *AC*, p. 159; *ALC*, p. 469; 'his body was brought to Áth Ísel': *AI*, p. 371; his son Richard (the Red Earl) was aged 12: Orpen, *Normans*, p. 405.

160 He broke his neck: *AMF*, p. 168; *AClyn*, p. 148; *Kilkenny chronicle*, p. 332; 'Killed by Ó Broin and a number of the Connachtmen': *AC*, p. 159; *ALC*, p. 471; *AClon*, p. 249; *AFM*, iii, p. 417; for maps showing the justiciar and royal service, 1252–1442, see Robin Frame, 'The defence of the English lordship, 1250–1450' in Thomas Bartlett and Keith Jeffery (eds), *A military history of Ireland* (Cambridge, 1996), pp 78–9.

161 *AMF*, p. 168; *AClyn*, p. 148. The first time that the word *capitalis* is used; it does not appear again until 1323 and is used just nine times in all. The title *capitalis* is not noted in *Admin. Ire.*, p. 81.

162 Chapter at York; Brother of Jean de Joinville, biographer of Louis IX of France; 'Geoffrey de Geneville came to Ireland from the Holy Land, a short time before the feast of blessed Francis [4 Oct.], and was made justiciar of Ireland, after the octave of Blessed Francis': *AMF*, p. 170; *CStM*, ii, pp 281, 293; *Admin. Ire.*, p. 81; Simon Lloyd, 'The Lord Edward's crusade, 1270–2: its setting and significance' in John Gillingham and J.C. Holt (eds), *War and government in the Middle Ages; essays in honour of J.O. Prestwich* (Cambridge, 1984), pp 120–33; Potterton, *Medieval Trim*, pp 80–91.

163 Another possible Dominican beginning: specific dates now begin to occur especially from 1282.

164 *Lanercost*, i, p. 8; *Chronica Buriensis*, p. 57; for inclusion of documents by chroniclers, see John Taylor, 'Fourteenth-century chroniclers' in idem, *English historical literature in the fourteenth century* (Oxford, 1987), pp 50–3; for his coronation, see Prestwich, *Edward I*, p. 90; Edward was crowned upon his return from the crusade; Kilwardby was consecrated in 1273 and crowned the new king and queen on 19 August 1274, a few days after his return from the General Council of Lyon: Hinnebusch, *English friars preachers*, pp 377–86; Kilwardby was provincial prior of the English (and therefore Irish Dominicans) from 1261 to 1272: ibid., p. 497.

165 I thank Professor Brian Scott for his advice in this translation; for a full discussion, see Bernadette Williams, 'The lost coronation oath of King Edward I: rediscovered in a Dublin manuscript?' in Seán Duffy (ed.), *Medieval Dublin IX* (Dublin, 2009), pp 84–90; 'Walter Winterbourne (Edward's confessor) may have acted as royal agent in Ireland in 1274': Hinnebusch, *English friars preachers*, p. 471.

166 John, son of Rohesia and Theobald: Hagger, *Fortunes*, p. 16.

167 Thomas de Clare married the daughter of Maurice fitz Maurice: *Kilkenny chronicle*, p. 332; he was younger brother of the earl of Gloucester, granted Thomond by Edward I in 1276: Orpen, *Normans*, p. 467.

168　In 1273, 'Geoffrey de Geneville and other nobles of Ireland went in to Glenmalure around the beginning of Lent': *AMF*, p. 172; 1274, 'The English were slaughtered at Glenmalure': *AClyn*, p. 148; *Kilkenny chronicle*, p. 332; the long vacancy of the archbishopric of Dublin may have been the cause of the tension: Lydon, 'A land of war', pp 256–9.
169　Possible reason for the army of Roscommon: Otway-Ruthven, 'Royal service' in Crooks (ed.), *Government*, p. 174.
170　Muirchertach Mac Murchada, king of Leinster; a Walter Lenfaunt buried with Dublin Dominicans, see below 1311; Walter Lenfaunt had kept guard (*c*.1272) at Ballymore Eustace: *36th rep. DKPRI*, p. 33; for Walter in Ballymore, see William Betham, 'The account of Thomas de Chaddisworth, custodee of the temporalities of the archbishop of Dublin from 1271–1276', *PRIA*, 5 (1850), 158–9; he was partially reimbursed 'for horses and arms lost in the king's service' *c*.1275–6: *IExP*, pp 13, 70, 108, 165; he was a justice itinerant in 1301: Connolly, 'Chancery files (C.260)', p. 5; for Walter's death, see s.a. 1311; for a later Walter, see s.a. 1345.
171　See above s.a.1268; appointed 17 June 1276: *Admin. Ire.*, pp 80, 81.
172　Chapter at Waterford; *Kilkenny chronicle*, p. 333; the Irish annals state that he had him drawn between horses: *AC*, p. 167; *ALC* p 481; *AI* p 373; captured treacherously by the son of the earl of Clare, 'after both had entered into *gossipred* with each other, and taken vows of mutual friendship: *AFM*, iii, p. 427; for *gossipred*, see Fiona Fitzsimons, 'Fosterage and gossiprid in late medieval Ireland: some new evidence' in Patrick J. Duffy, David Edwards and Elizabeth FitzPatrick (eds), *Gaelic Ireland, c.1250–c.1650: land, lordship and settlement* (Dublin, 2004), pp 138–49; for death of Ó Briain, Aoife Nic Ghiollamhaith, 'Dynastic warfare and historical writing in North Munster, 1276–1350', *Cambridge Medieval Celtic Studies*, 2 (1981), 83–4.
173　*AClyn*, p. 150; in 1277, *Kilkenny chronicle*, p. 333; justiciar 1266: Orpen, *Normans*, p. xliii.
174　Chapter at Mullingar; a later John de Cogan buried with Dublin Dominicans in 1311; *Kilkenny chronicle*, p. 333; Orpen, *Normans*, p. 388; for Cogan genealogy, see A. Gray, 'Kinaleghin: a forgotten Irish charterhouse of the thirteenth century', *JRSAI*, 89 (1959), 41–5, 56.
175　*Flores hist.*, p. 474; *Chronica Buriensis*, p. 70; in 1277 '*nova moneta fabricata est*', *Kilkenny chronicle*, p. 333; in 1279 Edward I decided on a major re-coinage in England and by 1281 Dublin and Waterford followed: R.H.M. Dolley, 'The Irish mints of Edward I in the light of the coin hoards from Ireland and Great Britain', *PRIA*, 66C (1968), 287–8; for Stephen de Fulbourne, bishop of Waterford, see Lydon, *The lordship of Ireland in the Middle Ages* (2nd ed., Dublin, 2003), pp 97–9; Lydon, 'The years of crisis', pp 191–3.
176　*Flores hist.*, p. 474; from the vigil of St Matthew and extending right up to the day after blessed Michael when a lion was led into the arena: *Kilkenny chronicle*, p. 333; for Edward I and his round tables, see Prestwich, *Edward I*, pp 120–1.
177　Identified as Lady Margery de Say: *AClyn*, p. 150.
178　Chapter at Dublin; for Cusack family in the east of Ireland, Hogan, *Llanthony*, pp 52–3; an Adam Cusack died in Roscommon in 1287: *AFM*, iii, pp, 435, 445.
179　Appointed 21 November 1281: *Admin. Ire.*, p. 81.
180　Priory at Arklow; *AClyn*, p. 150; *Kilkenny chronicle*, p. 333; *AFM*, iii, p. 437; this murder of the Mic Mhurchadha was listed in the Remonstrance of 1317, see *Scotichronicon of Walter Bower*, ed. D.E.R. Watt et al., vi (Aberdeen 1991), pp 394–5; killed by Henry de Pencoyt at the instigation of the justiciar: Robin Frame, 'The justiciar and the murder of the MacMurroughs in 1282', repr. in Frame, *Ire. & Brit.*, pp 241–7.

181 Roger de Mortimer, lord of Wigmore; see above *s.a.* 1219 where he acquired lands in Ireland (D.A. Carpenter, 'A noble in politics: Roger Mortimer in the period of baronial reform and rebellion, 1258–1265' in Anne Duggan (ed.), *Nobles and nobility in medieval Europe* (London, 2000), pp 183–203).

182 On 2 Jan. 1284 'within the walls', *AClyn*, p. 152; in 1282, *Kilkenny chronicle*, p. 333; *CStM*, ii, p. 290; in 1285 'after the burning of the city': *CARD*, p. 106; *AFM*, iii, p. 439; *Regs Christ Church*, p. 124; Roger Stalley, 'The architecture of the cathedral and priory buildings' in Milne, *Christ church*, pp 102–3.

183 *AClyn*, p. 152; Lea, principal Geraldine castle and caput of the Geraldine lordship of Offaly, was suffering a long minority and Orpen conjectures that Gerald Fitz Maurice III, fourth baron of Offaly was probably in Wales at this time: Orpen, 'Fitz Geralds, barons of Offaly', 110; for the importance of Lea castle, see Linzi Simpson, 'The early Geraldine castles of Ireland: some case studies' in Crooks and Duffy (eds), *The Geraldines*, pp 125–34; for the effect of a Welsh uprising on the Irish of Leinster, see Seán Duffy, 'Irish and Welsh responses to the Plantagenet empire in the reign of Edward I' in Peter Crooks et al. (eds) *The Plantagenet empire* (Donnington, 2016), pp 150–68.

184 *Flores hist.*, p. 479; 'Cont. Florence Worcester', p. 370; *AClyn*, p. 152; the third of Edward's sons to die: Prestwich, *Edward I*, pp 126–7; his heart to be buried with the London Dominicans: Hinnebusch, *English friars preachers*, p. 44.

185 In April 1285, Walter of Kilkenny OP went to Bologna to his general chapter: *CPR, 1281–1292*, p. 156.

186 *AClyn*, p. 152; Theobald, '*pincerna quartus*', died at Arklow, *Liber primus Kilkenniensis*, p. 62; *Kilkenny chronicle*, p. 333; credited with involvement in the foundation of the Dominican priory of Arklow; a statue erected to him in the church: James Ware, *The antiquities and history of Ireland* (Dublin, 1705), p. 80; Dermot Walsh, 'The Dominicans of Arklow (1264–1793)', *Reportorium Novum*, 3 (1964), 307.

187 'Called *Rochfalyaht*': *AClyn*, p. 152; Gerald Fitz Maurice III, fourth baron of Offaly came of age in 1285, *Red bk Kildare*, no. 136. Orpen, 'Fitz Geralds, barons of Offaly', 110.

188 The names Ralph and Roger can be found in the Petit family: Hogan, *Llanthony*, p. 55; Gilbert inserts the name Richard but leaves 'S.' and gives no reason: *CStM*, ii, p. 319.

189 Chapter Trim; for a Gilbert Doget, see *Reg. Alen*, p. 106; Gerald Doget: *IExP*, p. 4; for a John Doget: Lawlor, 'Liber Niger', 62; *Reg. St Thomas*, p; 182; a Roger Doget held lands in Colpe in 1303: Hogan, *Llanthony*, p. 334; Robert Doket witnessed two charters in the Dunbrody chartulary: *CStM*, ii, pp 185, 188.

190 In 1284, *Kilkenny chronicle*, p. 333; in connection with Baltinglass and Leinster: *IExP*, pp 15, 207; *39th rep. DKPRI*, p. 34.

191 Perhaps discussed at the Chapter at Beverly and General Chapter at Paris where both Edward I and Philip IV were present: Ernest Barker, *The Dominican order and convocation* (Oxford, 1913), p. 77; Eleanor of Provence, wife of Henry III; 'Her dower, which she was to have in perpetual possession in the kingdom of England, being confirmed to her by the supreme pontiff': *Flores hist.*, p. 482; 'Cont. Florence Worcester', pp 374; *Chronica Buriensis*, p. 87; *Chronicle of Lanercost 1272–1346*, trans H.E. Maxwell (Glasgow, 1913)), i, p. 51; in 23 Jan. 1286 'Grant to Eleanor the king's mother that although she should enter any religious order, whether professed or not, she shall retain all her possessions in England or Gascony ...'; one of the witnesses was the Dominican William de Hothum: *CPR, 1281–92*, pp 218–19, 220; Hothum had been Provincial Prior of the English (and therefore Irish Dominicans) from 1282 to 1287, and again in 1290–6, Hinnebusch, *English friars preachers*, pp 481–87, 497; J.C. Parsons, *Eleanor of Castile* (New York, 1995), p. 37.

192 An Calbhach Ó Conchobhair of the Uí Chonchobhair Failghe; Callan in Ossory was burnt; Calbhach was captured at Kildare: *AClyn*, p. 154; in 1286 he was imprisoned at Dublin castle: Orpen, *Normans*, pp 451–2.
193 Altschul, *The Clares*, pp 187–95, Table iii; died 29 August, ibid., p. 193; died 4 Sept. 1286, *Kilkenny chronicle*, p. 333; 29 August 1287; Orpen, *Normans*, pp 483–5.
194 Fulbourne died 3 July 1288; Sandford was justiciar from 7 July 1288: *Admin. Ire.*, pp 81–2.
195 For a similar account, *Flores hist.*, p. 483; for Tartar ambassadors to England, *Chronica Buriensis*, pp 63, 90; 'Cont. Florence Worcester', p. 376; the Hungarian royal family had Dominican links and King Stephen V was buried with them: Pál Engel, *The realm of St Stephen: a history of medieval Hungary, 895–1526* (London, 2001), pp 95–7; in 1272 Stephen V died and his 10-year-old son, Ladislas IV (1272–90), succeeded, but was a ward of his Cuman mother for five years: Z.J. Kosztolnyik, *Hungary in the thirteenth century* (New York, 1996), p. 255; in 1279 a papal legate was sent to Hungary: Engel, *The realm of St Stephen*, p. 109; in 1287 Honorius IV said that the king had kept pagan Cuman company (and even associated himself with the Mongols): Kosztolnyik, *Hungary in the thirteenth century*, pp 287, 294; in 1287 Ladislas was excommunicated and declared that 'he would "kill and drive the whole brood" – that is, the Christian clergy – "with Mongol swords as far as Rome"': Engel, *The realm of St Stephen*, p. 109; Istvan Vasary, *Cumans and Tatars* (Cambridge, 2005); for a MS in Trinity College Dublin mentioning the Tartars c.1255/78, see Marvin L. Colker, 'America rediscovered in the thirteenth century?', *Speculum*, 54 (1979), 712–26.
196 'He employed such cunning, that he treacherously convoked the chief nobles of his country to meet in a certain island, as if for the purpose of holding a parliament': *Flores hist.*, p. 483.
197 'Miramolin, the most powerful of the Saracen chiefs came upon them with twenty thousand warriors, and carried off the king by force, with all the Christians assembled in that place on the eve of the feast of St John the Baptist': *Flores hist.*, p. 484.
198 'As the Christians were proceeding on their way, the fine weather changed and became cloudy, and on a sudden, a violent hailstorm killed many thousands of that unbelieving and treacherous company; and the Christians returned to their own homes], no one going on with the Saracens except the apostate king; therefore, the Hungarians crowned his son and remained in the Catholic faith': *Flores hist.*, p. 484.
199 Dominican chapter York; the news might have come from there; 'Cont. Florence Worcester', p. 378; *Flores hist.*, p. 485; *Chronica Buriensis*, p. 93; for the fall of Tripoli in 1289, see Runciman, *Crusades*, iii, pp 405–8.
200 Annual entries become more pronounced from this point.
201 This information may have come from the chapter at Oxford; see above s.a. 1219. 'The noble daughters of the king/ Rich dowries to their husbands bring': *Flores hist.*, p. 485; Joan was married on the last day of April and Margaret was married on 10 July: 'Cont. Florence Worcester', p. 379; 9 July, *Kilkenny chronicle*, p. 333; *Lanercost*, i, p. 58; *Chronica Buriensis*, p. 94; for the relationship between Edward I and Gilbert de Clare, see Altschul, *The Clares*, pp 122–56; he was nearly fifty at the time of the marriage, ibid., p. 149; Prestwich, *Edward I*, pp 317, 348–9; Brabant was in Anglesey with Edward I in 1295: ibid., p. 387.
202 *Admin. Ire.*, p. 82; for the question of when powers took effect, see Peter Crooks, 'The structure of politics in theory and practice: colonial Ireland, 1210–1541' in Brendan Smith (ed.) *Cambridge history of Ireland: volume 1, 600–1550* (Cambridge, 2017), pp 455–6.
203 *AC* 1290: 'Cairpre Ó Mailsechlainn, king of Meath, was treacherously killed by Mac Cochlain and the Delbna'; *AFM*, iii, p. 451.

204 *Flores hist.*, p. 486; *Lanercost*, i, pp 102–3; Friday 4 May: *Chronica Buriensis*, pp 97–8; 'Cont. Florence Worcester', pp 381; died at Bannockburn, see below s.a. 1315.
205 For the similarity of Pembridge's account to that of a contemporary exchequer record, see Simms, 'O Hanlons, O Neills and Anglo-Normans', 87, n. 2; Irish annals focus, not on a southeast Ulster raid on Ó hAnluain, but de Burgh's activity in west Ulster: 'The Earl of Ulster led a great army into Tir Eogain and deposed Domnall son of Brian O Neill and set up Niall Culanach O Neill ... The Earl marched into Tir Conaill against Toirrdelbach O Domnaill and plundered the whole region, its churchmen and laymen, leaving neither altar-cloth nor missal nor chalice in any church of Cenel Conaill, and carried this booty into Connacht': *AC* 1291; *AFM*, iii, p. 453.
206 See above s.a. 1286; wife of Henry III; the same date, *Chronica Buriensis*, pp 87, 98; Eleanor died at Amesbury on 24 June 1291 and buried 9 September: *Lanercost*, i, pp 81–2, 85; on 25 June: 'Cont. Florence Worcester', pp 381–2; *Flores hist.*, p. 486; near Lincoln, *Kilkenny chronicle*, p. 333; her will left 100s to the five Dominican houses in Wales: R.C. Easterling, 'The friars in Wales', *Archaeologia Cambrensis*, 14 (1914), 335.
207 The Sultan with a great army came to Babylon and besieged it up to 18 May and destroyed 'the first city': *Kilkenny chronicle*, p. 333; 'Milcadar, the soldan of Babylon': *Flores hist.*, pp 486–7; *Chronica Buriensis*, p. 103; this information might have come via an embassy from the Tartars: 'Cont. Florence Worcester', pp 381, 397; the Patriarch took so many fugitives into the boat that she went down; Henry II, king of Cyprus and of Jerusalem, had embarked separately with his brother Almeric; 'Otto of Grandson ... all the soldiers he could rescue on board, and himself was the last to join them': Runciman, *Crusades*, iii, pp 405–8, 411–12, 416, 417–19, 420; Otto was involved with Ireland and also connected with William de Hothum, being envoys to the papal curia in 1289 and 1290: Prestwich, *Edward I*, p. 328; Esther Rowland Clifford, *A knight of great renown; the life and times of Otho de Grandson* (Chicago, 1961).
208 Also, in England: *Lanercost*, i, p. 86; 'Cont. Florence Worcester', p. 397; Prestwich, *Edward I*, pp 328–9; Maureen Jurkowski et al., *Lay taxes in England and Wales, 1188–1688* (Kew, 1998), pp xxvi–xxxiv.
209 Error of repetition, see above first entry for 1291; it is clear that the word is s*enex*, which typically means an old man but Gilbert de Clare was only 47 in 1291; it must mean Gilbert's 'older' (as in first-born) son though in the event his subsequent children were all girls.
210 Lionel Stones, 'English chroniclers and the affairs of Scotland, 1286–1296' in R.H.C. Davis and J.M. Wallace-Hadrill (eds), *The writing of history in the Middle Ages* (Oxford, 1981), pp 323–48.
211 'Peace was restored between the lord king and John de Baylol king of Scotland': *Kilkenny chronicle*, p. 333.
212 *Kilkenny chronicle*, p. 333; for full contemporary account and reasons, see *Chronica Buriensis*, pp 98–103, 115; *Lanercost*, i, pp 85–6; Norman Reid, 'The kingless kingdom: the Scottish guardianship of 1286–1306', *SHR*, 61 (1282), 105–29; there were 13 possible claimants, so Edward I was asked to arbitrate; however, Edward I intervened as 'feudal lord of Scotland': Michael Prestwich, 'England and Scotland during the wars of independence' in Michael Jones and Malcolm Vale (eds) *England and her neighbours 1066–1453: essays in honour of Pierre Chaplais* (London, 1989), p. 182; Prestwich, *Edward I*, pp 356, 360, 362, 370; Fiona Watson, *Under the hammer: Edward I and Scotland, 1286–1307* (2009); for Irish connection, see Seán Duffy, 'The Turnberry band' in idem. (ed.) *Princes, prelates and poets*, pp 124–38; for English overlordship, see A.A.M. Duncan, 'The process of Norham, 1291' in P.R. Coss and S.D. Lloyd (eds), *TCE 5* (Woodbridge, 1995), pp 207–30.

213 *Kilkenny chronicle*, p. 333; an assembly held at Dublin to consider the king's demand in 1292: Richardson and Sayles, 'The Irish Parliaments of Edward I', pp 144–5; for taxation on the church, see J.F. Lydon, 'The Irish church and taxation in the fourteenth century', *IER*, 5th ser., 103 (1965), 158–65.
214 Son and heir of Geoffrey and Matilda de Lacy; his daughter Joan married Roger Mortimer; Beth Hartland, 'Vaucouleurs, Ludlow and Trim: the role of Ireland in the career of Geoffrey de Geneville (*c.*1226–1314)', *IHS*, 32 (2001).
215 *Flores hist.*, p. 495; 'Cont. Florence Worcester', p. 398; 'He was dragged through the streets and perished by hanging': *Chronica Buriensis*, pp 113–14; *Lanercost*, i, p. 89; he was captured in April 1292 and executed at York for treason: *CCR, 1288–1296*, p. 267; A.D. Carr, 'Crown and communities: collaboration and conflict' in T. Herbert, and G.E. Jones (eds), *Edward I and Wales* (Cardiff, 1988), pp 125–6; Duffy, 'Irish and Welsh responses to the Plantagenet empire'.
216 The Cinque-Ports, Bayonne and Ireland: 'Cont. Florence Worcester', pp 400–1, 'Between English, Irish, and men of Bayonne on the one side and Normans on the other': *Chronica Buriensis*, p. 117; *Flores hist.* pp 495–6; *Lanercost*, i, pp 95–6.
217 T: *partibus;* Portibus is correct as, 'the barons of the Cinque ports were indignant and speedily equipped their ships with all necessary naval appointments, to avenge the injury done to the English': *Flores hist.* pp 495–7, 507; 'Cont. Florence Worcester', p. 401; *Lanercost*, i, pp 95–6, 104; *Chronica Buriensis*, pp 117, 119–21; in 1293 'A war arose between Edward king of England and Philip king of France for the land of Gascony': *Kilkenny chronicle*, p. 333; the fleet of the Cinque Ports defeated a Norman fleet off Cap Saint-Mathieu in Brittany and afterwards sacked La Rochelle in Poitou: Powicke, *The thirteenth century*, pp 644–5; the cause of this naval skirmish is unclear, Irish ships were also involved and the first battle was on 15 May: Prestwich, *Edward I*, pp 376–7.
218 Chapter at Lincoln; war arose over Gascony: *Kilkenny chronicle*, p. 333; for a different account, see 'Cont. Florence Worcester', p. 402; for the letter and the comment, 'because the king of England did not pay any attention to this command, he was presently ... pronounced a banished man', see *Flores hist.*, pp 497–500; 'Then the Cluniac monks were banished from our borders', *Lanercost*, i, p. 106; on 27 Oct., Edward I was formally summoned to appear in person in Paris in Jan. 1294 to answer the charges: Powicke, *The thirteenth century*, pp 646; Prestwich, *Edward I*, pp 378–9; Mark Kennedy Vaughn, '"Mount the war-horses, take your lance in your grip": logistics preparations for the Gascon campaign of 1294', *TCE 8* (2001), 97–112; the Dominican William de Hothum was among those sent to France to announce Edward's renunciation of his feudal allegiance: Hinnebusch, *English friars preachers*, p. 486.
219 Landed at Ross on Monday, 1 Nov.: *AClyn*, p. 154; *Kilkenny chronicle*, p. 333; Altschul, *The Clares*, pp 153–4.
220 William de Montfort was the 'procurator in the Roman court for the business connected with the tenth previously granted to the king of England for the defence of the Holy Land': *Chronica Buriensis*, pp 124; 'Cont. Florence Worcester', pp 406, 407; *Flores hist.*, pp 504–5; for background, see, Jeffrey H. Denton, *Robert Winchelsey and the Crown 1294–1313: a study in the defence of ecclesiastical liberty* (Cambridge 1980) pp 73–6; Prestwich, *Edward I*, pp 404–5; Vernon F. Snow, 'The evolution of proctorial representation in medieval England', *American Journal of Legal History*, 7 (1963), 319–39.
221 For Gascony in this period, see Malcolm Vale, 'Edward I and the French: rivalry and chivalry' in Peter Coss and Simon Lloyd (eds), *TCE 2* (1988), pp 165–76; Malcolm Vale 'The Gascon nobility and the Anglo-French war, 1294–98' in Gillingham and Holt (eds), *War and government*, pp 134–46; Powicke, *The thirteenth century*, pp 649–50; Prestwich, *Edward I*, pp 382–3.

222 The king 'sent the archbishop of Dublin and the bishop of Durham ... to the king of Germany': *Flores hist.*, pp 502, 503; there is an account of an embassy to France in 1294: Lawlor, 'Liber Niger', 3, 46; Colmán Ó Clabaigh, 'The *Liber Niger* of Christ Church cathedral, Dublin' in Raymond Gillespie and Raymond Refaussé (eds), *The medieval manuscripts of Christ Church cathedral, Dublin* (Dublin, 2006), pp 66–7; an English Dominican friar went as one of the king's ambassadors to France to protest against the seizure of Gascony: Gwynn, 'Black Book', 289–90; Hugh de Manchester OP: *CPR, 1293–1301*, p. 85; for relationship between England and Germany, see Michael Prestwich, 'Edward I and Adolf of Nassau' in *TCE 3* (1989), pp 127–36; Powicke, *The thirteenth century*, p. 660.
223 *CStM*, ii, p. 290.
224 *Liber primus Kilkenniensis*, p. 62; 'John de Sandford, archbishop of Dublin, having been attacked by a severe illness, went the way of all flesh': *Flores hist.*, pp 502, 503; Sandford died in Yarmouth: *Chronica Buriensis*, p. 124; 'Cont. Florence Worcester', p. 406; the canons of St Patrick's asked for his body, which was then buried in 1295 in St Patrick's cathedral.
225 Keeper and acting justiciar: *Admin. Ire.*, p. 82.
226 On such challenges, see Strickland, 'Provoking or avoiding battle?', pp 324–5.
227 'Non-appearance was judged an admission of guilt': Malcolm Vale, 'Aristocratic violence: trial by battle in the later Middle Ages' in R.W. Kaeuper (ed.), *Violence in medieval society* (Woodbridge, 2000), p. 166; this entry is erroneous since it was John Fitz Thomas who failed to appear: de Vescy was lord of the liberty of Kildare of which Offaly was part and therefore the lands of John fitz Thomas were administratively subject to de Vescy, who was unpopular (A.J. Otway-Ruthven, 'The medieval county of Kildare', *IHS*, 11 (1959), 192–3; Robin Frame, 'War and peace in the medieval lordship of Ireland', repr. in Frame, *Ire. & Brit.*, p. 237); strained relations between de Vescy and Fitz Thomas included the politics of Gaelic Connacht (Lydon, 'The years of crisis', pp 185–7); for the de Vescy family, see Keith Stringer, 'Nobility and identity in medieval Britain and Ireland: the de Vescy family, *c.*1120–1314' in Brendan Smith (ed.), *Britain and Ireland, 900–1300* (Cambridge, 1999), pp 199–239.
228 Rathangan co Kildare: *AClyn*, p. 154.
229 Landed at Ross, *AClyn*, p. 154; *Liber primus Kilkenniensis*, p. 63; for his problems with the king, see Altschul, *The Clares*, pp 145–55.
230 Lawlor gives date as 23 Edward [I]; this should be 24 Edward I; on Friday 9 December 1293 imprisoned in Ley castle and on Sunday following '[took] the castle of Kyldare': Lawlor, 'Liber Niger', 52.
231 'All Ireland was thrown into a state of disturbance': *AFM*, iii, p. 461.
232 Dominican house at Kilkenny; first mention of the Irish parliament.
233 Dominican house at Sligo; *AClyn*, p. 154; *Kilkenny chronicle*, p. 334; *Liber primus Kilkenniensis*, p. 63; for Lea, see Linzi Simpson, 'The early Geraldine castles of Ireland: some case studies' in Crooks and Duffy (eds), *The Geraldines*, pp 125–34; Lydon, 'Parliament and the community of Ireland' in idem (ed.), *Law and disorder in thirteenth-century Ireland: the Dublin parliament of 1297* (Dublin, 1997), pp 125–8; Richard de Burgh knighted by king at Rhuddlan in 1283: *CJRI, 1295–1303*, p. 452; de Burgh and fitz Thomas had both been part of the Irish army in Scotland in 1296: James Lydon, 'An Irish army in Scotland, 1296' in Crooks (ed.), *Government*, pp 182–8; de Burgh went to Connacht to assert his power there (*ALC*, p. 495); John Fitz Thomas was one of the largest landholders in Connacht (*Red bk Kildare*, no. 105); see also Cormac Ó Cléirigh, 'The problem of defence: a regional case-study' in Lydon (ed.), *Law and disorder*, pp 34–6; *Ir. parl.*, p. 333.

234 An Calbhach Ó Conchobhair of the Uí Chonchobhair Failghe: Orpen, *Normans*, p. 452; see s.a. 1285.
235 Therefore, written at least two years later; the 'greatest scarcity and many died from hunger': *AClyn*, p. 154; a statement in the margin of the Black Book of Christ Church declares, 'there was such a famine in Ireland during the winter of 1295 that the starving poor ate the bodies of men who had been hanged on the gibbets': Gwynn, 'Black Book', 296; Campbell and Ludlow, 'Climate, disease and society', 195.
236 Appointed justiciar 18 October 1294: *Admin. Ire.*, p. 82.
237 *Venedotia*, Latin for Gwynedd; 'War in Wales': *Kilkenny chronicle*, p. 334; 'Cont. Florence Worcester', pp 406–7; Prestwich, *The three Edwards: war and state in England, 1272–1377* (London, 1980), pp 12–13; for the cost of building Beaumaris castle, see J. Goronwy Edwards, 'Edward I's castle-building in Wales', *PBA*, 32 (1946), 24–30; Lydon, 'The years of crisis', p. 196; Beaumaris was the last and largest of the castles to be built: J.E. Morris, *The Welsh wars of King Edward the First* (Oxford, 1901), pp 268–70.
238 Madog ap Llywelyn; Madog surrendered to Havering, the justiciar of North Wales: Morris, *The Welsh wars*, pp 240–70, 308–9; Duffy, 'Irish and Welsh responses to the Plantagenet empire'.
239 'Died in office in April 1295': *Admin. Ire.*, p. 82.
240 *Admin. Ire.*, p. 82.
241 Pembridge does not always distinguish which Newcastle he means (see s.a. 1306, 1309, 1315, 1329, and 1332) but most probably Newcastle McKinegan, Co. Wicklow, is intended.
242 'Cont. Florence Worcester', p. 410; *Chronica Buriensis*, pp 128–9; *Flores hist.*, pp 511–12; *Lanercost*, i, p. 121; J.G. Edwards, 'The treason of Thomas Turberville, 1295' in Hunt et al. (eds), *Studies presented to F.M. Powicke*, pp 296–309; Prestwich *Edward I*, pp 382–3; J.G. Bellamy, *The law of treason in England in the later Middle Ages* (Cambridge, 2004) pp 16, 35.
243 The Scots 'having broken the covenant of peace which they had made with their liege lord the king of England, made another treaty with the king of France': *Flores hist.*, p. 511; Prestwich, 'England and Scotland during the wars of independence', pp 181–97; at the end of June a summons was issued by Edward demanding 'the personal service of the king of Scots, ten earls of Scotland, and sixteen barons': on 5 July 1295 the Scots sent embassy to negotiate alliance with French: Brown, *Wars of Scotland*, p. 348.
244 See above s.a. 1292; Brown, *Wars of Scotland*, pp 169–78.
245 An 'insult to the kingdom of England': *Flores hist.*, p. 511; 'a solemn parliament was held at Stirling': *Lanercost*, i, p. 114; Reid, 'The Scottish guardianship'.
246 *AFM*, iii, p. 467; 'A final summons was issued to John to meet Edward at Newcastle in early March': Brown, *Wars of Scotland*, p. 175; Hothum was involved in 'securing the acknowledgement of Edward's overlordship': Hinnebusch, *English friars preachers*, p. 485; for Irish involvement, see Lydon, 'An Irish army in Scotland, 1296'; Matthew Strickland, 'A law of arms or a law of treason? Conduct in war in Edward I's campaigns in Scotland, 1296–1307' in Kaeuper (ed.), *Violence in medieval society*, p. 40; James Lydon, 'The Dublin purveyors and the wars in Scotland, 1296–1324' in Gearóid Mac Niocaill and P.F. Wallace (eds), *Keimelia: studies in medieval archaeology and history in memory of Tom Delaney* (Galway, 1988), pp 435–48.
247 Possible benefactor of Dominicans of Athy: Coleman, *Ancient Dominican foundations*, p. 49; justiciar 1295–1308 and 1309–12; he brought a new continuity to Irish administration: *Admin Ire.*, pp 82–3
248 For the significance of the familial group, see Seán Duffy, 'The problem of degeneracy' in Lydon (ed.), *Law and disorder*, pp 87–106.

249 Before Christmas: 'Cont. Florence Worcester', p. 409; *Lanercost*, i, p. 126; *Chronica Buriensis*, p. 130; died 7 Dec. and buried at Tewkesbury abbey: Altschul, *The Clares*, p. 155.
250 The king of France took the opportunity of Edward's troubles in England to threaten the lands that Edward held in France: 'Cont. Florence Worcester', p. 411; *Flores hist.*, pp 513–14; *Lanercost*, i, pp 130–1; *Chronica Buriensis*, p. 130.
251 'Lord Edward king of England had moved with a great army against the Scots on 3 Kal April (30 March); the king took the city of Berwick': *Kilkenny chronicle*, p. 334; *Lanercost*, i, pp 134–5; 'Nine thousand Scotsmen': *Chronica Buriensis*, p. 131; Sixty thousand, of both sexes: *Flores hist.*, p. 517; for the 'form of homage rendered by John (Balliol), King of Scotland to Edward (I) at Berwyke on Twede': Lawlor, 'Liber Niger', 53; Barrow, *Robert Bruce*, pp 99–100.
252 At Monrose: *Kilkenny chronicle*, p. 334; *Flores hist.*, p. 518; 8,000 killed, *Chronica Buriensis*, p. 131; battle of Dunbar, 27 April: Brown, *Wars of Scotland*, p. 348.
253 At least 500 cavalry and 40,000 infantry and at least 10,000 fell in battle: *Flores hist.*, p. 518; Barrow, *Robert Bruce*, pp 101, 104; Brown, *Wars of Scotland*, p. 175; Prestwich, 'England and Scotland during the wars of independence', pp 190–1; Fiona J. Watson, 'Settling the stalemate: Edward I's peace in Scotland, 1303–1305' in Michael Prestwich et al. (eds), *TCE 6*, p. 129.
254 All Dominican benefactors; *AFM*, iii, p. 479; the Irish and the Welsh were summoned and came 'in great numbers ... like locusts': *Chronica Buriensis*, pp 131–2; the Irish were asked to muster at Whitehaven by 1 March, but much delayed not leaving until after 29 April; the eventual total of men was 3,157: Lydon, 'An Irish army in Scotland, 1296', p 183; idem, 'The Dublin purveyors and the wars in Scotland, 1296–1324', pp 447–8; John Wogan led 260 hobelars (soldiers mounted on small horses that were faster and more mobile than other mounted soldiers) with the contingent of Irish troops to Scotland, the first reference to the hobelar: Lydon, 'The hobelar: an Irish contribution to medieval warfare' in Crooks (ed.), *Government*, p. 178.
255 The records and regalia of the crown were sent to England during the summer: Brown, *Wars of Scotland*, p. 177.
256 The principal Dominican house in Scotland was Edinburgh and their first house was in Berwick: William Moir Bryce, *The Blackfriars of Edinburgh* (Edinburgh, 1911), p. 14; the date must refer to the nativity of John (Sunday 24 June (not 29 Aug.): *Lanercost*, i, pp 142, 144–5; *Chronica Buriensis*, pp 132–3; Barrow, *Robert Bruce*, p. 102.
257 *Kilkenny chronicle*, p. 334; 'John, formerly king of Scotland ... the area within a twenty-mile radius of London was assigned to him for hunting and hawking': *Chronica Buriensis*, p. 133; E.L.G. Stones, and M.N. Blount, 'The surrender of King John of Scotland to Edward I in 1296: some new evidence', *BIHR*, 48 (1975), 94–106.
258 'A valiant knight and noble, who was genial and merry, generous and pious': *Lanercost*, i, p. 146.
259 Chapter at Oxford; *Kilkenny chronicle*, p. 334; *Flores hist.*, pp 526–7; in 1297 Dominicans accompanied forty soldiers from Wales to Flanders: Hinnebusch, *English friars preachers*, p. 470; 'About the end of August Edward, king of England, came to the help of Count Guy and landed in Flanders; some Irish with the king in Flanders; a marriage was arranged between Edward son of King Edward and Philippa, the daughter of the count of Flanders, an enemy of the King of France: *Annales Gandenses: annals of Ghent*, ed. Hilda Johnstone (Oxford, 1985), pp 4, 6, 8; *Chronica Buriensis*, p. 137.
260 *Chronica Buriensis*, p. 137; Hothum was involved: Hinnebusch, *English friars preachers*, pp 484–6.

261 Truce in October lasted until Jan. 1300; 'In January (1298) the master-general of the Friars Preacher and the minister-general of the Friars Minor were sent by the pope to Ghent for the confirmation of the truce': *Annals of Ghent*, pp xvii, 8.

262 John de Warenne, earl of Surrey; while Edward was in Flanders, William Wallace with the Scots came to the bridge of Stirling and gave battle against lord John, earl of Warenne, and many were killed and drowned on both sides: *Kilkenny chronicle*, p. 334; *Chronica Buriensis*, pp 142–3; C.J. McNamee, 'William Wallace's invasion of Northern England in 1297', *Northern History*, 5 (1990), 40–58; Page and Page, 'Blackfriars of Stirling', p. 882.

263 McNamee, 'William Wallace's invasion of Northern England in 1297'; Brown, *Wars of Scotland*, pp 181–5.

264 *Kilkenny chronicle*, p. 334.

265 St Louis of Toulouse, also called Louis of Anjou, son of Charles II of Naples; *Flores hist.*, pp 527–8; *Chronica Buriensis*, p. 143.

266 The Dominican interest may be because they participated in King James I of Aragon's (1213–76) invasion of Majorca: D.S. Bachrach, 'The friars go to war: mendicant military chaplains, 1216–*c*.1300', *Catholic Historical Review*, 90 (2004), 628–30; Saint Louis of Toulouse, of the house of Anjou, was consecrated bishop of Toulouse 1296 and died in 1297; for his death, see Margaret Toynbee, *Saint Louis of Toulouse and the process of canonization in the fourteenth century* (Manchester, 1929), pp 129–32; Hugh the Illuminator and Simon Semeonis visited his shrine in 1323, *Itinerarium Symonis Semeonis ab Hybernia ad Terram Sanctam*, ed. Mario Esposito (Dublin, 1960), pp 32–3.

267 Sliabh Maircce, Co. Laois.

268 *AC* 1297: 'Cú Ulad Ó hAnluain and his brother, and Aengus Mag Mathgamna and many of their principal followers were killed by the Galls of Dundalk as they returned from [service with] the Earl, this same year'; *AFM*, iii, p. 469; *ALC*, p. 519; Simms, 'O Hanlons, O Neills and Anglo-Normans', 88.

269 Scribal error – *iiii* should be *viii*; Pope 24 December 1294 to death in 1303.

270 *Chronica Buriensis*, pp 143–7; the pope was 'appointed arbiter between the kings of England and France': *Flores hist.*, p. 528; for the full examination of the peace, see Prestwich *Edward I*, pp 395–7; for the financial problems associated with the war, see Prestwich, *The three Edwards*, pp 27–34.

271 *Kilkenny chronicle*, p. 334; *Chronica Buriensis*, pp 147, 148; around 3,000 plus cavalry and 25,700 infantry: Prestwich, 'England and Scotland during the wars of independence', p. 188.

272 Kilkenny has a full description; 'many without number killed, 60,000 and even more': *Kilkenny chronicle*, p. 334; 60,000 men fell: *Chronica Buriensis*, p. 150; 60,000–100,000 Scotsmen killed: *Lanercost*, i, p. 166; the number killed was 200 knights and 40,000 infantry: *Flores hist.* p. 527; in 1298 Edward I stayed at the Dominican priory of Stirling for fifteen days: Page and Page, 'Blackfriars of Stirling', p. 882; for Edward's conduct, Strickland, 'A law of arms or a law of treason?', p. 40; for the Scottish forces led by Wallace and his resignation of the Guardianship, see Barrow, *Robert Bruce*, pp 142–6; Brown, *Wars of Scotland*, pp 186–8.

273 This might refer to a comet which 'appeared in the north, emitting rays laterally towards the east, which vomited fire as it were, and it was visible for three days after sunset, which was an omen that great slaughter would take place in the ensuing year' in the aftermath of an earthquake in Rome and England: *Flores hist.*, p. 528; 'An extraordinary omen appeared on the sun and moon; they both appeared so red or rather blood coloured that they gave forth no rays to the earth except red- or blood-coloured ones … [then *c*.2 February 1299] a comet appeared, shooting out a radiant trail to the east': *Chronica*

Buriensis, pp 150, 151; Campbell and Ludlow, 'Climate, disease and society', 194; in 1301 on 28 Dec. there was an earthquake from the hour of nones': *Kilkenny chronicle*, p. 334.

274   For a list of forfeits, see Barrow, *Robert Bruce*, p. 147.

275   Out of sequence – but – in the East feast kept on 1 July.

276   This may be a repetition of the same year entry above or the comet of 1299: *Chronica Buriensis*, p. 151.

277   Maurice fitz Maurice died around 1 June: *Kilkenny chronicle*, p. 334; the common bench court was at Dublin (except 1362–94 when it was at Carlow); for Thomas Fitz Maurice, keeper of the land of Ireland and deputy justiciar, see *IExP*, pp 123, 125, 126 n.2; Robert Bagod, chief justice of the Dublin bench, can be traced in *IExP*, index; last mention of Robert Bagod is c.1281: *Admin. Ire.*, p. 140; for Robert Bagod c.1281, c.1282, 1313: *CCD*, pp 57, 58, 69; a Robert Bagod appears on the administrative scene in 1310: *Admin. Ire.*, p. 144; for a later Robert Bagod, son of Robert Bagod in 1329, see *CCD*, p. 146.

278   Rieti was the epicentre of the earthquake and a favourite papal seat in the Middle Ages; on 30 November 1298, an earthquake in Rome lasted three days: *Flores hist.*, p. 528; in 1298 'before daybreak there was a great earthquake': *Chronica Buriensis*, p. 151.

279   On 28 December 1301: *Kilkenny chronicle*, p. 334; earthquake on the vigil of the epiphany: *Flores hist.*, p. 528; *Chronica Buriensis*, p. 151.

280   Turvey is at Donabate, Co. Dublin; Wayney is Wetheney [Abington]; Chapter at Cork; see s.a. 1205.

281   *Lanercost*, ii, p. 169; *Chronica Buriensis*, p. 153; two days after the feast of the nativity (8 September): *Flores hist.*, p. 529; it was on 10 September 1299: Prestwich, *Edward I*, pp 483, 521; Seymour Phillips, *Edward II* (New Haven, 2010), pp 80–2, 91.

282   1299: *Flores hist.*, p. 531; *Chronica Buriensis*, p. 155; Ghazan Khan (1295–1304), the Mongol ruler of Persia: Peter Jackson, *The Mongols and the West, 1221–1410* (London, 2010), pp 170–76.

283   The year 1299 is repeated: did the copyist write twice by accident (eye skip)?

284   *Flores hist.*, pp 530–1.

285   This tall tale could have been heard at the chapter at Cork or Shrewsbury or even from a sailor; there is a forest in Guédelon, Burgundy; David Karunanithy, author of *Dogs of war: canine use in warfare from ancient Egypt to the 19th sentury Seminole wars* (London, 2008), very kindly replied to my email saying that, so far, he not come across any mention of this incident.

286   Annunciation Friday 25 March 1300; for Theobald de Verdun I, third son of John de Verdun, see Hagger, *Fortunes*, pp 16, 98–115; Orpen, *Normans*, p. 412 fn 29; Philomena Connolly, 'The enactments of the 1297 parliament' in Lydon (ed.), *Law and disorder* p. 151; for the descendants of Theobald, see Brendan Smith, *Crisis and survival in late medieval Ireland: the English of Louth and their neighbours, 1330–1450* (Oxford, 2013), p. 19.

287   General chapter at Marseilles where permission was given to Thomas de Jorz, Prior provincial of the Friars Preachers, to attend plus three friars: and also, Richard de Clyfford 'of the same order, going there with a confrere', March 1300: *CPR, 1292–1300*, p. 497. Richard de Clyfford may have been belonging to the Irish Dominicans as in 1301 he was sent by 'W. bishop of Emly ... beyond seas': *CPR, 1292–1301*, p. 584; *Chronica Buriensis*, p. 156.

288   In 1299 and 1300 'the island of England was polluted with base money, which is called crohard and pollard': *Flores hist.*, pp 529, 532–3; Harris, *Dublin*, pp 255–6; in 1279 an order 'to arrest and imprison all goldsmiths and other suspected of clipping or forging money': *Affairs Ire.*, pp 20–2. In 1352 clipping of coins was made treason: Bellamy, *The law of treason in England*, pp 17–18; for the regulation of currency in 1299, see *Stat. John–Hen V*, pp 213–15, 221–3.

289 *Lanercost*, ii, pp 171–2; in 1299 Pope Boniface VIII issued the bull, *Scimus Fili*, ordering Edward not to attack Scotland and to enter negotiations: Brown, *Wars of Scotland*, pp 192, 280; Pembridge's statement appears to imply that the king was acting legitimately; *Flores hist.*, pp 533, 537–8, 557–9; the king stayed at the Dominican priory at Pontefract in Jan. 1300 on route to Scotland while the queen remained at priory and later they spent Whitsuntide there: Hinnebusch, *English friars preachers*, pp 196–7; On 14 Oct. 1300, two Dominican friars, William de Maclesfeld and John de Shottesham, were given permission to go to the court of Rome 'on the affairs of their order': *CPR 1292–1300*, p. 540.

290 The first of three children: Prestwich, *Edward I*, p. 131; *Lanercost*, ii, p. 169; *Chronica Buriensis*, p. 158.

291 He left no children but 'an almost infinite amount of gold, silver and precious stones': *Chronica Buriensis*, p. 158; *Flores hist.*, p. 534; O.Cist., Gloucestershire; founded by Richard, earl of Cornwall, brother of Henry III, in 1245/6.

292 *Lanercost*, ii, pp 171–2; for a very detailed year by year account, see Fiona J. Watson, 'Edward I in Scotland: 1296–1305' (PhD, University of Glasgow, 1991).

293 In Feb. 1301, the king wrote to Wogan saying that he would need 'ten ships from Ireland'; it was here for the first time that 'also the mayors of Dublin Cork and Waterford, Drogheda and Limerick and the bailiffs of Ross and Kilkenny were requested to assist … by raising levies locally': Lydon, 'Irish levies in the Scottish wars, 1296–1302' in Crooks (ed.), *Government*, pp 191–2; this was Peter, third lord of Athenry (there was another Peter who was baron of Tethmoy); the Irish annals identify him as Mac Feorais; 'An army was led by the King of England into Scotland; Fitzgerald, Mac Feorais Bermingham, and all the other noble barons of Ireland, except the Earl of Ulster, accompanied him on this expedition' (*AFM*, iii, p. 475).

294 Lawlor, 'Liber Niger', 53; built of wattle and thatch: Harris, *Dublin*, p. 256; Gwynn, 'Black Book', 298; see 1304 below for another big fire, this time north of river Liffey; rolls were burnt: A.J. Otway-Ruthven, 'The medieval Irish chancery' in Crooks (ed.), *Government*, p. 107:

295 *recte* Edmund Mortimer: the Croxden Chronicle states that in 1302, de Verdun 'married the daughter of Lord Edmund Mortimer at Wigmore on 29 July'; the Croxden chronicle also records the children of the marriage and Matilda's death in 1312: Hagger, *Fortunes*, pp 115–16.

296 For defending the marches, see Áine Foley, *The royal manors of medieval Co. Dublin* (Dublin, 2013), pp 137–40; O'Byrne, 'MacMurroughs and the marches of Leinster', p. 181.

297 The source used by Pembridge for these years employs the unusual term *confectio* to mean a military victory (see, for example, his account of the Flemish victory over the French at Courtrai in the following year).

298 It is far from clear what the author means by *Bremorum* but Seán Duffy has suggested 'Berminghams' as the most likely explanation given the locus of the latter in Tethmoy, cheek by jowl with the Mac Fhaeláin family, descendants of the pre-Invasion kings of Uí Fhaeláin.

299 For the le Poer family, see Ciarán Parker, 'Pater familias and *parentela*: the Le Poer lineage in fourteenth-century Waterford', *PRIA*, 95 C (1995), 93–117.

300 Note the same entry below s.a. 1304.

301 Consecrated archbishop of Dublin 1 July 1299: Charles McNeill, 'The secular jurisdiction of the early archbishops of Dublin', *JRSAI*, 5 (1915), 81–108.

302 *Kilkenny chronicle*, p. 334; in 1302 'there began a painful and deadly war, long in incubation and incapable of appeasement': *Annals of Ghent*, p. 19: *Lanercost*, ii, pp 173–4. For doggerel verse, see *Flores hist.*, p. 560; for the battle of Courtrai, see ibid., pp 28–

33; J.F. Verbruggen, *The battle of the Golden Spurs (Courtrai, 11 July 1302)*, trans. David Richard Ferguson (Woodbridge, 2002); General chapter Bologne; safe conduct (23 Feb. 1302) for Nicholas de Stratton OP, with three fellow friars, to go to general chapter at Bologne: *CPR, 1301–1307*, p. 21.

303 *Annals of Ghent*, p. 31; *Flores hist.*, pp 560–1; see also the list of casualties in Verbruggen, *The battle of the Golden Spurs*, pp 117–18.

304 In 1302 he married for the second time, perhaps suggested by Edward I, Barrow, *Robert Bruce*, pp 174–5, 200, 411; J.A. Watt, 'The Anglo-Irish colony under strain, 1327–99', *NHI*, ii, pp 353–4; Robin Frame, 'A register of lost deeds relating to the earldom of Ulster, c.1230–1376' in Duffy (ed.), *Princes, prelates and poets*, p. 88; for other de Burgh marriages, see Frame, *Eng. lordship*, p. 50.

305 In 1303 'The province of Guienne, with all its rights and liberties, was restored to the king of England, in the same form': *Flores hist.*, p. 565; this is the result of the treaty of Paris in 1303; the king appointed John de Hastings his seneschal in Gascony: Malcolm Vale, *The origins of the hundred years war: the Angevin legacy, 1250–1340* (Oxford, 2000), pp 51, 68, 221.

306 Chapter Drogheda; *AClyn*, p. 156; *CStM*, ii, p. 291; *AFM*, iii, p. 475, 479; he knighted thirty-three in Dublin before leaving for Scotland: *Kilkenny chronicle*, p. 334; *AMisc.*, ii, p. 131; Lydon, 'Dublin purveyors and the wars in Scotland', pp 435–8; neither fitz Thomas, Bermingham nor Butler went to Scotland with the earl of Ulster: Lydon, 'Edward I, Ireland and the war in Scotland, 1303–1304' in Crooks (ed.), *Government*, pp 200–15; in 1304 Edward I stayed with the Dominicans of Stirling': Page and Page, 'Blackfriars of Stirling', p. 882.

307 Eldest son of John fitz Thomas, baron of Offaly; *AClyn*, p. 1303; 'around the feast of St Michael': *Kilkenny chronicle*, p. 334.

308 Decorated *E* (*Eodem*) beginning of sentence showing importance of the entry.

309 The Pope was captured, his treasury robbed, he was held for three days and then died: *Kilkenny chronicle*, p. 334; *Lanercost*, ii, p. 175; Pope Boniface excommunicated the king and queen of France and the children and placed the kingdom under interdict and revoked the privilege of the community of Paris: *Flores hist.*, pp 566–7, 568.

310 Wife of Richard Burke, earl of Ulster, and Walter de Burgo, heir of the same earl, died; *AFM*, iii, p. 401.

311 'The heirs of Walerand de Welleslay' mentioned in 1307: *Inquisitions & extents*, p. 73; there was an earlier Waleran de Wellesley, justice of king's bench, last mentioned in 1264, see index *Admin. Ire.*, p. 299; Connolly, 'Chancery files (C.260)', p. 6; holding by knight service of William de Vescy in 1297 with among others Robert Percival who was seneschal of William de Vescy: Orpen, *Normans*, p. 331.

312 Seán Duffy suggests that since the other places damaged in the fire – the Dominican priory and St Mary's Cistercian abbey – were north of the Liffey, it is possible that the fire was contained to the north of the river, and hence the *vicus pontis* is not Bridge Street (south of the Liffey) but Church Street, and the quays not Wood Quay on the south bank but a northside quay in the vicinity of Hammond Lane.

313 VI Ides June matches feast day; St Mary's Cistercian abbey 'with its suburb' and the Dominican priory burnt on 9 June: *AClyn*, p. 156; 'The abbey of Blessed Mary in Dublin and the convent of the Dominicans with the greater part of Dublin above the riverbank was burnt on the eve of St Columba abbot': *Kilkenny chronicle*, p. 334; St Mary's 'the depository of the records in chancery': Harris, *Dublin*, pp 256–7; 'Many of the chancery rolls and files were destroyed': Philomena Connolly, *Medieval record sources* (Dublin, 2002), p. 10; see above for burning south of river Liffey in 1301.

314 The Dominicans were loyal to the le Poers; in 1328, when Arnold le Poer died in Dublin castle he lay with the Dominicans without burial; they were evidently willing to take his body and hold it even though he was in disgrace.
315 Same date, 11 April, as original entry in 1302; incorrect date sequence may mean this one is incorrect.
316 *Capucii* a furred hood: *Account roll Holy Trinity*, p. 88.
317 Philip IV of France; Tuesday 18 August 1304; there is no mention of this particular incident in the Ghent annals: *Annals of Ghent*, pp 63–72; Kelly deVries, 'The battle of Courtrai', and 'The battle of Arques, 1304' and 'The battle of Mons-en-Pevelle, 1304' in Kelly deVries, *Infantry warfare in the early fourteenth century: discipline, tactics, and technology* (Woodbridge, 1996), pp 9–22, 23–31, 32–48.
318 Chapter Athy; interestingly, Pembridge (or his source) blames Jordan Comyn not de Bermingham, a Dominican benefactor; *AClyn*, p. 156; *Kilkenny chronicle*, p. 334; Peter de Bermingham was paid £100 for the beheading: *CJRI, 1305–1307*, p. 82; Peter de Bermingham was godfather for the Uí Chonchobhair Failghe children, plus the Uí Chonchobhair Failghe had been invited to Carbury castle: *AI*, pp 395–7; the Irish viewed it as 'hideous treachery': see *AC*, p. 207, *AClon*, p. 260, *AU*, p. 403; *AMisc.*, ii, p. 131; *ADR*; *AFM*, p. 481; this massacre was included by Domhnall Ó Néill in the Remonstrance in 1317 sent to Pope John XXII: *Scotichronicon*, vi, pp 392–5; Connolly, *IExP*, pp 182, 200; Cormac Ó Cléirigh, 'The O'Connor Faly lordship of Offaly, 1395–1513', *PRIA*, 96C (1996), 87–102; idem, 'The problem of defence', pp 46–52.
319 Seneschal of the liberty of Wexford: *CStM*, ii, p. 291; his widow Agatha later married David de Caunteton: *CJRI, 1308–1314*, pp 18–19, 60–1, 106–7, 159–60; Hamo le Gras was summoned to fight in Scotland: *CDI, 1302–1307*, p. 19; Hamon le Gras, killed at Skerries in 1315, was called 'that noble warrior': *AClyn*, p. 162.
320 *Flores hist.*, p. 583; *Lanercost*, ii, p. 176; John Comyn, lord of Badenoch (the Red Comyn), stabbed to death before the altar at the Franciscans in Dumfries: Alexander Grant, 'The death of John Comyn: what was going on?', *SHR*, 86 (2007), 176–224; Prestwich, 'England and Scotland during the wars of independence', p. 193; Matthew Strickland, 'Treason, feud and the growth of state violence: Edward I and the "war of the earl of Carrick" 1306–7' in Chris Given-Wilson et al. (eds), *War, government and aristocracy in the British Isles, c.1150–1500* (Woodbridge, 2008), p. 84.
321 *Flores hist.*, p. 584; 1306 March 25: *Lanercost*, ii, p. 176.
322 Pembridge has *Odymcy*, but Ó Duinn of Uí Riagáin is intended (see *AI* 1306: 'Amlaíb Ó Duinn, chief of Uí Riacáin, was slain by the Uí Dímusaig and by the foreigners'); for Geashill, see Linzi Simpson, 'The early Geraldine castles of Ireland: some case studies' in Crooks and Duffy (eds), *The Geraldines*, pp 114–25; Dominicans held a *congreatio* at Kilkenny this year, which may account for this entry.
323 *AI*; *AFM*.
324 *AI* ('Domnall Óc, son of Domnall Ruad Mac Carthaig, one fitted to be king by reason of good sense, piety, and purity, was taken prisoner by Domnall Cairprech Mac Carthaig and put to death in captivity on the eighth of the Kalends of October [September 24], and that was regarded as a shocking deed by the Gaedil and by the foreigners generally').
325 *AI* ('A defeat was inflicted by Ó Maíl Shechnaill on the foreigners and on Mac Feórais, and many of the foreigners were slain by Ó Maíl Shechnaill and by Mag Eochagáin').
326 Manor of the archbishopric of Dublin: *Account roll Holy Trinity*, p. 183; it had been profitable in 1271 (£1550–0–11¾): William Betham, 'The account of Thomas de Chaddisworth, custodee of the temporalities of the archbishop of Dublin from 1271–1276', *PRIA*, 5 (1850), 151–2; because of its position it was subject to raids by the Uí Thuathail and Uí Bhroin; for feoffees in 1249–52: Lawlor, 'Liber Niger', 60–2.

327 In 1287, a Henry Calf was a juror in Reyns, Co. Limerick: *Inquisitions & extents*, p. 37.
328 O'Byrne, 'MacMurroughs and the marches of Leinster', p. 181.
329 Possibly *Gleann Fhaídhle* (Glenealy, Co. Wicklow).
330 Quarrel over his burial between Friars Preachers and Friars Minor: Fitzmaurice and Little, *Franciscan province*, pp 104–5; *CPL* ii, 171; in 1296–7 a Thomas de Maundevyle was given payment of £20 for loss of horse in Scotland; he is mentioned again in connection with Scottish war in 1301; he is called knight in 1318: *IExP*, pp 139, 170, 195, 257; a Thomas de Mandeville, knight, accounts for lands in 1339–1340: *47th rep. DKPRI*, p. 19.
331 Thomas Quantock, chancellor Michaelmas 1291 to Christmas 1308: *Admin. Ire.*, p. 93; Lydon, 'Christ Church in the later medieval Irish world, 1300–1500' in Milne, *Christ church*, p. 90.
332 Died 17 Oct. 1306; on 23 Oct. licence sought to elect successor: Connolly, 'Chancery warrants (C81)', p. 142.
333 Elected March 1307, never consecrated, resigned 21 Nov. 1310; John Leche consecrated May 1311.
334 Chapter York; *Flores hist.*, pp 586–7; Feast of the Swans; on Whitsunday 1306 Edward I offered knighthood, robes and equipment to anyone who wished to be knighted on the same day and place as his son; among the estimated three hundred were Gilbert de Clare, Piers Gaveston and Roger Mortimer: see Constance Bullock-Davies, *Menestrellorum multitudo: minstrels at a royal feast* (Cardiff, 1978), pp ix–xxvii; Phillips, *Edward II*, pp 109–12; for group knighting, see s.a. 1361.
335 *Lanercost*, ii, pp 176, 180–1; for the sources, see Grant, 'The death of John Comyn'; Bruce was excommunicated by Pope Clement V: Barrow, *Robert Bruce*, pp 206–8, 211, 462; Rosalind Hill, 'Belief and practice as illustrated by John XXII's excommunication of Robert Bruce' in G.J. Cuming and Derek Barker (eds), *Popular belief and practice*, 8 (Cambridge, 1984), pp 135–8.
336 The missing name is undoubtedly Guy de Beauchamp, earl of Warwick, though his presence at the battle of Methven on 19 June 1306 is otherwise unattested; de Valence, who had been in Scottish campaigns from 1298 onwards, was brother-in-law of John Comyn (J.R.S. Phillips, *Aymer de Valence, earl of Pembroke, 1307–1324* (Oxford, 1972), p. 24), and was the king's special lieutenant in Scotland at the time of Methven, successfully commanding the English forces in the rout of Bruce's small following (Barrow, *Robert Bruce*, pp 216, 462).
337 'And there they engaged him in battle near the town of St John (which is called by another name Pert)': *Lanercost*, ii, p. 177.
338 For his precise movements, see Henry Gough, *Itinerary of King Edward the First throughout his reign, A.D. 1272–1307, exhibiting his movements so far as they are recorded*, vol. ii (Paisley, 1900), pp 262–4; on 21 Sept. he was in Newbrough: *Lanercost*, p. 181; Phillips, *Edward II*, p. 113; provisions and even Irishmen went through Dublin: Connolly, 'Memoranda rolls', 168–9, 171, 180.
339 *Lanercost*, ii, p. 178; the earl of Atholl was hanged but Fraser was a royal household knight who had changed sides and therefore received more severe punishment: Prestwich, 'England and Scotland during the wars of independence', p. 193; they were 'executed with the full ritual barbarity that the law could muster': Strickland, 'Edward I and the "war of the earl of Carrick"', p. 85.
340 Daughter of the earl of Ulster was sent to the royal manor of Burstwick; the others received very severe punishments: Prestwich, 'England and Scotland during the wars of independence', pp 193–4.

341 *Lanercost*, ii, p. 179; two brothers, 'Thomas and Alexander were captured in Galloway in February 1307', Phillips, *Edward II*, p. 113; Seán Duffy, 'The Bruce brothers and the Irish Sea world', *Cambridge Medieval Celtic Studies*, 21 (1991), 55–86; reprinted in idem (ed.), *Robert the Bruce's Irish wars: the invasions of Ireland, 1306–1329* (Stroud, 2002), p. 52.

342 For Richard McKyoghy Ó Tuathail of Cnoclorkan in Imaal, see Emmett O'Byrne, *War, politics and the Irish of Leinster, 1156–1606* (Dublin, 2003), pp 27, 65; it is possible that 'Lorcano Obony' is an Ó Broin; Thomas de Suytirby is found in 1294–5: *CStM*, i, p 295; keeper of Castlekevin in 1307: *CJRI, 1305–1307*, p. 336.

343 Chapter at Cashel; for the execution of Murchadh Ballach Mac Murchadha, see O'Byrne, *Irish of Leinster*, p. 65; 'Marton' is unidentified; a David de Caunteton was hanged, see below s.a. 1308; a David de Caunteton died 2 Oct. 1340, *Inquisitions & extents*, p. 188.

344 Unidentified.

345 *AC* 1307: 'All the Galls of Roscommon were killed by Donnchad Muimnech Ó Cellaig a little while before his death, at Ahascragh; here fell Philip Munter and Seoan Munter and Matthew Driu, and eighty others were killed or captured …'.

346 O'Byrne, *Irish of Leinster*, pp 81–2.

347 Chapter at London; 'The illustrious Edward king of England died at Karlex in Scotland on the seventh day of July aged 68 years in the 35th year of his reign and his son Edward of Carnarvon who married Isabella daughter of the king of France at Bononiam succeeded him. And in the same year on the day of the conversion of St Paul (25 Jan.) he was crowned in London': *Kilkenny chronicle*, p. 334; *AClyn*, p. 158; he died near Carlisle on 7 July 1307 and was buried in Westminster Abbey on 27 October;

348 *Flores hist.*, pp 595–6; the wedding had been arranged: *Lanercost*, ii, pp 182, 186; J.R.S. Phillips, 'Edward II and Ireland (in fact and in fiction)', *IHS*, 33 (2002), 6; Phillips, *Edward II*, pp 132–5; E.A.R. Brown, 'The political repercussions of family ties in the early fourteenth century: the marriage of Edward II and Isabelle of France', *Speculum*, 63 (1988), 573–95.

349 The Templars were seized in France and England: *Kilkenny chronicle*, p. 334.

350 *AClyn*, p 158; same date, *Kilkenny chronicle*, p. 334; first seized in France, 13 Oct. 1307; order was sent on 29 September 1309: *CCR 1307–1313*, p. 179; I thank Professor Helen Nicholson especially for her 'List of Irish religious involved in the trial of the Templars, 1310 [from Oxford, Bodleian Library, MS Bodley 454, fols 134r–153v]'; Helen Nicholson, 'The testimony of Brother Henry Danet and the trial of the Templars in Ireland' in Iris Shagrir et al. (eds), *In laudem hierosolymitani: studies in crusades and medieval culture in honour of Benjamin Z. Kedar* (Aldershot, 2008), pp 411–23; eadem, 'The trial of the Templars in Ireland' in eadem et al. (eds), *The debate on the trial of the Templars (1307–1314)* (Farnham, 2010), pp 225–35; Maeve Callan, *The Templars, the witch, and the wild Irish: vengeance and heresy in medieval Ireland* (Dublin, 2015).

351 See above s.a. 1305; on the eve of Easter: *Kilkenny chronicle*, p. 334; Peter Bermingham of Tethmoy; he was responsible for the murder of An Calbhach Ó Conchobhair: M. Hickey, 'Peter de Bermingham, lord of Tethmoy', *JCKAS*, 16 (1981–2), 232–8.

352 Son of the Walter Ó Tuathail who managed to retain substantial lands in Co. Kildare (O'Byrne, *Irish of Leinster*, pp 26–7); it is unclear whether he is the Baltor Ototheal found in Imaal (*Red bk Ormond*, p. 20; Lawlor, 'Liber Niger', 62–3); the William mac Walter of this entry may be a brother of Adam Dubh son of Walter Dubh Ó Tuathail who was burned for heresy in 1327 in Hoggen Green in Dublin.

353 Seán Duffy informs me that there is no obvious candidate to fit this name and that most likely an individual is not intended (hence, 'Otothiles', the plural found throughout these

annals, is used here rather than singular 'Otothil'); he suggests that the original annals contained a phrase like that used in 1327 in reference to a probable brother of William mac Walter, when we hear of 'Adam Duff, filius Walteri Duff de Lagenia *de cognatione Othothiles*', so that the 1308 entry should properly read something like 'Castlekevin was burnt, certain guards being killed, by William mac Walter of the surname Uí Thuathail and his accomplices'.

354 'Courcouley' is unidentified: Seán Duffy suggests perhaps Kilcoole.
355 In T.
356 For a 'Johannem Howelin', and a 'Johanni Howelyn', see Philomena Connolly, 'An account of a military expedition in Leinster, 1308', *AH*, 30 (1982), 4; he was a member of a family of mercenaries, possibly Welsh in origin, and hence the surname Mac Llywelyn, Mac Uigilin in Irish, later anglicized MacQuillan (Katharine Simms, *Gaelic Ulster in the Middle Ages: history, culture and society* (Dublin, 2020), pp 110, 122–3, 143).
357 Between 1306 and 1313 another John de Bretton was keeper of rolls of Dublin bench: *IExP*, pp 202, 205, 210, 218.
358 Tober bar; Talbotstown; Castlekevin was the archbishop of Dublin's manor and the O'Byrnes and O'Tooles were main tenants: Linzi Simpson, 'Dublin's southern frontier under siege: Kindlestown Castle, Delgany, County Wicklow' in Seán Duffy (ed.), *Medieval Dublin IV* (Dublin, 2003), pp 289–91; for a list of feoffees here in 1249–52, see Lawlor, 'Liber Niger', 62–3; O'Byrne, 'MacMurroughs and the marches of Leinster', pp 182–3; in addition to the 20 men at arms, 200 hobelars and 500 foot-soldiers were involved, Dublin, 18 October 1308 (CIRCLE, Close Roll 2 Edw II, §§41, 47, 52); also 128 foot-soldiers at Newcastle McKynegan to attack the Irish felons of the Leinster mountains, Dublin, 2 November 1308 (CIRCLE, Close Roll 2 Edw II, §43); Connolly, 'Military expedition in Leinster', 1–5; G.H. Orpen, '*Castrum Keyvini*, Castlekevin', *JRSAI*, 38 (1908), 17–27.
359 Peter, otherwise Piers: *Lanercost*, ii, pp 184, 186–7, 189; for Gaveston and Dominicans, see Röhrkasten, *Mendicant London*, pp 212, 360, 362, 530; J.S. Hamilton, *Piers Gaveston, earl of Cornwall, 1307–12* (London, 1988); Pierre Chaplais, *Piers Gaveston: Edward II's adoptive brother* (Oxford, 1994).
360 Gaveston 'who was called earl of Cornwall, came to Ireland': *Kilkenny chronicle*, p. 334; *Lanercost*, ii, pp 193–4; Gaveston was appointed as lieutenant in Ireland on 16 June 1308: *Admin. Ire.* p. 83; Phillips *Edward II*, pp 149–51; he married the king's niece, Margaret de Clare, sister of the earl of Gloucester: *Lanercost* ii, pp 186–7; Otway-Ruthven, 'Chief governors', p. 79, n.1.
361 William son of Walter Ó Tuathail; see above same year on 4 Id. May.
362 Gilbert, *History of the city of Dublin*, i (Dublin, 1854), pp 408–15; as early as 1228 the Dominicans had permission to receive part of the city water supply without damaging the bridge, their pipe to be the width of a man's little finger: *CARD*, pp 92, 101–2; H.F. Berry, 'Notes on an unpublished manuscript inquisition (A.D.1258), relating to the Dublin city watercourse, from the muniments of the earl of Meath', *PRIA*, 24C (1902–4), 39–46; for le Decer's fountain, see H.F. Berry, 'The water supply of ancient Dublin', *JRSAI*, Ser. 5, 1:2 (1891) 563–4; for grant to the Dominicans, ibid., p. 571; Gilbert, *Hist. & mun. docs*, pp 105–6; for mayors, see Seán Duffy, 'Town and crown: the kings of England and their city of Dublin' in Prestwich et al. (eds), *TCE 10*, pp 95–117; note use of *dominus* for mayor in this instance.
363 A house of Victorine canons near Celbridge, Co. Kildare (Gwynn and Hadcock, *MHRI*, p. 193); for medieval bridges, see Peter O'Keeffe and Tom Simington, *Irish stone bridges: history and heritage* (Dublin, 2016), pp 13–16, 165.
364 See s.a. 1332.

365 For this chapel of St Mary Magdalene, see Joseph Harbison and René Gapert, 'Before and after St John's hospital: evidence for a pre-Anglo-Norman cemetery on Thomas Street found on the shelves of Trinity College Dublin' in Seán Duffy (ed.), *Medieval Dublin XIX* (Dublin, 2023), pp 39, 49.

366 Constitutions of John Comyn (1186) stated that altars must be of stone: *The book of obits and martyrology of ... Christ Church, Dublin*, p. xxi, note; Harris (ed.), *Whole works of Sir James Ware, vol. I bishops*, p. 316; Harris, *Dublin*, pp 258–9; R.A. Sundt, '"*Mediocres domos et humiles habeant fratres nostri*": Dominican legislation on architecture and architectural decoration', *Journal of the Society of Architectural Historians*, 46 (1987), 394–407.

367 First indication of age of scribe here; this was primarily a penitential, religious, ascetic act and le Decer would have been fasting too, as it was a Friday; I thank Colmán Ó Clabaigh for this clarification.

368 *CStM*, ii, p. 293; Gaveston June 1308–May 1309 (deputy justiciar, William de Burgh), John Wogan 1309–12, Edmund Butler 1312–14 as keeper and acting justiciar: *Admin. Ire.*, p. 83.

369 *CStM*, ii, p. 293; *Kilkenny chronicle*, p. 334; important marriage as Joan was sole heir to the large inheritance of her grandfather, Geoffrey de Geneville; permission for the transfer in 1307: *CPR, 1307–13*, p. 33.

370 Paul Dryburgh, 'The career of Roger Mortimer, first earl of March (c.1287–1330)' (PhD, University of Bristol, 2002), p. 28.

371 Geoffrey de Geneville is assumed to be the founder of Trim but, if he had founded Trim, one would expect that it would be mentioned here; Thomas Case only states that he became a Friar Preacher at Trim: *CStM*, ii, p 281; not claimed by Ware fragment: *CStM*, ii, p. 293 or by Pembridge as is sometimes stated: Hugh Fenning, 'The Dominicans of Trim: 1263–1682', *Ríocht na Mídhe*, 2 (1961), 15.

372 *Servientes* are technically tenants under the rank of knight; *CStM*, ii, pp 291, 293; see also, *AC* 1308 ('Piers Gaveston, a knight and a high officer of the King of England, came to Ireland and he killed Ó Dimusaig this same year'); for Diarmuid Ó Díomusaigh and Isabella de Cadel who was living with him and charged with spying on the English, see *CJRI*, ii, p. 368; Margaret Murphy, 'Tullow, from medieval manor to market town' in Thomas McGrath (ed.), *Carlow: history and society* (Dublin, 2008), pp 235–58.

373 Dominican house at Trim.

374 Dominican house at Drogheda; Gilbert, *Viceroys*, pp 127–8, 524.

375 The earl of Gloucester married the daughter of the earl of Ulster: *Kilkenny chronicle*, p. 334.

376 *CStM*, ii, pp 281, 294; *CJI, 1308–14*, pp 159–61, 174–5.

377 In 1309 'Maurice Caunteton was killed and David [Caunteton] hanged': *AClyn*, p. 158; *Kilkenny chronicle*, p. 335; *CStM*, ii, p. 294; the Roches had a grievance because Maurice held two thirds of the lordship of Fermoy from Maurice de Carreu, but this created 'a mesne lord between Roche and Carreu': see Connolly, 'Ancient petitions (SC 8)', p. 93; Maurice and David allied themselves with the Leinster Irish and their downfall can be traced in *CJRI, 1308–14*, pp 19–21, 25, 145–6, 159–61, 200, 237, 247; John Wogan led an expedition 'to repress the malice and rebellion of Maurice de Caunteton and others of his *parentela*, felons because of the death of Richard Talun, who confederated with .... the Obrens' (*IExP*, pp 207, 211, 598; *39th rep. DKPRI*, p. 31).

378 See *AC* 1309: 'Aed son of Eogan son of Ruaidri son of Aed son of Cathal Croberg, king of Connacht and eligible for his nobility, valour, generosity, form and feature for the kingship of Ireland, was killed by Aed Brefnech son of Cathal Ruad Ó Conchobair at Coill in Chlachain in the territory of Brefne; many of the great men of Connacht were

killed with him …'; the O'Connors were Dominicans benefactors in Roscommon; Séan Duffy informs me that it is interesting that while the slain Aodh has his surname rendered in the standard nominative *Oconghir*, the source knows to reproduce the other Aodh, his slayer, in the genitive (he being Aodh *son of* Cathal Ó Conchobair), and hence the form *Yconghir*; another instance of the same is found below s.a. 1315.
379 Dominican priory at Athy but Athboy, Co. Meath, seems to be intented.
380 *CStM*, ii, p 281; 'Newcastle Mac Kinnegan was destroyed by Irish felons of that region so that for ten years it lay uncultivated and devastated': *53th rep. DKPRI*, p. 23; Piers de Gaveston 'went to rebuild and repair the castle of Castlekevin which had been knocked down by the Irish': Connolly, 'Memoranda rolls', 203; on Castlekevin, see Linzi Simpson, 'Anglo-Norman settlement in Uí Briúin Cualann, 1169–1350' in Ken Hannigan and William Nolan (eds), *Wicklow: history and society* (Dublin, 1994), pp 203–4, 219, 225.
381 Arrived at Chester 27 June: Phillips, *Edward II*, pp 153–8.
382 John de Burgh, son of Richard de Burgh married Elizabeth de Clare (known as Elizabeth de Burgh).
383 Dominican priory at Drogheda; *CStM*, ii, p. 294.
384 *CStM*, ii, p. 294; *AClyn*, p. 158; *Kilkenny chronicle*, p. 335; in 1308 John de Boneville was seneschal of the liberties of Kildare and Carlow and sent a writ to attend parliament at Kilkenny in 1310 (*Stat. John–Hen V*, p. 261), but was killed at that very point; in January 1310 the king had ordered Arnold le Poer to desist from besieging de Boneville in his castle in Co. Carlow (Brooks, *Knights' fees*, p. 87) but le Poer went ahead and killed him on 2 February, as our annalist reports, adding (under 1310) that le Poer was subsequently acquitted of murder.
385 Dominican house at Kilkenny; *CStM*, ii, p. 294.
386 This must be the February 1310 parliament at Kilkenny: *Ir. parl.*, p. 334; there was another held in Kildare after 24 March, ibid., p. 335; 'The 1310 Parliament was notable for the large number of magnates (eighty-seven) individually summoned and for the procedure adopted': Lydon, 'The impact of the Bruce invasion, 1315–27', *NHI*, ii, p. 278.
387 In previous three entries not called *dominus*; now called *dominus* as he had been knighted: *CStM*, ii, p. 295.
388 He left four daughters as heirs: Frame, *Eng. lordship*, p. 53; Hagger, *Fortunes*, pp 16, 98–115; for his descendants, see Smith, *Crisis and survival*, p. 19.
389 *Lanercost*, ii, p. 190; *CStM*, ii, p. 295; the campaign was fruitless even though Gaveston managed to reach as far north as Perth; there were 25 Irish hobelars at Berwick: Lydon, 'The hobelar: an Irish contribution to medieval warfare' in Crooks (ed.), *Government*, p. 180.
390 The first mention of crops and prices; Crannock was 'a measure for grain, peas, beans, woad, coals, salt, and other articles': Gilbert, *Hist. & mun. docs*, p. xxxiv; 'The greatest scarcity then in Ireland so that crannocks of grain were selling for thirty shillings: *Kilkenny chronicle*, p. 335; '20 shillings and more': *CStM*, ii, p. 295.
391 *CStM*, ii, p. 295; bread production was taken very seriously and the Dublin city ordinances declared that bakers must stamp their bread with their own names, unstamped breads to be forfeited and the bakers fined; also, after the third offence for faulty bread 'they shall stand in the pillory and swear to leave the city for a year and a day and if wishing to return could not be a baker again': *CARD*, pp 219, 221, 224; for bakers, Phyllis Gaffney and Yolande de Pontfarcy Sexton, '"The laws and usages of Dublin": a complete translation of *Les leys et les uages de la cite de Diveline*' in Seán Duffy (ed.), *Medieval Dublin XVII* (Dublin, 2019), pp 179–80.

392 For eulogy, see Ware fragment: *CStM*, ii, p. 295.
393 Held in Kildare after 24 March: *Ir. parl.*, p. 335; for the 1310 parliament, see M.V. Clarke, 'Irish parliaments in the reign of Edward II', *TRHS*, 9 (1926), 44–5; for John de Boneville's killing, see above s.a. 1309.
394 G.J. Hand, 'The rivalry of the cathedral chapters in medieval Dublin', *JRSAI*, 92 (1962), 193–206; K.W. Nicholls, 'Mediæval Irish cathedral chapters', *Arch. Hib.*, 31 (1973), 102–11; Lawlor, 'Liber Niger', 8–12, 16–17; canon of St Patrick's and treasurer of Ireland consecrated archbishop of Dublin Aug.1317; he preached a sermon against beggars in the city and suburbs of Dublin, following which the mayor of Dublin legislated against all beggars 'including the begging friars': *CStM*, ii, pp xiv–xv; J.F. Lydon, 'The enrolled account of Alexander Bicknor, treasurer of Ireland, 1308–1314', *AH*, 30 (1982), 7–46; idem, 'The case against Alexander Bicknor, archbishop and peculator' in Brendan Smith (ed.), *Ireland and the English world in the late Middle Ages* (Basingstoke, 2009), pp 103–11.
395 Chapter at Athenry; *AClyn*, p. 158; *Kilkenny chronicle*, p. 335; *Caithréim Thoirdhealbhaigh*, ed. S.H. O'Grady, ii (Irish Texts Soc., London, 1929), pp 6, 44–52; *AFM*, iii, p. 499; *AC* 1311 ('Great warfare ... between ... Sir Richard de Clare and Diarmait, son of Donnchad Ó Briain, on the one side ... opposed by Donnchad Ó Briain and the Tuadmumu, along with William de Burgo and many of the Connachta and of the foreigners of Mide. The latter came to Bun Raite on Ascension Thursday [May 20] ... and gave battle in ring formation to Sir Richard de Clare ... And although more of these last were slain, they were victorious, and Sir William de Burgo and about twelve or thirteen nobles of those northern foreigners were taken prisoner by them ...').
396 Lydon, 'Medieval Wicklow: "a land of war"' in Hannigan and Nolan (eds), *Wicklow: history and society*, pp 151–89; Margaret Murphy, 'The "key of the county": Saggart and the manorial economy of the Dublin March *c*.1200–1540' in Jennifer Ní Ghrádaigh and Emmett O'Byrne (eds), *The march in the islands of the medieval West* (Leiden, 2012), pp 53–78; Foley, *The royal manors of medieval Co. Dublin*, pp 175–6; Emmet O'Byrne, 'Cultures in contact in the Leinster and Dublin marches, 1170–1400' in Seán Duffy (ed.), *Medieval Dublin V* (Dublin, 2004), pp 129–30; for the boroughs of Rathcoole and Saggart, see John Bradley, 'The medieval boroughs of county Dublin' in Conleth Manning (ed.), *Dublin and beyond the Pale: studies in honour of Patrick Healy* (Bray, 1998), pp 136–7; James Lydon, 'The defence of Dublin in the Middle Ages' in Duffy (ed.), *Medieval Dublin IV*, pp 70–1.
397 The king stayed with Dominicans during the London parliament: Röhrkasten, *Mendicant London*, p. 515; *Lanercost* ii, p. 193; Michael Prestwich, 'The Ordinances of 1311 and the politics of the early fourteenth century' in John Taylor and Wendy Childs (eds), *Politics and crisis in fourteenth-century England* (Woodbridge, 1990), pp 1–18; Phillips, *Edward II*, pp 161–2, 171–80; for Ireland at this point, see James Lydon, 'Select documents XXIV: Edward II and the revenues of Ireland in 1311–12', *IHS*, 14 (1964), 39–57.
398 Kenneth Nicholls, 'Scottish mercenary kindreds in Ireland, 1250–1600' in Seán Duffy (ed.), *The world of the galloglass: kings, warlords and warriors in Ireland and Scotland, 1200–1600* (Dublin, 2007), pp 86–105; Lydon, 'The Scottish soldier in medieval Ireland: the Bruce invasion and the galloglass' in G.G. Simpson (ed.), *The Scottish soldier abroad, 1247–1967* (Edinburgh, 1992), pp 1–15.
399 Chapter at Gloucestor; he was ordered to leave on 1 November but left 3 November: Phillips, *Edward II*, pp 180–2.
400 Flanders, *Lanercost*, ii, pp 196–7; either northern France or Flanders: Phillips, *Edward II*, p. 181.

401 In 1310 John de Cogan died: *AClyn*, p. 158; Cogan founded the Franciscan friary at Claregalway, so perhaps it was only the other two who were buried with the Dominicans: Fitzmaurice and Little, *Franciscan province*, p. 62; *AI*, p. 411; in 1309, 'Walter Lenfaunt and his fellow justices': *Inquisitions & extents*, p. 90; Edmund Curtis, 'The fitz Rerys, Welsh lords of Cloghran, Co Dublin', *JLAHS*, 5 (1921–4), 13–17.

402 The Irish annals report instead for this year that 'Muirchertach Mór son of Congalach Mag Eochagáin, chieftain of Ceinéal Fhiachach [Kinaleagh, Co. Westmeath], was killed by the Galls' (*AC* 1311); no mention here of Ó Maoil Mhuaidh [of Fir Cheall in Co. Westmeath], whose head at this time was Donnchadh (*AC* 1316) but, as they were neighbours and rivals, Pembridge's account seems very plausible.

403 For a list of Roches at this period, see *CJRI, 1308–14*, pp 199–200; *AI*, p. 405.

404 Peter le Poer was killed by the Roaches and Eustace died 'before Easter': *AClyn*, p. 160; for le Poers, see Parker, 'Pater familias and *parentela*'; Eustace, a knight, was head of his lineage: James Lydon, 'Impact of the Bruce invasion', p. 278; he was itinerant justice for Limerick in 1279 and Dublin 1291–92: *Admin. Ire.*, pp 141, 143.

405 'Contemporary records use the terms "Uriel" and "Louth" interchangeably': Smith, *Crisis and survival*, p. 22; reported in Kilkenny; 'lord Nicholas de Avenell, Patrick de Roche and many Irish, were killed by lord Nicholas de Verdun and the burgesses of Dundalk, near Dundalk', on Monday 17 April: *AClyn*, p. 158; for an account of the proceedings, see *CStM*, ii, appendix iii, pp 417–23; Robert was the younger brother of Nicholas and Milo de Verdun and was killed defending Dundalk against the Uí Anluain in 1316: Brendan Smith, 'The Bruce invasion and county Louth, 1315–1318', *JLAHS* (1989), 10; for a full examination and the choice of 21 February, see Smith, *Colonisation and conquest*, pp 97–105; Lydon, 'Impact of the Bruce invasion', p. 280.

406 Interestingly, different strands in the Gaelic annals have a similarly damning view of Donnchadh's slaying: 'Murchad, son of Mathgamain, son of Domnall Connachtach Ó Briain, committed treachery against Donnchad son of Tairdelbach Ó Briain, king of Tuadmumu, and that crime was a great calamity, for he was a prominent person with a large retinue, destructive [to enemies], and of goodly worth ...' (*AI* 1311); 'Donnchad Ó Briain, king of Thomond and a good man for the kingship of Ireland, was treacherously killed by Murchad son of Mathgamain Ó Briain' (*AFM* 1311).

407 Chapter at Chester; first to Scarborough then York, then later Scarborough again: *Lanercost* ii, pp 196–8.

408 Phillips, *Aymer de Valence*, pp 32–37.

409 Gaveston captured and buried; Clyn, a Franciscan, does not mention where buried *AClyn*, p. 160; *Kilkenny chronicle*, p. 335; before 24 June in 1311, Flower, 'Manuscripts of Irish interest', 314–15 fn.3: he was buried at Langley; 'All this time the body ... remained above ground unburied with the Friars Preachers of Oxford ... receiving from the king half a mark for their trouble': *Lanercost*, ii, p. 203; Phillips, *Aymer de Valence*, pp 35–6; idem, *Edward II*, pp 240–2; the Dominicans 'gathered up Piers and sewing the head to the body they carried it to Oxford: 'but because he was excommunicate', they dared not bury the body in church': Chris Given-Wilson, '*Vita Edwardi Secundi*: memoir or journal?' in *TCE VI* (1996), p. 168.

410 See above s.a. 1311; Near Dundalk, *AClyn*, p. 158; Nicholas Avenell married Margaret Cruys, who held Naul, Co. Dublin: Brooks, *Knights' fees*, p. 164; *39th rep. DKPRI*, pp 41–2; Lydon, 'Impact of the Bruce invasion', p. 280; this is in connection with the 'Riot of Louth' early in 1312; Smith, *Colonisation and conquest*, pp 97–101; Theobald de Verdun [II] and Roger Mortimer 'bailed Robert de Verdun and another twelve named and 27 unnamed accomplices, who were to go and serve the king in the army in Scotland': Hagger, *Fortunes*, pp 117, 151, 215; Dryburgh, 'Roger Mortimer', pp 33–4, 35; see also *CStM*, ii, appendix iii, p. 419.

411 This entry is rubricated; *AClyn*, p. 160; under 1310, *Kilkenny chronicle*, p. 335; a new moon and eclipse and strange colours: *Lanercost*, ii, p. 198; the papal bull of 22 March 1312, *Vox in excelso*, suppressed the order.
412 *AClyn*, p. 160; *Lanercost*, ii, p. 200.
413 From 7 August 1312 to 18 June 1314, 'keeper and acting justiciar': *Admin. Ire.*, p. 83.
414 'Lord Maurice Fitz Thomas married Katherine, daughter of Richard, earl of Ulster, and there Edmund Butler made two knights': *AClyn*, p. 160; he died in 1356 (see below); for Desmond, see Robin Frame, 'Rebellion and rehabilitation: the first earl of Desmond and the English scene' in Crooks & Duffy (eds), *The Geraldines*, pp 194–222; Keith Alan Waters, 'The earls of Desmond in the fourteenth century' (PhD, University of Durham, 2004); this healed the rift between the Geraldines of Offaly and the de Burghs: ibid., pp 27–8.
415 See above 1309.
416 Thomas de Jorz of the same family had been provincial prior of the English (and therefore of Irish) Dominicans from 1297–1303/4, see note above s.a. 1300; there was also his brother Walter Jorz, archbishop of Armagh, in 1306: Hinnebusch, *English friars preachers*, pp 413, 414, 497; Bede Jarrett, *The English Dominicans* (New York, 1921), p. 219; three members of the family were Dominicans: Alison K. McHardy, 'The Great Bardney scandal' in W. Mark Ormrod (ed.), *Fourteenth century England VII* (Woodbridge, 2012), p. 40.
417 New page with special heading.
418 This highlights the controversy between the two archbishoprics as to which was the primate of Ireland; in 1345 the chapter of Dublin was summoned to defend the archbishop against the archbishop of Armagh regarding the title of primate: Lawlor, 'Liber Niger', 56; in 1368 there was a petition concerning the rivalry over cross-bearing between the two archbishops: *Affairs Ire.*, pp 227–8; Ware has a long discourse on the controversy: Harris (ed.), *Whole works of Sir James Ware, vol. I bishops*, pp 71–80; Tomás Ó Fiaich, 'The primacy in the Irish church', *Seanchas Ardmhacha*, 21 (2006), 3–8, 19–20.
419 They made promises 'which afterwards they did not observe': *Lanercost*, ii, pp 203–4.
420 E.A.R. Brown and N.F. Regalado, '*La grant feste*: Philip the Fair's celebration of the knighting of his sons in Paris at Pentecost of 1313' in Barbara Hanawalt and Kathryn Reyerson (eds.), *City and spectacle in medieval Europe* (Minneapolis,1994), pp 56–86; '*ut interesset ... in quo festo rex francie*' missing from L.
421 At Christmas, 'a great, sumptuous and peaceful feast' was held at Adare and he made Nicholas Fitz Maurice of Kerry a knight, and two others': *AClyn* p. 160; for a Nicholas son of Maurice in Limerick in 1307, see Robin Frame, 'Commissions of the peace in Ireland, 1302–1461', *AH*, 35 (1992), 14; K.W. Nicholls, 'The FitzMaurices of Kerry', *Kerry Arch. Soc.*, 3 (1970) 30–1, 33.
422 'galleys' supplied by L.
423 In 1313, 'Robert Bruce, king of Alba, came on the coast of Erinn': *ALC*, p. 561; in 1312, a 'great fleet-host came from Scotland': *AU*, p. 423; under leadership of Thomas Dun: Olive Armstrong, *Edward Bruce's invasion of Ireland* (London, 1923), pp 68, 69.
424 It was rebuilt in 1488: CIRCLE, Close Roll 4 Edw II, §26; Colm Lennon, 'The medieval manor of Clontarf, 1171–1540' in Seán Duffy (ed.), *Medieval Dublin XII* (Dublin, 2010), p. 199.
425 *CStM*, ii, p. 291.
426 Lydon, 'Christ Church in the later medieval Irish world', p. 75.
427 In 1317 Hothum was nominated to the mission to Avignon partly to secure the promotion of Bicknor as archbishop of Dublin, Hotham having deputized as treasurer of the Irish exchequer in the latter part of 1309; Phillips, *Edward II*, pp 284–7; Lydon, 'The case against Alexander Bicknor'.

428 Milo, brother of Theobald II, chief guardian of Irish lands: Hagger, *Fortunes*, p. 117; see above 1269; obit Richard: *CStM* i, 279; for Milo, see Smith, *Crisis and survival*, p. 27; Nicholas and Miles de Verdun in 1312: Frame, 'Commissions of the peace', 20.

429 'On the 18th of May, Lord Robert, king of Scotland, put in at Ramsay with a large number of ships ... and on Monday laid siege to the castle of Rushen, which was defended by the Lord Dungall MacDowyle': *Chronicon Manniae et Insularum (Chronicle of Man and the Isles), 1249–1374,* www.isle-of-man.com/manxnotebook/manxsoc/msvol22/index.htm); for 'Duncan O Dowell', otherwise Dungal Macdouall, the Galloway lord who had captured and executed Robert Bruce's brothers Thomas and Alexander in 1307, see Duffy, 'Bruce brothers' in idem, *Bruce's Irish wars*, p. 62.

430 Dominican house at Galway; around Pentecost [3 June]: *AClyn* p. 160.

431 Clyn gives the year as 1313 and the feast of blessed Michael [Saturday 29 September], when 'lord Edmund *Pincerna* [Butler] held a great feast in Dublin and he made thirty knights': *AClyn*, p. 160; thirty-one knights: *Kilkenny chronicle*, p. 335.

432 H.J. Nicholson, 'A long way from Jerusalem: the Templars and Hospitallers in Ireland, *c.*1172–25 1348' in Martin Browne and Colmán Ó Clabaigh (eds), *Soldiers of Christ: the Knights Hospitaller and the Knights Templar in medieval Ireland* (Dublin, 2015), p. 11; Wood, 'The Templars in Ireland', pp 359–60.

433 Dominican house at Drogheda; a John de Parys was rector of Dissard (Dysert, dio. Meath) in 1279–80: *IExP*, p. 40; a Peter Parys granted land in Termonfeckin in 1372: Smith, *Crisis and survival*, p. 9; a Peter de Parys, the king's mariner in 1290s: *IExP*, p 133; Paristown in Killua, bar. Delvin, Co. Westmeath: Hogan, *Llanthony*, p. 220.

434 19 June 1314 to 27 February 1315: *Admin. Ire.*, p. 83; he died in July 1316 after marrying Elizabeth, widow of John de Burgh, son of the earl of Ulster, in February 1316 without the king's permission: Hagger, *Fortunes*, p. 119.

435 An incorrect date is given for his death in the register of Athenry; this casts doubt on its comment about 12,000 marks: '*Obitus domini Galfridi de Genfyl qui fuit dominus Mediae et potuit expendere duodecim millia marcarum qui suis ultimus diebus factus est frater ordinis Praedicatorum in conventu de Truym*': Ambrose Coleman, '*Regestum monasterii fratrum Praedicatorum de Athenry*', *Archivium Hibernicum*, 1 (1912), p. 214.

436 Chapter at Mullingar, caput of de Verdun's lordship of west Meath: Orpen, *Normans*, p. 522; Smith, 'The Bruce invasion and county Louth', p. 8.

437 Justiciar from 28 February 1315 to 30 November 1317, then again from 27 Jan. 1318 to 4 April 1318: *Admin. Ire.*, p. 84.

438 On 23–4 June 1314; Clyn has the correct date and year: *AClyn*, p. 160; under 1313: *Kilkenny chronicle*, p. 335; Stirling castle, and 'a great ditch called Bannackburn', and the aforesaid battle near Stirling: *Lanercost*, ii, 207–8, 215); Michael Brown, *Bannockburn: The Scottish War and the British Isles, 1307–1323* (Edinburgh, 2008); for the death of Gilbert de Clare, see Kelley deVries, 'The battle of Bannockburn, 1314' in idem, *Infantry warfare in the early fourteenth century: discipline, tactics, and technology* (Woodbridge, 1996) pp 81–82; for Irish involvement with Northumberland (and for a Jack le Irish who led a contingent to Scotland), see Andy King, 'Bandits, robbers and *schavaldours*: war and disorder in Northumberland in the reign of Edward II' in Prestwich et al. (eds), *TCE IX* (Woodbridge, 2003), pp 115–29; for a possible Irish contingent of forty pardoned for de Verdun, see Dryburgh, 'Roger Mortimer', pp 33–4.

439 *Lanercost*, ii, pp 210, 212–13.

440 'Sir James Douglas, a bold and cautious knight, stationed himself ... on the west side opposite the place of the canons and the preaching friars [Dominicans]'; this mention of the Dominican priory may well be the source of Pembridge's knowledge: see *Lanercost*, vol. ii, p. 215; Brown, *Wars of Scotland*, pp 206, 208, 213–14; Douglas may have been crushed but he lived long afterwards.

441 Here, Pembridge provides a summary of the events of the Bruce invasion of Ireland, including the first three battles, and then begins again to describe events in normal annal format.

442 'They were not satisfied with their own frontiers': *Lanercost*, ii, p. 212; Pembridge (or his source) also gives the same reason as Barbour: 'Edward Bruce ... thought Scotland too small for his brother and himself': John Barbour, *The Brus*, in Duffy (ed.), *Bruce's Irish wars*, Appendix A, p. 163; Pembridge also has the same number (6,000); *AFM*, iii, pp 503–5; for Bruce invasion in general, see Duffy (ed.), *Bruce's Irish wars;* Armstrong, *Bruce's invasion;* Robin Frame, 'The Bruces in Ireland, 1315–1318', repr. in Frame, *Ire. & Brit.*, pp 71–98; J.R.S. Phillips, 'Documents on the early stages of the Bruce invasion of Ireland, 1315–1316', *PRIA*, 79C (1979), 247–70; Lydon, 'Impact of the Bruce invasion', pp 275–302; C.J. McNamee, *The wars of the Bruces: Scotland, England and Ireland 1306–1328* (East Linton, 1998).

443 The Scots landed in Ulster: *AClyn*, p. 162; *Kilkenny chronicle*, p. 335; the Cambridge manuscript (University Library, Additional 3392c), origin St Mary's O. Cist. Dublin, just gives '*applicuit in boriali plaga Ultonie*': Mac Niocaill, 'Cáipéisí', 33; there are many suggestions identifying the site: see Seán Duffy, 'The Bruce invasion of Ireland: a revised itinerary and chronology' in idem (ed.), *Bruce's Irish wars*, p. 10.

444 Pembridge (or his source) gives the same number as Barbour, *The Brus*, p. 164.

445 Thomas Randolph, earl of Moray, nephew of Bruce, later became Robert's chief military lieutenant: Brown, *Wars of Scotland*, pp 206, 213; John, brother of earl of Menteith, and cousin of Stewarts: Brown, *Wars of Scotland*, pp 195, 214; Barbour, *The Brus*, p. 163; Fergus of Ardrossen: Barrow, *Robert Bruce*, p. 427; Duffy, 'Revised itinerary', p. 11; for the Bissets, see Seán Duffy, 'The lords of Galloway, earls of Carrick, and the Bissets of the Glens: Scottish settlement in thirteenth-century Ulster' in David Edwards (ed.), *Regions and rulers in Ireland, 1100–1650* (Dublin, 2004), pp 39–42.

446 Thomas de Mandeville was Richard de Burgh's seneschal and leader of Ulster forces which include Logan and Savages: Duffy, 'Revised itinerary', p. 11; Barbour, *The Brus*, p. 164; Smith, 'The Bruce invasion and County Louth', p. 14; letter of Thomas de Mandeville to the king on 10 July 1315: Phillips, 'Documents', pp 260–1.

447 See above where Pembridge states 'landed at Clondonne': this may therefore indicate a different original source; 'Lord Edward Bruce entered Ireland', and 'Lord Robert de Bruce and lord Edward his brother entered Ireland and drawing up his troops journeyed to Knockfergus, through the middle of the English spoiling and burning the land right up to Nannath, they arrived opposite the strength of the English; after Easter lord Robert returned from Knockfergus to Scotland from where he had come': *Kilkenny chronicle*, p. 335; *AFM*, iii, p. 515.

448 Same date: *AClyn*, p. 162; Phillips, 'Documents', pp 251–3, 255–7.

449 'Only five of the English were killed but around seventy of the Scots': *AClyn*, p. 162; *Kilkenny chronicle*, p. 335; Phillips, *Edward II*, pp 255–6.

450 Bruce 'forcing himself as king of Ireland': *AClyn*, p. 162; 'Lord Edward, who claimed to be king of Ireland': *AI*, p. 425; Duffy, 'Revised itinerary', pp 12–13; for the possibility that in 1315 Edward Bruce proposed himself as king of the Irish, see Seán Duffy, 'The "Continuation" of the annals of Nicholas Trevet: a new source for the Bruce invasion', *PRIA*, 91C (1991), 303–15; the date is challenged by Duncan but both manuscripts are definite in their date (A.A.M. Duncan, 'The Scots' invasion of Ireland, 1315' in R.R. Davies (ed.), *The British Isles, 1100–1500* (Edinburgh, 1988), p. 109); the Cambridge manuscript also gives the date as the feast of Philip and James: Mac Niocaill, 'Cáipéisí', 33; J.R.S. Phillips, 'The mission of John de Hothum to Ireland, 1315–1316' in J.F. Lydon (ed.), *England and Ireland in the later Middle Ages* (Dublin, 1981), pp 69–75.

451 Most likely Greencastle, Co. Down, rather than Northburgh Castle, also known as Greencastle, built in 1305 by the earl of Ulster.
452 A 'diet' was a legal punishment: 'judgment was to be put to a diet and he died in prison', see s.a. 1318; also, in 1339, 'lord Maurice Fitz Nicholas was seized and imprisoned ... and ... died in prison on a starvation diet': *AClyn*, p. 226.
453 From this point, having summarized events thus far, Pembridge returns to the earliest stages of the invasion.
454 'The Scots, with the Irish, burnt Dundalk and the house of the friars and they plundered books, garments, chalices, vestments, and many were killed': *AClyn*, p. 162; Barbour, *The Brus*, pp 164–5; Mac Niocaill, 'Cáipéisí', 33; Dundalk had been established by de Verdun: Duffy, 'Revised itinerary', pp 14–15.
455 Duffy, 'Revised itinerary', p. 16; this is the first mention here of the Irish in relation to Bruce.
456 The earl of Ulster was also lord of Connacht. In 1315, 'When Richard Burke, Earl of Ulster, heard that Edward was approaching to attack him he brought together a great army from all sides to Roscommon at first, marching thence to Athlone and obliquely through Meath and Mag Breg, having with him Feidlim Ó Conchobair, king of Connacht, their numbers being about twenty battalions ... the earl saw coming to meet them Edmund Butler, Justiciar of Ireland but the Earl would not let him join his assembled force, for he trusted to himself and his own men to expel the Scots from Ireland': *AC*, pp 231–41; Duffy, 'Revised itinerary', pp 14–16; Armstrong, *Bruce's invasion*, pp 78–80; they converged south of Ardee: Duffy, 'Revised itinerary', pp 15–16; 'If the earl of Ulster is loyal there is nothing to be feared from their plots': *Vita Edwardi secondi*, p 107.
457 Near Coleraine where there was a Dominican priory; Lydon, 'The Bruce invasion of Ireland: an examination of some problems' in Duffy (ed.), *Bruce's Irish wars*, p. 80; Duffy, 'Revised itinerary, p. 16.
458 Duffy, 'Revised itinerary', pp 16–17.
459 William Liath de Burgh: Armstrong, *Bruce's invasion*, pp 82–3.
460 For date of Monday 1 September: Phillips, 'Documents', p. 264; John le Poer of Dunoil (Dunohill): Phillips, 'The mission of de Hothum', pp 72, 73, 74, 75.
461 Duffy, 'Revised itinerary', p. 18.
462 'William Burke and his knights ... were captured and the earl fled': *AC*, p. 235; Duffy, 'Revised itinerary', pp 17–18.
463 Thomas Randolph (earl of Moray) was made 'lord of Man' in 1316: Duffy, 'The Bruce brothers', pp 53, 59; idem, 'Revised itinerary', pp 17–18.
464 G.O. Sayles, 'The siege of Carrickfergus castle, 1315–16' in *Scripta Diversa* (London, 1982), pp 212–18.
465 This is Ruaidhrí son of Cathal Ruadh Ó Conchobhair, of the line of Muircheartach Muimhneach, who was challenging the reigning king, Feidhlim, of the line of Cathal Croibhdhearg.
466 Duffy, 'Revised itinerary', pp 17, 18.
467 L has 'a quodam Hibernico de midia occisus est'; the word '*a*' is missing in the TCD manuscript, which can result in a totally different sentence; Seán Duffy suggests that perhaps it is not that Richard de Lan de Ofervvill, a certain Irishman of Meath, was killed, but that Richard Dillon was killed *by* Ofervvill a certain Irishman of Meath, possibly Sefraidh (Geoffrey) son of Giolla na Naomh Ó Fearghail (O'Farrell) (d. 1318), lord of Anghaile (Annaly, Co. Longford); Dillon is found as de Delun, de Dilun, and also without the 'de'; the Uí Fhearghail were next door neighbours in Westmeath/Longford and both families were regularly involved in conflicts alongside and against each other.

468 I thank Seán Duffy for suggesting that this St Nicholas must refer to the feast of St Nicholas the Great (pope) (11 Nov.) and not St Nicholas (6 Dec.).
469 Duffy, 'Revised itinerary', p. 18.
470 Duffy, 'Revised itinerary', p. 21; Finnea (Cavan–Westmeath border); Granard/Abbeylara, O. Cist.; '*Granardo, quod quidem spo[lia] vit de omnibus bonis suis*': Mac Niocaill, 'Cáipéisí', 33–34; Seán Duffy has suggested that the *Novum Castrum* may possibly be Newcastle, parish of Lickbla, Co. Westmeath (*pers. comm.*).
471 Lough Sewdy, Co. Westmeath, a Verdun manor: Smith, 'The Bruce invasion and county Louth', p. 7; Duffy, 'Revised itinerary', p. 21.
472 Priory at Athy; '*Deinde rediens versus Ultoniam per Riban et Athy*': Mac Niocaill, 'Cáipéisí', 34; Duffy, 'Revised itinerary', pp 23–4; St Mary's had interests in Reban: *CStM* i, 390.
473 Duffy, 'Revised itinerary', pp 24–5.
474 'The battle of the Scots': *Kilkenny chronicle*, p. 335; for Hothum's report and a report by a royal clerk on the battle, see Phillips, 'Documents', pp 251–3, 255–7; Duffy, 'Revised itinerary', p. 24.
475 This is clearly after Christmas 1315 as Pembridge states above, so therefore the year 1316; the source of the text is Luke 11:14, 17; 'Only five of the English were killed but around seventy of the Scots' but 'the English abandoned the field to the Scots': *AClyn*, p. 162; *Kilkenny chronicle*, p. 335; Hothum was present so this information may have come from him: Phillips, 'Documents', pp 251–3, 255–7; idem 'The mission of de Hothum'; Duffy, 'Revised itinerary', p. 24.
476 'Here that noble warrior Hamon le Gras, and lord William Prendergast, and only three others, rested in the grave': *AClyn*, p. 162; Mac Niocaill, 'Cáipéisí', 34; only Prendergast is a named knight (*miles*) by both sources; another William de Prendergast, who died 1302, was called 'a young knight, of the best repute and liberality and disposition': *AU*, p. 407; a William and a Maurice Pindigast were buried on the north side of the altar in the Dominican Athenry priory: Rachel Moss, 'Records of art and architectural patronage at Athenry Friary' in eadem (ed.), *Art and architecture of Ireland*, i: *Medieval* (Dublin, 2015), p. 546.
477 Barrow, *Robert Bruce*, p. 427; after Bannockburn, Bruce restored his lands that had been confiscated by Edward and thereafter Ardrossan was a firm Bruce supporter.
478 It is not clear whether all the dead were buried by the Dominicans, or only the two named who might have been benefactors of the Dominicans of Scotland.
479 Belonging to John fitz Thomas: Duffy, 'Revised itinerary', p. 26.
480 L: Roger supplied.
481 'Bruce met and defeated Roger Mortimer, who as yet held no official position in Ireland … Roger's tenants were the de Lacys': Frame, 'The Bruces in Ireland', p. 93; Duffy, 'Revised itinerary', pp 19–21. Dryburgh, 'Roger Mortimer', pp 45–7.
482 Walter Cusack was making sure Trim did not fall into enemy hands: Duffy, 'Revised itinerary', pp 19, 25; a Walter Cusack was knighted by Lionel, see *s.a.* 1361; for Walter Cusack of Clonnortheran in Skreen in 1361; see Frame, 'Commissions of the peace', 24; in 1319 'John de Cusack claimed that 'his father, Sir Walter, and himself and their friends have been thrice burned and plundered by the Scots and the Lacys': Smith, 'The Bruce invasion and County Louth', p. 9.
483 There was great unrest in this period among the Irish; around July, 'there was a great slaughter of the Irish near the abbey of Baltinglass where around three hundred were killed' and 'this year all the Irish abandoned faith, faithfulness and fealty as, jointly, they placed themselves at war': *AClyn*, p 164; O'Byrne, 'Cultures in contact', pp 130–2; G.H. Orpen, 'Newcastle Mc Kynegan', *JRSAI*, 38 (1908), 120–40.

484 Priory at Athy; 'On 6 Jan. there was a great massacre of the Irish, namely of the Uí Mhórdha, and about three hundred of those men were killed near Balilethan': *AClyn*, p. 162; Ballilehan is between Athy and Castlecomer.
485 On 4 February 1316: Phillips, 'Documents', p. 253.
486 Arrived in Dublin 5 November 1315: Phillips, 'Documents', p. 249; idem, 'The mission of de Hothum'; for his wide powers, see ibid., p. 63; in 1316 'John Fitz Thomas and Arnold le Poer crossed to England to Edward 5 [II], giving hostages for keeping faith and fealty and the king gave the earldom of Kildare to John Fitz Thomas; and to Arnold he gave other lands for maintenance': *AClyn*, p. 164; Arnold le Poer received the manors of Castlewarden and Oughterard, Co. Kildare: Farker, 'Pater familias and *parentela*', 98; Connolly, 'Ancient petitions (SC 8)', p. 54; some of Pembridge's information about this period may have come via John de Hothum who may well have stayed with the Dominicans when in Dublin as he was the nephew of the distinguished Dominican scholar, William de Hothum, Dominican provincial in England and archbishop of Dublin, 1296–8: MacInerny, *History of the Irish Dominicans*, pp 378–476.
487 The earl of Ulster and the de Lacys were not there: Armstrong, *Bruce's invasion*, p. 90; for the pledge of loyalty and the list of names who swore, see Philips, 'Documents', 253–5; 'They agree that their bodies, lands and chattels shall be forfeited if they fail in their loyalty': *CCR, 1313–1318*, p. 333; Gilbert, *Viceroys*, pp 527–8.
488 See s.a. 1315 above; if he were a Dominican benefactor this would account for the interest.
489 Duffy, 'Revised itinerary', p. 26; for the New Town of Leys, see A.J. Otway-Ruthven, 'The medieval county of Kildare', *IHS*, 11 (1959), 181–99, at 183–4.
490 Probably Greencastle in Inishowen, built by the earl of Ulster in 1308: Duffy, 'Revised itinerary', p. 29; cf. Armstrong, *Bruce's invasion*, pp 92–3, n. 3.
491 *AC* 1316: 'Feidlim assembled a large army of Galls and Gaels ... to contest the kingship with ... Ruaidri ... son of Cathal Ó Conchobair ... They faced each other on the moor of the Tochar, and Ruaidri was overpowered by the greater force...and he fell there ... With him fell ... Donnchad Mac Ruaidri with a hundred galloglass ... These deeds were done on the twenty-fourth of February'; another instance (see also s.a. 1308 above) of the source being aware that if Irish surnames have an Ó in the nominative (which gives him his *Ochonchure* for Ó Conchobhair), this will become *Uí* in the genitive (which he expertly renders *Ychonghure*).
492 The younger brother of Robert; '*filium juniorem*.', *CStM*, i, p. 260; Smith, 'The Bruce invasion and county Louth', p. 14; defending Carrickfergus town: Armstrong, *Bruce's invasion*, p. 94.
493 John, rector of St Mary's, 'Corryton', d.c.1319, *NHI*, ix p. 278.
494 There was a Hugh de Anton' connected with the earl of Ulster in 1278–9: *IExP*, p. 33; a Richard de Anton, sheriff of Waterford in 1302; in 1304 Hugh de Anthony, son of Richard de Anthony; and in 1304, 'for good services in Scotland', pardon to 'Hugh de Anthony for 100*l* for debts for himself and his father Richard': *CDI, 1302–1307*, pp 27, 118–19.
495 Duffy, 'Revised itinerary', p. 26.
496 'Many afflictions in all parts of Ireland: very many deaths, famine and many strange diseases, murders, and intolerable storms as well': *AC*, p. 241; in 1330 the prior of Fore wrote to king that 'the Scots were in their house and did much damage to their charters there': Connolly, 'Chancery warrants (C81)', p. 147; Duffy, 'Revised itinerary', pp 26–7; Campbell and Ludlow, 'Climate, disease and society', 204–6; William Chester Jordan, *The great famine: northern Europe in the early fourteenth century* (Princeton, 1996); Ian Kershaw, 'The great famine and agrarian crisis in England, 1315–1322', *Past and Present*, 59 (1973), 3–50.

497 Presumably, the Kilkenny one of 1316: *Ir. parl.* p. 335; Clyn (*AClyn*, p. 162) gives this as 1315: 'At the beginning of June, a general parliament of the magnates of Ireland was held at Kilkenny to give aid and counsel against the Scots'; for an argument that this parliament was in fact the 1316 parliament held in Kilkenny (14 Feb.), see Otway-Ruthven, *Med. Ire.*, p. 226 fn.9; see also, J.A. Watt, 'The first recorded use of the word 'parliament' in Ireland?', *Irish Jurist*, n.s., 4 (1969), 123–6; Lydon, 'Parliament and the community of Ireland' in Lydon (ed.), *Law and disorder*, pp 125–9.

498 For an account of legal proceedings in 1316–17 of the charge that Walter and Hugh de Lacy had invited Edward Bruce to come and take Ireland, see *CStM*, ii, appendix ii pp 407–16.

499 'Here they were safe, if uncertain perhaps about what course to take next': Duffy, 'Revised itinerary', p. 27.

500 For Archebolds, Harolds, Walshes, Lawlesses and Howels, see Christopher Maginn, 'English marcher lineages in South Dublin in the late Middle Ages', *IHS*, 34 (2004), 113–36; for a list of malefactors, see James Mills, 'Notices of the manor of St Sepulchre in the fourteenth century', *JRSAI* 9 (1889), 39; idem, 'Notices of the manor of St Sepulchre in the fourteenth century: continuation', p. 119; Emmett O'Byrne, 'A much disputed land: Carrickmines and the Dublin marches' in Seán Duffy (ed.), *Medieval Dublin IV* (Dublin, 2003), p. 237; 'Contemporaries believed that it was the arrival of the Scots that produced the disorder': Duffy, 'Revised itinerary', pp 31–2.

501 Duffy, 'Revised itinerary', p. 27.

502 According to Barbour, captured at the battle of Connor: Duffy, 'Revised itinerary', p. 27; Alan fitz Warin was an Ulster tenant of Richard de Burgh: Orpen, *Normans*, p. 540 fn.4.

503 There is some confusion here; Finghin is not an Ó Conchobhair name and, as for Cathal Ruadh Ó Conchobhair, he had died in 1293; presumably, the persons intended are Feidhlim and Ruaidhrí son of Cathal Ruadh but, if so, Pembridge is here repeating (corruptly) an entry he had supplied earlier the same year; he does however supply one important additional piece of information: that around 300 others, including galloglass, were killed in the battle, something confirmed by *AC* 1316 ('a hundred gallowglasses, and many others gentle and simple').

504 Thomas Case's Dublin annals has a lacuna 1316 to 1368, and thus Pembridge becomes most important: *CStM*, ii, p. 282.

505 Dominican house at Drogheda; Duffy, 'Revised itinerary', pp 27–9.

506 Cambridge manuscript also gives death as 10 April: Mac Niocaill, 'Cáipéisí', 34; *Dominica Cananee* is the 2nd Sunday in Lent; it appears that there were two battles, 11 March and 10 April: Duffy, 'Revised itinerary', p. 29; Smith, 'The Bruce invasion and county Louth', p. 14; Sayles, 'The siege of Carrickfergus', p. 213; in 1317 in Avignon there was a quarrel over his burial, between the Franciscans of Carrickfergus and the Dominicans of Drogheda: Fitzmaurice and Little, *Franciscan Province*, pp 104–5.

507 Richard de Bermingham lord of Athenry; Richard de Clare was paid for his expenses: Connolly, 'Memoranda rolls', 185.

508 Dúnlaing was a brother of the then head of the dynasty, Murchadh son of Gerald Ó Broin (O'Byrne, *Irish of Leinster*, p. 68); a William Comyn, knight, with two of his brothers was killed on 24 June 1316: *AClyn*, p. 164; there is clearly a problem here between the two sources or there was more than one William Comyn, knight; perhaps there was a Kilkenny William Comyn and a Dublin William Conyn; in 1319 we find a William Comyn, knight, on the panel of inquisition about Bruce damage to Dublin in 1319: *CARD*, pp 150–1; in 1316 Gilbert, *Hist. & mun. docs*, pp 380–2; in 1356, forty years later (the same or another) William Comyn was escheator in Dublin: *Inquisitions & extents*, p. 191.

Notes to pages 133 to 135   245

509 Brother of Nicholas: Smith, *Crisis and survival*, p. 97; idem, 'The Bruce invasion and county Louth', p. 10.
510 Sayles, 'Siege of Carrickfergus', p. 215.
511 Armstrong, *Bruce's invasion*, pp 95–6; Carrickfergus became the base of Bruce's operation in Ireland as a most important port with connections to Scotland; for accusations against and trial of Henry of Thrapston (and his eventual pardon) for his part in the fall of Carrickfergus, see Sayles, 'Siege of Carrickfergus', pp 213–18; Duffy, 'Revised itinerary', p. 29.
512 Around 1 July 'there was a great slaughter of the Irish near the abbey of Baltinglass where around three hundred were killed': *AClyn*, p. 162; the leader of the defeated Irish forces was David, head of the Uí Thuathail of Fercullen and Imaal: O'Byrne, *Irish of Leinster*, p. 68.
513 In 1312 a group of English robbers rushed into a town and shouted in a loud voice, '*Fennok abo, Fennok abo*, which is the war cry of the O Totheles [Uí Thuathail], and by this cry of malice made all the men and women of the town fly out of their houses, and this done, robbed the said town': *CJRI, 1308–14*. p. 244; *CStM*, ii, p. 296; for a note on the war cry, see *CStM*, ii, p. cxiv n3.
514 Dominican priory at Drogheda; *CStM*, ii, p. 296
515 Armstrong, *Bruce's invasion*, p. 96; Duffy, 'Revised itinerary', p. 31; Sayles, 'Siege of Carrickfergus', p. 213.
516 *AC* 1316: 'Feidlim ... seized the kingship of Connacht ... He then set out to banish the Galls of West Connacht, burning Ballylahan and killing Stephen d'Exeter, Miles Gocan, William Prendergast, John Standon –these were knights – and William Lawless, slaughtering unnumbered people with them'; *CStM*, ii, p. 296; Stephen de Exonia had been in the entourage of William Liath de Burgh in 1308: Frame, *Eng. lordship*, p. 41; de Exonia involved in the foundation of Rathfran and Strade; the Barrys referred to may be Barretts; John de Cogan may have been buried with the Dublin Dominicans (1311).
517 *AC* 1316: 'Feidlim called upon his subjects to assemble an army ... and many more of the kings' and chieftains' sons of Ireland assembled to him; and they all marched to Athenry to oppose William Burke, Mac Feorais [de Bermingham], and the other Connacht Galls, and joined battle with them in front of the town; the Gaels were defeated and Feidlim Ó Conchobair, who was king of Connacht ... was killed there and Tadc Ó Cellaig, king of Uí Maine fell with him, together with twenty-eight men who were entitled to succeed to the kingship of Uí Maine [and 29 other named kings and lords of Connacht] ... Moreover it is hard to say how many of the men of Munster and of Meath and of Ireland generally were killed there ... These deeds were done on the day of St Laurence Martyr; Fedlimid was a man of twenty-three when he was killed...'.
518 The same date, 'according to common report 'five ... thousand in all, the number decapitated was one thousand five hundred': *AClyn*, p. 164; seven thousand: *ARoss*, p. 42; eight thousand killed by Richard de Bermingham and lord William de Burgh, *Kilkenny chronicle*, p. 336; 'on the day of St Laurence Martyr, *AC*, p. 247; the de Berminghams were the principal founders of the Dominican priory of Athenry: Coleman, '*Regestum monasterii fratrum praedicatorum de Athenry*', pp 204–5; H.T. Knox, 'The Bermingham family of Athenry', *JGAHS*, 10 (1917–18), 139–54; for significance of this battle, see Seán Duffy, *Ireland in the Middle Ages* (Basingstoke, 1997), pp 139–40.
519 *Carnifex* is executioner but the medieval translation is butcher; Hussees in Dublin from an early date (1200): Lawlor, 'Liber Niger', 50; a Walter Hussy held land in the parish of St Michan (near the Dominican priory): *CStM*, ii, pp 43, 56, 58; *CCD*, p. 124; Husses, with variant spellings, were involved in the subinfeudation of Meath: Daniel Brown, 'Select document: a charter of Hugh II de Lacy, earl of Ulster, to Hugh Hose (2 March

1207)', *IHS*, 38 (2013), 492–510; Hose lord of Deece in the de Lacy lordship of Meath; a William Husse was in the garrison of Roscommon and was a knight: *IExP*, pp 1, 4; Walter Hussey in Athenry in 1333: *Inquisitions & extents* p. 150.
520 Richard, supplied by L.
521 Athenry's fourteenth-century seal had, 'a rather grisly display of two severed and spiked heads, almost certainly those of the Connacht king Feidlim Ó Conchobair, and one of his lieutenants, perhaps Tadg Ó Cellaig, killed in open battle by the inhabitants of the town in 1316': Duffy, 'Ireland's Hastings', p. 74.
522 Both the de Bermingham and Hussee family were Dominican benefactors; this demonstrates a de Bermingham rewarding good feudal service and if John Hussey was related to the Dublin Husseys he would be of interest to a Dublin chronicler.
523 Simms, 'O Hanlons, O Neills and Anglo-Normans', 89.
524 Ranelagh; the original Cullenswood was 66 acres of wood: Mills, 'Notices of the manor of St Sepulchre', 33–4; a similar incident had happened before in 1209; 'as they had formerly done in 1209': Harris, *Dublin*, pp 153–4; Declan Johnston, 'Black Monday: the power of myth in medieval Dublin' in Seán Duffy (ed.), *Medieval Dublin XIII* (2013), p. 146.
525 Or miles: C.T. Martin, *The record interpreter* (London, 1892), p. 271; 2 miles from Dublin: Harris, *Dublin*, p. 153.
526 *CStM*, ii, p. 297; Comyn was sheriff of Dublin in 1361: Connolly, 'Chancery files (C.260)', p. 15.
527 'Around Christmas, lord Robert Bruce arrived, conducting himself as king of the Scots': *AClyn*, p. 166; 'Lord Robert de Brus and lord Edward his brother entered Ireland and drawing up his troops journeyed to Knockfergus, through the middle of the English spoiling and burning the land right up to Nannath', then 'after Easter lord Robert returned from Knockfergus to Scotland from where he had come': *Kilkenny chronicle*, p. 335; 'Lord Robert Bruce, who styled himself king of Scotland': *AI*, p. 425; 'Robert Bruce, King of Scotland, came to Ireland bringing many gallowglasses with him to help his brother Edward, and to expel the Galls from Ireland': *AC*, p. 249; *AFM*, iii, p. 515; Duffy, 'Revised itinerary', pp 29–30.
528 'Passing through the whole land of Ulster ... he crossed Ireland almost as far as Limerick burning, killing, destroying, and plundering vills, castles and even churches': *AClyn*, p. 166; Armstrong, *Bruce's invasion*, p. 101.
529 Armstrong, *Bruce's invasion*, pp 101–2.
530 Several years before 1315 the harvests were poor and a general rise in food prices and torrential floods which were noted in Ireland: H.S. Lucas, 'The great European famine of 1315, 1316, and 1317', *Speculum*, 5 (1930), 343–77; cannibalism was reported from many countries during this period of Continent-wide famine: ibid., p. 355; Campbell and Ludlow, 'Climate, disease and society', 205–6.
531 For the importance of Maynooth, see Linzi Simpson, 'The early Geraldine castles of Ireland: some case studies' in Crooks and Duffy (eds), *The Geraldines*, pp 108–14.
532 In 1316 'lord John Fitz Thomas and Arnold le Poer crossed to England to Edward 5 [II], giving hostages for keeping faith and fealty; and the king gave the earldom of Kildare to John Fitz Thomas; and to Arnold he gave other lands for maintenance': *AClyn*, p. 164; 'Lord John fitz Thomas died this year f... [first] earl of Kildare': *Kilkenny chronicle*, p. 335.
533 Armstrong, *Bruce's invasion*, p. 95.
534 It is not clear who the Irish victim was here, whose death does not seem to be recorded in the Irish annals.
535 *Regs Christ Church*, p. 124; Stalley, 'The architecture of the cathedral and priory buildings', pp 102–3.

536 *CStM*, ii, p. 298.
537 First cousin of Edward I, holder of five earldoms: J.R. Maddicott, *Thomas of Lancaster, 1307–1322: a study in the reign of Edward II* (Oxford, 1970), pp 318–34; Phillips, *Edward II*, chapter 7.
538 *CStM*, ii, pp 407–16.
539 First days of Lent or Septuagesima Sunday or Sexagesima Sunday; Colman Ó Clabaigh states that the feast is fluid, and it all depends on when abstention from meat began in preparation for Easter: in some cases it was two Sundays before Ash Wednesday (Septuagesima Sunday) or the Sunday before Ash Wednesday (Sexagesima Sunday); from Ash Wednesday the Lenten fast proper began and one abstained from eggs, cheese and other dairy products; when that was in Ireland, and specifically in the early fourteenth century, I have not been able to determine precisely.
540 L: *coram*: Armstrong, *Bruce's invasion*, p. 102.
541 'Richard, earl of Ulster, was captured by the burgesses of Dublin and was detained in the castle': *Kilkenny chronicle*, pp 335, 336; he was not popular in certain areas outside the city as, after the death of Edward Bruce, he was captured and beaten by his enemies: Connolly, 'Ancient petitions (SC 8)', p. 46; for date of Jan. 18, Gwynn, 'Black Book', p. 286: Duffy, 'Revised itinerary', p. 35.
542 'On Monday around the hour of vespers 18 February': Mac Niocaill, 'Cáipéisí', 34; Gilbert, *Hist. & mun. docs*, pp 397–402; 'If the earl of Ulster is loyal there is nothing to be feared from their plots': Chris Given-Wilson, '*Vita Edwardi Secundi*: memoir or journal?' in *TCE VI* (1996), p. 107; popular suspicion grew strong against the earl, who was Robert Bruce's father-in-law: Lydon, 'Bruce invasion: an examination of some problems', p. 80; Duffy, 'Revised itinerary', pp 33–5; Robert Nottingham was mayor for seven years between 1309 and 1322.
543 Castleknock *c.* 8km from Dublin with a clear view of Dublin: E. St J. Brooks, 'The grant of Castleknock to Hugh Tyrel', *JRSAI*, 4th ser., 63 (1933), 206–20: Duffy, 'Revised itinerary', p. 35: for a Richard, Hugh, David, Walter and Thomas Tyrell, see Áine Foley, 'The sheriff of Dublin in the fourteenth century' in Duffy (ed.), *Medieval Dublin XII*, pp 275, 283, 285, 287; in 1346–7 Walter Tyrell was prior of the Dominicans in Dublin and therefore one might assume that the Tyrell family were benefactors of the Dominicans: *IExP*, p. 444; these annals also mention a James, Robert, Joan and Matilda Tyrell: see below.
544 In 1318 the city was pardoned: *CPR, 1317–1321*, pp 192, 204.
545 On the following Friday the monastery '*idem maior spoliavit de omnibus bonis suis ad summam mille librorum et domicilia predicti monasterii flamis accendebat*': Mac Niocaill, 'Cáipéisí', 34; for the problems of defence confronting Dublin at this time, see Lydon, 'Dublin and the Scottish threat, 1315–18' in Seán Duffy (ed.), *Medieval Dublin XV* (Dublin, 2016), pp 282–4, 287–90.
546 The Latin used is *locus*, a smaller community with no constitutional rights: Hinnebusch, *Dominican order*, p. 252; clearly this is not intended here and therefore must mean heart or centre, sacred place, sanctuary'; Lydon, 'Dublin castle in the Middle Ages', p. 123: idem, 'The defence of Dublin in the Middle Ages', pp 74–5.
547 Burnt by the burgesses: *Kilkenny chronicle*, pp 335, 336; interestingly, William de Nottingham had the stone tower at Ostmans' Gate in 1284, and Robert de Nottingham surrendered this in 1322: *CARD*, p 103, 118; for a letter to king 1319 concerning burning the city: *CARD*, pp 149–50.
548 In 1312 a request was made for murage 'to rebuild the towers of the New Gate': Connolly, 'Ancient petitions (SC 8)', p. 13.

549 Harris, *Dublin*, pp 55–6, 263; in 1317 to 1319 we find information about the 'great labours and expenses in repairing walls and towers of the city' and repairing 'at the king's expense the belfry of the church of St Mary del Dam, near the castle in Dublin which had been taken down and its stones used for fortifying the latter against imminent peril': Gilbert, *Hist. & mun. docs*, pp 402–12; Duffy, 'Revised itinerary', p. 35: H.B. Clarke, 'Decolonisation and the dynamics of urban decline in Ireland, 1300–1550' in T.R. Slater (ed.), *Towns in decline, AD 100–1600* (Aldershot, 2000), p. 188 n.70.

550 Indicates that the information was written after 1316; in 1318 Edward II pardoned the mayor and citizens for taking 'cattle, corn, victuals from the people of the adjacent parts, for the use of the city during the recent hostile incursions of the Scots', and also a remission of rent: *CARD*, pp 11, 12.

551 'The last thing he needed was a siege that might pin his men down as long as that of Carrickfergus': Duffy, 'Revised itinerary', p. 36; Leixlip was the property of John de Hothum since 1302.

552 For Thomas Randolph, earl of Moray and nephew of Robert Bruce, see Brown, *Wars of Scotland*, pp 222–5.

553 Brother of the earl of Menteith: Michael Brown, *Wars of Scotland*, pp 195–6: Duffy, 'Revised itinerary', pp 31–2.

554 Brown, *Wars of Scotland*, p. 214.

555 For Naas, see Linzi Simpson, 'The early Geraldine castles of Ireland: some case studies' in Crooks and Duffy (eds), *The Geraldines*, pp 97–102: Dominicans were not in Naas until *c*.1354: *Inquisitions & extents*, pp 188–9.

556 See above s.a. Feb. 1317 where they gave their oath.

557 Hugh Canoun went to England on behalf of justiciar and council in Ireland: *IExP*, p. 231.

558 *CStM*, ii, p. 299.

559 The second time a Franciscan house is damaged: *AClyn*, p. 162: Duffy, 'Revised itinerary', p. 36.

560 Dominican house at Kilkenny.

561 Armstrong, *Bruce's invasion*, p. 108; royal banners had considerable legal significance: Strickland, 'A law of arms or a law of treason?', p. 56; in 1314–15, 'Symon Gernoun ... rose in war ... against the king and his faithful people bearing the king's banner'; in 1324–5, a royal banner was bought and delivered to John Darcy, justiciar of Ireland, going to the parts of Leinster to subdue the Irish felons of the king there: *IExP*, p. 303.

562 Dominican priory at Limerick.

563 'At Easter [3 April], there was a great gathering of the magnates ... near Limerick against the Scots; with the Scots being opposite them at Castleconnell': *AClyn*, p. 166: Ludden, southeast of Limerick and Castleconnell just north of Limerick; both the earl of Ulster and Butler had interests in Castleconnell: *COD, 1172–1350*, no. 179; the Scots hoped to benefit from an alliance with the Irish of Thomond: *AI*, pp 425–7; for the detailed record of Butler in Munster between 24 February and 17 April 1317, see Robin Frame, 'The campaign against the Scots in Munster, 1317', repr. in Frame, *Ire. & Brit.*, pp 99–112; Duffy, 'Revised itinerary', p. 38.

564 Priory at Kilkenny.

565 Priory at Cashel; Frame, 'The campaign against the Scots in Munster', pp 105–6.

566 Frame, *Eng. lordship*, pp 13–18.

567 Landed at Youghal with thirty-eight knights: *AClyn*, p. 166; before Easter and 'with 38 knights': *Kilkenny chronicle*, pp 335, 336; '*Rogerus de Mortuomari locum domini regis in Hibernia tenens*' landed at Waterford: Mac Niocaill, 'Cáipéisí', 34; on 23 November 1316 appointed justiciar of Ireland and with responsibility of defeating Bruce, quelling the

568 *AClyn*, p. 166.
569 Parliament held in Kilkenny Dominican priory: Philomena Connolly, '"The head and comfort of Leinster": Carlow as an administrative capital of Ireland, 1361–1394' in Thomas McGrath (ed.), *Carlow: history and society*(Dublin, 2008), p. 328 fn.46.
570 Dominican priory at Trim.
571 27 June 1317: *Ir. parl.*, pp 111, 335; Dublin had been intended but a letter of 7 June 1317 cautioned otherwise: *CCR, 1313–1318*, p. 476.
572 *CCR, 1313–18*, pp 404–5; Dryburgh, 'Mortimer and the governance of Ireland', p. 93.
573 *Ir. parl.*, p 335; Mac Niocaill, 'Cáipéisí', 34; often held in Christ Church: Lydon, 'Christ Church in the later medieval Irish world', p. 84; on 18 Jan. 1317, he was imprisoned and on 18 January 1317 'he was liberated by Sir Roger de Mortuo Mari "*post prandium*" 17 May': Lawlor, 'Liber Niger', 39; Gwynn, 'Black Book', pp 286, 337.
574 The word used is *infamierunt* but this is not in dictionaries even as *famuerunt*; so – were starving – *fames* hunger so *infames* in hunger? Campbell and Ludlow, 'Climate, disease and society', 205–6.
575 Dominican priories at Drogheda and Trim.
576 'He drove out all of the *natione* and *cognomine* of de Lacy from Ireland and in the summer he forced them to flee to Scotland': *AClyn*, p. 166; 'he expelled all the de Lacys from Meath and subjected their lands to himself': *Kilkenny chronicle*, pp 335, 336: Mac Niocaill, 'Cáipéisí', 34; see also *CStM*, ii, appendix II, pp 407–16; in 1332 Hugh de Lacy accused Mortimer of being motivated by a desire for de Lacy land: Connolly, 'Ancient petitions (SC 8)', pp 77–78; the de Lacys were suspected and accused of both inviting Edward Bruce to come to Ireland and acting as guide in Meath and Offaly: Orpen, *Normans*, p. 522; Frame, *Eng. lordship*, p. 160; Dryburgh, 'Roger Mortimer', pp 57–8; idem, 'Mortimer and the governance of Ireland', p. 93.
577 Phillips, *Aymer de Valence*, pp 111–17; idem, *Edward II*, pp 288–90.
578 This date is the Kilmainham one: *Ir. parl.*, p 335; Lydon, 'Christ Church in the later medieval Irish world, p. 84.
579 They stood surety to keep him out of prison upon the reliance that he would be available when needed.
580 'Thomas Dun, plunderer of many ships, destroyer, and cruel pirate': *AClyn*, p. 168: 'Cruel pirate of the Scots': *Kilkenny chronicle*, p. 336; a request was made (*c.*1317) to guard the coast of Wales against him: Connolly, 'Ancient petitions (SC 8)', p. 58; eadem, 'Memoranda rolls', 197' Athy, knight and former sheriff of Limerick and Kerry avoided arrest by fighting the Scots: Gilbert, *Hist. & mun. docs*, p, 373; Athy was to guard the seas, in company with Roger Mortimer: *CPR, 1313–1317*, p. 632; the mayor and bailiffs of Drogheda were ordered to supply shipping to fight Dun: Gilbert, *Hist. & mun. docs*, pp 377–8; the king's admiral: *CPR, 1317–1321*, pp 164, 165, 195; in March 1318 John of Athy was granted Dissard, Co. Meath for life: *CPR, 1317–1321*, p. 126; on 2 March 1319 Athy was given custody of Carrickfergus castle: *CPR, 1317–1321*, p. 311; Don, involved in siege of Carrickfergus and John de Athy was appointed admiral of the fleet in 1317 and on 2 July met and killed Thomas Don: Sayles, 'Siege of Carrickfergus', pp 214–17; his career can be followed in *IExP*, index; Dun raided Holyhead harbour and captured a royal ship: Phillips, 'The mission of de Hothum', p. 67; G.O. Sayles, 'The battle of Faughart' in *Scripta Diversa*, pp 271–2; See also W.S. Reid, 'Sea power in the Anglo-Scottish war, 1296–1328', *The Mariner's Mirror*, 46 (1960), 19.

581 'Two cardinals were sent to England to arrange peace between the English and the Scots, but they made no progress': *AClyn*, p. 168; s.a. 1318, *Kilkenny chronicle*, p. 336; *Regs Christ Church*, p. 124: Barrow, *Robert Bruce*, pp 348–50, 353–4, 424; Bruce was excommunicated as a subject of the king of England who had 'defected from his allegiance': Rosalind M.T. Hill, 'Belief and practice as illustrated by John XXII's excommunication of Robert Bruce' in G.J. Cuming and Derek Barker (eds), *Popular belief and practice. Studies in Church History, 8* (Cambridge, 1984), pp 135–8; Nicholas de Balscote was baron of the exchequer, chancellor of exchequer, clerk of wages, engrosser of exchequer and keeper of office of treasurer; his career can be followed in *IExP*, index.

582 For properties in Meath and Uriel taken into the king's hands, see *47th rep. DKPRI*, pp 29, 31; Frame, *Eng. lordship*, pp 159–60.

583 In *c*.1319 Drogheda asked for exemption from fee farm because of great expense in 'enclosing and defending the town' and the death of many burgesses: Connolly, 'Ancient petitions (SC 8)', p. 37.

584 Dominican priory at Drogheda: 'Many citizens of Ulster were killed near Drogheda, among whom William Savage was the chief of those killed; these, and other Ulstermen, had been expelled from their neighbourhood by the Scots': *AClyn*, p. 166.

585 Rathregan, co Meath; for John Blund, see index *IExP*, pp 640–1; for John White, see ibid., p. 716; the White family had a connection with Drogheda: Smith, *Crisis and survival*, p. 11.

586 O'Byrne, *Irish of Leinster*, p. 68; Dryburgh, 'Mortimer and the governance of Ireland', p. 94.

587 Parliament to meet at Lincoln on 27 Jan. 1318: Phillips, *Edward II*, pp 301, 308–9; Hilda Johnstone, 'The parliament of Lincoln of 1316', *EHR*, 36 (1921), 53–57.

588 Phillips, *Aymer de Valence*, pp 170–2.

589 Castlemartin lies about 15km southwest of Naas; Canon went to England in 1315: *Admin. Ire.* p 154n1, 155, 167, 242.

590 On 22 July 1317 according to Ware fragment: *CStM*, ii, p. 291; on Friday 29 Sept, Alexander Bicknor arrived from the Curia: *AClyn*, p. 170; *Regs Christ Church*, p. 124.

591 Chris Given-Wilson, '*Vita Edwardi Secundi*: memoir or journal?' in *TCE VI* (1996), p. 155.

592 Roger Mortimer evidently wished to create his own entourage of loyal supporters in Ireland; however, there is some confusion as to the number of men he knighted: see *AClyn*, pp 166, 168.

593 From 1 May to Autumn 1318, 'there was a great scarcity and famine': *AClyn*, p. 168; great famine through all the land: *Kilkenny chronicle*, p. 336; 'In Livonia and Estonia … starving mothers ate their children': Lucas, 'The great European famine', 364, 376.

594 Chapter at Oxford; Berwick was 1 to 2 April: Barrow, *Robert Bruce*, p. 463; the news arrived in Dublin on 22 April 1318; Edward I stayed there for 15 days in 1304: Page and Page, 'Blackfriars of Stirling', p. 882; in 1320 John Cadel sought the position of porter of Dublin castle as a reward for good services including Berwick: Connolly, 'Ancient petitions (SC 8)', pp 6–7.

595 Associated with Holy Trinity: *Account roll Holy Trinity*, pp 169–70; also linked with Bicknor: Lydon, 'The case against Alexander Bicknor', pp 103–7, 111 fn. 21; Robin Frame, 'Profits and perils of an Irish legal career: Sir Elias Ashbourne (d. 1356), chief justice and marcher lord' in T.R. Baker (ed.) *Law and society in later medieval England and Ireland* (London, 2017), p. 125.

596 In charge of the Dublin exchequer during the Bruce invasion: Frame, 'The campaign against the Scots in Munster, 1317', pp 99–100.

597 William fitz John, formerly bishop of Ossory, was keeper from May to November 1318; he was chancellor Feb-May 1314, Feb. 1316 to April 1322: *Admin. Ire.*, pp 84, 94.
598 Clyn has Thomas 'de Lees' rather than 'de Naas': *AClyn*, p. 170; T reads Naas; on balance it appears as if Clyn is correct as James and Henry de la Chappelle and Thomas de Lees were tenants of Richard de Clare: *38th rep. DKPRI*, p. 38 and 42, p. 20; a later Thomas de Lees was constable of Limerick castle *c.*1326–7: Connolly, *IExP*, p. 320; a Thomas de Lees knight gave evidence in Limerick as to the age of earl of Desmond's son: *Inquisitions & extents*, p. 193; 'Lord Richard de Clare, with four knights, and with many others was killed on 5 Ides May on Thursday morning': *Kilkenny chronicle*, pp 335, 336; 'On the sixth of the Ides of May Lord Richard de Clare is slain in Tuadmumu with four knights and many others by Muirchertach Ó Briain': *AI* 1318; for a detailed Irish account, see *Caithréim Thoirdhealbhaigh*, ed. S.H. O'Grady, ii (Irish Texts Soc., London, 1929), pp 126–30; Katharine Simms, 'The battle of Dysert O'Dea and the Gaelic resurgence in Thomond', *Dal gCais*, 5 (1979), 59–66.
599 Dominican house at Limerick; for a glowing eulogy, see *Kilkenny chronicle*, p. 335; in 1319 the earl of Kildare petitions for military aid in avenging the death of Richard de Clare: *Affairs Ire.*, p. 91.
600 Dominican house at Trim; Áine Foley, 'High status execution in fourteenth century Ireland' in James Bothwell and Gwilym Dodd (eds), *Fourteenth Century England IX* (Woodbridge, 2016), pp 136–7.
601 See Paul Dryburgh, '"The Mortimer has taken great pains to save and keep the peace": crown, city and community during the Bruce invasion and its aftermath' in Seán Duffy (ed.), *Medieval Dublin XVII* (Dublin, 2019, pp 222–36.
602 In 1316 'salt was selling in Ireland for 4 marks': *Kilkenny chronicle*, p. 335; for a similar sign of 'great hope', see Chris Given-Wilson, '*Vita Edwardi Secundi*: memoir or journal?' in *TCE VI* (1996), p. 167.
603 On Friday 29 Sept: *AClyn*, p. 170; *CStM*, ii, p. 291; *Kilkenny chronicle*, p. 336; justiciar and keeper Sept. 1318 to June 1319: *Admin. Ire.*, p. 84; Lydon, 'The case against Alexander Bicknor', pp 103–11.
604 The battle of Faughart; '*venit Edwardus Bruys cum domino Waltero de Lacy et domino Hugone de Lacy cum multitudine Scotorum et Hibernicorum versus villam de Dundalk*': Mac Niocaill, 'Cáipéisí', 35; *Liber primus Kilkenniensis*, p. 63; *AFM*, iii, p. 521; Sayles, 'Battle of Faughart' in *Scripta diversa*, pp 267–75 (also, in Duffy, *Bruce's Irish wars*, pp 107–18).
605 The White family were connected with Drogheda: Smith, *Crisis and survival*, p. 11.
606 For an account of the Scots present at Faughart, including Philip de Mowbray, John de Soules, John Alan and Walter Stewart, Hugo and Armoricus de Lacy and John Kermedyn, see Duffy, 'The "Continuation" of Nicholas Trevet', 314–15.
607 Lands in Killeen and connected with Cusack by marriage: Hogan, *Llanthony*, pp 52–3; land held by Richard and Nicholas de Cusack: *Inquisitions & extents*, p. 140; in *c.*1319, a Robert de Tuyt was praised for his good service at Dundalk: Connolly, 'Ancient petitions (SC 8)', p. 31.
608 'The Verdun barony of Upper Dundalk was especially affected by repeated Scottish and Irish incursions': Smith, 'The Bruce invasion and county Louth', p. 8; Nicholas and Milo fought against Bruce: Hagger, *Fortunes*, pp 216–17.
609 His reward was to be given a de Lacy manor: Smith, 'The Bruce invasion and County Louth', p. 15.
610 In 1323 he is recorded as holding land in Rathwire, Co. Meath, from Mortimer: *Inquisitions & extents*, pp 117, 120.
611 In 1319 John de Cusack asked for recompense for 'expenses and losses incurred at Dundalk', and at the same time an Adam de Cusack asks to be appointed constable of

Drogheda castle for 'his good service and expenses incurred at Dundalk': Connolly, 'Ancient petitions (SC 8)', pp 33–4, 34; sheriff of Louth 1328–9: Smith, *Crisis and survival*, p. 15.

612 He later served as escheator and was granted the manor of Ardee in 1325: Smith, 'The Bruce invasion and County Louth', p. 10.

613 Dominican house at Drogheda.

614 In this instance it must be an idiom meaning climbed the ladder of battle; *scalam* is a scaling ladder and there is a long and detailed description of how a scaling ladder was made in 1312: *Lanercost*, ii, pp 201–2.

615 '*Iohannes Mawpas*': Mac Niocaill, 'Cáipéisí', 35; for Peter de Maupas: Orpen, *Normans*, p. 200; for a Simon Maupas at Drogheda in 1334, see *Inquisitions & extents*, p. 136; John Barbour, *The Bruce*, ed. A.A.M. Duncan (Edinburgh, 1997), book 18, pp 672, 676.

616 '*Walterus vero de Lacy et Hugo de Lacy fugam inierunt et vix evaserunt versus Scociam, et ibidem cum Roberto Bruys longo tempore permanserunt*': Mac Niocaill, 'Cáipéisí', 35.

617 'Edward Bruce (usurping the name and making his men call him king of Ireland) was killed with many Scots at Dundalk by John de Bermingham and Milo de Verdun: *AClyn*, p. 170; *AU*, p. 433; Sayles, 'Battle of Faughart' in *Scripta Diversa*, pp 267–75; reported by the England chroniclers: Frame, *Eng. lordship*, pp 132–3; for an assessment of why the invasion failed, see Lydon, 'Dublin and the Scottish threat'.

618 'Lord Edward Bruce was killed by lord John de Bermingham and his body divided into four parts through the cities of the kingdom of England': *Kilkenny chronicle*, p. 335.

619 *CPR, 1317–1321*, pp 334–5; see also Smith, *Colonisation and conquest*, p. 114.

620 *Kilkenny chronicle*, pp 335–7.

621 Our chronicler seems almost exhausted after the trauma of the Bruce years: there are few entries and many items not specifically dated until 1326.

622 June 1319 to Dec. 1320: *Admin. Ire.*, p 84.

623 Chapter Salisbury.

624 Athassel Augustinian priory founded by William de Burgh in the late twelfth century and supported by the de Burgo family; Walter de Burgh earl of Ulster was buried there in 1271 and Richard de Burgh, earl of Ulster in 1326 (see below 1326).

625 The reward was because Bruce had himself crowned king of Ireland 'to the king's disinheritance': *CPR, 1317–1321*, pp 334–5; see also Smith, *Colonisation and conquest*, pp 113–14.

626 For an inquisition at Naas in 1326 where Master Maurice Jak makes a substantial gift to the Hospitallers: *Inquisitions & extents*, pp 130–1; Peter O'Keeffe and Tom Simington, *Irish stone bridges: history and heritage* (Dublin, 2016), pp 244–5.

627 The opening entry is very solemn, an indication of importance to Pembridge; however, Clyn is brief, very scathing and dismissive: 'a university as far as name, but if only it had been so in fact and reality': *AClyn*, p. 172; Harris (ed.), *Whole works of Sir James Ware, vol. I bishops*, p. 330; date 10 February 1320 and for the statutes of the university, see ibid., pp 242–5; a parliament at Dublin (27 April 1320) approved a university: Aubrey Gwynn, 'The medieval university of St Patrick's, Dublin', *Studies*, 27 (1938), 199–212, 437–54; Fergal McGrath, *Education in ancient and medieval Ireland* (Dublin, 1979), pp 216–19.

628 'Erected in St Patrick's church', and also Harris states that the Hardite, Cogry and the Dominican Kermerdyn were created doctors of divinity; and William Rodiart 'doctor of canon law': Harris, *Dublin*, pp 383–4; Adam de Kermerdyn, supervisor of collection of fifteenth in Munster: *IExP*, p. 125; Fitzmaurice and Little, *Franciscan province*, p. 108 fn.1; Ware states that 'there remained some footsteps of it in the reign of King Hen. VII': Harris (ed.), *Whole works of Sir James Ware, vol. II*, p. 245; by 1348 the prior of the

Augustinian order states that, as there is no university in Ireland, his friars should be allowed to go to England to study: Connolly. 'Chancery warrants (C81)', p. 158; *CPR, 1348–1350*, p. 94.
629 This is the last mention of Mortimer; Ian Mortimer, *The greatest traitor: the life of Sir Roger Mortimer, 1st earl of March, ruler of England, 1327–1330* (London, 2003).
630 See below s.a. 1320.
631 See above s.a. 1319; there was an earlier bridge on the site; it was defended by a tower erected in 1310 and repaired in 1347 by the Carmelites who were responsible for the safety of the bridge and of people using it: Connolly, 'Carlow as an administrative capital', pp 310, 320.
632 'About three hundred of the Uí Chonchobhair were killed by Andrew de Bermingham': *AClyn*, p. 172; 'A great defeat was inflicted by Andriu Mac Feorais, and by the Foreigners of Midhe, on the sons of kings of Uí Fhailghe': *ALC* 1321; Andrew was the head of the family forces in Tethmoy/Carbury: Frame, *Eng. lordship*, p. 33; he was killed in 1322 (see below and 1317 above); see also, *AU*, p. 37; *AFM*, iii, p. 527.
633 'On the eve of the Exaltation of the Holy Cross [Sunday 13 September], Edmund *Pincerna* [Butler] died in London and, on the day before the eve of blessed Martin, bishop and confessor [Monday 9 November], was buried at Gowran': *AClyn*, p. 174; he was in England in late 1320 and may have wanted to wait until spring to set off for Compostela; if he had reached Compostela, one would have expected Clyn, his great admirer, to mention that fact; Butler 'submitted a request to the archbishop of Dublin that he and his wife and son be absolved of their vow': Bernadette Cunningham, *Medieval Irish Pilgrims to Santiago de Compostela* (Dublin, 2018), p. 30; I thank Dr Colmán Ó Clabaigh OSB for this reference; James, his son and heir, was a minor in the king's custody: *Kilkenny chronicle*, p. 337; he died on 13 Sept. 1321 and buried on 9 Nov. in Gowran; for his will of 1321, see *COD, 1350–1413*, no. 431.
634 *AClyn*, p. 172; *Kilkenny chronicle*, p. 335, 337; August 1321 to August 1323; *Admin. Ire.*, p. 84.
635 No mention of Mortimer being imprisoned in the Tower of London or his escape the following year, however Clyn in Kilkenny does know about this: *AClyn*, p. 178; G.O. Sayles, 'The formal judgment of the traitors of 1322', repr. in *Scripta Diversa* (London, 1982), pp 81–7.
636 See above 1318; Saturday 16 Oct. 1322: *AClyn*, p. 176; there was an expedition headed by John de Bermingham, earl of Louth, against the Uí Nualláin between 2 Nov.1321 and 14 Jan.1322: *43th rep. DKPRI*, p. 43; Nicholas de Launde was constable of Drogheda castle on the side of Meath: *IExP*, p. 281.
637 In May, a thirteen-year truce was signed at York between Scotland and England: Phillips, *Edward II*, pp 431–6; the failure of supplies in 1322 was crucial: Michael Prestwich, 'Military logistics: the case of 1322' in Strickland (ed.), *Armies, chivalry and warfare*, pp 276–88.
638 Thursday 2 February 1324: *AClyn*, p. 178; justiciar 1324–7, 1329–31, 1333, 1334, 1335, 1336, and 1340–4: *Admin. Ire.*, pp 84, 85, 86, 87; Frame, *Eng. Lordship*, chap. III and passim.
639 He died in England in 1324 'having been given to the king as a hostage': *AClyn*, p. 178.
640 Simon de Geneville held lands in Meath from Roger Mortimer: *Reg. Gormanston*, pp 171–4; in 1331–41 he was seneschal of Trim: Connolly, 'Chancery files (C.260)', p. 8.
641 On 6 January 1326, 'there was the greatest wind and storm throwing down houses and buildings, laying bare churches and monasteries, breaking and tearing trees out by the roots and many bell-towers, scattering stooks of corn and barns': *AClyn*, p. 184.
642 In 1324 'A great plague [affecting] bulls and cows in many parts of Ireland': *AClyn*, p. 180; called, '*Maldow*', *ARoss*, p. 43; '*Maldouny*': *Kilkenny chronicle*, p. 337; 'A general

murrain': *CStM*, ii, p. 362; 'Mael Domnaig': *AC*, p. 259; *AI.*, p .435; *AClon.*, p. 284; '*Maeldomhnaigh*': *ALC*, p. 603; '*Maeldomnaigh*': *AU*, pp 437–4; Campbell and Ludlow, 'Climate, disease and society', 206–8; the murrain was in England in 1319–20: Mary C. Lyons, 'Weather, famine, pestilence, and plague in Ireland, 900–1500' in Crawford (ed.), *Famine*, p. 43.

643 The year is repeated, indicating use of a different source.
644 *AClyn*, p. 178; *Kilkenny chronicle*, p. 337; the translation of this whole entry concerning Alice Kyteler is taken from that of Walter Kudrycz, in L.S. Davidson and J.O. Ward (eds), *The sorcery trial of Alice Kyteler. A contemporary account 1324 together with related documents in English translation* (New York 1993), appendix VI, pp 82–3; for a full Latin account from the viewpoint of Richard Ledrede, see Thomas Wright (ed.), *A contemporary narrative of the proceedings against dame Alice Kyteler, prosecuted for sorcery in 1324, by Richard de Ledrede, bishop of Ossory*, Camden Soc. 1st ser., 24 (London, 1843); Anne Neary, 'The origins and character of the Kilkenny witchcraft case of 1324', *PRIA*, 83C (1983), 333–50; Bernadette Williams, '"She was usually placed with the great men and leaders of the land in the public assemblies": Alice Kyteler: a woman of considerable power' in Christine Meek (ed.), *Women in renaissance and early modern Europe* (Dublin, 2000), pp 67–83.
645 Dominican house at Kilkenny.
646 Pembridge has extra information about Kyteler not found in either Clyn or Ledrede's *Contemporary narrative against Dame Alice Kyteler;* e.g., Pembridge has the sweeping item which later became the doggerel 'Unto the house of William my son – Hie all the wealth of Kilkenny town' and only he reports that Alice put ointment on a stick called a *cowltre* which she could then ride on throughout the world; these details may be examples of how quickly rumour can distort truth.
647 No mention by Pembridge of the king being deposed; however, for full contemporary account as known in Kilkenny, see *AClyn*, pp 186–8; *Chronica Buriensis*, p. 164; *Lanercost*, ii, pp 255–6; no mention of possibility of Edward escaping to Ireland: Phillips, 'Edward II and Ireland (in fact and in fiction)', pp 13–14; there is also a lack of information about Despenser in Pembridge: Nigel Saul, 'The Despensers and the downfall of Edward II', *EHR*, 99:390 (1984), 1–33.
648 Dominican house at Kilkenny
649 This is the only reference to this parliament: *Ir. parl.*, p. 336.
650 'A skilled knight, courteous, rich, and wise and full of days': *AClyn*, p. 184; died around 1 August: *Kilkenny chronicle*, p. 338; 'The choicest of all the English in Ireland': *AFM*, iii, p. 533; *AC*, p. 261; many de Burghs were buried there in the Augustinian priory.
651 The heir, his grandson William '[son of] his son John de Burgh and the daughter of the earl of Gloucester': *AClyn*, pp 184–6; for William's arrival in Ireland, see 1328, and for his murder, see 1333.
652 Dominican Chapter in London; the new king was proclaimed in England 25 Jan; in Ireland 13 May: Phillips, 'Edward II and Ireland (in fact and in fiction)', pp 16–18; for Edward III, see W.M. Ormrod, *The reign of Edward III: crown and political society in England, 1327–1377* (London, 1990); Frame, *Eng. lordship*, pp 139, 174–82.
653 This was reported in full by Clyn and the Kilkenny chronicler; it was a serious war 'between the Geraldines the Butlers and the de Berminghams on the one side against the le Poers and the de Burghs on the other side': *Kilkenny chronicle*, p. 338; *AClyn*, p. 188; William de Bermingham was the brother of the murdered earl of Louth; Eustace le Poer, knight, held Castle Grace: *COD, 1172–1350*, no. 418; *Red bk Ormond*, p. 145; the le Poers held Kells and there was a long-standing relationship between the le Poer and de Burgh: Parker, 'Pater familias and *parentela*', 103–4, 111; for the le Poer allegiance to

Notes to pages 157 to 159

de Burgh in the aftermath of the deposition of Edward II and the rise of Mortimer, see Frame, *Eng. lordship*, pp 174–95; attacks on the Poer lands in Munster and Ossory followed: Sayles, 'The rebellious first earl of Desmond' in Watt et al. (eds), *Medieval studies presented to Aubrey Gwynn*, pp 209–10.

654 *Kilkenny chronicle*, p. 338; perhaps 'the point of Arnold's insult was that composing harmless *vers de salon* was all that Maurice was fit for': Evelyn Mullally, 'Hiberno-Norman literature and its public' in John Bradley (ed.), *Settlement and society in medieval Ireland: studies presented to F.X. Martin* (Kilkenny, 1988), pp 332–3; for different interpretation of the insult implied by the word *rymoure*, see Frame, 'Rebellion and rehabilitation', p. 200, fn. 28; Katharine Simms, 'The Geraldines and Gaelic culture' in Crooks & Duffy (eds), *The Geraldines*, p. 265; Maurice fitz Thomas, earl of Desmond; Thomas de Clare died in February 1321 and Maurice fitz Thomas took control of all the Clare lands causing friction in the area of Dungarvan: Waters, 'The earls of Desmond', pp 45–50; Sayles, 'The rebellious first earl of Desmond', pp 209–10.

655 Dominican house at Waterford.
656 *AClyn*, p. 188.
657 10 May: *Ir. parl.*, p. 336; *Parls and councils*, pp 6–7, 202–3.
658 Outlawe was chancellor from 1322; for a full account, see Eithne Massey, *Prior Roger Outlaw of Kilmainham, 1314–1344* (Dublin, 2000).
659 *Admin. Ire.*, pp 156, 169, fn. 4; for Nicholas Fastolf and his life as an administrator, see *IExP*, index; in 1329 Fastolf was given permission to bring a water supply to all his houses in St Nicholas's parish, provided that he paved and repaired the streets afterwards: *CARD*, i, p. 119.
660 Dominican house at Kilkenny.
661 This may have been an Irish reaction to the events in England, based perhaps on a belief that the deposition of Edward II had removed the legitimacy of English rule in Ireland: Phillips, 'Edward II and Ireland (in fact and in fiction)', p. 14 fn.67; Frame, 'Two kings in Leinster: the crown and the MicMhurchadha in the fourteenth century' in *Colony and frontier*, pp 155–75; it is unusual that Pembridge does not mention the advent of a new king in 1327 (in England 25 Jan.; in Ireland 13 May).
662 Order to pay Henry Traharne £40 for the capture of 'Donenaldus McMurghuth McUeth, Irish felon, and for expenses in fighting the Irish of name of McMurghuthes in the marches of Leinster' (Dublin, 20 July 1322): CIRCLE, Close Roll 18 Edw II, §5; *IExP*, pp 295, 334, 353
663 In 1327 John de Wellesley and Milo de Rocheford, knights, were witnesses to a Christ Church grant: *CCD*, p. 75; Lawlor, 'Liber Niger', 18; for John and William, knights, in connection with the lands of the earl of Kildare: *47th rep. DKPRI*, pp 45, 53.
664 Re-named College Green in the 1600s; Bernadette Williams, 'Heresy in Ireland in the thirteenth and fourteenth centuries' in Duffy (ed.), *Princes, prelates and poets*, pp 346–8; *Red bk Ormond*, 15–16; *CJRI, 1295–1303*, p. 271.
665 Died at Maynooth on 5 April: *AClyn*, p. 188; same date, *Kilkenny chronicle*, p. 338; buried with the Franciscans where his son Richard, who died at Rathmegan in 1331 without male heirs (see 1331) was also buried: *Red bk Kildare*, no. 118; he built the lady chapel of the Franciscans at Kildare and was buried there with his wife, Joan, daughter of Richard de Burgh, earl of Ulster: Fitzmaurice and Little, *Franciscan province*, p. 131.
666 Outlawe deputy justiciar July to Oct. 1324 and for a few days in May 1327 and acting justiciar April 1328; then deputy justiciar in 1330–1; later in 1335, 1336–7 and again 1340–41: *Admin. Ire.*, pp 85, 86, 87; Massey, *Prior Roger Outlaw*.
667 The Tholsel was the city court held before the mayor and bailiffs; Ashbourn not knighted until *c.*1335; for a full examination of his career, see Frame, 'Ashbourne', p. 129; for links

with Hothum, ibid., pp 124–5; for his lands in proximity to the Uí Thuathail, and his other lands, see ibid., pp 130–3; he died *c.*1356 and his heir Thomas de Asshebourne aged *c.*30 was also a knight, *Inquisitions & extents*, pp 191–2; Fastolf, justice of the common bench and justice of the justiciar's bench with Elias Ashbourne in 1327–1329: *Admin. Ire.*, pp 156, 169; *CCD*, pp 160–6; Gilbert, *History of Dublin*, i, p. 239 states: 'Among the MSS. of Trinity College, Dublin, is a grant made by the Corporation in 1305 to Roger de Asheburn and his heirs, of a certain ditch (*quoddam fossatum*) without the city walls, near Bertram's court (*curia Bertrami*), extending from the tenements near the New-gate as far as the ground near St Patrick's gate towards the south, and lying in breadth between the place where the fairs are held and the wall of the city of Dublin'.

668 Williams, 'Heresy in Ireland', p. 347; O'Byrne, 'Cultures in contact in the Leinster and Dublin marches', p. 133; *CCD*, p. 141.

669 'Peter Poer, son and heir of the baron of Dunohill was killed with around twelve others of his *cognomine*, by the *familia* of lord Maurice Fitz Thomas; And on that day lord John Fitz Gerald was killed in the same conflict': *AClyn*, pp 188–90.

670 In 1328, 'William de Burgh, earl of Ulster, having been brought up in England came to Ireland with his wife Matilda, daughter of lord Henry, earl of Lancaster, and his kinswoman; they had been betrothed by papal dispensation because they were in the third and fourth degree of affinity; he was the son of John de Burgh, son of Richard, and Elizabeth, daughter of Gilbert de Clare; to him came a third part of the lands of the earl of Gloucester through his mother Elizabeth': *AClyn*, p. 190.

671 'Edward ... made his brother ... earl of Cornwall, made lord Roger de Mortimer earl of March, and made lord James Butler, earl of Ormond': *AClyn*, p. 190; *Kilkenny chronicle*, p. 338; Pembridge does not mention Mortimer becoming earl of March.

672 Chapter at London; Treaty of Northampton acknowledged Scottish independence and Robert Bruce as king.

673 In 1328 'William de Burgh earl of Ulster, the son of lord John, the son of the lord earl Richard came to Ireland with his wife, namely the daughter of the earl of Lancaster, who was in the third and fourth degree of consanguinity, from which there was a dispensation from the pope': *Kilkenny chronicle*, pp 338–9.

674 For a rather complicated scenario at this time, see Ranald Nicholson, 'A sequel to Edward Bruce's invasion of Ireland', *SHR*, 42 (1963–4), 30–40; Phillips, 'Edward II and Ireland (in fact and in fiction)', p. 16.

675 15 August: *Ir. parl.*, p 336.

676 The following two entries again follow, very substantially, the translation in *Sorcery trial of Alice Kyteler*, appendix VI, p. 84; for the petition of bishop of Ossory complaining of Arnold le Poer, see *Affairs Ire.*, pp 132–4.

677 Mid-Lent 1329: *Ir. parl.*, p 337; for compurgation in parliament, see *Parls and councils*, 202–3; Lydon, 'Christ Church in the later medieval Irish world', pp 75–94.

678 In 1341 the bishop of Ossory was still complaining to the king: *Affairs Ire.*, pp 173–7.

679 Áine Foley, 'Violence and authority: the sheriff and seneschal in late medieval Ireland', *PRIA*, 117C (2017), 185–206.

680 Acting as treasurer of the deputy, chief justice of the Dublin bench: *IExP*, pp 332, 336, 337, 341

681 Chamberlain of exchequer, 1314–1317: *Admin. Ire.*, p. 120; *IExP*, pp 225, 228, 232, 235, 237, 241, 245; Adam Laweles had land in Ostmantown: *CARD*, i, p. 94.

682 Peter de Wylebi, official of Dublin court in 1325: *CCD*, pp 75, 151; called Master in 1328: ibid., pp 145, 148; *Alan's register*, p. 203; a Robert de Wylleby/Willeby was provost of Dublin late 1200s to 1313 at least: *CStM*, i, pp 447, 448.

683 The same date: *AClyn*, p. 192; *Kilkenny chronicle*, p. 339; a continuation of the Kyteler saga; Ledrede had once more accused le Poer and Outlawe of heresy; le Poer was left unburied 'in accordance with the fifteenth article in the constitutions of Bishop Ledrede, which declares that anyone who (inter alia) "impedes the jurisdiction of the bishop" shall not receive ecclesiastical burial, and if buried in ignorance they should be exhumed and cast on a dunghill: H.J. Lawlor, 'Calendar of the *Liber Ruber* of the diocese of Ossory', *PRIA*, 27 C (1908), 168; for the petition of Ledrede to the king complaining of Arnold (1328), see *Sorcery trial of Alice Kyteler*, appendix IX, pp 89–91; for the 1329 letter from Edward III to the pope warning him against Ledrede, ibid., appendix X, p. 92; the prior of Holy Trinity was Robert de Gloucester: Milne, *Christ church*, p. 391.

684 Pembridge was prior of the Dublin Dominicans, 1329–33.

685 This may refer to the same parliament: *Ir. parl.* p 337; 'On 17 May 1333, the new justiciar, John Darcy, the mayor and other important officials, in a formal ceremony in the choir of Holy Trinity, before the high altar, witnessed the earl of Desmond make solemn promises in the presence of God, the holy gospels, the sacred cross and the *baculum beati Patricii* (the staff of blessed Patrick) and other relics': *Account Roll Holy Trinity*, p. xv.

686 He was not earl until August.

687 For a very full account, see *AClyn*, pp 95–6, 192–4; 'with 16 or more': *Kilkenny chronicle*, p. 339; *AFM*, iii, pp 539–41; the earldom ceased; he left no son only daughters; for a full discussion and all the names involved, see James Lydon, 'The Braganstown Massacre, 1329', *JLAHS*, 19 (1977–80), 5–16; all the names mentioned above are in the inquisition, ibid. p. 12; for pardons, see Connolly, 'Chancery warrants (C81)', p. 147; in 1346 there was a request to the king that Irish scholars at Oxford should be arrested in reprisal for the killing of 150 men by their relatives in Co. Louth: Connolly, 'Ancient petitions (SC 8)', p. 66; the reply was '*La peticion nest pas resonable*': *Affairs Ire.*, pp 186–7; Smith, *Colonisation and conquest*, pp 113–21; idem, *Crisis and survival*, p. 25; William Bermingham became the accepted head of the lineage, he was lord of Carbury: Frame, *Eng. lordship*, pp 32–4.

688 Simon de Geneville held lands in Meath from Roger Mortimer: *Reg. Gormanston*, pp 171–4; Matthew Devitt, 'Carbury and the Bermingham's country', *Kildare Arch. Soc. Jn.* (1896–9) 85–110.

689 Louth had been a centre of disorder: Brendan Smith, 'The murder of Richard Gernon, sheriff of Louth, 1311', *JLAHS*, 4 (1988), 391–3; in 1312 there was the Verdun rebellion (see above s.a. 1312); Roger, sheriff of Louth: *IExP*, p. 302; and John had held many administrative posts: *IExP*, index.

690 Dominican priory Mullingar; 'Thomas Butler was killed near Mullingar with around a hundred others by Mac Eochagáin': *AClyn*, p. 196; 'Lord Thomas Butler, with many others, was killed on the eve of blessed Lawrence by Mchokegan': *Kilkenny chronicle*, p. 339; William Gallda Mag Eochagáin, dux of Ceinéal Fhiachach, died in 133: *AC*; Ardnurcher, now Horseleap on Westmeath Offaly border; Hugh Tyrell, keeper of castle of Ardnurcher: *IExP*, p. 284; Foley, 'The sheriff of Dublin in the fourteenth century', p 285; Thomas, lord of Dunboyne, brother of Edmund Butler, and uncle of the earl of Ormond.

691 Lucy, daughter of Roger, married Cusack: Hogan, *Llanthony*, p. 52

692 Founded Mullingar, Hugh Fenning, 'Founders of Irish Dominican friaries: an unpublished list of c.1647', *Collectanea Hibernica*, 44/5 (2002–3), 60.

693 In 1375–6, a David Naungle was called a felon and rebel: *IExP*, p. 535.

694 The family would be known to Pembridge as they held Castleknock and a Stephen Tyrell, was abbot of St Thomas, Dublin, and Walter Tyrell was prior of Dublin Dominicans in 1350s: *IExP*, p. 444

695 White may appear in sources as Albus or White or even Blund; perhaps Nicholas Blund who held lands in Rathregan, Co. Meath, from Roger Mortimer: *Reg. Gormanston*, p. 139.
696 'The English sustained a great defeat from Mageoghegan, three thousand five hundred of them being slain in the contest, together with some of the Daltons, and the son of the Proud Knight': *AFM* 1328.
697 Brother of Edmund Butler was killed 'defending his wife's interests in Meath': Frame, 'The campaign against the Scots in Munster, 1317', p. 109 fn. 39.
698 Philip de Staunton, clerk of wages: *IExP*, pp 15, 207, 215, 598.
699 On 21 November, lord Henry Traharne and Lawrence, brother of lord James Butler, were captured by the Uí Nualláin': *AClyn*, p. 196; *Kilkenny chronicle*, p. 339; Treharne, assisting the justiciar, captured Domhnall, son of Art Mac Murchadha, king of Leinster: see above 1327; *IExP*, pp 295, 334, 353.
700 'Whereupon lord James *Pincerna* [Butler] on the Thursday after Lucy, virgin [14 December], gathered an army of nobles and on the following Friday [15 December] wasted their lands and very nearly all their neighbourhood by fire': *AClyn*, p. 196; Connolly, 'Chancery warrants (C81)', p. 149; the barony of Forth, Co. Carlow (from Irish Fotharta), was the heartland of Uí Nualláin territory.
701 Gilbert has *Locum* and assumes this is Laweles but gives no reason: *CStM*, p. 271; however, on the same line the scribe had just written Lawless which was very different and very easy to read; however, for a Robert Lawless in Carlow in 1346, see Frame, 'Commissions of the peace', 11; *IExP*, 483.
702 O'Byrne, 'Carrickmines and the Dublin marches', p. 237; idem, 'Cultures in contact', pp 126-7.
703 Created earl in 1329: Sayles, 'The rebellious first earl of Desmond'; see s.a.1330.
704 [extra word = nns ?].
705 The castle of Ley was captured by the Uí Dhíomusaigh and in the same year was restored by lord Maurice fitz Thomas: *Kilkenny chronicle*, p. 339; in September 1329, the castle of Lea was captured by Uí Dhíomusaigh: *AClyn*, p. 196; *IExP* p. 335; Sayles, 'The rebellious first earl of Desmond', p. 245.
706 But he does not mention the similar attempt by William de Bermingham on the 2 July 1332; the explanation must lie in the praise and the lament for the execution of William de Bermingham in 1332, see below s.a. 1332; Lydon, 'Dublin castle in the Middle Ages', p. 124 fn. 52; another David Naungle was a felon and rebel in 1375-6: *IExP*, p. 535; Frame, 'Two kings in Leinster', pp 163.
707 It should be noted that Clyn gives the information that 'before Christmas, Roger de Mortimer, earl of March, was condemned to death': *AClyn*, p. 200; this lack of information indicates the state of mind of Pembridge.
708 These next entries are all concerned with bad weather: see Campbell and Ludlow, 'Climate, disease and society', 209-10; reported also in Kilkenny and according to Clyn, the weather was bad from May to February, 'excessively wet, full of rain and wind so that summer and autumn seemed almost to have become the winter period'; there was also 'a violent and dreadful wind' that dispersed haycocks, destroyed houses and caused much damage and many perished from hunger': *AClyn*, p. 200; 'The year was most rainy and hostile to all men and the summer was costly and the autumn seemed to be converted into winter storms, many perished from hunger': *Kilkenny chronicle*, p. 339; a single span is all that remains of the 'once massive eleven-span bridge ... about 2.5km downstream of Navan': Peter O'Keeffe and Tom Simington, *Irish stone bridges: history and heritage* (Dublin, 2016), p. 15; M.T. Flanagan suggests that Babe is closer to the twelfth-century version of the name as it comes from John le Baub: *Reg. St Thomas*, pp 12, 27, 28, 242, 247, 263, 275, 279; I thank Prof. Flanagan for this information and reference; there is

no mention of damage to the Dominican houses of Trim or Drogheda; 'While the famine of 1330–2 was severe it may have been confined to Leinster and the south west, as it was not recorded in any of the Gaelic annals': Lyons, 'Weather, famine, pestilence, and plague in Ireland', p. 44.

709 In 1330 'William de Burgh, earl of Ulster, gathered a large army of men of Ulster and Connacht': *AClyn*, p. 198; 'a large army of Ulstermen and with many others; and lord James Butler with his army; and the prior of Kilmainham then justiciar (with the king's army) against Bren O'Bren and nothing was achieved': *Kilkenny chronicle*, p. 339; Waters, 'The earls of Desmond', p. 56.

710 Dominican house at Kilkenny: *Ir. parl.*, p. 337.

711 In 1326 Walter, son of William de Burgh: Frame, 'Commissions of the peace', 8.

712 Priories at Kilkenny and Cashel; in 1330 'William de Burgh, earl of Ulster ... and lord James Butler [led] his army against Brian Ó Briain; this was because he [Brian] had destroyed their lands and their neighbourhood; all of them made little headway against him on that occasion but they returned without great gain or damage, disgrace or honour to their [own lands]': *AClyn*, p. 198; Ormond claimed that he maintained 500 horse and 1,000 foot against Ó Briain in 1330: Frame, *Eng. lordship*, p. 40; Brian had attacked the manor of Raymond Ercedeakne and burned Ardmayle and Moyaliffe in Co. Tipperary, and Roger Outlaw, as deputy justiciar, took prompt action: Sayles, 'The rebellious first earl of Desmond', p. 210.

713 Waters, 'The earls of Desmond', pp 226–9.

714 1329, 'Maurice Fitz Thomas was created earl of Desmond in the same year by the same [king]': *AClyn*, p. 196; also granted Kerry as a liberty: Frame, *Eng. lordship*, p. 188.

715 Priory at Limerick; Waters, 'The earls of Desmond', pp 44, 55–60.

716 Perhaps Pembridge was appointed at the general chapter at Vitry in 1331: see *CCR, 1330–1333*, p. 283; dates now day and month rather than feast.

717 Perhaps to be appointed as lieutenant: see Otway-Ruthven, 'Chief governors', p. 79 fn. 1.

718 Priory at Arklow.

719 For the archbishop's palace and castle at Tallaght, see John Bradley, 'The medieval boroughs of county Dublin', pp 141–2; Paul MacCotter 'The church lands of the diocese of Dublin: reconstruction and history' in Duffy (ed.), *Medieval Dublin XIII*, pp 81–107; for a later Richard White, knight, and Nicholas Houth knight, see James Lydon, 'William of Windsor' in Crooks (ed.), *Government*, p. 103.

720 The name of the district granted by the Lord John to Archbishop Cumin in the 1180s, which appears to have been in the present parishes of Blessington and Kilbride: Liam Price, *The place-names of Co. Wicklow*, iv (Dublin, 1983), pp 245–6.

721 *AClyn*, p. 204; *Kilkenny chronicle*, p. 340.

722 At Thurles on Wednesday 22 May 1331, 'William Hacket, with others of the neighbourhood, killed around fifty of the men of Brian Ó Briain and other Irishmen, and William was himself killed on the same day and in the same place', *AClyn*, p. 202.

723 Finnea, Co. Westmeath; *AFM* 1330: 'An army was led by Ualgarg O'Rourke to Fiodhan-atha, whereupon the English of that town rose up against him. O'Rourke's people were defeated; and Art O'Rourke, a materies of a chief lord of Breifny, Rory Magauran, and many others, were slain by the English'.

724 *Hedis* plural of *hed*, Middle-English variant spelling of 'heed' which derives from Anglo-Saxon *heafod*, meaning head; *Thurl* is the alternative Middle-English spelling of the Anglo-Saxon word *Þurl* means hole; so together it is 'hole-heads'; whale was usually *hwael* (Anglo-Saxon) but maybe *tharlhedis* is a colloquial term for whales: I thank Emma Williams for this suggestion; whales cast upon the land, belonged to the king; in 1295 Robert de Clohulle of Kerry kept one cast up on his land and the decision was 'unless

such fish are specially mentioned in the charter, the king ought to have it': *CJRI, 1295–1303*, pp 29, 54.

725 Le Connyng may be a rabbit-warren, possibly Sandymount. Reported in Kilkenny as Monday 24 June 1331, 'many large marine fish were washed ashore in the harbour of Dublin near the town … they were forty feet long, some thirty; so that some of them could scarcely be dragged from the place by the power of men or the strength of beasts and some were of such a height that when two large men were standing around one long fish neither was able to see the other on the other side of the belly': *AClyn*, p. 204; during excavation in Dublin, 'a skull of an immature pilot whale (*Globicephala melaena*) was recovered …. The skull displayed butchery marks. Adult pilot whales can grow up to 28 feet long but are generally about 20ft in length … [and] have a tendency to become beached'; Claire Walsh is tempted to identify this skull with the 1331 report: eadem, *Archaeological excavations at Patrick, Nicholas and Winetavern Streets Dublin* (Dingle, 1997), pp 205–6; I am indebted to Dr Margaret Murphy for this reference.

726 Mayor 1330, 1331: Eoin C. Bairéad, 'The bailiffs, provosts and sheriffs of the city of Dublin' in Seán Duffy (ed.), *Medieval Dublin XIV* (Dublin, 2015), p. 215.

727 In 1295 Robert de Clohulle appropriated 'a certain great whale' that had been cast up on his land 'in prejudice of the crown'; he claimed that his father's charter included wreck of the sea; the decision was that unless such fish were specifically mentioned in the charter, great whales cast upon the land were not wreck of the sea: *CJRI, 1295–1303*, pp 29, 54–5; in 1246 a whale was stranded in Carbury, at Cuil Irra, which brought great relief and joy to the countryside: *AC*, p. 87; for the importance of stranded whales in medieval times, see Arthur E.J. Went, 'Whaling from Ireland', *JRSAI*, 98 (1968), 31.

728 *Ir. parl.*, pp 29, 338.

729 Dominican priory at Kilkenny; *Ir. parl.*, p. 337.

730 'Maurice Fitz Thomas, earl of Desmond, and William de Bermingham, made peace … And having touched the gospels and relics of the saints and, after the body of Christ having been brought, they swore that they would keep peace and fealty to the lord king and serve the people henceforth': *AClyn*, p. 204; 'taking the holy Gospel and the holy relics and the body of Christ they contracted and swore fidelity to the lord king and to observe the peace of the faithful vassals for the future': *Kilkenny chronicle*, p. 340.

731 D.P. Sweetman, 'Archaeological excavations at Ferns Castle, Co. Wexford', *PRIA*, 79C (1979) 217–45.

732 Dominican priory at Limerick.

733 'Maurice Fitz Thomas, within fifteen days of peace having been granted to him by the same justiciar, was captured at Limerick and detained in his custody'; afterwards, in November 1331, 'Katherine de Burgh, wife of Maurice Fitz Thomas, died in Dublin': *AClyn*, p. 206; she was presumably in Dublin because the earl of Desmond was in prison in Dublin castle; for second wife, Aneline (daughter of Nicholas fitz Maurice of Kerry), see *NHI*, ix, p. 168; fifteen days after the peace he was captured by the Justiciar at Limerick and held in his custody; then at Clonmel he seized lord William Bremegham and lord Walter his son': *Kilkenny chronicle*, p. 340; Desmond stayed imprisoned until 1333, see s.a 1333; Sayles, 'The rebellious first earl of Desmond', pp 249–53; idem, 'The legal proceedings against the first earl of Desmond', *AH*, 23 (1966), 1–47; the whole episode is discussed by Frame, *Eng. lordship*, pp 209–16; idem, 'Rebellion and rehabilitation', pp 195–7.

734 Justice of common bench 1334–8: *Admin. Ire.*, pp 156, 158, 160; he accounted for Gormanston manor: *44th rep. DKPRI*, p. 12; in 1332, the earl of Ulster wrote to the king stating that Henry de Mandeville 'committed homicide, robberies and other crimes': Connolly, 'Chancery warrants (C81)', p. 148; Friar Alexander Laweles of the Dublin

Dominicans went to Ulster 'by order of the justiciar and council, with the king's writs directed to Henry de Mandeville: *IExP*, p. 379; 'The felons of Ulster recently besieged Greencastle in Ulster, intending to knock it down; and for this reason, Henry Mandeville proceeded there on two occasions with many men-at-arms, hobelars and foot and recovered the castle by force at his own expense; it was agreed that for this Henry should have 20m of the K.'s gift from the issues of the lands and tenements in Ulster that belonged to William Burgh, late earl of Ulster, in the K.'s hand because of the minority of his heir; ORDER to pay this sum to Henry; and the K. will grant him [William Logan] allowance for this in his account at the Ex': CIRCLE, Close Roll 8 Edw III, §58; J.R.H. Greeves, 'Robert I and the de Mandevilles of Ulster', *Trans Dumfriesshire and Galloway Natural History Soc.*, 3rd ser. 34 (1957–8), 59–73

735 In 1328 the castle of Carrickfergus was restored to William de Burgh, earl of Ulster: Connolly, 'Chancery warrants (C81)', p. 144; Walter de Burgh, eldest son of William Liath de Burgh (1324 above) and first cousin of the earl of Ulster (Orpen, *Normans*, p. 554) with two of his brothers were taken prisoner in Connacht in November and in the following February were taken to Greencastle where Walter died in prison; Walter and the earl had clashed in Connacht: Orpen, *Normans*, p. 555; according to Clyn, this affair led to the murder of the earl of Ulster (1333 below): *AClyn*, p. 210.

736 T and L: Arabic 19

737 *Kilkenny chronicle*, p. 340; *AClyn*, p. 206; for the allegations of conspiracy and Walter's claim of benefit of clergy, see Philomena Connolly, 'An attempted escape from Dublin castle: the trial of William and Walter de Bermingham, 1332', *IHS*, 29 (1994), 100–8; Sayles, 'The legal proceedings against the first earl of Desmond', *AH*, 23 (1966), 6, 12; no mention is made of the attempted escape, see Philomena Connolly, '"Devices made by magic": an attempted escape from Dublin castle in 1332', *History Ireland*, 3 (1995), 19–23; Leona C. Gabel, *Benefit of clergy in England in the later Middle Ages* (repr. New York, 1969), p. 33; Frame, *Eng. lordship*, pp 209–16.

738 Freynestown, midway between Dunlavin and Baltinglass, Co. Wicklow.

739 This incident may be the source of the complaint from the justiciar and council of Ireland to the pope in 1331, 'even though the holiest body of our Lord Jesus Christ was certainly known to be present there, and with the priests in their sacerdotal vestments holding the eucharist in their hands in front of the said malefactors, for the sake of protection and refuge (against the malefactors who were) pressing (them) violently back into the fires': *Sorcery trial of Alice Kyteler*, appendix VIII, pp 87–9; Lydon, 'Medieval Wicklow: "a land of war"', p. 173.

740 The Dublin Dominican, Friar Richard Ó Cormacáin, was the person chosen to execute the excommunication against Ó Tuathail: *IExP*, p. 347

741 Seán Duffy suggests that L's reading, 'Carcarne', indicates this is Carn Curnáin, which gives its names to Carne, bar. Forth, Co. Wexford, and Carnsore Point: Pádraig Ó Riain et al. (eds), *Historical dictionary of Gaelic placenames*, fasc. 3 (ITS, London, 2008), p. 69.

742 In 1306 a Richard le Whyte was called a merchant of Cork: Connolly, 'Memoranda rolls', 171; in 1320 Richard White of Waterford was accused of seizing a ship in Bordeaux: Connolly, 'Ancient petitions (SC 8)', p. 92; in 1386 a Richard White was prior of the hospital but also a Richard White was an administrator: *IExP*, p. 545, index.

743 There was a proposal that king should come to Ireland, but the Scottish wars intervened.

744 Walter was not freed until 1334, and therefore this entry was written on or after 1334; On 11 July, 'William de Bermingham, a vigorous and military knight, bold and intrepid, was hanged in Dublin': *AClyn*, p. 208; *Kilkenny chronicle*, p. 340; Walter may have escaped death by claiming benefit of clergy, see Connolly, 'An attempted escape from Dublin castle', p. 102; Lydon 'Dublin castle in the Middle Ages', pp 124–5; Lucy held

an inquisition in Dublin into the attempt by William and Walter, prisoners in Dublin castle, to escape by means of sorcery and bribery: Connolly, 'Chancery files (C.260)', pp 8, 9.

745 'On the feast of blessed Pius martyr (Pope Pius I, 11 July) lord William Bremegham ... was hanged in Dublin by lord Anthony de Lucy Justiciar': *Kilkenny chronicle*, p. 340; he was lord of Carbury in County Kildare and married to the widow of Richard de Clare, lord of Thomond; his brother John, earl of Louth, had been justiciar in 1321–3 and William had served as John's deputy for six months during that period; however, in the years since then, William had become associated with Maurice fitz Thomas, and this association lead to his downfall.

746 Clyn called Bunratty impregnable: *AClyn*, p. 208; the earl of Desmond had appointed John Fitz Maurice as constable of Bunratty in 1331: Sayles, 'The rebellious first earl of Desmond', pp 212–14.

747 Priory at Arklow; castle rebuilt autumn 1333: *AClyn*, p. 208; *IExP*, pp 347, 351, 352, 353; the justiciar was at Clonmore from 3 May to 4 Aug. and at Arklow from 5 to 24 August; for the accounts of de Lucy (including payments for the troops of Fulk de la Freigne, Walter de Valle and Laoiseach Ó Mórdha): *43th rep. DKPRI*, pp 54–5.

748 T and L Arabic numeral 1

749 Correct date: *Admin. Ire.*, p. 85.

750 'The earl of Ormond, the Geraldines and the de Burghs, ... made war against Brian Ó Briain; and a great many of his men were killed and they took great plunder from him and his men': *AClyn*, p. 208; at the parliament at Dublin, 17 August 1332, it was decided to 'summon those owing military service to meet at Limerick on 5 Oct. 1332': *Parls and councils*, pp 9–10.

751 Perhaps Decer died of measles? See next entry; Harris states that 'this generous magistrate in a time of great scarcity raised a vast sum of money, and furnished out three ships to France, which returned in two months laden with corn, and that he bestowed one ... on the lord justice and militia, another on the Dominican and Augustin seminaries, and reserved a third for the exercise of his own hospitality and bounty; at the same time the prior of Christ-church, being destitute of corn, and having no money to buy it, sent to this worthy mayor a pledge of plate to the value of 40*l*; but he returned the plate and sent the prior a present of 20 barrels of corn; these beneficent actions moved the Dominicans to insert the following prayer in their litany, viz. "*Orate pro salute majoris, ballivorum, et communitatis de omni civitate Dubliniensi, optimorum benefactorum huic ordini tuo, nunc et in hora mortis.*"': Harris, *Dublin*, pp 258–9.

752 Measles? In the ninth century, a Persian doctor, Rhazes, published one of the first written accounts of measles; there was an increasing number of descriptions of measles in the eleventh and twelfth centuries: W. McNeil, *Plagues and peoples* (New York, 1976); no mention by W.P. MacArthur, in 'The identification of some pestilences recorded in the Irish annals', *IHS*, 6 (1948–49), 169–88.

753 Dominican house at Limerick; in *c.* 1328 there was a request that Limerick castle and the prison should be rebuilt: Connolly, 'Ancient petitions (SC 8)', p. 44.

754 Earl of Ormond acquired Tipperary as a liberty in 1328 and his lands were centred round Nenagh and Thurles.

755 John Bradley, 'The medieval boroughs of county Dublin', p. 136; K.J. Edwards, F.W. Hamond and Anngret Simms. 'The medieval settlement of Newcastle Lyons, County Dublin, an interdisciplinary approach', *PRIA*, 83C (1983), 351–76; for a useful map, see James Mills, 'Norman settlement in Leinster: the cantreds near Dublin', *JRSAI*, 24 (1894), 160; for Newcastle Lyons, ibid., p. 173; in 1344 the inhabitants stated that the manor had been burned and devastated many times: *Account Roll Holy Trinity*, pp 153–4.

756 Perhaps Aghancon, Co. Offaly.
757 For the list of mainpernors, see *Parls and councils*, pp 13; G.O. Sayles, 'The rebellious first earl of Desmond' in *Scripta Diversa* (London, 1982) p. 214; he swore his oath in Christ Church cathedral: Lydon, 'Christ Church in the later medieval Irish world', p. 85; *Account Roll Holy Trinity*, p. xv; Frame, 'Rebellion and rehabilitation', p. 195.
758 Richard de Mandeville and Giles his wife were also involved, and 100 marks was offered for their capture: Connolly, 'Chancery warrants (C81)', p. 152; *AFM*, iii, p. 551.
759 Aged 20; for an equally dramatic account, see *AClyn*, p. 210; in 1339 a query was sent to the Dublin exchequer asking on what day William de Burgh earl of Ulster died, and the return was that he died on 6 June 1333: Connolly, 'Chancery files (C.260)', p. 9.
760 This hurried exit from Ireland was repeated when she was the wife of Ufford: see *s.a.*1344.
761 *Ir. parl.*, p 337; *Parls and councils*, pp 12–17.
762 The warehouse of Holy Trinity stored French wine for the king in Scotland: Roger Stalley 'The construction of the medieval cathedral, *c.*1039–1250' in Milne, *Christ church*, p. 63.
763 'Murchadh Nicol Ó Tuathail was killed in Dublin when he was walking among many in a crowd; afterwards the unknown murderer fled secretly concealed in the tumult; this was in accord with the just judgment of God; he [Ó Tuathail] himself previously had evilly killed many faithful men': *AClyn*, p. 210; for a list of those present at the parliament: *Parls and councils*, pp 12–17; Ó Tuathail was a supporter of Ormond and the justiciar: 'Morth, son of Nicholas Otothel, for his labours and expenses on various occasions in the king's service in the company of the justiciar in subduing certain felons of the Leinster mountains': *IExP*, p. 335; Ó Tuathail could have been murdered by either the Geraldine or de Burgh factions, or by the Irish: he is among those named with the Anglo-Irish who were paid for going from Dublin to Kilkenny 'to establish peace between the said magnates' and also to suppress malice of O'Brynnrs, Omorthes and O'Dymsiis': *43th rep. DKPRI*, pp 28–9; 'Irish and strong in arms': *ARoss*, p. 45.
764 Walter claimed benefit of clergy: Lydon, 'Dublin castle in the Middle Ages', pp 124–5; Connolly, 'An attempted escape from Dublin castle', pp 100–8.
765 See above 1316 for similar occurrence; the peck, in use since the early fourteenth century, was a measure for flour.
766 There is a gap for the years 1334, 1335, 1336; during these years, chapters were held in England in Leicester, London (general chapter) and Cambridge (provincial chapter), and there were also general chapters at Limoges and Bruges: G.R. Galbraith, *The constitution of the Dominican order, 1216 to 1360* (Manchester, 1925), p. 265; was Pembridge, as prior, away reporting at one of these?
767 *Perdix perdix* (grey partridge), is ground-nesting, usually on the edges of fields and only flies a short distance; the surprise must have been the height to which the birds arose as Christ Church was the highest point in the medieval city: Stalley, 'The architecture of the cathedral and priory buildings', pp 111, 126.
768 This piece of Irish marginalia is at the bottom of the page but in the same hand; I thank Professor Pádraig Ó Macháin of UCC for this following note: 'The transcription of the marginalium is as follows: *Niroibh ar dhacorp a coimdhe cneadh arnem asnarsil cru. fuil as da taeb oguin / ghallga saeib is nac duil tharla thu*; this is a quatrain from a religious bardic poem that I have not been able to identify so far; the second line is corrupt, but the general sense is clear enough; arranged as a verse it would look like this: *Niroibh ar dhacorp a coimdhe /cneadh arnem as nar sil cru. fuil as da taeb oguin ghallga /saeib is nac duil tharla thu*'.

769 For the crisis of 1341–2, see Robin Frame, 'English policies and Anglo-Irish attitudes in the crisis of 1341–1342' in J.F. Lydon (ed.), *England and Ireland in the later Middle Ages* (Dublin, 1981), pp 86–103.
770 *AClyn*, p. 222; Otway-Ruthven, 'Chief governors', p. 81; *Admin. Ire.*, p. 86; Frame, *Eng. lordship*, pp 236–42; he was a friend of Mortimer: Dryburgh, 'Roger Mortimer', p. 27.
771 15 October: *Admin. Ire.*, pp, 95, 102.
772 Two hundred Welsh archers: *AClyn*, p. 222; for wages paid to the Welshmen: *CCR, 1337–1339*, p. 314; Frame, *Eng. lordship*, pp 236–42.
773 *CStM*, ii, p. 292.
774 On 14 Jan.: *Ir. parl.*, p. 338; the archbishop of Armagh was represented by proctors; 'Nothing ... would induce the archbishop of Armagh to attend a parliament in the province of Dublin': *Ir. parl.*, p. 123; *CStM*, ii, p. 292; an order to the archbishop of Dublin and a similar one to the mayor and bailiffs of Dublin in 1338, 'not to interfere with the archbishop of Armagh in the bearing of his cross in that diocese, on his way to the parliament at Dublin': *CCR, 1337–1339*, p. 286; MacInerny, *History of the Irish Dominicans*, pp 194–210; the king had expressly forbidden Bicknor to offer him any opposition; Friar Richard de Bochampton, vicar of the Dominican order in Ireland, going to the king and council in England to further and expedite very important business touching the state of the land of Ireland,1337–9: *IExP*, p. 392; in 1345 'the chapter of Dublin was summoned to defend the archbishop in the proceedings instituted against him by the archbishop of Armagh in regard to the title of Primate': Lawlor, 'Liber Niger', 56.
775 David Mág Oireachtaigh died 16 May 1346; Richard FitzRalph, dean of Lichfield elected July 1346.
776 T and L: Arabic 1Λ for 17; Gilbert did not identify: *CStM*, ii, p. 381 fn. 3.
777 Problem with date here; Clyn has xii Kal. March [18 Feb.]: *AClyn*, p. 222; the *Annals of Nenagh* has 'kalandis ... Martii': Dermot F. Gleeson, 'The Annals of Nenagh', *AH*, 12 (1943), 159; his son and heir was a minor and custody of Butler lands in Tipperary and Limerick went to Desmond: C.A. Empey, 'The Butler lordship', *Butler Society Journal*, 3 (1970–1), 178.
778 June 1338 to April 1340: *Admin. Ire.*, p. 86; *CCR, 1337–9*, pp 389, 422–3, 464.
779 An entry in Clyn demonstrates the situation on the ground; in October 'the le Poers, after [taking] an oath and a fixed day chosen between them, killed Walter de Valle with thirteen of his *sanguine* and *familia* returning from his court held near Clonmel, outside the vill, even though he was then sheriff of Tipperary: *AClyn*, p. 234; for an earlier Walter de Valle, see above 1324; in 1327 a Walter de Valle and Henry Traharne were rewarded for the capture of Domhnall son of Art Mac Murchadha: *IExP*, pp 334–5; Walter brought a contingent of men to Clonmore in 1332: *43th rep. DKPRI*, p. 55; for Walter, son of Walter de Valle in 1332, see Sayles, 'Legal proceedings', p. 6; he was sheriff in Tipperary: *47th rep. DKPRI*, p. 24.
780 For a description of extraordinary weather, see *AClyn*, p. 224; Harris includes bear dancing: Harris, *Dublin*, pp 266–7.
781 No mention of the eclipse of sun on 7 July: Lawlor, 'Liber Niger', 67.
782 In Meath: *AFM*, iii, p. 565.
783 *AClyn*, p. 224; Sayles, 'Legal proceedings', pp 21, 42–3.
784 Lord Maurice Fitz Nicholas 'was seized and imprisoned by Maurice Fitz Thomas, then earl of Desmond ... he died in prison on a starvation diet': *AClyn*, p. 226; Maurice Fitz Nicholas of Kerry, knight, possibly brother-in-law of Desmond, was imprisoned at Castleisland: Sayles, 'The rebellious first earl of Desmond', p. 216 n.82; Foley, 'High status execution in Ireland', pp 137–8; Sayles, 'Legal proceedings', pp 21, 42–3; Maurice son of Nicholas was 'against the king's peace' and in alliance with Brian Ó Briain in

1336–7: *IExP*, p. 385; the earl of Desmond was accused (1331) of '*extraxit oculos*' of a William fitz Nicholas, Sayles, 'Legal proceedings', pp 9, 42.
785   A 'great slaughter was made upon Uí Dhíomasaigh': *AClyn*, p. 224.
786   Idrone, Co. Carlow.
787   *Admin. Ire.*, p. 87; Massey, *Prior Roger Outlaw*.
788   For Outlawe eulogy, see *AClyn*, p. 228; Massey, *Prior Roger Outlaw*, p. 54.
789   *Admin. Ire.*, p. 87
790   Pembridge again prior of Dublin, 1341–3.
791   *Admin. Ire.*, p. 87; a new group of officials came to Dublin: Frame *Eng. lordship*, pp 243–50.
792   T has forty-three days, but the reading in L is preferable.
793   Pembridge may have heard this at the Dominican chapter at Warwick or the general chapter in Avignon in 1341; Henry Knighton states: 'In the summer … 1340, there occurred a repugnant and widespread illness almost everywhere in England, and especially in Leicestershire, during which men emitted a sound like dogs barking, and suffered almost unbearable pain while it lasted; and a great many people were infected': *Henry Knighton Chronicle 1337–1396*, ed. G.H. Martin (Oxford, 1995), pp 37–8; Ergotism has been suggested: Charles Creighton, *A history of epidemics in Britain* (Cambridge, 1894), i, pp 59–64; perhaps whooping cough sounds more similar? Pertussis, also known as 100-day cough, is highly contagious.
794   This occurred in July 1341 and was a 'resumption of all grants made since 8 July 1307'; 'This horrendous proposal threatened the foundations of many a noble family in Ireland': Lydon, 'Ireland and the English crown, 1171–1541' in Crooks (ed.), *Government*, pp 73, 77; 'An unprecedented crisis': Robin Frame, 'The crisis of 1341–1342' in Lydon (ed.), *England and Ireland*, p. 86; Frame, *Eng. lordship*, pp 248–9; on 24 July; *Cal. Fine Rolls 1337–1347*, p 234; J.S. Bothwell, 'Edward III, the English peerage, and the 1337 earls: estate redistribution in fourteenth century England' in idem (ed.) *The age of Edward III* (Woodbridge, 2002), pp 35–53.
795   Frame, 'England and Ireland, 1171–1299' in Jones and Vale (eds), *England and her neighbours*, pp 151–2; Robin Frame, 'The crisis of 1341–1342', pp 86–103; Lydon, 'Ireland and English crown', pp 73, 77; Frame, *Eng. lordship*, pp 248–9.
796   *Ir. parl.*, pp 77n21, 338; October 1341: Frame, 'The crisis of 1341–1342'.
797   The beginning of Desmond's rebellion: Waters, 'The earls of Desmond', pp 74–85.
798   L supplies 'and the English in the land of Ireland'; James Lydon, 'The middle nation', repr. in Crooks (ed.), *Government;* Frame, '"*Les Engleys nées en Irlande*": the English political identity in medieval Ireland', repr. in Robin Frame, *Ire. & Brit.*, p. 142; on 14 June 1364 the same language is used: 'the king's subjects born in England or in Ireland': *CCR, 1364–1368*, p. 63; for the situation on the ground, see Brendan Smith, 'Lionel of Clarence and the English of Meath', *Peritia*, 10 (1996), 297–302.
799   *Ir. parl.*, pp 77, fn. 21, 338; when the prior went to attend a parliament at Kilkenny in 1346 it cost 22s. 6d.: Lydon, 'Christ Church in the later medieval Irish world', p. 80.
800   Dominican house at Kilkenny.
801   Messengers were John Larcher, prior of Hospitallers, and Thomas Wogan; they were sent by the prelates, earls, barons and community of Ireland with other articles which the king ordained should be diligently examined by the council and answer made': *CCR, 1341–1343*, pp 508–16; 'Thomas Wogan seems to have been the son and heir of John Wogan', justiciar: *Account roll Holy Trinity*, pp 151–2; Frame, 'The crisis of 1341–1342'.
802   Lydon, 'Ireland and the English crown', p. 73; part of a series of complaints to England: Peter Crooks, '"Hobbes", "Dogs" and politics in the Ireland of Lionel of Antwerp', *Haskins Society Journal*, 16 (2005), 129, fn. 50; Gwilym Dodd, 'Petitions from the king's dominions: Wales, Ireland and Gascony, *c.*1290–1350' in Crooks et al. (eds), *The Plantagenet empire*, pp 187–215.

803 Keith Busby, *French in medieval Ireland, Ireland in medieval French: the paradox of two worlds* (Turnhout, 2017); I wish to thank Professor Busby, for his great kindness in dealing with this difficult entry; he considers that someone at some point in the transmission has failed to understand some of the French and informs me that, even given the vagaries of Law French and its common failure to decline, conjugate, and make adjectives and nouns agree, some of this is corrupt.

804 'The petitions from the prelates, earls, barons and commons ... were presented to the king early in 1342': *Ir. parl.*, p. 77; *Affairs Ire.*, pp 178–80, 181–3; *CCR, 1341–43*, pp 508–16.

805 *AClyn*, p. 230; Matilda of Lancaster, widow of the murdered earl of Ulster (see above 1328 and 1333); her mother was Elizabeth de Clare; for a full account of Ufford in Ireland, see Robin Frame, 'The justiciarship of Ralph Ufford: warfare and politics in 14th century Ireland', *Studia Hibernica*, 13 (1973), 7–47; Smith, *Crisis and survival*, pp 32, 35–6; Otway-Ruthven, 'Chief governors', p. 87.

806 Referring to the English of Ireland here.

807 Uses *consorte* again.

808 'Ralph de Ufford ... repaired the crossing of Ymerdoylan and made it passable': *AClyn*, p. 230; 'In medieval documents the Moiry Pass is generally called "Humberdoylan", "Endulan" or "Aberdullan"': Frame, 'Ralph Ufford', pp 23 n.100, 24; Connolly, 'Chancery files (C.260)', p. 10; Duffy, 'Revised itinerary', p. 14.

809 For this expedition, see Frame, 'Ralph Ufford', pp 7–26.

810 On Tuesday 22 February 1345 'there was a parliament held at Callan and Maurice Fitz Thomas came to that with many thousands of men because he believed, why I know not, that the magnates of the land would come over to him; but the king, fearing such suspicious gatherings, and that more harm than good would come from this, prohibited all to come by royal writ; and because of this, the magnates of the land excused themselves to the aforesaid Maurice and stayed at home': *AClyn*, p. 230; *Ir. parl.*, pp 75–6, 338; for a full account, see Waters, 'The earls of Desmond', p. 83.

811 'There was war between Ralph de Ufford, justiciar of Ireland, and Maurice Fitz Thomas, earl of Desmond, and the justiciar deprived him of his lands namely Clonmel, Kilsheelan, Kilfeackle, Connello, Kerry and Desmond, and confiscated his goods, plunders, lordships and possessions into the hand and use of the king': *AClyn*, p. 232; for a map of his campaigns in 1345, see Frame, 'Defence of the English lordship', p. 93.

812 Sayles, 'The rebellious first earl of Desmond', p. 222; for lands see, C.A. Empey, 'The settlement of the kingdom of Limerick' in J.F. Lydon (ed.), *England and Ireland in the later Middle Ages* (Dublin, 1981), pp 1, 6, 12, 19, fn. 20; for John Coterel, see Frame, *Eng. lordship*, pp 271–2, 274; John Coterel was escheator of the king in Co. Kerry: *47th rep. DKPRI*, p. 63; for earlier relationship between the le Grant and le Poer, see Parker, 'Pater familias and *parentela*', 99, 103; it was inevitable that the le Poers would join with Desmond because of the situation between the le Poers and Ufford: Parker, 'Pater familias and *parentela*', 112–13; the earl escaped and found refuge with the Irish until he arranged to go to the king in England and answer charges there; he did not return to Ireland until 1350: Sayles, 'The rebellious first earl of Desmond', p. 224; for the escheated lands see 1346; Frame, 'Rebellion and rehabilitation', pp 201–2.

813 The 4th earl had succeeded his brother Richard in 1331 at age 9 and got his livery in 1342 and died 1390.

814 In October 1344, the pope had given permission for Kildare to marry Desmond's daughter, and it seems likely that Ufford feared an alliance between them; in *c.*1346–8 there was a request for the restoration of the liberty of Kildare and in 1369 there is a

815 request to the king to examine the record of the seizure of the liberty of Kildare by Ufford: Connolly, 'Ancient petitions (SC 8)', pp 74, 83.
815 Ufford may have believed that Kildare would support Desmond as a marriage alliance was being sought between Desmond with Kildare: Waters, 'The earls of Desmond', p. 85; in 1346 and 1347 Walter de Bermingham is asking for more information about Kildare and Burton 'asking reason for seizure of liberty of Kildare' and the answer was that Ufford had kept the record of indictment; also Burton was accused of forgery: Connolly, 'Chancery files (C.260)', pp 11–12, 14.
816 Askeaton seized on Friday 30 September 1345 and Castleisland on Friday 21 October 1345; 'the justiciar ... raised, extended and lifted up the king's banner, and attacked, destroyed and entered Castleisland with a strong and bold force': *AClyn*, p. 232.
817 For John Coterel, see Frame, *Eng. lordship*, pp 271–2, 274; John Coterel was escheator of the king in Co. Kerry: *47th rep. DKPRI*, p. 63.
818 It is worth noting that Clyn, much nearer the action in Kilkenny, has a different angle to this even. Earlier that year the justiciar deprived him of his lands namely Clonmel, Kilsheelan, Kilfeackle, Connello, Kerry and Desmond, and confiscated his goods, plunders, lordships and possessions into the hand and use of the king': *AClyn*, p. 232; then 'John Coterel, the earl's seneschal (who was said to have practised, held and invented many oppressive, foreign and intolerable laws), [was] judicially hanged, beheaded and his intestines burnt and divided limb from limb, and his quarters ordered to be sent to various places in the province as a memorial to his tyranny, and to serve as an example to others ... Eustace le Poer and William le Grant, ... were drawn and hanged and their lands were taken into the hands of the king and forfeited': *AClyn*, p. 234; but Clyn did not approve of all Ufford's actions: 'lord Maurice Fitz Philip died in the castle of Dublin having been previously captured by the justiciar and detained there; he was a bountiful and generous man, although not very rich or powerful', ibid., p. 236; the earl escaped and found refuge with the Irish until he arranged to go to the king in England and answer charges there; he did not return to Ireland until 1350: Sayles, 'The rebellious first earl of Desmond', p. 224.
819 From a list of 1333: *Parls. and councils* p. 13; see also other mainpernors in 1346: *CCR, 1346–49*, p. 140; in 1348, order to deliver the earl to the king within 8 days: *CCR, 1346–49*, p. 494.
820 *Parls and councils*, p. 13.
821 Large, decorated *A* with trail.
822 'Ralph de Ufford, justiciar of Ireland, died at Kilmainham and was later brought to England for burial': *AClyn*, p. 236; on 5 Idus Junii; the earl of Desmond was in hiding, the earl of Kildare was in prison and Eustace le Poer and others of his lineage hanged; also several inoffensive lords, such as Fulk de la Freigne, were under threat of forfeiture because of their participation in Desmond's mainprise of 1333; in 1348 Fulk was asking the king for restoration of his forfeited property: Connolly, 'Chancery warrants (C81)', p. 157; *CPR, 1348–1350*, pp 19–20.
823 *Uxor* now used here.
824 He died at Kilmainham: *AClyn*, p. 236; his wife, the widow of murdered earl of Ulster (see above 1333), now widowed again, became a nun.
825 Appointed by the council in Ireland on 10 April 1346: *Admin. Ire.*, p. 87; this may possibly be at the *tractatus* of 1346: *Ir. Parl.*, pp 101–2.
826 [23–9 April], 'castles of Lea, Kilmohide and Balylethan were captured; and on the Thursday following the feast of Holy Cross [Thursday 4 May Assuming the feast is the Finding of the Holy Cross], they were broken by Uí Mhórdha, Uí Chonchobhair, and

Uí Dhíomusaigh': *AClyn*, p. 238; Seán Duffy informs me that 'Balylethan' is Ballylehane, Co. Laois, and that Kilmohide appears to be Adamstown (https://www.logainm.ie/128.aspx).

827 Trinity says lord John fitz Maurice: L omits *fitz*; error probably because of familiarity with name fitz Maurice; John Morice on 16 May: *Admin. Ire.*, p. 87; *NHI*, ix, p. 473.

828 From the parliamentary list of 1333, *Parls and councils*, p. 13; it took place in Holy Trinity, ibid., p. 14.

829 Around 24 June, 'four hundred of the men of Uriel and Dundalk were killed by the Irish': *AClyn*, p. 238.

830 *AClyn*, p. 238; according to John Morice this appointment of Walter was not well received in Ireland: *Affairs Ire.*, pp 184–5; 29 June 1346 to 27 November 1347 and 27 April 1348 to 27 Oct. 1349: *Admin. Ire.*, p. 88.

831 Dominican house at Youghal; Frame, 'Rebellion and rehabilitation', pp 197, 202, 204; for his words in 1355 in claiming against injustices, see ibid., pp 213–14.

832 He was granted £356 a year: Frame, 'Rebellion and rehabilitation', p. 204; in July 1346, *CCR 1346–49*, p. 140, and 1348: ibid., p. 494.

833 'A war between the English, namely, W[alter] de Bermingham, and the earl of Kildare, and Uí Mhórdha and Uí Dhíomusaigh, and they attacked and burnt their lands; they killed few men however': *AClyn*, p. 240.

834 Priory at Athy. In *c.*1309–15. Kylmehyge is listed with Balyhethan and Leys: see *COD, 1172–1350*, no. 426; see also Kilmohede, Co. Carlow, where Edward I gave free warren to Eustace le Poer in 1302: *COD, 1350–1413*, p. 330; Ballylehane is midway between Athy and Castlecomer.

835 'Maurice Fitz Thomas, earl of Kildare, and lord Fulk de la Freigne ... entered France': *AClyn*, p. 242; a force of at least 100 men led by Kildare and Fulk: Frame, *Eng. lordship*, p. 153; the siege of Calais was 4 September 1346 to 1 August 1347; for English grievances against France, see Michael Jones, 'Relations with France, 1333–1399' in Jones and Vale (eds), *England and her neighbours*, pp 240–2.

836 For a military viewpoint, see C.L. Lambert, 'Edward III's siege of Calais: a reappraisal', *Journal of Medieval History*, 37 (2011), 245–56; Calais remained in English hands until 1558.

837 See above 1310 where John de Boneville was buried with the Dominicans.

838 William Wellesley was a commissioner in 1346: Frame, 'Commissions of the peace', 14; John and William, knights, in connection with the lands of the earl of Kildare: *47th rep. DKPRI*, pp 45, 53, 65–6; William, Demore Manor, co. Meath: *53th rep. DKPRI*, p. 56.

839 There was an outbreak of dysentery during the winter: Lambert, 'Edward III's siege of Calais', 252–6.

840 They 'were treacherously killed by their kinsmen; they were warlike and cunning men and oppressive attackers of the peace and of peacekeeping men and because of their death there was peace for a time, the peace-loving population rested, and society thrived': *AClyn*, p. 244; Frame, 'Two kings in Leinster', p. 164.

841 'At Christmas ... they burnt and destroyed the town of Nenagh and the whole neighbourhood and all the Ormond castles except the castle of Nenagh': *AClyn*, p. 244; for agreement between Ó Ceinnéidigh and Ormond: *COD, 1315–1413*, no. 34; in 1345 it was reported that the land around Thurles was wasted by war: C.A. Empey, 'Medieval Thurles: origins and development' in William Corbett and William Nolan (eds), *Thurles: the cathedral town* (Dublin, 1989), pp 35–6; in 1358 Edmund Ó Ceinnéidigh was among the entourage of the earl of Ormond: Frame '"Les Engleys nées en Irlande"', p. 148.

842 T (f. 34r) ends with these words, in the same hand, not present in L, and hence not noted in Gilbert's edition: Walter Harris was, however, aware that Pembridge ends here (Harris, *Dublin*, p. 56).
843 Perhaps a victim of the plague: Simon de Geneville held lands in Meath from Roger Mortimer, *Reg. Gormanston*, pp 172, 173; this may have been an additional and later entry, before the new continuator began.
844 Apart from noting his regnal years, the continuator has no interest in Edward III; in the general chapter 1348 Adam Guarin was now vicar general.
845 *AClyn*, pp 246–52; Maria Kelly, *A history of the Black Death in Ireland* (Stroud, 2001); Maria Kelly, *The great dying: the Black Death in Dublin* (Dublin, 2003); Campbell and Ludlow, 'Climate, disease and society', 211.
846 Chief Justiciar 27 April 1348–27 October 1349: *Admin. Ire.*, p. 88.
847 This proves that the Dominican continuator had Pembridge in front of him.
848 'The barony and lordship of Kells ... was assigned to lord Walter de Bermingham ... lands of lord William le Grant ... to lord Fulk de la Freigne': *AClyn*, p. 238; le Poer's lands of Castlewarden and Oughterard were taken into the king's hands: *54th rep. DKPRI*, p. 62; lands had previously been leased to Thomas Smothe who wrote to the king in 1347 asking for their restoration: Connolly, 'Chancery warrants (C81)', pp 156, 157; Connolly, 'Ancient petitions (SC 8)', p. 52.
849 Berminghams were Dominican benefactors; see below died 1350.
850 Called deputy justiciar, 3 Oct. 1349–19 December 1349: *Admin. Ire.*, p. 88; Frame, *Eng. lordship*, pp 165–6; he was associated with Matilda of Lancaster, countess of Ulster: CIRCLE Patent Roll 20 Edw III, §24.
851 Appointed 20 December 1349–4 March 1352: *Admin. Ire.* p. 88; Gilbert, *Viceroys*, pp 205–8; an unusual appointment: Robin Frame, 'Thomas Rokeby, sheriff of Yorkshire, justiciar of Ireland', *Peritia*, 10 (1996), 279–81; A.J. Otway-Ruthven, 'Ireland in the 1350s: Sir Thomas de Rokeby and his successors', *JRSAI*, 97 (1967), 47–59; Otway-Ruthven, 'Chief governors', p. 83.
852 Report of his death by 1350; the age of Walter his son and heir unknown as he lives in England: *Inquisitions & extents*, pp 182–3; left a minor as heir: Frame, *Eng. Lordship*, pp 31–37; Preston married Margaret de Bermingham, who was heiress of her brother Walter de Bermingham, see below.
853 Bairéad, 'The bailiffs, provosts and sheriffs of the city of Dublin', p. 286; he was mentioned in *Account roll Holy Trinity*, pp 103, 161, 181, and also in J.G. Smyly, 'Old (Latin) deeds in the library of Trinity College', *Hermathena* (ii), 67 (1946), 18.
854 In 1319 'William, the glassmaker of Dublin' gets lands in Oxmantown: *CCD*, p. 140; Archbishop John de St Paul (1349–62) who built the 'long quire' of Christ Church cathedral is also listed as erecting three windows: Stalley, 'The architecture of the cathedral and priory buildings', pp 97–8.
855 Colmán Ó Clabaigh thinks that he probably retired to the monastery infirmary as the end approached and died there; the bell tower or campanile generally marked the division between the choir and nave in a mendicant church; a door in the north wall of the cloister also provided the internal access for the friars from the friary to the church; turning left they could enter the choir, turning right, the nave; by being buried here Sherman was ensuring that the friars were reminded of him each time they entered the church for prayers or to preach; it also associated him with the most prominent architectural feature of the church and meant that he was buried just underneath the Rood: see Ó Clabaigh, *The Friars in Ireland*, pp 110–12.
856 This was the usual bequest in medieval wills, see Margaret Murphy, 'The high cost of dying: an analysis of *pro anima* bequests in medieval Dublin', *Studies in Church History*, 24 (1987), 111–23.

857 The first mention of the Savage family; in 1317 it was Clyn who reported the death of William Savage: *AClyn*, p. 166; after the murder of the earl of Ulster in 1333, Robert Savage rose in prominence; he was the chief juror in the inquisition into the earl's lands in Carrickfergus and Antrim: *Inquisitions & extents*, pp 142, 144, 145, 148, 155; CIRCLE Close Roll 8 Edw III, §56; for the suggestion that Lissanoure castle was the principal residence of Robert Savage and for a mistake of 1342 for 1352, see G.F. Savage-Armstrong, *A genealogical history of the Savage family in Ulster* (London, 1906) pp 37–41; for Robert Savage II, see T.E. McNeill, *Anglo-Norman Ulster. the history and archaeology of an Irish barony, 1177–1400* (Edinburgh, 1980), pp 79–80, 118, 123–4; Katharine Simms, 'The Ulster revolt of 1404 – an anti-Lancastrian dimension?' in Smith (ed.), *Ireland and the English world*, pp 142–4, 157; on the Savage family, see notes by K.W. Nicholls, 'Anglo-French Ireland and after', *Peritia*, 1 (1982), 386, 386 fn. 3; Frame, *Eng. lordship*, pp 67, 134, 137; idem, 'Thomas Rokeby', 292–3.

858 In 1374 Henry Savage, knight, was summoned to Parliament: CIRCLE Close Roll 48 Edw III, §158.

859 Arpad Steiner, 'The vernacular proverb in mediaeval Latin prose', *American Journal of Philology*, 65 (1944), 37–68; this is possibly a biblical reference and could refer to Numbers, 1:52 or Numbers 2:2.

860 Therefore, the continuator was writing later than 1352; McNeill, *Anglo-Norman Ulster*, pp 118–19.

861 The years 1353 and 1354 are missing in which there were general chapters at Besançon and Narbonne, though no record exists of English chapters.

862 Dublin helped Rokeby: *CARD*, i, pp 18–19; CIRCLE Close Roll 29 Edw III, §99; he led a force against the Uí Bhroin in 1353, but the continuator has no interest: Frame, 'Defence of the English lordship', pp 84–5, 89–90; Maginn, 'English marcher lineages in South Dublin', 123–4.

863 Rokeby justiciar again on 15 June 1352–9 Aug. 1355, 31 December 1356–23 April 1357: *Admin. Ire.*, pp 88–9; Maurice fitz Thomas, earl of Desmond, was justiciar 17 Aug. 1355–25 Jan. 1356: *Admin. Ire.*, p. 88; for the aftermath of Desmond's rebellion, see A.F. O'Brien, 'The territorial ambitions of Maurice Fitz Thomas, first earl of Desmond, with particular reference to the barony and manor of Inchiquin, Co. Cork', *PRIA*, 82C (1982), 74–80; he was now elderly having been born *c.* 1293 and had a chequered career especially at the time of the justiciars Lucy in 1331 and Ralph Ufford in 1345 (see above): see Frame, 'Rebellion and rehabilitation', pp 194–222; Keith Waters, 'The earls of Desmond and the Irish of south-western Munster', *Journal of Medieval History*, 32 (2006), 54–68

864 First earl of Desmond, see s.a 1326; also, on Conversion of St Paul, *Annals of Nenagh*, p. 161.

865 Geoffrey fitz Eustace to give 12 acres and appurtenances to Dominicans to construct a church and residence in Naas, 15 June 1354: *Inquisitions & extents*, pp 188–9.

866 'In 1353 Rokeby ... with the royal standard, subdued to himself Munster and Thomond and the kings of these parts, namely McDermound and Mckilmar and the castle of Bunratty (Benrat) was restored': *Kilkenny chronicle*, p. 336; Gilbert points out that there is an old political song (which, according to Wright, is from the reign of Edward I) that refers to the same idea; Wright translates it as 'If the king would take my advice, I would praise him then, to take the vessels of silver, and make money of them;-it would be better to eat out of wood, and to give money for victuals—than to serve the body with silver, and pay with wood;-It is a sign of vice, to pay for victuals with wood': Thomas Wright (ed.), *The political songs of England* (London, 1839), p. 186; *CStM*, ii, p. cxxxviii, n. 2; Gilbert, *Viceroys*, p. 205–6, 541–2; for a long list of horses lost to the value of £186 10s 6d, see *IExP*, p. 435; Otway-Ruthven, 'Ireland in the 1350s', pp 45–59.

867 April 1357: *Annals of Nenagh*, p. 161.
868 Amaury de St Amand acquired property in Dublin in 1220s and in 1230s was granted Gormanston which the family held until 1363 when he sold his Irish property to Sir Robert Preston, chief justice of the Dublin bench, ancestor of the viscounts Gormanston: Frame, 'England and Ireland, 1171–1299', p. 142; idem, *Eng. lordship*, pp 59, 88.
869 He had preached a sermon at the Dominican General Chapter at Avignon in 1342; Michael Dunne and Simon Nolan (eds), *Richard FitzRalph: his life, times and thought* (Dublin, 2013); Michael Dunne, 'Richard FitzRalph of Dundalk (*c*.1300–1360) and the new world', *Archivium Hibernicum*, 58 (2004), 243–58; Janet Coleman, 'FitzRalph's antimendicant '*proposicio*' (1350) and the politics of the papal court at Avignon', *Journal of Ecclesiastical History*, 35 (1984), 376–90; M.J. Haren, 'Friars as confessors: the canonist background to fourteenth-century controversy', *Peritia*, 3 (1984), 503–16.
870 No mention here of a new university in Dublin, see Linne R. Mooney, 'An English record of the founding of a university in Dublin in 1358', *IHS*, 28:111 (1993), 225–7; CIRCLE Patent Roll 32 Edw III, §32; neither is there a mention of the death of Maurice 2nd earl of Desmond drowned at sea.
871 Appointed 16 Feb. 1359: *CPR, 1358–1361*, pp 176, 572; Lydon, 'Ireland and the English Crown', p. 67, n. 14.
872 For obituary (*s.a.*1359) and gifts to Kildare friary, see *Annals of Nenagh*, p. 162; again, *consort* instead of *uxor*.
873 In 1360 messengers were sent to England about the desperate situation: Connolly, 'Carlow as an administrative capital', pp 307–8; *Parls and councils*, pp 19–22; no mention of treaty of Bretigny.
874 Smith, *Crisis and survival*, p 161; many of FitzRalph's family were Franciscans: Aubrey Gwynn, 'Richard Fitzralph, archbishop of Armagh', *Studies*, 22 (1933), 389–405.
875 See above 1352.
876 In 1360 'Sir Robert Savadge and Dermot O'Hanly died' and 'Art, son of Gillareagh Magennis, was treacherously slain by the sons of Savadge and the son of Murtough Riaganagh Magennis': *AFM*, iii, pp 617, 619; this burial of one of the Savage family among the Dominicans is of interest and gives weight to the statement by O'Heyne that the Savages founded the Dominican priory of Newtownards: Coleman, *Ancient Dominican foundations*, p. 19, appendix, p. 9; Gwynn & Hadcock, *MRHI*, p. 228; however, if he had founded Newtownards, one would expect him to be buried there.
877 On 16 March 1361: *CPR 1358–1361*, p. 572.
878 Richardson and Sayles state the dates of Thomas Burley as chancellor as 5 August 1359–5 November 1360 (then a gap of a year), 5 November 1361–24 October 1364: *Admin. Ire.*, p. 96; but, a letter of 14 April 1361 lists Thomas de Burle, prior of St John of Jerusalem in Ireland, as chancellor of Ireland: *CPR, 1358–1361*, pp 580–1.
879 Regnal year 25 Jan. 1361–24 January 1362; this is missing from *Admin. Ire.*, p. 89; Butler was appointed 16 Feb. 1359; Kildare appointed 16 March 1361: *CPR, 1358–1361*, pp 176, 572.
880 No regnal year.
881 Neither Clyn nor Pembridge reported the betrothal in 1341 of Lionel to Elizabeth de Burgh, sole heiress of the earl of Ulster and lord of Connacht but this could have been because Lionel was only 4 years and it might not have come to fruition; it was arranged at the request of the Anglo-Irish who had 'insistently' asked for the marriage: Frame, *Eng. lordship*, p. 51; for Lionel, see Philomena Connolly, 'Lionel of Clarence and Ireland, 1361–1366' (PhD, University of Dublin, 1977); Peter Crooks, 'Factionalism and noble power in English Ireland, *c.*1361–1423' (PhD, University of Dublin, 2007), pp 75–103.

882   15 September 1361–22 April 1364: *Admin. Ire.*, p. 89; he came as *tenens locum Domini Regis* not *justiciarius*; 'with the title of king's lieutenant': Connolly, 'Carlow as an administrative capital', p. 2; eadem, 'The financing of English expeditions to Ireland, 1361–1376' in Lydon (ed.), *England and Ireland in the later Middle Ages*, pp 104–21.

883   'He landed near Dublin': *Annals of Nenagh*, p. 162; Peter Crooks, '"Hobbes"', 117–48; he stayed at Dublin castle: Lydon, 'Dublin castle in the Middle Ages', pp 123–4; David Green, 'Lordship and principality: colonial policy in Ireland and Aquitaine in the 1360s', *Journal of British Studies*, 47 (2008), 8–10, 14–15, 17, 20–21.

884   Campbell and Ludlow, 'Climate, disease and society', 215–7; for *pestis secunda* and *pestis tertia* (1370), see MacArthur, 'Pestilences recorded in the Irish Annals', pp 178, 180.

885   Chapter at Northampton; Roger Mortimer, second earl of March, died in France, February 1360, but the other two died in England; Henry, duke of Lancaster, ob. March 1361, was the second man in England to be given the title duke (Edward the Black Prince was the first): Kenneth A. Fowler, *The king's lieutenant: Henry of Grosmont, first duke of Lancaster, 1310–1361* (London, 1969); William de Bohun, first earl of Northampton, died September 1360; this entry must have been written after March 1361.

886   See above 1361 where Kendrick Sherman had glazed the window in the chapter choir; Walter Harris states that he was twice sheriff (1353, 1354) but never mayor: Harris, *Dublin*, pp 271–2; for a Maurice Duncreen (variant spellings) in antiquarian lists, see Bairéad, 'The bailiffs, provosts and sheriffs of the city of Dublin', pp 216, 233, 243, 262, 286.

887   Married 1353 at age 13, so she was now 21 years of age: James Moynes, 'The Prestons of Gormanston, c.1300–1532: an Anglo-Irish gentry family', *Ríocht na Mídhe*, 14 (2003), 33; Robert was a knight, *Ir. parl.*, p. 304.

888   His age unknown in 1350 as he lived in England: *Inquisitions & extents*, p. 183; *Reg. Gormanston*, pp viii–ix; his wife's inheritance now gave Robert Preston property on the borders of Meath, Kildare and Offaly ... contested by the cadet branch of the Bermingham family, Smith, *Crisis and survival*, p. 66; see below s.a. 1367, 1368.

889   For Lionel's army in Ireland, 1361–6, see Connolly, 'Lionel of Clarence and Ireland', pp 134–165; for his itinerary, ibid., pp 319–24.

890   *quod nullus nativus de Hibernia appropinquaret exercitui suo;* this line missing from T; Connolly, 'Lionel of Clarence and Ireland', pp 152–3; Crooks, 'Factionalism and noble power', pp 69–74; Crooks, '"Hobbes"', 123.

891   'Most retinues relied on Gaelic element': Crooks, '"Hobbes"', 121, fn. 20, 122, 123, fn. 27.

892   Smith, *Crisis and survival*, p. 39; the last page of L has the following information in what appears to be a different hand: *Iste liber constat Domino Willelmo Preston, Vicecomiti de Gormanstoun.*

893   Baron of the exchequer: Connolly, 'Carlow as an administrative capital', pp 311, 318–9; Crooks, '"Hobbes"', pp 125, 127, 133; Frame, *Eng. lordship*, 101–2; there was a Friar Henry Holywode in the Dublin priory in mid-1330s: *IExP*, pp 379, 623; colonial administrator who bought the de Ferrers portion of de Verdun inheritance from William de Ferrers: Smith, 'Lionel of Clarence and the English of Meath', 301; Robert was remembrancer of the Dublin exchequer in 1357 and was called knight by 1369: Connolly, 'Ancient petitions (SC 8)', pp 16, 69; *Ir. parl.*, p. 304.

894   Joan Tuyt married her cousin Walter Cusack, justice of the peace in Skreen: Smith, 'Lionel of Clarence and the English of Meath', 298; Smith, *Crisis and survival*, pp 47–8; Walter Cusack of Clonnortheran: Frame, 'Commissions of the peace', 24.

895   Patrick de la Freigne was seneschal of Kilkenny in 1348: *54th rep. DKPRI*, p 57; *Affairs Ire.*, pp 198–201 (no. 218 (ii), called 291 (ii), by error in index); Patrick de la Freigne,

knight, was also seneschal of Kilkenny in 1375: *Red bk Ormond*, p. 140; Patrick and Robert de la Freigne, knights, are mentioned at parliament of Castledermot of 1378: *Parls and councils*, p. 101; the family were particularly important in Kilkenny area: see *AClyn*, pp 74–85.

896 It was difficult for the revenue needed for King Edward to reach Dublin; Carlow castle was in the king's hand with a royal appointee as constable and the county was a royal shire; a stone wall was built to surround the town; the exchequer appears to have been there by 1361. For a full analysis, see Connolly, 'Carlow as an administrative capital', pp 307–29; Connolly, 'Lionel of Clarence and Ireland', p. 134.

897 T: three letters *S*, *l* and *f* larger than normal. Campbell and Ludlow, 'Climate, disease and society', 168; Stalley, 'The architecture of the cathedral and priory buildings', pp 102–3.

898 John Sextyn/Sextyne was tenant in Patrick Street and New Street in the fourteenth century: Mills, 'Notices of the manor of St Sepulchre', 120, 121; if John de Sexton was responsible for the fire he would be liable to severe punishment: Gaffney and de Pontfarcy Sexton, '"The laws and usages of Dublin"', p. 193.

899 Butler was called 'keeper', 25 April 1364 to 25 Jan. 1365: *Admin. Ire.*, p. 90; for relationship of Lionel and Ormond, see Crooks, '"Hobbes"', 134–8, 144.

900 L: 8th day; Lionel, duke of Clarence, Mid December 1365–7 November 1366: *Admin. Ire.*, p. 90.

901 'The last great charter of liberties granted to Dublin in this age, issued by Edward III at Westminster on 22 November 1363, was a confirmation of a grant made by his son Lionel, duke of Clarence, while at Dublin two months earlier: Duffy, 'Town and crown: the kings of England and their city of Dublin', p. 117.

902 *AFM*, iii, p. 631; from 7 Nov. 1366–22 April 1367: *Admin. Ire.*, p. 90; Thomas de la Dale: *IExP*, pp 510, 515, 519, 520, 535.

903 See above s.a. 1361; inherited it through his de Bermingham wife.

904 April 1367 to June 1369: *Admin. Ire.*, p. 90.

905 This could be the meeting 'at Burgage in the marches of Co. Dublin in autumn 1368' which involved men from Co. Meath: Connolly, 'Carlow as an administrative capital', p. 33.

906 In 1309 men from Carbury invaded 'parts of Trym, committing manslaughter, destroying by fires and [causing] other damages': *CCR, 1307–13*, p. 188; in 1368 the territory of 'Carbury was partitioned equally between the son of Manus and Donnnell': *AFM*, iii, p. 641.

907 Dominican house at Trim; Moynes, 'Prestons of Gormanston', pp 33–5.

908 This must refer to St Mary's Augustinian friary; in these annals a Dominican church is always the 'church of the Friars Preachers', 'the church of the Order of Preachers', 'choir of the Friars Preachers', 'convent of the Friar Preachers', 'campanile of the Friars Preachers', 'cemetery of the Preachers'; Fr Hugh Fenning said that as the Dominicans priory was referred to as *conventus* not *monasterium*, however the Dominican continuator also refers to the Augustinians as having a *conventus* in 1368,(see s.a. 1368): Fenning, 'The Dominicans of Trim, 1263–1682', p. 17.

909 His wife was the daughter of Galeazzo Visconti, lord of Pavia; chapter at Sudbury; Lionel died 16 October 1368; his heir, Phillipa aged 14, married Edmund Mortimer, earl of March: *Inquisitions & extents*, p. 199; his heart and bones returned to England for burial with his first wife Elizabeth de Burgh at Clare Priory in Suffolk: K.W. Barnardiston, *Clare Priory* (Cambridge, 1962), pp 16, 20–1.

910 On 20 June 1369: *Admin. Ire.*, p. 90; William of Windsor did not long remain a man to be admired: Crooks, 'Negotiating authority in a colonial capital: Dublin and the Windsor

crisis, 1369–78' in Duffy (ed.), *Medieval Dublin IX*, pp 134–51; Crooks, 'Factionalism and noble power', pp 104–25; Lydon 'William of Windsor', pp 90–105; Otway-Ruthven, 'Chief governors', pp 81, 83.

911 Campbell and Ludlow, 'Climate, disease and society', 241–2.

912 Monasteranenagh: T.J. Westropp, 'History of the abbey and battles of Monasteranenagh, Croom, Co. Limerick, 1148–1603', *JRSAI*, 9 (1889), 234; *AFM*, iii, p. 649; *AC*, p. 282.

913 Dominican house at Limerick.

914 Death of whole family probably indicated the plague. An earlier (or the same?) Scholastica, widow of Adam de Houth, received her dower lands in 1334–5: *44th rep. DKPRI*, p. 37; a Nicholas de Houth was sheriff of Dublin 1356–58: *IExP*, p. 483; Nicholas Houth (d. 1404) and Richard White, knights: Lydon 'William of Windsor', pp 103–4; Peter Crooks, 'Representation and dissent: "Parliamentarianism" and the structure of politics in colonial Ireland, *c*.1370–1420', *EHR*, 125 (2010), 18.

915 Fleming died 13 September 1370, and his son and heir Thomas was aged 12 years: *Inquisitions & extents*, p. 200; Fleming went to Westminster with Maurice fitz Thomas, John Husee, Richard Plunket and Richard White 'bearing grievances': Crooks, '"Hobbes"', 126, 129, 132; for Simon and also John Fleming, see Frame, 'Commissions of the peace', 23, 24; Smith, *Crisis and survival*, pp 46–7, 49, 66, 184.

916 Culmullin, Co. Meath; for Cusack, see Frame, 'Commissions of the peace', 24; John, son and heir of lord Walter de Cusack of Kilmessen, *CStM*, i, p. 278; for members of the Cusack family, see Smith, *Crisis and survival*, index; he served with Rokeby in 1352; Frame, 'Defence of the English lordship', p. 85; a John de Cusack had custody of the Tuyt manor of Killeen after 1351; Smith, 'Lionel of Clarence and the English of Meath', 298; in 1281 a John de Cusack and a Simon le Fleming were both jurors: *Inquisitions & extents*, p. 57.

917 In John Taillour's long will of 2 July 1370 (a dying will?) he left ten pounds of silver to the Friars Preachers and to the other mendicant orders (but twenty to Augustinians); he held land in Oxmantown and was buried in St Mary's: *CStM*, i, pp 16–21; see also index, *IExP*; Murphy, 'The high cost of dying', p. 211; he owned the houses in which the pleas of the exchequer and Dublin bench were held from at least 1346 to 1365 at £4 p. a.: *Account roll Holy Trinity*, pp 123–4; a Thomas Tailleur held lands in Meath from Roger Mortimer: *Reg. Gormanston*, pp 96–7; William le Taillour merchant of Dublin 1305: Connolly, 'Ancient petitions (SC 8)', p. 82.

APPENDIX

Marginal illustrations

Annal	Folio in T	Description
1180	f. 1v	First head: side face and conical hat with swirl at top. Highlighting the archbishops of Dublin, the first of many faces in T[1]
1193	f. 2r	Face: emphasizing the capture of King Richard and the sale of the chalices
1198	f. 2r	Face: emphasizing the foundation of the Dominicans
1219	f. 4v	Face: lines descending from face represent either a beard or, just possibly, a family tree. Emphasizing the importance of the Marshal family
1240 [recte 1241]	f. 5v	Rubricated head may be highlighting de Lacy or de Geneville (Fig. 2)
1243	f. 5v	First flourish: rubricated trailing *A*, possibly highlighting de Lacy
1250	f. 5v	Rubricated trailing *A*, may be highlighting Holy Land
1255	f. 5v	Rubricated trailing *A*.
1261	f. 6r	IHC [Christogram]
1262	f. 6r	Long trailing *I* over 5 lines
1264	f. 6r	Long trailing *A*
1269	f. 6r	Long trailing *A*

1 For similar heads, see Philomena Connolly and Geoffrey Martin (eds), *The Dublin guild merchant roll, c.1190–1265* (Dublin, 1992), pp 57, 72, 73; see also the face in a Giraldus MS, in Meehan, 'A fourteenth-century historical compilation from St Mary's', p. 373; for an Irish plea roll, AD 1281–2 containing a contemporary outline sketch of a man's head in profile partly covered by a tight-fitting cap, see Gilbert, *Hist. & mun. docs*, p. xxxvii, fn. 2; the *chaperon* (hood covering head and draped over shoulders) with a long *liripipe* (long, trailing point often added to a hood) attached is typical of the 1300s.

Annal	Folio in T	Description
1275	f. 6v	Flourish
1278	f. 6v	Flourish
1280	f. 6v	Flourish
1282	f. 6v	Rubrication highlighting the significance of the year's events
1284	f. 6v	Head: drawn as part of the initial *A* of *Anno*, indicates a particular interest in this event
1285	f. 6v	Manicule: level with word 'captured', **T**.
1286	f. 7r	IHC
1287	f. 7r	Slightly rubricated E
1289	f. 7r	Two cc are slightly rubricated
1290	f. 7r	Slightly rubricated *E*
1294	f. 7v	High flourish to letter f
1294	f. 8	Decorated box edge and note, both rubricated
1294	f. 8	Box and note, both in black
1295	f. 8v	IHC
1296	f. 9r	Decorated box edge and note, both rubricated
1302	f. 10v	Face and hat with fleur de lis on top. Emphasizing the significance of one or both of these obits (Margaret, wife of John Wogan; Matilda, wife of Geoffrey de Geneville)
1302	f. 10v	IHC
1302	f. 10v	Initial letter *I* is long and decorated
1302	f. 10v	IHC
1302	f. 10v	Head: bearded face added to the initial *A* of 'Anno', with a possible crown on the head. Emphasizing Robert Bruce's significance
1303	f. 11r	IHC
1306	f. 11v	Head: hat with 3 tassels on end and hair on chin. Unclear why the copyist would choose to highlight this entry with an illustrated initial
1307	f. 12v	IHC
1308	f. 12v	IHC

Appendix: List of marginal illustrations

Annal	Folio in T	Description
1310	f. 14r	IHC
1311	f. 14v	IHC
1313	f. 15r	IHC
1315	f. 15v	Head: face has a beard and same hat as once before (some of the more complicated men's hats were actually hoods with a long strip of fabric in the back that could be wound around the head). The illustrated initial marks the significance of the death of Gloucester.
1315	f. 16v	Second manicule: *nö discordia* at the fingertip
1316	f. 18r	IHC
1316	f. 19r	IHC
1316	f. 19r	Decorated box and text both rubricated
1316	f. 19v	IHC
1321	f. 24	Face
1321	f. 24v	IHC
1325	f. 25r	IHC
1327	f. 26r	IHC
1328	f. 26r	flourish or decoration
1328	f. 26r	IHC
1329	f. 28v	IHC
1330	f. 29r	IHC
1331	f. 29v	IHC
1332	f. 30r	IHC
1338	f. 31r	head
1339	f. 31v	IHC
1341	f. 32r	Long red mark
1342	f. 32r	Red mark
1343	f. 32r	Red mark
1343	f. 32v	Significant flourish
1345	f. 33r	IHC
1346	f. 33v	Long tailed decorated A
1346	f. 34r	IHC

Annal	Folio in T	Description
1347	f. 34r	Face with beard
1347	f. 34v	Flourish or decoration
1351	f. 34v	Flourish or decoration
1352	f. 34v	Flourish or decoration
1352	f. 35r	IHC
1356	f. 35r	Flourish or decoration
1357	f. 35r	Flourish or decoration
1357	f. 35r	Head
1361	f. 36r	Historiated initial, with zoomorphic extensions into the margin partly rubricated
1361	f. 36v	IHC
1362	f. 36v	Historiated initial, with zoomorphic extensions into the margin (Fig. 4)
1368	f. 36v	Historiated initial, with zoomorphic extensions into the margin (Fig. 4)
1370	f. 37r	Last face: the style of the hat is later than those depicted in the earlier faces within the portion of the annals attributable to Pembridge: it is no longer a chaperon (hood covering head and draped over shoulders) but a long liripipe (long, trailing point often added to a hood)

Index

(items listed by year; figures in **bold** refer to page numbers in the introduction)

Abbeydorney (Kyrie Eleison),
    Co. Kerry, 1186
Abbeylara, Co. Longford (Granard), **39**
Abbeyleix (*Lex Dei*), Co. Laois, 1183
Abbeymahon (*Fons Vivus*) abbey, 1172
Abbeyshrule abbey (*Flumen Dei*),
    Co. Longford, 1200
abjuration, 1311
Acre, Israel, 1291
abduction, 1167
Abington (Wetheney) abbey,
    Co. Limerick, 1205
Adare, Co. Limerick, 1313
Airghialla, kingdom, 1297
Alba, Piedmont, Italy, **43**, 1368
Albus (White, *see also* Blound), John
    (d. 1329), 1329
    Nicholas (d. 1329), 1329
ale, 1360
Alexander III, king of Scots (1249–86),
    24, 1251
Alexander III, pope (1159–81), 1177
Almeric, king of Jerusalem (1163–74),
    1167
Alnwick, Northumberland, England,
    1175
Alphonso (d. 1284), e. Chester, **24**,
    1284
Amesbury Priory, 1286, 1291
*Annales Monasterii Beate Marie
    Virginis, juxta Dublin*, **50–1**

Antona, Hugo de, 1315
Apilgard, Adam de, 1318
appurtenances, 1343
Aquitaine, France, 1306
Archdeacon, Hamund (d. 1331), 1331
    Raymond (d. 1333), 1333
Archebold, lineage, 1315, 1317
Archer, John, prior of the hospital of St
    John of Jerusalem in Ireland,
    deputy justiciar of Ireland, 1348
Ardee, Co. Louth, 1318
Ardnurcher, battle of, 1329
Ardrossan, Fergus de, 1315
Ards, Co. Down, **44**
Ardscull, Co. Kildare, **41**, 1286, 1309,
    1315
Arklow, Co. Wicklow, 1282, 1315
    castle, **34**, 1285, 1331, 1332
    Dominican priory of, **6**, **38**
    army, 1291, 1311, 1315, 1317, 1330,
    1361
arson, 1191, 1283, 1284, 1286, 1301,
    1307, 1314, 1315, 1331, 1343, 1347,
    1362
Arthur I (d. 1203), dk Brittany and 4th
    e. Richmond, 1199, 1204
Artysson, Robyn, demon, 1325
Ashbourne, Elias, justice of the
    Common Bench, 1328
Askeaton, Co. Limerick, 1345
Assisi, Italy, 1206

Athassel, Co. Tipperary, 1319, 1326
Athenry, Co. Galway, **48**, 1316
    battle of, **7**
    priory, **7, 28, 38**
Athlone, Co. Westmeath, 1211
    castle, 1315
Athy, Co. Kildare, 1308, 1315
    church of the Friars Preachers, **38**, 1309, 1315
Athy, John de, 1317
Audley, James de, justiciar of Ireland, 1270, 1272
Augustinian order, **11, 45**
Avenal, Nicholas, 1312
Avignon, France, **13**, 1360

Babylon, 1167, 1289, 1291, 1298
Badlesmere, Bartholomew de (d. 1322), 1st Baron Badlesmere, 1316
Bagod, Robert, chief justice of the Common Bench, 1298
bakers, 1310
Ballyboggan (Balibegan), Co. Meath, 1321
Ballybough, Co. Dublin, 1313
Ballymore Eustace, Co. Kildare, 1306
Balscote, Nicholas de, **40**, 1317
Balybragan, *see* Braganstown
Bann, river, **40**, 1315, 1360
Bannockburn, battle of (1314), 1315
barley, 1330
Barrett, William, 1281
Barrow, river, 1339
Barry, lineage, 1316
    David de (d. 1278), 1278
        justiciar of Ireland, 1267
    David de, 1345
    Robert, 1345
battle, 1234, 1293, 1315, 1329
beans, 1330
Beatitude monastery, *see* Bective abbey
Beauchamp, Guy de (d. 1315), 10th e. Warwick, 1306, 1312
Beaumaris castle, Anglesey, Wales, 1295

Beaumont, Isabel de, w. of Gilbert de Clare, 1169
Becket, Thomas, abp Canterbury (1162–70), 1162, 1170
    translation of, 1220
Bective (Beatitude) abbey, Co. Meath, 1195
Bedford castle, Bedford, England, 1224
beggars, 1317
Benedictines, religious order, 1204
benefices, 1294
Berkeley, Henry, 1345
Bermingham, family, **6–7, 14, 28**, 1301
    Andrew, 1317
    Basilia, **7**
    Catherine, wife of Christopher Plunket of Finglas **49**
    Edmund, 1318
    Elizabeth, of Athenry, wife of Christopher St Lawrence, 1st Baron Howth, **48**
    Henry (d. 1329), of Connacht, 1329
    James, 1368
    John de, e. Louth 1318, 1319, 1329
        justiciar of Ireland, 1321
    John (d. 1329), s. of Richard, lord of Athenry, 1329
    Margaret (d. 1361), w. of Robert Preston, **7, 27–8**, 1361
    Meiler, **7**
    Peter (d. 1308), lord of Tethmoy, **7**, 1301, 1305, 1306, 1308
    Peter (d. 1329), bro. of John, e. Louth, 1329
    Peter (d. 1329), of Connacht, s. of James, 1329
    Richard, 1316
    Richard, lord of Athenry, **7**, 1316, 1329
    Robert (d. 1329), bro. of John, e. Louth, 1329
    Simon (d. 1329), s. of William Fynn, 1329

Index

Thomas (d. 1329), of Connacht, s. of Robert, 1329
Walter, 1318
   justiciar of Ireland (d. 1350), 7, 27, 31, 1346, 1348, 1349
Walter, s. of Walter (d. 1361), 1361
Walter, s. of William, 34, 1331, 1332, 1333
William, 1318
William (d. 1332), bro. of John, e. Louth, 6–7, 34, 1327, 1329, 1330, 1331, 1332, 1333
William Fynn (d. 1329), 1329
Berminghams of Carbury, 1333, 1367, 1368
Bernard of Clairvaux, saint, 1186
Bernard's Catalogue, 14
Berwick, England, 36, 1296, 1318, 1328
Bicknor, Alexander, abp Dublin (1317–49), 4, 10, 38, 1310, 1313, 1317, 1320, 1330, 1331, 1337
   justiciar of Ireland, 1318
   treasurer of Ireland, 1313
Bigod, Hugh (d. 1225), 3rd e. Norfolk, 1219
   John (d. 1305), 1219
   Ralph (d. 1260), 1219
   Roger (d. 1306), earl marshal, 5th e. Norfolk, 1297
birds, 1360
Bisset, Hugh, 1316
   John, 1315
Black Death, the, 34, 1348
Blound (White), John, of Rathregan, 1317
Bodleian Library, Oxford, *see* L (Laud Miscellaneous MS 526)
Bohun, Eleanor (d. 1363), countess of Ormond, dau. of Humphrey, 1328
   Humphrey (d. 1322), 4th e. Hereford, 1328
   William de, (d. 1360), 1st e. Northampton, 1361

Boneville, John (d. 1310), 1309, 1310
   Walter (d. 1347), 1347
Boniface VIII, pope (1294–1303), 1298, 1300, 1302, 1303
Book of Howth, 48–50
Bordeaux, France, 1294, 1302
Bosco, John de, 1315
Boulogne, France, 1307
Boyne, river, 1330
Braganstown, Co. Louth (Balybragan), 1329
Braose, de, family, 10
Braose, William de, 10
Bray, Co. Wicklow, 1315
bread, 1318
Bretton, John de, 1308
bridge, 1304, 1308, 1313, 1325, 1330
Briouze, Eleanor (d. 1251), w. of Humphrey de Bohun, 1219
   Eve (d. 1255), w. of William de Cantilupe, 1219
   Matilda (d. 1301), w. of Roger Mortimer, 1st Baron Mortimer of Wigmore, 1219
   William de (d. 1211), 4th lord of Bramber, 1208
   William de (d. 1230), lord of Abergavenny, 1219
Bristol(l), John de, prior provincial of the friars preachers in England, 31
Brittany, France, 1199
Brotherton, Yorkshire, England, 1300
Bruce (Brus), Edward (d. 1318), e. Carrick, bro. of Robert, king of Scots, 33, 41, 1315, 1316, 1318
   Robert (d. 1295), 5th lord of Annandale, 1219
   Robert (d. 1304), 6th lord of Annandale, 1292
   e. Carrick, 1292
Bruce invasion (1315–18), 11, 33–4, 38–41
Bruges, Belgium, 31

Brun, Nigel le, escheator of Ireland, 1310
Bryt, Philip, 1331
Bunratty, Co. Clare, 1311, 1332
Burgh, lineage, 1327, 1328
    Edmund (d. 1338), s. of Richard Óg, 1345
    Elizabeth de (d. 1327), w. of Robert the Bruce, king of Scots, 1302, 1306
    Elizabeth de (d. 1363), duchess of Clarence and countess of Ulster, **43**, 1361
    Hubert de (d. 1243), e. Kent, chief justiciar of England and Ireland, 1230
    Joan (Johanna) de (d. 1359), w. of Thomas fitz John, 2nd e. Kildare and John Darcy, **24**, 1312, 1329, 1330, 1359
    John de (d. 1313), s. of Richard Óg, 1309, 1312, 1313
    Katherine de (d. 1331), w. of Maurice fitz Thomas, 1st e. Desmond, 1312
    Margaret de (d. 1303), w. of Richard Óg, 2nd e. Ulster, 1303
    Maud de, w. of Gilbert de Clare, 8th e. Gloucester, 1308
    Richard de, 1243
    Richard Óg de (d. 1326), 2nd e. Ulster, **24**, 1291, 1294, 1295, 1296, 1298, 1302, 1303, 1306, 1308, 1309, 1311, 1312, 1313, 1315, 1316, 1317, 1326
    Thomas (d. 1316), s. of Richard Óg, 1316
    Thomas, treasurer of Ireland, 1333
    Thomas de Lees, 1345
    Walter de, 1330
    Walter de (d. 1271), 1st e. Ulster, 1243, 1271
    William Donn (d. 1333), 3rd e. Ulster, 1326, 1328, 1329, 1330, 1331, 1333, 1345, 1361
    William Liath (d. 1324), 1311, 1315, 1316
    justiciar of Ireland, 1308
    William Liath (d. 1332), 1331
    William of Connacht, 1330
Burghersh, Bartholomew de (d. 1355), 1347
    Elizabeth, w. of Maurice fitz Thomas, 4th e. Kildare, 1347
Burley, Thomas de, prior of the hospital of St John of Jerusalem in Ireland, chancellor of Ireland, 1360, 1368
Burton, William, 1345
Butler (*Pincerna*), Edmund (d. 1321), e. Carrick, **42**, 1302, 1307, 1309, 1313, 1320, 1321
    deputy justiciar of Ireland, 1312
    justiciar of Ireland, 1314, 1315, 1316, 1317
    James (d. 1338), 1st e. Ormond, 1327, 1328, 1329, 1330, 1333, 1337
    James (d. 1382), 2nd e. Ormond, 1345, 1359, 1364
    justiciar of Ireland, 1360
    Theobald (d. 1206), s. of Walter, lord of Carrick, 1205
    Theobald (d. 1285), 4th chief butler of Ireland, **6**, 1264, 1285
    Theobald (d. 1299), 5th chief butler of Ireland, 1296
    Thomas (d. 1329), 1st Baron Dunboyne, **7**, 1329

Calais, France, 1347
Calf, Henry (d. 1306), 1306
    William (d. 1347), 1347
Callan, Co. Kilkenny, 1316
Cambrensis, Giraldus (Gerald of Wales), **25**, **37**, 1167 fn. 205, 1179

Index

Camden, William, 25–6, 46–9
Canoun (Canon), Hugh (d. 1317), 1316, 1317
Canterbury, 1179, 1298
   abp, 1162
   Holy Trinity monastery (Christ Church), 1179
Cantilupe, Millicent (d. 1299), w. of John de Mohun, 1219
Cantok, Thomas, bp Emly (1306–9), 1306
   chancellor of Ireland, 1306
Capella, Henry de, 1318
Carbury, Co. Kildare, 1305, 1329, 1333
   castle of, 1367
Carew, George (d. 1629), e. Totnes, 25–6
   John de, justiciar of Ireland, 1349
Carlisle, Cumbria, England, 40, 1306, 1315
Carlow, Co., 1200
Carlow, town, exchequer at, 1361
Carnsore Point, Co. Wexford, 1331
Carrick, Carbury, Co. Kildare, 1305
Carrick, Co. Tipperary, 1205
Carrickfergus, Co. Antrim, 41, 1315, 1316, 1328, 1333
   convent of Friars Minor, 1243
Carthusian, religious order, 1186
Case, Thomas, 37, 50–3
Cashel, Co. Tipperary, 38, 1195, 1316, 1330
Cassanus, king of Tartars, 1299
Castleconnell (Connell), Co. Limerick, 1316
Castledermot (Tristeldermot), Co. Kildare, 1264, 1315, 1316
   Friars Minor, friary of, 1316
Castleisland, Co. Kerry, 1345, 1348
Castlekevin, Co. Wicklow, 1308, 1309
Castleknock, Co. Dublin, 1316
Castlemartin, Co. Kildare, 1317
castles, 1352
Castrum Dei (Fermoy) abbey, 1170
cattle, 1325, 1333, 1339
Caunteton, lineage, 1317
   David (d. 1308), 1307, 1308
   James, 1318
   John, 1318
   Maurice (d. 1308), 1308
Chamberlin (Camerarius), John (d. 1331), 1331
Chancery of Ireland, 28
Charles II (d. 1309), king of Naples, 1297
Charlton, John, justiciar of Ireland, 1337, 1338
   Thomas, bp Hereford (1327–44), chancellor of Ireland, 1337
   justiciar of Ireland, 1338, 1339, 1340
Charroux, France, 1199
charters, 1211
Chartularies of St Mary's Abbey, Dublin: with the Register of its house at Dunbrody, and Annals of Ireland, 50
Chepstow, Monmouthshire, Wales, 1169
Chester, black monks (Benedictines) of, 1204
Chorus Benedicti, see Jerpoint
Chronica Buriensis, 35
churches, 1204
Cinque ports, 1293
Cistercian, religious order, 5, 29, 37, 51, 1194
Clairvaux abbey, 1186, 1192, 1194
Clare, Amicia (d. 1287), w. of Baldwin de Redvers, 6th e. Devon, 1219
   Basilia, dau. of Gilbert, 1169 fn. 208
   Elizabeth (d. 1360), w. of John de Burgh, 1309, 1312
   Gilbert de (d. 1230), 5th e. Gloucester, 1219
   Gilbert de (d. 1295), 7th e. Gloucester, 1290, 1291, 1293, 1294, 1295

Clare, Amicia (*continued*)
  Gilbert de (d. 1314), 8th e.
    Gloucester, 1291, 1308, 1315
  Gilbert de (d. 1148), 1st e.
    Pembroke, 1169
  Gilbert de (d. 1241), 4th e.
    Pembroke (2nd creation), 1219
  Isabel (d. 1220), 4th countess of
    Pembroke and Striguil, dau. of
    Richard, 1200, 1219
  Isabella (d. 1240), w. of Gilbert, 4th
    e. Pembroke, 1219
  Isabelle (d. 1264), w. of Robert de
    Brus, 5th lord of Annandale,
    1219
  Margaret (d. 1342), w. of Piers
    Gaveston, e. Cornwall, 1308
  Richard de (d. 1262), 6th e.
    Gloucester, 1219, 1262
  Richard de (d. 1176), 2nd e.
    Pembroke (Strongbow), 1169,
    1177, 1185, 1200, 1219
  Richard de (d. 1318), **42**, 1315, 1316,
    1317, 1318
    s. of Thomas, 1311
  Thomas de (d. 1287), lord of
    Thomond, 1274, 1286
Clare Priory, Suffolk, England, **43**, 1368
Clement V, pope (1305–14), 1306
Clohull, Robert, 1313
Clondonne, unidentified, Ulster, **40**,
  1315
Clonee, Co. Meath, 1317
Clonmel, Co. Tipperary, 1331
Clontarf, Co. Dublin, 1313
clothes, 1343
Clyn, John (d. 1349?), Franciscan friar,
  8, **11**, **34–5**
  annals of, **9**, **15**, **25**, **45**, **50**
Cogan, John (d. *c*.1278), 1264, 1278
  John (d. 1311), 1311
  Milo (d. 1316), 1316
Cogry, Henry, friar minor, master of
  Dublin university, 1320

Coillach, 1331
coinage, 1279, 1300
Coleraine, Co. Derry, **38**, 1360
  Dominicans of, **45**
Collis Victoriae, see Knockmoy
Common pleas, court of, 1302
Comyn (Cumin), John, abp Dublin
  (1181–1212), 1180, 1195, 1211
  John (d. 1302) II of Badenoch,
    1292
  John (d. 1305) Rede ('the Red') III
    of Badenoch, 1305, 1306
  Jordan, 1305
  William, 1316
Connacht, **38**, 1317, 1327, 1328, 1330,
  1331
  kingdom, 1200, 1202, 1281, 1308,
    1315, 1316
  lordship, 1204, 1294, 1307
Connell, see Castleconnell
Connor, Co. Antrim, 1315
Connyng, le, 1331
Constance (d. 1198), queen of Sicily,
  Holy Roman empress, 1193
Constitutions, **3**
Corcomroe abbey, Co. Clare, 1199
Cork, **38**
  city, mayor of, 1328
corn, 1318
Cornwall, Richard de, 1296
coronation, 1199
Coterel, John (d. 1345), 1345
Coulrach, Robert de (d. 1315), 1315
Courcy, John de, 1204
Courson, John de, lord of Raheny and
  Kilbarrack, 1210
Courtrai, battle of, 1302
Craddock, Philip, 1331
Croft, Hugo de (d. 1317), 1317
Croxden abbey, Staffordshire, England,
  1176
Cullen, wood of (Cullenswood,
  Ranelagh), Co. Dublin, 1316
Cumin, see Comyn

Cusack, Adam, the younger, 1281
    John, 1318
    John (d. 1370), Baron of Culmullin, 43, 1370
    Walter, 1315, 1361

Dale, Thomas, justiciar of Ireland, 1365
Damietta, Egypt, 1213
Dan, Adam (d. 1307), 1307
Dangan (Dengle), lordship, Co. Meath, 1210
Darcy, John, 1330
    justiciar of Ireland, 1323, 1329, 1332, 1333, 1340, 1341
    Roger, justiciar of Ireland, 1346
    William, s. of John, 1330
David (d. 1219), e. Huntingdon, 1169
Decer, John le (d. 1332), citizen of Dublin, 6, 11, 33, 38, 1313, 1332
    mayor of Dublin, 1308
Deddington, Oxfordshire, England, 1312
demons, 1325
Dene, William (d. 1261), justiciar of Ireland, 1260, 1261
Derbforgaill, w. of Tigernán Ó Ruairc, 1167
Desmond, lordship, 1261
Despenser, Hugh le (d. 1326), 1st Baron Despenser, 1316
Dillon, see Lan, de
Dodder, river, 1331
d'Oddingeseles, William, justiciar of Ireland, 1294
Doget, S., 1285
dogs, 1299
Dominic (d. 1221), saint, 1198
Dominican continuator, 1, 12–14, 16–17, 28, 33, 42–6, 50, 53
    see also Pembridge, John de
Dominicans, 1, 3–4, 6–8, 10, 12–14, 35, 37
Don, Thomas (d. 1317), sea-captain, 1317

Doncref, Maurice (d. 1361), citizen of Dublin, 13, 1361
Dowling, Thady (d. 1628), annalist, 50
Downpatrick, Co. Down, 1204, 1259
    monastery of Blessed Patrick, 1316
    church, 1204
dowry, 1286
Douglas, James de (d. 1330), lord of Douglas, 40, 1315
Drogheda, counties Meath and Louth, 34, 41, 1308, 1309, 1314, 1316, 1317, 1318
    Friars Minor of, 1330
    Friars Preachers of (Dominicans), 7, 27–8, 38, 41, 1361
    mayor of, 1328
drowning, 1313
Dublin, 5, 7, 12, 34, 1311, 1315, 1327, 1342, 1361
    administration, 44
    aqueduct, 1308
    bakers, 1310
    bridge, 5, 39, 1304, 1308
    Carmelites of, 1333
    castle, 5–6, 14, 1211, 1303, 1313, 1315, 1316, 1317, 1318, 1327, 1328, 1329, 1331, 1333, 1338, 1355
    prison in, 1312
    chapel of Blessed Mary Magdalen, 1316
    Christ Church cathedral (Priory of Holy Trinity), 5, 44–5, 1177, 1211, 1225, 1283, 1306, 1316
    account roll of, 45
    brew-house of, 5, 1337
    prior of, 1328
    cistern, 1308
    citizens of, 4–5, 1317, 1320, 1331, 1337
    city, 1170, 1177, 1191, 1283, 1301, 1304, 1308, 1316, 1317, 1318, 1327, 1329, 1331, 1332, 1337, 1346
    mayor of, 1328

Dublin (*continued*)
  clerics of, 1180
  court at, 1308
  exchequer, 1361
  Friars Minor of, 1310, 1332
  Friars Preachers of (Dominicans), 1,
    6–7, 14, 24, 28, 34, 47, 1308,
    1311, 1329, 1332, 1351, 1355,
    1361
  Hoggen Green, 1327
  men of, 1315, 1316
  parliament at, 1317, 1328, 1329,
    1331, 1333, 1337, 1341, 1345
  port of, 1331, 1337
  prison of, 1333, 1346
  quays, 1304
  St Audeon's church, 1316
  St John's church 1316
  St Mary of the Friars Minor, chapel
    of, 1308
  St Mary of the Hospital of St John,
    chapel of, 1308
  St Mary's abbey, 5, 37–9, 48, 50–2,
    1316, 1337
    abbot of, 1328
  St Patrick's Cathedral, 10, 1180,
    1211, 1294, 1316, 1320, 1328,
    1329, 1362
  St Saviour's priory, 3, 5–7, 9, 13,
    16–17, 37, 41, 1304
    church of, 7, 1316
  St Thomas's abbey, 1195, 1310,
    1343
    abbot of, 1328
  St Thomas's street, 1316
  St Werburgh's church, 1301
  suburbs of, 37, 1316
  university of, 8, 10–11, 1320
  walls of, 41, 1316
  Tholsel, 1328
  Winetavern Street, gate of, 1316
Duiske abbey (abbey of St Saviour),
  Co. Kilkenny, 1203
Dumfries, Scotland, 1305

Dunbar, Patrick IV (d. 1308), e. March,
  1292
Dunbar castle, Scotland, 1296
Dunbrody abbey, Co. Wexford, 1179
Dundalk, Co. Louth, 41, 1315, 1316,
  1318
  St Nicholas's church of, 13, 1360
Dunlavin, Co. Wicklow, 1308
Dunoil (Dunohill), Baron of, *see* Poer

earthquakes, 1246, 1298
eclipse, 1312
Edinburgh, Scotland, 14, 1296
Edmund (d. 1300), 2nd e. Cornwall,
  1300
Edmund (d. 1296), 1st e. Lancaster,
  1295, 1296
Edward I, king of England
  (1272–1307), 24, 35, 38, 1274,
  1284, 1286, 1290, 1291, 1292,
  1293, 1294, 1295, 1296, 1297,
  1298, 1300, 1301, 1302, 1303, 1306,
  1307
Edward II, king of England (1307–27),
  4, 8, 1306, 1307, 1310, 1313, 1315,
  1316, 1317, 1320, 1341
Edward III, king of England (1327–77),
  12, 1312, 1339, 1341, 1345
Eleanor of Provence (d. 1291), queen of
  England, 1286, 1291
Emerdullan (Moiry Pass, Co. Armagh),
  1343
England, 8, 1193, 1199, 1208, 1279,
  1280, 1281, 1286, 1293, 1294,
  1298, 1308, 1311, 1318, 1319, 1320,
  1327, 1328, 1330, 1346, 1347, 1348,
  1358, 1360
Ethergonyll (?Aghancon), Co. Offaly,
  1333
Eugene III, pope (1145–53), 1186
Evesham, Worcestershire, England,
  1180
exchequer, Irish, 1361, 1367
excommunication, 1303, 1306, 1317

Index

execution, **6–7, 34**, 1199, 1204, 1210, 1295, 1306, 1308, 1312, 1315, 1317, 1318, 1325, 1327, 1328, 1329, 1332, 1339, 1345, 1355
Exeter (Exonia), Jordan de, 7
   Richard de (d. 1287), itinerant justice, 1269
   Richard (d. 1327), 1313
   Stephen (d. 1316), 1316
expedition, military, 1167, 1291, 1306
   royal, 1185, 1210

Falkirk, Scotland, 1298
famine, **33**, 1271, 1315, 1317, 1331
Fastolf, Nicholas, justice of the Common Bench, 1327, 1328
Faughart, Co. Louth, **41**, 1318
felonies, 1294
Fenlys, William de, 1302
Ferings, Richard de, abp Dublin (1299–1306), 1302, 1306
Fermoy, Co. Cork, 1170 fn. 213
Ferns, Co. Wexford, 1171
   castle, 1331
Ferrers, Agatha (d. 1306), w. of Hugh de Mortimer of Chelmarsh, 1219
   Agnes (d. 1290), w. of William de Vesci, 1219
   Eleanor (d. 1274), w. of Roger de Quincy, 2nd e. Winchester, 1219
   Isabella (d. before 1260), 1219
   Joan (d. 1267), w. of John de Mohun, 1219
   Matilda (d. 1298), lady of Carbury, w. Simon de Kyme, 1219
   Sibyl, w. of Francis de Bohun, lord of Midhurst, 1219
   William de (d. 1254), 5th e. Derby, 1219
feudal aid, 1345
fifteenth, tax, 1292
Finglas, Co. Dublin, **49**
Finnea, Co. Westmeath, 1315, 1331

fish, 1318, 1331
Fishamble Street (Preston's Inns), Dublin, **27–8**
fitz Acory (Alured), John, 1210
fitz Amand, Almeric de, justiciar of Ireland, 1357, 1358
fitz Geoffrey, John, 1219
   justiciar of Ireland, 1248
FitzGerald, John fitz Thomas (d. 1316), 1st e. Kildare, 1294, 1295, 1296, 1298, 1301, 1302, 1307, 1309, 1312, 1313, 1315, 1316
   Gerald (d. 1303), s. of John, 1303
   Gerald fitz Maurice (d. 1398), 3rd e. Desmond, 1370
     justiciar of Ireland, 1367, 1369
   Gerald fitz Maurice (d. 1432), 5th e. Kildare, **25**
   John (d. 1323), s. of Thomas, 2nd e. Kildare, 1323
   John fitz Thomas, bro. of Maurice, 1st e. Desmond, 1319
   Maurice (d. 1257), 2nd lord of Offaly, 1255
   Maurice (d. 1331), Hospitaller, 1331
   Maurice, 1345
   Maurice fitz Thomas (d. 1356), 1st e. Desmond, **14**, 1312, 1316, 1319, 1327, 1328, 1329, 1330, 1331, 1333, 1339, 1341, 1345, 1346, 1348, 1355
   Maurice fitz Thomas (d. 1390), 4th e. Kildare, **14, 24**, 1345, 1346, 1347
     justiciar of Ireland, 1360
   Thomas fitz John (d. 1328), 2nd e. Kildare, **24**, 1312, 1316, 1317, 1323, 1359
     deputy justiciar of Ireland, 1320
     justiciar of Ireland, 1327
   William, 1345
fitz Henry, Matthew, 1345
   Meiler, 1202, 1220
   Richard, 1331

fitz John, Thomas, 1370
   William, abp Cashel (1317–26), 1318
      justiciar of Ireland, 1318
      keeper of Ireland, 1318
fitz Leon, Joanna (d. 1348), w. of Simon de Geneville, 6, 1347
fitz Maurice, Gerald, 24, 1243, 1264, 1285
   John, justiciar of Ireland, 1346
   Maurice, 1264, 1268
   Maurice, justiciar of Ireland, 1272
   Maurice fitz Nicholas (d. 1339), lord of Kerry, 1339
   Nicholas, 1313
   Robert, 1345
   Thomas, 1298, 1317
      justiciar of Ireland, 1295
fitz Nicholas, John, 1370
fitz Ralph, Richard, abp Armagh (1346–60), 12, 31, 1337, 1357, 1360
   dean of Lichfield, 1337
fitz Rery, John, 1311
   Simon, justice of the Common Bench, 1331
fitz Richer, John, sheriff of Meath, 1368
fitz Roger, William, prior of the hospital of St John of Jerusalem in Ireland, 1274
fitz Stephen, Ralph, 1179
   Robert (d. before 1192), 1168, 1185
fitz Thomas, John, *see also* fitz Gerald, 1261
   Maurice, s. of John, 1261
fitz Warin, Alan, 1315
   Fulk, 1317
Flanders, Belgium, 1297, 1302, 1304
Flattisbury, Philip, 48–9
Fleming, Johanna (d. 1361), w. of Geoffrey Travers, 1361
   Simon (d. 1370), Baron of Slane, 43, 1370
Flemings, 1302, 1304
flood, 1330, 1346

Flore (Flotte), Peter de (d. 1302), chancellor of France, 1302
Florence, Italy, 44
Florence V (d. 1296), count of Holland, 1292
Flumen Dei, see Abbeyshrule
Foley catalogue, 14
Fons Vivus, see Abbeymahon
Fontevrault (Fontevraud) abbey, France, 1189, 1199
footsoldiers, 1296
Forth, Co. Carlow, 1329
Four Courts, Dublin, 1
fowl, 1360
France, 3, 15, 50, 1199, 1204, 1210, 1293, 1294
Francis (d. 1226) of Assisi, saint, 1206
Franciscan, religious order (friars minor), 4, 10, 34–5, 1206, 1297
Fraser, Simon (d. 1306), 1306
Freigne, Fulk de la, 1345
   John de, 1361
   Patrick de, 1361
   Robert de, 1361
   William (d. 1329), 1329
French, 1302
Freynestown, Co. Wicklow, 1331
Friars Minor, religious order, 1243, 1316, 1318
Friars Preachers (Black Friars), religious order, 1, 3–4, 7, 1198, 1231, 1234, 1274, 1285, 1304, 1308, 1316
Fulbourne, Stephen, abp Tuam (1286–8), 1287
   bp Waterford (1274–86), 30, 1279
   justiciar of Ireland, 1281
Furnivall, Bertha (d. 1279), 1219

Gainsborough, William, bp Worcester (1302–7), 1306
gallowglasses, 1315
Galway, town, 38, 1313
Gandon, James, architect, 1

Gascony, France, 1294, 1295
Gaveston, Piers (Peter) de (d. 1312), 1st e. Cornwall, **39**, 1308, 1309, 1310, 1311, 1312
Geashill castle, Co. Offaly, 1306, 1307, 1315
Gelasius (Gilla Meic Liac mac Diarmata) abp Armagh (1137–74), 1174
Geneville, **7**
   Geoffrey de (d. 1314), 1st Baron Geneville, **6**, 1240 (1241), 1276, 1301, 1304, 1308, 1314
      justiciar of Ireland, 1273
   Joan (d. 1356), 2nd Baroness Geneville, w. of Roger Mortimer, 1st e. March, 1301, 1308
   Maud (Matilda) de Lacy (d. 1304), w. of Geoffrey, **6**, 1240 (1241), 1302, 1304
   Nicholas (d. 1325), s. of Simon, **6**, 1325
   Peter (d. 1292), lord of Ludlow, 1292, 1301
   Simon, s. of Geoffrey, **6**, 1325, 1329, 1347
Geoffrey II (d. 1186), dk of Brittany and 3rd e. Richmond, 1199
Germany, 1317
Gernon, John, 1329
   Roger, 1329
Ghent Annals, **36**
Gilbert, J.T., **50–3**
Gillebertus (Gilbert), *see* Ó Caráin, Gilla an Choimded
Glendalough, Co. Wicklow, 1274, 1309
   abb. of, **36**, 1162
Glenealy, Co. Wicklow, 1317
Glenfell (poss. Glenealy, Co. Wicklow), 1306
Glenmalure, Co. Wicklow, 1308, 1311, 1312

Godfrey of Brabant (d. 1302), lord of Aarschot and Vierzon, 1302
Gormanston, Viscount, **2**, **26**
Gourdon, Bertrand de, 1199
Gowran, Co. Kilkenny, 1316, 1321, 1337
Grace, Hamon de, 1305
   James, **25**, **48**, **50**
Grace Dieu, priory of, Co. Dublin, 1313
grain, 1318
   shortage of, 1310, 1330
Granard, Co. Longford, 1315
   monastery of, **37**, **39**, 1211
Grandmont, religious order, 1186
Grant, William (d. 1345), 1345
Gras, Hamon le, 1315
Great Connell (Greatconnell; house of St Mary), Priory, Co. Kildare, 1202, 1220
Greencastle, Co. Donegal, 1260, 1315, 1328
Gregory, abp Dublin (1152–62), **36**, 1162
Grey Abbey (*Jugum Dei*), Co. Down, 1193
Gros, Raymond le, 1169
Guédelon (Genelon) castle, Burgundy, 1299
Guy IV of Châtillon (d. 1317), count of St-Pol, 1302
Guy I of Clermont (d. 1302), lord of Breteuil, marshal of France, 1302
Guzman, Dominic de, **3**
Gwynedd, Wales, 1295

Hailes abbey, Gloucestershire, England, 1300
Hampton, England, 1298
Hardits, William de, friar preacher, master of Dublin university, **4**, 1320
Harolds, lineage, 1315
Harris, Walter, **4**, **15**, **47**
Hastings, John de, 1st Baron Hastings, 1292, 1302

Havering, John de, 1295
  Richard de, abp elect Dublin (1307–10), 1306
Hay, William de la, justiciar of Ireland, 1294
Henry III, duke of Saxony (1142–80), 1193
Henry VI, Holy Roman emperor (1191–7), 1193
Henry II, king of England (1154–89), 48, 1172, 1185, 1189, 1199
Henry III, king of England (1216–72), 1230, 1251, 1274
Henry VIII, king of England (1491–1547), 26
Henry of Almain (d. 1271), 1271
Henry of Grosmont (d. 1361), duke of Lancaster, 1361
Herefordshire, 9–10
heresy, 7–8, 1307, 1325, 1327
herring, 1338
Hogelyn, John, 1308
Hollywood (Holywood), Co. Wicklow, 1302
Holy Land, 6, 1190, 1193, 1273, 1291
Holywood, Robert, 1361
homage, 1204, 1292
horsemen, 1296, 1299
horses, 1272, 1306, 1343
Hospitallers, *see* Knights Hospitallers
hostages, 1315, 1316, 1317, 1329, 1332
Hothum (Hotham), John de (d. 1337), 39–40, 1315
  bp Ely (1316–37), 1316
  William de, provincial prior of the Irish Dominicans, 39
Houth, Scholastica, w. of Robert Tyrell, Baron of Castleknock, 1370
Hovenden, Roger de, 35
Howard, Thomas (d. 1554), dk. Norfolk, lord lieutenant of Ireland, 26, 46
  William (d. 1640), 26, 47
Howth, Co. Dublin, 38, 1313

Huntingdon, Henry of, 35
Hussey (Husse), family, 7
  John, the butcher of Athenry, 7, 1316
Hyde, James de la, 1361

Idrone, Co. Carlow, 1339
Imaal, Irish of, 1316, 1317
imprisonment, 1204, 1230, 1307, 1315
Inch abbey, Co. Down, 1187
Inns Quay, Dublin, 1
inquisition, 1316, 1317
interdict, 1208, 1315
Ireland, 8
  invasion of, 1169
Isabella of France (d. 1358), queen of England, 1307
Istlip, Walter de, treasurer of Ireland, 1318
Italy, 1298

Jak, Maurice, canon of the cathedral church of Kildare, 1319, 1320
James II (d. 1327), king of Aragon, 1302
  king of Majorca, 1297
James of Aragon (monk, d. 1334), 1297
Jerpoint (*Chorus Benedicti*) abbey, Co. Kilkenny, 1180
Jerusalem, 1186
Joan (Joanna) of Acre (d. 1307), 1290, 1291
Joan I of Navarre (d. 1305), queen of France, 1303
John, bp Connor (1292–1319), 1315
John, count of Mortain, 1199
  king of England (1199–1216), 1199, 1204, 1208, 1210
  lord of Ireland, 1185, 1199
John II (d. 1312), duke of Brabant, 1290
John XXII, pope (1316–34), 3, 1319, 1320
John de Balliol (d. 1314), e. Galloway, 1292
  king of Scots, 1292, 1295, 1296

Index

John of Avesnes (d. 1302), count of Ostrevent, son of John II, count of Hainaut, 1302
John II of Brienne (d. 1302), count of Eu, 1302
John I of Ponthieu (d. 1302), count of Aumale, 1302
John of Strathbogie (d. 1306), 9th e. Athol, 1306
John of Vierzon (d. 1302), s. of Godfrey of Brabent, 1302
John son of Gerald, prior of the Dominican priory of Dublin, **25**
Jorz (Jorse), Roland, abp Armagh (1311–22), **38**, 1313, 1318
Jugum Dei, see Grey Abbey

keepers of the peace, 1316
Kells, Co. Kilkenny, **31**, **40**, 1316, 1327, 1348
Kells, Co. Meath, 1315
Kenilworth, Warwickshire, England, 1279
Kent, Peter (d. 1329), 1329
Kermedyn, John, 1318
Kermerdyn, Edmund de, friar, master of Dublin university, **4**, **10**, 1320
Kerry, Co., 1339, 1345
Kilbarrack, Co. Dublin, 1210
Kilbeg, 1329
Kilcullen, Co. Kildare, 1319
Kildare, **24**
    castle, 1294
    cathedral church of, 1319
    Co., 1200, 1234, 1315, 1317
    earls of, **18**, **24–5**, **28**, **46**
    English of, 1339
    Friars Minor of, 1316, 1359
    lordship, 1294
    parliament at, 1294, 1326
Kilkea castle, Co. Kildare, 1356
Kilkenny (Ossory), **8**, **34**, **38**, **42**, **48**, 1327, 1348
    castle, prison of, 1325
    Co., 1200
    parliament at, 1330, 1331, 1341
    town, 1325
    Friars Preachers of, 1231, 1234, 1316, 1317
    parliament at (1310), 1309, 1326
Kilkenny Chronicle, **4**
Kilmainham, Co. Dublin, 1345
    hospital of St John of Jerusalem at, 1329
    parliament at, **42**, 1317
Kilmohide (?Ballyadams), Co. Laois, 1346
Kilwardby, Robert, abp Canterbury (1273–8), **38**, 1274
Kington, Herefordshire, **10**
Knights Hospitallers, military order, 1183, 1274, 1314
Knights Templars, military order, **7–8**, 1183, 1312, 1314
    suppression of, 1307
Knockmoy, Co. Galway, 1189
    abbey, 1200
Kyrie Eleison, see Abbeydorney
Kyteler, Alice de, **8–9**, 1325

L (Laud Miscellaneous MS 526, Bodleian Library, Oxford), **1**, **28–33**, **43**, **48**, **49**
Lacy, Armoricus, 1318
    Henry de (d. 1311), 5th e. Lincoln, 1251, 1310
    Hugh (Hugo) de, 1302, 1308, 1317, 1318, 1331
    Hugh de (d. 1186), lord of Meath, 1172, 1186, 1195, 1210
    Hugh de (d. 1242), 1st e. Ulster, 1204, 1210, 1243
    Isabella, 1219
    John (d. 1318), 1318
    John, s. of Walter, 1311
    Margery (Margaret), w. of John de Verdun, lord of Westmeath, 1240 (1241)

Lacy, Armoricus (*continued*)
   Maud (Matilda, d. 1304), w. of
      Geoffrey de Geneville, **30**, 1240
      (1241), 1302, 1304
   Maud, w. of Walter de Burgh, 1st e.
      Ulster, 1243
   Robert, 1318
   Walter de (d. 1241), lord of Meath,
      1210, 1240 (1241)
   Walter de, 1308, 1311, 1315, 1317,
      1318
Lacy family, **50**, 1316, 1317
Ladislas IV, king of Hungary
   (1272–90), 7, 1287
Laghynerthy, 1330
Lamberton, William de, bp St Andrews
   (1297–1328), 1305
Lan, Richard de, 1315
Lanercost, Chronicle of, **40**
Laois, 1250
Laraghbryan, Co. Kildare, 1316
Laud, William, abp Canterbury (1633–
   45), **26, 46**
Laweles, 1329
   Elias, 1328
   Raymond (d. 1330), 1330
Lawless, lineage, 1316
Lea castle (Lega; Ley), Co. Laois, 1284,
   1294, 1307, 1315, 1329, 1346
Lecale, Co. Down, **44**
Leche, John de, abp Dublin (1311–13),
   1306, 1313
Ledewiche, John (d. 1329), 1329
   Roger (d. 1329), 1329
   Thomas (d. 1329), 1329
Ledrede, Richard, bp Ossory (1317–
   61), 8, 1325, 1328
Ledrede's *Narrative*, **9**
Leicester, England, 1341
Leighlin, Co. Carlow, 1297, 1320
Leinster, **38**, 1295, 1301, 1311, 1315,
   1339
   English of, 1306
   Irish of, 1306, 1327, 1331, 1370
   lord of, 1200
   men of, 1321
Leixlip (Salmon Leap), Co. Kildare,
   39, 1225, 1316, 1327
Lenfaunt, John, 1345
   Walter (d. 1311), 1275, 1311
   Walter, 1345
Lent, **12, 33, 42**
Leominster, Herefordshire, **10**
Leopold V, duke of Austria (1177–94),
   1193
Lex Dei, *see* Abbeyleix
Liffey, river, **1, 5, 41**, 1308, 1338
Limerick, **38**
   castle, 1332
   constable of, 1332
   city, 1331
   citizens of, 1332
   Friars Minor of, 1318
   Irish of, 1370
   marshal of, 1330
   mayor of, 1328
Limousin, France, 31
Lincoln, Lincolnshire, England,
   1306
   parliament at, 1317
Lionel of Antwerp (d. 1368), duke of
   Clarence and e. Ulster, lord
   lieutenant of Ireland, **43**, 1361,
   1364, 1365, 1368
Lismore, Co. Waterford, 1179
Locun, Robert, 1329
Logan, lineage, 1315
   John, 1316
   Milo, 1317
London, England, 31, 1295, 1296,
   1312
   parliament at, 1308, 1311, 1313
London, Elizabeth, w. of Christopher
   Preston, 27
   Henry, abp Dublin (1213–28), **49**,
   1211, 1225
   William de, 1213
   William de, Baron of Naas, **27**

Longespée, Stephen (d. 1260), justiciar of Ireland, 1259, 1260
William de, 1250
Lough Sewdy, Co. Westmeath, 1314, 1315
Louis IX, king of France (1226–70), 1250
Louis of Toulouse (d. 1297), saint, bishop of Toulouse, 1297
Low Countries, **15**
Lucy, Anthony de, justiciar of Ireland, 1331, 1332
Ludden, Co. Limerick, 1316
Lune (Luyn), Baron of, 1213
Lyon catalogue, **14**

Mac Artáin, 1343
Mac Cárthaigh (McCarthy), 1261, 1318, 1332
Domhnall Óg, 1306
Domhnall Ruadh (d. 1306), king of Desmond, 1306
Mac Conmara, of Thomond, 1370
Macdouall (O Dowell), Duncan, 1313
Mac Giollaphádraig, Donnchadh, son of Anmchadh, son of Donnchadh, of Ossory (Mac Anmchadha, the son of Belial), 1250
McKele, Conghor, 1316
Mac Mathghamhna, Aonghus, 1297
Mac Murchadha (MacMurrough), Art (d. 1282), bro. of Muirchertach, 1282, 1327, 1329, 1347
Diarmait (d. 1171), king of Leinster, 1167, 1171, 1200
Domhnall (d. c.1338), king of Leinster, **5–6**, 1327, 1329, 1347
Domhnall (d. 1347), king of Leinster, 1347
Eva, dau. of Diarmait and w. of Richard de Clare, 1169, 1200
Muirchertach (d. 1282), king of Leinster, 1275, 1282
Murchadh Ballach (d. 1307), 1307

Madog ap Llywelyn (d. 1312), 1295
Mag Eochagáin (MacGeoghegan), 1330
John, 1311
William, 1329
Mág Oireachtaigh, David, abp Armagh (1334–46), 1337
Maidstone, Walter, bp Worcester (1313–17), 1316
Majorca, 1297
Malachy (d. 1148), saint, abp Armagh (1132–36/7), 1192, 1194
Malcolm IV, king of Scots (1153–65), 1169
Malmesbury, William of, **35**
Man, Isle of, 1313
Mandeville, Henry, 1331
Martin de, 1262, 1333
Robert, s. of Martin, 1333
Thomas de, **41**, 1306, 1315, 1316
William (d. 1315), 1315
Margaret of England (d. aft. 1333), duchess of Brabant, 1290
Margaret of England (d. 1275), queen of Scots, 1251
Margaret of France (d. 1318), queen of England, 1300
Marianus Scotus, **35**
Marisco, Geoffrey de (d. 1245), 1208
Marshal, Anselm (d. 1245), 5th e. Pembroke (2nd creation), 1219
Eva (d. 1246), w. of William de Briouze, 1219
Gilbert (d. 1241), 4th e. Pembroke, **24**, 1219
Isabella (d. 1240), w. of Gilbert de Clare, 1219
Joan, (d. 1234), w. of Warin de Munchensi, lord of Swanscombe, 1219
Matilda (d. 1248), w. of Hugh Bigod, 1219
Richard (d. 1234), earl Marshal and 3rd e. Pembroke, 1219, 1234

Marshal, Anselm (*continued*)
   Sibyl (d. 1245), w. of William de
     Ferrers, 5th e. Derby, 1219
   Walter (d. 1245), 5th e. Pembroke,
     1219
   William (d. 1219), earl Marshal and
     1st e. Pembroke, 1200, 1219
   William (d. 1231), earl Marshal and
     2nd e. Pembroke, 1219, 1231
Marton, unidentified, 1307
massacre, 1329, 1332, 1339, 1346
Mathilda, empress of Germany (d.
   1167), 1167, 1189
Matilda of Lancaster (d. 1377),
   countess of Ulster, 1343, 1346
Maupass, John, 41, 1318
Maynooth, Co. Kildare, 1316
Meath, Co., **5**, 1306
   English of, 1330
   men of, 1315, 1321
Meath, liberty, 1314
Meath, lordship, 1172, 1195, 1308
Mellifont monastery, Co. Louth, 1168,
   1194
mendicants, 1357
Menteith, John de, bro. of Alan, earl of
   Menteith, 1316
messengers, 1317
Messet, Peter, Baron of Luyn (Lune),
   1213
Midia, Basilia, dau. of Petronilla, 1325
   Petronilla, maid of Alice de Kyteler,
     1325
Milkadar, sultan of Babylon, 1291
mill, 1330
mill-pond, 1313
Miramomelius, Saracen, 1287
Monasteranenagh abbey (Maigue;
   Maio), Co. Limerick, 1370
Monasterevin and Assaroe (Rosea
   Vallis; Rosglas) abbey, 1178
money, 1343
Montfort, William de (d. 1294), dean of
   St Paul's, London, 1294

moon, 1342
Morris, John, justiciar of Ireland, 1341
Mortimer, Edmund (d. 1304), 2nd
   Baron Mortimer of Wigmore,
   1219, 1301
   Maud, dau. Edmund, 2nd Baron
     Mortimer of Wigmore, 1301
   Roger (d. 1282), 1st Baron
     Mortimer of Wigmore, **10**,
     1219, 1279, 1282
   Roger (d. 1330), 1st e. March, **12**,
     14, **42**, 1301, 1308, 1309, 1310,
     1315, 1317, 1318
     justiciar of Ireland, 1317, 1319,
       1320
   Roger (d. 1360), 2nd e. March, 1361
Mortimer family, **10**
Mowbray, Philip (d. 1318), 1316, 1318
Muireadhach III (d. 1332), e. Menteith,
   1328
Multyfarnham, annals of, **4**
Munchensi, Joan (d. 1307), w. of
   William de Valence, 1219
   Warin de (d. 1255), 1219
Munster, 1208, 1301, 1315, 1316, 1327,
   1330, 1332, 1338, 1345, 1370
murrain, 1325

Naas, Co. Kildare, **38**, 1316, 1317
Naas, Thomas de, 1318
Naungle, Adam (d. 1329), 1329
   David (d. 1329), 1329
   John (d. 1329), 1329
Nenagh, Co. Tipperary, 1316, 1332,
   1347
Newark, Nottinghamshire, England,
   1306
Newcastle, Co. Westmeath, 1315
Newcastle Lyons, Co. Dublin, 1332
Newcastle McKinegan, Co. Wicklow,
   1295, 1306, 1309, 1315, 1329
Newcastle upon Tyne, England, 1292
Newtown (Newtownabbey),
   Co. Antrim, 1333

Index 295

New Town of Leys, Co. Laois, 1315
Nicholas IV, pope (1288–92), **30**, 1291
Nobber, Co. Meath, 1315
Normandy, duchy of, France, 1199, 1293
Normans, 1293
Norragh, Co. Kildare, 1275, 1286
Northampton, England, parliament at, 1328
Northon, John de, 1308
Northburgh, Co. Donegal, 1315
  castle, 1331
Northumberland, England, **40**, 1315
Notre Dame, church of, Boulogne, France, 1307
Nottingham, Robert de, mayor of Dublin, **34**, **39**, 1316
Nuremberg (Tordran), Germany, 1294

oats, 1318
Ó Briain (O'Brien), 1370
Ó Briain (d. 1277), 1277
Ó Briain (d. 1306), king of Thomond, 1306
  Brian, 1329, 1330, 1331, 1332
  Donnchadh (d. 1311), king of Thomond, 1311
  Muirchertach (d. 1343), king of Thomond, 1318
Ó Broin (O'Byrne), Dúnlaing (d. 1316), 1316
  Lorcán (d. 1307), 1306
  Murchadh, 1317, 1329
Ó Caráin, Gilla an Choimded (Gilbert; Gillebertus), abp Armagh (1175–80), 1174
Ó Ceallaigh (O'Kelly), **7**, 1316
Ó Cerbaill, Donnchadh (d. 1168/9), king of Airgialla, 1168
Ó Conchobhair (Ua Conchobhair; Uí Chonchobhair), **40**, 1306, 1316, 1321, 1333
  Aodh (d. 1308), king of Connacht, 1308

Aodh, s. of Cathal, 1308
Calbhach (d. 1305), 1286, 1294, 1305
Crobderg, 1200, 1202
Cathal Ruadh, 1315
Feidhlim, king of Connacht (d. 1316), 1315, 1316
Finghin, 1315
Muircheartach, king of Offaly, 1305
Ruadhrí (d. 1315), s. of Cathal Ruadh, 1315
Ruaidrí (d. 1198), high king of Ire., 1166
  king of Connacht, 1166
Ó Connairche, Gille Críst (Christian), Mellifont, 1186
  bp Lismore (1151–86), 1186
  legate of Ireland, 1186
Ó Díomusaigh (O'Dempsey), 1329
  Diarmuid (d. 1308), 1308
O Dowell, *see* Macdouall
Ó Duinn, chief of the Uí Riagáin, 1306
Ó Fearghail (O'Farrell), 1315, 1317
Offaly, 1307
  Irish of, **24**, 1285
  kinglets of, 1284
Ó hAnluain, 1291, 1316
  Cú Uladh, 1297
Ó hÉanna, Matthew, abp Cashel (*a*.1185–1206), 1195
Ó Mailsechlainn, Cairpre (d. 1290), king of Meath, 1290
Ó Maoil Mhuaidh, 1311
Ó Mórdha, 1346
Ó Néill, Brian (d. 1260), king of Tír Eoghain, 1259
Ó Nualláin, Philip, 1329
Orte, Italy, 1298
Ó Riagáin (Uí Riagáin), 1306
Ó Ruairc, Tigernán (d. 1172), king of Bréifne, 1167
Ossory, *see also* Kilkenny, **31**, 1327
Otto IV (d. 1218), Holy Roman Emperor, 1199

Ó Tuathail (O'Toole), 1370
   Adam Dubh (d. 1328), heretic, 1327
   Cuygnismio, 1308
   David, 1331
   David (d. 1328), 1316, 1327, 1328
   Laurence (d. 1180), abb.
      Glendalough, 36, 1162
      abp Dublin (1162–80), 36, 1162, 1180
   Murchadh (Maurice) (d. 1333), s. of Nicholas, 1333
   Nicholas, 1333
   Richard (Mac Eochaidh, d. 1307), 1306
   Walter Dubh, 1327
   William mac Walter, 1308
Outlaw (Outlawe), Roger (d. 1341), prior of Kilmainham, chancellor of Ireland, 1327, 1328
      justiciar of Ireland, 1328, 1329, 1330, 1340
   William, s. of Alice de Kyteler, 1325
outlawry, 1311
oxen, 1325, 1360
Oxmantown, Dublin, 5

palfrey, 1333
papal bull, 1317
parchment, 14–15
Paris, France, 1295
   university of, 1303
parlement of France, 1199, 1293
parley, 1368
partridges, 1337
Parys, John (d. 1314), 1314
Patrick, saint, 1174
peas, 1330
Pembridge, John de, *see also* 'Dominican continuator', 1, 5, 7–12, 16, 31, 33–8, 41–2, 45, 47, 50, 53
   Richard, 9
Pembridge, Herefordshire, 10
Pembridge Castle, Herefordshire, 9–10
Pembridge family, 9
Pembridge manor, 10
'Pembridge's annals', 1, 6, 11, 13, 15–16, 28, 47–52; *see also* T (Trinity College Dublin, MS 583) ; L (Laud Miscellaneous MS 526, Bodleian Library, Oxford)
Percival, Robert de, 1303
pestilence, 1294, 1317
Petit, Meiler (d. 1329), 1329
   R., 1285
   Simon (d. 1329), 1329
   William, 1213
petitions, 1317
Philip II, king of France (1180–1223), 1190, 1204
Philip IV, king of France (1285–1314), 1293, 1294, 1295, 1297, 1298, 1303, 1304, 1313
Philip of Slane, friar, 44
pilgrimage, 1204
pillories, 1210, 1295
Pippard, Roger, 1225
   William, lord of Salmon Leap (Leixlip), 1225
pirates, 1313, 1315, 1317
plague, 13, 27, 34, 42–3, 1271, 1348, 1361, 1370
plunder, 1301, 1315, 1317, 1339, 1343
plunderers, 1307
Plunket, Christopher, 49
   John, 49
Plunket family, 48
Poer, lineage, 6, 1328
   Arnold (d. 1329), 6, 1309, 1310, 1315, 1316, 1317, 1327, 1328
      seneschal of Co. Kilkenny, 1325
   Eustace le (d. 1311), 6, 1303, 1304, 1311
   Eustace (d. 1345), 1338, 1345, 1348
   John le (d. *c*.1331), Baron of Dunoil, 1315, 1317
   John, s. of Robert, 1345
   John, uncle of Eustace, 1338

Index

Robert, 1345
Roger, 1345
Walter, 1301
pollard, *see* coinage
ports, 1331
　English, 1315
Portus St Marie abbey, *see* Dunbrody
poultry, 1360
Prendergast, William, 1315
Preston, family, 1, 26–8, 46
Preston, Christopher, 25, 27–8
　Elizabeth, 49
　Robert, 7, 27, 1361
　　chief Baron of the exchequer, 1367
　Robert (d. 1503), 1st Viscount Gormanston, 27
　William (d. 1532), 2nd Viscount Gormanston, 26–7, 29
prison, 1318, 1325, 1339
Pulle, Walter de la, 41, 1318
punishment, 1310

Raheny, Co. Dublin, 1210
Randolph, Thomas (d. 1332), 1st e. Moray, 1315, 1316
　Thomas (d. 1332), 2nd e. Moray, 1315
ransom, 1368
Raoul of Clermont-Nesle (d. 1302), lord of Nesle, constable of France, 1302
Rathangan, Co. Kildare, 1315
　lordship, 1294
Rathcoole, Co. Dublin, 1311
Rathdown, vill of, Co. Dublin, 1301
Rathregan, Co. Meath, 1317
Ratoath, Co. Meath, 1285
Reban, Co. Kildare, 1315
rebels, 1298
Red Book of the Earls of Kildare, 48
Redvers, Baldwin de (d. 1245), 6th e. Devon, 1219
Rheims, siege of (1295), 1295

Rhys, John, treasurer of Ireland, 1337
Rhys ap Maredudd (d. 1292), 1292
Richard I, king of England (1189–99), 30, 48, 1189–90, 1193, 1199
Rieti, Italy, 1298
Rindoon castle, Co. Roscommon, 1315
Robert II (d. 1302), count of Artois, 1302
Robert the Bruce (d. 1329), e. Carrick, 1302, 1305
　king of Scots, 34, 40, 1219, 1305, 1306, 1313, 1315, 1316, 1317, 1319, 1323, 1328
robbers, 1311
robbery, 1343
Roche, George de, 1315, 1345
　John, s of George, 1345
　Patrick de, 1312
　William de, 1311
Rocheford, Gerald, 1345
　Maurice de, 1317, 1345
Rochelle, Richard de la, justiciar of Ireland, 1261, 1264
　Richard, 1345
Roches, 1308
Rodyard, William de, dean of St Patrick's cathedral, Dublin, 1320, 1328
　master of Dublin university, 1320
Rokeby, Thomas (d. 1356), kt, justiciar of Ireland, 14, 1350, 1355, 1356
Roman church, 1302
Roman Curia, 1297, 1300, 1316, 1317
Rome, Italy, 5
Roscommon castle, Co. Roscommon, 1269, 1275
Rosea Vallis (Rosglas), *see* Monasterevin and Assaroe
Ross, William de (d. 1316), 1st Baron Ross, 1292
Rouen, France, 1199
　abp, 1199
Roxburgh castle, Scotland, 1296

Saggart, Co. Dublin, 1311
sailors, 1315
St Amand, Amaury, **27**
St James de Compostela, Spain, 1320
St Kevin, of Glendalough, 1162, 1309
St Lawrence, Christopher, 1st Baron Howth, sheriff of Dublin, **48**
    Christopher, 7th Baron Howth, **48**
St Lawrence family, **48**
St Mary, house of, *see* Great Connell
St Mary of Eu, Normandy, France, 1180
St Omer, vill of, Flanders, 1317
St Peter, church, Westminster, *see* Westminster abbey
St-Pol, James de (Jacques de Châtillon), 1302
St Saviour's abbey, *see* Duiske abbey
St Stephen at Monte Celio, Rome, Italy, 1177
St Taurin abbey, Évreux, Normandy, France, 1210
St Wolstan's (Wolfstan) Priory, Celbridge, Co. Kildare, 1308
Saladin (d. 1193), sultan of Egypt and Syria, 1186
Salmon Leap, *see* Leixlip
salt, 1318
Samaria abbey, 1178
Sandal, John, 1316
Sandford, John, abp Dublin (1286–94), 1287, 1294
Saracens, **7**, 1186, 1250, 1287, 1291, 1298, 1299
Savage, Henry, s. of Robert, 1352
    John, brother, **45–6**
    Robert, **31, 42, 44–5**, 1352, 1360
    William, **45**
Savage family, **45–6**
Say, Margery de (d. 1280), w. of Robert d'Ufford, 1280
Scarborough castle, North Yorkshire, England, 1312

Scone, Scotland, 1305
Scotland, **35**, 1292, 1295, 1300, 1303, 1305, 1306, 1308, 1316, 1328, 1333
    wars in, 1295, 1298, 1301, 1310, 1315
Scots, **36, 40–2**, 1296, 1297, 1315, 1316, 1317, 1318
Sexton, John, 1362
sheep, 1360
Sherman, Kendrick (d. 1351), mayor of Dublin, **13**, 1351
ships, **41**, 1315
siege, of castle, 1312
silver, 1343
Skerries, Co. Kildare, **40**, 1315
Slane, Co. Meath, **43**, 1316
Slaney, river, 1331
Slievemargy, Co. Laois, 1297
Sligo, 1294
Soules, Nicholas II de, lord of Liddesdale and butler of Scotland, 1292
    Walter de, 1318
Stafford, Thomas, **26**
stags, 1360
Stanihurst, Richard, **49**
Stanton (Staunton), John de, 1315
    Philip, clerk of wages, 1286, 1329
Stewart, Alan, 1316, 1318
    John, 1316
Stirling bridge, battle of, **40**, 1297
Stirling Castle, Scotland, **14**
Strade, Co. Mayo, **7**
Sutton, Gilbert, seneschal of Wexford, 1305
    Herbert, 1318

T (Trinity College Dublin, MS 583), **1–2, 13–25, 28–33, 43, 46, 48–9, 51–3**
Taillour, John (d. 1370), mayor of Dublin, **43**, 1370

Index 299

Talbot, Michael, 1213
   Richard (d. 1329), of Malahide, 1329
   Thomas, 1361
Tallaght, Co. Dublin, 1331
Talon, Richard, 1308
Templars, *see* Knights Templars
tenants, 1211
Tethmoy, Co. Offaly, 1315
thieves, 1316
Thomas (d. 1322), 2nd e. Lancaster, 1316, 1317
Thomas of Brotherton (d. 1338), 1st e. Norfolk, 1300
Thomond, 1370
   Irish of, 1332
   kingdom, 1272, 1306, 1311
Thornbury, Walter (d. 1313), chancellor of Ireland, 1313
Thurles, Co. Tipperary, 1208, 1330, 1331
Tintern abbey, Co. Wexford, 1200
tithes, 1294, 1302
Tober, Co. Wicklow, 1308
Tordran, *see* Nuremberg
Toulouse, France, **44**, 1198
Tower of London, London, England, 1295
Tracton, Co. Cork, Cistercian house of, 37
Tralee, Co. Kerry, Friars Preachers of, **14**, 1355
treason, 1294, 1295, 1368
treasury, 1199
Treharne (Traharne), Henry, 1327, 1329, 1345
Trim, Co. Meath, 1213, 1308, 1317, 1318
   castle, 1224, 1315, 1368
   Dominican priory and Friars Preachers of, **6**, **13**, 1308, 1314, 1325
   Friars Minor of, 1330
   St Mary's church, **13**, 1368

Trinity College Dublin, 1
   see also T (Trinity College Dublin, MS 583)
Tripoli, Libya, 1289
Tristeldermot, *see* Castledermot
Tullow, Co. Carlow, 1316
Turberville, Thomas de, 1295
Turpilton, Hugo de, 1318
Tuyt, Richard, 1211, 1318, 1345
Tyrell, Hugh, lord of Castleknock, 1316
   James (d. 1329), 1329
   Joan, sister of Robert, 1370
   Matilda, sister of Robert, 1370
   Robert (d. 1331), 1331
   Robert (d. 1370), Baron of Castleknock, 1368, 1370

Ufford, Ralph (d. 1346), justiciar of Ireland, **12**, **14**, **34**, **42**, 1343, 1345, 1346, 1348
   Robert d', 1279, 1281
   justiciar of Ireland, 1268, 1276, 1280
Uí Bhroin, 1309, 1311, 1312, 1315, 1329, 1361
Uí Cheallaigh, 1307
Uí Cheinnsealaigh, **34**, 1331
Uí Chonaill, 1345
Uí Dhíomasaigh, 1306, 1339
Uí Fhaeláin, 1301
Uí Mháil, *see* Imaal
Uí Mhórdha, 1315, 1329
Uí Thuathail, 1311, 1315, 1331, 1332
Ulster, **5**, **45**, 1187, 1210, 1291, 1313, 1315, 1317, 1330, 1343, 1352, 1360
   earldom of, **39**, 1204, 1243
   Irish of, 1346
   manors of, **44**
   men of, **12**, 1313, 1317
Ulster, annals of, **4**
Uriel, Co., *see also* Louth, 1311, 1329
   English of, 1346

Ussher, James, abp Armagh (1625–56), 47, 49
Ussher catalogue, 14

Valence, Aymer de (d. 1324), 2nd e. Pembroke (3rd creation), 1306, 1312, 1317
Valle, Stephen de, bp Meath (1369–79), 13, 1360
Venedotians, 1295
Verdun, Bertram de, 1176
　John de, 1240 (1241),
　John de (d. 1274), 1274
　John de, bro. of Nicholas (d. 1271), 1271
　Milo de, 1313, 1318, 1330
　Nicholas de (d. 1271), 1271
　Nicholas de, 1345
　Robert de (d. 1316), 1311, 1312, 1316
　Theobald de (d. 1309), 1st Baron Verdun, 1309
　Theobald de (d. 1316), 2nd Baron Verdun, 1299, 1301
　　justiciar of Ireland, 1314
Vernoyl, Henry de, 1213
　Hugh de, 1302
Vescy, John, 1292
　William (d. 1297), justiciar of Ireland, 1290, 1291, 1294
Vienna, Austria, 31
villeins, 1211
Vitry, France, 31
Vivian, cardinal priest, papal legate, 1177

Waleys, Richard, 1345
Wallace, William, 1297
Ware, Sir James (d. 1666), 10, 25, 37, 46–7, 49–53
Warenne, Isabel (d. 1282), countess of Arundel, w. of Hugh d'Aubigny, 5th e. Arundel, 1219
　John de (d. 1304), 6th e. Surrey, 1219, 1297
　William de (d. 1240), 5th e. Surrey, 1219
Waring, John (d. 1329), 1329
wars, 1301, 1339
Waterford, 38, 1327
　city, 1172, 1179
　mayor of, 1328
weather, 1325, 1330, 1333, 1338, 1343, 1346, 1361
Wellesley, John le, 1345
　Walerand, 1303
　William (d. 1347), 1347
Welsh, 1296, 1337
Welsh Marches, 9
Welsh Newton, Herefordshire, 9
Westminster abbey, London, England, 1199
　church, 1274, 1290, 1307
Wetheney, *see* Abington
Wexford, town, burgesses of, 1331
　Co., 1200, 1331
　seneschal of, 1305
whales, 1331
wheat, 1315, 1317, 1330, 1332, 1333
White, Richard, 1331
　Wadin, 1316
　Walter, 1318
Wicklow, town, Co. Wicklow, 1301, 1315, 1329, 1330
Wigmore, Herefordshire, England, 1301
Wileby, Peter, 1328
William I, king of Scots (1165–1214), 1169, 1175
Windsor, William, justiciar of Ireland, 44, 1369
Windsor castle, Berkshire, England, 1312
wine, 1318, 1360

Index

Wishart, Robert, bp Glasgow (1271–1316), 1305
witchcraft, 1325
Wogan, John (d. 1321), **30**, 1317, 1321
    justiciar of Ireland, 1295, 1296, 1301, 1304, 1308, 1309, 1312
    Margaret (d. 1304), w. of John, **30**, 1302, 1304

Woodlock, Henry, bp Winchester (1305–16), 1306
writ, royal, 1325

York, England, 1251, 1292, 1311
Youghal, Co. Cork, **38**, 1317, 1318
    port of, 1346

Zouche, Alan de la, justiciar of Ireland, 1255